Praise for *The Rails Way*

For intermediates and above, I strongly recommend adding this title to your technical bookshelf. There is simply no other Rails title on the market at this time that offers the technical depth of the framework than *The Rails™ 3 Way*.

—Mike Riley, *Dr. Dobb's Journal*

I highly suggest you get this book. Software moves fast, especially the Rails API, but I feel this book has many core API and development concepts that will be useful for a while to come.

—Matt Polito, software engineer and member of Chicago Ruby User Group

This book should live on your desktop if you're a Rails developer. It's nearly perfect in my opinion.

—Luca Pette, developer

The Rails™ 3 Way is likely to take you from being a haphazard poke-a-stick-at-it programmer to a deliberate, skillful, productive, and confident RoR developer.

—Katrina Owen, JavaRanch

I can positively say that it's the single best Rails book ever published to date. By a long shot.

—Antonio Cangiano, software engineer and technical evangelist at IBM

This book is a great crash course in Ruby on Rails! It doesn't just document the features of Rails, it filters everything through the lens of an experienced Rails developer—so you come out a pro on the other side.

—Dirk Elmendorf, cofounder of Rackspace Inc. and Rails developer

The key to *The Rails Way* is in the title. It literally covers the "way" to do almost everything with Rails. Writing a truly exhaustive reference to the most popular web application framework used by thousands of developers is no mean feat. A thankful community of developers that has struggled to rely on scant documentation will embrace *The Rails Way* with open arms. A tour de force!

—Peter Cooper, editor, *Ruby Inside: The Ruby Blog*

In the past year, dozens of Rails books have been rushed to publication. A handful are good. Most regurgitate rudimentary information easily found on the Web. Only this book provides both the broad and deep technicalities of Rails. Nascent and expert developers, I recommend you follow *The Rails Way*.

—Martin Streicher, chief technology officer, McClatchy Interactive, former editor in chief of *Linux Magazine*

Hal Fulton's *The Ruby Way* has always been by my side as a reference while programming Ruby. Many times I had wished there was a book that had the same depth and attention to detail, only focused on the Rails framework. That book is now here and hasn't left my desk for the past month.

—Nate Klaiber, Ruby programmer

I knew soon after becoming involved with Rails that I had found something great. Now, with Obie's book, I have been able to step into Ruby on Rails development coming from .NET and be productive right away. The applications I have created I believe to be a much better quality due to the techniques I learned using Obie's knowledge.

—Robert Bazinet, InfoQ.com, .NET, and Ruby community editor and founding member of the Hartford Ruby Brigade

Extremely well written; it's a resource that every Rails programmer should have. Yes, it's that good.

—Reuven Lerner, *Linux Journal* columnist

THE RAILS™ 5 WAY

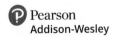

THE RAILS™ 5 WAY

Obie Fernandez

✦✦Addison-Wesley

Boston • Columbus • Indianapolis • New York • San Francisco • Amsterdam • Cape Town
Dubai • London • Madrid • Milan • Munich • Paris • Montreal • Toronto • Delhi • Mexico City
São Paulo • Sydney • Hong Kong • Seoul • Singapore • Taipei • Tokyo

To my son Liam—may I someday be as cool as you

Contents

Foreword
(to *The Rails™ 5 Way*)

Why are you even reading this book? Rails is old and busted. Everybody knows that Node.js is the new hotness.

Just kidding. Rubyists and Rails programmers alike could learn a lot from Node, but Rails is a slow burn, an old hotness that hasn't petered out yet.

Really, the question isn't "Why are you even reading this book?" The horrifying thing about this book is that you probably won't read it. The question, really, is "Why *aren't* you reading it?" What I hear is that this book's supposed to be a reference for intermediate to expert Rails programmers. This is not how I approached it at all.

I got started in Rails in December of 2005, when it was brand spanking new, but by 2010 or so, I had forgotten a lot of what I knew, and Rails had changed a lot. So I read an earlier edition of this book cover-to-cover, and I was kind of embarrassed about it, because I figured it was a book for newbies to read like that. I thought every Rails newbie was doing what I was doing.

I somehow forgot that in the tech industry, learning how something works *before* you use it is exotic and wizardly. In the exacting, demanding Rails school that I would run if I had nothing better to do with my life, you would be required to read this book cover-to-cover, along with *Rails Anti-Patterns*, another book in this series, before you were ever allowed to write a line of code. You'd even have to memorize parts of it. Of course, nobody does that before they build Rails apps, and few people do it at all.

Unfortunately, this means that the more you learn about Rails, the more you'll see people using it wrong. But the upside is that reading this book is actually a really good idea. It's weird that I should have to say this, but while buying this book is a good first step, you're not done yet. Reading it is also a very good idea.

It's not just me. If you read Steve Klabnik's foreword for the previous edition of this book, you'll see that he also read an edition of this book cover-to-cover, and that this was sufficient to catapult him from Rails newbie to superstar hacker overlord.

I don't mean to diminish his work, of course; he's also done a ton of open source work on Rails, far more than I have, and he's since developed and shared expertise in REST and Rust. (Presumably, when a technology comes along named Rist, Rast, or Rost, he'll be an expert in that too. It's an odd specialty, but he's clearly got it locked down.) But I do want to suggest a controversial possibility: maybe the standards of expertise in our industry are so low that all you have to do, to radically outpace every Rails programmer you know, is actually *read* this book, start to finish.

I know it's over 1,000 pages, but every single book in George RR Martin's *A Song of Ice and Fire* is longer than that, and I know at least half the people who buy this book will have read that entire series. If you can sit through an endless list of pheasant pies and random food involving persimmons, as if anyone even knows what a persimmon is, you can sit down and invest some time in actually getting good at the thing that you do for a living. Stranger things have happened.

Rails is often seen as a newbie-friendly shorthand for building web apps. Unwise people say that it makes building web apps so simple that anybody can do it. I'm going to recommend that you regard that point of view as utter bullshit. Here's an alternative paradigm: Rails is a user interface for web development which streamlines complex tasks. It doesn't take the complexity away. It streamlines your interaction with that complexity. There are two things you should really watch out for here.

The first is that in programming, all abstractions are ultimately leaky abstractions. For example, it's irresponsible to write any kind of code which handles money and currency if you don't understand the basics of floating-point math, including the reasons why computers can't actually *do* floating-point math. It's literally impossible to represent many decimal fractions as binary fractions, and computers represent everything in binary because they ultimately run everything through logic gates. This means that it's impossible to accurately represent certain numerical values as floating-point numbers, and people can take that mathematical impossibility quite personally when it affects the accuracy of their bank account balances. In other words, the realities of calculation in silicon are very important when you're doing financial transactions. That's just an example, but in every case, if you've got a system which makes complex stuff simple, it's still a really good idea to know what those underlying complexities ultimately are.

The second thing you should understand, to avoid the majority of pitfalls in Rails, is that building a good user interface is a lot of work. Every project out there will encounter the tricky situation where you get the first 90% of the problem out of the way, and then you discover that the remaining 10% of the problem—all the random little edge cases and details—will take as much code as the first 90% did. User interface code is all about that remaining 10%. And Rails really is a user interface for web development. So entire libraries within Rails, such as Active Relation, are dedicated to that little 10%.

One solution to both these problems is to read this book cover to cover. It's certainly not the only solution, and it might not even be the best. The best solution is probably to win the lottery and spend all your time smoking weed, but there are quite a few practical obstacles to implementing this solution, so you might end up choosing to read this book instead.

Long story short, you bought this book. Good idea. Now read it.

—**Giles Bowkett**

Foreword
(to *The Rails™ 4 Way*)

A long time ago, I was an intern at a technology company. We had "deploy week," meaning that after deploying, we took an entire week to fight fires. Moving our code to the production environment would inevitably cause unexpected changes. One day, I read a blog post titled "Unit Testing with Ruby on Rails," and my life was forever changed. I excitedly went and told my team that we could write code to check whether our code worked before deploying, but they weren't particularly interested. A few months later, when a friend asked me to be the CTO of his startup, I said, "Only if I can do it in Ruby on Rails."

My story was fairly typical for that period. I didn't know anything about Ruby, but I *had* to write my application in Rails. I figured out enough Ruby to fake it and cobbled together an application in record time. There was just one problem: I didn't really understand how it actually *worked*. This is the deal everyone makes with Rails at the start. You can't think about the details too much because you're flying to the sky like a rocket.

This book, however, isn't about that. When I read *The Rails Way* for the first time, I felt like I truly understood Rails for the first time. All those details I didn't fully understand were now able to be grokked. Every time someone said, "Rails is magic," I would smile to myself. If Rails was magic, I had peered behind the curtain. One day, I decided that I should write some documentation to help dispel those kinds of comments. One comment became two; two became twenty. Eventually, I was a large contributor in my own right. Such a long way for someone who had just a few short years earlier never heard of a unit test!

As Rails has changed, so has *The Rails Way*. In fact, one criticism you could make of this book is that it's not actually "the Rails way"; after all, it teaches you HAML instead of ERb! I think that this criticism misses the mark. After all, it's not 2005 anymore. To see what I mean, go read the two forewords from the previous edition. They appear right after this one … I'll wait.

Done? David's foreword was quite accurate for both Rails 2 and *The Rails Way*. At that time, Rails was very much "not as a blank slate equally tolerant of every kind of expression." Rails was built for what I call the "Omakase Stack": you have no choice, you get exactly what Chef David wants to serve you.[1]

Yehuda's foreword was also quite accurate—but for Rails 3 and *The Rails*™ *3 Way*. "We brought this philosophy to every area of Rails 3: flexibility without compromise." With Rails 3, you get the Omakase stack by default, but you are free to swap out components: if you don't like sushi, you can substitute some sashimi.

There was a lot of wailing and gnashing of teeth during the development of Rails 3. Jeremy Ashkenas called it "by far the worst misfortune to ever happen to Rails." Rails 3 was an investment in the future of Rails, and investments can take a while to pay off. At the release of Rails 3, it seemed like we had waited more than a year for no new features. Rails was a little better but mostly the same. The real benefit was where it couldn't be seen: in the refactoring work. Rails 1 was "red-green." Rails 2 was "red-green." Rails 3 was "refactor." It took a little while for gem authors to take advantage of this flexibility, but eventually, they did.

And that brings us to Rails 4 and *The Rails*™ *4 Way*. This book still explains quite a bit about how Rails works at a low level but also gives you an alternate vision from the Omakase Stack, based on the experience and talent of Hashrocket. In many ways, *The Rails*™ *4 Way*, *Agile Web Development with Rails*, and *Rails 4 in Action* are all "the Rails way." Contemporary Rails developers get the best of both worlds: They can take advantage of the rapid development of convention over configuration, but if they choose to follow a different convention, they can. And we have many sets of conventions to choose from. It's no longer "David's way or the highway," though David's way is obviously the default, as it should be.

It has been an amazing few years for Rails, and it has been a pleasure to take a part in its development. I hope that this book will give you the same level of insight and clarity into Rails as it did for me, years ago, while also sparking your imagination for what Rails will undoubtedly become in the future.

—Steve Klabnik

---

1. *Omakase* is a Japanese term used at sushi restaurants to leave the selection to the chef. To learn more about the Omakase stack, read http://words.steveklabnik.com/rails-has-two-default-stacks

Foreword
(to *The Rails*™ *3 Way*)

Rails is more than programming framework for creating web applications. It's also a framework for thinking about web applications. It ships not as a blank slate equally tolerant of every kind of expression. On the contrary, it trades that flexibility for the convenience of "what most people need most of the time to do most things." It's a designer straightjacket that sets you free from focusing on the things that just don't matter and focuses your attention on the stuff that does.

To be able to accept that trade, you need to understand not just how to do something in Rails but also why it's done like that. Only by understanding the why will you be able to consistently work with the framework instead of against it. It doesn't mean that you'll always have to agree with a certain choice, but you will need to agree to the overachieving principle of conventions. You have to learn to relax and let go of your attachment to personal idiosyncrasies when the productivity rewards are right.

This book can help you do just that. Not only does it serve as a guide in your exploration of the features in Rails, but it also gives you a window into the mind and soul of Rails. Why we've chosen to do things the way we do them and why we frown on certain widespread approaches. It even goes so far as to include the discussions and stories of how we got there—straight from the community participants that helped shape them.

Learning how to do Hello World in Rails has always been easy to do on your own, but getting to know and appreciate the gestalt of Rails, less so. I applaud Obie for trying to help you on this journey. Enjoy it.

—**David Heinemeier Hansson**
creator of Ruby on Rails

Foreword
(to *The Rails™ 3 Way*)

From the beginning, the Rails framework turned web development on its head with the insight that the vast majority of time spent on projects amounted to meaningless sit-ups. Instead of having the time to think through your domain-specific code, you'd spend the first few weeks of a project deciding meaningless details. By making decisions for you, Rails frees you to kick off your project with a bang, getting a working prototype out the door quickly. This makes it possible to build an application with some meat on its bones in a few weekends, making Rails the web framework of choice for people with a great idea and a full-time job.

Rails makes some simple decisions for you, like what to name your controller actions and how to organize your directories. It also gets pretty aggressive and sets development-friendly defaults for the database and caching layer you'll use, making it easy to change to more production-friendly options once you're ready to deploy.

By getting so aggressive, Rails makes it easy to put at least a few real users in front of your application within days, enabling you to start gathering the requirements from your users immediately rather than spending months architecting a perfect solution only to learn that your users use the application differently than you expected.

The Rails team built the Rails project itself according to very similar goals. Don't try to overthink the needs of your users. Get something out there that works and improve it based on actual usage patterns. By all accounts, this strategy has been a smashing success, and with the blessing of the Rails core team, the Rails community leveraged the dynamism of Ruby to fill in the gaps in plugins. Without taking a close look at Rails, you might think that Rails' rapid prototyping powers are limited to the 15-minute blog demo but that you'd fall off a cliff when writing a real app. This has never been true. In fact, in Rails 2.1, 2.2, and 2.3, the Rails team looked closely at common usage patterns reflected in very popular plugins, adding features that would further reduce the number of sit-ups needed to start real-life applications.

By the release of Rails 2.3, the Rails ecosystem had thousands of plugins, and applications like Twitter started to push the boundaries of the Rails defaults. Increasingly, you might build your next Rails application using a nonrelational database or deploy it inside a Java infrastructure using JRuby. It was time to take the tight integration of the Rails stack to the next level.

Over the course of 20 months, starting in January 2008, we looked at a wide range of plugins, spoke with the architects of some of the most popular Rails applications, and changed the way the Rails internals thought about its defaults.

Rather than starting from scratch, trying to build a generic data layer for Rails, we took on the challenge of making it easy to give any ORM the same tight level of integration with the rest of the framework as Active Record. We accepted no compromises, taking the time to write the tight Active Record integration using the same APIs that we now expose for other ORMs. This covers the obvious, such as making it possible to generate a scaffold using DataMapper or Mongoid. It also covers the less obvious, such as giving alternative ORMs the same ability to include the amount of time spent in the model layer in the controller's log output.

We brought this philosophy to every area of Rails 3: flexibility without compromise. By looking at the ways that an estimated million developers use Rails, we could hone in on the needs of real developers and plugin authors, significantly improving the overall architecture of Rails based on real user feedback.

Because the Rails 3 internals are such a departure from what's come before, developers building long-lived applications and plugin developers need a resource that comprehensively covers the philosophy of the new version of the framework. *The Rails*™ *3 Way* is a comprehensive resource that digs into the new features in Rails 3 and perhaps, more important, the rationale behind them.

—**Yehuda Katz**
Rails Core Team Alumni

Introduction

It's an exciting time for the Rails community. Our mainstream adoption is as strong as ever. More than 10 years since DHH made the initial Rails releases, we have cemented our place as the standard bearer amongst web frameworks.

While Rails 5 does not bring a huge leap forward in features like its predecessor did, it does give us a level of fit and finish that surpasses any major technology framework that most of us have ever worked with. Everything. Just. Works. Maybe it's just that I'm getting older, but as I've worked my way through the comprehensive revision/rewrite cycle for this edition, I marveled at how little digging and debugging I had to do, even for new features. Truly, with maturity and community depth, we have acquired strength beyond what anyone could have imagined at the start when we were the radicals.

This particular revision of *The Rails Way* was much less of a team exercise than earlier ones. This time around it was me, sitting in my cabin outside Atlanta, with my dog Daisy at my feet and copious amounts of research at my fingertips. During this revision cycle, I fell in love with Rails all over again, and banged out a couple of side projects just for the sheer fun of it. I couldn't be prouder of how it's come together. I pored over every line, and tightened up the writing in every single chapter. I checked every bit of sample code, and changed lots of it to reflect more modern techniques.

About This Book

As with previous editions, this book is not a tutorial or basic introduction to Ruby or Rails. The idea is for the full-time Rails developer to give it a once over straight through at first, then use it as a day-to-day reference. The more confident reader might be able to get started in Rails using just this book, extensive online resources, and his wits, but there are other publications that are more introductory in nature and might be a wee bit more appropriate for beginners.

Historically, every contributor to this book has worked with Rails on a full time basis. We do not spend our days writing books or training other people, although that is certainly something that we enjoy doing on the side.

This book was originally conceived for myself, because I hate having to use online documentation, especially API docs, which need to be consulted over and over again. Since the API documentation is liberally licensed (just like the rest of Rails), there are some sections of the book that draw from the API documentation. But in practically all of those cases, the API documentation has been expanded and/or corrected, supplemented with additional examples and enhanced with commentary drawn from practical experience.

Hopefully you are like me—I really like books that I can keep next to my keyboard, scribble notes in, and fill with bookmarks and dog-ears. When I'm coding, I want to be able to quickly refer to API documentation, in-depth explanations, and relevant examples.

Book Structure

I attempted to give the material a natural structure while meeting the goal of being the best-possible Rails reference book. To that end, careful attention has been given to presenting holistic explanations of each subsystem of Rails, including detailed API information where appropriate. Every chapter is slightly different in scope, and I suspect that Rails is now too big a topic to cover the whole thing in depth in just one book.

Believe me, it has not been easy coming up with a structure that makes perfect sense for everyone. Particularly, I have noted surprise in some readers when they notice that Active Record is not covered first. Rails is foremost a web framework and, at least to me, the controller and routing implementation is the most unique, powerful, and effective feature, with Active Record following a close second.

Sample Code and Listings

The domains chosen for the code samples should be familiar to almost all professional developers. They include time and expense tracking, auctions, regional data management, and blogging applications. I don't spend pages explaining the subtler nuances of the business logic for the samples or justify design decisions that don't have a direct relationship to the topic at hand. Following in the footsteps of my series colleague Hal Fulton and *The Ruby Way*, most of the snippets are not full code listings—only the relevant code is shown. Ellipses (…) often denote parts of the code that have been eliminated for clarity.

Whenever a code listing is large and significant, and I suspect that you might want to use parts of it verbatim in your own code, I supply a listing heading. There are not too many of those. The whole set of code listings will not add up to a complete working system, nor are there 30 pages of sample application code in an appendix. The code listings should serve as inspiration for your production-ready work, but keep in mind that it often lacks touches necessary in real-world work. For example, examples of controller code are often missing pagination and access control logic, because it would detract from the point being expressed.

Some of the source code for my examples can be found at https://github.com/ obie/tr5w_time_and_expenses. Note that it is not a working nor complete application. It just made sense at times to keep the code in the context of an application and hopefully you might draw some inspiration from browsing it.

Concerning Third-Party RubyGems and Plugins

Whenever you find yourself writing code that feels like plumbing, by which I mean completely unrelated to the business domain of your application, you're probably doing too much work. I hope that you have this book at your side when you encounter that feeling. There is almost always some new part of the Rails API or a third-party RubyGem for doing exactly what you are trying to do.

As a matter of fact, part of what sets this book apart is that I never hesitate in calling out the availability of third-party code, and I even document the RubyGems and plugins that I feel are most crucial for effective Rails work. In cases where third-party code is better than the built-in Rails functionality, we don't cover the built-in Rails functionality (pagination is a good example).

An average developer might see his productivity double with Rails, but I've seen serious Rails developers achieve gains that are much, much higher. That's because we follow the Don't Repeat Yourself (DRY) principle religiously, of which Don't

Reinvent The Wheel (DRTW) is a close corollary. Reimplementing something when an existing implementation is good enough is an unnecessary waste of time that nevertheless can be very tempting, since it's such a joy to program in Ruby.

Ruby on Rails is actually a vast ecosystem of core code, official plugins, and third-party plugins. That ecosystem has been exploding rapidly and provides all the raw technology you need to build even the most complicated enterprise class web applications. My goal is to equip you with enough knowledge that you'll be able to avoid continuously reinventing the wheel.

David Heinemeier Hansson (aka DHH)

Regarding David Heinemeier Hansson a.k.a. DHH. I had the pleasure of establishing a friendship with David, creator of Rails, in early 2005, before Rails hit the mainstream and he became an International Web 2.0 Superstar. My friendship with David is a big factor in why I'm writing this book today. David's opinions and public statements shape the Rails world, which means he gets quoted a lot when we discuss the nature of Rails and how to use it effectively.

I don't know if this is true anymore, but back when I wrote the original edition of this book, David had told me on a couple of occasions that he hates the "DHH" moniker that people tend to use instead of his long and difficult-to-spell full name. For that reason, in this book I try to always refer to him as "David" instead of the ever-tempting "DHH." When you encounter references to "David" without further qualification, I'm referring to the one-and-only David Heinemeier Hansson.

There are a number of notable people from the Rails world who are also referred to on a first-name basis in this book. Those include:

- *Yehuda* Katz
- *Jamis* Buck
- *Xavier* Noria
- *Tim* Pope

Goals

As already stated, I hope to make this your primary working reference for Ruby on Rails. Over time I hope this book gives you as an application developer/programmer greater confidence in making design and implementation decisions while working on your day-to-day tasks. After spending time with this book, your understanding of the fundamental concepts of Rails coupled with hands-on experience should leave you feeling comfortable working on real-world Rails projects, with real-world demands.

If you are in an architectural or development lead role, this book is not targeted to you but should make you feel more comfortable discussing the pros and cons of Ruby on Rails adoption and ways to extend Rails to meet the particular needs of the project under your direction.

Finally, if you are a development manager, you should find the practical perspective of the book and our coverage of testing and tools especially interesting and hopefully get some insight into why your developers are so excited about Ruby and Rails.

Prerequisites

The reader is assumed to have the following knowledge:

- Basic Ruby syntax and language constructs such as blocks
- Solid grasp of object-oriented principles and design patterns
- Basic understanding of relational databases and SQL
- Familiarity with how Rails applications are laid out and function
- Basic understanding of network protocols such as HTTP and SMTP
- Basic understanding of JSON and web services
- Familiarity with transactional concepts such as ACID properties

As noted in the section "Book Structure," this book does not progress from easy material in the front to harder material in the back. Some chapters do start out with fundamental, almost introductory material, and push on to more advanced coverage. There are definitely sections of the text that experienced Rails developers will gloss over. However, I believe that there is new knowledge and inspiration in every chapter, for all skill levels.

Rails Essentials

Previous editions of this book included a final appendix called "Rails Essentials," containing a list of tools and third-party RubyGems that we find useful for Rails development. Since that kind of information goes out-of-date often, we've made a strategic decision to remove the appendix and make it available as an online resource on the book's InformIT page (informit.com/title/9780134657677).

Required Technology

A late-model Apple MacBookPro running Mac OS X. Just kidding, of course. Linux is pretty good for Rails development also. Microsoft Windows—well, let me just put it this way—your mileage may vary. I'm being nice and diplomatic in saying that. We specifically do not discuss Rails development on Microsoft platforms in this book. It's common knowledge that the vast majority of working Rails professionals develop and deploy on non-Microsoft platforms.

Register your copy of *The Rails*™ *5 Way* at informit.com/register for convenient access to downloads, updates, and/or corrections as they become available (you must log in or create a new account). Enter the product ISBN (9780134657677) and click Submit. Once the process is complete, you will find any available bonus content under "Registered Products." If you would like to be notified of exclusive offers on new editions and updates, please check the box to receive email from us.

Acknowledgments

This edition probably has the greatest amount of edits and changes in the history of the title, by the smallest team: Looking back on the effort involved in bringing *The Rails™ 5 Way* to fruition, I'd like to first thank my lovely bride Tamara for her patience and understanding when I sacrifice family time for writing and other creative pursuits. Second, I must express tremendous gratitude to my loyal friend and mentor Debra Williams Cauley, Executive Editor at Addison-Wesley. It seems like every edition of this book brings fresh opportunities for me to test her patience.

I'd also like to thank (not necessarily in order of importance): My team at Kickass Consulting, Luis Miguel Delgado, Tim Pope, and Wilson Bilkovich. Kevin Faustino and the rest of the team from the last edition, for their initial work helping me get this edition off the ground. Prathamesh Sonpatki Janmejay Rai provided invaluable and detailed knowledge about changes in Rails 5. Anthony Lombardi and Jeremy Hamel provided early technical review. Chris Zahn, our copyeditor extraordinaire. Julie Nahil and Kim Boedigheimer, and the rest of the team at Pearson. Jason Swett and the Ruby Rogues, for having me on their podcast to promote the book.

Last, but not least, I'd like to thank Peter Armstrong and his team at Leanpub, and my Leanpub readers, many of whom took the time to give me detailed feedback and bug reports that let me fix errors and omissions that would not have been caught otherwise.

About the Author

Obie Fernandez has been hacking computers since he got his first Commodore VIC-20 in the eighties, and found himself in the right place and time as a programmer on some of the first Java enterprise projects of the mid-nineties. He moved to Atlanta in 1998, where he founded the Extreme Programming (later Agile Atlanta) User Group and was that group's president and organizer for several years. In 2004, he joined world-renowned consultancy Thought-Works and made a name for himself tackling high-risk, progressive projects in the enterprise, including some of the first enterprise projects in the world utilizing Ruby on Rails. He also gained a reputation and fan following for being one of the fledgling framework's loudest evangelists.

In 2007, Obie leveraged his position in the community to launch Hashrocket, a firm specializing in Ruby on Rails development. Over the course of three years it grew to almost 50 employees, $7 million in revenue, and recognition as one of the world's best web design and development consultancies. At Hashrocket, Obie specialized in orchestrating the creation of large-scale, web-based applications, both for startups and mission-critical enterprise projects.

At the end of 2010, Obie sold his stake in Hashrocket and has been either founding or consulting technology startups ever since. His last startup, Andela, has received close to $40 million in funding, including a $24 million, Series B round–led Chan Zuckerberg initiative. With Andela, Obie is helping to transform the technology sphere by training 100 thousand brilliant young Africans how to become world-class technology leaders.

Today, in addition to working with clients at Kickass Consulting, composing electronic music, and writing, Obie maintains a variety of technical side projects that keep him coding on a daily basis. Other books he has authored include *How to Eat Nachos and Influence People*, *The Lean Enterprise*, and *Serverless*. Learn more at http://obiefernandez.com.

CHAPTER 1

Rails Configuration and Environments

[Rails] gained a lot of its focus and appeal because I didn't try to please people who didn't share my problems. Differentiating between production and development was a very real problem for me, so I solved it the best way I knew how.

—David Heinemeier Hansson

Rails applications have always been preconfigured with three standard modes of operation: development, test, and production. These modes are basically execution environments and have a collection of associated settings that determine things such as which database to connect to and whether the classes of your application should be reloaded with each request. It is simple to create your own custom environments if necessary.

The current environment can be specified via the environment variable `RAILS_ENV`, which names the desired mode of operation and corresponds to an environment definition file in the `config/environments` folder. You can also set the environment variable `RACK_ENV`, or as a last resort you may rely on the default being `development`. Since this environment setting governs some of the most fundamental aspects of Rails, such as class loading, in order to really understand the Rails way you should understand its environment settings.

The most fundamental aspect of your application settings is its list of external libraries that it depends on. Therefore, we kick off this chapter by covering Bundler, a tool that manages RubyGem dependencies for Ruby applications. It takes a manifest file as input and is able to fetch, download, and install the gems in the manifest, plus any and all child dependencies. A little later in the chapter we move on to how Rails starts up and handles requests, by examining scripts such as `boot.rb` and

1

`application.rb` and the settings that make up the three standard environment settings (modes). We also cover some of the basics of defining your own environments, and why you might choose to do so.

Note that this book is not written with absolute newcomers to Rails in mind. To make the most out of this book, you should already be at least somewhat familiar with how to bootstrap a Rails application and the MVC (Model-View-Controller) architectural pattern. If you are not, I recommend that you first take advantage of the excellent Ruby on Rails Tutorial website[1] by Michael Hartl, a fellow Addison-Wesley Professional Ruby Series author.

API Mode

Instead of using Rails to generate HTML on the server side, an ongoing trend in web development is to write rich client applications that execute in the browser using technologies such as Angular or React. These client applications treat their Rails backends as just an API server and generally communicate via JSON.

Rails 5 introduces an "API Mode" for bootstrapping new applications that will *not* be used for serving traditional HTML-based browser applications. We cover the details of API Mode in Appendix C, "Rails API."

1.1 Bundler

Bundler[2] is not a technology that is specific to Rails, but it *is* the preferred way to manage your application's RubyGem dependencies. Applications generated with Rails use Bundler automatically, and you should not need to install the `bundler` gem separately since it's a dependency of Rails itself.

Since we believe that it is silly to not use Bundler, figuring out how to do so is left as an exercise for adventurous and/or nonconformist readers.

One of the most important things that Bundler does is dependency resolution on the full list of gems specified in your configuration, all at once. This differs from the one-at-a-time dependency resolution approach employed by RubyGems and previous versions of Rails, which can (and often did) result in the following hard-to-fix problem.

---

1. https://www.railstutorial.org/
2. http://bundler.io

Assume that your system had the following RubyGem versions installed:

```
activesupport 4.0.2
activesupport 3.2.11
activemerchant 1.29.3
rails 3.2.11
```

It turns out that `activemerchant 1.29.3` depends on `activesupport >= 2.3.14`. Therefore, when you load it using the `gem` command (from the Ruby-Gems library) like this

```
gem 'activemerchant', '1.29.3'
```

it results in the loading of `activemerchant`, as well as the latest compatible versions of its dependencies, including the `activesupport 4.0.2` gem, since it is greater than or equal to version 2.3.14. Subsequently, trying to load Rails itself with

```
gem 'rails', '3.2.11'
```

results in the following exception at runtime:

```
can't activate activesupport (= 3.2.11, runtime)
for ["rails-3.2.11"], already activated
activesupport-4.0.2 for ["activemerchant-1.29.3"]
```

The exception happens because `activemerchant` has a broader dependency that results in the activation of a version of Active Support that does not satisfy the more narrow dependency of the older version of Rails. Bundler solves this problem by evaluating all dependencies at once and figuring out exactly the right versions of gems to load.

For an interesting perspective concerning the way that Bundler was conceived, make sure to read Yehuda's blog post on the subject.[3]

1.1.1 Gemfile

The root of your Rails project directory contains a Ruby-based gem manifest file named simply `Gemfile`, with no filename extension. The `Gemfile` specifies all dependencies of your Rails app, including the version of Rails being used. The basic syntax for the `Gemfile` is super simple:

```
gem 'kaminari'
gem 'nokogiri'
```

---

3. http://yehudakatz.com/2010/04/21/named-gem-environments-and-bundler/

To load a dependency only in a specific environment, place it in a group block specifying one or more environment names as symbols:

```
group :development do
  gem 'byebug'
end

group :test do
  gem 'capybara'
  gem 'database_cleaner'
end

group :development, :test do
  gem 'rspec-rails'
  gem 'factory_girl_rails'
end
```

The `gem` directive takes an optional second argument describing the version of the RubyGem desired. Leaving the version argument off will simply get the latest available *stable* version, which may not be the latest version available. To include a release candidate or a pre-release gem you'll need to specify the version explicitly.

The format of the version argument matches the RubyGem versioning scheme to which you should already be accustomed:

```
gem 'nokogiri', '1.5.6'
gem 'pry-rails', '> 0.2.2'
gem 'decent_exposure', '~> 2.0.1'
gem 'draper', '1.0.0.beta6'
```

You can find full instructions on how to craft a version string in the RubyGems documentation.[4]

Occasionally, the name of the gem that should be used in a `require` statement is different than the name of that gem in the repository. In those cases, the `:require` option solves this simply and declaratively right in the `Gemfile`:

```
gem 'webmock', require: 'webmock/rspec'
```

---

4. http://docs.rubygems.org/read/chapter/16

1.1.1.1 Loading Gems Directly from a Git Repository

Until now we have been loading our gems from https://rubygems.org. It is possible to specify a gem by its source repository as long as it has a `.gemspec` file in the root directory. Just add a `:git` option to the call to `gem`:

```
gem 'carrierwave', git: 'git@github.com:carrierwaveuploader/carrierwave.git'
```

If the gem source repository is hosted on GitHub and is public, you can use the `:github` shorthand:

```
gem 'carrierwave', github: 'carrierwaveuploader/carrierwave'
```

Gemspecs with binaries or C extensions are also supported:

```
gem 'nokogiri', git: 'git://github.com/tenderlove/nokogiri.git'
```

If there is no `.gemspec` file at the root of a gem's git repository, you must tell Bundler which version to use when resolving its dependencies:

```
gem 'deep_merge', '1.0', git: 'git://github.com/peritor/deep_merge.git'
```

It's also possible to specify that a git repository contains multiple `.gemspec` files and should be treated as a gem source. The following example does just that for the most common git repository that fits the criteria, the Rails codebase itself. (Note: You should never actually need to put the following code in a `Gemfile` for one of your Rails applications!)

```
git 'git://github.com/rails/rails.git'
gem 'railties'
gem 'action_pack'
gem 'active_model'
```

Additionally, you can specify that a git repository should use a particular ref, branch, or tag as options to the `git` directive:

```
git 'git://github.com/rails/rails.git',
  ref: '4aded'

git 'git://github.com/rails/rails.git',
  branch: '3-2-stable'

git 'git://github.com/rails/rails.git',
  tag: 'v3.2.11'
```

Specifying a ref, branch, or tag for a git repository specified inline uses the same option syntax:

```
gem 'nokogiri', git: 'git://github.com/tenderlove/nokogiri.git', ref: '0eec4'
```

1.1.1.2   Loading Gems from the File System

You can use a gem that you are actively developing on your local workstation using the `:path` option:

```
gem 'nokogiri', path: '~/code/nokogiri'
```

1.1.2   Installing Gems

Every time you modify the `Gemfile`, or more specifically, if you introduce dependencies not yet installed, invoke the `install` command to ensure that all the dependencies in your `Gemfile` are available to your Rails application.[5]

```
$ bundle install
Fetching gem metadata from https://rubygems.org/..........
Fetching version metadata from https://rubygems.org/..
Fetching dependency metadata from https://rubygems.org/.
Resolving dependencies...
Using rake 11.3.0
Using concurrent-ruby 1.0.2
Using i18n 0.7.0
Using minitest 5.9.1
Using thread_safe 0.3.5
Using builder 3.2.2
Using erubis 2.7.0
Using mini_portile2 2.1.0
Using rack 2.0.1
Using nio4r 1.2.1
Using websocket-extensions 0.1.2
Using mime-types-data 3.2016.0521
Using arel 7.1.4
Using bundler 1.13.6
Using byebug 9.0.6
Using coffee-script-source 1.10.0
Using execjs 2.7.0
Using method_source 0.8.2
Using thor 0.19.1
Using debug_inspector 0.0.2
Using ffi 1.9.14
Using multi_json 1.12.1
```

---

5. rbenv allows you to easily install, manage and work with multiple Ruby versions and it's a must-have tool for modern Rails developers. https://github.com/sstephenson/rbenv

Config

```
Using rb-fsevent 0.9.8
Using puma 3.6.0
Using sass 3.4.22
Using tilt 2.0.5
Using sqlite3 1.3.12
Using turbolinks-source 5.0.0
Using tzinfo 1.2.2
Using nokogiri 1.6.8.1
Using rack-test 0.6.3
Using sprockets 3.7.0
Using websocket-driver 0.6.4
Using mime-types 3.1
Using coffee-script 2.4.1
Using uglifier 3.0.3
Using rb-inotify 0.9.7
Using turbolinks 5.0.1
Using activesupport 5.0.0.1
Using loofah 2.0.3
Using mail 2.6.4
Using listen 3.0.8
Using rails-dom-testing 2.0.1
Using globalid 0.3.7
Using activemodel 5.0.0.1
Using jbuilder 2.6.0
Using spring 2.0.0
Using rails-html-sanitizer 1.0.3
Using activejob 5.0.0.1
Using activerecord 5.0.0.1
Using spring-watcher-listen 2.0.1
Using actionview 5.0.0.1
Using actionpack 5.0.0.1
Using actioncable 5.0.0.1
Using actionmailer 5.0.0.1
Using railties 5.0.0.1
Using sprockets-rails 3.2.0
Using coffee-rails 4.2.1
Using jquery-rails 4.2.1
Installing web-console 3.4.0
Using rails 5.0.0.1
Using sass-rails 5.0.6
Bundle complete! 15 Gemfile dependencies, 62 gems now installed.
Use `bundle show [gemname]` to see where a bundled gem is installed.
```

The `install` command updates all dependencies named in your `Gemfile` to the latest versions that do not conflict with other dependencies. It is invoked automatically upon bootstrapping a new Rails application using the `rails new` command in your terminal.

The first time you run `bundle install` no `Gemfile.lock` file exists yet. (We'll talk about gem locking in the next section.) Bundler will start by fetching all remote sources, resolving dependencies and installing needed gems.

Re-running `bundle install` without updating the `Gemfile` will cause Bundler to re-fetch all remote sources but use the dependencies specified in the `Gemfile.lock` instead of resolving dependencies again. Under normal circumstances, this doesn't change anything about your configuration.

The most common situation is that a `Gemfile.lock` does exist, and you have updated your `Gemfile` by adding or modifying a dependency. When running `bundle install` the dependencies specified in `Gemfile.lock` will be used for gems that did not change, but dependencies will be re-resolved for any gems that were updated.

1.1.3   Gem Locking

Every time you run `bundle install` or `bundle update`, Bundler calculates the dependency tree for your application and stores the results in a file named `Gemfile.lock` that looks a little like this:

```
GEM
  remote: https://rubygems.org/
  specs:
    actioncable (5.0.0.1)
      actionpack (= 5.0.0.1)
      nio4r (~> 1.2)
      websocket-driver (~> 0.6.1)
    actionmailer (5.0.0.1)
      actionpack (= 5.0.0.1)
      actionview (= 5.0.0.1)
      activejob (= 5.0.0.1)
      mail (~> 2.5, >= 2.5.4)
      rails-dom-testing (~> 2.0)
```

Once a lock file is created, Bundler will only load specific versions of gems that you were using at the moment that the `Gemfile` was locked, the idea being that you *lock* your configuration down to using versions of dependencies that you know will work well with your application.

> **ⓘ Note**
>
> The `Gemfile.lock` file should always be checked into version control, to ensure every machine running the application uses the exact same versions of gems.[6]
>
> To illustrate the importance of this, imagine the `Gemfile.lock` is missing and the application is being deployed to production. Since the dependency tree is non-existent, Bundler has to resolve all of the gems from the `Gemfile` on that machine. This in result may install newer gem versions than you tested against, causing unforeseen issues.

1.1.4 Packaging Gems

You can package up all your gems in the `vendor/cache` directory inside of your Rails application:

```
$ bundle package
```

Running `bundle install --local` in an application with packaged gems will use the gems in the package and skip connecting to rubygems.org or any other gem sources. You can use this to avoid external dependencies at deploy time or if you depend on private gems that are not available in any public repository.

> **ⓘ Making Gem Dependencies Available to Non-Rails Scripts**
>
> Non-Rails scripts must be executed with `bundle exec` in order to get a properly initialized RubyGems environment:
>
> ```
> $ bundle exec guard
> ```

1.1.5 Binstubs

Bootstrapping a new application will result in the creation of binstubs for Rails executables, located in the `bin` folder. A *binstub* is a script containing an executable that runs in the context of the bundle. This means one does not have to prefix `bundle exec` each time a Rails specific executable is invoked. Binstubs are first-class citizens of your project and should be added into your version control system like any other source code file.

By default, the following stubs are available on every new Rails project:

---

6. http://yehudakatz.com/2010/12/16/clarifying-the-roles-of-the-gemspec-and-gemfile/

- `bin/bundle`

- `bin/rails`

- `bin/rake`

- `bin/setup`

- `bin/spring`

- `bin/update`

To add a *binstub* of a commonly used executable in your bundle, invoke `bundle binstubs some-gem-name`. To illustrate, consider the following example,

```
$ bundle binstubs guard
```

which creates a binstub for `guard` in the `bin` folder:

```
#!/usr/bin/env ruby
#
# This file was generated by Bundler.
#
# The application 'guard' is installed as part of a gem, and
# this file is here to facilitate running it.
#

require 'pathname'
ENV['BUNDLE_GEMFILE'] ||= File.expand_path("../../Gemfile",
  Pathname.new(__FILE__).realpath)

require 'rubygems'
require 'bundler/setup'

load Gem.bin_path('guard', 'guard')
```

Using binstubs, scripts can be executed directly from the `bin` directory:

```
$ bin/guard
```

1.2 Startup Scripts

Whenever you start a process to handle requests with Rails (such as with `rails server`), one of the first things that happens is that `config/boot.rb` is loaded.

There are three files involved in setting up the entire Rails stack.

1.2.1 `config/environment.rb`

This file loads `application.rb`, then runs initializer scripts.

```
# Load the Rails application.
require_relative 'application'

# Initialize the Rails application.
Rails.application.initialize!
```

1.2.2 `config/boot.rb`

This file is required by `application.rb` to set up Bundler and load paths for RubyGems.

```
ENV['BUNDLE_GEMFILE'] ||= File.expand_path('../Gemfile', __dir__)
require 'bundler/setup' # Set up gems listed in the Gemfile.
```

`Bundler.setup` will add all your gems to the Rails load path but won't actually require them. This is referred to as a "lazy-loading" setup. More about that in "The Rails Class Loader" section later in the chapter.

1.2.3 `config/application.rb`

Now we get into the meat of configuration. This script loads the Ruby on Rails gems and gems for the specified `Rails.env` and configures the application. Let's go step by step through the settings provided in the default `config/application.rb` file that you'll find in a newly created Rails application. As you're reading through the following sections, make a mental note to yourself that changes to these files require a server restart to take effect.

```
require_relative 'boot'
```

Note that the boot script is generated as part of your Rails application, but you don't (usually) need to edit it.

Next, the Rails gems are loaded.

```
require 'rails/all'
```

By replacing this line you can easily cherry-pick only the components needed by your application:

```
# To pick the frameworks you want, remove 'require "rails/all"'
# and list only the framework railties that you want:
```

```
#
# require "active_model/railtie"
# require "active_record/railtie"
# require "action_controller/railtie"
# require "action_mailer/railtie"
# require "action_view/railtie"
# require "sprockets/railtie"
# require "rails/test_unit/railtie"
```

The main configuration of our application follows, which gets its own module and class:

```
module TimeAndExpenses
  class Application < Rails::Application
    # Settings in config/environments/* take precedence over those
    # specified here. Application configuration should go into files
    # in config/initializers
    # -- all .rb files in that directory are automatically loaded.
```

As opposed to the simpler assumptions of earlier Rails versions, the creation of a module specifically for your application lays a foundation for running multiple Rails applications in the same executable Ruby process.

1.3   Default Initializers

The `config/initializers` directory contains a set of default initializer scripts. In this section, we'll take a walk through them and briefly cover their functions. Remember that you need to restart your server when you modify any of these files—by their nature, they are only loaded once at server startup.

Also note that you can (and should) add configuration settings for your own application by adding your own Ruby scripts to the initializers directory. The following ten initializers are included by default in all Rails applications.

1.3.1   `config/initializers/application_controller_renderer.rb`

View rendering is covered in depth in Chapter 10, "Action View." For now, what you should know is that Rails 5 introduces the `ActionController::Renderer` class as a utility for rendering arbitrary templates' absent controller actions (for example, to render a PDF report in a background job).

Templates are rendered in a context with supplementary data. For example, if a view template needs to create a URL, how will it know what hostname to use or whether to use SSL or not?

The `application_controller_renderer.rb` script provides a place for setting those kinds of defaults.

```
# ApplicationController.renderer.defaults.merge!(
#   http_host: 'example.org',
#   https: false
# )
```

1.3.2   config/initializers/assets.rb

The Asset Pipeline has a number of settings that allow you to customize its behavior. These settings are covered in detail in Asset Pipeline Configuration.

```
# Version of your assets, change this if you want to expire all your assets.
Rails.application.config.assets.version = '1.0'

# Add additional assets to the asset load path
# Rails.application.config.assets.paths << Emoji.images_path

# Precompile additional assets.
# application.js, application.css, and all non-JS/CSS in app/
# assets folder are already added.
# Rails.application.config.assets.precompile += %w( search.js )
```

1.3.3   config/initializers/backtrace_silencers.rb

Nobody likes really long exception backtraces, except maybe Java programmers. (Kidding!) Rails actually gives you a built-in mechanism for reducing the size of back-traces by eliminating lines that don't really add anything to your debugging effort.

```
# You can add backtrace silencers for libraries that you're using
# but don't wish to see in your backtraces.
# Rails.backtrace_cleaner.add_silencer { |line| line =~ /my_noisy_
# library/ }
```

The `backtrace_silencers.rb` initializer lets you modify the way that back-traces are shortened. I've found it useful to remove backtrace entries for noisy librar-ies, but removing all silencers is usually never needed during normal application development.

```
# You can also remove all the silencers if you're trying to debug
# a problem that might stem from framework code.
# Rails.backtrace_cleaner.remove_silencers!
```

1.3.4 `config/initializers/cookies_serializer.rb`

Since browser cookies are simply string-based key-value pairs, then storing anything other than strings requires serialization. This setting controls how Rails handles that serialization behavior.

```
# Specify a serializer for the signed and encrypted cookie jars.
# Valid options are :json, :marshal, and :hybrid.
Rails.application.config.action_dispatch.cookies_serializer = :json
```

Note that applications created before Rails 4.1 use Ruby's built-in `Marshal` class to serialize cookie values into the signed and encrypted cookie jars. If you are upgrading to Rails 5 and want to transparently migrate your existing Marshal-serialized cookies into the new JSON-based format, you can set the `cookies_serializer` to `:hybrid`:

```
Rails.application.config.action_dispatch.cookies_serializer = :hybrid
```

When using the `:json` or `:hybrid` serializer, you should beware that not all Ruby objects can be natively serialized as JSON. For example, Date and Time objects will be serialized as strings, and Hashes will have symbolic keys stringified.

```
class CookiesController < ApplicationController
  def set_cookie
    cookies.encrypted[:expiration_date] = Date.tomorrow # => Thu, 20 Mar 2014
    redirect_to action: 'read_cookie'
  end

  def read_cookie
    cookies.encrypted[:expiration_date] # => "2014-03-20"
  end
end
```

It's advisable that you only store simple data (strings and numbers) in cookies. If you have to store complex objects, you will need to handle the conversion manually when reading the values on subsequent requests. If you use the cookie session store (the default case), then this advice applies to the session and flash hashes also.

1.3.5 `config/initializers/filter_parameter_logging.rb`

When a request is made to your application, by default Rails logs details such as the request path, HTTP method, IP address, and parameters. If an attacker somehow gained access to your logs, they may be able to view sensitive information, like passwords and credit card numbers.

The `filter_parameter_logging.rb` initializer let's you specify what request parameters should be filtered from your log files. If Rails receives a request parameter included in the `filter_parameters` collection, it will mark it as [FILTERED] in your logs.

```
# Configure sensitive parameters which will be filtered from the log file.
Rails.application.config.filter_parameters += [:password]
```

1.3.6 `config/initializers/inflections.rb`

Rails has a class named `Inflector` whose responsibility is to transform strings (words) from singular to plural, class names to table names, modularized class names to ones without, and class names to foreign keys, etc. (Some of its operations have funny names, such as `dasherize`.)

The default inflections for pluralization and singularization of uncountable words are kept in an interesting file inside the Active Support gem, named `inflections.rb`.

Most of the time the `Inflector` class does a decent job of figuring out the pluralized table name for a given class, but occasionally it won't. This is one of the first stumbling blocks for many new Rails users, but it is not necessary to panic. With a little ad hoc testing beforehand, it's easy to find out how `Inflector` will react to certain words. We just need to use the Rails console, which by the way is one of the best things about working in Rails.

You fire up the console from your terminal with the `rails console` command:

```
$ rails console
>> ActiveSupport::Inflector.pluralize "project"
=> "projects"
>> ActiveSupport::Inflector.pluralize "virus"
=> "viri"
>> "pensum".pluralize # Inflector features are mixed into String
   by default
=> "pensums"
```

As you can see in the example, `Inflector` tries to be smart, pluralizing *virus* as *viri*; but if you know your Latin, you have already noticed that the plural *pensum* should actually be *pensa*. Needless to say, the inflector does not know Latin.[7]

---

7. Comically, the Rails inflection of virus is also wrong. See http://en.wikipedia.org/wiki/Plural_form_of_words_ending_in_-us#Virus

However, you can teach the inflector new tricks by adding new pattern rules, by pointing out an exception, or by declaring certain words unpluralizable. The preferred place to do that is inside the `config/initializers/inflections.rb` file, where a commented example is already provided:

```
ActiveSupport::Inflector.inflections(:en) do |inflect|
  inflect.plural /^(ox)$/i, '\1en'
  inflect.singular /^(ox)en/i, '\1'
  inflect.irregular 'person', 'people'
  inflect.uncountable %w( fish sheep )
end
```

The file `activesupport/test/inflector_test_cases.rb`[8] has a long list of pluralizations correctly handled by `Inflector`. I found some of them pretty interesting, such as the following:

```
"datum"    => "data",
"medium"   => "media",
"analysis" => "analyses"
```

1.3.7 `config/initializers/mime_types.rb`

Rails supports a standard set of MIME types (*/*, text/html, text/plain, text/javascript, text/css, text/calendar, text/csv, application/xml, application/rss+xml, application/atom+xml, application/x-yaml, multipart/form-data, application/x-www-form-urlencoded, application/json).

Short Name	respond_to Symbol	Aliases and Explanations
text/html	`:html, :xhtml`	application/xhtml+xml
text/plain	`:text, :txt`	
text/javascript	`:js`	application/javascript, application/x-javascript
text/css	`:css`	Cascading style sheets
text/calendar	`:ics`	iCalendar format for sharing meeting requests and tasks
text/csv	`:csv`	Comma-separated values
application/xml	`:xml`	text/xml, application/x-xml
application/rss+xml	`:rss`	Really Simple Syndication format for web feeds

---

8. https://github.com/rails/rails/blob/master/activesupport/test/inflector_test_cases.rb

Short Name	respond_to Symbol	Aliases and Explanations
application/ atom+xml	`:atom`	Atom Syndication Format for web feeds
application/ x-yaml	`:yaml`	text/yaml—The human-readable data serialization format
application/ x-www-form- urlencoded	`:url_encoded_form`	The default content type of HTML forms
multipart/ form-data	`:multipart_form`	Used for HTML forms that contain files, non-ASCII data, and binary data
application/json	`:json`	text/x-json, application/ jsonrequest—JavaScript Object Notation

If your application needs to respond to other MIME types, you can register them in the `mime_types.rb` initializer

```
# Add new mime types for use in respond_to blocks:
# Mime::Type.register "text/richtext", :rtf
```

1.3.8 `config/initializers/new_framework_defaults.rb`

This initializer contains migration options that promise to ease migration to Rails 5 from earlier versions. The script is reproduced here, but descriptions of what these settings do is covered in their related chapters.

```
# Enable per-form CSRF tokens. Previous versions had false.
Rails.application.config.action_controller.per_form_csrf_tokens = true

# Enable origin-checking CSRF mitigation. Previous versions had false.
Rails.application.config.action_controller.forgery_protection_origin_check = true

# Make Ruby 2.4 preserve the timezone of the receiver when calling `to_time`.
# Previous versions had false.
ActiveSupport.to_time_preserves_timezone = true

# Require `belongs_to` associations by default. Previous versions had false.
Rails.application.config.active_record.belongs_to_required_by_default = true

# Do not halt callback chains when a callback returns false. Previous versions had true.
ActiveSupport.halt_callback_chains_on_return_false = false

# Configure SSL options to enable HSTS with subdomains. Previous versions had false.
Rails.application.config.ssl_options = { hsts: { subdomains: true } }
```

1.3.9 `config/initializers/session_store.rb`

Rails session cookies are encrypted by default using something called an encrypted cookie store. The `session_store.rb` initializer configures the session store of the application, by setting its session store type and key.

```
Rails.application.config.session_store :cookie_store,
  key: '_example_session'
```

The session cookies are signed using the `secret_key_base` set in the `config/secrets.yml` configuration file. If you are really paranoid, you can change the secret key in `config/secrets.yml` or run `rake secret` to generate a new one automatically.

1.3.10 `config/initializers/wrap_parameters.rb`

Introduced in Rails 3.1, the `wrap_parameters.rb` initializer configures your application to work with many JavaScript frameworks out of the box.

```
# Be sure to restart your server when you modify this file.

# This file contains settings for ActionController::ParamsWrapper which
# is enabled by default.

# Enable parameter wrapping for JSON. You can disable this by setting
# :format to an empty array.
ActiveSupport.on_load(:action_controller) do
  wrap_parameters format: [:json]
end

# To enable root element in JSON for ActiveRecord objects.
# ActiveSupport.on_load(:active_record) do
#   self.include_root_in_json = true
# end
```

When submitting JSON parameters to a controller, Rails will *wrap* the parameters into a nested hash, with the controller's name being set as the key. In that way, the controller can treat JavaScript clients and HTML forms identically.

To illustrate, consider the following JSON:

```
{"title": "The Rails 4 Way"}
```

If a client submitted the preceding JSON to a controller named `ArticlesController`, Rails would nest the `params` hash under the key "article". This ensures the setting of model attributes from request parameters is consistent with the convention used when submitting from Rails form helpers.

```
{"title": "The Rails 4 Way", "article" => {"title": "The Rails 4 Way"}}
```

1.4 Other Common Initializers

While the following settings are not included in the Rails boilerplate, we feel they are sufficiently common as to be worth mentioning.

1.4.1 Time Zones

The default time zone for Rails applications is UTC. If the business domain of your application is sensitive to knowing exactly what time zone the server is in, add an initializer script with the following setting to override the default:

```
# Set Time.zone default to the specified zone and make Active Record
# auto-convert to this zone.
# Run "rake -D time" for a list of tasks for finding time zone names.
config.time_zone = 'Central Time (US & Canada)'
```

💬 Juanito says . . .

`rake time:zones:all` will list all the time zones Rails knows about.

1.4.2 Localization

Rails features localization support via locale files, behavior that is covered in great detail in Chapter 11, "All about Helpers," in the "TranslationHelper and I18n API" section.

The default locale is `:en`. Both it and the location of your locale files can be overridden in an initializer.

```
config.i18n.default_locale = :de
config.i18n.load_path += Dir[Rails.root.join('config','sprechen','*.{rb,yml}')]
```

1.4.3 Generator Default Settings

Rails generator scripts make certain assumptions about your tool chain. Setting the correct values here means having to type fewer parameters on the command line.

For instance, to use RSpec without fixtures and Haml as the template engine, our settings would look like the following:

```
# Configure generators values. Many other options are available,
# be sure to check the documentation.
config.generators do |g|
  g.template_engine :haml
  g.test_framework :rspec, fixture: false
end
```

Note that RubyGems such as `rspec-rails` and `factory_girl_rails` handle this particular configuration for you automatically.

1.4.4   Load Path Modifications

By default, Rails looks for code in a number of standard directories, including all nested directories under app, such as app/models. This is referred to collectively as the load path. It's exceedingly rare to need to do so, but it is possible to add other directories to the load path using the following code:

```
# Custom directories with classes and modules you want to be autoloadable
# config.autoload_paths += %W(#{config.root}/extras)
```

In case you didn't know, the `%W` functions as a whitespace-delimited array literal and is used quite often in the Rails codebase for convenience.

1.4.5   Log-Level Override

The default log level is `:debug`, and you can override it if necessary.

```
# Force all environments to use the same logger level
# (by default production uses :info, the others :debug)
config.log_level = :debug
```

This book covers use of the Rails logger in-depth later on in this chapter.

1.4.6   Schema Dumper

Every time you run tests, Rails dumps the schema of your development database and copies it to the test database using an auto-generated schema.rb script. It looks very similar to an Active Record migration script; in fact, it uses the same API.

You might find it necessary to revert to the older style of dumping the schema using SQL, if you're doing things that are incompatible with the schema dumper code (see the comment).

```
# Use SQL instead of Active Record's schema dumper when creating the
# test database. This is necessary if your schema can't be completely
# dumped by the schema dumper, for example, if you have constraints
# or db-specific column types
config.active_record.schema_format = :sql
```

1.4.7   Console

It's possible to supply a block to `console` to be evaluated when the Rails environment is loaded via the terminal. This enables you to set console-specific configurations. I like saving some typing with helper methods like this one.

```
console do
  def obie
    User.where(email: "obiefernandez@gmail.com").first
  end
end
```

1.5   Spring Application Preloader

Rails ships with an application preloader named Spring.[9] Unless you disable it, during development your application process will keep running in the background continuously. This speeds up development by eliminating the need to boot up Rails *from scratch* every time you execute tests or run a `rake` task.

While running, Spring monitors folders `config` and `initializers` for changes. If a file within those folders is changed, Spring will automatically restart your application. Spring will also restart if any gem dependencies are changed during development.

To demonstrate the speed increase Spring provides, let's run the same `rake` task in both Rails 4.0 and and a preloaded 4.1 application:

```
# Rails 4.0
$ time bin/rake about
  ...
  bin/rake about 1.20s user 0.36s system 22% cpu 6.845 total

# Rails 4.1
$ time bin/rake about
```

---

9. https://github.com/rails/spring

```
  . . .
  bin/rake about  0.08s user 0.04s system 32% cpu 0.370 total
```

The preloaded Rails environment using Spring provided a savings of over 6 seconds. Those kinds of time savings can add up, especially if you practice TDD.

You can tweak settings for files that Spring monitors for reloading behavior in `config/spring.rb`

```
%w(
  .ruby-version
  .rbenv-vars
  tmp/restart.txt
  tmp/caching-dev.txt
).each { |path| Spring.watch(path) }

-
```

Remember we said that the value of the `RAILS_ENV` environment variable dictates which additional environment settings are loaded next? So now let's review the default settings for each of Rails' standard modes.

1.6   Development Mode

Development is Rails' default mode and the one in which you will spend most of your time as a developer. This section contains an in-depth explanation of each setting in `config/environments/development.rb`.

```
Rails.application.configure do
  # Settings specified here will take precedence over those in
  # config/application.rb.
```

Note that configuration settings specified in these environment scripts also take precedence over those set in initializers.

1.6.1   Automatic Class Reloading

One of the signature benefits of using Rails is the quick feedback cycle offered by its development mode. Make changes to your code, hit Reload in the browser, and like magic, the changes are reflected in your application. This behavior is governed by the `config.cache_classes` setting:

```
# In the development environment your application's code is reloaded on
# every request. This slows down response time but is perfect for
# development since you don't have to restart the web server when you
```

```
# make code changes.
config.cache_classes = false
```

Without getting into too much nitty-gritty detail, when the `config.cache_classes` setting is `true`, Rails will use Ruby's `require` statement to do its class loading, and when it is `false`, it will use `load` instead.

When you require a Ruby file, the interpreter executes and caches it. If the file is required again (as in subsequent requests), the interpreter ignores the require statement and moves on. When you load a Ruby file, the interpreter executes the file again, no matter how many times it has been loaded before.

Now it's time to examine the Rails class-loading behavior a bit more in depth, because sometimes you won't be able to get certain things to reload automatically, and it will drive you crazy unless you understand how class loading works!

1.6.1.1   The Rails Class Loader

In plain old Ruby, a script file doesn't need to be named in any particular way that matches its contents. In Rails, however, you'll notice that there's almost always a direct correlation between the name of a Ruby file and the class or module contained within. Rails takes advantage of the fact that Ruby provides a callback mechanism for missing constants. When Rails encounters an undefined constant in the code, it uses a class loader routine based on file-naming conventions to find and require the needed Ruby script.

How does the class loader know where to search? Rails has the concept of load paths, and the default load paths include the base directories of just about anywhere you would think of adding code to your Rails application.

Want to see the contents of your project's load path? Just fire up the console and type `$LOAD_PATH`.

```
$ rails console
Loading development environment.
>> $LOAD_PATH
=> ["/usr/local/lib/ruby/... # about 20 lines of output
```

I snipped the console output to save space. A typical Rails project load path will usually have 60 or more items in its load path. Try it and see.

1.6.1.2 Rails, Modules, and Auto-Loading Code

Normally in Ruby, when you want to include code from another file in your application, you have to include a require statement. However, Rails enhances Ruby's default behavior by establishing a simple convention that enables Rails to automatically load your code in most cases. If you've used the Rails console at all, you've already seen this behavior in action: You never have to explicitly `require` anything!

This is how it works: If Rails encounters a class or module in your code that is not already defined, Rails uses the following convention to guess which files it should require to load that module or class.

If the class or module is not nested, insert an underscore between the constant's names and require a file of this name. For example,

- `EstimationCalculator` becomes `require "estimation_calculator"`.

- `KittTurboBoost` becomes `require "kitt_turbo_boost"`.

If the class or module is nested, Rails inserts an underscore between each of the containing modules and requires a file in the corresponding set of subdirectories. For example,

- `MacGyver::SwissArmyKnife` becomes `require "mac_gyver/swiss_army_knife"`.

- `Example::ReallyRatherDeeply::NestedClass` becomes `require "example/really_rather_deeply/nested_class"` and if not already loaded, Rails would expect to find it in a file called `nested_class.rb`, in a directory called `really_rather_deeply`, itself in the directory `example` which can be found somewhere in Ruby's load path (e.g., one of the `app` subdirectories, `lib`, or a plugin's `lib` directory).

The bottom line is that you should rarely need to explicitly load Ruby code in your Rails applications (using `require`) if you follow the naming conventions.[10]

---

10. If you want to learn more about this topic, Benjamin Fleischer has written about using Rails-style `autoload` versus `require` versus `require_relative` at http://www.benjaminfleischer.com/2013/07/18/ruby-requires-confusion/.

1.6.2   Eager Load

To speed up the boot time of starting a Rails server during development, your project code and libraries are not eager loaded into memory. Instead, they are loaded on an as-needed basis (aka "lazy-loading"). This behavior is governed by the `config.eager_load` setting:

```
# Do not eager load code on boot.
config.eager_load = false
```

In your production environment, you will want this set to `true`, as it copies most of your application into memory. This provides a performance increase to web servers that copy on write, such as Unicorn.

1.6.3   Error Reports

Requests from localhost, like when you're developing, generate useful error messages that include debugging information such as a line number where the error occurred and a backtrace. Setting `consider_all_requests_local` to true causes Rails to display those developer-friendly error screens even when the machine making the request is remote. This is admittedly a bit of an edge-case.

```
config.consider_all_requests_local = true
```

1.6.4   Caching

You normally do not want caching behavior when you're in development mode. The only time you do want it is if you're actually testing caching, and we discuss that at length in Chapter 17, "Caching and Performance."

```
# Enable/disable caching. By default caching is disabled.
if Rails.root.join('tmp/caching-dev.txt').exist?
  config.action_controller.perform_caching = true
  config.cache_store = :memory_store
  config.public_file_server.headers = {
    'Cache-Control' => 'public, max-age=172800'
  }
else
  config.action_controller.perform_caching = false
  config.cache_store = :null_store
end
```

In earlier versions of Rails, you merely set the `perform_caching` property to `true` or `false`. Now, as you can see in the code listing, caching behavior is determined by the presence of `tmp/caching-dev.txt`. This is done this way to help ensure that you don't accidentally leave caching on. Unexpected caching behavior can be subtle and tricky to diagnose.

1.6.5 Action Mailer Settings

Rails assumes that you don't want Action Mailer to raise delivery exceptions in development mode, so based on the `config.action_mailer.raise_delivery_errors` settings, it will swallow those exceptions. That's fine because mailing capabilities don't necessarily work in an average development workstation, particularly on Windows and other platforms that lack `sendmail`.

```
# Don't care if the mailer can't send.
config.action_mailer.raise_delivery_errors = false
```

If you actually want to send mail while in development mode as part of debugging or ad-hoc testing, then you probably should toggle this setting to `true`.

💬 Xavier says . . .

I find it handy to set `config.action_mailer.perform_deliveries = false` in development. No delivery attempt is performed, but you can still see the mail in the log file to check that it looks good, copy account activation URLs, etc.

```
config.action_mailer.perform_caching = false
```

This line of code should probably be part of the caching section. Setting it to `true` tells Action Mailer to not ignore `cache` methods called in mailer view templates.

1.6.6 Deprecation Notices

Deprecations warnings are very useful for lettting you know when you should stop using a particular piece of functionality. The configuration setting `config.active_support.deprecation` enables you to set how you would like to receive deprecation warnings. In development mode, by default all deprecation warnings will appear in the development log.

```
# Print deprecation notices to the Rails logger.
config.active_support.deprecation = :log
```

1.6.7   Pending Migrations Error Page

In previous versions of Rails, if pending migrations needed to be run, the web server would fail to start. As of Rails 4, a new error page is displayed instead, indicating to developers that they should run `rake db:migrate RAILS_ENV=development` to resolve the issue.

```
# Raise an error on page load if there are pending migrations
config.active_record.migration_error = :page_load
```

1.6.8   Assets Debug Mode

Rails 3.1 introduced us to the Asset Pipeline, a framework to concatenate and minify JavaScript and other static assets. By default in development mode, JavaScript and CSS files are served separately in the order they were specified in their respective manifest files. Setting `config.assets.debug` to `false` would result in Sprockets concatenating and running preprocessors on all assets, making it a lot harder to debug errors when they occur.

```
# Debug mode disables concatenation and preprocessing of assets.
config.assets.debug = true

# Suppress logger output for asset requests.
config.assets.quiet = true
```

Development mode also omits logger output for asset requests, because they aren't normally very useful. You can turn them on here for debugging if necessary.

1.6.9   Missing Translations

Rails views normally just print the key for missing translations, since that's what you want when you're developing prior to translation activities taking place.

```
# Raises error for missing translations
# config.action_view.raise_on_missing_translations = true
```

This property is uncommented in test mode, which we're about to cover.

1.7   Test Mode

Whenever you run Rails in test mode, that is, the value of the `RAILS_ENV` environment value is `test`, then the following settings are in effect (`config/environments/test.rb` reproduced here for reference purposes):

```
Rails.application.configure do
  # Settings specified here will take precedence over those in
  # config/application.rb.

  # The test environment is used exclusively to run your application's
  # test suite. You never need to work with it otherwise. Remember that
  # your test database is "scratch space" for the test suite and is wiped
  # and recreated between test runs. Don't rely on the data there!
  config.cache_classes = true

  # Do not eager load code on boot. This avoids loading your whole
  # application just for the purpose of running a single test. If you
  # are using a tool that preloads Rails for running tests, you may
  # have to set it to true.
  config.eager_load = false

  # Configure public file server for tests with Cache-Control for performance
  config.public_file_server.enabled = true
  config.public_file_server.headers = {
    'Cache-Control' => 'public, max-age=3600'
  }

  # Show full error reports and disable caching.
  config.consider_all_requests_local       = true
  config.action_controller.perform_caching = false

  # Raise exceptions instead of rendering exception templates.
  config.action_dispatch.show_exceptions = false

  # Disable request forgery protection in the test environment.
  config.action_controller.allow_forgery_protection = false
  config.action_mailer.perform_caching = false

  # Tell Action Mailer not to deliver emails to the real world.
  # The :test delivery method accumulates sent emails in the
  # ActionMailer::Base.deliveries array.
  config.action_mailer.delivery_method = :test

  # Print deprecation notices to the stderr.
  config.active_support.deprecation = :stderr

  # Raises error for missing translations
  # config.action_view.raise_on_missing_translations = true
end
```

Most people get by without ever needing to modify their test environment settings.

ⓘ Custom Environments

If necessary, you can create additional environments for your Rails app to run by cloning one of the existing environment files in the `config/environments` directory of your application. The most common use case for custom environments is in setting up additional production configurations, such as for staging and QA deployments. Do you have access to the production database from your development workstation? Then a triage environment might make sense. Use the normal environment settings for development mode, but point its database connection to a production database server. It's a potentially life-saving combination when you need to quickly diagnose issues in production.

1.8 Production Mode

Finally, production mode is what you want your Rails application running in whenever it is deployed to its hosting environment and serving public requests. There are a number of significant ways that production mode differs from the other modes, not least of which is the speed boost you get from not reloading all of your application classes for every request.

Here is `config/environments/production.rb`:

```
Rails.application.configure do
  # Settings specified here will take precedence over those in
  # config/application.rb.

  # Code is not reloaded between requests.
  config.cache_classes = true

  # Eager load code on boot. This eager loads most of Rails and
  # your application in memory, enabling both threaded web servers
  # and those relying on copy on write to perform better.
  # Rake tasks automatically ignore this option for performance.
  config.eager_load = true

  # Full error reports are disabled and caching is turned on.
  config.consider_all_requests_local       = false
  config.action_controller.perform_caching = true

  # Disable serving static files from the `/public` folder by default since
  # Apache or NGINX already handles this.
  config.public_file_server.enabled = ENV['RAILS_SERVE_STATIC_FILES'].present?

  # Compress JavaScripts and CSS.
```

```
config.assets.js_compressor = :uglifier
# config.assets.css_compressor = :sass

# Do not fall back to the assets pipeline if a precompiled asset is missed.
config.assets.compile = false

# `config.assets.precompile` and `config.assets.version` have moved to
# config/initializers/assets.rb.

# Enable serving of images, stylesheets, and JavaScripts from an asset server.
# config.action_controller.asset_host = 'http://assets.example.com'

# Specifies the header that your server uses for sending files.
# config.action_dispatch.x_sendfile_header = 'X-Sendfile' # for Apache
# config.action_dispatch.x_sendfile_header = 'X-Accel-Redirect' # for NGINX

# Mount Action Cable outside main process or domain
# config.action_cable.mount_path = nil
# config.action_cable.url = 'wss://example.com/cable'
# config.action_cable.allowed_request_origins = [ 'http://example.com',
# /http:\/\/example.*/ ]

# Force all access to the app over SSL, use Strict-Transport-Security, and
# use secure cookies.
# config.force_ssl = true

# Use the lowest log level to ensure availability of diagnostic information
# when problems arise
config.log_level = :debug

# Prepend all log lines with the following tags.
config.log_tags = [ :request_id ]

# Use a different cache store in production.
# config.cache_store = :mem_cache_store

# Use a real queuing backend for Active Job (and separate queues per
# environment)
# config.active_job.queue_adapter     = :resque
# config.active_job.queue_name_prefix = "auction_#{Rails.env}"
config.action_mailer.perform_caching = false

# Ignore bad email addresses and do not raise email delivery errors.
# Set this to true and configure the email server for immediate
# delivery to raise delivery errors.
# config.action_mailer.raise_delivery_errors = false

# Enable locale fallbacks for I18n (makes lookups for any locale fall
# back to the I18n.default_locale when a translation cannot be found).
```

```
config.i18n.fallbacks = true

# Send deprecation notices to registered listeners.
config.active_support.deprecation = :notify

# Use default logging formatter so that PID and timestamp are not suppressed.
config.log_formatter = ::Logger::Formatter.new

# Use a different logger for distributed setups.
# require 'syslog/logger'
# config.logger = ActiveSupport::TaggedLogging.new(Syslog::Logger.new
# 'app-name')

if ENV["RAILS_LOG_TO_STDOUT"].present?
  logger           = ActiveSupport::Logger.new(STDOUT)
  logger.formatter = config.log_formatter
  config.logger = ActiveSupport::TaggedLogging.new(logger)
end

# Do not dump schema after migrations.
config.active_record.dump_schema_after_migration = false
end
```

1.8.1   Assets

In production mode, assets are by default precompiled by the Asset Pipeline. All files included in `application.js` and `application.css` asset manifests are compressed and concatenated into their respective files of the same name, located in the `public/assets` folder.

If an asset is requested that does not exist in the `public/assets` folder, Rails will throw an exception. To enable live asset compilation fallback on production, set `config.assets.compile` to `true`.

The `application.js` and `application.css` manifest files are the only JavaScript/Stylesheets included during the Asset Pipeline precompile step. To include additional assets, specify them using the `config.assets.precompile` configuration setting.

```
config.assets.precompile += %w( admin.css )
```

1.8.2   Asset Hosts

By default, Rails links to assets on the current host in the public folder, but you can direct Rails to link to assets from a dedicated asset server. The `config.action_controller.asset_host` setting is covered in detail in Chapter 11, "All about Helpers," in the "Using Asset Hosts" section.

1.9   Configuring a Database

The file `database.yml` found in the `config` folder specifies all the configuration settings required by Active Record to connect to a database. When a new application is bootstrapped, Rails automatically generates boilerplate sections for each environment.

The following is an example of a generated `config/database.yml` file configured to work with PostgreSQL:

```
default: &default
  adapter: postgresql
  encoding: unicode
  pool: 5
  username: example
  password:

development:
  <<: *default
  database: example_development

  # Connect on a TCP socket. Omitted by default since the client uses a
  # domain socket that doesn't need configuration. Windows does not have
  # domain sockets, so uncomment these lines.
  # host: localhost

  # The TCP port the server listens on. Defaults to 5432.
  # If your server runs on a different port number, change accordingly.
  #port: 5432

  # Schema search path. The server defaults to $user,public.
  #schema_search_path: myapp,sharedapp,public

  # Minimum log levels, in increasing order:
  #   debug5, debug4, debug3, debug2, debug1,
  #   log, notice, warning, error, fatal, and panic
  # Defaults to warning.
  #min_messages: notice

# Warning: The database defined as "test" will be erased and
# re-generated from your development database when you run "rake".
# Do not set this db to the same as development or production.
test:
  <<: *default
  database: example_test

production:
  <<: *default
```

```
database: example_production
```

An old best practice within the Rails community has been not to store `config/database.yml` in version control. First and foremost, if a hacker gained access to the application repository, they would have all the connection settings to your production database. Secondly, developers on the team could potentially have different development and test database settings. New to Rails 4.1 is the capability to configure Active Record with an environment variable `DATABASE_URL`. This allows each developer working on the project to have their own copy of `config/database.yml` that is not stored in version control. The production environment of the Rails application would just need to have `DATABASE_URL` set with a valid connection string to be configured correctly.

1.10   Configuring Application Secrets

There is also a `secrets.yml` file found within the `config` folder. This file is meant to store your application's sensitive data, such as access keys and passwords that are required for external APIs. At a minimum, Rails requires that `secret_key_base` is set for each environment of your application. This is the property that used to be set in the `secret_token.rb` initializer in older versions of Rails.

```
# config/secrets.yml

# Be sure to restart your server when you modify this file.

# Your secret key is used for verifying the integrity of signed cookies.
# If you change this key, all old signed cookies will become invalid!

# Make sure the secret is at least 30 characters and all random,
# no regular words or you'll be exposed to dictionary attacks.
# You can use `rake secret` to generate a secure secret key.

# Make sure the secrets in this file are kept private
# if you're sharing your code publicly.

development:
  secret_key_base: 7aed4bcb28...

test:
  secret_key_base: a4b717a2a8...

production:
  secret_key_base: 39a63892bd...
```

💬 Kevin says . . .

I would strongly advise not storing any production secret values in version control. Like `database.yml`, if a hacker gained access to the application repository, they could use these values to exploit your application. Instead, set all production secret values to environment variables. The environment variables will only be set on your production machine.

```
# config/secrets.yml
...
production:
  secret_key_base: <%= ENV['SECRET_KEY_BASE'] %>
```

A hash of all the secrets defined in `config/secrets.yml` can be accessed via `Rails.application.secrets`.

```
>> Rails.application.secrets
=> {:secret_key_base=>"7aed4bcb28..."}
   To access a specific secrets, pass X to
```

An accessor for each secret key is also provided. For example, to access the secret for `secret_key_base`, invoke `Rails.application.secrets.secret_key_base`. This will return the value of `secret_key_base` for the current environment.

```
>> Rails.env
=> "development"
>> Rails.application.secrets.secret_key_base
=> "7aed4bcb28..."
```

Secret Token

Certain types of hacking involve modifying the contents of cookies without the server knowing about it. By digitally signing all cookies sent to the browser, Rails can detect whether they were tampered with. Rails signs cookies using the value of `secret_key_base`, found in `config/secrets.yml`, which is randomly generated along with your app.

1.11 Logging

Most programming contexts in Rails (models, controllers, view templates) have a `logger` attribute, which holds a reference to a logger conforming to the interface of `Log4r` or the default Ruby 1.8+ `Logger` class. Can't get a reference to `logger`

Config

somewhere in your code? The `Rails.logger` method references a logger that you can use anywhere.

It's really easy to create a new `Logger` in Ruby, as shown in the following example:

```
$ pry
> require 'logger'
=> true

> logger = Logger.new STDOUT
=> #<Logger:0x00000106c795f0 @progname=nil, @level=0, ...>

> logger.warn "do not want!!!"
W, [2013-11-02T18:34:30.281003 #54844]  WARN -- : do not want!!!
=> true

> logger.info "in your logger, giving info"
I, [2013-11-02T18:34:57.186636 #54844]  INFO -- : in your logger, giving info
=> true
```

Typically, you add a message to the log using the logger whenever the need arises, using a method corresponding to the severity of the log message. The standard logger's severities are (in increasingly severe order):

debug Use the debug level to capture data and application state useful for debugging problems later on. This level is not usually captured in production logs.

info Use info level to capture informational messages. I like to use this log level for time-stamping non-ordinary events that are still within the bounds of good application behavior.

warn Use the warn level to capture things that are out of the ordinary and might be worth investigating. Sometimes I'll throw in a logged warning when guard clauses in my code keep a client from doing something they weren't supposed to do. My goal is to alert whoever's maintaining the application about a malicious user or bug in the user interface, as in the following example:

```
def create
  begin
    group.add_member(current_user)
    flash[:notice] = "Successfully joined #{scene.display_name}"
  rescue ActiveRecord::RecordInvalid
    flash[:error] = "You are already a member of #{group.name}"
    logger.warn "A user tried to join a group twice. UI should
                 not have allowed it."
```

```
    end

    redirect_back(fallback_location: group_path)
  end
```

error Use the error log level to capture information about error conditions that don't require a server restart.

fatal The worst-case imaginable has happened—your application is now dead and manual intervention is necessary to restart it.

1.11.1   Rails Log Files

The log folder of your Rails application holds three log files corresponding to each of the standard environments. Log files can grow very large over time. A rake task is provided for easily clearing the log files:

```
$ rake log:clear # Truncates all *.log files in log/ to zero bytes
```

The contents of log/development.log are very useful while you're working. Many Rails coders leave a terminal window open with a continuous tail of the development log open while they're coding:

```
$ tail -f log/development.log

  Article Load (0.2ms)  SELECT "articles".* FROM "articles" WHERE
    "articles"."id" = $1 LIMIT 1  [["id", "1"]]
```

All sorts of valuable information is available in the development log. For instance, every time you make a request, a bunch of useful information about it shows up in the log. Here's a sample from one of my projects.

```
Started GET "/userphotos/1" for 127.0.0.1 at 2007-06-06 17:43:13
  Processing by UserPhotosController#show as HTML
  Parameters: {"/users/8-Obie-Fernandez/photos/406"=>nil,
  "action"=>"show", "id"=>"406", "controller"=>"userphotos",
  "user_id"=>"8-Obie-Fernandez"}
  User Load (0.4ms) SELECT * FROM users WHERE (users.'id' = 8)
  Photo Load (0.9ms) SELECT * FROM photos WHERE (photos.'id' = 406
  AND (photos.resource_id = 8 AND photos.resource_type = 'User'))
  CACHE (0.0ms) SELECT * FROM users WHERE (users.'id' = 8)
Rendered adsense/_medium_rectangle (1.5ms)
  User Load (0.5ms) SELECT * FROM users WHERE (users.'id' = 8)
  LIMIT 1
  SQL (0.4ms) SELECT count(*) AS count_all FROM messages WHERE
  (messages.receiver_id = 8 AND (messages.'read' = 0))
Rendered layouts/_header (25.3ms)
```

```
Rendered adsense/_leaderboard (0.4ms)
Rendered layouts/_footer (0.8ms)
Rendered photos/show.html.erb within layouts/application.html.erb (38.9ms)
Completed in 99ms (Views: 37.4ms | ActiveRecord: 12.3ms) with 200
```

This is a list of all the data items contained in that chunk of log output:

- The controller and action that were invoked

- The remote IP address of the computer making the request

- A timestamp indicating when the request happened

- The session ID associated with the request

- The hash of parameters associated with the request

- Database request information including the time and the SQL statement executed

- Query cache hit info including time and the SQL statement triggering results from the cache instead of a roundtrip to the database

- Rendering information for each template involved in rendering the view output and time consumed by each

- Total time used in completing the request with corresponding request-per-second figures

- Analysis of the time spent in database operations versus rendering

- The HTTP status code and URL of the response sent back to the client

1.11.2 Tagged Logging

Log files can contain an extensive amount of information, making tracking down issues or particular requests difficult. To alleviate this issue, Rails 3.2 introduced the capability to prepend information to each of your log messages.

To add "tagged" information to your logs, pass an array of one or many method names that respond to the `request` object to the `config.log_tags` configuration setting.

To illustrate, assuming we want to track the subdomain that each request is made from; we can achieve this by setting `config.log_tags` to `[:subdomain]`. When Rails writes to the log, it will prefix the output of `request.subdomain`, resulting in a log message like the following:

```
[some_subdomain] Started GET "/articles" for 127.0.0.1 at 2013-02-01 11:49:09 -0500
```

1.11.3   Log File Analysis

A number of informal analyses can be easily performed using just the development log output and some common sense.

Performance   One of the more obvious analyses would be a study of the performance of your application. The faster your requests execute, the more requests you can serve with a given Rails process. That's why performance figures are often expressed in terms of requests per second. Find the queries and rendering sections that are taking a long time and figure out why.

It's important to realize that the times reported by the logger are not super-accurate. In fact, they're wrong more often than not, if simply for the reason that it's very difficult to measure the timing of something from within itself. Add up the percentage of rendering and database times for any given request and it will not always be close to 100%.

However, despite not being accurate in a purely objective sense, the reported times are perfect for making subjective comparisons within the same application. They give you a way of gauging whether an action is taking longer than it used to or whether it is relatively faster or slower than another action, and so on.

SQL queries   Active Record not behaving as expected? The fact that SQL generated by Active Record is logged can often help you debug problems caused by complicated queries.

Identification of N+1 select problems   Whenever you are displaying a record along with an associated collection of records, there's a chance that you will have a so-called N+1 select problem. You'll recognize the problem by a series of many SELECT statements, with the only difference being the value of the primary key.

For example, here's a snippet of some log output from a real Rails application showing an N+1 select issue in the way that FlickrPhoto instances are being loaded:

```
FlickrPhoto Load (1.3ms) SELECT * FROM flickr_photos WHERE
(flickr_photos.resource_id = 15749 AND flickr_photos.resource_type =
'Place' AND (flickr_photos.'profile' = 1)) ORDER BY updated_at desc
LIMIT 1
FlickrPhoto Load (1.7ms) SELECT * FROM flickr_photos WHERE
(flickr_photos.resource_id = 15785 AND flickr_photos.resource_type =
'Place' AND (flickr_photos.'profile' = 1)) ORDER BY updated_at desc
LIMIT 1
FlickrPhoto Load (1.4ms) SELECT * FROM flickr_photos WHERE
```

Config

```
(flickr_photos.resource_id = 15831 AND flickr_photos.resource_type =
'Place' AND (flickr_photos.'profile' = 1)) ORDER BY updated_at desc
LIMIT 1
```

and so on and so forth, for pages and pages of log output. Look familiar?

Luckily, each of those database queries is executing very quickly, around 0.0015 seconds each. That's because 1) MySQL is extraordinarily fast for small SELECT statements and 2) my Rails process is on the same physical machine as the database.

Still, accumulate enough of those N queries and they add up quickly to eat away at performance. Absent the mitigating factors I mentioned, I would have a serious performance problem to address. The problem would be especially severe if the database was on a separate machine, giving me network latency to deal with on each of those queries.

N+1 select issues are not the end of the world. A lot of times all it takes is proper use of the includes method on a particular query to alleviate the problem.

ℹ Separation of Concerns

A well-designed model-view-controller application follows certain protocols related to which logical tier does database operations (that would be the model) versus rendering tasks (the view). Generally speaking, you want your controller to cause the loading of all of the data that is going to be needed for rendering from the database. In Rails, it is accomplished by controller code that queries the model for needed data and makes that data available to the view.

Database access during rendering is usually considered a bad practice. Calling database methods directly from template code violates proper separation of concerns and is a maintainability nightmare.[11]

However, there are plenty of opportunities for implicit database access during view rendering to creep into your codebase, encapsulated by the model, and perhaps triggered by lazy loading of associations. Can we conclusively call it a bad practice? It's hard to say so definitively. There are cases (such as usage of fragment caching) where it makes sense to have database operations happening during view rendering.

---

11. Practically every PHP application ever written has this problem.

ⓘ Using Alternate Logging Schemes

It's easy! Just assign a class compatible with Ruby's Logger to one of the various `logger` class variables, such as `ActiveRecord::Base.logger`. A quick hack based on the capability to swap loggers is one demonstrated by David at various events, including his keynote at Railsconf 2007. During a console session, assign a new `Logger` instance pointing to `STDOUT` to `ActiveRecord::Base.logger` in order to see the SQL being generated right in your console. Jamis has a complete write-up of the technique and more at http://weblog.jamisbuck.org/2007/1/31/more-on-watching -activerecord.

1.11.4 `Rails::Subscriber.colorize_logging`

This tells Rails whether to use ANSI codes to colorize the logging statements. The colors make it much easier to read the logs (except on Windows) and may complicate matters if you use software like syslog. Defaults to `true`. Change to `false` if you view your logs with software that doesn't understand the ANSI color codes.

Here's a snippet of log output with the ANSI codes visible:

```
^[[4;36;1mSQL (0.0ms)^[[0m  ^[[0;1mMysql::Error: Unknown table
'expense_reports': DROP TABLE expense_reports^[[0m
  ^[[4;35;1mSQL (3.2ms)^[[0m  ^[[0mCREATE TABLE expense_reports ('id'
int(11) DEFAULT NULL auto_increment PRIMARY KEY, 'user_id' int(11))
```

💬 Wilson says . . .

Almost nobody I meet seems to know how to display colorized logs in a pager. The -R option tells `less` to output "raw" control characters to the screen.

ⓘ Syslog

UNIX-like systems have a system service called `syslog`. For various reasons, it might be a better choice for production logging of your Rails applications.

- Finer-grained control over logging levels and content.
- Consolidation of logger output for multiple Rails applications.
- If you're using remote syslog capabilities of many systems, consolidation of logger output for multiple Rails application servers is possible. Contrast this with having to handle individual log files on each application server box separately.

You can use Eric Hodel's SyslogLogger[12] to interface your Rails application to `syslog`.

1.12   Conclusion

We've kicked off our Rails journey by covering Bundler in fairly good detail and then reviewing Rails initialization step-by-step, along with the different environments in which Rails executes and how it loads its dependencies, including your application code. An in-depth look at Rails mode variants revealed how we can customize Rails behavior to our taste.

Next up we delve into one of the configuration files that we skipped over in this section, the one that controls what URLs will be available in your Rails-based web application: `config/routes.rb`.

---

12. http://docs.seattlerb.org/SyslogLogger

CHAPTER 2

Routing

I dreamed a thousand new paths . . . I woke and walked my old one.

—Chinese proverb

The routing system in Rails is the system that examines the URL of an incoming request and determines what action should be taken by the application. And it does a good bit more than that. Rails routing can be a bit of a tough nut to crack. But it turns out that most of the toughness resides in a small number of concepts. After you've got a handle on those, the rest falls into place nicely.

This chapter introduces you to the principal techniques for defining and manipulating routes. The next chapter builds on this knowledge, helping you to explore the facilities Rails offers in support of writing applications that comply with the principles of Representational State Transfer (REST). As you'll see, those facilities can be of tremendous use to you even if you're not planning to scale the heights of REST theorization. Both chapters assume at least a basic knowledge of the Model-View-Controller (MVC) pattern and Rails controllers.

Some of the examples in these two chapters are based on a small auction application. The examples are kept simple enough that they should be comprehensible on their own. The basic idea is that there are auctions and each auction involves auctioning off an item. There are users and they submit bids. That's it.

The triggering of a controller action is the main event in the life cycle of a connection to a Rails application. So it makes sense that the process by which Rails determines which controller and which action to execute must be very important. That process is embodied in the routing system.

The routing system maps URLs to actions. It does this by applying rules that you specify using a special syntax in the `config/routes.rb` file. Actually it's just plain Ruby code, but it uses special methods and parameters, a technique sometimes referred to as an internal domain-specific language (DSL). If you're using Rails generators, code gets added to the routes file automatically, and you'll get some reasonable behavior. But it doesn't take much work to write custom rules and reap the benefits of the flexibility of the routing system.

2.1   The Two Purposes of Routing

The routing system does two things: It maps requests to controller action methods, and it enables the dynamic generation of URLs for you to use as arguments to methods like `link_to` and `redirect_to`.

Each rule—or to use the more common term, route—specifies a pattern, which will be used both as a template for matching URLs and as a blueprint for creating them. The pattern can be generated automatically based on conventions, such as in the case of REST resources. Patterns can also contain a mixture of static substrings, forward slashes (mimicking URL syntax), and positional *segment key* parameters that serve as "receptors" for corresponding values in URLs.

A route can also include one or more hardcoded segment keys, in the form of key/value pairs accessible to controller actions in a hash via the `params` method. A couple of keys (`:controller` and `:action`) determine which controller and action gets invoked. Other keys present in the route definition simply get stashed for reference purposes.

Putting some flesh on the bones of this description, here's a sample route:

```
get 'recipes/:ingredient' => "recipes#index"
```

In this example, you find the following:

- static string (`recipes`)
- slash (`/`)
- segment key (`:ingredient`)
- controller action mapping (`"recipes#index"`)
- HTTP verb constraining method (`get`)

Routes have a pretty rich syntax—this one isn't by any means the most complex (nor the most simple)—because they have to do so much. A single route, like the one in this example, has to provide enough information both to match an existing URL and to manufacture a new one. The route syntax is engineered to address both of these processes.

2.2   The `routes.rb` File

Routes are defined in the file `config/routes.rb`, as shown in Listing 2.1. This file is created when you bootstrap a Rails application.

Listing 2.1   The default `routes.rb` file

```
Rails.application.routes.draw do
  # For details on the DSL available within this file,
  # see http://guides.rubyonrails.org/routing.html
end
```

The whole file consists of a single call to the method `draw` of `Rails.application.routes`, which takes a block.

At runtime, the block is evaluated inside of an instance of the class `ActionDispatch::Routing::Mapper`. Through it you configure the Rails routing system.

The routing system has to find a pattern match for a URL it's trying to recognize or a parameters match for a URL it's trying to generate. It does this by going through the routes in the order in which they're defined; that is, the order in which they appear in `routes.rb`. If a given route fails to match, the matching routine falls through to the next one. As soon as any route succeeds in providing the necessary match, the search ends.

The router code in Rails 5 is based on work by Aaron Patterson (aka Tenderlove) in https://github.com/rails/journey.

2.2.1   Regular Routes

The basic way to define a route is to supply a URL pattern plus a controller class/ action method mapping string with the special `:to` parameter.

```
get 'products/:id', to: 'products#show'
```

Since this is so common, a shorthand form is provided:

```
get 'products/:id' => 'products#show'
```

David has publicly commented on the design decision behind the shorthand form, when he said that it drew inspiration from two sources:[1]

> 1) the pattern we've been using in Rails since the beginning of referencing controllers as lowercase without the "Controller" part in `controller: "main"` declarations and 2) the Ruby pattern of signaling that you're talking about an instance method by using #. The influences are even part mixed. Main #index would be more confusing in my mind because it would hint that an object called Main actually existed, which it doesn't. MainController#index would just be a hassle to type out every time—exactly the same reason we went with `controller: "main"` versus `controller: "MainController"`. Given these constraints, I think `"main#index"` is by far the best alternative . . .

The information in this part of the chapter is mostly academic. You should be defining the vast majority of your routes in a RESTful fashion, as covered extensively in Chapter 3, "REST, Resources, and Rails."

2.2.2 Constraining Request Methods

As of Rails 4, it's recommended to limit the HTTP method used to access a route. If you are using the match directive to define a route, you accomplish this by using the `:via` option:

```
match 'products/:id' => 'products#show', via: :get
```

Rails provides a shorthand way of expressing this particular constraint, by replacing match with the desired HTTP method (get, post, patch, etc.).

```
get 'products/:id' => 'products#show'
post 'products' => 'products#create'
```

If, for some reason, you want to constrain a route to more than one HTTP method, you can pass :via an array of verb names.

```
match 'products/:id' => 'products#show', via: [:get, :post]
```

Defining a route without specifying an HTTP method will result in Rails raising a `RuntimeError` exception.

---

1. Full comments at http://yehudakatz.com/2009/12/26/the-rails-3-router-rack-it-up.

It used to be possible to make a route match *any* HTTP method by passing
:any to the :via option, but it was removed in favor of forcing the developer to
be more explicit. Note that providing that option doesn't error out or raise
a deprecation warning, it just sets your route to respond to a (non-existent)
ANY HTTP method.

```
match 'products' => 'products#index', via: :any
            # doesn't do what you think it does
```

2.2.3 URL Patterns

Keep in mind that there's no necessary correspondence between the number of
fields in the pattern string, the number of segment keys, and the fact that every connection needs a controller and an action. For example, you could write a route like

```
get ":id" => "products#show"
```

which would recognize a URL like

```
http://localhost:3000/8
```

The routing system would set the value of params[:id] in your controller action
to 8 (based on the position of the :id segment key, which matches the position of
8 in the URL), and it would execute the show action of the products controller.
Of course, this is a bit of a stingy route, in terms of visual information. On the other
hand, the following example route contains a static string, products/, inside the
URL pattern:

```
match 'products/:id' => 'products#show'
```

This string anchors the recognition process. Any URL that does not contain the
static string products/ in its leftmost slot will not match this route.

As for URL generation, static strings in the route simply get placed within the URL
that the routing system generates. The URL generator uses the route's pattern string
as the blueprint for the URL it generated. The pattern string stipulates the substring
products.

As we go, you should keep the dual purpose of recognition/generation in mind,
which is why it was mentioned several times so far. There are two principles that are
particularly useful to remember:

Routes

- The same rule governs both recognition and generation. The whole system is set up so that you don't have to write rules twice. You write each rule once, and the logic flows through it in both directions.

- The URLs that are generated by the routing system (via `link_to` and friends) only make sense to the routing system. The resulting URL, http://example .com/products/19201, contains not a shred of a clue as to what's supposed to happen when a user follows it—except insofar as it maps to a routing rule. The routing rule then provides the necessary information to trigger a controller action. Someone looking at the URL without knowing the routing rules won't know which controller and action the URL maps to.

2.2.4   Segment Keys

The URL pattern string can contain parameters (denoted with a colon) referred to as *segment keys*. In the following route declaration, `:id` is a segment key:

```
get 'products/:id' => 'products#show'
```

When this route matches a request URL, the `:id` portion of the pattern acts as a type of matcher, and picks up the value of that segment. For instance, using the same example, the value of id for the following URL would be `4`: `http://example .com/products/4`.

This route, when matched, will always take the visitor to the product controller's show action. You'll see techniques for matching controller and action based on segments of the URL shortly. The symbol `:id` inside the quoted pattern in the route is a segment key (that you can think of as a type of variable). Its job is to be latched onto by a value.

What that means in the example is that the value of `params[:id]` will be set to the string `"4"`. You can access that value inside your `products/show` action.

When you generate a URL, you have to supply values that will attach to the segment keys inside the URL pattern string. The simplest to understand (and original) way to do that is using a hash, like this:

```
link_to "Products",
  controller: "products",
  action: "show",
  id: 1
```

As you probably know, it's actually more common nowadays to generate URLs using what are called *named routes*, versus supplying the controller and action parameters explicitly in a hash. However, right now we're reviewing the basics of routing.

In the call to `link_to`, we've provided values for all three parameters of the route. Two of them are going to match the hard-coded, segment keys in the route; the third, `:id`, will be assigned to the corresponding segment key in the URL pattern.

It's vital to understand that the call to `link_to` doesn't *know* whether it's supplying hard-coded or segment values. It just knows (or hopes!) that these three values, tied to these three keys, will suffice to pinpoint a route and therefore a pattern string—and therefore a blueprint for generating a URL dynamically.

ℹ Hardcoded Parameters

It's always possible to insert additional hardcoded parameters into route definitions that don't have an effect on URL matching but are passed along with the normal expected `params`.

```
get 'products/special' => 'products#show', special: 'true'
```

Mind you, I'm not suggesting that this example is a good practice. It would make more sense to me (as a matter of style) to point at a different action rather than inserting a clause. Your mileage may vary.

```
get 'products/special' => 'products#special'
```

2.2.5   Spotlight on the `:id` Field

Note that the treatment of the `:id` field in the URL is not magic; it's just treated as a value with a name. If you wanted to, you could change the rule so that `:id` was `:blah` but then you'd have to do the following in your controller action:

```
@product = Product.find(params[:blah])
```

The name `:id` is simply a convention. It reflects the commonness of the case in which a given action needs access to a particular database record. The main business of the router is to determine the controller and action that will be executed.

The `id` field ends up in the `params` hash, already mentioned. In the common, classic case, you'd use the value provided to dig a record out of the database:

```
class ProductsController < ApplicationController
  def show
    @product = Product.find(params[:id])
  end
end
```

2.2.6   Optional Segment Keys

Rails 3 introduced a syntax for defining optional parts of the URL pattern. The easiest way to illustrate this syntax is by taking a look at the *legacy default controller route*, found in old versions of Rails at the bottom of a default `config/routes.rb` file:

```
match ':controller(/:action(/:id(.:format)))', via: :any
      # doesn't work in Rails 5
```

Note that parentheses are used to define optional segment keys, kind of like what you would expect to see when defining optional groups in a regular expression.

2.2.7   Defining Defaults

You can define default parameters in a route by supplying a hash for the `:defaults` option. This even applies to parameters that you do not specify as dynamic segments in the route itself.

```
get 'photos/:id', to: 'photos#show', defaults: {format: 'jpg'}
```

In the preceding example, Rails would match `http://example.com/photos/12` to the `show` action of `PhotosController`, and set `params[:format]` to `"jpg"`.

⚠ For security reasons, you cannot override defaults by changing the values in the params object.

2.2.8   Redirect Routes

It's possible to code a redirect directly into a route definition, using the redirect method:

```
get "/foo", to: redirect('/bar')
```

The argument to redirect can contain either a relative URL or a full URI.

```
get '/google', to: redirect('https://google.com/')
```

Rails lets you use a basic string interpolation in the supplied redirect argument to easily relay parameters, like this:

```
get 'docs/:article', to: redirect('/wiki/%{article}')
```

The `redirect` method can also take a block, which receives the request params as its argument. This enables you to, for instance, do quick versioning of web service API endpoints. Just remember that the do end syntax for the redirect block wouldn't work, as Ruby would pass the block to match instead of redirect. Use curly braces instead.[2]

```
match "/api/v1/:api",
  to: redirect { |params| "/api/v2/#{params[:api].pluralize}" },
  via: [:get, :post]
```

If you need it, the redirect method also accepts parameters, such as :status. (Rails uses a 301 status code for redirects by default.)

```
match "/api/v1/:api", to:
  redirect(status: 302) { |params| "/api/v2/#{params[:api].pluralize}" },
  via: [:get, :post]
```

All the other options that would work with a call to url_for will work with a redirect (:host, :port, etc.).

For example, it's possible to pass a path parameter, which in conjunction with a wildcard and interpolation, enables you to supply only the parts of the URL that need to change.

```
get 'stores/:name',        to: redirect(status: 302, path: '/%{name}')
get 'stores/:name(*all)', to: redirect(status: 302, path: '/%{name}%{all}')
```

Finally, an object that responds to call can be supplied as the last (or only) parameter to redirect, enabling you to encapsulate commonly used redirection code in objects. The call method must accept two arguments, params and request, and return a string.

```
get 'accounts/:name' => redirect(SubdomainRedirector.new('api'))
```

If you return a path without a leading slash, then the URL is prefixed with the current SCRIPT_NAME environment variable. This is typically a forward slash but may be different in a mounted engine or where the application is deployed to a subdirectory of a website.

2.2.9 The Format Segment

Let's revisit a legacy-style default route again:

---

2. Examples drawn from Yehuda Katz' excellent blog post about generic actions in Rails 3 routes at http://yehudakatz.com/2009/12/20/generic-actions-in-rails-3/.

Routes

```
get ':controller(/:action(/:id(.:format)))'
```

The `.:format` at the end matches a literal dot and a "format" segment key after the id field. That means it will match, for example, a URL like the following:

```
http://localhost:3000/products/show/3.json
```

Here, the value of `params[:format]` will be set to `json`. The `:format` field is also special; it has an effect inside the controller action. That effect is related to the behavior of a method called `respond_to`.

The `respond_to` method enables you to write your action so that it will return different results, depending on the requested format. Here's a `show` action for the products controller that offers either HTML or JSON:

```
def show
  @product = Product.find(params[:id])
  respond_to do |format|
    format.html
    format.json { render json: @product.to_json }
  end
end
```

The `respond_to` block in this example has two clauses. The HTML clause just consists of `format.html`. A request for HTML will be handled by the usual rendering of a view template. The JSON clause includes a code block; if JSON is requested, the block will be executed and the result of its execution will be returned to the client.

Here's a command-line illustration, using `curl` (slightly edited to reduce line noise):

```
$ curl http://localhost:3000/products/show/1.json -i
HTTP/1.1 200 OK
Content-Type: application/json; charset=utf-8
Content-Length: 81
Connection: Keep-Alive

{"created_at":"2013-02-09T18:25:03.513Z",
"description":"Keyboard",
"id":"1",
"maker":"Apple",
"updated_at":"2013-02-09T18:25:03.513Z"}
```

The `.json` on the end of the URL results in `respond_to` choosing the *json* branch, and the returned document is a JSON representation of the product.

Requesting a format that is not included as an option in the `respond_to` block will not generate an exception. Rails will return a `406 Not Acceptable` status, to indicate that it can't handle the request.

If you want to set up an *else* condition for your `respond_to` block, you can use the `any` method, which tells Rails to catch any other formats not explicitly defined.

```ruby
def show
  @product = Product.find(params[:id])
  respond_to do |format|
    format.html
    format.json { render json: @product.to_json }
    format.any
  end
end
```

Just make sure that you explicitly tell `any` what to do with the request or have view templates corresponding to the formats you expect. Otherwise, you'll get a `MissingTemplate` exception.

```
ActionView::MissingTemplate (Missing template products/show,
  application/show with {:locale=>[:en], :formats=>[:xml],
  :handlers=>[:erb, :builder, :raw, :ruby, :jbuilder, :coffee]}.)
```

2.2.10   Routes as Rack Endpoints

You'll see usage of the `:to` option in routes throughout this chapter. What's most interesting about `:to` is that its value is what's referred to as a *Rack Endpoint*. To illustrate, consider the following simple example:

```ruby
get "/hello", to: proc { |env| [200, {}, ["Hello world"]] }
```

The router is very loosely coupled to controllers! The shorthand syntax (like `"items#show"`) relies on the `action` method of controller classes to return a Rack endpoint that executes the action requested.

```
>> ItemsController.action(:show)
=> #Proc:0x01e96cd0@...
```

The capability to dispatch to a Rack-based application, such as one created with Sinatra,[3] can be achieved using the `mount` method. The `mount` method accepts an `:at` option, which specifies the route to which the Rack-based application will map.

---

3. http://www.sinatrarb.com

```
class HelloApp < Sinatra::Base
  get "/" do
    "Hello World!"
  end
end

Rails.application.routes.draw do
  mount HelloApp, at: '/hello'
end
```

Alternatively, a shorthand form is also available:

```
mount HelloApp => '/hello'
```

2.2.11   Accept Header

You can also trigger a branching on `respond_to` by setting the `Accept` header in the request. When you do this, there's no need to add the `.:format` part of the URL. (However, note that out in the real world, it's difficult to get this technique to work reliably due to HTTP client/browser inconsistencies.)

Here's a `curl` example that does not specify a `.json` format, but does set the `Accept` header to `application/json`:

```
{lang=text, linenos=off}
$ curl -i -H "Accept: application/json" http://localhost:3000/
      products/show/1 HTTP/1.1 200 OK Content-Type:
      application/json; charset=utf-8 Content-Length:
      81 Connection: Keep-Alive
{"created_at":"2013-02-09T18:25:03.513Z",
"description":"Keyboard",
"id":"1",
"maker":"Apple",
"updated_at":"2013-02-09T18:25:03.513Z"}
```

The result is exactly the same as in the previous example.

2.2.12   Segment Key Constraints

Sometimes you want not only to recognize a route but to recognize it at a finer-grained level than just what components or fields it has. You can do this through the use of the `:constraint` option (and possibly regular expressions).

For example, you could route all show requests so that they went to an error action if their `id` fields were non-numerical. You'd do this by creating two routes, one that handled numerical ids, and a fall-through route that handled the rest:

```
get ':controller/show/:id' => :show, constraints: {:id => /\d+/}
get ':controller/show/:id' => :show_error
```

---

❶ Implicit Anchoring

The example constraint we've been using

```
constraints: {:id => /\d+/}
```

seems like it would match "foo32bar". It doesn't because Rails implicitly anchors it at both ends. Adding explicit anchors \A and \z causes exceptions to be raised.

It's so common to set constraints on the :id param that Rails lets you shorten our previous example to simply

```
get ':controller/show/:id' => :show, id: /\d+/
get ':controller/show/:id' => :show_error
```

Regular expressions in routes can be useful, especially when you have routes that differ from each other only with respect to the patterns of their components. But they're not a full blown substitute for data-integrity checking. You probably still want to make sure that the values you're dealing with are usable and appropriate for your application's domain.

From the example, you might conclude that :constraints checking applies to elements of the params hash. However, you can also check a grab-bag of other request attributes that return a string, such as :subdomain and :referrer. Matching methods of request that return numeric or boolean values are unsupported and will raise a somewhat cryptic exception during route matching.

```
# only allow users admin subdomain to do old-school routing
get ':controller/:action/:id' => :show, constraints: {subdomain: 'admin'}
```

If for some reason you need more powerful constraints checking, you have full access to the request object, by passing a block or any other object that responds to call as the value of :constraints like the following:

```
# protect records with id under 100
get 'records/:id' => "records#protected",
  constraints: proc { |req| req.params[:id].to_i < 100 }
```

2.2.13 The Root Route

A root route is a rule specifying what should happen when someone connects to the "root" of your website (or routing namespace).

```
http://example.com # Note the lack of "/anything" at the end!
```

The root route says, "I don't want any values; I want nothing, and I already know what controller and action I'm going to trigger!"

Here are some examples of fairly common empty route rules:

```
root to: "welcome#index"
root to: "pages#home"

# Shorthand syntax
root "user_sessions#new"
```

Defining the empty route gives people something to look at when they connect to your site with nothing but the domain name. You might be wondering why you see something when you view a newly generated Rails application that still has its root route commented out.

The answer is that if a root route is not defined, by default, Rails will route to an internal controller `Rails::WelcomeController` and render a welcome page instead.

In previous versions of Rails, this was accomplished by including the file `index.html` in the public directory of newly generated applications. Any static content in the public directory hierarchy matching the URL scheme that you come up with for your app results in the static content being served up instead of triggering the routing rules. Actually, the web server will serve up the content without involving Rails at all.

---

❶ A Note on Route Order

Routes are consulted, both for recognition and for generation, in the order they are defined in `routes.rb`. The search for a match ends when the first match is found, meaning that you have to watch out for false positives.

2.3 Route Globbing

In some situations, you might want to grab one or more components of a route without having to match them one by one to specific positional parameters. For example, your URLs might reflect a directory structure. If someone connects to

```
/items/list/base/books/fiction/dickens
```

you want the `items/list` action to have access to all four remaining fields. But sometimes there might be only three fields:

```
/items/list/base/books/fiction
```

or five:

```
/items/list/base/books/fiction/dickens/little_dorrit
```

So you need a route that will match (in this particular case) everything after the second URI component. You define it by *globbing* the route with an asterisk.

```
get 'items/list/*specs', controller: 'items', action: 'list'
```

Now, the `products/list` action will have access to a variable number of slash-delimited URL fields, accessible via `params[:specs]`:

```
def list
  specs = params[:specs] # e.g, "base/books/fiction/dickens"
end
```

ⓘ Globbing Key-Value Pairs

Route globbing might provide the basis for a general mechanism for fielding ad hoc queries. Let's say you devise a URI scheme that takes the following form:

```
http://localhost:3000/items/q/field1/value1/field2/value2/...
```

Making requests in this way will return a list of all products whose fields match the values, based on an unlimited set of pairs in the URL.

In other words, `http://localhost:3000/items/q/year/1939/material/wood` could generate a list of all wood items made in 1939. The route that would accomplish this would be

```
get 'items/q/*specs', controller: "items", action: "query"
```

Of course, you'll have to write a `query` action like this one to support the route:

```
def query
  @items = Item.where(Hash[*params[:specs].split("/")])
  if @items.empty?
    flash[:error] = "Can't find items with those properties"
  end
  render :index
end
```

How about that square brackets class method on `Hash`, eh? It converts a one-dimensional array of key/value pairs into a hash! This is further proof that in-depth knowledge of Ruby is a prerequisite for becoming an expert Rails developer.

2.4 Named Routes

The topic of named routes almost deserves a chapter of its own. In fact, what you learn here will feed directly into our examination of REST-related routing in Chapter 3.

The idea of naming a route is basically to make life easier on you, the programmer. There are no outwardly visible effects as far as the application is concerned. When you name a route, a new method gets defined for use in your controllers and views; the method name follows a convention like `name_url` (with name being the name you gave the route), and calling the method, with appropriate arguments, results in a URL string being generated that will trigger the route. In addition, a method called `name_path` also gets created; this method generates just the path part of the URL, without the protocol and host components.

2.4.1 Creating a Named Route

The way you name a route is by using the optional `:as` parameter in a rule:

```
get 'help' => 'help#index', as: 'help'
```

In this example, you'll get methods called `help_url` and `help_path`, which you can use wherever Rails expects a URL or URL components:

```
link_to "Help", help_path
```

And, of course, the usual recognition and generation rules are in effect. The pattern string consists of just the static string component `help`. Therefore, the path you'll see in the hyperlink will be

```
/help
```

When someone clicks on the link, the `index` action of the `help` controller will be invoked.

🗩 Xavier says . . .

You can test named routes in the console directly using the special `app` object.

```
>> app.clients_path
=> "/clients"

>> app.clients_url
=> "http://www.example.com/clients"
```

Named routes save you some effort when you need a URL generated. A named route zeros in directly on the route you need, bypassing the matching process that would be needed otherwise. That means you don't have to provide as much detail as you otherwise would, but you still have to provide values for any segment keys in the route's pattern string that cannot be inferred.

2.4.2   `name_path` versus `name_url`

When you create a named route, you're actually creating at least two route helper methods. In the preceding example, those two methods are `help_url` and `help_path`. The difference is that the `_url` method generates an entire URL, including protocol and domain, whereas the `_path` method generates just the path part (sometimes referred to as an *absolute path* or a *relative URL*).

According to the HTTP spec, redirects should specify a URI, which can be interpreted (by some people) to mean a fully qualified URL.[4] Therefore, if you want to be pedantic about it, you probably should always use the `_url` version when you use a named route as an argument to `redirect_` to in your controller code.

Other than redirects, permalinks, and a handful of edge cases, it's the Rails way to use `_path` instead of `_url`. It produces a shorter string, and the user agent (browser or otherwise) should be able to infer the fully qualified URL whenever it needs to do

---

4. http://www.w3.org/Protocols/rfc2616/rfc2616-sec10.html

so, based on the HTTP headers of the request, a base element in the document, or the URL of the request.

💬 Prathamesh says . . . .

Using `_path` in mailer templates is deprecated; use `_url` instead. Over the years, I have seen many times where using `_path` helpers in mailer templates was the root cause of hard to diagnose issues.

As you read this book and as you examine other code and other examples, the main thing to remember is that `help_url` and `help_path` are basically doing the same thing. I tend to use the `_url` style in general discussions about named route techniques but to use `_path` in examples that occur inside view templates (for example, with `link_to` and `form_for`). It's mostly a writing-style thing, based on the theory that the URL version is more general and the path version more specialized. In any case, it's good to get used to seeing both and getting your brain to view them as very closely connected.

ℹ️ Using Literal URLs

You can, if you wish, hard-code your paths and URLs as string arguments to `link_to`, `redirect_to`, and friends. For example, instead of

```
link_to "Help", controller: "main", action: "help"
```

you can write

```
link_to "Help", "/main/help"
```

However, using a literal path or URL bypasses the routing system. If you write literal URLs, you're on your own to maintain them. (You can, of course, use Ruby's string interpolation techniques to insert values, if that's appropriate for what you're doing, but really stop and think about why you are reinventing Rails functionality if you go down that path.)

2.4.3   What to Name Your Routes

As you'll learn in Chapter 3, the best way to figure out what names you should use for your routes is to follow REST conventions, which are baked into Rails and simplify things greatly. Otherwise, you'll need to think top-down; that is, think about what you want to write in your application code, and then create the routes that will make it possible.

Take, for example, this call to `link_to`:

```
link_to "Auction of #{item.name}",
  controller: "items",
  action: "show",
  id: item.id
```

The routing rule to match that path is (a generic route):

```
get "item/:id" => "items#show"
```

It sure would be nice to shorten that `link_to` code. After all, the routing rule already specifies the controller and action. This is a good candidate for a named route for items:

```
get "item/:id" => "items#show", as: "item"
```

Lets improve the situation by introducing `item_path` in the call to `link_to`:

```
link_to "Auction of #{item.name}", item_path(id: item.id)
```

Giving the route a name is a shortcut; it takes us straight to that route, without a long search and without having to provide a thick description of the route's hard-coded parameters.

2.4.4 Argument Sugar

In fact, we can make the argument to `item_path` even shorter. If you need to supply an id number as an argument to a named route, you can just supply the number, without spelling out the `:id` key:

```
link_to "Auction of #{item.name}", item_path(item.id)
```

And the syntactic sugar goes even further: You can and should provide objects and Rails will grab the id automatically by calling `to_param` on it. (Active Record objects and almost everything else in Rails come with `to_param` methods by default.)

```
link_to "Auction of #{item.name}", item_path(item)
```

This principle extends to other segment keys in the pattern string of the named route. For example, if you've got a route like

```
get "auction/:auction_id/item/:id" => "items#show", as: "item"
```

you'd be able to call it like

```
link_to "Auction of #{item.name}", item_path(auction, item)
```

and you'd get something like this as your path (depending on the exact id numbers):

```
/auction/5/item/11
```

Here, we're letting Rails infer the ids of both an auction object and an item object, which it does by calling `to_param` on whatever non-hash arguments you pass into named route helpers. As long as you provide the arguments in the order in which their ids occur in the route's pattern string, the correct values will be dropped into place in the generated path.

2.4.5   A Little More Sugar with Your Sugar?

Furthermore, it doesn't have to be the id value that the route generator inserts into the URL. As alluded to a moment ago, you can override that value by defining a `to_param` method in your model.

Let's say you want the description of an item to appear in the URL for the auction on that item. In the `item.rb` model file, you would override `to_param`; here, we'll override it so that it provides a "munged" (stripped of punctuation and joined with hyphens) version of the description, courtesy of the `parameterize` method added to strings in Active Support.

```
def to_param
  description.parameterize
end
```

Subsequently, the method call `item_path(auction, item)` will produce something like

```
/auction/3/item/cello-bow
```

Of course, if you're putting things like "cello-bow" in a path field called `:id`, you will need to make provisions to dig the object out again. Blog applications that use this technique to create *slugs* for use in permanent links often have a separate database column to store the munged version of the title that serves as part of the path. That way, it's possible to do something like

```
Item.where(munged_description: params[:id]).first!
```

to unearth the right item. (And yes, you can call it something other than `:id` in the route to make it clearer!)

💬 Courtenay says . . . .

Why shouldn't you use numeric IDs in your URLs? First, your competitors can see just how many auctions you create. Numeric consecutive IDs also enable people to write automated spiders to steal your content. It's a window into your database. And finally, words in URLs just look better.

2.5   Scoping Routing Rules

Rails gives you a variety of ways to bundle together related routing rules concisely. They're all based on usage of the scope method and its various shortcuts. For instance, let's say that you want to define the following routes for auctions:

```
get 'auctions/new' => 'auctions#new'
get 'auctions/edit/:id' => 'auctions#edit'
post 'auctions/pause/:id' => 'auctions#pause'
```

You could DRY up your routes.rb file by using the scope method instead:

```
scope controller: :auctions do
  get 'auctions/new' => :new
  get 'auctions/edit/:id' => :edit
  post 'auctions/pause/:id' => :pause
end
```

Then you would DRY it up again by adding the :path argument to scope:

```
scope path: '/auctions', controller: :auctions do
  get 'new' => :new
  get 'edit/:id' => :edit
  post 'pause/:id' => :pause
end
```

2.5.1   Controller

The scope method accepts a :controller option (or it can interpret a symbol as its first argument to assume a controller). Therefore, the following two scope definitions are identical:

```
scope controller: :auctions do
scope :auctions do
```

To make it more obvious what's going on, you can use the controller method instead of scope, in what's essentially syntactic sugar:

```
controller :auctions do
```

2.5.2 Path Prefix

The `scope` method accepts a `:path` option (or it can interpret a string as its first parameter to mean a path prefix). Therefore, the following two scope definitions are identical:

```
scope path: '/auctions' do
scope '/auctions' do
```

The `:path` option also understands symbols instead of strings. The following scope definition

```
scope :auctions, :archived do
```

will scope all routes nested under it to the `/auctions/archived` path.

2.5.3 Name Prefix

The `scope` method also accepts a `:as` option that affects the way that named route URL helper methods are generated. The route

```
scope :auctions, as: 'admin' do
  get 'new' => :new, as: 'new_auction'
end
```

will generate a named route URL helper method called `admin_new_auction _url`.

2.5.4 Namespaces

URLs can be grouped by using the `namespace` method, which is syntactic sugar that rolls up module, name prefix and path prefix settings into one declaration. The implementation of the `namespace` method converts its first argument into a string, which is why in some example code you'll see it take a symbol.

```
namespace :auctions do
  get 'new' => :new
  get 'edit/:id' => :edit
  post 'pause/:id' => :pause
end
```

2.5.5 Bundling Constraints

If you find yourself repeating similar segment key constraints in related routes, you can bundle them together using the `:constraints` option of the `scope` method:

```
scope controller: :auctions, constraints: {:id => /\d+/} do
  get 'edit/:id' => :edit
```

```
    post 'pause/:id' => :pause
end
```

It's likely that only a subset of rules in a given scope need constraints applied to them. In fact, routing will break if you apply a constraint to a rule that doesn't take the segment keys specified. Since you're nesting, you probably want to use the `constraints` method, which is just more syntactic sugar to tighten up the rule definitions.

```
scope path: '/auctions', controller: :auctions do
  get 'new' => :new
  constraints id: /\d+/ do
    get 'edit/:id' => :edit
    post 'pause/:id' => :pause
  end
end
```

To enable modular reuse, you may supply the `constraints` method with an object that has a `matches?` method.

```
class DateFormatConstraint
  def self.matches?(request)
    request.params[:date] =~ /\A\d{4}-\d\d-\d\d\z/ # YYYY-MM-DD
  end
end
```

```
# in routes.rb
constraints(DateFormatConstraint) do
  get 'since/:date' => :since
end
```

In this particular example (`DateFormatConstraint`) if an errant or malicious user input a badly formatted date parameter via the URL, Rails will respond with a 404 status instead of causing an exception to be raised.

2.5.6   Direct Routes

Rails 5.1 added the direct method to the routing DSL. It supports the creation of custom URL helpers that link to a static URL, like this:

```
direct(:apple) { "http://www.apple.com" }
```

The name of the direct route is used to create its helper method:

```
>> apple_url
=> "http://www.apple.com"
```

Direct routes have the advantage of being available everywhere that URL helpers are available, unlike similar functionality implemented in helper modules.

2.6   Listing Routes

A handy route listing utility can be invoked by typing `rails routes` in your application directory. For example, here is the output for a routes file containing just a single `resources :products` rule:

```
$ rails routes
    Prefix Verb    URI Pattern                 Controller#Action
  products GET     /products(.:format)         products#index
           POST    /products(.:format)         products#create
new_product GET    /products/new(.:format)     products#new
edit_product GET   /products/:id/edit(.:format) products#edit
   product GET     /products/:id(.:format)     products#show
           PATCH   /products/:id(.:format)     products#update
           PUT     /products/:id(.:format)     products#update
           DELETE  /products/:id(.:format)     products#destroy
```

The output is a table with four columns. The first two columns are optional and contain the name of the route and HTTP method constraint, if they are provided. The third column contains the URL mapping string. Finally, the fourth column indicates the controller and action method that the route maps to, plus constraints that have been defined on that route's segment keys (if any).

Note that the routes task checks for an optional controller parameter.

```
$ rails routes -c products
```

would only list the routes related to ProductsController.

💬 Juanito says . . .

While you have a server up and running on the development environment, you could visit `/rails/info/routes` to get a complete list of routes of your Rails application.

2.7   Conclusion

The first half of the chapter helped you to fully understand the generic routing rules of Rails and how the routing system has two purposes:

- Recognizing incoming requests and mapping them to a corresponding controller action, along with any additional variable receptors.

- Recognizing URL parameters in methods such as `link_to` and matching them up to a corresponding route so that proper HTML links can be generated.

We built on our knowledge of generic routing by covering some advanced techniques such as using regular expressions and globbing in our route definitions, plus the bundling of related routes under shared scope options.

Finally, before moving on, you should make sure that you understand how named routes work and why they make your life easier as a developer by allowing you to write more concise view code. As you'll see in the next chapter, once we start defining batches of related named routes, we're on the cusp of delving into REST.

Routes

CHAPTER 3

REST, Resources, and Rails

Before REST came, I (and pretty much everyone else) never really knew where to put stuff.

—Jonas Nicklas on the Ruby on Rails mailing list

What I've come to embrace is that being almost fundamentalistic about when I create a new controller to stay adherent to REST has served me better every single time. Every single time I've regretted the state of my controllers, it's been because I've had too few of them. I've been trying to overload things too heavily.

—DHH interview on Full Stack Radio http://www.fullstackradio.com/32

Representational State Transfer (REST) is a complex topic in information theory, and a comprehensive exploration of it is well beyond the scope of this chapter.[1] However, we'll touch on some of the keystone concepts.

The reason that we devote an entire chapter to REST is that one of the inherent problems that all web developers face is deciding how to name and organize the resources and actions of their application. And it just so happens that the vast majority of Rails applications are backed by databases and fit well into the REST paradigm (aka "RESTful design").

---

1. For those interested in a complete description of REST, the canonical text is Roy Fielding's dissertation, which you can find at http://www.ics.uci.edu/~fielding/pubs/dissertation/top.htm. In particular, you'll probably want to focus on Chapters 5 and 6 of the dissertation, which cover REST in relation to HTTP.

3.1   REST in a Rather Small Nutshell

REST is described by its creator, Roy T. Fielding, as a network *architectural style*, specifically the style manifested in the architecture of the World Wide Web. Indeed, Fielding is not only the creator of REST but also one of the authors of the HTTP protocol itself. REST and the web have a very close relationship.

Fielding defines REST as a series of constraints imposed upon the interaction between system components. Basically, you start with the general proposition of machines that can talk to each other, and you start ruling some practices in and others out by imposing constraints that include (among others):

- Use of a client-server architecture

- Stateless communication

- Explicit signaling of response cacheability

- Use of HTTP request methods such as GET, POST, PUT and DELETE

(We'll get into what each of those bullet points mean later in the chapter.)

Systems that adhere to REST constraints are said to be *RESTful*. Much of the web itself uses REST-compliant communication, but notably, it has plenty of room for violations of REST principles. REST constraints have to be purposely built into a system by its designer.

To get the most out of this chapter, the most important thing you have to understand is that REST is designed to help you provide services using the native idioms and constructs of HTTP. It used to be that you'd find, if you looked for it, lots of discussion comparing REST to, for example, SOAP—with the thrust of the pro-REST argument being that HTTP already enables you to provide services, so you don't need a semantic layer on top of it. Just use what HTTP already gives you.

One of the allures of REST is that it scales relatively well for big systems, like the web. Another is that it encourages—mandates, even—the use of stable, long-lived identifiers (URIs). Machines talk to each other by sending requests and responses labeled with these identifiers. Messages consist of *representations* (manifestations in text, XML, graphic format, and so on) of *resources* (high-level, conceptual descriptions of content) or simply HTTP headers.

Ideally at least, when you ask a machine for a JSON representation of a resource—say, Romeo and Juliet—you'll use the same identifier every time and the same request metadata indicating that you want JSON, and you'll get the same response. And if it's not the same response, there's a reason—like, the resource you're retrieving is a changeable one ("The current transcript for Student #3994," for example).

3.2   Resources and Representations

The REST style characterizes communication between system components (where a component is, say, a web browser or a server) as a series of requests to which the responses are representations of resources.

A resource, in this context, is a "conceptual mapping" (Fielding). Resources themselves are not tied to a database, a model, or a controller. Examples of resources include

- The current time of day
- A library book's borrowing history
- The entire text of *The Little Prince*
- A map of Jacksonville Beach, Florida
- The inventory of a store

A resource may be singular or plural, changeable (like the time of day) or fixed (like the text of *The Little Prince*). It's basically a high-level description of the thing you're trying to get hold of when you submit a request.

A resource may also be ephemeral, like the result of authenticating to a server or a temporary filtering of tabular data.

Whether permanent, subject to change or ephemeral, the point is that resources are nouns.

Next, it's important to realize that what you actually get from a RESTful server is never the resource itself but a representation of it. This is where REST unfolds onto the myriad content types and actual deliverables that are the stuff of the web. A resource may, at any given point, be available in any number of representations (or none at all). Thus your site might offer a text version of *The Little Prince* but also an audio version. Those two versions would be understood as the same resource and would be retrieved via the same identifier (URI). The difference in content type— one representation versus another—would be negotiated separately in the request.

3.3   REST in Rails

The REST support in Rails consists of methods to define resources in the routing system, designed to impose a particular style, order, and logic on your controllers and, consequently, on the way the world sees your application. There's more to it than just a set of naming conventions (though there's that too). In the larger scheme of things, the benefits that accrue to you when you use Rails' REST support fall into two categories:

- Convenience and automatic best practices for you
- A RESTful interface to your application's services for everyone else

You can reap the first benefit even if you're not concerned with the second. In fact, that's going to be our focus here: what the REST support in Rails can do for you in the realm of making your code nicer and your life as a Rails developer easier.

I don't mean to minimize the importance of REST itself, nor the seriousness of the endeavor of providing REST-based services. Rather, it's an expedient; we can't talk about everything, and this section of the book is primarily about routing and how to do it, so we're going to favor looking at REST in Rails from that perspective.

Getting back to practical matters, the focus of the rest of this chapter will be showing you how the REST support in Rails opens the door to further study and practice, including the study of Fielding's dissertation and the theoretical tenets of REST. Again, we won't cover everything about REST here, but what we do cover will be onward compatible with the wider topic.

It all starts with CRUD . . .

3.4   Routing and CRUD

The acronym CRUD (create read update delete) is the classic summary of the spectrum of database operations. It's also a kind of rallying cry for Rails practitioners. Because we address our databases through abstractions, we're prone to forget how simple it all is. This manifests itself mainly in excessively creative names for controller actions.

If you're ignorant of RESTful design, then there's a strong temptation to name your actions `add_item` and `replace_email_address` and things like that. But we needn't, and usually shouldn't, do this. True, the controller does not map to the database, the way the model does. But things get simpler when you name your actions after CRUD operations—or as close to the names of those operations as you can get.

The routing system does not force you to implement your app's CRUD functionality in any consistent manner. You can create a route that maps to any action, whatever the action's name. Choosing CRUD names is a matter of discipline. Except . . . when you use the REST facilities offered by Rails, it happens automatically.

Another way of looking at it is that REST in Rails involves standardization of action names. In fact, the heart of the Rails' REST support is a technique for creating bundles of named routes automatically—named routes that are bundled together to point to a specific, predetermined set of actions.

Here's the logic. It's good to give CRUD-based names to your actions. It's convenient and elegant to use named routes. The REST support in Rails gives you named routes that point to CRUD-based action names. Therefore, using the REST facilities gives you a shortcut to some best practices.

Shortcut hardly describes how little work you have to do to get a big payoff. If you put

```
resources :auctions
```

into your `config/routes.rb` file, you will have created four named routes, which, in a manner to be described in this chapter, connect to seven controller actions. And those actions have nice CRUD-like names, as you will see.

3.4.1   REST Resources and Rails

Like most of Rails, support for RESTful applications is "opinionated"; that is, it offers a particular way of designing a REST interface, and the more you play along, the more convenience you reap from it. Most Rails applications are database-backed, and the Rails take on REST tends to associate a resource very closely with an Active Record model or a model/controller stack.

In fact, you'll hear people using the terminology fairly loosely. For instance, they'll say that they have created a *Book resource*. What they mean, in most cases, is that they have created a Book model, a book controller with a set of CRUD actions, and some named routes pertaining to that controller (courtesy of `resources :books`). You can have a Book model and controller, but what you actually present to the world as your resources, in the REST sense, exists at a higher level of abstraction: *The Little Prince*, borrowing history, and so on.

The best way to get a handle on the REST support in Rails is by going from the known to the unknown. In this case, from the topic of named routes to the more specialized topic of REST.

3.4.2   From Named Routes to REST Support

When we first looked at named routes, we saw examples where we consolidated things into a route name. By creating a route like

```
get 'auctions/:id' => "auction#show", as: 'auction'
```

you gain the capability to use nice helper methods in situations like

```
link_to item.description, auction_path(item.auction)
```

The route ensures that a path will be generated that will trigger the `show` action of the auctions controller. The attraction of this kind of named route is that it's concise and readable.

Now, think in terms of CRUD. The named route `auction_path` is a nice fit for a `show` (the R in CRUD) action. What if we wanted similarly nicely named routes for the `create, update,` and `delete` actions?

Well, we've used up the route name `auction_path` on the `show` action. We could make up names like `auction_delete_path` and `auction_create_path`, but those are cumbersome. We really want to be able to make a call to `auction_path` and have it mean different things, depending on which action we want the URL to point to.

We could differentiate between the singular (`auction_path`) and the plural (`auctions_path`). A singular URL makes sense, semantically, when you're doing something with a single, existing auction object. If you're doing something with auctions in general, the plural makes more sense.

The kinds of things you do with auctions in general include creating. The `create` action will normally occur in a form such as the following:

```
form_tag auctions_path
```

It's plural because we're not saying "perform an action with respect to a particular auction", but rather "with respect to the collection of auctions, perform the action of creation." Yes, we're creating one auction, not many. But at the time we make the call to our named route, `auctions_path,` we're addressing auctions in general.

Another case where you might want a plural named route is when you want an overview of all of the objects of a particular kind, or at least, some kind of general view, rather than a display of a particular object. This kind of general view is usually handled with an `index` action. These `index` actions typically load a lot of data into one or more variables, and the corresponding view displays it as a list or table (possibly more than one).

Here again, we'd like to be able to say the following:

```
link_to "Click here to view all auctions", auctions_path
```

Already, though, the strategy of breaking `auction_path` out into singular and plural has hit the wall: We've got two places where we want to use the plural named route. One is create; the other is index. But they're both going to look like

```
/auctions
```

How is the routing system going to know that when we use `auctions_path` as a link versus using it in a form that we mean the `create` action and not `index`? We need another qualifier, another flag, another variable on which to branch.

Luckily, we've got a perfect candidate.

3.4.3 Reenter the HTTP Verb

Form submissions are POSTs by default. Index actions are GETs. That means that we need to get the routing system to realize that

```
/auctions submitted in a GET request!
```

versus

```
/auctions submitted in a POST request!
```

are two different things. We also have to get the routing system to generate the same URL—/auctions—but with a different HTTP request method, depending on the circumstances.

This is what the REST facility of Rails routing does for you. It allows you to stipulate that you want /auctions routed differently, depending on the HTTP request method. It lets you define named routes with the same name, but with intelligence about their HTTP verbs. In short, it uses HTTP verbs to provide that extra data slot necessary for achieving everything you want to achieve in a concise way.

The way you do this is by using a special routing method: `resources`. Here's what it would look like for auctions:

```
resources :auctions
```

That's it. Making this one call inside `routes.rb` is the equivalent of defining four named routes. And if you mix and match those four named routes with a variety of HTTP request methods, you end up with seven useful permutations.

3.5   The Standard RESTful Controller Actions

Calling `resources :auctions` involves striking a kind of deal with the routing system. The system hands you four named routes. Between them, these four routes point to seven controller actions, depending on HTTP request method. In return, you agree to use very specific names for your controller actions: index, create, show, update, destroy, new, edit.

It's not a bad bargain, since a lot of work is done for you and the action names you have to use are nicely CRUD-like.

Table 3.1 summarizes what happens. It's a kind of "multiplication table" showing you what you get when you cross a given RESTful named route with a given HTTP request method. Each box (the nonempty ones, that is) shows you, first, the URL that the route generates and, second, the action that gets called when the route is recognized. (Table 3.1 lists _path methods rather than _url ones, but you get both.)

Table 3.1   RESTful Routes Table Showing Helpers, Paths, and the Resulting Controller Action

Helper Method	GET	POST	PATCH	DELETE
`client_path` `(client)`	/clients/1 show		/clients/1 update	/clients/1 destroy
`clients_path`	/clients index	/clients create		
`edit_client_` `path(client)`	/clients/1/edit edit			
`new_client_` `path`	/clients/new new			

(The `edit` and `new` actions have unique named routes, and their URLs have a special syntax.)

Since named routes are now being crossed with HTTP request methods, you'll need to know how to specify the request method when you generate a URL so that your GET'd `clients_url` and your POST'd `clients_url` don't trigger the same controller action. Most of what you have to do in this regard can be summed up in a few rules:

1. The default request method is GET.

2. In a `form_tag` or `form_for` call, the POST method will be used automatically.

3. When you need to (which is going to be mostly with PATCH and DELETE operations), you can specify a request method along with the URL generated by the named route.

An example of needing to specify a DELETE operation is a situation when you want to trigger a destroy action with a link:

```
link_to "Delete", auction_path(auction), method: :delete
```

Depending on the helper method you're using (as in the case of `form_for`), you might have to put the method inside a nested hash:

```
form_for "auction", url: auction_path(auction),
  html: {method: :patch } do |f|
```

That last example, which combined the singular named route with the PATCH method, will result in a call to the update action when submitting the form (as per row 1, column 4 of Table 3.1). You don't normally have to program this functionality specifically, because as we'll see later in the book, Rails automatically figures out whether you need a POST or PATCH if you pass an object to form helpers.

3.5.1   PATCH versus PUT

If you are coming from a previous version of Rails, you may be wondering why the update action of a RESTful route is mapped to the HTTP verb PATCH instead of PUT. In the HTTP standards document RFC 5789,[2] it outlines that a PUT request to a given resource is meant to completely replace it on the origin server. However, when updating a resource in Rails, rarely, if ever, do you replace an entire resource when performing an update. For example, when updating an Active Record model, Rails sets the attribute `updated_at` timestamp, not the requesting client.

Therefore, to better implement HTTP semantics, Rails uses the HTTP verb PATCH for updates. PATCH make possible both full and partial updates of a resource and is more suited to how Rails updates resources.

If you are upgrading an existing Rails application, the HTTP verb PUT will still map to the update action in RESTful routes, but it's recommended to use PATCH instead.

---

2. http://tools.ietf.org/html/rfc5789

3.5.2   Singular and Plural RESTful Routes

As you may have noticed, some of the RESTful routes are singular; some are plural. The logic is as follows:

1. The routes for `show`, `new`, `edit`, and `destroy` are singular because they're working on a particular resource.

2. The rest of the routes are plural. They deal with collections of related resources.

The singular RESTful routes require an argument because they need to be able to figure out the id of the member of the collection referenced.

```
item_url(item) # show, update, or destroy, depending on HTTP verb
```

You don't have to call the `id` method on `item`. Rails will figure it out (by calling `to_param` on the object passed to it.)

3.5.3   The Special Pairs: `new/create` and `edit/update`

As Table 3.1 shows, `new` and `edit` obey somewhat special RESTful naming conventions. The reason for this has to do with `create` and `update` and how `new` and `edit` relate to them.

Typically, `create` and `update` operations involve submitting a form. That means that they really involve two actions—two requests—each:

1. The action that results in the display of the form

2. The action that processes the form input when the form is submitted

The way this plays out with RESTful routing is that the `create` action is closely associated with a preliminary `new` action, and `update` is associated with `edit`. These two actions, `new` and `edit`, are really assistant actions: All they're supposed to do is show the user a form, as part of the process of creating or updating a resource.

Fitting these special two-part scenarios into the landscape of resources is a little tricky. A form for editing a resource is not, itself, really a resource. It's more like a *pre-resource*. A form for creating a new resource is sort of a resource, if you assume that being new—that is, nonexistent—is something that a resource can do and still be a resource!

That line of reasoning might be a little too philosophical to be useful. The bottom line, as implemented in RESTful Rails, is the following: The `new` action is understood to be giving you a new, single (as opposed to plural) resource. However, since the logical verb for this transaction is GET, and GETting a single resource is already spoken for by the `show` action, `new` needs a named route of its own.

That's why you have to use

```
link_to "Create a new item", new_item_path
```

to get a link to the `items/new` action.

The `edit` action is understood not to be giving you a full-fledged representation of a resource, exactly, but rather a kind of edit *flavor* of the `show` resource. So it uses the same URL as `show`, but with a kind of modifier, in the form of `/edit`, hanging off the end, which is consistent with the URL form for `new`:

```
items/5/edit
```

The corresponding named route is `edit_item_url(@item)`. As with `new`, the named route for `edit` involves an extra bit of name information, to differentiate it from the implied `show` of the existing RESTful route for GETting a single resource.

3.5.4   The PATCH and DELETE Cheat

We have just seen how Rails routes PATCH and DELETE requests. Modern HTTP clients are able to use said verbs, but forms in older web browsers can't be submitted using anything other than a POST. Rails provides a hack that is nothing to worry about, other than being aware of what's going on.

A PATCH or DELETE request originating in a browser, in the context of REST in Rails, is actually a POST request with a hidden field called `_method` set to either `"patch"` or `"delete"`. The Rails application processing the request will pick up on this and route the request appropriately to the `update` or `destroy` action.

You might say, then, that the REST support in Rails is ahead of its time. REST components using HTTP should understand all of the request methods. They don't, so Rails forces the issue. As a developer trying to get the hang of how the named routes map to action names, you don't have to worry about this little cheat. And hopefully some day it won't be necessary any more.

3.5.5   Limiting Routes Generated

It's possible to add `:except` and `:only` options to the call to `resources` in order to limit the routes generated.

```
resources :clients, except: [:index]
resources :clients, only: [:new, :create]
```

If you make the leap from thinking of resources as strictly *things that are stored in a database* to *concepts in my application*, then it begins to make sense why the only limitation is useful. There are concepts that only require a couple of routes. A common example is authentication: when you sign in to the application, you are *creating* a session, and when you sign out, you are *destroying* it. That can be (and is) modeled in a RESTful fashion by libraries such as Devise.

3.6   Singular Resource Routes

In addition to `resources`, there's also a singular (or *singleton*) form of resource routing: `resource`. It's used to represent a resource that only exists once in its given context.

A singleton resource route at the top level of your routes can be appropriate when there's only one resource of its type for the whole application, perhaps something like a per-user profile.

```
resource :profile
```

You get almost the full complement of resource routes, all except the collection route (index). Note that the method name `resource`, the argument to that method, and all the named routes generated are in the singular.

```
$ rake routes
      profile POST    /profile(.:format)        profiles#create
  new_profile GET     /profile/new(.:format)    profiles#new
 edit_profile GET     /profile/edit(.:format)   profiles#edit
              GET     /profile(.:format)        profiles#show
              PATCH   /profile(.:format)        profiles#update
              PUT     /profile(.:format)        profiles#update
              DELETE  /profile(.:format)        profiles#destroy
```

It's assumed that you're in a context where it's meaningful to speak of *the profile*—the one and only—because there's a user to which the profile is scoped. The scoping itself is not automatic; you have to authenticate the user and retrieve the profile from (and/or save it to) the database explicitly. There's no real magic or mind-reading here; it's just an additional routing technique at your disposal if you need it.

3.7   Nested Resources

Let's say you want to perform operations on bids: create, edit, and so forth. You know that every bid is associated with a particular auction. That means that whenever you do anything to a bid, you're really doing something to an auction/bid pair—or, to look at it another way, an auction/bid nest. Bids are at the bottom of a drill-down hierarchical structure that always passes through an auction.

What you're aiming for here is a URL that looks like

```
auctions/3/bids/5
```

What it does depends on the HTTP verb it comes with, of course. But the semantics of the URL itself are: the resource that can be identified as bid 5, belonging to auction 3.

Why not just go for `bids/5` and skip the auction? For a couple of reasons. First, the URL is more informative—longer, it's true, but longer in the service of telling you something about the resource. Second, thanks to the way RESTful routes are engineered in Rails, this kind of URL gives you immediate access to the auction id in the controller, via `params[:auction_id]`.

To created nested resource routes, put this in `routes.rb`:

```
resources :auctions do
resources :bids
end
```

What that tells the routing mapper is that you want RESTful routes for auction resources; that is, you want `auctions_url`, `edit_auction_url`, and all the rest of it. You also want RESTful routes for bids: `auction_bids_url`, `new_auction_bid_url`, and so forth.

However, the nested resource command also involves you in making a promise. You're promising that whenever you use the bid named route helpers, you will provide an auction resource in which they can be nested. In your application code, that translates into an argument to the named route method:

```
link_to "See all bids", auction_bids_path(auction)
```

When you make that call, you enable the routing system to add the `/auctions/3` part before the `/bids` part. And, on the receiving end—in this case, in the action `bids/index`, which is where that URL points—you'll find the id of `auction` in `params[:auction_id]`. (It's a plural RESTful route, using GET. See Table 3.1 again if you forgot.)

You can nest to any depth. Each level of nesting adds one to the number of arguments you have to supply to the nested routes. This means that for the singular routes (`show`, `edit`, `destroy`), you need at least two arguments:

```
link_to "Delete this bid", auction_bid_path(auction, bid), method: :delete
```

REST

This will enable the routing system to get the information it needs (essentially `auction.id` and `bid.id`) in order to generate the route.

Alternatively, instead of specifying the route to be used in a view helper, such as `link_to`, you can simply pass an object.

```
link_to "Delete this bid", [auction, bid], method: :delete
```

Since the object in the preceding example is an `Array`, Rails infers that the route is nested. And, based on the order and class names of the objects in the Array, Rails will use the `auction_bid_path` helper behind the scenes.

3.7.1 RESTful Controller Mappings

Something we haven't yet explicitly discussed is how RESTful routes are mapped to a given controller. It was just presented as something that happens automatically, which in fact it does, based on the name of the resource.

Going back to our recurring example, given the following nested route

```
resources :auctions do
resources :bids
end
```

there are two controllers that come into play, the `AuctionsController` and the `BidsController`.

3.7.2 Considerations

Is nesting worth it? For single routes, a nested route usually doesn't tell you anything you wouldn't be able to figure out anyway. After all, a bid belongs to an auction.

That means you can access `bid.auction_id` just as easily as you can `params [:auction_id]`, assuming you have a bid object already.

Furthermore, the bid object doesn't depend on the nesting. You'll get `params[:id]` set to 5, and you can dig that record out of the database directly. You don't need to know what auction it belongs to.

```
Bid.find(params[:id])
```

A common rationale for judicious use of nested resources, and the one most often issued by David, is the ease with which you can enforce permissions and context-based constraints. Typically, a nested resource should only be accessible in the context of its parent resource, and it's really easy to enforce that in your code based on the way that you load the nested resource using the parent's Active Record association.

```
auction = Auction.find(params[:auction_id])
bid = auction.bids.find(params[:id])  # prevents auction/bid mismatch
```

If you want to add a bid to an auction, your nested resource URL would be

```
http://localhost:3000/auctions/5/bids/new
```

The auction is identified in the URL rather than having to clutter your new bid form data with hidden fields or resorting to non-RESTful practices.

3.7.3 Deep Nesting?

Jamis Buck is a very influential figure in the Rails community, almost as much as David himself. In February 2007, via his blog,[3] he basically told us that deep nesting was a bad thing and proposed the following rule of thumb: Resources should never be nested more than one level deep.

That advice is based on experience and concerns about practicality. The helper methods for routes nested more than two levels deep become long and unwieldy. It's easy to make mistakes with them and hard to figure out what's wrong when they don't work as expected.

Assume that in our application example, bids have multiple comments. We could nest comments under bids in the routing like this:

```
resources :auctions do
  resources :bids do
  resources :comments
  end
end
```

Instead, Jamis would have us do the following:

```
resources :auctions do
  resources :bids
end

resources :bids do
  resources :comments
end

resources :comments
```

---

3. http://weblog.jamisbuck.org/2007/2/5/nesting-resources

Notice that each resource (except auctions) is defined twice, once in the top-level namespace, and one in its context. The rationale? When it comes to parent-child scope, you really only need two levels to work with. The resulting URLs are shorter and the helper methods are easier to work with.

```
auctions_path              # /auctions
auctions_path(1)           # /auctions/1
auction_bids_path(1)       # /auctions/1/bids
bid_path(2)                # /bids/2
bid_comments_path(3)       # /bids/3/comments
comment_path(4)            # /comments/4
```

I personally don't follow Jamis' guideline all the time in my projects, but I have noticed something about limiting the depth of your nested resources. It helps with the maintainability of your codebase in the long run.

💬 Courtenay says

Many of us disagree with the venerable Jamis. Want to get into fisticuffs at a Rails conference? Ask people whether they believe routes should be nested more than one layer deep.

3.7.4   Shallow Routes

As of Rails 2.3, resource routes accept a :shallow option that helps to shorten URLs where possible. The goal is to leave off parent collection URL segments where they are not needed. The end result is that the only nested routes generated are for the :index, :create, and :new actions. The rest are kept in their own *shallow* URL context.

It's easier to illustrate than to explain, so let's define a nested set of resources and set :shallow to true:

```
resources :auctions, shallow: true do
  resources :bids do
    resources :comments
  end
end
```

Alternatively coded, it looks as follows (if you're block-happy):

```
resources :auctions do
  shallow do
    resources :bids do
      resources :comments
```

```
      end
    end
end
```

The resulting routes are:

```
   bid_comments GET      /bids/:bid_id/comments(.:format)
                POST     /bids/:bid_id/comments(.:format)
new_bid_comment GET      /bids/:bid_id/comments/new(.:format)
   edit_comment GET      /comments/:id/edit(.:format)
        comment GET      /comments/:id(.:format)
                PATCH    /comments/:id(.:format)
                PUT      /comments/:id(.:format)
                DELETE   /comments/:id(.:format)
   auction_bids GET      /auctions/:auction_id/bids(.:format)
                POST     /auctions/:auction_id/bids(.:format)
new_auction_bid GET      /auctions/:auction_id/bids/new(.:format)
       edit_bid GET      /bids/:id/edit(.:format)
            bid GET      /bids/:id(.:format)
                PATCH    /bids/:id(.:format)
                PUT      /bids/:id(.:format)
                DELETE   /bids/:id(.:format)
       auctions GET      /auctions(.:format)
                POST     /auctions(.:format)
    new_auction GET      /auctions/new(.:format)
   edit_auction GET      /auctions/:id/edit(.:format)
        auction GET      /auctions/:id(.:format)
                PATCH    /auctions/:id(.:format)
                PUT      /auctions/:id(.:format)
                DELETE   /auctions/:id(.:format)
```

If you analyze the routes generated carefully, you'll notice that the nested parts of the URL are only included when they are needed to determine what data to display.

3.8   Routing Concerns

One of the fundamental principles Rails developers follow is Don't Repeat Yourself (DRY). Even though this is the case, the `config/routes.rb` file can be prone to having repetition in the form of nested routes that are shared across multiple resources. For example, let's assume in our recurring example, that both auctions and bids can have comments associated with them.

```
resources :auctions do
  resources :bids
  resources :comments
  resources :image_attachments, only: :index
end
```

```
resources :bids do
  resources :comments
end
```

To eliminate code duplication and to encapsulate shared behavior across routes, Rails 4 introduced the routing method `concern`.

```
concern :commentable do
  resources :comments
end
```

```
concern :image_attachable do
  resources :image_attachments, only: :index
end
```

To add a routing concern to a RESTful route, pass the concern to the `:concerns` option.

```
resources :auctions, concerns: [:commentable, :image_attachable] do
  resources :bids
end
```

```
resources :bids, concerns: :commentable
```

The `:concerns` option can accept one or more routing concerns.

3.9   RESTful Route Customizations

Rails' RESTful routes give you a pretty nice package of named routes, mapped to useful, common, controller actions—the CRUD superset you've already learned about. Sometimes, however, you want to customize things a little more, while still taking advantage of the RESTful route naming conventions and the *multiplication table* approach to mixing named routes and HTTP request methods.

The techniques for doing this are useful when, for example, you've got more than one way of viewing a resource that might be described as *showing*. You can't (or shouldn't) use the `show` action itself for more than one such view. Instead, you need to think in terms of different perspectives on a resource and create URLs for each one.

3.9.1   Extra Member Routes

For example, let's say we want to make it possible to retract a bid. The basic nested route for bids looks like this:

```
resources :auctions do
  resources :bids
end
```

We'd like to have a `retract` action that shows a form (and perhaps does some screening for retractability). The `retract` isn't the same as `destroy`; it's more like a portal to `destroy`. It's similar to `edit`, which serves as a form portal to `update`. Following the parallel with `edit`/`update`, we want a URL that looks like

```
auctions/3/bids/5/retract
```

and a helper method called `retract_auction_bid_url`. The way you achieve this is by specifying an extra `member` route for the `bids`, as in Listing 3.1.

Listing 3.1   Adding an extra member route
```
resources :auctions do
  resources :bids do
    member do
      get :retract
    end
  end
end
```

Then you can add a retraction link to your view using

```
link_to "Retract", retract_bid_path(auction, bid)
```

and the URL generated will include the `/retract` modifier. That said, you should probably let that link pull up a retraction form (and not trigger the retraction process itself!). The reason I say that is because, according to the tenets of HTTP, GET requests should not modify the state of the server; that's what other requests methods like POST are for.

So how do you trigger an actual retraction? Is it enough to add a :method option to `link_to`?

```
link_to "Retract", retract_bid_path(auction,bid), method: :post
```

Not quite. Remember that in Listing 3.1 we defined the retract route as a `get`, so a POST will not be recognized by the routing system. The solution is to define an extra member route with `post`, like this:

```
resources :auctions do
  resources :bids do
    member do
      get :retract
      post :retract
    end
  end
end
```

If you're handling more than one HTTP verb with a single action, you should switch to using a single match declaration and a :via option, like this:

```
resources :auctions do
  resources :bids do
    member do
      match :retract, via: [:get, :post]
    end
  end
end
```

Thanks to the flexibility of the routing system, we can tighten it up further using match with an :on option, like

```
resources :auctions do
  resources :bids do
    match :retract, via: [:get, :post], on: :member
  end
end
```

which would result in a route like this (output from rake routes):

```
retract_auction_bid GET|POST
/auctions/:auction_id/bids/:id/retract(.:format) bids#retract
```

3.9.2   Extra Collection Routes

You can use the same routing technique to add routes that conceptually apply to an entire collection of resources:

```
resources :auctions do
  collection do
    match :terminate, via: [:get, :post]
  end
end
```

In its shorter form:

```
resources :auctions do
```

```
  match :terminate, via: [:get, :post], on: :collection
end
```

This example will give you a `terminate_auctions_path` method, which will produce a URL mapping to the `terminate` action of the auctions controller. (A slightly bizarre example, perhaps, but the idea is that it would enable you to end all auctions at once.)

Thus you can fine-tune the routing behavior—even the RESTful routing behavior—of your application, so that you can arrange for special and specialized cases while still thinking in terms of resources.

3.9.3   Custom Action Names

Occasionally, you might want to deviate from the default naming convention for Rails RESTful routes. The `:path_names` option allows you to specify alternate name mappings. The example code shown changes the new and edit actions to Spanish-language equivalents.

```
resources :projects, path_names: { new: 'nuevo', edit: 'cambiar' }
```

The URLs change (but the names of the generated helper methods do not).

```
GET     /projects/nuevo(.:format)        projects#new
GET     /projects/:id/cambiar(.:format)  projects#edit
```

3.9.4   Mapping to a Different Controller

You may use the `:controller` option to map a resource to a different controller than the one it would do so by default. This feature is occasionally useful for aliasing resources to a more natural controller name.

```
resources :photos, controller: "images"
```

3.9.5   Routes for New Resources

The routing system has a neat syntax for specifying routes that only apply to new resources, ones that haven't been saved yet. You declare extra routes inside of a nested new block, like this:

```
resources :reports do

  new do
    post :preview
  end
end
```

The declaration above would result in the following route being defined:

```
preview_new_report POST    /reports/new/preview(.:format) reports#preview
```

Refer to your new route within a view form by altering the default `:url`.

```
= form_for(report, url: preview_new_report_path) do |f|
...
= f.submit "Preview"
```

3.9.6   Considerations for Extra Routes

Referring to extra member and collection actions, David has been quoted as saying, "If you're writing so many additional methods that the repetition is beginning to bug you, you should revisit your intentions. You're probably not being as RESTful as you could be."

The last sentence is key. Adding extra actions corrupts the elegance of your overall RESTful application design because it leads you away from finding all of the resources lurking in your domain.

Keeping in mind that real applications are more complicated than code examples in a reference book, let's see what would happen if we had to model retractions strictly using resources. Rather than tacking a `retract` action onto the `BidsController`, we might feel compelled to introduce a retraction resource, associated with bids, and write a `RetractionController` to handle it.

```
resources :bids do
  resource :retraction
end
```

`RetractionController` could now be in charge of everything having to do with retraction activities, rather than having that functionality mixed into `Bids-Controller`. And if you think about it, something as weighty as bid retraction would eventually accumulate quite a bit of logic. Some would call breaking it out into its own controller proper separation of concerns or even just good object-orientation.

David says he doesn't put extra methods on his controllers anymore. For a detailed explanation of how and why he breaks out extras into their own (sub-)resource controllers, read this great blog post: http://jeromedalbert .com/how-dhh-organizes-his-rails-controllers/.

3.10   Controller-Only Resources

Resources are high-level abstractions of what's available through your web application. Database operations just happen to be one of the ways that you store and retrieve the data you need to generate representations of resources. But a REST resource doesn't necessarily have to map directly to a controller, either, at least not in theory. You could, if you wanted to, provide REST services whose public identifiers (URIs) did not match the names of your controllers at all.

What all of this adds up to is that you might have occasion to create a set of resource routes, and a matching controller, that don't correspond to any model in your application at all. There's nothing wrong with a full resource/controller/model stack where everything matches by name. But you may find cases where the resources you're representing can be encapsulated in a controller but not a model.

An example in the auction application is a sessions controller, which we alluded to earlier in the chapter. Assume a `routes.rb` file containing this line:

```
resource :session
```

It maps the URL /session to a `SessionController` as a singleton resource, yet there's no Session model. (By the way, it's properly defined as a singleton resource because from the user's perspective there is only one session.)

Why go the RESTful style for authentication? If you think about it, user sessions can be created and destroyed. The creation of a session takes place when a user logs in; when the user logs out, the session is destroyed. The RESTful Rails practice of pairing a new action and view with a `create` action can be followed! The user login form can be the session-creating form, housed in the template file such as `session/new.html.haml`.

```
%h1 Log in
= form_for :user, url: session_path do |f|
  %p
    = f.label :login
    = f.text_field :login
  %p
    = f.label :password
    = f.password_field :password
  %p
    = f.submit "Log in"
```

When the form is submitted, the input is handled by the `create` method of the sessions controller:

```
def create
  if user.try(:authorize, params[:user][:password])
   redirect_to home_url, notice: "Welcome, #{user.first_name}!"
  else
   redirect_to action: "new", flash: { error: "Login invalid." }
  end
end

protected
def user
  @user ||= User.find_by(login: params[:user][:login])
end
```

Nothing is written to any database table in this action, but it's worthy of the name `create` by virtue of the fact that it creates a session. Furthermore, if you did at some point decide that sessions should be stored in the database, you'd already have a nicely abstracted handling layer.

It pays to remain open-minded, then, about the possibility that CRUD as an action-naming philosophy and CRUD as actual database operations may sometimes occur independently of each other and the possibility that the resource-handling facilities in Rails might usefully be associated with a controller that has no corresponding model. Creating a session on the server isn't a REST-compliant practice, since REST mandates stateless transfers of representations of resources. But it's a good illustration of why, and how, you might make design decisions involving routes and resources that don't implicate the whole application stack.

💬 Xavier says . . .

Whether sessions are REST-compliant or not depends on the session storage. What REST disallows is not the idea of application state in general but rather the idea of client state stored in the server. REST demands that your requests are complete. For example, putting an `auction_id` in a hidden field of a form or in its action path is fine. There is state in that request that the edit action wants to pass to the update action, and you dumped it into the page, so the next request to update a bid carries all of what's needed. That's RESTful.

Now, using hidden fields and such is not the only way to do this. For example, there is no problem using a `user_id` cookie for authentication. Why? Because a cookie is part of a request. Therefore, I am pretty sure that cookie-based sessions are considered to be RESTful by the same principle. That kind of storage makes your requests self-contained and complete.

Sticking to CRUD-like action names is, in general, a good idea. As long as you're doing lots of creating and destroying anyway, it's easier to think of a user logging in as the creation of a session than to come up with a whole new semantic category for it. Rather than the new concept of *user logs in,* just think of it as a new occurrence of the old concept, *session gets created.*

3.11   Different Representations of Resources

One of the foundations of REST is that the components in a REST-based system exchange *representations* of resources. The distinction between resources and their representations is vital. We mentioned that at the beginning of the chapter, but didn't expound on it until now.

As a client or consumer of REST services, you don't actually retrieve a resource from a server; you retrieve representations of that resource. You also provide representations: A form submission, for example, sends the server a representation of a resource, together with a request—for example, PATCH—that this representation be used as the basis for updating the resource. Representations are the exchange currency of resource management.

3.11.1   The `respond_to` Method

The capability to return different representations in RESTful Rails practice is based on the `respond_to` method in the controller, which, as you've seen in the previous chapter, enables you to return different responses depending on what the client wants. Moreover, when you create resource routes you automatically get URL recognition for URLs ending with a dot and a `:format` parameter.

For example, assume that you have `resources :auctions` in your routes file and some `respond_to` logic in the `AuctionsController` like

```
def index
  @auctions = Auction.all
  respond_to do |format|
   format.html
   format.xml { render xml: @auctions }
  end
end
```

which will let you to connect to this URL: `/auctions.xml`.

The resource routing will ensure that the `index` action gets executed. It will also recognize the `.xml` at the end of the route and interact with `respond_to` accordingly, returning the XML representation.

REST

3.11.2   Responders Gem

The Responders[4] Gem features functionality that was removed from Rails 4.2 offering a more concise way of responding to a variety of formats in the same controller.

```
class AuctionsController < ApplicationController
  respond_to :html, :xml, :json
  def index
    @auctions = Auction.all
    respond_with(@auctions)
  end
end
```

Here we've told our controller, at the class level, that it should expect to respond to html, xml, and json so that each action will automatically return the appropriate content.

When the request comes in, the responder would attempt to do the following (given a `.json` extension on the URL):

- Attempt to render an associated view with a `.json` extension
- If no view exists, call `to_json` on the object passed to `responds_with`
- If the object does not respond to `to_json`, call `to_format` on it

For nested and namespaced resources, you must pass dependencies to the `respond _to` method similarly to the way you would generate a route.

```
respond_with(@user, :managed, @client)
```

3.11.3   Formatted Named Routes

So far we've covered how Rails recognizes different formats. But what if you want to generate a link to the XML representation of a resource? You can achieve it by passing an extra argument to the RESTful named route:

```
link_to "XML version of this auction", auction_path(@auction, :xml)
```

This will generate the following HTML:

```
<a href="/auctions/1.xml">XML version of this auction</a>
```

---

4. https://github.com/plataformatec/responders

When followed, this link will trigger the XML clause of the `respond_to` block in the `show` action of the auctions controller. The resulting XML may not look like much in a browser, but the named route is there if you want it.

The circuit is now complete: You can generate URLs that point to a specific response type, and you can honor requests for different types by using `respond_to`. All told, the routing system and the resource-routing facilities built on top of it give you quite a set of powerful, concise tools for differentiating among requests and, therefore, being able to serve up different representations.

3.12   The RESTful Rails Action Set

Rails REST facilities, ultimately, are about named routes and the controller actions to which they point. The more you use RESTful Rails, the more you get to know each of the seven RESTful actions. How they work across different controllers (and different applications) is of course somewhat different. Still, perhaps because there's a finite number of them and their roles are fairly well-delineated, each of the seven tends to have fairly consistent properties and a characteristic *feel* to it.

Now we're going to take a closer look at each of the seven actions, with examples and comments. You'll encounter all of them again, particularly in Chapter 4, "Working with Controllers," but here you'll get some backstory and start to get a sense of the characteristic usage of them and issues and choices associated with them.

3.12.1   Index

Typically, an `index` action provides a representation of a plural (or collection) resource. However, to be clear, not all resource collections are mapped to the `index` action. Your default index representations will usually be generic, although admittedly that has a lot to do with your application-specific needs. But in general, the `index` action shows the world the most neutral representation possible. A very basic `index` action looks like

```
class AuctionsController < ApplicationController
  def index
    @auctions = Auction.all
  end
end
```

The associated view template will display information about each auction, with links to specific information about each one, and to profiles of the sellers.

You'll certainly encounter situations where you want to display a representation of a collection in a restricted way. In our recurring example, users should be able to see a listing of all their bids, but maybe you don't want users seeing other people's bids.

There are a couple of ways to do this. One way is to test for the presence of a logged-in user and decide what to show based on that. But that's not going to work here. For one thing, the logged-in user might want to see the more public view. For another, the more dependence on server-side state we can eliminate or consolidate, the better.

So let's try looking at the two bid lists, not as public and private versions of the same resource, but as different index resources. The difference can be reflected in the routing like the following:

```
resources :auctions do
  resources :bids do
    get :manage, on: :collection
  end
end
resources :bids
```

We can now organize the bids controller in such a way that access is nicely layered, using action callbacks only where necessary and eliminating conditional branching in the actions themselves:

```
class BidsController < ApplicationController
  before_action :check_authorization, only: :manage

  def index
    @bids = Bid.all
  end

  def manage
    @bids = auction.bids
  end

  protected

  def auction
   @auction ||= Auction.find(params[:auction_id])
  end

  def check_authorization
    auction.authorized?(current_user)
  end
end
```

There's now a clear distinction between `/bids` and `/auctions/1/bids/manage` and the role that they play in your application.

On the named route side, we've now got `bids_url` and `manage_auction_bids_url`. We've thus preserved the public, stateless face of the `/bids` resource, and quarantined as much stateful behavior as possible into a discrete member resource, `/auctions/1/bids/manage`. Don't fret if this mentality doesn't come to you naturally. It's part of the REST learning curve.

🗨 Lark says . . .

If they are truly different resources, why not give them each their own controllers? Surely there will be other actions that need to be authorized and scoped to the current user.

3.12.2 Show

The RESTful `show` action is the singular flavor of a resource. That generally translates to a representation of information about one object, one member of a collection. Like `index`, `show` is triggered by a GET request.

A typical—one might say classic—`show` action looks like

```
class AuctionController < ApplicationController
  def show
    @auction = Auction.find(params[:id])
  end
end
```

As with index actions, it's good to make your show actions as public as possible and offload the administrative and privileged views onto either a different controller or a different action.

3.12.3 Destroy

Destroy actions are good candidates for administrative safeguarding, though of course it depends on what you're destroying. You might want something like this to protect the `destroy` action.

```
class ProductsController < ApplicationController
  before_action :admin_required, only: :destroy
```

A typical `destroy` action might look like

```
def destroy
  product.destroy
  redirect_to products_url, notice: "Product deleted!"
end
```

This approach might be reflected in a simple administrative interface like

```
%h1 Products
- products.each do |product|
  %p= link_to product.name, product
  - if current_user.admin?
    %p= link_to "delete", product, method: :delete
```

That delete link appears depending on whether current user is an admin.

The Rails UJS (unobtrusive JavaScript) API greatly simplifies the HTML emitted for a `destroy` action, using CSS selectors to bind JavaScript to (in this case) the "delete" link. See Chapter 20, "Ajax on Rails," for much more information about how it works.

`DELETE` submissions are dangerous. Rails wants to make them as hard as possible to trigger accidentally—for instance, by a crawler or bot sending requests to your site. So when you specify the `DELETE` method, JavaScript that submits a form is bound to your "delete" link, along with a `rel="nofollow"` attribute on the link. Since bots don't submit forms (and shouldn't follow links marked "nofollow"), this gives a layer of protection to your code.

3.12.4 `new` and `create`

As you've already seen, the `new` and `create` actions go together in RESTful Rails. A "new resource" is really just an entity waiting to be created. Accordingly, the `new` action customarily presents a form, and `create` creates a new record, based on the form input.

Let's say you want a user to be able to create (that is, start) an auction. You're going to need

1. A `new` action, which will display a form
2. A `create` action, which will create a new Auction object based on the form input, and proceed to a view (`show` action) of that auction

The `new` action doesn't have to do much. In fact, it has to do nothing. Like any empty action, it can even be left out. Rails will still figure out which view to render. However, your controller will need an auction helper method, like

```
protected

def auction
  @auction ||= current_user.auctions.build(params[:auction])
end
helper_method :auction
```

If this technique is alien to you, don't worry. We'll describe it in detail in the section "Decent Exposure."

A simplistic `new.html.haml` template might look like Listing 3.2.

Listing 3.2   A new auction form
```
%h1 Create a new auction
= form_for auction do |f|
  = f.label :subject
  = f.text_field :subject
  %br
  = f.label :description
  = f.text_field :description
  %br
  = f.label :reserve
  = f.text_field :reserve
  %br
  = f.label :starting_bid
  = f.text_field :starting_bid
  %br
  = f.label :end_time
  = f.datetime_select :end_time
  %br
  = f.submit "Create"
```

Once the information is filled out by a user, it's time for the main event: the `create` action. Unlike new, this action has something to do.

```
def create
  if auction.save
    redirect_to auction_url(auction), notice: "Auction created!"
  else
    render :new
  end
end
```

3.12.5   `edit` and `update`
Like new and `create`, the `edit` and `update` actions go together: `edit` provides a form, and `update` processes the form input.

The form for editing a record appears similar to the form for creating one. (In fact, you can put much of it in a partial template and use it for both; that's left as an exercise for the reader.)

The `form_for` method is smart enough to check whether the object you pass to it has been persisted or not. If it has, then it recognizes that you are doing an edit and specifies a PATCH method on the form.

3.13   Conclusion

In this chapter, we tackled the tough subject of using REST principles to guide the design of our Rails applications, mainly as they apply to the routing system and controller actions. We learned how the foundation of RESTful Rails is the `resources` method in your routes file and how to use the numerous options available to make sure that you can structure your application exactly how it needs to be structured.

By necessity, we've already introduced many controller-related topics and code examples in our tour of the routing and REST features. In the next chapter, we'll cover controller concepts and the Action Controller API in depth.

CHAPTER 4

Working with Controllers

Remove all business logic from your controllers and put it in the model. (My) instructions are precise, but following them requires intuition and subtle reasoning.

—Nick Kallen

Like any computer program, your Rails application involves the flow of control from one part of your code to another. The flow of program control gets pretty complex with Rails applications. There are many bits and pieces in the framework, many of which execute each other. And part of the framework's job is to figure out, on the fly, what your application files are called and what's in them, which of course varies from one application to another.

The heart of it all, though, is pretty easy to identify: It's the controller. When someone connects to your application, what they're basically doing is asking the application to execute a controller action. Sure, there are many different flavors of how this can happen and edge cases where it doesn't exactly happen at all. But if you know how controllers fit into the application life cycle, you can anchor everything else around that knowledge. That's why we're covering controllers before the rest of the Rails APIs.

Controllers are the C in MVC. They're the first port of call, after the dispatcher, for the incoming request. They're in charge of the flow of the program: They gather information and make it available to the views.

Controllers are also very closely linked to views, more closely than they're linked to models. It's possible to write the entire model layer of an application before you create a single controller or to have different people working on the controller and model layers who never meet or talk to each other. However, views and controllers are more tightly coupled to one another. They share a lot of information and the names you choose for your variables in the controller will have an effect on what you do in the view.

In this chapter, we're going to look at what happens on the way to a controller action being executed and what happens as a result. In the middle, we'll take a long look at how controller classes themselves are set up, particularly in regard to the many different ways that we can render views. Then we'll wrap up the chapter with a couple of additional topics related to controllers: action callbacks and streaming.

First, though, let's look at the underpinnings of the Rails controller, and almost every other Ruby web framework out there.

4.1 Rack

Rack is a modular interface for handling web requests, written in Ruby, with support for many different web servers. It abstracts away the handling of HTTP requests and responses into a single, simple `call` method that can be used by anything from a plain Ruby script all the way to Rails itself.

Listing 4.1   HelloWorld as a Rack application

```
class HelloWorld
  def call(env)
    [200, {"Content-Type" => "text/plain"}, ["Hello world!"]]
  end
end
```

An HTTP request invokes the call method and passes in a hash of environment variables, akin to the way that CGI works. The call method should return a three-element array consisting of the status, a hash of response headers, and finally, the body of the request.

Newer web developers may have never heard of CGI (Common Gateway Interface). It is a specification dating back to the 1990's about how a web server should communicate with executable scripts and programs to serve up dynamic content. https://www.w3.org/CGI/

As of Rails 2.3, request handling was moved to Rack and the concept of middleware was introduced. Classes that satisfy Rack's call interface can be chained together as filters. Rack itself includes a number of useful filter classes that do things such as logging and exception handling.

Rails 3 took this one step further and was re-architected from the ground up to fully leverage Rack filters in a modular and extensible manner. A full explanation of Rails' Rack underpinnings are outside the scope of this book, especially since Rack does not really play a part in day-to-day development of applications. However, it is essential Rails knowledge to understand that much of Action Controller is implemented as Rack middleware modules. Want to see which Rack filters are enabled for your application? There's a rake task for that!

```
$ rake middleware
use Rack::Runtime
use Rack::MethodOverride
use ActionDispatch::RequestId
use Rails::Rack::Logger
use ActionDispatch::ShowExceptions
use ActionDispatch::DebugExceptions
use ActionDispatch::RemoteIp
use ActionDispatch::Reloader
use ActionDispatch::Callbacks
use ActiveRecord::Migration::CheckPending
use ActiveRecord::ConnectionAdapters::ConnectionManagement
use ActiveRecord::QueryCache
use ActionDispatch::Cookies
use ActionDispatch::Session::CookieStore
use ActionDispatch::Flash
use ActionDispatch::ParamsParser
use Rack::Head
use Rack::ConditionalGet
use Rack::ETag
run Example::Application.routes
```

What's checking for pending Active Record migrations have to do with serving requests anyway?

```
module ActiveRecord
  class Migration
    class CheckPending
      ...
      def call(env)
        ActiveRecord::Base.logger.silence do
          ActiveRecord::Migration.check_pending!
        end
        @app.call(env)
      end
```

```
      end
    end
end
```

Ahh, it's not that pending Active Record migrations has anything specifically to do with serving requests. It's that Rails is designed in such a way that different aspects of its behavior are introduced into the request call chain as individual Rack middleware components or *filters*.

4.1.1   Configuring Your Middleware Stack

Your application object enables you to access and manipulate the Rack middleware stack during initialization, via `config.middleware` like

```
# config/application.rb
module Example
  class Application < Rails::Application
    ...
    # Rack::ShowStatus catches all empty responses the app it
    # wraps and replaces them with a site explaining the error.
    config.middleware.use Rack::ShowStatus
  end
end
```

Rack Lobster

As I found out trying to experiment with the hilariously named `Rack::Lobster`, your custom Rack middleware classes need to have an explicit initializer method, even if they don't require runtime arguments.

The methods of `config.middleware` give you very fine-grained control over the order in which your middleware stack is configured. The `args` parameter is an optional hash of attributes to pass to the `initializer` method of your Rack filter.

- `config.middleware.insert_after(existing_middleware, new_middleware, args)`—Adds the new middleware after the specified existing middleware in the middleware stack.

- `config.middleware.insert_before(existing_middleware, new_middleware, args)`—Adds the new middleware before the specified existing middleware in the middleware stack.

- `config.middleware.delete(middleware)`—Removes a specified middleware from the stack.

- `config.middleware.swap(existing_middleware, new_middleware, args)`—Swaps a specified middleware from the stack with a new class.

- `config.middleware.use(new_middleware, args)`—Takes a class reference as its parameter and just adds the desired middleware to the end of the middleware stack.

For an example of a very useful Rack middleware implemented as a RubyGem, check out https://github.com/cyu/rack-cors. It elegantly provides support for Cross-Origin Resource Sharing (CORS).

4.2 Action Dispatch: Where It All Begins

Controller and view code in Rails has always been part of its Action Pack framework. As of Rails 3, dispatching of requests was extracted into its own sub-component of Action Pack called Action Dispatch. It contains classes that interface the rest of the controller system to Rack.

4.2.1 Request Handling

The entry point to a request is an instance of `ActionDispatch::Routing::RouteSet`, the object on which you can call `draw` at the top of `config/routes.rb`.

The route set chooses the rule that matches, and calls its *Rack endpoint*. So a route like

```
get 'foo', to: 'foo#index'
```

has a dispatcher instance associated to it, whose `call` method ends up executing

```
FooController.action(:index).call
```

Prior to Rails 4, the RouteSet would convert its path data into an array of regular expressions. When a request needed to be dispatched, it would iterate through the array and try to match the given URLs one by one. It worked, but it was relatively slow. Nowadays, the core routing module in ActionDispatch is called Journey. It uses some advanced computer science techniques to do its thing, like a generalized transition graph (GTG) and non-deterministic finite automata (NFA). If you dig into its codebase, you'll find a Yacc grammar file for parsing route definitions!

As covered in the section "Routes as Rack Endpoints," the route set can call any other type of Rack endpoint, like a Sinatra app, a redirect macro or a bare lambda. In those cases no dispatcher is involved.

All of this happens quickly, behind the scenes. It's unlikely that you would ever need to dig into the source code of ActionDispatch; it's the sort of thing that you can take for granted to just work. However, to really understand the Rails way, it is important to know what's going on with the dispatcher. In particular, it's important to remember that the various parts of your application are just bits (sometimes long bits) of Ruby code and that they're getting loaded into a running Ruby interpreter.

4.2.2   Getting Intimate with the Dispatcher

Just for the purpose of learning, let's trigger the Rails dispatching mechanism manually. We'll do this little exercise from the ground up, starting with a new Rails application:

```
$ rails new dispatch_me --skip-turbolinks --skip-spring --skip-action-cable
```

Now create a single controller demo, with an index action (Note that Haml is set up as our template language):

```
$ cd dispatch_me/
$ rails generate controller demo index
  create  app/controllers/demo_controller.rb
   route  get "demo/index"
  invoke  haml
  create    app/views/demo
  create    app/views/demo/index.html.haml
  invoke  test_unit
  create    test/controllers/demo_controller_test.rb
  invoke  helper
  create    app/helpers/demo_helper.rb
  invoke    test_unit
  create      test/helpers/demo_helper_test.rb
  invoke  assets
  invoke    coffee
  create      app/assets/javascripts/demo.js.coffee
  invoke    scss
  create      app/assets/stylesheets/demo.css.scss
```

If you take a look at app/controllers/demo_controller.rb, you'll see that it has an index action:

```
class DemoController < ApplicationController
  def index
```

```
    end
end
```

There's also a view template file, `app/views/demo/index.html.haml` with some placeholder language. Just to see things more clearly, let's replace it with something we will definitely recognize when we see it again. Replace the contents of `index.html.haml` with

```
Hello!
```

Not much of a design accomplishment, but it will do the trick.

Now that we've got a set of dominos lined up, it's just a matter of pushing over the first one: the dispatcher. To do that, start by firing up the Rails console from your Rails application directory.

```
$ rails console
Loading development environment (Rails 5.0.0.1)
>>
```

There are some variables from the web server that Rack expects to use for request processing. Since we're going to be invoking the dispatcher manually, we have to set those variables like this in the console (output ommited for brevity)

```
>> env = {}
>> env['REMOTE_ADDR'] = '127.0.0.1'
>> env['REQUEST_METHOD'] = 'GET'
>> env['PATH_INFO'] = '/demo/index'
>> env['rack.input'] = StringIO.new
```

Now that we've replicated an HTTP environment, we're now ready to fool the dispatcher into thinking it's getting a request. Actually, it is getting a request. It's just that it's coming from someone sitting at the console, rather than from a proper web server. (Note that we edited the output HTML a bit to make it easier to read. The actual console will spit it out all in a big concatenated string, including a bunch of META tag gibberish.)

```
>> rack_body_proxy = DispatchMe::Application.call(env).last
=> #<Rack::BodyProxy:0x007f8163bb8be0 @
         body=#<Rack::BodyProxy:0x007f8163bb8c30 @
         body=#<Rack::BodyProxy:0x007f8163bb8e88 @
         body=#<Rack::BodyProxy:0x007f816b911330 @
         body=#<Rack::BodyP\ roxy:0x007f816b912aa0 @
         body=["<!DOCTYPE html>...
>> rack_body_proxy.last
```

```
=> "<!DOCTYPE html>
    <html>
      <head>...</head>
      <body><h1>Demo#index</h1>
        <p>Find me in app/views/demo/index.html.erb</p>
      </body>
    </html>
```

If you want to see everything contained in the `ActionDispatch::Response`
object returned from `call` then try the following code:

```
>> y DispatchMe::Application.call(env)
```

The handy y method formats its argument as a YAML string, making it a lot easier
to understand. We won't reproduce the output here because it's huge, but it includes
things like HTTP headers.

Getting back to the dispatching process, up to now we've executed the `call` method
of our Rails application and as a result, the `index` action got executed and the index
template (such as it is) got rendered and the results of the rendering got wrapped in
some HTTP headers and returned.

Just think: If you were a web server, rather than a human, and you had just done the
same thing, you could now return that document, headers and "Hello!" and all, to
a client.

You can follow the trail of bread crumbs even further by diving into the Rails source
code, but for purposes of understanding the chain of events in a Rails request and
the role of the controller, the peek under the hood we've just done is sufficient.

💬 Tim says . . .

Note that if you give Rack a path that resolves to a static file, it will be served
directly from the web server without involving the Rails stack. As a result,
the object returned by the dispatcher for a static file is different than what
you might expect.

4.3 Render unto View . . .

The goal of the typical controller action in a traditional web application is to render
a view template—that is, to fill out the template and hand the results, usually an
HTML document, back to the server for delivery to the browser. Oddly—at least it

might strike you as a bit odd, though not illogical—you don't actually need to define a controller action, as long as you've got a template that matches the action name.

You can try this out in under-the-hood mode. Go into `app/controller/demo_controller.rb`, and delete the `index` action so that the file will look empty, like this:

```
class DemoController < ApplicationController
end
```

Don't delete `app/views/demo/index.html.haml`, and then try the console exercise (`DispatchMe::Application.call(env)` and all that) again. You'll see the same result.

By the way, make sure you reload the console when you make changes—it doesn't react to changes in source code automatically. The easiest way to reload the console is simply to type `reload!`. But be aware that any existing instances of Active Record objects that you're holding on to will also need to be reloaded (using their individual `reload` methods). Sometimes it's simpler to just exit the console and start it up again.

4.3.1 When in Doubt, Render

People love saying that Rails is magical. This is the sort of thing they're talking about: Rails knows that when it gets a request for the `index` action of the demo controller, what really matters is handing something back to the server. So if there's no `index` action in the controller file, Rails shrugs and says, "Well, let's just assume that if there were an `index` action, it would be empty anyway, and I'd just render `index.html.haml`. So that's what I'll do."

You can learn something from an empty controller action, though. Let's go back to this version of the demo controller:

```
class DemoController < ApplicationController
  def index
  end
end
```

What you learn from seeing the empty action is that, at the end of every controller action, if nothing else is specified, the default behavior is to render the template whose name matches the name of the controller and action, which in this case means `app/views/demo/index.html.haml`.

Controllers

In other words, every controller action has an implicit `render` command in it. And `render` is a real method. You could write the preceding example like this:

```
def index
  render "demo/index"
end
```

You don't have to, though, because it's assumed that it's what you want, and that is part of what Rails people are talking about when they discuss *convention over configuration*. Don't force the developer to add code to accomplish something that can be assumed to be a certain way.

4.3.2   Explicit Rendering

Rendering a template is like putting on a shirt: If you don't like the first one you find in your closet—the default, so to speak—you can reach for another one and put it on instead.

If a controller action doesn't want to render its default template, it can render a different one by calling the `render` method explicitly. Any template file in the `app/views` directory tree is available. (Actually, that's not exactly true. Any template on the whole system is available!) But why would you want your controller action to render a template other than its default? There are several reasons, and by looking at some of them, we can cover all of the handy features of the controller's `render` method.

🐞 If you want to capture a call to `render` without automatically sending it to the browser, you can call `render_to_string` instead. It takes exactly the same options as `render`, but it returns a string instead of triggering a response.

4.3.3   Rendering Another Action's Template

A common reason for rendering an entirely different template is to redisplay a form, when it gets submitted with invalid data and needs correction. In such circumstances, the usual web strategy is to redisplay the form with the submitted data and trigger the simultaneous display of some error information, so that the user can correct the form and resubmit.

The reason that process involves rendering another template is that the action that processes the form and the action that displays the form may be—and often are— different from each other. Therefore, the action that processes the form needs a way to redisplay the original (form) template, instead of treating the form submission as successful and moving on to whatever the next screen might be.

Wow, that was a mouthful of an explanation. Here's a practical example:

```
class EventController < ActionController::Base
  def new
    # This (empty) action renders the new.html.haml template, which
    # contains the form for inputting information about the new
    # event record and is not actually needed.
end

def create
  # This method processes the form input. The input is available via
  # the params hash, in the nested hash keyed to :event
  @event = Event.new(params[:event])
  if @event.save
    # ignore the next line for now
    redirect_to dashboard_path, notice: "Event created!"
    else
      render action: 'new' # doesn't execute the new method!
    end
  end
end
```

On failure, that is, if `@event.save` does not return `true`, we render the "new" template. Assuming `new.html.haml` has been written correctly, this will automatically include the display of error information embedded in the new (but unsaved) `Event` object.

Note that the template itself doesn't "know" that it has been rendered by the `create` action rather than the `new` action. It just does its job: It fills out and expands and interpolates, based on the instructions it contains and the data (in this case, `@event`) that the controller has passed to it.

4.3.4   Rendering a Different Template Altogether

In a similar fashion, if you are rendering a template for a different action, it is possible to render any template in your application by calling `render` with a string pointing to the desired template file. The `render` method is very robust in its capability to interpret which template you're trying to refer to.

```
render template: '/products/index.html.haml'
```

A couple of notes: It's not necessary to pass a hash with `:template` because it's the default option. Also, in our testing, all of the following permutations worked identically when called from `ProductsController`:

```
render '/products/index.html.haml'
render 'products/index.html.haml'
render 'products/index.html'
render 'products/index'
render 'index'
render :index
```

The `:template` option only works with a path relative to the template root (`app/views`, unless you changed it, which would be extremely unusual).

💬 Tim says . . .

Use only enough to disambiguate. The content type defaults to that of the request, and if you have two templates that differ only by template language, you're Doing It Wrong.

Under rare circumstances, you can use the `render` method to access templates that are entirely outside of your application using the `:file` option.

```
render file: "/u/apps/warehouse_app/current/app/views/products/show"
```

Provide an absolute file-system path to the desired template. It will render using the current layout for your controller.

⚠ Using the `:file` option in combination with users' input can lead to security problems since an attacker could use this action to access sensitive files.

4.3.5   Rendering a Partial Template

Another option is to render a partial template (usually referred to simply as a *partial*). Usage of partial templates allows you to organize your template code into small files. Partials can also help you to avoid clutter and encourage you to break your template code up into reusable modules.

There are a few ways to trigger partial rendering. The first, and most obvious, is using the `:partial` option to explicitly specify a partial template. Rails has a convention of prefixing partial template file names with an underscore character, but you never include the underscore when referring to partials.

```
render partial: 'product' # renders app/views/products/_product.html.haml
```

Leaving the underscore off of the partial name applies, even if you're referring to a partial in a different directory than the controller that you're currently in!

```
render partial: 'shared/product'
# renders app/views/shared/_product.html.haml
```

The second way to trigger partial rendering depends on convention. If you pass `render :partial` to an object, Rails will use its class name to find a partial to render. You can even omit the `:partial` option, as in the following example code:

```
render partial: @product
render @product
render 'product'
```

All three lines render the `app/views/products/_product.html.haml` template.

Partial rendering from a controller is mostly used in conjunction with XHR calls that need to dynamically update segments of an already displayed page. The technique, along with generic use of partials in views, is covered in greater detail in Chapter 10, "Action View."

4.3.6   Rendering HTML

It's a poor practice, but you can send an HTML string back to the browser by using the `:html` option.

```
render html: "<strong>Not Found</strong>".html_safe
```

Make sure to mark it safe, or Rails will complain about a potential security vulnerability.

4.3.7   Rendering Inline Template Code

Occasionally, you may want to send the browser a snippet of HTML generated using template code that is too small to merit its own partial. This practice is contentious because it is a flagrant violation of proper separation of concerns between MVC layers. Still, if you want to flaunt the rules, you can use `render inline: '....`

Rails treats the inline code exactly as if it were a view template. The default type of view template processing is ERb, but passing an additional `:type` option allows you to choose Haml.

```
render inline: "%span.foo #{@foo.name}", type: "haml"
```

💬 Courtenay says . . .

If you were one of my employees, I'd reprimand you for using view code in the
controller, even if it is only one line. Keep your view-related code in the views!

4.3.8   Accessing Helpers in the Controller

If you've decided to use inline template code in your controllers despite our advice
to the contrary, then you might as well have access to your view helpers too. Rails
gives you access via the `helpers` method of the base controller class. It returns a
module containing all the helper methods available to the view.

```
module UsersHelper
  def full_name(user)
    user.first_name + user.last_name
  end
end

class UsersController < ApplicationController

  def update
    @user = User.find params[:id]
    if @user.update(user_params)
      notice = "#{helpers.full_name(@user) is successfully updated}"
      redirect_to user_path(@user), notice: notice
    else
      render :edit
    end
  end
end
```

As shown in the preceding example, using helpers inside your controllers is
occasionally very useful for generating dynamic flash messages.

4.3.9   Rendering JavaScript

Rails can execute arbitrary JavaScript expressions in your browser.

```
render js: "alert('Hello world!')"
```

The supplied string will be sent to the browser with a MIME type of `text/`
`javascript`.

4.3.10 Rendering Text

What if you simply need to send plain text back to the browser, particularly when responding to XHR and certain types of web service requests?

```
render plain: 'Submission accepted'
```

4.3.11 Rendering Raw Body Output

You can send a raw content back to the browser, without setting any content type, by using the `:body` option.

```
render body:
```

This option should be used only if you don't care about the content type of the response. Using `:plain` or `:html` is usually more appropriate. Unless overridden, the response returned from this render option will be `text/html`.

4.3.12 Rendering Other Types of Structured Data

The `render` command also accepts a series of (convenience) options for returning structured data such as JSON or XML. The content-type of the response will be set appropriately and additional options apply.[1]

4.3.12.1 `:json`

JSON[2] is a small subset of JavaScript selected for its usability as a lightweight data-interchange format. It is mostly used as a way of sending data down to JavaScript code running in a rich web application via Ajax calls. Active Record has built-in support for conversion to JSON, which makes Rails an ideal platform for serving up JSON data, as in the following example:

```
render json: @record
```

As long as the parameter responds to `to_json`, Rails will call it for you, which means you don't have to call it yourself with Active Record objects.

Any additional options passed to `render :json` are also included in the invocation of `to_json`.

```
render json: @projects, include: :tasks
```

---

1. Yehuda has written an excellent description of how to register additional rendering options at https://blog.engineyard.com/2010/render-options-in-rails-3/.
2. For more information on JSON go to http://www.json.org/.

Additionally, if you're doing JSONP, you can supply the name of a callback function to be invoked in the browser when it gets your response. Just add a `:callback` option with the name of a valid JavaScript method.

```
render json: @record, callback: 'updateRecordsDisplay'
```

4.3.12.2   `:xml`

Active Record also has built-in support for conversion to XML, as in the following example:

```
render xml: @record
```

As long as the parameter responds to `to_xml`, Rails will call it for you, which means you don't have to call it yourself with Active Record objects.

Any additional options passed to `render :xml` are also included in the invocation of `to_xml`.

```
render xml: @projects, include: :tasks
```

4.3.13   Default Rendering Policies

Template lookup for rendering takes into account the action name, locales, format, variant, template handlers, etc. We'll discuss how these parameters are specified momentarily.

If templates exist for the controller action, *but not in the right format (or variant, etc.)*, then an `ActionController::UnknownFormat` is raised, which may result in **204 No Content** being returned to the client. This is a signficant departure from older Rails behavior of just picking a default template to render. The reason for the change is that the list of available templates is assumed to be a complete enumeration of all the possible formats (or variants) wanted by the developer. In other words, having only JSON templates defined is your way of indicating that the controller action is, for instance, not meant to handle HTML or XML requests.

Now if you are in development mode, and the current request is an "interactive" browser request, meaning that you got there by entering the URL in the address bar, submitting a form, clicking on a link, etc. as opposed to an XHR or non-browser API request, then the raising of `ActionView::UnknownFormat` should result in a helpful error message being displayed in the browser.

A lot of times, the reason Rails is not finding a suitable template to render for your action is because you forgot to end your method with a call to `re-direct_to`.

In any case, if Rails cannot find a template to render, remember that it will respond to the request with "204 No Content." The tricky thing about that particular status code is that many browsers will simply ignore it and do nothing. If you're not paying attention to what's going on (particularly the Rails server console), you might think that the previous page re-rendered, especially if it contained an error status or message. Don't say we didn't warn you.

4.3.14   Rendering Nothing

If you really don't want to render anything at all, don't just omit your action templates. Explicitly indicate your intention by using the `head` method. It takes a symbol corresponding to the desired status code.

```
head :ok
```

A common use of this technique is to block unauthorized access.

```
head :unauthorized
```

The `head` method also accepts an options hash that is interpreted as header names and values to be included with the response. To illustrate, consider the following example, which returns an empty response with a status of 201 and also sets the `Location` header:

```
head :created, location: auction_path(@auction)
```

4.3.15   Rendering Options

Most calls to the `render` method accept additional options. Here they are in alphabetical order.

4.3.15.1 `:content_type`

All content flying around the web is associated with a MIME type.[3] For instance, HTML content is labeled with a content-type of `text/html`. However, there are

---

3. MIME is specified in five RFC documents, so it is much more convenient to point you to a rather good description of MIME provided by Wikipedia at http://en.wikipedia.org/wiki/MIME.

Controllers

occasions where you want to send the client something other than HTML. Rails doesn't validate the format of the MIME identifier you pass to the `:content_ type` option, so make sure it is valid.

4.3.15.2 `:layout`

By default, Rails has conventions regarding the layout template it chooses to wrap your response in, and those conventions are covered in detail in Chapter 10, "Action View." The `:layout` option makes it possible for you to specify whether you want a layout template to be rendered if you pass it a boolean value or the name of a layout template, if you want to deviate from the default.

```
render layout: false      # disable layout template
render layout: 'login'  # a template app/views/layouts is assumed
```

4.3.15.3 `:status`

The HTTP protocol includes many standard status codes[4] indicating a variety of conditions in response to a client's request. Rails will automatically use the appropriate status for most common cases, such as `200 OK` for a successful request.

The theory and techniques involved in properly using the full range of HTTP status codes would require a dedicated chapter, perhaps an entire book. For your convenience, Table 4.1 demonstrates some codes that I've occasionally found useful in my day-to-day Rails programming.

Table 4.1 Common HTTP status codes

Status Code	Description
200 OK	Everything is fine and here is your content.
201 Created	A new resource has been created and its location can be found in the Location HTTP response header.

---

4. For a list of all the HTTP status codes supported in Rails (all 59 of them!), consult the documentation for Rack at http://www.rubydoc.info/github/rack/ rack/Rack/Utils. The fully documented, official list of status codes is available in this RFC: http://www.w3.org/Protocols/rfc2616/rfc2616-sec10.html.

Table 4.1 Common HTTP status codes (*continued*)

Status Code	Description
307 Temporary Redirect	The requested resource resides temporarily under a different URI.
	Occasionally, you need to temporarily redirect the user to a different action, perhaps while some long-running process is happening or while the account of a particular resource's owner is suspended.
	This particular status code dictates that an HTTP response header named `Location` contain the URI of the resource that the client redirects to. Since the `render` method doesn't take a hash of response header fields, you have to set them manually prior to invoking `render`. Luckily, the `response` hash is in scope within controller methods, as in the following example:

```
def paid_resource
  if current_user.account_expired?
  response.headers['Location'] =
  account_url(current_user)
    render text: "Account expired",
    status: 307
    end
end
```

401 Unauthorized	Sometimes a user will not provide credentials to view a restricted resource or authentication and/or authorization will fail.
	Assuming using a Basic or Digest HTTP Authentication scheme, when that happens you should probably return a `401`.
403 Forbidden The server understood the request, but is refusing to fulfill it.	I like to use `403` in conjunction with a short `render :text` message in situations where the client has requested a resource that is not normally available via the web application's interface.
	In other words, the request appears to have happened via artificial means. A human or robot, for reasons innocent or guilty (it doesn't matter), is trying to trick the server into doing something it isn't supposed to do.
	For example, my current Rails application is public-facing and is visited by the GoogleBot on a daily basis. Probably due to a bug existing at some point, the URL /favorites was indexed.
	Unfortunately, /favorites is only supposed to be available to logged-in users. However, once Google knows about a URL it will keep coming back for it in the future. This is how I told it to stop:

```
def index
  return render nothing: true,
    status: 403 unless logged_in?
    @favorites = current_user.favorites.all
end
```

(*continued*)

Controllers

Table 4.1   Common HTTP status codes (*continued*)

Status Code	Description
404 Not Found The server cannot find the resource you requested.	You may choose to use 404 when a resource of a specific given ID does not exist in your database (whether due to it being an invalid ID or due to the resource having been deleted). For example, "GET /people/2349594934896107" doesn't exist in our database at all, so what do we display? Do we render a show view with a flash message saying no person with that ID exists? Not in our RESTful world. A 404 would be better. Moreover, if we happen to be using something like paranoia and we know that the resource used to exist in the past, we could respond with 410 Gone.
500 Internal Server Error	The server encountered an unexpected condition that prevented it from fulfilling the request. You probably know by now, this is the status code that Rails serves up if you have an error in your code.
503 Service Unavailable The server is temporarily unavailable.	The 503 code comes in very handy when taking a site down for maintenance, particularly when upgrading RESTful web services.

4.4   Additional Layout Options

You can specify layout options at the controller class level if you want to reuse layouts for multiple actions.

```
class EventController < ActionController::Base
  layout "events", only: [:index, :new]
  layout "global", except: [:index, :new]
end
```

The layout method can accept either a String, Symbol, or boolean, with a hash of arguments after.

String Determines the template name to use.

Symbol Call the method with this name, which is expected to return a string with a template name.

true Raises an argument error.

false Do not use a layout.

The optional arguments are either :only or :except and expect an array of action names that should or should not apply to the layout being specified.

4.5   Redirecting

The life cycle of a Rails application is divided into requests. Rendering a template, whether the default one or an alternate one—or, for that matter, rendering a partial or some text or anything—is the final step in the handling of a request. Redirecting, however, means terminating the current request and asking the client to initiate a new one.

Look at this example of a form-handling `create` method:

```
def create
  if @event.save
    redirect_to :index, notice: "Event created!"
  else
    render :new
  end
end
```

If the save operation succeeds, we `redirect_to` a different action along with a notice message for the flash hash. In this case, it's the `index` action. The logic here is that if the new `Event` record gets saved, the next order of business is to take the user back to the top-level view.

The main reason to redirect rather than just render a template after creating or editing a resource (really a POST action) has to do with browser reload behavior. If you didn't redirect, the user would be prompted to re-submit the form if they hit the back button or reload.

💬 Sebastian says . . .

Which redirect is the right one? When you use Rails' `redirect_to` method, you tell the user agent (i.e., the browser) to perform a new request for a different URL. That response can mean different things, and it's why modern HTTP has four different status codes for redirection. The old HTTP 1.0 had two codes: 301 aka *Moved Permanently* and 302 aka *Moved Temporarily*.

A permanent redirect meant that the user agent should forget about the old URL and use the new one from now on, updating any references it might have kept (i.e., a bookmark or in the case of Google, its search databases). A temporary redirect was a *one-time only* affair. The original URL was still valid, but for this particular request the user agent should fetch a new resource from the redirection URL.

But there was a problem: If the original request had been a POST, what method should be used for the redirected request? For permanent redirects it

Controllers

was safe to assume the new request should be a GET, since that was the case in all usage scenarios. But temporary redirects were used both for redirecting to a view of a resource that had just been modified in the original POST request (which happens to be the most common usage pattern) and also for redirecting the entire original POST request to a new URL that would take care of it.

HTTP 1.1 solved this problem with the introduction of two new status codes: 303 meaning *See Other* and 307 meaning *Temporary Redirect*. A 303 redirect would tell the user agent to perform a GET request, regardless of what the original verb was, whereas a 307 would always use the same method used for the original request. These days, most browsers handle 302 redirects the same way as 303, with a GET request, which is the argument used by the Rails Core team to keep using 302 in `redirect_to`. A 303 status would be the better alternative because it leaves no room for interpretation (or confusion), but I guess nobody has found it annoying enough to push for a patch.

If you ever need a 307 redirect, say, to continue processing a POST request in a different action, you can always accomplish your own custom redirect by assigning a path to `response.header["Location"]` and then rendering with `render status: 307`.

4.5.1   The `redirect_to` Method

The `redirect_to` method takes two parameters:

```
redirect_to(target, response_status = {})
```

The `target` parameter takes one of several forms.

Hash   The URL will be generated by calling `url_for` with the argument provided.

```
redirect_to action: "show", id: 5
```

Active Record object   The URL will be generated by calling `url_for` with the object provided, which should generate a named URL for that record.

```
redirect_to post
```

String starting with protocol like http://   Used directly as the target URL for redirection.

```
redirect_to "http://www.rubyonrails.org"
redirect_to articles_url
```

String not containing a protocol The current protocol and host is prepended to
the argument and used for redirection.

```
redirect_to "/"
redirect_to articles_path
```

Redirection happens as a "302 Moved" header unless otherwise specified. The
`response_status` parameter takes a hash of arguments. The code can be specified by name or number, as in the following examples:

```
redirect_to post_url(@post), status: :found
redirect_to :atom, status: :moved_permanently
redirect_to post_url(@post), status: 301
redirect_to :atom, status: 302
```

It is also possible to assign a flash message as part of the redirection. There are two
special accessors for commonly used flash names `alert` and `notice`, as well as a
general purpose `flash` bucket.

```
redirect_to post_url(@post), alert: "Watch it, mister!"
redirect_to post_url(@post), status: :found, notice: "Pay attention to the road"
redirect_to post_url(@post), status: 301, flash: { updated_post_id: @post.id }
redirect_to :atom, alert: "Something serious happened"
```

As of Rails 4, you can register your own flash types by using the `ActionControl-`
`ler::Flash.add_flash_types` macro-style method.

```
class ApplicationController
  ...
  add_flash_types :error
end
```

When a flash type is registered, a special flash accessor, similar to `alert` and
`notice`, becomes available to be used with `redirect_to`.

```
redirect_to post_url(@post), error: "Something went really wrong!"
```

💬 Courtenay says . . .

Remember that redirect and render statements don't magically halt execution of your controller action method. To prevent `DoubleRenderError`,
consider explicitly calling return after `redirect_to` or render like this:

```
def show
  @user = User.find(params[:id])
```

Controllers

```
    if @user.activated?
      render :activated and return
    end
    ...
  end
```

4.5.2 The `redirect_back` Method

You can use `redirect_back` to return the user to the page they just came from, a very useful technique in traditional web applications. The location to "go back to" is pulled from the HTTP_REFERER header. Since it isn't guaranteed to be set by the browser, you must provide a `fallback_location` parameter.

```
redirect_back fallback_location: root_path
```

If you're upgrading from earlier versions of Rails, this technique used to work with the magic symbol `:back`.

```
redirect_to :back # doesn't work in Rails 5
```

4.6 Controller/View Communication

When a view template is rendered, it generally makes use of data that the controller has pulled from the database. In other words, the controller gets what it needs from the model layer and hands it off to the view.

The way Rails implements controller-to-view data handoffs is through instance variables. Typically, a controller action initializes one or more instance variables. Those instance variables can then be used by the view.

There's a bit of irony (and possible confusion for newcomers) in the choice of instance variables to share data between controllers and views. The main reason that instance variables exist is so that objects (whether `Controller` objects, `String` objects, and so on) can hold on to data that they don't share with other objects. When your controller action is executed, everything is happening in the context of a controller object—an instance of, say, `DemoController` or `EventController`. *Context* includes the fact that every instance variable in the code belongs to the controller instance.

When the view template is rendered, the context is that of a different object, an instance of `ActionView::Base`. That instance has its own instance variables and does not have access to those of the controller object.

So instance variables, on the face of it, are about the worst choice for a way for two objects to share data. However, it's possible to make it happen—or make it appear to happen. What Rails does is to loop through the controller object's variables and, for each one, create an instance variable for the view object, with the same name and containing the same data.

It's kind of labor-intensive for the framework: It's like copying over a grocery list by hand. But the end result is that things are easier for you, the programmer. If you're a Ruby purist, you might wince a little bit at the thought of instance variables serving to connect objects, rather than separate them. On the other hand, being a Ruby purist should also include understanding the fact that you can do lots of different things in Ruby—such as copying instance variables in a loop. So there's nothing really un-Ruby-like about it. And it does provide a seamless connection, from the programmer's perspective, between a controller and the template it's rendering.

Controllers

💬 Stephen says . . .

I'm a cranky old man, and dammit, Rails is wrong, wrong, wrong. Using instance variables to share data with the view sucks. If you want to see how my Decent Exposure library helps you avoid this horrible practice, skip ahead to the section "Decent Exposure."

4.7   Action Callbacks

Action callbacks enable controllers to run shared pre- and post-processing code for their actions. These callbacks can be used to do authentication, caching, or auditing before the intended action is performed. Callback declarations are macro-style class methods, that is, they appear at the top of your controller method, inside the class context, before method definitions. We suggest omitting the parentheses around the method arguments, to emphasize their declarative nature, like this:

```
before_action :require_authentication
```

As with many other macro-style methods in Rails, you can pass as many symbols as you want to the callback method:

```
before_action :security_scan, :audit, :compress
```

Or you can break them out into separate lines, like this:

```
before_action :security_scan
before_action :audit
before_action :compress
```

You should make your action callback methods `protected` or `private`; otherwise, they might be callable as public actions on your controller (via the default route).

● Tim says . . .

In addition to `protected` and `private`, we can declare that a method should never be dispatched with the more intention-revealing `hide_action`.

Importantly, action callbacks have access to `request`, `response`, and all the instance variables set by other callbacks in the chain or by the action (in the case of `after` callbacks). Action callbacks can set instance variables to be used by the requested action and often do so.

4.7.1   Action Callback Inheritance

Controller inheritance hierarchies share action callbacks *downward*. Your average Rails application has an `ApplicationController` from which all other controllers inherit, so if you wanted to add action callbacks that are always run no matter what, that would be the place to do so.

```
class ApplicationController < ActionController::Base
  after_action :compress
```

Subclasses can also add and/or skip already defined action callbacks without affecting the superclass. For example, consider the two related classes in Listing 4.2, and how they interact.

Listing 4.2   A pair of cooperating `before` callbacks
```
class BankController < ActionController::Base
  before_action :audit

  protected

  def audit
    # record this controller's actions and parameters in an audit log
  end

end

class VaultController < BankController
```

```
before_action :verify_credentials

protected

def verify_credentials
  # make sure the user is allowed into the vault
end

end
```

Any actions performed on `BankController` (or any of its subclasses) will cause the `audit` method to be called before the requested action is executed. On the `VaultController`, first the `audit` method is called, followed by `verify_credentials`, because that's the "downwards" order in which the callbacks were specified, as per the inheritance hierarchy. (Callbacks are executed in the class context where they're declared, and the `BankController` has to be loaded before `VaultController`, since it's the parent class.)

If the audit method happens to call `render` or `redirect_to` for whatever reason, `verify_credentials` and the requested action are never called. This is called *halting the action callback chain* (see "Action Callback Chain Halting" section).

4.7.2 Action Callback Types

An action callback can take one of three forms: method reference (symbol), external class, or block. The first is by far the most common and works by referencing a protected method somewhere in the inheritance hierarchy of the controller. In the bank example in Listing 4.2, both `BankController` and `VaultController` use this form.

4.7.2.1 Action Callback Classes

Using an external class makes for more easily reused generic callbacks, such as output compression. External callback classes are implemented by having a static callback method on any class and then passing this class to the action callback method, as in Listing 4.3. The name of the class method should match the type of callback desired (for example, before, after, around).

Listing 4.3 An output compression action callback
```
class OutputCompressionActionCallback
  def self.after(controller)
    controller.response.body = compress(controller.response.body)
  end
end
```

Controllers

```
class NewspaperController < ActionController::Base
  after_action OutputCompressionActionCallback
end
```

The method of the *action callback* class is passed the controller instance it is running in. It gets full access to the controller and can manipulate it as it sees fit. The fact that it gets an instance of the controller to play with also makes it seem like feature envy, and frankly, I haven't had much use for this technique.

4.7.2.2   Inline Method

The inline method (using a block parameter to the action method) can be used to quickly do something small that doesn't require a lot of explanation or just as a quick test.

```
class WeblogController < ActionController::Base
  before_action do
    redirect_to new_user_session_path unless authenticated?
  end
end
```

The block is executed in the context of the controller instance, using `instance_eval`. This means that the block has access to both the request and response objects complete with convenience methods for params, session, template, and assigns.

4.7.3   Action Callback Chain Ordering

Using `before_action` and `after_action` appends the specified callbacks to the existing chain. That's usually just fine, but sometimes you care more about the order in which the callbacks are executed. When that's the case, you can use `prepend_before_action` and `prepend_after_action`. Callbacks added by these methods will be put at the beginning of their respective chain and executed before the rest, like the example in Listing 4.4.

Listing 4.4   An example of prepending before action callbacks
```
class ShoppingController < ActionController::Base
  before_action :verify_open_shop

class CheckoutController < ShoppingController
  prepend_before_action :ensure_items_in_cart, :ensure_items_in_stock
```

The action callback chain for the `CheckoutController` is now `:ensure_items_in_cart`, `:ensure_items_in_stock`, `:verify_open_shop`. So if either of the `ensure` callbacks halts execution, we'll never get around to seeing if the shop is open.

You may pass multiple action callback arguments of each type as well as a block. If a block is given, it is treated as the last argument.

4.7.4   Around Action Callbacks

Around action callbacks wrap an action, executing code both before and after the action that they wrap. They may be declared as method references, blocks, or objects with an `around` class method.

To use a method as an `around_action`, pass a symbol naming the Ruby method. Use `yield` within the method to run the action.

For example, Listing 4.5 has an `around` callback that logs exceptions (not that you need to do anything like this in your application; it's just an example).

Listing 4.5   An around action callback to log exceptions

```
around_action :catch_exceptions

private

def catch_exceptions
  yield
rescue => exception
  logger.debug "Caught exception! #{exception}"
  raise
end
```

To use a block as an `around_action`, pass a block taking as args both the controller and the action parameters. You can't call `yield` from blocks in Ruby, so explicitly invoke `call` on the action parameter:

```
around_action do |controller, action|
  logger.debug "before #{controller.action_name}"
  action.call
  logger.debug "after #{controller.action_name}"
end
```

To use an action callback object with `around_action`, pass an object responding to `:around`. With an action callback method, yield to the block like this:

```
around_action BenchmarkingActionCallback

class BenchmarkingActionCallback
```

```
  def self.around(controller)
    Benchmark.measure { yield }
  end
end
```

4.7.5 Action Callback Chain Skipping

Declaring an action callback on a base class conveniently applies to its subclasses, but sometimes a subclass should skip some of the action callbacks it inherits from a superclass:

```
class ApplicationController < ActionController::Base
  before_action :authenticate
  around_action :catch_exceptions
end

class SignupController < ApplicationController
  skip_before_action :authenticate
end

class HackedTogetherController < ApplicationController
  skip_action_callback :catch_exceptions
end
```

4.7.6 Action Callback Conditions

Action callbacks may be limited to specific actions by declaring the actions to include or exclude, using :only or :except options. Both options accept single actions (such as only: :index) or arrays of actions (except: [:foo, :bar]).

```
class Journal < ActionController::Base
  before_action :authorize, only: [:edit, :delete]

  around_action except: :index do |controller, action_block|
    results = Profiler.run(&action_block)
    controller.response.sub! "</body>", "#{results}</body>"
  end

  private

  def authorize
    # Redirect to login unless authenticated.
  end
end
```

4.7.7 Action Callback Chain Halting

The before_action and around_action methods may halt the request before the body of a controller action method is run. This is useful, for example, for denying access to unauthenticated users. As mentioned earlier, all you have to do to halt the before action chain is call render or redirect_to. After action callbacks will not be executed if the before action chain is halted.

Around action callbacks halt the request unless the action block is called. If an around action callback returns before yielding, it is effectively halting the chain and any after action callbacks will not be run.

4.8 Streaming

Rails has built-in support for streaming binary content back to the requesting client, as opposed to its normal duties rendering view templates.

4.8.1 `ActionController::Live`

Rails 4 introduced the ActionControler::Live module, a controller mixin that enables the controller actions to stream on-the-fly generated data to the client. It adds an I/O like interface object named stream to the response object. Using stream, you can call write, to immediately stream data to the client, and close, to explicitly close the stream. The response object is equivalent to what you'd expect in the context of the controller and can be used to control various things in the HTTP response, such as the Content-Type header.

The following example demonstrates how you can stream a large amount of on-the-fly generated data to the browser:

```
class StreamingController < ApplicationController
  include ActionController::Live

  # Streams about 180 MB of generated data to the browser.
  def stream
    response.headers["Content-Type"] = "text/event-stream"
    10_000_000.times do |i|
      response.stream.write "Event #{i} just happened\n"
    end
  ensure
    response.stream.close
  end
end
```

When using live streaming, there are a couple of things to take into consideration:

- All actions executed from `ActionController::Live` enabled controllers are run in a separate thread. This means the controller action code being executed must be threadsafe.

- A concurrent Ruby web server, such as puma,[5] is required to take advantage of live streaming.

- Headers must be added to the response before anything is written to the client.

- Streams must be closed once finished, otherwise a socket may be left open indefinitely.

For an interesting perspective on why live streaming was added into Rails and how to utilize it to serve Server-Sent Events, make sure to read Aaron Patterson's blog post on the subject.[6]

4.8.2   Support for EventSource

Live streaming is most useful with a relatively new W3C recommendation for Server-Sent Events,[7] commonly known as the EventSource API. For many applications, it presents a simple and compelling alternative to XHR polling and web sockets, with the limitation that the client can only listen to updates; it cannot publish anything. It seems perfect for things like updating read-only views (like dashboards) with real-time statistics, social media updates, etc.

🐞 Due to incomplete browser support, try using my friend Aslak's EventSource[8] JavaScript library, as opposed to trying to use the API directly.

`EventSource` and live streaming (together with Redis) make it trivial to implement things like chat functionality. Given a server with functionality like this:

```
class ChatChannelController < ApplicationController
  include ActionController::Live

  def show
    response.headers["Content-Type"] = "text/event-stream"
    redis = Redis.new
    redis.psubscribe("channel-#{params[:id]}:*") do |on|
      on.pmessage do |subscription, event, data|
        response.stream.write "data: #{data}\n\n"
```

---

5. Puma Web Server http://puma.io/

6. http://tenderlovemaking.com/2012/07/30/is-it-live.html

7. https://www.w3.org/TR/eventsource/

8. https://www.npmjs.com/package/eventsource

```
      end
    end
  rescue IOError
    # Client disconnected
  ensure
    redis.quit
    response.stream.close
  end
end
```

Here's essential JavaScript on the browser side:

```
source = new EventSource(chat_channel_url(id));
source.addEventListener("message", function(e) {
  appendChatMessage(e.data)
});
```

There are some additional features of this API that you should know about.

An optional `id` field represents the unique id of the message just sent. If available, then when EventSource automatically reestablishes a lost connection, it will include a header (Last-Event-ID) in its request to the server, enabling you to pick up where you left off.

You can send different events by specifying an `event` type in your stream. Here is a stream that has two event types, "add" and "remove":

```
event: add
data: 73857293
event: remove
data: 2153
event: add
data: 113411
```

The script to handle such a stream would look like this (where `addHandler` and `removeHandler` are functions that take one argument, the event):

```
var source = new EventSource('updates.cgi');
source.addEventListener('add', addHandler);
source.addEventListener('remove', removeHandler);
```

If you just send data without an event specified, the default type is "message."

For a complete description of this spec, go to https://html.spec.whatwg.org/multipage/comms.html#server-sent-events.

Controllers

4.8.3   Streaming Templates

By default, when a view is rendered in Rails, it first renders the template, and then the layout of the view. When returning a response to a client, all required Active Record queries are run, and the entire rendered template is returned all in one burst.

Introduced in version 3.2, Rails added support for streaming views to the client. This enables views to be rendered as they are processed, including only running Active Record scoped queries when they are needed. In order to achieve this, Rails reverses the normal rendering order. The layout is rendered first instead of last, then each part of the template is processed.

To enable view streaming, pass the option `stream` to the `render` method.

```
class EventController < ActionController::Base
  def index
    @events = Events.all
    render stream: true
  end
end
```

This approach can only be used to stream view templates. To stream other types of data, such as JSON, take a look at the section "`ActionController::Live`."

4.8.4   Streaming Buffers and Files

Rails also supports sending buffers and files with two methods in the `Action-Controller::Streaming` module: `send_data` and `send_file`.

4.8.4.1   `send_data(data, options = {})`

The `send_data` method enables you to send textual or binary data in a buffer to the user as a named file. You can set options that affect the content type and apparent filename and alter whether an attempt is made to display the data inline with other content in the browser or the user is prompted to download it as an attachment.

OPTIONS

The `send_data` method has the following options:

`:filename` Suggests a filename for the browser to use.

`:type` Specifies an HTTP content type. Defaults to `'application/octet -stream'`.

`:disposition` Specifies whether the file will be shown inline or downloaded. Valid values are `inline` and `attachment` (default).

:status Specifies the status code to send with the response. Defaults to '200 OK'.

Usage Examples
Creating a download of a dynamically generated tarball:

```
send_data my_generate_tarball_method('dir'), filename: 'dir.tgz'
```

Sending a dynamic image to the browser, like, for instance, a captcha system:

```
require 'RMagick'

class CaptchaController < ApplicationController

  def image
    # create an RMagic canvas and render difficult to read text on it
    ...

    img = canvas.flatten_images
    img.format = "JPG"

    # send it to the browser
    send_data img.to_blob, disposition: 'inline', type: 'image/jpg'
  end
end
```

4.8.4.2 send_file(path, options = {})
The send_file method sends an existing file down to the client using Rack::Sendfile middleware, which intercepts the response and replaces it with a webserver specific X-Sendfile header. The web server then becomes responsible for writing the file contents to the client instead of Rails. This can dramatically reduce the amount of work accomplished in Ruby and takes advantage of the web servers optimized file delivery code.[9]

Options
Here are the options available for send_file:

:filename Suggests a filename for the browser to use. Defaults to File .basename(path).

---

9. More information, particularly about webserver configuration available at http://rack.rubyforge.org/doc/Rack/Sendfile.html

Controllers

:type Specifies an HTTP content type. Defaults to `'application/octet -stream'`.

:disposition Specifies whether the file will be shown inline or downloaded. Valid values are `'inline'` and `'attachment'` (default).

:status Specifies the status code to send with the response. Defaults to `'200 OK'`.

:url_based_filename Should be set to `true` if you want the browser to guess the filename from the URL, which is necessary for I18n filenames on certain browsers (setting `:filename` overrides this option).

There's also a lot more to read about `Content-*` HTTP headers[10] if you'd like to provide the user with additional information that Rails doesn't natively support (such as `Content-Description`).

SECURITY CONSIDERATIONS

Note that the `send_file` method can be used to read any file accessible to the user running the Rails server process, so be extremely careful to sanitize[11] the `path` parameter if it's in any way coming from untrusted users.

If you want a quick example, try the following controller code:

```
class FileController < ActionController::Base
  def download
    send_file(params[:path])
  end
end
```

Give it a route

```
get 'file/download' => 'file#download'
```

then fire up your server and request any file on your system:

```
$ curl http://localhost:3000/file/download?path=/etc/hosts
##
# Host Database
#
# localhost is used to configure the loopback interface
# when the system is booting. Do not change this entry.
```

---

10. See the official spec at http://www.w3.org/Protocols/rfc2616/rfc2615-sec14.html.

11. Heiko Webers has an old, yet still useful write-up about sanitizing filenames at http://www.rorsecurity .info/2007/03/27/working-with-files-in-rails/.

```
##
127.0.0.1    localhost
255.255.255.255 broadcasthost
::1             localhost
fe80::1%lo0 localhost
```

● Courtenay says . . .

There are few legitimate reasons to serve static files through Rails. Unless you are protecting content, I strongly recommend you cache the file after sending it. There are a few ways to do this. Since a correctly configured web server will serve files in `public/` and bypass `rails`, the easiest is to just copy the newly generated file to the `public` directory after sending it:

```
public_dir = File.join(Rails.root, 'public', controller_path)
FileUtils.mkdir_p(public_dir)
FileUtils.cp(filename, File.join(public_dir, filename))
```

All subsequent views of this resource will be served by the web server.

USAGE EXAMPLES

Here's the simplest example, just a simple zip file download:

```
send_file '/path/to.zip'
```

Sending a JPG to be displayed inline requires specification of the MIME content-type:

```
send_file '/path/to.jpg',
          type: 'image/jpeg',
          disposition: 'inline'
```

This will show a 404 HTML page in the browser. We append a `charset` declaration to the MIME type information:

```
send_file '/path/to/404.html,
          type: 'text/html; charset=utf-8',
          status: 404
```

How about streaming an FLV file to a browser-based Flash video player?

```
send_file @video_file.path,
          filename: video_file.title + '.flv',
          type: 'video/x-flv',
          disposition: 'inline'
```

Controllers

Regardless of how you do it, you may wonder why you would need a mechanism to send files to the browser anyway, since it already has one built in— requesting files from the `public` directory. Well, many times a web application will front files that need to be protected from public access. (For example, it's a common requirement for membership-based adult websites.)

4.9   Variants

Rails 4.1 gave Action Pack a feature called *variants,* the capability to render different HTML, JSON, and XML templates based on some criteria. To illustrate, assuming we have an application that requires specific templates to be rendered for iPhone devices only, we can set a request variant in a `before_action` callback.

```ruby
class ApplicationController < ActionController::Base
  before_action :set_variant

  protected

  def set_variant
    request.variant = :mobile if request.user_agent =~ /iPhone/i
  end
end
```

ⓘ Note

Note that `request.variant` can be set based on any arbitrary condition, such as the existence of certain request headers, subdomain, current user, API version, etc.

Next, in a controller action, we can explicitly respond to variants like any other format. This includes the capability to execute code specific to the format by supplying a block to the declaration.

```ruby
class PostsController < ApplicationController
  def index
    ...
    respond_to do |format|
      format.html do |html|
        html.mobile do # renders app/views/posts/index.html+mobile.haml
          @mobile_only_variable = true
        end
      end
    end
  end
end
```

By default, if no `respond_to` block is declared within your action, Action Pack will automatically render the correct variant template if one exists in your views directory.

Variants are a powerful new feature in Action Pack that can be utilized for more than just rendering views based on a user agent. Since a variant can be set based on any condition, it can be utilized for a variety of use cases, such as rolling out features to a certain group of application users or even A/B testing a template.

4.10   Conclusion

In this chapter, we covered concepts at the very core of how Rails works: the request dispatcher and how controllers render views. Importantly, we covered the use of rendering and controller action callbacks, which you will use constantly, for all sorts of purposes. The Action Controller API is fundamental knowledge, which you need to understand well along your way to becoming an expert Rails programmer.

Moving on, we'll leave Action Pack and head over to the other major component API of Rails: Active Record.

Controllers

CHAPTER 5
Working with Active Record

An object that wraps a row in a database table or view, encapsulates the database access, and adds domain logic on that data.

—Martin Fowler, *Patterns of Enterprise Architecture*

The *Active Record pattern*, identified by Martin Fowler in his seminal work, *Patterns of Enterprise Architecture*, maps one domain class to one database table, and one instance of that class to each row of that database. It is a simple approach that, while not perfectly applicable in all cases, provides a powerful framework for database access and object persistence in your application.

The Rails Active Record framework is an implementation of the pattern and includes mechanisms for representing models and their relationships, CRUD (create, read, update, and delete) operations, complex searches, validations, callbacks, and many more features.

As with the rest of Rails, Active Record relies heavily on *convention over configuration.* It's easy to use it when you start a project with a new database schema following those conventions. However, Active Record also provides configuration settings that let you adapt it to work well with legacy database schemas that don't necessarily conform to Rails conventions.

According to Martin Fowler, delivering the keynote address at the inaugural Rails conference in 2006, Ruby on Rails has successfully taken the Active Record pattern much further than anyone imagined it could go. It shows you what you can achieve when you have a single-minded focus on a set of ideals, which in the case of Rails is simplicity.

Active
Record

5.1   The Basics

For the sake of completeness, let's briefly review the basics of how Active Record works. In order to create a new model class, the first thing you do is to declare it as a subclass of `ApplicationRecord`, using Ruby's class extension syntax:

```
class Client < ApplicationRecord
end
```

ⓘ `ApplicationRecord` is the default parent model for all other models starting from Rails 5. It is an abstract class inheriting from `ActiveRecord::Base`. If you are coming from earlier versions, don't worry, your models inheriting from `ActiveRecord::Base` will still work.

By convention, an Active Record class named `Client` will be automatically mapped to the `clients` table. Rails understands pluralization, as covered in the section "Pluralization" in Chapter 11.

Also by convention, Active Record will expect an `id` column to use as primary key. It should be an integer, and incrementing of the key should be managed automatically by the database server when creating new records. Note how the class itself makes no mention of the table name, columns, or their datatypes.[1]

Each instance of an Active Record class provides access to the data from one row of the backing database table, in an object-oriented manner. The columns of that row are represented as attributes of the object, using straightforward type conversions (i.e., Ruby strings for varchars, Ruby dates for dates, and so on), and with no default data validation. Attributes are inferred from the column definition pertaining to the tables with which they're linked. Adding, removing, and changing attributes and their types are done by changing the columns of the table in the database.

When you're running a Rails server in development mode, changes to the database schema are reflected in the Active Record objects immediately, via the web browser. However, if you make changes to the schema while you have your Rails console running, the changes will not be reflected automatically. Pick up changes manually by typing `reload!` at the console.

---

1. The useful Annotate gem can automatically maintain schema information in a comment at the top of your model (and other relevant) source files. Check it out at https://github.com/ctran/annotate_models.

● Courtenay says . . .

Active Record is a great example of the Rails "Golden Path." If you keep within its limitations, you can go far, fast. Stray from the path, and you might get stuck in the mud. This Golden Path involves many conventions, like naming your tables in the plural form ("users"). It's common for new developers to Rails and rival web-framework evangelists to complain about how tables must be named in a particular manner, how there are no constraints in the database layer, that foreign keys are handled all wrong, enterprise systems must have composite primary keys, and more. Get the complaining out of your system now, because all these defaults are simply defaults, and in most cases can be overridden with a single line of code or a plugin.

5.2   Macro-Style Methods

Most of the important classes you write while coding a Rails application are configured using what I call *macro-style method invocations* (also known in some circles as a domain-specific language or DSL). Basically, the idea is to have a highly readable block of code at the top of your class that makes it immediately clear how it is configured.

Macro-style invocations are usually placed at the top of the file, and for good reason. Those methods declaratively tell Rails how to manage instances, perform data validation and callbacks, and relate with other models. Many of them involve metaprogramming, meaning that they participate in adding behavior to your class at runtime, in the form of additional instance variables and methods.

5.2.1   Relationship Declarations

For example, look at the `Client` class with some relationships declared. We'll talk about associations extensively in Chapter 7, "Active Record Associations." All I want to do now is to illustrate what I'm talking about when I say macro-style:

```
# app/models/client.rb
class Client < ApplicationRecord
  has_many :billing_codes
  has_many :billable_weeks
  has_many :timesheets, through: :billable_weeks
end
```

As a result of those three has_many declarations, the Client class gains at least three new attributes, proxy objects that let you manipulate the associated collections interactively.

I still remember the first time I sat with an experienced Java programmer friend of mine to teach him some Ruby and Rails. After minutes of profound confusion, an almost visible light bulb appeared over his head as he proclaimed, "Oh! They're methods!"

Indeed, they're regular old method calls, in the context of the class object (rather than one of its instances). We leave the parentheses off to emphasize the declarative intention.

When the Ruby interpreter loads client.rb, it executes those has_many methods that are defined as class methods of Active Record's Base class. They are executed in the context of the Client class, adding attributes that are subsequently available to Client instances. It's a programming model that is potentially strange to newcomers but quickly becomes second nature to the Rails programmer.

5.2.2   Convention over Configuration

Convention over configuration is one of the guiding principles of Ruby on Rails. If we follow Rails conventions, very little explicit configuration is needed, which stands in stark contrast to the reams of configuration that are required to get even a simple application running in other technologies.

It's not that a newly bootstrapped Rails application comes with default configuration in place already, reflecting the conventions that will be used. It's that the conventions are baked into the framework, actually hard-coded into its behavior, and you need to override the default behavior with explicit configuration when applicable.

It's also worth mentioning that most configuration happens in close proximity to what you're configuring. You will see associations, validations, and callback declarations at the top of most Active Record models.

I suspect that the first explicit configuration (over convention) that many of us deal with in Active Record is the mapping between class name and database table, since by default Rails assumes that our database name is simply the pluralized form of our class name.

5.2.3 Setting Names Manually

The `table_name` and `primary_key` setter methods let you use any table and primary names you'd like, but you'll have to specify them explicitly in your model class.

```
class Client < ApplicationRecord
  self.table_name = "CLIENT"
  self.primary_key = "CID"
end
```

It's only a couple of extra lines per model, but don't do it if you don't absolutely need it. An example of needing it is in large organizations where you are not at liberty to dictate the naming guidelines for your database schema. In many such places, a separate DBA group controls all database schemas. But if you do have flexibility to choose your schema standards, you should really just follow Rails conventions. They might not be what you're used to, but following them will save you time and unnecessary headaches.

5.2.4 Legacy Naming Schemes

If you are working with legacy schemas, you may be tempted to automatically set `table_name` everywhere, whether you need it or not. Before you get accustomed to doing that, learn the additional options available that might just be more DRY and make your life easier.

Let's assume you need to turn off table pluralization altogether; you would set the following attribute in an initializer, perhaps `config/initializers/legacy_settings.rb`:

```
Rails.application.config.active_record.pluralize_table_names = false
```

There are various other useful attributes of `ActiveRecord::Base`, provided for configuring Rails to work with legacy naming schemes. We'll cover them here for the sake of completeness, but 90% or more of Rails developers never have to worry about this stuff.

`primary_key_prefix_type` Accessor for the prefix type that will be prepended to every primary key column name. If `:table_name` is specified, Active Record will look for `tableid` instead of `id` as the primary column. If `:table_name_with_underscore` is specified, Active Record will look for `table_id` instead of `id`.

Active
Record

table_name_prefix Some departments prefix table names with the name of the database. Set this attribute accordingly to avoid having to include the prefix in all of your model class names.

table_name_suffix Similar to prefix, but adds a common ending to all table names.

5.3 Defining Attributes

The list of attributes associated with an Active Record model class is not declared explicitly, unless you have a reason to do so.[2] At runtime, the Active Record model class reads its attribute information directly from the database definition. Adding, removing, and changing attributes and their type is done by manipulating the database definition itself via Active Record migrations.

The practical implication of the Active Record pattern is that you have to define your database table structure and make sure it exists in the database prior to working with your persistent models. Some people may have issues with that design philosophy, especially if they're coming from a background in top-down design.

> The Rails way is undoubtedly to have model classes that map closely to your database schema. On the other hand, remember you can have models that are simple Ruby classes and do not inherit from `ApplicationRecord`. Among other things, it is common to use non–Active Record model classes to encapsulate data and logic for the view layer.

5.3.1 Default Attribute Values

Migrations let you define default attribute values by passing a `:default` option to the `column` method. However, I feel like default values are part of your domain logic and should be kept together with the rest of the domain logic of your application, in the model layer, instead of being spread around the codebase.

A common example is the case when your model should return the string "n/a" instead of a `nil` (or empty) string for an attribute that has not been populated yet. It's super easy to implement this behavior declaratively using the new Rails 5 Attributes API.

```
class TimesheetEntry < ApplicationRecord
  attribute :category, :string, default: 'n/a'
end
```

---

2. Chapter 9, "Advanced Active Record," fully covers the new Rails 5 Attributes API, including how and when to use it.

But what if you're stuck on an older version of Rails or want the value of the default to depend on the value of other attributes at runtime? The case presents a good way to learn how attributes exist in model objects at runtime.

To begin with, since we're getting into more than just a line of declarative code, let's whip up a quick spec describing the behavior we want. This is often referred to as *test-driven development* (or *TDD,* for short).

```
describe TimesheetEntry do
  it "has a category of 'n/a' if not available" do
    entry = TimesheetEntry.new
    expect(entry.category).to eq('n/a')
  end
end
```

If we run this spec it should fail.

Going back to our model, we note that attribute accessors are usually handled "magically" by Active Record's internals. In this case, we're implementing the default value behavior by overriding the built-in magic with an explicit getter method. All we need to do is to define a method with the same name as the attribute and use Ruby's `||` operator, which will "short-circuit" if `@category` is not nil. If it is nil, then it will return the right-hand value.

```
class TimesheetEntry < ApplicationRecord
  def category
    @category || 'n/a'
  end
end
```

Now we run the spec and it passes. Great. Are we done? Not quite. We should test a case when the real category value should be returned. I'll insert an example with a not-nil category.

```
describe TimesheetEntry do
  it "returns category when available" do
    entry = TimesheetEntry.new(category: "TR5W")
    expect(entry.category).to eq("TR5W")
end

  it "has a category of 'n/a' if not available" do
    entry = TimesheetEntry.new
    expect(entry.category).to eq('n/a')
  end
end
```

Active
Record

Uh-oh. The first spec fails. Seems our default 'n/a' string is being returned no matter what. Which means that the @category instance variable must not be getting set when we thought it was. Should we even know that it is getting set or not? It is an implementation detail of Active Record, is it not?

The fact that Rails does not use instance variables like @category to store the model attributes is in fact an implementation detail. But model instances have a couple of methods, write_attribute and read_attribute, conveniently provided by Active Record for the purposes of overriding default accessors, which is exactly what we're trying to do. Using them, we don't have to know about the implementation details of how the model object uses instance variables. Phew!

Let's fix our TimesheetEntry class.

```
class TimesheetEntry < ApplicationRecord
  def category
    read_attribute(:category) || 'n/a'
  end
end
```

Now the spec passes, and we learned how to use read_attribute. How about a simple example of using its sister method, write_attribute?

```
class SillyFortuneCookie < ApplicationRecord
  def message=(txt)
    write_attribute(:message, txt + ' in bed')
  end
end
```

Alternatively, both of these examples could have been written with the shorter forms of reading and writing attributes, using square brackets.

```
class TimesheetEntry < ApplicationRecord
  def category
    self[:category] || 'n/a'
  end
end

class SillyFortuneCookie < ApplicationRecord
  def message=(txt)
    self[:message] = txt + ' in bed'
  end
end
```

5.4   CRUD: Creating, Reading, Updating, Deleting

The four standard operations of a database system combine to form a popular acronym: CRUD. It sounds somewhat negative, because as a synonym for *garbage* or *unwanted accumulation* the word *crud* in English has a rather bad connotation. However, in Rails circles, use of the word CRUD is benign. In fact, as in earlier chapters, designing your app to function primarily as RESTful CRUD operations is considered a best practice!

5.4.1   Creating New Active Record Model Instances

The most straightforward way to create a new instance of an Active Record model is by using a regular Ruby constructor, the class method `new`. New objects can be instantiated as either empty (by omitting parameters) or pre-set with attributes but not yet saved. Just pass a hash with key names matching the associated table column names. In both instances, valid attribute keys are determined by the column names of the associated table—hence you can't have attributes that aren't part of the table columns.

You can find out if an Active Record object is saved by looking at the value of its id, or programmatically, by using the methods `new_record?` and `persisted?`:

```
>> c = Client.new
=> #<Client id: nil, name: nil, code: nil>
>> c.new_record?
=> true
>> c.persisted?
=> false
```

Active Record constructors take an optional block, which can be used to do additional initialization. The block is executed after any passed-in attributes are set on the instance:

```
>> c = Client.new do |client|
?> client.name = "Nile River Co."
>> client.code = "NRC"
>> end
=> #<Client id: 1, name: "Nile River Co.", code: "NRC">
```

Active Record has a handy-dandy `create` class method that creates a new instance, persists it to the database, and returns it in one operation:

```
>> c = Client.create(name: "Nile RIver, Co.", code: "NRC")
=> #<Client id: 1, name: "Nile River, Co.", code: "NRC" ...>
```

Active
Record

The `create` method takes an optional block, just like `new`.

5.4.2   Reading Active Record Objects

Finding an existing object by its primary key is very simple and is probably one of the first things we all learn about Rails when we first pick up the framework. Just invoke `find` with the key of the specific instance you want to retrieve. Remember that if an instance is not found, a `RecordNotFound` exception is raised.

```
>> first_project = Project.find(1)
=> #<Project id: 1 ...>
>> boom_client = Client.find(99)
ActiveRecord::RecordNotFound: Couldn't find Client with ID=99

>> all_clients = Client.all
=> #<ActiveRecord::Relation [#<Client id: 1, name: "Paper Jam Printers",
   code: "PJP" ...>, #<Client id: 2, name: "Goodness Steaks",
   code: "GOOD_STEAKS" ...>]>

>> first_client = Client.first
=> #<Client id: 1, name: "Paper Jam Printers", code: "PJP" ...>
```

By the way, it is entirely common for methods in Ruby to return different types depending on the parameters used, as illustrated in the example. Depending on how `find` is invoked, you will get either a single Active Record object or an array of them.

For convenience, `first`, `last`, and `all` also exist as syntactic sugar wrappers around the find method.

```
>> Product.last
=> #<Product id: 1, name: "leaf", sku: nil,
   created_at: "2010-01-12 03:34:41", updated_at: "2010-01-12 03:34:41">
```

Since the underlying pattern is so common, the `first_or_initialize` method wraps `first`, and defaults to initializing a new instance with the provided parameters if the result set is empty.

```
>> Event.delete_all
  SQL (9.2ms)  DELETE FROM "events"
=> 5
>> Event.all
  Event Load (0.1ms)  SELECT "events".* FROM "events"
=> #<ActiveRecord::Relation []>
>> e = Event.first_or_initialize(starts_at: Date.today)
```

```
   Event Load (0.1ms)  SELECT  "events".* FROM "events" ORDER BY
         "events"."id" ASC LIMIT ? [["LIMIT", 1]]
=> #<Event id: nil, starts_at: "2016-11-28", ...>
>> e.save
   (0.1ms)  begin transaction
   SQL (0.2ms)  INSERT INTO "events" ...
>> Event.first_or_initialize(starts_at: 1.year.ago)
   Event Load (0.1ms)  SELECT  "events".* FROM "events" ORDER BY
         "events"."id" ASC LIMIT ? [["LIMIT", 1]]
=> #<Event id: 6, starts_at: "2016-11-28", ...>
```

Finally, the `find` method also understands arrays of ids, and raises a `RecordNot-Found` exception if it can't find all of the ids specified:

```
>> Product.find([1, 2])
ActiveRecord::RecordNotFound: Couldn't find all Products with IDs
      (1, 2) (found 1 results, but was looking for 2)
```

A lesser known cousin of `find` is named `take` (since v4.0.2). It returns a record (or N records if a parameter is supplied) without any implied order, instead relying on whatever order is provided by the database implementation. If an order is supplied (even though it would be nonsensical to do so) it will be respected.

```
# returns an object fetched by SELECT * FROM people LIMIT 1
Person.take

# returns 5 objects fetched by SELECT * FROM people LIMIT 5
Person.take(5)
```

5.4.3   Reading and Writing Attributes

After you have retrieved a model instance from the database, you can access each of its columns in several ways. The easiest (and clearest to read) is simply with dot notation:

```
>> first_client.name
=> "Paper Jam Printers"
>> first_client.code
=> "PJP"
```

The private `read_attribute` method of Active Record, covered briefly in an earlier section, is useful to know about and comes in handy when you want to override a default attribute accessor. To illustrate, while still in the Rails console, I'll go ahead and reopen the `Client` class on the fly and override the name accessor to return the value from the database but reversed:

```
>> class Client < ApplicationRecord
>>   def name
>>     read_attribute(:name).reverse
>>   end
>> end
=> nil
>> first_client.name
=> "sretnirP maJ repaP"
```

Hopefully, it's not too painfully obvious for me to demonstrate why you need read_
attribute in that scenario. Recursion is a bitch if it's unexpected:

```
>> class Client < ApplicationRecord
>>   def name
>>     self.name.reverse
>>   end
>> end
=> nil
>> first_client.name
SystemStackError: stack level too deep
        from (irb):21:in 'name'
        from (irb):21:in 'name'
        from (irb):24
```

As can be expected by the existence of a read_attribute method (and as we
covered earlier in the chapter), there is also a write_attribute method that lets
you change attribute values. Just as with attribute getter methods, you can override
the setter methods and provide your own behavior:

```
class Project < ApplicationRecord
  # The description for a project cannot be changed to a blank string
  def description=(new_value)
    write_attribute(:description, new_value) unless new_value.blank?
  end
end
```

The preceding example illustrates a way to do basic validation, since it checks to
make sure that a value is not blank before allowing assignment. However, as we'll see
in Chapter 8, "Validations," there are better ways to do this.

5.4.3.1   Hash Notation

Yet another way to access attributes is using the [attribute_name] operator,
which lets you access the attribute as if it were a regular hash.

```
>> first_client['name']
=> "Paper Jam Printers"
```

```
>> first_client[:name]
=> "Paper Jam Printers"
```

String versus Symbol

Many Rails methods accept symbol and string parameters interchangeably, and that is potentially very confusing. Which is more correct? The general rule is to use symbols when the string is a name for something and a string when it's a value. You should probably be using symbols when it comes to keys of options hashes and the like.

5.4.3.2 The `attributes` Method

There is also an `attributes` method that returns a hash with each attribute and its corresponding value as returned by `read_attribute`. If you use your own custom attribute reader and writer methods, it's important to remember that `attributes` will not use custom attribute readers when accessing its values, but `attributes=` (which lets you do mass assignment) does invoke custom attribute writers.

```
>> first_client.attributes
=> {"name"=>"Paper Jam Printers", "code"=>"PJP", "id"=>1}
```

Being able to grab a hash of all attributes at once is useful when you want to iterate over all of them or pass them in bulk to another function. Note that the hash returned from `attributes` is not a reference to an internal structure of the Active Record object. It is a copy, which means that changing its values will have no effect on the object it came from.

```
>> atts = first_client.attributes
=> {"name"=>"Paper Jam Printers", "code"=>"PJP", "id"=>1}
>> atts["name"] = "Def Jam Printers"
=> "Def Jam Printers"
>> first_client.attributes
=> {"name"=>"Paper Jam Printers", "code"=>"PJP", "id"=>1}
```

To make changes to an Active Record object's attributes in bulk, it is possible to pass a hash to the `attributes` writer.

5.4.4 Accessing and Manipulating Attributes Before They Are Typecast

The Active Record connection adapters, classes that implement behavior specific to databases, fetch results as strings and Rails takes care of converting them to other datatypes if necessary, based on the type of the database column. For instance, integer types are cast to instances of Ruby's `Fixnum` class, and so on.

Even if you're working with a new instance of an Active Record object and have passed in constructor values as strings, they will be typecast to their proper type when you try to access those values as attributes.

Sometimes you want to be able to read (or manipulate) the raw attribute data without having the column-determined typecast run its course first, and that can be done by using the *attribute*_before_type_cast accessors that are automatically created in your model.

For example, consider the need to deal with currency strings typed in by your end users. Unless you are encapsulating currency values in a currency class (highly recommended, by the way; see the "Money Gem" section) you need to deal with those pesky dollar signs and commas. Assuming that our Timesheet model had a rate attribute defined as a :decimal type, the following code would strip out the extraneous characters before typecasting for the save operation:

```
class Timesheet < ApplicationRecord
  before_validation :fix_rate

  def fix_rate
    self[:rate] = rate_before_type_cast.tr('$,','')
  end
end
```

5.4.5 Reloading

The reload method does a query to the database and resets the attributes of an Active Record object. The optional options argument is passed to find when reloading so you may do, for example, record.reload(lock: true) to reload the same record with an exclusive row lock. (See the section "Database Locking" later in this chapter.)

5.4.6 Cloning

Producing a copy of an Active Record object is done simply by calling clone, which produces a shallow copy of that object. It is important to note that for the sake of memory efficiency, no associations will get copied, even though they are stored internally as instance variables. Accessing associations on the clone will re-query the database.

5.4.7 The Query Cache

By default, Rails attempts to optimize performance by turning on a simple query cache. It is a hash stored on the current thread, one for every active database connection. (Most Rails processes will have just one.)

Whenever a `find` (or any other type of select operation) happens and the query cache is active, the corresponding result set is stored in a hash with the SQL that was used to query for them as the key. If the same SQL statement is used again in another operation, the cached result set is used to generate a new set of model objects instead of hitting the database again.

You can enable the query cache manually by wrapping operations in a `cache` block, as in the following example:

```
User.cache do
  puts User.first
  puts User.first
  puts User.first
end
```

Check your `development.log` and you should see the following entries:

```
User Load (0.1ms)  SELECT "users".* FROM "users" ORDER BY "users"."id"
ASC LIMIT 1
CACHE (0.0ms)  SELECT "users".* FROM "users" ORDER BY "users"."id"
ASC LIMIT 1 LIMIT 1
CACHE (0.0ms)  SELECT "users".* FROM "users" ORDER BY "users"."id"
ASC LIMIT 1
```

The database was queried only once. Try a similar experiment in your own console without the `cache` block, and you'll see that three separate `User Load` events are logged.

ⓘ Save and delete operations result in the cache being cleared, to prevent propagation of instances with invalid states. If you find it necessary to do so for whatever reason, call the `clear_query_cache` class method to clear out the query cache manually.

5.4.7.1 Logging

The log file indicates when data is being read from the query cache instead of the database. Just look for lines starting with CACHE instead of a Model Load.

Active Record

```
Place Load (0.1ms)  SELECT * FROM places WHERE (places.id = 15749)
CACHE (0.0ms)  SELECT * FROM places WHERE (places.id = 15749)
CACHE (0.0ms)  SELECT * FROM places WHERE (places.id = 15749)
```

5.4.7.2 Default Query Caching in Controllers

For performance reasons, Active Record's query cache is turned on by default for the processing of controller actions.

5.4.7.3 Limitations

The Active Record query cache was purposely kept very simple. Since it literally keys cached model instances on the SQL that was used to pull them out of the database, it can't connect multiple `find` invocations that are phrased differently but have the same semantic meaning and results.

For example, "select foo from bar where id = 1" and "select foo from bar where id = 1 limit 1" are considered different queries and will result in two distinct cache entries.

5.4.8 Updating

The simplest way to manipulate attribute values is to treat your Active Record object as a plain old Ruby object, meaning via direct assignment using `myprop=(some_value)`.

There are a number of other different ways to update Active Record objects, as illustrated in this section. First, let's look at how to use the `update` class method of `ActiveRecord::Base`.

```
class ProjectController < ApplicationController
  def update
    Project.update(params[:id], params[:project])
    redirect_to projects_path
  end

  def mass_update
    Project.update(params[:projects].keys, params[:projects].values)
    redirect_to projects_path
  end
end
```

The first form of `update` takes a single numeric id and a hash of attribute values, while the second form takes a list of ids and a list of values and is useful in scenarios where a form submission from a web page with multiple updateable rows is being processed.

The update class method does invoke validation first and will not save a record that fails validation. However, it returns the object whether or not the validation passes. That means that if you want to know whether or not the validation passed, you need to follow up the call to update with a call to valid?.

```
class ProjectController < ApplicationController
  def update
    project = Project.update(params[:id], params[:project])
    if project.valid? # uh-oh, do we want to run validate again?
      redirect_to project
    else
      render 'edit'
    end
  end
end
```

A problem is that now we are calling valid? twice, since the update call also called it. Perhaps a better option is to use the update instance method once as part of an if statement:

```
class ProjectController < ApplicationController
  def update
    project = Project.find(params[:id])
    if project.update(params[:project])
      redirect_to project
    else
      render 'edit'
    end
  end
end
```

And of course, if you've done some basic Rails programming, you'll recognize that pattern, since it is used in the generated scaffolding code. The update method takes a hash of attribute values and returns true or false depending on whether the save was successful or not, which is dependent on validation passing.

5.4.9   Updating by Condition

Active Record has another class method useful for updating multiple records at once: update_all. It maps closely to the way that you would think of using a SQL update...where statement. The update_all method takes two parameters: the set part of the SQL statement and the conditions, expressed as part of a where clause. The method returns the number of records updated.

I think this is one of those methods that is generally more useful in a scripting context than in a controller method, but you might feel differently. Here is a quick example of how I might go about reassigning all the Rails projects in the system to a new project manager.

```
Project.update_all({manager: 'Ron Campbell'}, technology: 'Rails')
```

The `update_all` method also accepts string parameters, which enables you to leverage the power of SQL!

```
Project.update_all("cost = cost * 3", "lower(technology) LIKE '%microsoft%'")
```

5.4.10   Updating a Particular Instance

The most basic way to update an Active Record object is to manipulate its attributes directly and then call `save`. It's worth noting that `save` will insert a record in the database if necessary or update an existing record with the same primary key.

```
>> project = Project.find(1)
>> project.manager = 'Brett M.'
>> project.save
=> true
```

The `save` method will return `true` if it was successful or `false` if it failed for any reason. There is another method, `save!`, that will use exceptions instead. Which one to use depends on whether you plan to deal with errors right away or delegate the problem to another method further up the chain.

It's mostly a matter of style, although the non-bang save and update methods that return a boolean value are often used in controller actions, as the clause for an if condition:

```
class StoryController < ApplicationController
  def points
    story = Story.find(params[:id])
    if story.update_attribute(:points, params[:value])
      render text: "#{story.name} updated"
    else
      render text: "Error updating story points"
    end
  end
end
```

5.4.11   Updating Specific Attributes

The instance methods `update_attribute` and `update` take one key/value pair or hash of attributes, respectively, to be updated on your model and saved to the database in one operation.

The `update_attribute` method updates a single attribute and saves the record, but updates made with this method are not subjected to validation checks! In other words, this method allows you to persist an Active Record model to the database even if the full object isn't valid. Model callbacks are executed, but the `updated _at` is still bumped.

> 💬 **Lark says . . .**
>
> I feel dirty whenever I use `update_attribute`.

On the other hand, `update` is subject to validation checks and is often used on update actions and passed the params hash containing updated values.

Active Record also provides an instance method `update_column`, which accepts a single key/value pair. Although similar to `update_attribute`, the `update_ column` method not only skips validations checks but also does not run callbacks and skips the bumping of the `updated_at` timestamp.

Rails 4 introduced an `update_columns` method, which works exactly the same as `update_column`, except that instead of accepting a single key/value pair as a parameter, it accepts a hash of attributes.

> 💬 **Courtenay says . . .**
>
> If you have associations on a model, Active Record automatically creates convenience methods for mass assignment. In other words, a `Project` model that `has_many :users` will expose a `user_ids` attribute writer, which gets used by its `update` method. This is an advantage if you're updating associations with check boxes because you just name the check boxes `project[user_ids][]` and Rails will handle the magic. In some cases, allowing the user to set associations this way would be a security risk.

5.4.12   Saving without Updating Timestamp

Rails 5 adds a `touch` option to `save`, which gives you the option of doing an update operation without updating the record's `updated_at` timestamp. Simply

Active
Record

pass `touch: false` and remember that it only works on update, not when inserting a new record.

```
>> user = User.first
>> user.updated_at
=> Wed, 16 Mar 2016 09:12:44 UTC +00:00

>> user.notes = "Hide this note from auditors"
>> user.save(touch: false)
  UPDATE "users" SET "notes" = ? WHERE "users"."id" = ?
    [["notes", "Hide this note from auditors"], ["id", 12]]
=> true
```

Like quite a few smaller features in Rails, I find it difficult to imagine how "no-touch" could be useful.

5.4.13 Convenience Updaters

Rails provides a number of convenience update methods in the form of `increment`, `decrement`, and `toggle`, which do exactly what their names suggest with numeric and boolean attributes. Each has a bang variant (such as `toggle!`) that additionally invokes `update_attribute` after modifying the attribute.

5.4.14 Touching Records

There may be certain cases where updating a time field to indicate a record was viewed is all you require, and Active Record provides a convenience method for doing so in the form of `touch`. This is especially useful for cache auto-expiration, which is covered in Chapter 17, "Caching and Performance."

Using this method on a model with no arguments updates the `updated_at` timestamp field to the current time without firing any callbacks or validation. If a timestamp attribute is provided it will update that attribute to the current time along with `updated_at`.

```
>> user = User.first
>> user.touch # => sets updated_at to now.
>> user.touch(:viewed_at) # sets viewed_at and updated_at to now.
```

If a `:touch` option is provided to a belongs to relation, it will touch the parent record when the child is touched.

```
class User < ApplicationRecord
  belongs_to :client, touch: true
```

```
end
```

```
>> user.touch # => also calls user.client.touch
```

5.4.15 Readonly Attributes

Sometimes you want to designate certain attributes as read-only, which prevents them from being updated after the parent object is created. The feature is primarily for use in conjunction with calculated attributes. In fact, Active Record uses this method internally for `counter_cache` attributes, since they are maintained with their own special SQL update statements.

The only time that read-only attributes may be set are when the object is not saved yet. The following example code illustrates usage of `attr_readonly`. Note the potential gotcha when trying to update a read-only attribute.

```
class Customer < ApplicationRecord
  attr_readonly :social_security_number
end
```

```
>> customer = Customer.new(social_security_number: "130803020")
=> #<Customer id: 1, social_security_number: "130803020", ...>
>> customer.social_security_number
=> "130803020"
>> customer.save
```

```
>> customer.social_security_number = "000000000" # Note, no error raised!
>> customer.social_security_number
=> "000000000"
```

```
>> customer.save
>> customer.reload
>> customer.social_security_number
=> "130803020" # the original readonly value is preserved
```

The fact that trying to set a new value for a read-only attribute doesn't raise an error bothers my sensibilities, but I understand how it can make using this feature a little bit less code-intensive.

You can get a list of all read-only attributes via the class method `readonly_attributes`.

```
>> Customer.readonly_attributes
=> #<Set: {"social_security_number"}>
```

5.4.16   Deleting and Destroying

Finally, if you want to remove a record from your database, you have two choices. If you already have a model instance, you can destroy it:

```
>> bad_timesheet = Timesheet.find(1)

>> bad_timesheet.destroy
=> #<Timesheet id: 1, user_id: "1", submitted: nil,
   created_at: "2006-11-21 05:40:27", updated_at: "2006-11-21 05:40:27">
```

The destroy method will both remove the object from the database and prevent you from modifying it again:

```
>> bad_timesheet.user_id = 2
RuntimeError: can't modify frozen Hash
```

Note that calling save on an object that has been destroyed will fail silently. If you need to check whether an object has been destroyed, you can use the destroyed? method.

The destroy method also has a complimentary bang method, destroy!. Calling destroy! on an object that cannot be destroyed will result in an Active-Record::RecordNotDestroyed exception being raised.

You can also call destroy and delete as class methods, passing the id(s) to delete. Both variants accept a single parameter or array of ids:

```
Timesheet.delete(1)
Timesheet.destroy([2, 3])
```

The naming might seem inconsistent, but it isn't. The delete method uses SQL directly and does not load any instances (hence it is faster). The destroy method does load the instance of the Active Record object and then calls destroy on it as an instance method. The semantic differences are subtle but come into play when you have assigned before_destroy callbacks or have dependent associations—child objects that should be deleted automatically along with their parent object.

5.5   Database Locking

Locking is a term for techniques that prevent concurrent users of an application from overwriting each other's work. Active Record doesn't normally use any type of database locking when loading rows of model data from the database. If a given Rails application will only ever have one user updating data at the same time, then you don't have to worry about it.

However, when more than one user may be accessing and updating the exact same data simultaneously, then it is vitally important for you as the developer to think about concurrency. Ask yourself, what types of collisions or race conditions could happen if two users were to try to update a given model at the same time?

There are a number of approaches to dealing with concurrency in database-backed applications, two of which are natively supported by Active Record: optimistic and pessimistic locking. Other approaches exist, such as locking entire database tables. Every approach has strengths and weaknesses, so it is likely that a given application will use a combination of approaches for maximum reliability.

5.5.1   Optimistic Locking

Optimistic locking describes the strategy of detecting and resolving collisions if they occur, and is commonly recommended in multi-user situations where collisions should be infrequent. Database records are never actually locked in optimistic locking, making it a bit of a misnomer.

Optimistic locking is a fairly common strategy, because so many applications are designed such that a particular user will mostly be updating with data that conceptually belongs to him and not other users, making it rare that two users would compete for updating the same record. The idea behind optimistic locking is that since collisions should occur infrequently, we'll simply deal with them only if they happen.

5.5.1.1   Implementation

If you control your database schema, optimistic locking is really simple to implement. Just add an integer column named `lock_version` to a given table, with a default value of zero.

```
class AddLockVersionToTimesheets < ActiveRecord::Migration

  def change
    add_column :timesheets, :lock_version, :integer, default: 0
  end

end
```

Simply adding that `lock_version` column changes Active Record's behavior. Now, if the same record is loaded as two different model instances and saved differently, the first instance will win the update, and the second one will cause an `Active-Record::StaleObjectError` to be raised.

We can illustrate optimistic locking behavior with a simple spec:

```
describe Timesheet do
  it "locks optimistically" do
    t1 = Timesheet.create
    t2 = Timesheet.find(t1.id)

    t1.rate = 250
    t2.rate = 175

    expect(t1.save).to be_true
    expect { t2.save }.to raise_
        error(ActiveRecord::StaleObjectError)
  end
end
```

The spec passes because calling `save` on the second instance raises the expected `ActiveRecord::StaleObjectError` exception. Note that the `save` method (without the bang) returns `false` and does not raise exceptions if the save fails due to validation, but other problems, such as locking in this case, can indeed cause it to raise exceptions.

To use a database column named something other than `lock_version`, change the setting using `locking_column`. To make the change globally, add the following line to an initializer:

```
Rails.application.config.active_record.locking_column =
  :alternate_lock_version
```

Like other Active Record settings, you can also change it on a per-model basis with a declaration in your model class:

```
class Timesheet < ApplicationRecord
  self.locking_column = :alternate_lock_version
end
```

5.5.1.2   Handling `StaleObjectError`

Now of course, after adding optimistic locking, you don't want to just leave it at that, or the end user who is on the losing end of the collision would simply see an application error screen. You should try to handle the `StaleObjectError` as gracefully as possible.

Depending on the criticality of the data being updated, you might want to invest time into crafting a user-friendly solution that somehow preserves the changes that the loser was trying to make. At minimum, if the data for the update is easily re-creatable, let the user know why their update failed with controller code that looks something like the following:

```
def update
  timesheet = Timesheet.find(params[:id])
  timesheet.update(params[:timesheet])
  # redirect somewhere
rescue ActiveRecord::StaleObjectError
  redirect_to [:edit, timesheet], flash: { error: "Timesheet was
        modified while you were editing it." }
end
```

There are some advantages to optimistic locking. It doesn't require any special feature in the database, and it is fairly easy to implement. As you saw in the example, very little code is required to handle the `StaleObjectError`.

The main disadvantages to optimistic locking are that update operations are a bit slower because the lock version must be checked and the potential for bad user experience, since they don't find out about the failure until after they've potentially lost data.

5.5.2   Pessimistic Locking

Pessimistic locking requires special database support (built into the major databases) and locks down specific database rows during an update operation. It prevents another user from reading data that is about to be updated, in order to prevent them from working with stale data.

Pessimistic locking works in conjunction with transactions as in the following example:

```
Timesheet.transaction do
  t = Timesheet.lock.first
  t.approved = true
  t.save!
end
```

It's also possible to call `lock!` on an existing model instance, which simply calls `reload(lock: true)` under the covers. You wouldn't want to do that on an instance with attribute changes since it would cause them to be discarded by the reload. If you decide you don't want the lock anymore, you can pass `false` to the `lock!` method.

Pessimistic locking takes place at the database level. The `SELECT` statement generated by Active Record will have a `FOR UPDATE` (or similar) clause added to it, causing all other connections to be blocked from access to the rows returned by the select statement. The lock is released once the transaction is committed. There are theoretically situations (Rails process goes boom mid-transaction?!) where the lock would not be released until the connection is terminated or times out.

5.5.3   Considerations

Web applications scale best with optimistic locking, which as we've discussed doesn't really use any database-level locking at all. However, you have to add application logic to handle failure cases. Pessimistic locking is a bit easier to implement, but can lead to situations where one Rails process is waiting on another to release a database lock, that is, waiting and not serving any other incoming requests. Remember that Rails processes are typically single-threaded.

In my opinion, pessimistic locking should not be super dangerous as it is on other platforms, since in Rails we don't ever persist database transactions across more than a single HTTP request. In fact, it would be impossible to do that in a shared-nothing architecture. (If you're running Rails with JRuby and doing crazy things like storing Active Record object instances in a shared session space, all bets are off.)

A situation to be wary of would be one where you have many users competing for access to a particular record that takes a long time to update. For best results, keep your pessimistic-locking transactions small and make sure that they execute quickly.

5.6   Querying

In mentioning Active Record's `find` method earlier in the chapter, we didn't look at the wealth of options available in addition to querying by primary key and the `first`, `last`, and `all` methods. Each method discussed here returns an `Active-Record::Relation`—a chainable object that is lazy evaluated against the database only when the actual records are needed.

Active Record's querying and relationship behavior are implemented using the Arel[3] relational algebra gem, which is considered part of Rails and maintained by the Rails core team. We attempt to provide you with a complete overview in this chapter, but note that full coverage and explanation of everything possible with Arel would require a book of its own.

Note that I have attempted to order the method list by relative importance to daily coding tasks.

---

3. https://github.com/rails/arel

5.6.1   `where(*conditions)`

It's very common to need to filter the result set of a find operation (just a SQL SELECT under the covers) by adding conditions (to the WHERE clause). Active Record gives you a number of ways to do just that with the `where` method.

The conditions parameter can be specified as a string or a hash. Parameters are automatically sanitized to prevent SQL-injection attacks.

Passing a hash of conditions will construct a `where` clause containing a union of all the key/value pairs. If all you need is equality, versus, say LIKE criteria, I advise you to use the hash notation, since it's arguably the most readable of the styles.

```
Product.where(sku: params[:sku])
```

The hash notation is smart enough to create an IN clause if you associate an array of values with a particular key.

```
Product.where(sku: [9400,9500,9900])
```

The simple string form can be used for statements that don't involve data originating outside of your app. It's most useful for doing LIKE comparisons, as well as greater-than/less-than and the use of SQL functions not already built into Active Record, like those needed for querying into Hstore and JSON columns in PostgreSQL.

If you do choose to use the string style, additional arguments to the `where` method will be treated as query variables to insert into the `where` clause.

```
Product.where('description like ? and color = ?', "%#{terms}%", color)
Product.where('sku in (?)', selected_skus)
User.where('preferences @> ?', {newsletter: true}.to_json)
```

Note that dates, booleans, and arrays like `selected_skus` are coerced into their SQL expression representations correctly and automatically.

`where.not`

The Active Record query interface for the most part abstracts SQL from the developer. However, there is a condition that always requires using pure string conditions in a `where` clause, specifying a NOT condition with <> or !=, depending on the database. Starting in Rails 4, the query method `not` has been added to rectify this.

To use the new query method, it must be chained to a `where` clause with no arguments:

```
Article.where.not(title: 'Rails 3')
# >> SELECT "articles".* FROM "articles"
#    WHERE ("articles"."title" != 'Rails 3')
```

The not query method can also accept an array to ensure multiple values are not in a field:

```
Article.where.not(title: ['Rails 3', 'Rails 5'])
# >> SELECT "articles".* FROM "articles"
#    WHERE ("articles"."title" NOT IN ('Rails 3', 'Rails 5'))
```

5.6.1.1   Bind Variables

When using multiple parameters in the conditions, it can easily become hard to read exactly what the fourth or fifth question mark is supposed to represent.

In those cases, you can resort to named bind variables instead. That's done by replacing the question marks with symbols and supplying a hash with values for the matching symbol keys as a second parameter.

```
Product.where("name = :name AND sku = :sku AND created_at > :date",
              name: "Space Toilet", sku: 80800, date: '2009-01-01')
```

During a quick discussion on IRC about this final form, Robby Russell gave me the following clever snippet:

```
Message.where("subject LIKE :foo OR body LIKE :foo", foo: '%woah%')
```

In other words, when you're using named placeholders (versus question mark characters) you can use the same bind variable more than once. Like, whoa!

Simple hash conditions like this are very common and useful, but they will only generate conditions based on equality with SQL's AND operator.

```
User.where(login: login, password: password).first
```

If you want logic other than AND, you'll have to use one of the other forms available.

5.6.1.2   Boolean Conditions

It's particularly important to take care in specifying conditions that include boolean values. Databases have various different ways of representing boolean values in columns. Some have native boolean datatypes, and others use a single character, often 1 and 0 or T and F (or even Y and N). Rails will transparently handle the data conversion issues for you if you pass a Ruby boolean object as your parameter:

```
Timesheet.where('submitted = ?', true)
```

5.6.1.3 Nil Conditions

Rails expert Xavier Noria reminds us to take care in specifying conditions that might be nil. Using a question mark doesn't let Rails figure out that a `nil` supplied as the value of a condition should probably be translated into `IS NULL` in the resulting SQL query.

Compare the following two find examples and their corresponding SQL queries to understand this common gotcha. The first example does not work as intended, but the second one does work:

```
>> User.where('email = ?', nil)
User Load (151.4ms)  SELECT * FROM users WHERE (email = NULL)

>> User.where(:email => nil)
User Load (15.2ms)  SELECT * FROM users WHERE (users.email IS NULL)
```

5.6.2 `order(*clauses)`

The `order` method takes one or more symbols (representing column names) or a fragment of SQL, specifying the desired ordering of a result set:

```
Timesheet.order('created_at desc')
```

The SQL spec defaults to ascending order if the ascending/descending option is omitted, which is exactly what happens if you use symbols.

```
# first two timesheets ever created
Timesheet.order(:created_at).take(2)
```

As of Rails 4, `order` can also accept hash arguments, eliminating the need to write SQL for descending order clauses.

```
Timesheet.order(created_at: :desc)
```

🔊 Wilson says . . .

The SQL spec doesn't prescribe any particular ordering if no "order by" clause is specified in the query. That seems to trip people up, since the common belief is that "ORDER BY id ASC" is the default.

The value of the :order option is not validated by Rails, which means you can pass any code that is understood by the underlying database, not just column/direction tuples. An example of why that is useful is when wanting to fetch a random record:

```
# MySQL
Timesheet.order('RAND()')

# Postgres
Timesheet.order('RANDOM()')

# Microsoft SQL Server
Timesheet.order('NEWID()') # uses random uuids to sort

# Oracle
Timesheet.order('dbms_random.value').first
```

Remember that ordering large datasets randomly is known to perform terribly on most databases, particularly MySQL.

● Tim says . . .

A clever, performant and portable way to get a random record is to generate a random offset in Ruby.

```
Timsheet.limit(1).offset(rand(Timesheet.count)).first
```

5.6.3 `take(number)` and `skip(number)`

The `take` (aliased to `limit`) method takes an integer value establishing a limit on the number of rows to return from the query. It's companion, the `skip` (aliased to `offset`) method, which must be chained to `take`, specifies the number of rows to skip in the result set and is 0-indexed. (At least it is in MySQL. Other databases may be 1-indexed.) Together these options are used for paging results.

⚬ Don't do pagination of your models manually. Use the Kaminari gem at https://github.com/amatsuda/kaminari.

For example, a call to find for the second page of 10 results in a list of timesheets is:

```
Timesheet.take(10).skip(10)
```

Depending on the particulars of your application's data model, it may make sense to always put some limit on the maximum number of Active Record objects fetched in any one specific query. Letting the user trigger unbounded queries pulling thousands of Active Record objects into Rails at one time is a recipe for disaster.

5.6.4 `select(*clauses)`

By default, Active Record generates `SELECT * FROM` queries, but it can be changed if, for example, you want to do a join but not include the joined columns. Or if you want to add calculated columns to your result set, like this:

```
>> b = BillableWeek.select("mon_hrs + tues_hrs as two_day_total").first
=> #<BillableWeek ...>
>> b.two_day_total
=> 16
```

Now, if you actually want to fully use objects with additional attributes that you've added via the select method, don't forget the `*` clause:

```
>> b = BillableWeek.select(:*, "mon_hrs + tues_hrs as two_day_total").first
=> #<BillableWeek id: 1...>
```

Keep in mind that columns not specified in the query, whether by `*` or explicitly, will not be populated in the resulting objects! So, for instance, continuing the first example, trying to access `created_at` on b has unexpected results:

```
ActiveModel::MissingAttributeError: missing attribute: created_at
```

The reason that the attribute is missing is because the result set returned from the database governs what attributes are created on Active Record objects. They are *that* tightly bound to the database schema.

5.6.5 `from(*tables)`

The `from` method enables you to modify the table name(s) portion of the SQL statements generated by Active Record.

You can provide a custom value if you need to include extra tables for joins or to reference a database view or subquery.

```
>> Topic.select('title').from(Topic.approved).to_sql
=> "SELECT title FROM (SELECT * FROM topics WHERE approved = 't')"
```

You can also use it to override the generated aliases with your own, which is probably not super useful but could yield some readability benefits in certain situations involving complex joins.

```
>> Topic.select('a.title').from(Topic.approved, :a).to_sql
=> "SELECT a.title FROM (SELECT * FROM topics WHERE approved = 't')"
```

The capability to control the FROM clause means you can easily make all or part of it dynamic. Here's an example from an application that enables tagging on a variety of different models:

```
def self.find_tagged_with(list)
  select("#{table_name}.*").
    from("#{table_name}, tags, taggings").
    where("#{table_name}.#{primary_key} = taggings.taggable_id
        and taggings.tag_id = tags.id
        and tags.name IN (?)",
        Tag.parse(list))
end
```

ⓘ This example code is mixed into a target class using Ruby modules. Learn how to use that technique yourself in the section "Modules for Reusing Common Behavior" from Chapter 9, "Advanced Active Record."

5.6.6 `group(*args)`

group specifies a GROUP BY SQL-clause to add to the query generated by Active Record. Generally, you'll want to combine :group with the :select option, since valid SQL requires that all selected columns in a grouped SELECT be either aggregate functions or columns.

```
>> users = Account.select('name, SUM(cash) as money').group('name').to_a
=> [#<User name: "Joe", money: "3500">, #<User name: "Jane", money: "9245">]
```

Keep in mind that those extra columns you bring back might sometimes be strings if Active Record doesn't try to typecast them. In those cases, you'll have to use to_i and to_f to explicitly convert the string to numeric types.

```
>> users.first.money > 1_000_000
ArgumentError: comparison of String with 1000000 failed
  from (irb):8:in '>'
```

5.6.7 `distinct`

If you need to perform a query with a 'DISTINCT SQL'-clause, you can use the distinct method.

```
>> User.select(:login).distinct
User Load (0.2ms) SELECT DISTINCT login FROM "users"
```

5.6.8 `having(*clauses)`

If you need to perform a group query with a SQL `HAVING` clause, you use the `having` method.

```
>> User.group("created_at").having(["created_at > ?", 2.days.ago])
=> [#<User name: "Joe", created_at: "2013-03-05 19:30:11">]
```

5.6.9 `includes(*associations)`

Active Record has the capability to eliminate "N+1" queries by letting you specify what associations to eager load using the `includes` method or option in your finders. Active Record will load those relationships with the minimum number of queries possible.

To eager load first-degree associations, provide `includes` with an array of association names. When accessing these later in the same request cycle, further database queries will not be needed.

```
>> users = User.where(login: "mack").includes(:billable_weeks)
=> [#<User login: "mack">]
>> users.first.billable_weeks.each { |week| puts week }
=> #<Week start_date: "2008-05-01 00:00:00">
```

For second degree associations, provide a hash with the array as the value for the hash key.

```
>> clients = Client.includes(users: [:avatar])
=> [#<Client id: 1, name: "Hashrocket">]
```

You may add more inclusions following the same pattern.

```
>> Client.includes(
     users: [:avatar, { timesheets: :billable_weeks }]
   )
=> [#<Client id: 1, name: "Hashrocket">]
```

If possible, `includes` uses `LEFT OUTER JOIN` to grab all the data it needs in one query. When that happens, it delegates to `eager_load`. Otherwise, it will use at least two separate queries and delegate to `preload`.

If you know you want one approach versus the other, you can ensure you get it by using `eager_load` or `preload` directly with the same syntax.

Active Record

5.6.10 `eager_load(*associations)`

As mentioned already, `eager_load` grabs all data together in a single query using joins, instead of using separate queries like `preload` does.

5.6.11 `preloads(*associations)`

As mentioned already, `preloads` uses separate queries to preload associated data rather than attempting to bring all data back together in a single query using joins like `eager_load` does.

We didn't talk about this too much in our description of `includes`, so I'll provide an example.

```
>> User.preload(:auctions).to_a
  User Load (0.1ms) SELECT "users".* FROM "users"
  Auction Load (0.2ms)  SELECT "auctions".* FROM "auctions"
  WHERE "auctions"."user_id" IN (1, 2)
```

Notice the two separate SQL queries. Logically, since the queries are separate, you can't refer to a preloaded table in a query expression the way that you can using `includes`.

5.6.12 `references(*table_names)`

The query method `references` is used to indicate that a related table is referenced by some part of the SQL expression under construction. It's only needed in cases where Active Record can't figure out which table to join on its own, like in the following example:

```
>> User.includes(:auctions).where('auctions.name = ?','Lumina')
   User Load (0.2ms)  SELECT "users".* FROM
        "users" WHERE (auctions.name = 'Lumina')
        ActiveRecord::StatementInvalid: SQLite3::SQLException:
        no such column: auctions.name
   ...
```

You might be wondering why Active Record couldn't figure out that it needed the `auctions` table based on the call to `includes`. I'm not sure either and couldn't find a good answer. I do know that to get the above example to work, you need to use `references` with the name of the table to join.

```
User.includes(:auctions)
     .where('auctions.name = ?','Lumina')
     .references(:auctions)
```

A much better and more concise alternative to use of `references` is available *if you are able to use hash syntax* instead of a string for your `where` conditions, as in the following example. It automatically generates a `LEFT OUTER JOIN` using table name aliases:

```
>> User.includes(:auctions)
      .where(auctions: {name: 'Lumina'})
SQL (0.2ms)   SELECT "users"."id" AS t0_r0, "users"."email" AS t0_r1,
"users"."password_digest" AS t0_r2, "users"."password_reset_token" AS
t0_r3, "users"."name" AS t0_r4, "users"."created_at" AS t0_r5,
"users"."updated_at" AS t0_r6, "users"."token" AS t0_r7,
"auctions"."id" AS t1_r0, "auctions"."name" AS t1_r1,
"auctions"."description" AS t1_r2, "auctions"."ends_at" AS t1_r3,
"auctions"."created_at" AS t1_r4, "auctions"."updated_at" AS t1_r5,
"auctions"."closes_at" AS t1_r6, "auctions"."user_id" AS t1_r7 FROM
"users" LEFT OUTER JOIN "auctions" ON "auctions"."user_id" =
"users"."id" WHERE "auctions"."name" = ?  [["name", "Lumina"]]
```

> 🔑 Note that `includes` and its sister methods work with association names, while `references` needs actual table names.

5.6.13 `joins(expression)`

`joins` works similarly to `includes` using an `INNER JOIN` in the resulting SQL query. One of the key bits of knowledge to understand about inner joins is they return only the set of records that match the tables being joined. If a row on either side of the join is missing its corresponding row on the other side, neither will be returned in the result set.

```
>> User.joins(:auctions).to_sql
=> "SELECT users.* FROM users INNER JOIN auctions ON auctions.user_id = users.id"
```

The query in the example returns not only the row in the users table that contains the user's information, it also brings back the corresponding rows that will populate the `user.auctions` association. When that association is accessed later within the same request cycle, it will not result in additional database queries, just like with `includes`.

The `joins` method also understands multiple joins, as well as nested association joins, using hash notation.

```
>> User.joins(auctions: [:bids]).to_sql
=> "SELECT users.* FROM users INNER JOIN auctions ON auctions.user_id
       = users.id INNER JOIN bids ON bids.auction_id = auctions.id"
```

While the `joins` method normally takes symbols corresponding to table names and can figure out the ON clause based on association metadata, if you want to provide a more complex expression, then write the clause yourself and pass it in as a string.

```
Buyer.select(:*, 'count(carts.id) as cart_count')
    .joins('left outer join carts on carts.buyer_id = buyers.id')
    .group('buyers.id')
```

> By far the most common usage of the `joins` method is to eager-fetch data for associated objects in a single SELECT statement in order to prevent so-called *N+1 queries*.
>
> Note that LEFT JOIN queries are popular enough that they get their own method `left_outer_join` in Rails 5.

5.6.14 `left_outer_join`

As mentioned previously, LEFT OUTER JOIN is popular enough that it gets its own method in Rails 5.

```
>> User.select(:*, 'count(bids.id) as bid_count)')
    .left_outer_joins(auctions: [:bids])
    .group('users.id').to_sql
=> "SELECT *, count(bids.id) as bid_count) FROM users LEFT OUTER
    JOIN auctions ON auctions.user_id = users.id LEFT OUTER JOIN
    bids ON bids.auction_id = auctions.id GROUP BY users.id"
```

The method is aliased to `left_joins` for those of you who prefer shorter names.

> I can only imagine using `joins` and `left_outer_join` in circumstances where I need the join for querying purposes alone, and not for eager loading an association, because otherwise I would use `includes` instead. This part of the API might seem overly confusing, but I think it is designed in such a way as to help you write the most intention-revealing code as possible.

5.6.15 `find_or_create_by(attributes, &block)`

`find_or_create_by` finds the first record using the relation and given attributes, or if none are found, saves a new record using the provided attributes and where clause values of the relation.

This silly example looks for active users named Buster and creates a matching record if it doesn't find one.

```
User.active.find_or_create_by(first_name: 'Buster', ...)
```

Assuming that the `active` scope does the obvious thing, that code is identical to the following:

```
User.find_or_create_by(active: true, first_name: 'Buster', ...)
```

If you're playing with this technique, it's also worth taking a look at `create_with`, which gives you the option of explicitly specifying attribute values to use for creation (but not the query).

Notice the slight difference in behavior in this example compared to the last two:

```
>> User.create_with(active: true)
      .find_or_create_by(first_name: 'Buster', ...)
```

What this code does is to search for *any* users (whether active or not), and if not found, creates an active user named Buster.

If for whatever reason you need it, you can pass a block to `find_or_create_by`. In the case of generating a new record, it will be yielded to the block prior to saving to the database. This technique looks something like this:

```
User.find_or_create_by(first_name: 'Scarlett') do|user|
  user.last_name = 'Johansson'
end
```

Note that the behavior of `find_or_create_by` *is not atomic*. First it executes a `SELECT`, and if there are no results, then an `INSERT` is attempted. If there are other threads or processes, a race condition could result in two similar records being saved to the database.

As is usually the case in these situations, if the record you are trying to create has a `UNIQUE` constraint at the database level, then you can catch the resulting exception and `retry`, like this:

```
begin
  CreditAccount.transaction(requires_new: true) do
    CreditAccount.find_or_create_by(user_id: user.id)
  end
rescue ActiveRecord::RecordNotUnique
  retry
end
```

The `find_or_create_by` is similar to regular `create` in that if validation fails, it will not try to save to the database and will return an unsaved record. Unsurprisingly, there's also a version of this method called `find_or_create_by!` that (like `create!`) will raise an exception if validation fails.

5.6.16 `find_or_initialize_by(attributes, &block)`
`find_or_initialize_by` is very similar to `find_or_create_by` but calls `new` instead of `create` under the covers.

5.6.17 `new(attributes, &block)`
`new` is very similar to `find_or_initialize_by` but without the find operation.

```
>> active_users = User.where(active: true)
>> active_users.new
=> #<User id: nil, active: true, created_at: nil, updated_at: nil>
```

5.6.18 `create_with`
See `find_or_create_by`.

5.6.19 `reload`
See the "Reloading" section of this chapter.

5.6.20 `reset`
`reset` blows away all of the relation's settings and contents. It is used to ensure that the *next* access of a relation (if needed) hits the database again instead of using cached values. Contrast it with `reload`, which always hits the database again no matter what.

5.6.21 `explain`
`explain` runs EXPLAIN on the query or queries triggered by this relation and returns the result as a string. Note that this method can actually run queries as part of its operation since the results are needed when eager loading is involved.

```
> User.includes(:auctions).where(auctions: {name: 'Foo'}).explain
  SQL (0.2ms)  SELECT "users"."id" AS t0_r0, ...
=> EXPLAIN for: SELECT "users"."id" AS t0_r0 ...
0|0|0|SCAN TABLE users
0|1|1|SEARCH TABLE auctions USING AUTOMATIC COVERING INDEX
 (name=? AND user_id=?)
```

5.6.22 `extending(*modules, &block)`

`extending` specifies one or many modules with methods that will extend the scope with additional methods. It returns a relation object, for further chaining or extension.

```
module Pagination
  def page(number)
    # pagination code
  end
end

scope = Model.all.extending(Pagination)
scope.page(params[:page])
```

You can pass more than one module to `extending` and it also takes an optional block (essentially acting as an anonymous module).

```
# same example extended with a block
scope = Model.all.extending(Pagination) do
  def per_page(number)
    # pagination code goes here
  end
end
```

5.6.23 `exists?`

`exists` takes arguments to those of `find` and instead of returning records returns a boolean for whether or not the query has results.

```
>> User.create(login: "mack")
=> #<User id: 1, login: "mack">
>> User.exists?(1)
=> true
>> User.exists?(login: "mack")
=> true
```

Of course, it can also be chained off of a relation.

```
>> User.where(login: "mack").exists?
=> true
```

5.6.24 `any?`

`any` is the opposite of `empty`.

5.6.25 `empty?`

If the relation is loaded, `empty` returns `true` if no records are present. If the relation is not loaded, it does a count under the covers to derive a return value.

```
# File activerecord/lib/active_record/relation.rb
def empty?
  return @records.empty? if loaded?

  if limit_value == 0
    true
  else
    c = count(:all)
    c.respond_to?(:zero?) ? c.zero? : c.empty?
  end
end
```

5.6.26 `many?`

`many` returns `true` if the relation returns more than one record. It is implemented
using `SELECT COUNT` as seen in the example.

```
>> User.where(id: 1).many?
   (0.1ms)  SELECT COUNT(*) FROM "users" WHERE "users"."id" = ?  [["id", 1]]
=> false
```

5.6.27 `one?`

`one?` returns `true` if the relation returns exactly one record.

5.6.28 `none`

Introduced in Rails 4, `ActiveRecord::QueryMethods.none` is a chainable
relation that causes a query to return zero records. The query method returns `Active-
Record::NullRelation`, which is an implementation of the Null Object pat-
tern. It is to be used in instances where you have a method that returns a relation,
but there is a condition in which you do not want the database to be queried. All
subsequent chained conditions will work without issue, eliminating the need to continuously check whether the object your are working with is a relation.

```
def visible
  case role
  when :reviewer
    Post.published
  when :bad_user
    Post.none
  end
end
```

```
# If chained, the following code will not break for users
# with a :bad_user role
posts = current_user.visible.where(name: params[:name])
```

5.6.29 `lock`

`lock` specifies locking settings for the query. It is described earlier in this chapter in the "Database Locking" section.

5.6.30 `readonly`

Chaining the `readonly` method marks returned objects as read-only. You can change their attributes, but you won't be able to save them back to the database.

```
>> c = Comment.readonly.first
=> #<Comment id: 1, body: "Hey beeyotch!">
>> c.body = "Keep it clean!"
=> "Keep it clean!"
>> c.save
ActiveRecord::ReadOnlyRecord: ActiveRecord::ReadOnlyRecord
```

5.6.31 `reorder`

Using `reorder`, you can replace any existing defined order on a given relation.

```
>> Member.order('name DESC').reorder(:id)
Member Load (0.6ms) SELECT "members".* FROM "members" ORDER BY
"members"."id" ASC
```

Any subsequent calls to `order` will be appended to the query.

```
>> Member.order('name DESC').reorder(:id).order(:name)
Member Load (0.6ms) SELECT "members".* FROM "members" ORDER BY
"members".name ASC, "members"."id" ASC
```

5.6.32 `reverse_order`

`reverse_order` is a convenience method for reversing an existing order clause on a relation.

```
>> Member.order(:name).reverse_order
Member Load (0.4ms)  SELECT "members".* FROM "members" ORDER BY
"members".name DESC
```

5.6.33 `rewhere(conditions)`

`rewhere` enables changing a previously set `where` condition for a given attribute, instead of appending to that condition. (Rarely used.)

🔍 In the console and unsure what conditions are in effect on a scope or relation? Try calling `where_values_hash` and it will tell you.

5.6.34 `scoping(&block)`

`scoping` defines a scope for all queries in the provided block.

```
Comment.where(post_id: 1).scoping do
  Comment.first
end
# SELECT * FROM comments WHERE comments.post_id = 1 LIMIT 1
```

5.6.35 `unscope(*args)`

The `unscope` query method is useful when you want to remove an unwanted relation without reconstructing the entire relation chain. For example, to remove an order clause from a relation, add `unscope(:order)`:

```
>> Member.order('name DESC').unscope(:order)
SELECT members.* FROM members
```

Additionally, one can pass a hash as an argument to unscope specific `:where` values. This will cause only the value specified to not be included in the `where` clause.

```
Member.where(name: "Tyrion", active: true).unscope(where: :name)
```

is equivalent to

```
Member.where(active: true)
```

The following is a listing of the query methods `unscope` accepts:

- `:from`
- `:group`
- `:having`
- `:includes`
- `:joins`
- `:limit`
- `:lock`
- `:offset`
- `:order`

- `:readonly`
- `:select`
- `:where`

5.6.36 `merge(other)`

`merge` merges in the conditions from an `other` relation or array. If passed an `ActiveRecord::Relation`, then the return value is a merged relation. If passed an array, it returns an array representing the intersection of the resulting records with the `other` array.

I can't immediately think of a use for array intersection using this method, but I do find its other form useful for composing elegant query code.

```
# Find recent posts with comments highlighted by the editor
Post.recent.joins(:comments).merge(Comment.where(editor_pick: true))
```

Interestingly, `other` can also be a `Proc`, whose evaluation context is the relation that you're merging into. According to the docs this is most useful for associations.

```
# Find recent comments on a given post highlighted by the editor
editor_pick = -> { where(editor_pick: true) }
post.comments.latest.merge(editor_pick)
```

I suspect there's no good reason to do something like that last example, unless `editor_pick` was some more complex bit of logic that you've extracted into its own object and want to share across different contexts.

5.6.37 `only(*onlies)`

`only` limits a relation to specified components. Pass one or more symbols representing the part of the query to include.

```
# only keep the scope's where clause, discard anything else
Post.latest.only(:where)
```

5.6.38 `except(*skips)`

`except` removes part of the query. Pass one or more symbols representing the part of the query to skip. (It is probably very rare to need to do this.)

```
# discards any order condition that might be on the scope
Post.latest.except(:order)
```

5.6.39 `or(other)`

You can generate OR expressions in your SQL queries by chaining Arel nodes together using the `or` method.

```
Member.where(name: "Tyrion").or(Member.where(family: 'Lannister').first)

# => SELECT * FROM members WHERE members.name = 'Tyrion'
                             OR members.family = 'Lannister'
```

Compare this to a logical AND, which doesn't require an explicit method call and is Arel's default behavior upon chaining.

```
Member.where(name: "Tyrion").where(family: 'Lannister')

# => SELECT * FROM members WHERE members.name = 'Tyrion'
                             AND members.family = 'Lannister'
```

5.6.40 `load`

`load` loads the relation from the database and returns the relation. Used in extremely rare cases where it is necessary to load a relation during its construction. The return value is the relation itself, not the records.

5.6.41 `to_a`

`to_a` loads the relation from the database and returns the resulting Active Record objects in an `Array` (instead of wrapped in a relation).

5.6.42 `to_sql`

As demonstrated in numerous examples throughout this section, calling `to_sql` on a relation will dump the generated SQL. It is most useful for debugging complicated joins.

5.6.43 `to_json` and friends

The results of relations can be serialized to a variety of textual formats using `to_json`, `to_yaml`, and `to_xml`. They use the Psych gem in conjunction with `encode_with(coder)` under the covers.

```
>> User.where(id: 1).to_json
   User Load (0.1ms)  SELECT users.* FROM users ...
=> "[{"id":1,"email":"obiefernandez@gmail.com", ...}]"
```

5.6.44 `arel_table`

For cases in which you want to generate custom SQL yourself through Arel, you may use the `arel_table` method to gain access to the `Table` instance for the class.

```
>> users = User.arel_table
>> users.where(users[:login].eq("mack")).to_sql
=> "SELECT `users`.`id`, `users`.`login` FROM `users`
   WHERE `users`.`login` = 'mack'"
```

As we mentioned at the opening of this section, the Arel API is quite complex. You should consult the Arel documentation[4] to learn how to construct custom queries using its DSL.

5.6.45 `cache_key`

`cache_key` returns a cache key that can be used to identify the records fetched by this query.

```
>> Product.where("name like ?", "%Cosmic Encounter%").cache_key
=> "products/query-1850ab3d302391b85-1-20150714212553907087000"
```

A full description of this method and how to use it is presented in Chapter 17, "Caching and Performance."

5.7 Ignoring Columns

Active Record handles automatic schema introspection and mapping but has not traditionally exposed an abstraction for the table definition itself or allowed it to be altered. The attitude of the core team with regard to that policy is gradually changing with the introduction of the Attributes API and the capability to ignore specified columns using `ActiveRecord::Base.ignored_columns`.

If you find yourself working with legacy tables containing inconveniently named columns or in a situation[5] where you need to make one or more columns temporarily invisible to Active Record, simply add them to the `ignored_column` array.

```
class User < ApplicationRecord
  self.ignored_columns = %w(associations)
end
```

---

4. https://github.com/rails/arel/

5. It's common to need to ignore columns during online schema changes using tools like https://github.com/soundcloud/lhm.

5.8   Connections to Multiple Databases in Different Models

Connections are created via `ActiveRecord::Base.establish_connec-tion` and retrieved by `ActiveRecord::Base.connection`. All classes inheriting from `ActiveRecord::Base` will use this connection. What if you want some of your models to use a different connection? You can add class-specific connections.

For example, let's say you need to access data residing in a legacy database apart from the database used by the rest of your Rails application. We'll create a new base class that can be used by models that access legacy data. Begin by adding details for the additional database under its own key in `database.yml`. Then call `establish_connection` to make `LegacyProjectBase` and all its subclasses use the alternate connection instead.

```
class LegacyProjectBase < ApplicationRecord
  establish_connection :legacy_database
  self.abstract_class = true
  ...
end
```

Incidentally, to make this example work with subclasses, you must specify `self.abstract_class = true` in the class context. Otherwise, Rails considers the subclasses of `LegacyProject` to be using single-table inheritance (STI), which we discuss at length in Chapter 9, "Advanced Active Record."

💬 Xavier says . . .

You can easily point your base class to different databases depending on the Rails environment like this:

```
class LegacyProjectBase < ApplicationRecord
  establish_connection "legacy_#{Rails.env}"
  self.abstract_class = true
  ...
end
```

Then just add multiple entries to `database.yml` to match the resulting connection names. In the case of our example, that is `legacy_development`, `legacy_test`, etc.

The `establish_connection` method takes a string (or symbol) key pointing to a configuration already defined in `database.yml`. Alternatively, you can pass it a literal hash of options, although it's messy to put this sort of configuration data right into your model file instead of `database.yml`.

```
class TempProject < ApplicationRecord
  establish_connection adapter: 'sqlite3', database: ':memory:'
  ...
end
```

Rails keeps database connections in a connection pool inside the `ActiveRecord::Base` class instance. The connection pool is simply a `Hash` object indexed by the Active Record class. During execution, when a connection is needed, the `retrieve_connection` method walks up the class-hierarchy until a matching connection is found.

5.9 Using the Database Connection Directly

It is possible to use Active Record's underlying database connections directly, and sometimes it is useful to do so from custom scripts and for one-off or ad-hoc testing.

Access the connection via the connection attribute of any Active Record class. If all your models use the same connection, then use the connection attribute of `ActiveRecord::Base`.

```
ActiveRecord::Base.connection.execute("show tables").values
```

The most basic operation that you can do with a connection is simply to `execute` a SQL statement from the `DatabaseStatements` module. For example, Listing 5.1 shows a method that executes a SQL file statement by statement.

Listing 5.1 Execute a SQL file line by line using active record's connection
```
def execute_sql_file(path)
  File.read(path).split(';').each do |sql|
    begin
      ActiveRecord::Base.connection.execute(#{sql}\n") unless sql.blank?
    rescue ActiveRecord::StatementInvalid
      $stderr.puts "warning: #{$!}"
    end
  end
end
```

If for some reason you want to execute methods directly on the underlying Ruby-based database driver library, you can access it via `raw_connection`.

```
rc = ActiveRecord::Base.connection.raw_connection
```

```
rc.prepare('some_name', "SELECT FROM my_table WHERE id = $1")
st = connection.exec_prepared('some_name', [ id ])
```

5.9.1   The **DatabaseStatements** Module

The   `ActiveRecord::ConnectionAdapters::DatabaseStatements`
module mixes a number of useful methods into the connection object that make it
possible to work with the database directly instead of using Active Record models.
I've purposely left out some of the methods of this module because they are used
internally by Rails to construct SQL statements dynamically, and I don't think they're
of much use to application developers.

For the sake of readability in the `select_` examples below, assume that the connection object has been assigned to `conn`, like this:

```
conn = ActiveRecord::Base.connection
```

begin_db_transaction() Begins a database transaction manually (and turns
   off Active Record's default autocommitting behavior).

commit_db_transaction() Commits the transaction (and turns on Active
   Record's default autocommitting behavior again).

delete(sql_statement) Executes a SQL DELETE statement provided and
   returns the number of rows affected.

execute(sql_statement) Executes the SQL statement provided in the context of this connection. This method is abstract in the DatabaseState-
   ments module and is overridden by specific database adapter implementations. As such, the return type is a result set object corresponding to the
   adapter in use.

insert(sql_statement) Executes a SQL INSERT statement and returns the
   last autogenerated ID from the affected table.

reset_sequence!(table, column, sequence = nil) Used in Oracle
   and Postgres; updates the named sequence to the maximum value of the specified table's column.

rollback_db_transaction() Rolls back the currently active transaction (and
   turns on auto-committing). Called automatically when a transaction block raises an exception or returns `false`.

select_all(sql_statement) Returns an array of record hashes with the
   column names as keys and column values as values.

```
conn.select_all("select name from businesses limit 5")
=> [{"name"=>"Hopkins Painting"}, {"name"=>"Whelan & Scherr"},
{"name"=>"American Top Security Svc"}, {"name"=>"Life Style Homes"},
{"name"=>"378 Liquor Wine & Beer"}]
```

select_one(sql_statement) Works similarly to `select_all` but returns only the first row of the result set, as a single hash with the column names as keys and column values as values. Note that this method does not add a limit clause to your SQL statement automatically, so consider adding one to queries on large datasets.

```
>> conn.select_one("select name from businesses")
=> {"name"=>"New York New York Salon"}
```

select_value(sql_statement) Works just like `select_one`, except that it returns a single value: the first column value of the first row of the result set.

```
>> conn.select_value("select * from businesses limit 1")
=> "Cimino's Pizza"
```

select_values(sql_statement) Works just like `select_value`, except that it returns an array of the values of the first column in all the rows of the result set.

```
>> conn.select_values("select * from businesses limit 5")
=> ["Ottersberg Christine E Dds", "Bally Total Fitness", "Behboodikah,
Mahnaz Md", "Preferred Personnel Solutions", "Thoroughbred Carpets"]
```

update(sql_statement) Executes the update statement provided and returns the number of rows affected. Works exactly like `delete`.

5.9.2   Other Connection Methods

The full list of methods available on `connection`, which returns an instance of the underlying database adapter, is fairly long. Most of the Rails adapter implementations define their own custom versions of these methods. That makes sense, since all databases have slight variations in how they handle SQL and very large variations in how they handle extended commands, such as for fetching metadata.

A peek at `abstract_adapter.rb` shows us the default method implementations:

```
...

# Returns the human-readable name of the adapter. Use mixed case - you
# can always use downcase if needed.
def adapter_name
  'Abstract'
```

```
end

# Does this adapter support migrations? Backend specific, as the
# abstract adapter always returns +false+.
def supports_migrations?
  false
end

# Can this adapter determine the primary key for tables not attached
# to an Active Record class, such as join tables? Backend
# specific, as the abstract adapter always returns +false+.
def supports_primary_key?
  false
end

...
```

In the following list of method descriptions and code samples, I'm accessing the connection of our sample `time_and_expenses` application in the Rails console, and again I've assigned `connection` to a local variable named `conn`, for convenience.

active? Indicates whether the connection is active and ready to perform queries.

adapter_name Returns the human-readable name of the adapter, as in the following example:

```
>> conn.adapter_name
=> "SQLite"
```

disconnect! and reconnect! Closes the active connection or closes and opens a new one in its place, respectively.

raw_connection As mentioned earlier, this method provides access to the underlying database connection. Useful for when you need to execute a proprietary statement or you're using features of the Ruby database driver that aren't necessarily exposed in Active Record. (In trying to come up with a code sample for this method, I was able to crash the Rails console with ease. There isn't much in the way of error checking for exceptions that you might raise while mucking around with `raw_connection`.)

supports_count_distinct? Indicates whether the adapter supports using DISTINCT within COUNT in SQL statements. This is `true` for all adapters except SQLite, which therefore requires a workaround when doing operations such as calculations.

supports_migrations? Indicates whether the adapter supports migrations.

tables Produces a list of tables in the underlying database schema. It includes
tables that aren't usually exposed as Active Record models, such as `schema`
`_info` and `sessions`.

```
>> conn.tables
=> ["schema_migrations", "users", "timesheets", "expense_reports",
"billable_weeks", "clients", "billing_codes", "sessions"]
```

verify!(timeout) Lazily verify this connection, calling `active?` only if it
hasn't been called for `timeout` seconds.

5.10   Custom SQL Queries

Active Record's `find_by_sql` class method takes a SQL query string and returns
an array of Active Record objects based on the results. It predates `Relation` and
practically everything else in Rails.

Here's a barebones example, which you would never actually need to do in a real
application:

```
>> Client.find_by_sql("select * from clients")
=> [#<Client id: 1, name: "Paper Jam Printers",
    code: "PJP" ...>, #<Client id: 2, name: "Goodness Steaks",
    code: "GOOD_STEAKS" ...>]
```

You should take care to use `find_by_sql` only when you really need it! And
thanks to the power of Arel, nowadays it's rare to need it. The problem with using
SQL directly starts with reduced database portability. When you use Active Record's
normal find operations, Rails takes care of handling differences between the underlying databases for you.

Active Record also already has a ton of built-in functionality abstracting queries.
In fact, half of this chapter was dedicated to listing those abstractions as they
exist in Arel. It would be unwise to reinvent that functionality in your application code.

There are cases where it might seem that you might need to use `find_by_sql`, but
you actually don't. A common one is a LIKE query:

```
>> Client.find_by_sql("select * from clients where code like 'A%'")
=> [#<Client id: 1, name: "Amazon, Inc" ...>]
```

Turns out that you can easily pass that LIKE clause to a `where` method:

```
>> param = "A"
>> Client.where("code like ?", "#{param}%")
=> [#<Client id: 1, name: "Amazon, Inc" ...>]
```

Preventing SQL Injection Attacks

Under the covers, Rails sanitizes[6] your SQL code, provided that you parameterize your query. Active Record executes your SQL using the `connection.select_all` method, iterating over the resulting array of hashes and invoking your Active Record's `initialize` method for each row in the result set.

What would this section's example look like un-parameterized?

```
>> Client.where("code like '#{params[:code]}%'")
=> [#<Client id: 1, name: "Amazon, Inc" ...>] # NOOOOO!
```

Notice the missing question mark as a variable placeholder. Always remember that interpolating user-supplied values into a SQL fragment of any type is very unsafe! Just imagine what would happen to your project if a malicious user called that unsafe find with `params[:code]` set to

```
"Amazon'; DELETE FROM users;'
```

This particular example might fail in your own experiments. The outcome is very specific to the type of database/driver that you're using. Some popular database drivers may even have features that help to prevent SQL injection. I still think it's better to be safe than sorry.

Chapter 15, "Security," covers this topic in-depth.

The `count_by_sql` method works in a manner similar to `find_by_sql`.

```
>> Client.count_by_sql("select count(*) from clients")
=> 132
```

Again, you should have a special reason to be using it instead of the abstractions provided by Active Record and Arel.

---

6. Sanitization prevents SQL injection attacks. For more information about SQL injection and Rails see http://guides.rubyonrails.org/security.html#sql-injection.

5.11   Other Configuration Options

In addition to the configuration options used to instruct Active Record on how to handle naming of tables and primary keys, there are a number of other settings[7] that govern miscellaneous functions. Set them in an initializer, if needed.

default_timezone Tells Rails whether to use `Time.local` (using `:local`) or `Time.utc` (using `:utc`) when pulling dates and times from the database. Defaults to `:local`.

```
Rails.application.config.active_record.default_timezone = :utc
```

logger Accepts a logger conforming to the interface of Log4r or the default Ruby `Logger` class, which is then passed on to any new database connections made. You can retrieve this logger by calling `logger` on either an Active Record model class or instance. Set to `nil` to disable logging.

primary_key UUIDs are becoming a popular alternative to auto-incrementing integer primary keys. (Not supported in all databases, though.)

```
Rails.application.config.active_record.primary_key = :uuid
```

schema_format Specifies the format to use when dumping the database schema with certain default rake tasks. Use the `:sql` option to have the schema dumped as potentially database-specific SQL statements. Just beware of incompatibilities if you're trying to use the `:sql` option with different databases for development and testing. The default option is `:ruby`, which dumps the schema as an `ActiveRecord::Schema` file that can be loaded into any database that supports migrations.

```
Rails.application.config.active_record.schema_format = :sql
```

schema_migrations_table_name Lets you set a string to be used as the name of the schema migrations table.

store_full_sti_class Specifies whether Active Record should store the full constant name including namespace when using single-table inheritance (STI), covered in Chapter 9, "Advanced Active Record."

warn_on_records_fetched_greater_than This configuration setting helps you find queries that return a result set with a number of rows larger than the set limit.

```
...config.active_record.warn_on_records_fetched_greater_than = 1000
```

---

7. This section does not contain an exhaustive list of Active Record configuration options. For a complete, always up-to-date list see http://edgeguides.rubyonrails.org/configuring.html#configuring-active-record.

If the result set loaded is greater than the limit, a warning is posted in the log. (Grep the log for "Query fetched".) The warning can help you find cases where a poorly scoped operation is loading too many objects into memory at a time.

ⓘ Looking for `config.active_record.auto_explain_threshold` `_in_seconds`? This cool feature, which would automatically log `EXPLAIN` output for long-running queries was removed in Rails 4, and many of us will definitely miss it. Its removal solved a long-running issue with database connections failing during asset compilation. Fortunately, you can still invoke `explain` manually on a query that you suspect might be problematic.

5.12   Conclusion

This chapter covered the fundamentals of Active Record, the framework included with Ruby on Rails for creating database-bound model classes. We've learned how Active Record expresses the convention over configuration philosophy that is such an important part of the Rails way and how to make settings manually that override the conventions in place.

We've also looked at the methods provided by `ActiveRecord::Base`, the parent class of all persistent models in Rails, which include everything you need to do basic CRUD operations: create, read, update, and delete. Finally, we reviewed how to drill through Active Record to use the database connection whenever you need to do so.

In the next chapter, we continue our coverage of Active Record by learning how migrations help evolve an application's database schema.

CHAPTER 6

Active Record Migrations

Baby step to four o'clock. Baby step to four o'clock.

—Bob Wiley

It's a fact of life that the database schema of your application will evolve over the course of development. Tables are added, names of columns are changed, things are dropped—you get the picture. Without strict conventions and process discipline for the application developers to follow, keeping the database schema in proper lock-step with application code is traditionally a very troublesome job.

Migrations are Rails' way of helping you to evolve the database schema of your application (also known as its DDL) without having to drop and re-create the database each time you make a change. And not having to drop and recreate the database each time a change happens means that you don't lose your development data. That may or may not be that important, but is usually very convenient. The only changes made when you execute a migration are those necessary to move the schema from one version to another, whether that move is forward or backward in time.

Of course, being able to evolve your schema without having to recreate your databases and the loading/reloading of data is an order of magnitude more important once you're in production.

6.1   Creating Migrations

Rails provides a generator for creating migrations.

```
$ rails generate migration
Usage:
rails generate migration NAME [field[:type][:index]...] [options]
```

At minimum, you need to supply a descriptive name for the migration in CamelCase (or underscored_text—both work) and the generator does the rest. Other generators, such as the model and scaffolding generators, also create migration scripts for you, unless you specify the `--skip-migration` option.

The descriptive part of the migration name is up to you, but most Rails developers that I know try to make it match the schema operation (in simple cases) or at least allude to what's going on inside (in more complex cases).

✎ If you change the classname of your migration to something that doesn't match its filename, you will get an `uninitialized constant` error when that migration gets executed.

The whole workflow starts with generating a new migration, editing its source (if necessary), then running `rails db:migrate` from your terminal.

6.1.1 Generator Magic

If the migration name is of the form "CreateXXX" and is followed by a list of column names and types, then a migration creating the table XXX with the columns listed will be generated. For example:

```
$ rails g migration CreateProducts name:string part_number:string
```

generates

```
class CreateProducts < ActiveRecord::Migration[5.0]
  def change
    create_table :products do |t|
      t.string :name
      t.string :part_number
    end
  end
end
```

If the migration name is of the form "AddXXXToYYY" or "RemoveXXXFromYYY" and is followed by a list of column names and types then a migration containing the appropriate `add_column` and `remove_column` statements will be created.

```
$ rails g migration AddPartNumberToProducts part_number:string
```

will generate

```
class AddPartNumberToProducts < ActiveRecord::Migration[5.0]
  def change
```

```
    add_column :products, :part_number, :string
  end
end
```

If you'd like to add an index on the new column, you can do that as well:

```
$ bin/rails generate migration AddPartNumberToProducts
  part_number:string:index
```

will generate

```
class AddPartNumberToProducts < ActiveRecord::Migration[5.0]
  def change
    add_column :products, :part_number, :string
    add_index :products, :part_number
  end
end
```

Add as many columns as you need.

```
$ rails g migration AddDetailsToProducts part_number:string price:decimal
```

generates

```
class AddDetailsToProducts < ActiveRecord::Migration[5.0]
  def change
    add_column :products, :part_number, :string
    add_column :products, :price, :decimal
  end
end
```

The migration generator will produce join tables if "JoinTable" is part of the name.

```
$ rails g migration CreateJoinTableCustomerProduct customer product
```

will produce the following migration:

```
class CreateJoinTableCustomerProduct < ActiveRecord::Migration[5.0]
  def change
    create_join_table :customers, :products do |t|
      # t.index [:customer_id, :product_id]
      # t.index [:product_id, :customer_id]
    end
  end
end
```

6.1.2 Sequencing

Originally, Rails migrations were sequenced via a simple numbering scheme baked into the name of the migration file and automatically managed by the migration generator. Each migration simply received a sequential number. There were many inconveniences inherent in that approach, especially in team environments where two developers could check in a migration with the same sequence number. Thankfully those issues were eliminated by using timestamps to sequence migrations instead.

A record of migrations that have already been run is kept in a special hidden database table that Rails maintains. It is named `schema_migrations` and only has one column:

```
mysql> desc schema_migrations;
+----------+--------------+------+-----+---------+-------+
| Field    | Type         | Null | Key | Default | Extra |
+----------+--------------+------+-----+---------+-------+
| version  | varchar(255) | NO   | PRI | NULL    |       |
+----------+--------------+------+-----+---------+-------+
1 row in set (0.00 sec)
```

The first thing that `rails db:migrate` does is to check the `schema_migrations` table and execute any migrations on your file system that have not yet run (even if they have earlier timestamps than any you've added yourself in the interim).

6.1.3 The **change** Method

Rails pushes you toward defining reversible migrations. In older versions, each migration class had two instance methods named `up` and `down`. The `up` method included the logic of what to change in the database for the migration, while the `down` method specified how to revert/roll back that change.

While it's still possible to use `up` and `down`, nowadays we usually use the `change` method. For most operations, Rails is smart enough to figure out how to roll back automatically.

The following migration file `20130313005347_create_clients.rb` illustrates creating a new simple table named `clients`:

```ruby
class CreateClients < ActiveRecord::Migration[5.0]
  def change
    create_table :clients do |t|
      t.string :name
      t.string :code
      t.timestamps
```

```
      end
    end
end
```

If we go to the command line in our project folder and type `rails db:migrate`, then the `clients` table will be created. Rails gives us informative output during the migration process so that we see what is going on:

```
$ rails db:migrate
== CreateClients: migrating ==========================================
-- create_table(:clients)
   -> 0.0448s
== CreateClients: migrated (0.0450s) =================================
```

ℹ Wondering what that [5.0] is doing at the end of the migration's base class? It turns out that there are slight differences in the Migration API's behavior between Rails 5 and older versions, for instance the way that it automatically adds NOT NULL to timestamps.

The changes mean that if you were to upgrade an old Rails application to version 5 and re-run old migrations, you'd get a different schema than you were expecting. The problem is avoided by the introduction of a compatibility layer, which is where that version tagging with the square brackets comes in. If [5.0] is not present on a migration class, it will be run with legacy behavior. However, Rails will raise a warning asking you to add the appropriate version tag to the old migrations.

6.1.4   Rolling Back

It's easy to roll back changes if you made a mistake in development.

```
$ rails db:rollback
== 20161123170510 CreateEvents: reverting =========================
-- drop_table(:events)
   -> 0.0009s
== 20161123170510 CreateEvents: reverted (0.0111s) ==============
```

If you ever need to roll back to an earlier version of the schema, just pass it a version number to roll back to, as in `rails db:migrate VERSION=20161123170510`.

6.1.5   Redo

It's actually super common to forget to add something to a migration. Rails gives you `rails db:migrate:redo` as a convenient way to rollback and re-migrate in one command.

6.1.6   Reversible Operations

If a migration is very complex, Active Record may not be able to reverse it without some additional information from you.

The `reversible` method acts very similarly to the old school up and down migration methods, that were common in previous versions of Rails. Using `reversible`, you can specify operations to perform when running a migration and others when reverting it.

In the following example, the `reversible` method passes logic in a block to methods, up and down, to create a new function in a PostgreSQL database:

```
def change
  reversible do |dir|
    dir.up do
      execute <<-END
        CREATE FUNCTION add(integer, integer) RETURNS integer
          AS 'select $1 + $2;'
          LANGUAGE SQL
          IMMUTABLE
          RETURNS NULL ON NULL INPUT;
      END
    end

    dir.down do
      execute "DROP FUNCTION add"
    end
  end
end
```

The Migrations API doesn't know anything about custom functions, which is why in the example we have to drop down to talking to the database connection directly, using the `execute` method.

6.1.7   Irreversible Operations

Some transformations are destructive in a manner that cannot be reversed. Migrations of that kind should raise an `ActiveRecord::IrreversibleMigration` exception in their reversible down block.

For example, what if someone on your team made a silly mistake and defined the telephone column of your clients table as an integer? You can change the column to a string and the data will migrate cleanly, but going from a string to an integer? Not so much.

```
def change
  reversible do |dir|
    dir.up do
      # Phone number fields are not integers, duh!
      change_column :clients, :phone, :string
    end

    dir.down { raise ActiveRecord::IrreversibleMigration }
  end
end
```

6.1.8 `create_table(name, options, &block)`

The `create_table` method needs at minimum a name for the table and a block containing column definitions. Why do we specify identifiers with symbols instead of strings? Both will work, but symbols require one less keystroke.

The `create_table` method makes a huge, but usually true, assumption that we want an auto-incrementing, integer-typed, primary key. That is why you don't see it declared in the list of columns. If that assumption happens to be wrong, it's time to pass `create_table` some options in a hash.

For example, how would you define a simple join table consisting of two foreign key columns and not needing its own primary key? Just pass the `create_table` method an `:id` option set to `false` as a boolean, not a symbol! It will stop the migration from auto-generating a primary key altogether:

```
create_table :ingredients_recipes, id: false do |t|
  t.column :ingredient_id, :integer
  t.column :recipe_id, :integer
end
```

Alternatively, the same functionality can be achieved using the `create_join_table` method, covered later in the chapter.

If all you want to do is change the name of the primary key column from its default of 'id', pass the `:id` option a symbol instead. For example, let's say your corporation mandates that primary keys follow the pattern tablename_id. Then the earlier example would look as follows:

Active Record

```
create_table :clients, id: :clients_id do |t|
  t.column :name, :string
  t.column :code, :string
  t.column :created_at, :datetime
  t.column :updated_at, :datetime
end
```

6.1.8.1   Options

The `force: true` option tells the migration to go ahead and drop the table being defined if it exists. Be careful with this one, since it will produce (possibly unwanted) data loss when run in production. As far as I know, the `:force` option is mostly useful for making sure that the migration puts the database in a known state but isn't all that useful on a daily basis.

The `:options` option enables you to append custom instructions to the SQL `CREATE` statement and is useful for adding database-specific commands to your migration. Depending on the database you're using, you might be able to specify things such as character set, collation, comments, min/max sizes, and many other properties using this option.

The `temporary: true` option specifies creation of a temporary table that will only exist during the current connection to the database. In other words, it only exists during the migration. In advanced scenarios, this option might be useful for migrating big sets of data from one table to another but is not commonly used.

> ● **Sebastian says . . .**
>
> A little known fact is that you can remove old migration files (while still keeping newer ones) to keep the `db/migrate` folder to a manageable size. You can move the older migrations to a `db/archived_migrations` folder or something like that. Once you do trim the size of your migrations folder, use the `rake db:reset` task to (re)create your database from `db/schema.rb` and load seed data into your development environment.

6.1.9   `change_table(table_name, &block)`

This method works just like `create_table` and accepts the same kinds of column definitions.

6.1.10 `create_join_table(*table_names)`

In Rails 4, a new migration method `create_join_table` was added to easily create `has_and_belongs_to_many`-style join tables. The `create_join_table` accepts at minimum the names of two tables.

```
create_join_table :ingredients, :recipes
```

The preceding code example will create a table named 'ingredients_recipes' with no primary key.

6.1.10.1 Options

`:table_name` If you do not agree with the Rails convention of concatenating both tables names with an underscore, the `:table_name` option enables you to override it explicitly.

`:column_options` Add any extra options to append to the foreign key column definitions. For example, you might need to use UUID keys instead of integers.

```
class CreateJoinTableUserAuction < ActiveRecord::Migration[5.0]
  def change
    create_join_table(:users, :auctions, column_options: {type: :uuid})
  end
end
```

`:options`, `:temporary`, and `:force` Accept the same interface as the equivalent options found in `create_table`.

6.1.11 API Reference

This section details the methods that are available in the context of `create_table` and `change_table` methods within a migration class.

6.1.11.1 `change(column_name, type, options = {})`

Changes the column's definition according to the new options. The options hash optionally contains a hash with arguments that correspond to the options used when adding columns.

```
t.change(:name, :string, limit: 80)
t.change(:description, :text)
```

6.1.11.2 `change_default(column_name, default)`

Sets a new default value for a column.

```
t.change_default(:qualification, 'new')
t.change_default(:authorized, 1)
```

Active Record

6.1.11.3 `column(column_name, type, options = {})`
Adds a new column to the named table.

```
t.column(:name, :string)
```

Note that you can also use the short-hand version by calling it by type. This adds a column (or columns) of the specified type.

```
t.string(:goat)
t.string(:goat, :sheep)
t.integer(:age, :quantity)
```

The basic column types supported by most all database adapters are listed in Table 6.1.

Table 6.1   Column Types Most Commonly Used with Rails[1]

Column Type	Description
`:string`	Limited to 255 characters by default. Might be case-sensitive depending on database.
`:text`	Generally unlimited length depending on database. Usually can't be indexed like regular strings.
`:integer`	Whole number, in contrast to `:decimal` or `:float`.
`:decimal`	Stored with specified precision. Use for math that requires accuracy.
`:float`	Floating-point decimal number with fixed precision depending on platform. Do *not* use for math that requires accuracy due to rounding errors.
`:boolean`	`True` or `false`.
`:binary`	Raw chunks of data saved in database-specific way.
`:date`	Year, month and day (no time).
`:time`	Hours, minutes, seconds (no date).
`:datetime`	Date and time stored together.
`:timestamp`	Exactly the same as `:datetime` on Rails.[1]

Learn more about defining columns a little later on in the chapter.[1]

---

1. This stackoverflow question features a great explanation of `:datetime` versus `:timestamp`: http://stackoverflow.com/questions/3928275/in-ruby-on-rails-whats-the-difference-between -datetime-timestamp-time-and-da.

6.1.11.4 `index(column_name, options = {})`

Adds a new index to the table. The `column_name` parameter can be one symbol or an array of symbols referring to columns to be indexed. The `name` parameter lets you override the default name that would otherwise be generated.

```
# a simple index
t.index(:name)

# a unique index
t.index([:branch_id, :party_id], unique: true)

# a named index
t.index([:branch_id, :party_id], unique: true, name: 'by_branch_party')
```

Rails has built-in support for PostgreSQL partial indices (see https://www.postgresql .org/docs/7.0/static/partial-index.htm). You can specify them in your migration by adding a `:where` option to the normal index declaration. The main benefit is reduction of the size of indexes on commonly used queries within an application.

For example, let's assume your application queries constantly for clients that have a status of "active" within the system. Instead of creating an index on the status column for every client record, we can include only those records that meet the specified criteria:

```
add_index(:clients, :status, where: 'active')
```

Rails also has built-in support for PostgreSQL expression indexes, with optional operator classes (see https://www.postgresql.org/docs/9.4/static/indexes-opclass .html). Take note of the SQL expression and operator on line 3.

```
1 def change
2   add_index :users,
3             'lower(last_name) varchar_pattern_ops',
4             name: "index_users_on_name_unique",
5             unique: true
6 end
```

Instead of a column name, there's a SQL expression specifying that the value of the index should be a lower-case representation of the user's last name.

The `varchar_pattern_ops` operator class (also on line 3) is especially useful for fields that you know you will be doing `LIKE` or regexp queries on. It changes the way that the index analyzes the column from being based on locale-specific collation to a character-by-character B-tree. Just be careful to also create normal indexes if needed, or some of your queries might end up doing full table scans and run really slowly.

6.1.11.5 `belongs_to(*args)` and `references(*args)`

These two methods are aliases to each other. They add a foreign key column to another model, using Active Record naming conventions. Optionally, it adds a `_type` column if the `:polymorphic` option is set to `true`.

```
create_table :accounts do
  t.belongs_to(:person)
end

create_table :comments do
  t.references(:commentable, polymorphic: true)
end
```

A common best practice is to create an index for each foreign key in your database tables. It's so common, that Rails 5 automatically does it for you.

If you're on an older version of Rails or want to disable auto-indexing, you can use the `:index` option of `references` and `belongs_to` methods. It accepts a boolean value or the same hash options as the `index` method, covered in the preceding section.

```
create_table :accounts do
  t.belongs_to :person, index: false
end
```

6.1.11.6 `remove(*column_names)`

Removes the column(s) specified from the table definition.

```
t.remove(:qualification)
t.remove(:qualification, :experience)
```

6.1.11.7 `remove_index(options = {})`

Removes the given index from the table. Specify the index to remove either by its columns or explicitly by its name.

```
# remove the accounts_branch_id_index from the accounts table
t.remove_index column: :branch_id

# remove the accounts_branch_id_party_id_index from the accounts table
t.remove_index column: [:branch_id, :party_id]
```

```
# remove the index named by_branch_party in the accounts table
t.remove_index name: :by_branch_party
```

6.1.11.8 `remove_references(*args)` and `remove_belongs_to`

Removes a reference. Optionally removes a `type` column if marked as polymorphic.

```
t.remove_belongs_to(:person)
t.remove_references(:commentable, polymorphic: true)
```

6.1.11.9 `remove_timestamps`

You will never use this method. It removes `created_at` and `updated_at` columns.

6.1.11.10 `rename(old_column_name, new_column_name)`

Renames a column. The old name comes first, a fact that I usually can't remember. I try to remember it as renaming *this* to *that*.

```
t.rename :description, :name
```

6.1.11.11 `revert`

If you have ever wanted to revert a specific migration file explicitly within another migration, now you can. The `revert` method can accept the name of a migration class, which when executed, reverts the given migration.

```
revert CreateProductsMigration
```

The revert method can also accept a block of directives to reverse on execution.

6.1.11.12 `timestamps`

Adds Active Record–maintained timestamp (`created_at` and `updated_at`) columns to the table.

```
t.timestamps
```

As of Rails 5, timestamps are automatically marked as `NOT NULL`.

6.2 Defining Columns

Columns can be added to a table using either the `column` method, inside the block of a `create_table` statement, or with the `add_column` method. Other than taking the name of the table to add the column to as its first argument, the methods work identically.

```
create_table :clients do |t|
  t.column :name, :string
end

add_column :clients, :code, :string
add_column :clients, :created_at, :datetime
```

The first (or second) parameter obviously specifies the name of the column, and the second (or third) obviously specifies its type. The SQL92 standard defines fundamental data types, but each database implementation has its own variation on the standards.

Rails has its own generalized names for column types, which we summarized earlier in this chapter in Table 6.1. If you're familiar with database column types, when you examined that table it might have struck you as a little weird that there is a database column declared as type `:string`, since databases don't have string columns—they have char or varchars types.

6.2.1   Column Type Mappings

The reason for declaring a database column as type string is that Rails migrations are meant to be database-agnostic. That's why you could (as I've done on occasion) develop using Postgres as your database and deploy in production to Oracle.

A complete discussion of how to go about choosing the right data type for your application needs is outside the scope of this book. However, it is useful to have a reference for how migration's generic types map to database-specific types. The mappings for the databases most commonly used with Rails are in Table 6.2.

Table 6.2   Column Mappings for the Databases Most Commonly Used with Rails

Migration Type	MySQL	Postgres	SQLite	Oracle	Ruby Class
`:binary`	`blob`	`bytea`	`blob`	`blob`	`String`
`:boolean`	`tinyint(1)`	`boolean`	`boolean`	`number(1)`	`Boolean`
`:date`	`date`	`date`	`date`	`date`	`Date`
`:datetime`	`datetime`	`timestamp`	`datetime`	`date`	`Time`
`:decimal`	`decimal`	`decimal`	`decimal`	`decimal`	`Big-Decimal`
`:float`	`float`	`float`	`float`	`number`	`Float`
`:integer`	`int(11)`	`integer`	`integer`	`number(38)`	`Fixnum`
`:string`	`varchar (255)`	`character-varying (255)`	`varchar (255)`	`varchar (255)`	`String`

Table 6.2 Column Mappings for the Databases Most Commonly Used with Rails (*continued*)

Migration Type	MySQL	Postgres	SQLite	Oracle	Ruby Class
:text	text	text	text	clob	String
:time	time	time	time	date	Time
:timestamp	datetime	timestamp	datetime	date	Time

6.2.1.1 Native Database Column Types

Each connection adapter class has a `native_database_types` hash which establishes the mapping described in Table 6.2. If you need to look up the mappings for a database not listed in Table 6.2, you can pop open the adapter Ruby code and find the `native_database_types` hash, like the following one inside the `PostgreSQLAdapter` class within `postgresql_adapter.rb`:

```
NATIVE_DATABASE_TYPES = {
    primary_key: "serial primary key",
    string:      { name: "character varying" },
    text:        { name: "text" },
    integer:     { name: "integer" },
    float:       { name: "float" },
    decimal:     { name: "decimal" },
    datetime:    { name: "timestamp" },
    time:        { name: "time" },
    date:        { name: "date" },
    daterange:   { name: "daterange" },
    numrange:    { name: "numrange" },
    tsrange:     { name: "tsrange" },
    tstzrange:   { name: "tstzrange" },
    int4range:   { name: "int4range" },
    int8range:   { name: "int8range" },
    binary:      { name: "bytea" },
    boolean:     { name: "boolean" },
    xml:         { name: "xml" },
    tsvector:    { name: "tsvector" },
    hstore:      { name: "hstore" },
    inet:        { name: "inet" },
    cidr:        { name: "cidr" },
    macaddr:     { name: "macaddr" },
    uuid:        { name: "uuid" },
    json:        { name: "json" },
    jsonb:       { name: "jsonb" },
    ltree:       { name: "ltree" },
    citext:      { name: "citext" },
    point:       { name: "point" },
    line:        { name: "line" },
```

Active
Record

```
    lseg:         { name: "lseg" },
    box:          { name: "box" },
    path:         { name: "path" },
    polygon:      { name: "polygon" },
    circle:       { name: "circle" },
    bit:          { name: "bit" },
    bit_varying:{ name: "bit varying" },
    money:        { name: "money" },
}
```

You might have noticed that the PostgreSQL adapter includes a large number of column type mappings that are not available in other databases. You can specify these column types in your migration and they'll work just fine, but you'll, of course, lose database portability.

 ✎ The easiest way to peek at the adapter code is on Github.[2]

We delve into why you might want to use extended column types such as `hstore` and `array` in Chapter 9, "Advanced Active Record."

6.2.2   Column Options

For many column types, just specifying type is not enough information. All column declarations accept the following options:

default: value Sets a default to be used as the initial value of the column for new rows. You don't ever need to explicitly set the default value to `null`. Just leave off this option to get a `null` default value. It's worth noting that MySQL 5.x ignores default values for binary and text columns.

limit: size Adds a size parameter to string, text, binary, or integer columns. Its meaning varies depending on the column type that it is applied to. Generally speaking, limits for string types refers to number of characters, whereas for other types it specifies the number of bytes used to store the value in the database.

null: false Makes the column required at the database level by adding a `not null` constraint.

index: true Adds an ordinary generated index for the column.

comment: text Adds a comment for the column that will be visible in `schema .rb` and certain kinds of database management software.

---

2. https://github.com/rails/rails/tree/master/activerecord/lib/active_record/connection_adapters

⚷ The `comment` option is new to Rails 5 and especially useful on larger teams where it's not always possible to keep up with exactly what every new column added to the database does. Currently only MySQL and PostgreSQL allow comments.

6.2.2.1   Decimal Precision

Columns declared as type `:decimal` accept the following options:

precision: number Precision is the total number of digits in a number.

scale: number Scale is the number of digits to the right of the decimal point. For example, the number 123.45 has a precision of 5 and a scale of 2. Logically, the scale cannot be larger than the precision.

❶ Note

Decimal types pose a serious opportunity for data loss during migrations of production data between different kinds of databases. The default precisions between Oracle and SQL Server can cause the migration process to truncate and change the value of your numeric data if it doesn't have precision details specified.

6.2.3   Column Type Gotchas

The choice of column type is not necessarily a simple choice and depends on both the database you're using and the requirements of your application.

:binary Depending on your particular usage scenario, storing binary data in the database can cause very significant performance problems. Active Record doesn't generally exclude any columns when it loads objects from the database, and putting large binary attributes on commonly used models will increase the load on your database server significantly. If you must put binary content in a commonly used class, take advantage of the `:select` method to only bring back the columns you need.

:boolean The way that boolean values are stored varies from database to database. Some use 1 and 0 integer values to represent true and false, respectively. Others use characters such as T and F. Rails handles the mapping between Ruby's true and false very well, so you don't need to worry about the underlying scheme yourself. Setting attributes directly to database values such as 1 or F may work correctly but is considered an anti-pattern.

:datetime and :timestamp The Ruby class that Rails maps to `datetime` and `timestamp` columns is `Time`. In 32-bit environments, `Time` doesn't work for dates before 1902. Ruby's `DateTime` class does work with year values prior to 1902, and Rails falls back to using it if necessary. It doesn't use `DateTime` to begin for performance reasons. Under the covers, `Time` is implemented in C and is very fast, whereas `DateTime` is written in pure Ruby and is comparatively slow.

:time It's very, very rare that you want to use a `:time` datatype—perhaps if you're modeling an alarm clock. Rails will read the contents of the database as hour, minute, and second values into a `Time` object with dummy values for the year, month, and day.

:decimal Older versions of Rails (prior to 1.2) did not support the fixed-precision `:decimal` type and as a result many old Rails applications incorrectly used `:float` datatypes. Floating-point numbers are by nature imprecise, so it is important to choose `:decimal` instead of `:float` for most business-related applications.

● Tim says . . .

If you're using a float to store values that need to be precise, such as money, you're a jackass. Floating point calculations are done in binary rather than decimal, so rounding errors abound in places you wouldn't expect.

```
>> 0.1+0.2 == 0.3
=> false
>> BigDecimal('0.1') + BigDecimal('0.2') == BigDecimal('0.3')
=> true
```

:float Don't use floats to store currency values, or more accurately, any type of data that needs fixed precision. Since floating-point numbers are pretty much approximations, any single representation of a number as a float is probably okay. However, once you start doing mathematical operations or comparisons with float values, it is ridiculously easy to introduce difficult to diagnose bugs into your application.

:integer and :string There aren't many gotchas that I can think of when it comes to integers and strings. They are the basic data building blocks of your application, and many Rails developers leave off the size specification, which results in the default maximum sizes of 11 digits and 255 characters, respectively. You should keep in mind that you won't get an error if you try to store values that exceed the maximum size defined for the database column, which again, is 255 characters by default. Your string will simply get truncated. Use validations to make sure that user-entered data does not exceed the maximum size allowed.

:text There have been reports of text fields slowing down query performance on some databases, enough to be a consideration for applications that need to scale to high loads. If you must use a text column in a performance-critical application, put it in a separate table.

⚲ Preserving Custom Data Types

If use of database-specific datatypes (such as `:double`, for higher precision than `:float`) is critical to your project, use the `config.active_record.schema_format = :sql` setting in `config/application.rb` to make Rails dump schema information in native SQL DDL format rather than its own cross-platform compatible Ruby code, via the `db/schema.rb` file.

6.2.4   "Magic" Timestamp Columns

Rails does magic with datetime columns, if they're named a certain way. Active Record will automatically timestamp create operations if the table has columns named `created_at` or `created_on`. The same applies to updates when there are columns named `updated_at` or `updated_on`.

Note that `created_at` and `updated_at` should be defined as `datetime`, but if you use `t.timestamps` then you don't have to worry about what type of columns they are.

Automatic timestamping can be turned off globally, by setting the following variable in an initializer.

```
ActiveRecord::Base.record_timestamps = false
```

The preceding code turns off timestamps for all models, but `record_timestamps` is class-inheritable, so you can also do it on a case-by-case basis by setting `self.record_timestamps` to `false` at the top of specific model classes.

6.2.5   More Command-Line Magic

A number of commonly used column type modifiers can be passed directly on the command line. They are enclosed by curly braces and follow the field type.

For instance, running:

```
$ rails g migration AddDetailsToProducts 'price:decimal{5,2}'
  supplier:references{polymorphic}
```

will produce a migration that looks like this:

```
class AddDetailsToProducts < ActiveRecord::Migration[5.0]
  def change
    add_column :products, :price, :decimal, precision: 5, scale: 2
    add_reference :products, :supplier, polymorphic: true
  end
end
```

This particular magic is not a well documented area of Rails. It's "dark magic" if you will and fun to experiment with.

6.3 Transactions

Rails normally tries to execute your migration inside of a transaction, if that functionality is supported by your database. (Most do.) Occasionally, this can cause an issue if you try to do something that doesn't work inside of a transaction (like adding certain kinds of indexes[3]).

If you run into this kind of issue, you can turn off transactions for a particular migration using the `disable_ddl_transaction!` class method.

```
class AddConcurrentIndexToBids < ActiveRecord::Migration[5.0]
  disable_ddl_transaction!
  def change
    reversible do |dir|
      dir.up do
        execute "CREATE INDEX CONCURRENTLY index_auction_id
                ON bids(auction_id)"
      end
      dir.down do
        execute "DROP INDEX index_auction_id"
      end
```

6.4 Data Migration

So far we've only discussed using migration files to modify the schema of your database. Inevitably, you will run into situations where you also need to perform data migrations, whether in conjunction with a schema change or not.

---

3. https://www.postgresql.org/docs/9.1/static/sql-createindex.html#SQL-CREATEINDEX
-CONCURRENTLY

6.4.1   Using SQL

In most cases, you should craft your data migration in raw SQL using the `execute` command that is available inside a migration class.

For example, say you had a `phones` table that kept phone numbers in their component parts and later wanted to simplify your model by just having a `number` column instead. You'd write a migration similar to this one:

```
class CombineNumberInPhones < ActiveRecord::Migration
  def change
    add_column :phones, :number, :string
    reversible do |dir|
      dir.up do
        execute "UPDATE phones SET number =
                CONCAT(area_code, prefix, suffix)"
      end
      dir.down do
        # code to undo that update, ugh...
        # might want to make this one Irreversible
      end
    end

    remove_column :phones, :area_code
    remove_column :phones, :prefix
    remove_column :phones, :suffix
  end
end
```

There is a naive alternative to using SQL in the example above that would be more lines of code and significantly slower.

```
Phone.find_each do |p|
  p.number = p.area_code + p.prefix + p.suffix
  p.save
end
```

I suppose a better Ruby-based solution would be to use Active Record's `update_all` method.

```
Phone.update_all("set number = concat(area_code, prefix, suffix)")
```

While I admit that it's tempting to do that instead of hacking some SQL that you might not be as comfortable with, the danger comes down the road as your schema and model design continues to evolve. Although it's unlikely in this example, `Phone` might not have the same configuration and behavior in the future as it does today.

In the next section, we delve into how you protect yourself from that situation by writing a simple, stand-alone `Phone` model in the migration script itself.

I can actually tell you from experience that introducing migration-specific models can get messy and hard to debug very quickly. I strongly advise sticking to raw SQL in data migrations whenever possible.

6.4.2 Migration Models

If you declare an Active Record model inside of a migration script, it'll be namespaced to that migration class.

```
class HashPasswordsOnUsers < ActiveRecord::Migration
  class User < ActiveRecord::Base
  end

  def change
    reversible do |dir|
      dir.up do
        add_column :users, :hashed_password, :string
        User.reset_column_information
        User.find_each do |user|
          user.hashed_password = Digest::SHA1.hexdigest(user.password)
          user.save!
        end
        remove_column :users, :password
      end

      dir.down { raise ActiveRecord::IrreversibleMigration }
    end
  end
end
```

Why not use just your application model classes in the migration scripts directly? As your schema evolves, older migrations that use model classes directly can and will break down and become unusable. Properly namespacing migration models prevent you from having to worry about name clashes with your application's model classes or ones that are defined in other migrations.

💬 Durran says . . .

Note that Active Record caches column information on the first request to the database, so if you want to perform a data migration immediately after a migration you may run into a situation where the new columns have not yet been loaded. This is a case where using `reset_column_information` can come in handy. Simply call this class method on your model, and everything will be reloaded on the next request.

6.4.3   Database Adapter Helper Methods

The database adapter has a number of methods that facilitate data analysis without involving the overhead of loading Active Record objects. Since they can be called directly in the context of your migration, they can be pretty convenient.

⚠ None of the following methods do any kind of typecasting for you. All values returned will be in the form of a string.

6.4.3.1   `select_all(sql)`

Returns an `ActiveRecord::Result` on which you can call `to_a` to have an array of hashes.

```
>> select_all("SELECT * FROM users").to_a
=> [ { 'id' => '1', 'name' => 'Obie Fernandez' }...
```

6.4.3.2   `select_rows(sql)`

Similar to `select_all`, but returns an array of arrays (tuples) containing the contents of each row in the result set.

```
>> select_rows("SELECT id, name FROM users")
=> [["1","obie"],["2","bob"],["3","cam"]]
```

6.4.3.3   `select_one(sql)`

Similar to `select_all`, but returns one row as a hash.

6.4.3.4   `select_values(sql)`

Returns an array of the first column in a select.

```
>> select_values("SELECT * FROM users")
=> [ '1', '2', ... ] # returns id column since it is first
```

6.4.3.5   `select_value(sql)`

Similar to `select_values`, but returns only the first value as a string. Useful for executing functions, querying counts and doing other kinds of calculations that return a single value.

```
>> select_value("SELECT answer FROM secret(life, universe, everything))
=> '42'
```

🔑 You might be wondering how to use these helper methods *outside* of migrations. They're available on `connection`, which is a class method of every Active Record model.

6.5   Database Schema

The file `db/schema.rb` is generated every time you migrate and reflects the latest status of your database schema. The top of a schema file looks something like this.

```
ActiveRecord::Schema.define(version: 20161123170510) do

  create_table "auctions", force: :cascade do |t|
    t.string   "name"
    t.text     "description"
    t.datetime "ends_at"
    t.datetime "created_at", null: false
    t.datetime "updated_at", null: false
    t.datetime "closes_at"
    t.integer  "user_id"
end
```

It looks very similar to a migration!

Indeed, `schema.rb` uses the same API as migrations. However, you should never edit `db/schema.rb` by hand because this file is auto-generated from the current state of the database every time you do a migration.

Instead of editing `schema.rb` directly, you use the migrations feature of Active Record described in this chapter to incrementally modify your database, which has the side effect of regenerating this schema definition.

Rails' schema definition provides the authoritative record of truth for the latest version of your database schema. If you need to recreate your database on another server, you should be using `db:schema:load`, not running all the migrations from scratch.

It's strongly recommended to check `schema.rb` into your version control system. First of all, it helps to have one definitive schema definition around for reference. Secondly, it gives you the capability to run `rake db:schema:load` to create your database schema from scratch without having to run all migrations from the beginning. That's especially important because old migrations have a tendency to break in difficult to understand ways.

6.6   Database Seeding

The automatically created file db/seeds.rb is a default location for creating seed
data for your database. It was introduced in order to stop the practice of inserting
seed data in individual migration files, which makes sense if you accept the premise
that migrations should never be used for seeding example or base data required by
your application. It is executed with the rake db:seed task (or created alongside
the database when you run rake db:setup).

At its simplest, the contents of seed.rb is simply a series of create! statements
that generate baseline data for your application, whether it's default or related to
configuration. For example, let's add an admin user and some billing codes to our
time and expenses app:

```
User.create!(login: 'admin',
             email: 'admin@example.com',
             :password: '123', password_confirmation: '123',
             authorized_approver: true)

client = Client.create!(name: 'Workbeast', code: 'BEAST')
client.billing_codes.create!(name: 'Meetings', code: 'MTG')
client.billing_codes.create!(name: 'Development', code: 'DEV')
```

Why use the bang version of the create methods? Because otherwise you won't find
out if you had errors in your seed file. An alternative would be to use first_or_
create methods to make seeding idempotent.

```
c = Client.where(name: 'Workbeast', code: 'BEAST').first_or_create!
c.billing_codes.where(name: 'Meetings', code: 'MTG').first_or_create!
c.billing_codes.where(name: 'Development', code: 'DEV').first_or_create!
```

Another common seeding practice worth mentioning is calling delete_all prior
to creating new records, so that seeding does not generate duplicate records. This
practice avoids the need for idempotent seeding routines and lets you be very secure
about exactly what your database will look like after seeding.)

```
User.delete_all
User.create!(login: 'admin', ...

Client.delete_all
client = Client.create!(name: 'Workbeast', ...
```

Active Record

● Carlos says . . .

I typically use the `seed.rb` file for data that is essential to **all** environments, including production.

For dummy data that will be only used on development or staging, I prefer to create custom rake tasks under the `lib/tasks` directory, for example `lib/tasks/load_dev_data.rake`. This helps keep `seed.rb` clean and free from unnecessary conditionals, like `unless Rails.env .production?`.

6.7 Database-Related Tasks

The following command-line tasks are included by default in boilerplate Rails projects.

6.7.1 `db:create` and `db:create:all`

Create the database defined in `config/database.yml` for the current `Rails .env`. If the current environment is development, Rails will create both the local development and test databases. (Or create all of the local databases defined in `config/database.yml` in the case of `db:create:all`.)

6.7.2 `db:drop` and `db:drop:all`

Drops the database for the current `RAILS_ENV`. If the current environment is development, Rails will drop both the local development and test databases. (Or drops all of the local databases defined in `config/database.yml` in the case of `db:drop:all`.)

6.7.3 `db:forward` and `db:rollback`

The `db:rollback` task moves your database schema back one version. Similarly, the `db:forward` task moves your database schema forward one version and is typically used after rolling back.

6.7.4 `db:migrate`

Applies all pending migrations. If a `VERSION` environment variable is provided, then `db:migrate` will apply pending migrations through the migration specified, but no further. The `VERSION` is specified as the timestamp portion of the migration file name.

```
# example of migrating up with param
$ rails db:migrate VERSION=20130313005347
```

```
== CreateUsers: migrating ========================================
-- create_table(:users)
   -> 0.0014s
== CreateUsers: migrated (0.0015s) ===============================
```

If the VERSION provided is older than the current version of the schema, then this task will actually roll back the newer migrations.

```
# example of migrating down with param
$ rails db:migrate VERSION=20130312152614
== CreateUsers: reverting ========================================
-- drop_table(:users)
   -> 0.0014s
== CreateUsers: reverted (0.0015s) ===============================
```

6.7.5   `db:migrate:down`

This task will invoke the down method of the specified migration only. The VERSION is specified as the timestamp portion of the migration file name.

```
$ rails db:migrate:down VERSION=20130316172801
== CreateClients: reverting ======================================
-- drop_table(:clients)
   -> 0.0028s
== CreateClients: reverted (0.0054s) =============================
```

6.7.6   `db:migrate:up`

This task will invoke the up method of the specified migration only. The VERSION is specified as the timestamp portion of the migration file name.

```
$ rails db:migrate:up VERSION=20130316172801
== CreateClients: migrating ======================================
-- create_table(:clients)
   -> 0.0260s
== CreateClients: migrated (0.0261s) =============================
```

6.7.7   `db:migrate:redo`

Executes the down method of the latest migration file, immediately followed by its up method. This task is typically used right after correcting a mistake in the up method or to test that a migration is working correctly.

```
$ rails db:migrate:redo
== AddTimesheetsUpdatedAtToUsers: reverting ======================
-- remove_column(:users, :timesheets_updated_at)
   -> 0.0853s
== AddTimesheetsUpdatedAtToUsers: reverted (0.0861s) =============
```

```
== AddTimesheetsUpdatedAtToUsers: migrating ======================
-- add_column(:users, :timesheets_updated_at, :datetime)
   -> 0.3577s
== AddTimesheetsUpdatedAtToUsers: migrated (0.3579s) ============
```

6.7.8 `db:migrate:reset`

Resets your database for the current environment using your migrations (as opposed to using `schema.rb`).

6.7.9 `db:migrate:status`

Displays the status of all existing migrations in a nicely formatted table. It will show up for migrations that have been applied, and down for those that haven't.

This task is useful in situations where you might want to check for recent changes to the schema before actually applying them (right after pulling from the remote repository, for example).

```
$ rails db:migrate:status

database: timesheet_development

 Status   Migration ID    Migration Name
--------------------------------------------------
   up     20130219005505  Create users
   up     20130219005637  Create timesheets
   up     20130220001021  Add user id to timesheets
  down    20130220022039  Create events
```

6.7.10 `db:reset` and `db:setup`

The `db:setup` creates the database for the current environment, loads the schema from `db/schema.rb`, then loads the seed data. It's used when you're setting up an existing project for the first time on a development workstation. The similar `db:reset` task does the same thing except that it drops and recreates the database first.

6.7.11 `db:schema:dump`

Creates a `db/schema.rb` file that can be portably used against any DB supported by Active Record. Note that creation (or updating) of `schema.rb` happens automatically any time you migrate.

6.7.12 `db:schema:load`

Loads `schema.rb` file into the database for the current environment.

6.7.13 `db:seed`

Loads the seed data from `db/seeds.rb` as described in this chapter's section "Database Seeding."

6.7.14 `db:structure:dump`

Dumps the database structure to a SQL file containing raw DDL code in a format corresponding to the database driver specified in `database.yml` for your current environment.

```
$ rake db:structure:dump

$ cat db/development_structure.sql
CREATE TABLE `avatars` (
  `id` int(11) NOT NULL AUTO_INCREMENT,
  `user_id` int(11) DEFAULT NULL,
  `url` varchar(255) COLLATE utf8_unicode_ci DEFAULT NULL,
  PRIMARY KEY (`id`)
) ENGINE=InnoDB DEFAULT CHARSET=utf8 COLLATE=utf8_unicode_ci;

...
```

I've rarely needed to use this task. It's possible that some Rails teams working in conjunction with DBAs that exercise strict control over their application's database schemas will need this task on a regular basis.

6.7.15 `db:test:prepare`

Checks for pending migrations and loads the test schema by doing a `db:schema:dump` followed by a `db:schema:load`.

This task gets used very often during active development whenever you're running specs or tests without using Rake. (Standard spec-related Rake tasks run `db:test:prepare` automatically for you.)

6.7.16 `db:version`

Returns the timestamp of the latest migration file that has been run. Works even if your database has been created from `db/schema.rb`, since it contains the latest version timestamp in it:

Active Record

```
ActiveRecord::Schema.define(version: 20130316172801)
```

6.8   Conclusion

This chapter covered the fundamentals of Active Record migrations. In the next chapter, we continue our coverage of Active Record by learning about how model objects are related to each other and interact via associations.

CHAPTER 7

Active Record Associations

Any time you can reify something, you can create something that embodies a concept, it gives you leverage to work with it more powerfully. That's exactly what's going on with has_many :through.

—Josh Susser

Active Record associations let you declaratively express relationships between model classes. The power and readability of the Associations API is an important part of what makes working with Rails so special.

This chapter covers the different kinds of Active Record associations available while highlighting use cases and available customizations for each of them. We also take a look at the classes that give us access to relationships themselves.

7.1 The Association Hierarchy

Associations typically appear as methods on Active Record model objects. For example, the method timesheets might represent the timesheets associated with a given user.

```
user.timesheets
```

People used to get confused about the type of objects returned by these association methods because they have a way of masquerading as plain old Ruby objects and arrays. Rails 4 dropped the charade. Inspecting any association now reveals that it is in fact a proxy object.

```
>> user.timesheets
=> #<ActiveRecord::Associations::CollectionProxy []>
```

225

The `CollectionProxy` acts like a middleman between the object that owns the association and the actual associated object. Fortunately, it's not the Ruby way to care about the actual class of an object. What messages an object responds to is a lot more significant.

But before we get any deeper into the details of the association proxies, let's talk about the relationships that Active Record lets you model, starting with the most common kind.

7.2   One-to-Many Relationships

An example of one-to-many relationships in our sample code is the association between the `User`, `Timesheet`, and `ExpenseReport` classes:

```
class User < ActiveRecord::Base
  has_many :timesheets
  has_many :expense_reports
end
```

Timesheets and expense reports should be linked in the opposite direction as well, so that it is possible to reference the `user` to which a timesheet or expense report belongs.

```
class Timesheet < ActiveRecord::Base
  belongs_to :user
end

class ExpenseReport < ActiveRecord::Base
  belongs_to :user
end
```

When these relationship declarations are executed, Rails uses some metaprogramming magic to dynamically add code to your models. In particular, proxy collection objects are created that let you manipulate the relationship easily.

⚠ Don't create associations that have the same name as instance methods of `ActiveRecord::Base`. Since the association adds a method with that name to its model, it will override the inherited method and break things. For instance, `attributes` and `connection` would make really bad choices for association names.

If I whip up the Rails console I should be able to add a new blank timesheet to my user and then check to make sure it's there:

```
>> obie = User.find(1)
=> #<User id: 1...>
>> obie.timesheets << Timesheet.new
=> #<ActiveRecord::Associations::CollectionProxy [#<Timesheet id: 1 ...]>
>> obie.timesheets
=> #<ActiveRecord::Associations::CollectionProxy [#<Timesheet id: 1 ...]>
```

7.2.1 Adding Associated Objects to a Collection

Notice that the `Timesheet` object gains an `id` immediately. Appending an object to a `has_many` collection automatically saves that object, that is, unless the parent object (the owner of the collection) is not yet stored in the database. Let's make sure that's the case using Active Record's `reload` method, which re-fetches the attributes of an object from the database:

```
>> obie.timesheets.reload
=> #<ActiveRecord::Associations::CollectionProxy [#<Timesheet id:
        1, user_id: 1 ...]>
```

There it is. The foreign key, `user_id`, was automatically set by the `<<` method. It takes one or more association objects to add to the collection, and since it flattens its argument list and inserts each record, `push` and `concat` behave identically.

I could have used a `create` method on the association proxy, and it would have worked essentially the same way:

```
>> obie.timesheets.create
=> #<ActiveRecord::Associations::CollectionProxy [#<Timesheet id:
        1, user_id: 1 ...]>
```

7.3 Belongs to Associations

The `belongs_to` class method expresses a relationship from one Active Record object to a single associated object for which it has a foreign key attribute. The trick to remembering whether a class "belongs to" another one is considering which has the foreign key column in its database table.

Assigning an object to a `belongs_to` association will set its foreign key attribute to the owner object's id but will not save the record to the database automatically, as in the following example:

```
>> timesheet = Timesheet.create
=> #<Timesheet id: 1409, user_id: nil...>
>> timesheet.user = obie
=> #<User id: 1, login: "obie"...>
>> timesheet.user.login
```

Active Record

```
=> "obie"
>> timesheet.reload
=> #<Timesheet id: 1409, user_id: nil...>
```

7.3.1   Methods

Defining a `belongs_to` relationship on an Active Record class creates accessor methods with the same name on its model instances, plus a handful of useful additional methods.

7.3.1.1   Reloading

Just invoking the association method will query the database (if necessary) and return an instance of the related object. If you want to explicitly reload the related object from the database, Active Record provides a `reload_<association_name>` method for that purpose.

In the following capture from my console, I query for a timesheet and take a peek at the `object_id` of its related `user`. Notice that the second time I invoke the association via `user` on line 5, the `object_id` remains the same because the related object has been cached. However, invoking `reload_user` on line 7 reloads the relationship, and I get a new instance of `user`.

```
1 >> ts = Timesheet.first
2 => #<Timesheet id: 3, user_id: 1...>
3 >> ts.user.object_id
4 => 70279541443160
5 >> ts.user.object_id
6 => 70279541443160
7 >> ts.reload_user && ts.user.object_id
8 => 70279549419744
```

7.3.1.2   Building and Creating Related Objects via the Association

Besides the accessor and reload methods, during the `belongs_to` method's metaprogramming it also adds factory methods for creating new instances of the related class and attaching them via the foreign key automatically.

Following a common pattern, the `build_<association_name>` method does not save the new object, but the `create_<association_name>` method does. Both methods take an optional hash of attribute parameters with which to initialize the newly instantiated objects. Both are essentially one-line convenience methods, which I don't find particularly useful. It just doesn't usually make sense to create instances in that direction!

To illustrate, I'll simply show the code for building a User from a Timesheet or creating a Client from a BillingCode, neither of which would ever happen in real code because it just doesn't make sense to do so:

```
>> ts = Timesheet.first
=> #<Timesheet id: 3, user_id: 1...>

>> ts.build_user
=> #<User id: nil, email: nil...>

>> bc = BillingCode.first
=> #<BillingCode id: 1, code: "TRAVEL"...>

>> bc.create_client
=> #<Client id: 1, name=>nil, code=>nil...>
```

You'll probably find yourself creating instances of belonging objects from the has_many side of the relationship much more often.

7.3.2   Options

The following options can be passed in a hash to the belongs_to method to customize the behavior of the association.

7.3.2.1   `autosave`

Whether to automatically save the owning record whenever this record is saved. Defaults to false, because this behavior is usually not necessary. With the exception of counter cache columns, changing a child does not generally mean changes on the parent object.

If true, always save the associated object or destroy it if marked for destruction, when saving the parent object. If false, never save or destroy the associated object.

By default, associated objects are only saved if they are new records.

7.3.2.2   `class_name`

Assume for a moment that we wanted to establish another belongs_to relationship from the Timesheet class to User, this time modelling the relationship to the approver of the timesheet. You might start by adding an approver_id column to the timesheets table and an authorized_approver column to the users table via a migration. Then you would add a second belongs_to declaration to the Timesheet class:

```
class Timesheet < ActiveRecord::Base
  belongs_to :approver
  belongs_to :user
  ...
```

Active Record won't be able to figure out what class you're trying to link with just the information provided because you've (legitimately) acted against the Rails convention of naming a relationship according to the related class. It's time for a :class_ name parameter.

```
class Timesheet < ActiveRecord::Base
  belongs_to :approver, class_name: 'User'
  belongs_to :user
  ...
```

7.3.2.3 `counter_cache`

Use this option to make Rails automatically update a counter field on the associated object with the number of belonging objects. The option value can be `true`, in which case the pluralized name of the belonging class plus `_count` is used, or you can supply your own column name to be used:

```
counter_cache: true
counter_cache: :number_of_children
```

If a significant percentage of your association collections will be empty at any given moment, you can optimize performance at the cost of some extra database storage by using counter caches liberally. The reason is that when the counter cache attribute is at zero, Rails won't even try to query the database for the associated records!

⚠️ The value of the counter cache column must be set to zero by default in the database! Otherwise the counter caching won't work at all. It's because the way that Rails implements the counter caching behavior is by adding a simple callback that goes directly to the database with an UPDATE command and increments the value of the counter. If you're not careful, and neglect to set a default value of 0 for the counter cache column on the database, or misspell the column name, the counter cache will still seem to work! There is a magic method on all classes with has_many associations called col-lection_count, just like the counter cache. It will return a correct count value based on the in-memory object, even if you don't have a counter cache option set or the counter cache column value is null!

In the case that a counter cache was altered on the database side, you may tell Active Record to reset a potentially stale value to the correct count via the class method `reset_counters`. Its parameters are the id of the object and a list of association names.

```
Timesheet.reset_counters(5, :weeks)
```

> ⚠ It might feel a little more intuitive to put the `counter_cache` option on the `has_many` side of the association. However, doing so (at least in Rails 5.0.1) will result in a cryptic error message like `ActiveModel::Missing-AttributeError: can't write unknown attribute 'true'`. Worse, it is raised from the bowels of Active Record and not from the line in your code where you made the mistake. Same goes for other invalid options. Just something to file away in the back of your mind in case it happens to you.

7.3.2.4 `dependent`

Specifies a rule that the associated owner record should be destroyed or just deleted from the database, depending on the value of the option being `:destroy` or `:delete`, respectively.

The `:destroy` option will cause the dependent's callbacks to fire, whereas `:delete` will not.

Usage of this option *might* make sense in a `has_one/belongs_to` pairing. However, it is really unlikely that you want this behavior on `has_many/belongs_to` relationship; it just doesn't seem to make sense to code things that way.

> ⚠ If an owner record has its `:dependent` option set on the corresponding `has_many` association, then destroying one associated record will have the ripple effect of destroying all of its siblings.

7.3.2.5 `foreign_key`

Specifies the name of the foreign key column that should be used to find the associated object. Rails will normally infer this setting from the name of the association, by adding `_id` to it. You can override the inferred foreign key name with this option if necessary.

```
# without the explicit option, Rails would guess administrator_id
belongs_to :administrator, foreign_key: 'admin_user_id'
```

Active
Record

7.3.2.6 `inverse_of`

Explicitly declares the name of the inverse association in a bi-directional relationship. Considered an optimization, use of this option enables Rails to return the same instance of an object no matter which side of the relationship it is accessed from.

Covered in detail in the section "`inverse_of: name_of_belongs_to_association`."

7.3.2.7 `optional`

See the "`required`" section.

7.3.2.8 `polymorphic`

Set the `:polymorphic` option to `true` in order to specify that an object is related to its association in a *polymorphic* way. That is the Rails way of saying that the type (class name) of the related object is stored in the database along with its foreign key. Making a `belongs_to` relationship polymorphic abstracts the association so that any compatible model in the system can fill it.

In a sense, polymorphic associations let you trade relational integrity for convenience in child relationships that are reused across your application. Common examples are models such as photo attachments, comments, notes, line items, and so on.

One developer's sense of convenience is another's sense of abuse.

Let's illustrate by writing a `Comment` class that attaches to its subjects polymorphically. We'll associate it to both expense reports and timesheets. Listing 7.1 has the schema information in migration code, followed by the code for the classes involved. Notice the `:subject_type` column, which stores the class name of the associated class.

Listing 7.1   Comment class using polymorphic belongs to relationship

```
create_table :comments do |t|
  t.text :body
  t.references :subject, polymorphic: true

  # references can be used as a shortcut for following two statements
  # t.integer :subject_id
  # t.string  :subject_type

  t.timestamps
end
```

```
class Comment < ActiveRecord::Base
  belongs_to :subject, polymorphic: true
end

class ExpenseReport < ActiveRecord::Base
  belongs_to :user
  has_many :comments, as: :subject
end

class Timesheet < ActiveRecord::Base
  belongs_to :user
  has_many :comments, as: :subject
end
```

As you can see in the `ExpenseReport` and `Timesheet` classes of Listing 7.1, there is a corresponding syntax where you give Active Record a clue that the relationship is polymorphic by specifying `as: :subject`. We haven't covered `has_many`'s options yet in this chapter, and polymorphic relationships have their own section in Chapter 9, "Advanced Active Record."

7.3.2.9 `primary_key`

You should never need to use this option, except perhaps with strange legacy database schemas. It enables you to specify a surrogate column on the owning record to use as the target of the foreign key, instead of the usual primary key.

7.3.2.10 `required`

Require associated object to be present. (Defaults to `true`.)

In Rails 5, `belongs_to` associations automatically add a validation requiring the associated record to be present. This makes sense in the vast majority of cases—you don't want to save an *orphan* record to the database. It's also becoming more and more acceptable in the Rails world to put foreign-key constraints on relationships, which means that trying to save an object with a missing belongs to association could trigger a failure at the database level.

If you're modeling an optional belongs to association then remember to set this option to `false` (or set `optional: true`.)

Interestingly, this option was introduced in Rails 4 but defaulted to `false`. You could also get the same behavior on older versions of Rails but had to opt in by using `validates_presence_of` and referencing the association name.

⚲ If you're migrating a large application to Rails 5 and really want to turn off this behavior, you're in luck. Go into `config/initializers/new_framework_defaults.rb` and set `config.active_record.belongs_to_required_by_default` to `false`.

7.3.2.11 `touch`

If set to `true`, *touches* the owning record's `updated_at` timestamp.

```
class Timesheet < ActiveRecord::Base
  belongs_to :user, touch: true
...
```

Also works with a specific timestamp column specified by `column_name` if it is supplied. This option is helpful for caching schemes where timestamps are used to invalidate cached view content. The `column_name` option is particularly useful here if you want to do fine-grained fragment caching of the owning record's view.

For example, let's set the foundation for doing just that with the `User/Timesheet` association:

```
$ rails generate migration AddTimesheetsUpdatedAtToUsers timesheets_updated_at:datetime
    invoke  active_record
      create    db/migrate/20130413175038_add_timesheets_updated_at_to_users.rb

$ rake db:migrate
== AddTimesheetsUpdatedAtToUsers: migrating ===================================
-- add_column(:users, :timesheets_updated_at, :datetime)
   -> 0.0005s
== AddTimesheetsUpdatedAtToUsers: migrated (0.0005s) ==========================


class Timesheet < ActiveRecord::Base
  belongs_to :user, touch: 'timesheets_updated_at'
  ...
```

Learn about caching in Chapter 17, "Caching and Performance."

⚲ Note that the touch operation is a *straight to the database* `UPDATE` operation. Since it doesn't rely on normal Active Record update operations, you can't rely on touch behavior to trigger validations or passively save other attributes you may have changed on the associated object.

7.3.2.12 `validate`

Defaults to `false` on `belongs_to` associations, contrary to its counterpart setting on `has_many`. Tells Active Record to validate the owner record but *only in circumstances where it would normally save the owning record,* such as when the record is new and a save is required in order to get a foreign key value.

💬 Tim says . . .

Use `validates_associated` if you want association validation outside of automatic saving.

7.3.3   Scopes

Sometimes the need arises to have a relationship that must satisfy certain conditions in order for it to be valid. To facilitate this, Rails allows us to supply query criteria, or a *scope*, to a relationship definition as an optional second block argument. Active Record scopes are covered in detail in Chapter 9.

7.3.3.1 `where(*conditions)`

To illustrate supplying a condition to a `belongs_to` relationship, let's assume that the `users` table has a column named `approver`:

```
class Timesheet < ActiveRecord::Base
  belongs_to :approver,
    -> { where(approver: true) },
    class_name: 'User'
  ...
end
```

Now in order for the assignment of a user to the `approver` field to work, that user must be authorized. I'll go ahead and add a spec that both indicates the intention of my code and lets me show it in action. First, I turn my attention to `spec/models/timesheet_spec.rb`.

```
require 'spec_helper'

describe Timesheet do
  subject(:timesheet) { Timesheet.create }

  describe '#approver' do
    it 'may have a user associated as an approver' do
```

Active Record

```
        timesheet.approver = User.create(approver: true)
      expect(timesheet.approver).to be
    end
  end
end
```

It's a good start, but I also want to make sure something happens to prevent the system from assigning a non-authorized user to the `approver` field, so I add another spec:

```
it 'cannot be associated with a non-authorized user' do
  timesheet.approver = User.create(approver: false)
  expect(timesheet.approver).to_not be
end
```

I have my suspicions about the validity of that spec, though, and as I half-expected, it doesn't really work the way I want it to work:

```
1) Timesheet#approver cannot be associated with a non-authorized user
     Failure/Error: expect(timesheet.approver).to_not be
       expected #<User id: 1, approver: false ...> to evaluate to false
```

The problem is that Active Record (for better or worse, probably worse) allows me to make the invalid assignment. The `scope` option only applies during the query to get the association back from the database. I'll have some more work ahead of me to achieve the desired behavior, but I'll go ahead and prove out Rails' actual behavior by fixing my specs. I'll do so by leveraging `reload_<association>`, which tells the parent of the association to reload its target object:

```
describe Timesheet do
  subject(:timesheet) { Timesheet.create }

  describe '#approver' do
    it 'may have a user associated as an approver' do
      timesheet.approver = User.create(approver: true)
      timesheet.save
      timesheet.reload_approver
      expect(timesheet.approver(true)).to be
    end

    it 'cannot be associated with a non-authorized user' do
      timesheet.approver = User.create(approver: false)
      timesheet.save
      timesheet.reload_approver
      expect(timesheet.approver(true)).to_not be
    end
```

```
    end
end
```

Those two specs do pass, but note that I went ahead saved the `timesheet`, since just assigning a value to it will not save the record.

The takeaway is that providing a `scope` on relationships never affects the assignment of associated objects, only how those objects are read back from the database. To enforce the rule that a timesheet approver must be authorized, you'd need to add a `before_save` callback to the `Timesheet` class itself. Callbacks are covered in detail at the beginning of Chapter 9, "Advanced Active Record."

7.3.3.2 `includes`

In previous versions of Rails, relationship definitions had an `:include` option, that would take a list of second-order association names (on the owning record) that should be eagerly loaded when the current object was loaded. As of Rails 4, the way to do this is supplying the `includes` clause as part of the scope argument.

```
belongs_to :post, -> { includes(:author) }
```

In general, this technique is used to knock N+1 select operations down to N plus the number of associations being included. It is rare to use this technique on a `belongs_to`, rather than on the `has_many` side.

If necessary, due to conditions or orders referencing tables other than the main one, a SELECT statement with the necessary LEFT OUTER JOINS will be constructed on the fly so that all the data needed to construct a whole object graph is queried in one big database request.

With judicious use of using a relationship scope to include second-order associations and careful benchmarking, you can sometimes improve the performance of your application dramatically, mostly by eliminating N+1 queries. On the other hand, pulling lots of data from the database and instantiating large object trees can be very costly, so using an `includes` scope is no "silver bullet." As they say, your mileage may vary.

7.3.3.3 `select`

Replaces the SQL select clause that normally is generated when loading this association, which usually takes the form `table_name.*`. This just provides additional flexibility that it normally never needed.

7.3.3.4 `readonly`

Locks down the reference to the owning record so that you can't modify it. Theoretically, this might make sense in terms of constraining your programming contexts very specifically, but I've never had a use for it. Still, for illustrative purposes, here is an example where I've made the `user` association on `Timesheet` read-only:

```
class Timesheet < ActiveRecord::Base
  belongs_to :user, ~> { readonly }
  ...
```

```
>> t = Timesheet.first
=> #<Timesheet id: 1, submitted: nil, user_id: 1...>
```

```
>> t.user
=> #<User id: 1, login: "admin"...>
```

```
>> t.user.save
ActiveRecord::ReadOnlyRecord: ActiveRecord::ReadOnlyRecord
```

7.4   Has Many Associations

Just like it sounds, the `has_many` association enables you to define a relationship in which one model has many other models that belong to it. The sheer readability of code constructs such as `has_many` is a major reason that people fall in love with Rails.

The `has_many` class method is often used without additional options. If Rails can guess the type of class in the relationship from the name of the association, no additional configuration is necessary. This bit of code should look familiar by now:

```
class User < ActiveRecord::Base
  has_many :timesheets
  has_many :expense_reports
```

The names of the associations can be singularized and match the names of models in the application, so everything works as expected.

7.4.1   Methods

Fundamentally, `has_many` association proxies are fancy wrappers around a Ruby array and have all of a normal array's methods. Named scopes and all of `Active-Record::Base`'s class methods and Arel relations are also available on association collections, including `find`, `order`, `where`, etc.

```
user.timesheets.where(submitted: true).order('updated_at desc')
user.timesheets.late # assuming a scope :late defined on the Timesheet class
```

The following methods of `CollectionProxy` are available to `has_many` association collections.

7.4.1.1   `<<(*records)` and `create(attributes = {})`

Both methods will add either a single associated object or many, depending on whether you pass them an array or not. They both also trigger the `:before_add` and `:after_add` callbacks (covered in this chapter's options section for `has_many`).

Finally, the return value behavior of both methods varies wildly. The `create` method returns the new instance created, which is what you'd expect given its counterpart in `ActiveRecord::Base`. On the other hand, the `<<` method returns the association proxy, which enables chaining and is also natural behavior for a Ruby array.

⚠ Somewhat unfortunately, the `<<` method will return `false` and not itself if any of the records being added causes the operation to fail. Therefore, you shouldn't depend on the return value of `<<` being something on which you can continue chaining additional methods.

7.4.1.2   `any?` and `many?`

The `any?` method behaves like its Enumerable counterpart if you give it a block, otherwise it's the opposite of `empty?`. Its companion method `many?`, which is an Active Support extension to Enumerable, returns `true` if the size of the collection is greater than one, or if a block is given, if two or more elements match the supplied criteria.

7.4.1.3   `average(column_name, options = {})`

Convenience wrapper for `calculate(:average, ...)`.

7.4.1.4   `build(attributes={}, &block)`

Traditionally, the `build` method has corresponded to the `new` method of Active Record classes, except that it automatically sets the owner's foreign key and appends it to the association collection in one operation. However, as of Rails 2.2, the `new` method has the same behavior and probably should be used instead of `build`.

Active Record

```
user.timesheets.build(attributes)
user.timesheets.new(attributes) # same as calling build
```

⚷ One possible reason to still use `build` is that as a convenience, if the `attributes` parameter is an array of hashes (instead of just one), then `build` executes for each one. However, you would usually accomplish that kind of behavior using `accepts_nested_attributes_for` on the owning class, covered in Chapter 11, "All about Helpers," in the section about `fields_for`.

7.4.1.5 `calculate(operation, column_name, options = {})`

Provides aggregate (`:sum`, `:average`, `:minimum`, and `:maximum`) values within the scope of associated records. Covered in detail in Chapter 9, "Advanced Active Record," in the section "Calculation Methods."

7.4.1.6 `clear`

The `clear` method is similar to invoking `delete_all`, but instead of returning an array of deleted objects, it is chainable.

7.4.1.7 `count(column_name=nil, options={})`

Counts all associated records in the database. The first parameter, `column_name` gives you the option of counting on a column instead of generating COUNT(*) in the resulting SQL. If the `:counter_sql` option is set for the association, it will be used for the query; otherwise you can pass a custom value via the options hash of this method.

Assuming that no `:counter_sql` or `:finder_sql` options are set on the association, nor passed to `count`, the target class's count method is used, scoped to only count associated records.

7.4.1.8 `create(attributes, &block)` and `create!(attributes, &block)`

Instantiates a new record with its foreign key attribute set correctly, adds the new record to the association collection, and then saves it, all in one method call. The bang variant raises `Active::RecordInvalid` if saving fails, while the non-bang variant returns `true` or `false`, as you would expect it to based on the behavior of create methods elsewhere in Active Record.

The owning record must be saved in order to use create, otherwise an `Active-Record::RecordNotSaved` exception is raised.

```
>> User.new.timesheets.create
ActiveRecord::RecordNotSaved: You cannot call create unless the parent is saved
```

If a block is passed to `create` or `create!`, it will yield the newly created instance after the passed-in attributes are assigned but before saving the record to the database.

7.4.1.9   `delete(*records)` and `delete_all`

The `delete` and `delete_all` methods are used to sever specified associations or all of them, respectively. Both methods operate transactionally.

Invoking `delete_all` executes a `SQL UPDATE` that sets foreign keys for all currently associated objects to nil, effectively disassociating them from their parent.

⚠ The names of the `delete` and `delete_all` methods can be misleading. By default, they don't delete anything from the database—they only sever associations by clearing the foreign key field of the associated record. This behavior is related to the `:dependent` option, which defaults to `:nullify`. If the association is configured with the `:dependent` option set to `:delete` or `:destroy`, then the associated records will actually be deleted from the database.

7.4.1.10   `destroy(*records)` and `destroy_all`

The `destroy` and `destroy_all` methods are used to remove specified associations from the database or all of them, respectively. Both methods operate transactionally.

The `destroy_all` method takes no parameters; it's an all or nothing affair. When called, it begins a transaction and invokes `destroy` on each object in the association, causing them all to be deleted from the database with individual `DELETE` SQL statements.

⚠ There are load issues to consider if you plan to use `destroy_all` with large association collections, since many objects will be loaded into memory at once.

Active Record

7.4.1.11 `empty?`
Simply calls `size.zero?`.

7.4.1.12 `find(id)`
Find an associated record by `id`, a really common operation when dealing with nested RESTful resources. Raises an `ActiveRecord::RecordNotFound` exception if either the id or foreign key of the owner record is not found.

7.4.1.13 `first(*args)`
Returns the first associated record. Passing `first` an integer argument mimics the semantics of Ruby's `Array#first`, returning that number of records.

```
>> c = Client.first
=> #<Client id: 1, name: "Taigan", ...>
>> c.billing_codes.first(2)
=> [#<BillingCode id: 1, client_id: 1, code: "MTG"...>,
    #<BillingCode id: 2, client_id: 1, code: "DEV"...>]
```

🔑 If you're a Rails 5 hipster, you can use this method's cooler alias `take`.

7.4.1.14 `ids`
Returns an array of primary keys for the associated objects by hitting the database with a pluck operation.

7.4.1.15 `include?(record)`
Checks to see if the supplied record exists in the association collection and that it still exists in the underlying database table.

7.4.1.16 `last(*args)`
Returns the last associated record. Refer to the description of `first` earlier in this section for more details—it behaves exactly the same except for the obvious.

7.4.1.17 `length`
Returns the size of the collection by loading it (if necessary) and calling `size` on the array.

7.4.1.18 `maximum(column_name, options = {})`
Convenience wrapper for `calculate(:maximum, ...)`. Covered in detail in Chapter 9, "Advanced Active Record," in the section "Calculation Methods."

7.4.1.19 `minimum(column_name, options = {})`

Convenience wrapper for `calculate(:minimum, ...)`. Covered in detail in Chapter 9, "Advanced Active Record," in the section "Calculation Methods."

7.4.1.20 `new(attributes, &block)`

Instantiate a new record with its foreign key attribute set to the owner's id and add it to the association collection, in one method call.

7.4.1.21 `pluck(*column_names)`

Returns an array of attribute values. Covered in detail in Chapter 9, "Advanced Active Record," in the section "Calculation Methods."

7.4.1.22 `replace(other_array)`

Replaces the collection of records currently inside the proxy with `other_array`. Works by deleting objects that exist in the current collection, but not in `other_array`, and inserting (using `concat`) objects that don't exist in the current collection but do exist in `other_array`.

7.4.1.23 `select(select=nil, &block)`

The `select` method enables the specification of one or more columns to be selected for an association result set.

```
>> user.timesheets.select(:submitted).to_a
=> [#<Timesheet id: nil, submitted: false>,
   #<Timesheet id: nil, submitted: true>]
>> user.timesheets.select([:id,:submitted]).to_a
=> [#<Timesheet id: 1, submitted: false>,
   #<Timesheet id: 2, submitted: true>]
```

Only attributes specified will be populated in the resulting objects! For instance, continuing the first example, trying to access `updated_at` on any of the returned timesheets results in an `ActiveModel::MissingAttributeError` exception being raised.

```
>> timesheet = user.timesheets.select(:submitted).first
=> #<Timesheet id: nil, submitted: false>
>> timesheet.updated_at
ActiveModel::MissingAttributeError: missing attribute: updated_at
```

One of the main reasons to use this method is to perform calculations in the database. If you're doing that and still need a complete object to work with, pass `:*` as the first argument.

Active Record

```
>> user.timesheets.select(:*, "calc_something(col1, col2) as delta").to_a
=> [#<Timesheet id: 1, ..., delta: 1234>,
```

Alternatively, passing a block to the select method behaves similarly to `Array#select`. The result set from the database scope is converted into an array of objects and iterated through using `Array#select`, including only objects where the specified block returns `true`.

7.4.1.24 `size`

If the collection has already been loaded or its owner object has never been saved, the `size` method simply returns the size of the current underlying array of associated objects.

Otherwise, a `SELECT COUNT(*)` query is executed to get the size of the associated collection without having to load any objects.

⚠️ A number of configuration options can affect the behavior of the `size` method. For instance, the query is bounded to the `:limit` option of the association, if there is any set. Also, if there is a `counter_cache` option set on the association, then the value of the counter cache attribute on the parent is used instead of executing a database query.

When you know that you are starting from an unloaded state and it's likely that there are associated records in the database that you will need to load no matter what, it's more efficient to use `length` instead of `size`.

Some association options, such as `:group` and `:uniq`, come into play when calculating size—basically they will always force all objects to be loaded from the database so that the resulting size of the association array can be returned.

7.4.1.25 `sum(column_name, options = {})`

Convenience wrapper for `calculate(:sum, ...)`. Covered in detail in Chapter 9, "Advanced Active Record," in the section "Calculation Methods."

7.4.1.26 `uniq`

Iterates over the target collection and populates an `Array` with the unique values present. Keep in mind that equality of Active Record objects is determined by identity, meaning that the value of the `id` attribute is the same for both objects being compared.

7.4.2   Options
Despite the ease of use of has_many, there is a surprising amount of power and customization possible for those who know and understand the options available.

7.4.2.1   **after_add**
Called after a record is added to the collection via the << method. It is not triggered by the collection's create method, so careful consideration is needed when relying on association callbacks. A lambda callback will get called directly, versus a symbol, which correlates to a method on the owning record, which takes the newly added child as a parameter. It's also possible to pass an array of lambda or symbols.

Add callback method options to a has_many by passing one or more symbols corresponding to method names or Proc objects. See Listing 7.2 in the :before_add option for an example.

7.4.2.2   **after_remove**
Called after a record has been removed from the collection with the delete method. A lambda callback will get called directly, versus a symbol, which correlates to a method on the owning record, which takes the newly added child as a parameter. It's also possible to pass an array of lambda or symbols. See Listing 7.2 in the :before_add option for an example.

7.4.2.3   **as**
Specifies the polymorphic belongs_to association to use on the related class. (See Chapter 9, "Advanced Active Record," for more about polymorphic relationships.)

7.4.2.4   **autosave**
Whether to automatically save *all modified records* in an association collection when the parent is saved. Defaults to false, but note that normal Active Record behavior is to save *new* association records automatically when the parent is saved.

If true, associated objects are destroyed if marked for destruction when saving the parent object.

7.4.2.5   **before_add**
Triggered when a record is added to the collection via the << method. (Remember that concat and push are aliases of <<.)

A lambda callback will get called directly, versus a symbol, which correlates to a method on the owning record, which takes the newly added child as a parameter. It's also possible to pass an array of lambda or symbols.

Active Record

Raising an exception in the callback will stop the object from getting added to the collection. (Basically, this is because the callback is triggered right after the type mismatch check, and there is no rescue clause to be found inside <<.)

Listing 7.2   A simple example of `:before_add` **callback usage**

```
has_many :unchangable_posts,
         class_name: "Post",
         before_add: :raise_exception

private

def raise_exception(object)
  raise "You can't add a post"
end
```

Of course, that would have been a lot shorter code using a `Proc` since it's a one liner. The `owner` parameter is the object with the association. The `record` parameter is the object being added.

```
has_many :unchangable_posts,
  class_name: "Post",
  before_add: ->(owner, record) { raise "Can't do it!" }
```

One more time, with a lambda, which doesn't check the arity of block parameters:

```
has_many :unchangable_posts,
  class_name: "Post",
  before_add: lambda { raise "You can't add a post" }
```

7.4.2.6 `before_remove:` callback

Called before a record is removed from a collection with the `delete` method. See `before_add` for more information. As with `:before_add`, raising an exception stops the remove operation.

```
class User < ActiveRecord::Base
  has_many :timesheets,
           before_remove: :check_timesheet_destruction,
           dependent: :destroy

  protected

  def check_timesheet_destruction(timesheet)
    if timesheet.submitted?
      raise TimesheetError, "Cannot destroy a submitted timesheet."
```

```
      end
  end
```

Note that this is a somewhat contrived example, because it violates my sense of good object-oriented principles. The `User` class shouldn't really be responsible for knowing when it's okay to delete a timesheet or not. The `check_timesheet_destruction` method would more properly be added as a `before_destroy` callback on the `Timesheet` class.

7.4.2.7 `class_name`

The `:class_name` option is common to all of the associations. It allows you to specify, as a string, the name of the class of the association and is needed when the class name cannot be inferred from the name of the association itself.

```
has_many :draft_timesheets, -> { where(submitted: false) },
  class_name: 'Timesheet'
```

7.4.2.8 `dependent`

The default behavior when deleting a record that `has_many` associations is to leave the associated records in the database alone. Their foreign key fields will still point at the record that was deleted. That's ehrm, not great, so this is an option that is almost always worth considering.

`:nullify` Active Record will attempt to nullify, or clear, the foreign key that joins the parent record to the associations. Note that nullification can fail due to foreign key constraints.

`:destroy` Associated objects are destroyed along with the parent object, by iteratively calling their `destroy` methods.

`:delete_all` Associated objects are deleted in one fell swoop at the database level using a single SQL command. Note: While this option is much faster than `:destroy`, it doesn't trigger any destroy callbacks on the associated objects—you should use this option very carefully. It should only be used on associations that depend solely on the parent object.

`:restrict_with_exception` If associated objects are present when you attempt to destroy a parent object, Rails raises an `ActiveRecord::DeleteRestrictionError` exception.

`:restrict_with_error` An error is added to the parent object if any associated objects are present, rolling back the deletion from the database.

7.4.2.9 `foreign_key`

Overrides the convention-based foreign key column name that would normally be used in the SQL statement that loads the association. Normally it would be the owning record's class name with `_id` appended to it.

7.4.2.10 `inverse_of`

Explicitly declares the name of the inverse association in a bi-directional relationship. Considered an optimization, use of this option enables Rails to return the same instance of an object no matter which side of the relationship it is accessed from.

Consider the following, using our recurring example, *without* usage of `inverse_of`.

```
>> user = User.first
>> timesheet = user.timesheets.first
=> <Timesheet id: 1, user_id: 1...>
>> timesheet.user.equal? user
=> false
```

We use `equal?` instead of `==` because we purposely want to check object equality, not identity. As you see in the example, there are two instances of the same user in memory.

If we add `:inverse_of` to the association objection on `User`, like

```
has_many :timesheets, inverse_of: :user
```

then `timesheet.user.equal?` user will be `true`. Try something similar in one of your apps to see it for yourself.

7.4.2.11 `primary_key`

Specifies a surrogate key to use instead of the owning record's primary key, whose value should be used when querying to fill the association collection.

7.4.2.12 `source` and `source_type`

Used exclusively as additional options to assist in using `has_many :through` associations with polymorphic `belongs_to`. Covered in detail later in this chapter.

7.4.2.13 `through`

Creates an association collection via another association. See the section "has_many :through."

7.4.2.14 `validate`

In cases where the child records in the association collection would be automatically saved by Active Record, this option (`true` by default) dictates whether to ensure that they are valid. If you always want to check the validity of associated records when saving the owning record, then use `validates_associated :association_name`.

7.4.3 Scoping

The `has_many` association provides the capability to customize the query used by the database to retrieve the association collection. This is achieved by passing a scope block to the `has_many` method definition using any of the standard Active Record query methods, as covered in Chapter 5, "Working with Active Record."

In this section, we'll cover the most common scope methods used with `has_many` associations.

7.4.3.1 `where(*conditions)`

Using the query method `where`, you could add extra conditions to the Active Record-generated SQL query that brings back the objects in the association.

You can apply extra conditions to an association for a variety of reasons. How about approval of comments?

```
has_many :comments,
```

Plus, there's no rule that you can't have more than one `has_many` association exposing the same two related tables in different ways. Just remember that you'll probably have to specify the class name too.

```
has_many :pending_comments, -> { where(approved: true) },
  class_name: 'Comment'
```

7.4.3.2 `extending(*extending_modules)`

Specifies one or many modules with methods that will extend the association collection proxy. Used as an alternative to defining additional methods in a block passed to the `has_many` method itself. Discussed in the section "Association Extensions."

7.4.3.3 `group(*args)`

Adds a GROUP BY SQL clause to the queries used to load the contents of the association collection.

7.4.3.4 `having(*clauses)`

Must be used in conjunction with the `group` query method and adds extra conditions to the resulting SQL query used to load the contents of the association collection.

7.4.3.5 `includes(*associations)`

Takes an array of second-order association names (as an array) that should be eager-loaded when this collection is loaded. With judicious use of the `includes` query method and careful benchmarking, you can sometimes improve the performance of your application dramatically.

To illustrate, let's analyze how `includes` affects the SQL generated while navigating relationships. We'll use the following simplified versions of `Timesheet`, `BillableWeek`, and `BillingCode`:

```
class Timesheet < ActiveRecord::Base
  has_many :billable_weeks
end

class BillableWeek < ActiveRecord::Base
  belongs_to :timesheet
  belongs_to :billing_code
end

class BillingCode < ActiveRecord::Base
  belongs_to :client
  has_many :billable_weeks
end
```

First, I need to set up my test data, so I create a `timesheet` instance and add a couple of billable weeks to it. Then I assign a billable code to each billable week, which results in an object graph (with four objects linked together via associations).

Next, I do a fancy one-line `collect`, which gives me an array of the billing codes associated with the timesheet:

```
>> Timesheet.find(3).billable_weeks.collect(&:code)
=> ["TRAVEL", "DEVELOPMENT"]
```

Without the `includes` scope method set on the `billable_weeks` association of `Timesheet`, that operation cost me the following four database hits (copied from `log/development.log`, and prettied up a little):

```
Timesheet Load (0.3ms)  SELECT timesheets.* FROM timesheets WHERE
```

```
(timesheets.id = 3) LIMIT 1
BillableWeek Load (1.3ms)  SELECT billable_weeks.* FROM billable_weeks WHERE
(billable_weeks.timesheet_id = 3)
BillingCode Load (1.2ms)  SELECT billing_codes.* FROM billing_codes WHERE
(billing_codes.id = 7) LIMIT 1
BillingCode Load (3.2ms)  SELECT billing_codes.* FROM billing_codes WHERE
(billing_codes.id = 8) LIMIT 1
```

This demonstrates the so-called "N+1 select" problem that inadvertently plagues many systems. Anytime I need one billable week, it will cost me N select statements to retrieve its associated records. Now let's provide the `billable_weeks` association a scope block using `includes`, after which the `Timesheet` class looks as follows:

```
class Timesheet < ActiveRecord::Base
  has_many :billable_weeks, -> { includes(:billing_code) }
end
```

Simple! Rerunning our test statement yields the same results in the console:

```
>> Timesheet.find(3).billable_weeks.collect(&:code)
=> ["TRAVEL", "DEVELOPMENT"]
```

But look at how different the generated SQL is:

```
Timesheet Load (0.4ms)  SELECT timesheets.* FROM timesheets WHERE
(timesheets.id = 3) LIMIT 1
BillableWeek Load (0.6ms)  SELECT billable_weeks.* FROM billable_weeks WHERE
(billable_weeks.timesheet_id = 3)
BillingCode Load (2.1ms)  SELECT billing_codes.* FROM billing_codes WHERE
(billing_codes.id IN (7,8))
```

Active Record smartly figures out exactly which `BillingCode` records it will need and pulls them in using one query. For large datasets, the performance improvement can be dramatic!

It's generally easy to find N+1 select issues just by watching the log scroll by while clicking through the different screens of your application. (Of course, make sure that you're looking at realistic data or the exercise will be pointless.) Screens that might benefit from eager loading will cause a flurry of single-row `SELECT` statements, one for each record in a given association being used.

If you're feeling particularly daring (perhaps masochistic is a better term) you can try including a deep hierarchy of associations by mixing hashes into your `includes` query method, like in this fictional example from a bulletin board:

```
has_many :posts, -> { includes([:author, {comments: {author: :avatar }}]) }
```

That example snippet will grab not only all the comments for a `Post` but all their authors and avatar pictures as well. You can mix and match symbols, arrays, and hashes in any combination to describe the associations you want to load.

The biggest potential problem with so-called "deep" includes is pulling too much data out of the database. You should always start out with the simplest solution that will work, then use benchmarking and analysis to figure out if optimizations such as eager-loading help improve your performance.

💬 Wilson says . . .

Let people learn eager loading by crawling across broken glass, like we did. It builds character!

7.4.3.6 `limit(integer)`

Appends a `LIMIT` clause to the SQL generated for loading this association. This option is potentially useful in capping the size of very large association collections. Use in conjunction with the order query method to make sure you are grabbing the most relevant records.

7.4.3.7 `offset(integer)`

An integer determining the offset from where the rows should be fetched when loading the association collection. I assume this is here mostly for completeness, since it's hard to envision a valid use case.

7.4.3.8 `order(*clauses)`

Specifies the order in which the associated objects are returned via an `ORDER BY` SQL fragment, such as `"last_name, first_name DESC"`.

7.4.3.9 `readonly`

Sets all records in the association collection to read-only mode, which prevents saving them.

7.4.3.10 `select(expression)`

By default, this is * as in `SELECT * FROM` but can be changed if, for example, you want to add additional calculated columns or "piggyback" additional columns from joins onto the associated object as it's loaded.

7.4.3.11 `distinct`

Strips duplicate objects from the collection. Sometimes useful in conjunction with `has_many :through`.

7.5   Many-to-Many Relationships

Associating persistent objects via a join table can be one of the trickier aspects of object-relational mapping to implement correctly in a framework. Rails has a couple of techniques that let you represent many-to-many relationships in your model. We'll start with the older and simpler `has_and_belongs_to_many` and then cover the newer `has_many :through`.

I must clear my conscience with a disclaimer. As far as I can tell, the Rails Core Team is reluctantly maintaining support for `has_and_belongs_to_many` (habtm for short), and it is practically obsolete in the minds of many Rails developers. Using `has_many :through` to establish first-class join models *should* make your life easier. However, `habtm` is still a fact of life in legacy applications and may even be occasionally useful in new ones. We think the following section also contains some example code that enlightens the reader about nuances of Active Record behavior.

7.5.1   `has_and_belongs_to_many`

The `has_and_belongs_to_many` method establishes a link between two associated Active Record models via an intermediate join table. Unless the join table is explicitly specified as an option, Rails guesses its name by concatenating the table names of the joined classes, in alphabetical order and separated with an underscore.

For example, if I was using `has_and_belongs_to_many` (or `habtm` for short) to establish a relationship between `Timesheet` and `BillingCode`, the join table would be named `billing_codes_timesheets`, and the relationship would be defined in the models. Both the migration class and models are listed:

```
class CreateBillingCodesTimesheets < ActiveRecord::Migration
  def change
    create_join_table :billing_codes, :timesheets do |t|
      t.index [:billing_code_id, :timesheet_id]
      t.index [:timesheet_id, :billing_code_id]
    end
  end
end

class Timesheet < ActiveRecord::Base
```

```
  has_and_belongs_to_many :billing_codes
end

class BillingCode < ActiveRecord::Base
  has_and_belongs_to_many :timesheets
end
```

The `create_join_table` method takes care of creating the table without a primary key automatically. It also specifies that the foreign keys can't be null. We add indexes for the foreign keys in both directions, to make sure that queries are optimized.

7.5.1.1   Self-Referential Relationships

What about self-referential many-to-many relationships? Let's create a join table and establish a link between related `BillingCode` objects.

```
class CreateRelatedBillingCodes < ActiveRecord::Migration
  def change
    create_table :related_billing_codes, id: false do |t|
      t.column :first_billing_code_id, :integer, null: false
      t.column :second_billing_code_id, :integer, null: false
    end
  end
end
```

This time I was not able to use `create_join_table` since I'm doing something out of the ordinary. Accordingly, the association declaration needs a bunch of explicit options because I've stepped outside the realm of convention.

```
class BillingCode < ApplicationRecord
  has_and_belongs_to_many :related,
    join_table: 'related_billing_codes',
    foreign_key: 'first_billing_code_id',
    association_foreign_key: 'second_billing_code_id',
    class_name: 'BillingCode'
```

`BillingCode` objects now have a related collection of billing codes that you can treat as you would an array.

7.5.1.2   Bidirectionality

It's worth noting that the `related` relationship of the `BillingCode` is not automatically *bidirectional*. Just because you associate two objects in one direction does not mean they'll be associated in the other direction. But what if you do want to automatically establish a bidirectional relationship? It's not too hard.

First, let's write a spec for the `BillingCode` class to prove our solution. When we add bidirectionality we don't want to break the normal behavior, so at first my spec example will establish that the normal `habtm` relationship works correctly:

```
describe BillingCode do
  let(:travel_code) { BillingCode.create(code: 'TRAVEL') }
  let(:dev_code) { BillingCode.create(code: 'DEV') }

  it "has a working related habtm association" do
    travel_code.related << dev_code
    expect(travel_code.reload.related).to include(dev_code)
  end
end
```

I run the spec and it passes.

Now I can proceed to modify the example in order to prove that the bidirectional behavior that we're going to add works. It ends up looking very similar to the first example.

```
describe BillingCode do
  let(:travel_code) { BillingCode.create(code: 'TRAVEL') }
  let(:dev_code) { BillingCode.create(code: 'DEV') }

  before do
   travel_code.related << dev_code
  end

  it "has a working related habtm association" do
    expect(travel_code.reload.related).to include(dev_code)
  end

  it "should have a bidirectional habtm association" do
    expect(travel_code.related).to include(dev_code)
    expect(dev_code.reload.related).to include(travel_code)
  end
end
```

Of course, the new version fails, since we haven't added the new behavior yet.

7.5.1.3 Association Callbacks

How will we implement this behavior? (Older editions of this book tackled the problem with messy custom SQL options that aren't supported anymore.) Luckily, associations like `has_and_belongs_to_many` have collections callbacks:

- `before_add`
- `after_add`
- `before_remove`
- `after_remove`

🔑 If any of the `before_add` callbacks throw an exception, the object will not be added to the collection. Similarly, if any of the `before_remove` callbacks throw an exception, the object will not be removed from the collection.

It looks like `after_add` and `after_remove` will fit our needs. As usual with callbacks, you can pass a symbol pointing a to an instance method, a Proc, or even an array. In this case, I'll add a method.

```ruby
class BillingCode < ApplicationRecord
  has_and_belongs_to_many :related,
    join_table: 'related_billing_codes',
    foreign_key: 'first_billing_code_id',
    association_foreign_key: 'second_billing_code_id',
    class_name: 'BillingCode',
    after_add: :reciprocate

  def reciprocate(other_billing_code)
    unless other_billing_code.related.include?(self)
      other_billing_code.related << self
    end
  end
end
```

The spec passes! Make sure to note that the conditional on line 10 prevents infinite recursion.

While we're at it, let's make sure that reciprocal links are cleaned up when a related billing code is removed from the collection. I'll test drive this too.

```ruby
describe BillingCode do
  ...

  it "has a working related habtm association" do ...

  it "should have a bidirectional habtm association" do ...

  it "should clean up reciprocal relationship on removal" do
    travel_code.related.delete(dev_code)
```

```
    expect(travel_code.related).to_not include(dev_code)
    expect(dev_code.reload.related).to_not include(travel_code)
  end
end
```

When I run this spec it fails on line 11, as expected. The first link was broken but not the second. I'll make the spec pass by adding an `after_remove` callback.

```
class BillingCode < ApplicationRecord
  has_and_belongs_to_many :related,
    join_table: 'related_billing_codes',
    foreign_key: 'first_billing_code_id',
    association_foreign_key: 'second_billing_code_id',
    class_name: 'BillingCode',
    after_add: :reciprocate,
    after_remove: :cleanup

  def reciprocate(other_billing_code)
    unless other_billing_code.related.include?(self)
      other_billing_code.related << self
    end
  end

  def cleanup(other_billing_code)
    if other_billing_code.related.include?(self)
      other_billing_code.related.delete(self)
    end
  end
end
```

Here is the complete code that passes the spec successfully. The `reciprocate` and `cleanup` methods mirror themselves nicely.

```
$ rails spec
...

Finished in 0.0618 seconds (files took 1.2 seconds to load)
3 examples, 0 failures
```

7.5.1.4   Extra Columns on **has_and_belongs_to_many** Join Tables

Rails has never had a problem with you adding as many extra columns as you want to habtm's join table. The extra attributes will be read in and added onto model objects accessed via the habtm association. However, speaking from experience, the severe annoyances you will deal with in your application code make it really unattractive to go that route.

What kind of annoyances? For starters, records returned from join tables with additional attributes will be marked as read-only because it's not possible to save changes to those additional attributes.

The way that Rails makes those extra columns of the join table available might cause problems in other parts of your codebase. Having extra attributes appear magically on an object is kind of cool, but what happens when you try to access those extra properties on an object that wasn't fetched via the `habtm` association? Kaboom! Get ready for some potentially bewildering debugging exercises.

Methods of the `habtm` proxy act just as they would for a `has_many` relationship. Similarly, `habtm` shares options with `has_many`; only its `:join_table` option is unique. It allows customization of the join table name.

To sum up, `habtm` is a simple way to establish a many-to-many relationship using a join table. As long as you don't need to capture additional data about the relationship, everything is fine. The problems with `habtm` begin once you want to add extra columns to the join table, after which you'll want to upgrade the relationship to use `has_many :through` instead.

7.5.1.5 "Real Join Models" and **habtm**

The Rails documentation advises readers that: "It's strongly recommended that you upgrade any [has_and_belongs_to_many] associations with attributes to a real join model." Use of `has_and_belongs_to_many`, which was one of the original innovative features in Rails, fell out of favor once the capability to create real join models was introduced via the `has_many :through` association.

Realistically, `has_and_belongs_to_many` is not going to be removed from Rails, for a couple of sensible reasons. First of all, plenty of legacy Rails applications need it. Second, `has_and_belongs_to_many` provides a way to join classes without a primary key defined on the join table, which is occasionally useful. But most of the time you'll find yourself wanting to model many-to-many relationships with `has_many :through`.

As of Rails 4.1, `has_and_belongs_to_many` doesn't even have its own implementation anymore. If you dig into the Active Record source code you'll note that it's just a layer over a specially configured `has_many` association.

7.5.2 `has_many :through`

My old friend (and world-famous Ruby Rogue) Josh Susser used to be considered the expert on Active Record associations, to the extent that his blog was called "has_ many :through." I still can't do better than his description of the `:through` option for `has_many`, written back in 2006 when the feature was originally introduced in Rails 1.1.

> The `has_many :through` association enables you to specify a one-to-many relationship indirectly via an intermediate join table. In fact, you can specify more than one such relationship via the same table, which effectively makes it a replacement for `has_and_belongs_to_many`. The biggest advantage is that the join table contains full-fledged model objects complete with primary keys and ancillary data [. . .] *join models* just work the same way all your other Active Record models do.[1]

7.5.2.1 Join Models

To illustrate the `has_many :through` association, we'll set up a Client model so that it has many `Timesheet` objects, through a normal `has_many` association named `billable_weeks`.

```
class Client < ActiveRecord::Base
  has_many :billable_weeks
  has_many :timesheets, through: :billable_weeks
end
```

The `BillableWeek` class was already in our sample application and is ready to be used as a join model:

```
class BillableWeek < ActiveRecord::Base
  belongs_to :client
  belongs_to :timesheet
end
```

We can also set up the inverse relationship, from timesheets to clients, like this:

```
class Timesheet < ActiveRecord::Base
  has_many :billable_weeks
  has_many :clients, through: :billable_weeks
end
```

Notice that `has_many :through` is always used in conjunction with a normal `has_many` association. Also, notice that the normal `has_many` association will

---

1. Josh Susser: http://blog.hasmanythrough.com/2006/2/28/association-goodness

often have the same name on both classes that are being joined together, which means the :through option will read the same on both sides.

```
through: :billable_weeks
```

How about the join model—will it always have two belongs_to associations? Nope.

7.5.2.2 More Than a **has_and_belongs_to_many** Replacement

You can also use has_many :through to easily aggregate has_many or has_one associations on a join model. Forgive me for switching to a completely non-realistic domain for a moment—it's only intended to clearly demonstrate what I'm trying to describe:

```
class Grandparent < ApplicationRecord
  has_many :parents
  has_many :grand_children, through: :parents, source: :children
end

class Parent < ActiveRecord::Base
  belongs_to :grandparent
  has_many   :children
end
```

For the sake of clarity in later chapters, I'll refer to this usage of has_many :through as aggregating.

💬 Courtenay says . . .

We use has_many :through so much! It has pretty much replaced the old has_and_belongs_to_many, because it enables your join models to be upgraded to full objects. It's like when you're just dating someone and they start talking about the Relationship (or, eventually, Our Marriage). It's an example of an association being promoted to something more important than the individual objects on each side.

7.5.2.3 Aggregating Associations

When you're using has_many :through to aggregate multiple child associations, there are more significant limitations—essentially you can query to your hearts content using find and friends, but you can't append or create new records through them.

For example, let's add a `billable_weeks` association to our sample `User` class. (Note: For the sake of clarity, I've hidden the options for `timesheets`.)

```
class User < ActiveRecord::Base
  has_many :timesheets, ...
  has_many :billable_weeks, through: :timesheets
  ...
```

The `billable_weeks` association aggregates all the billable week objects belonging to all of the user's timesheets.

```
class Timesheet < ActiveRecord::Base
  belongs_to :user
  has_many :billable_weeks, -> { includes(:billing_code) }
  ...
```

Now let's go into the Rails console and set up some example data so that we can use the new `billable_weeks` collection (on `User`).

```
>> admin = User.first
>> obie = User.second
>> client = Client.first

>> obie.timesheets
=> #<ActiveRecord::Associations::CollectionProxy []>

>> ts1 = obie.timesheets.create(approver: admin)
=> #<Timesheet id: 1 ...>

>> ts2 = obie.timesheets.create(approver: admin)
=> #<Timesheet id: 2 ...>

>> ts1.billable_weeks.create(start_date: 1.week.ago, client: client)
=> #<BillableWeek id: 1, timesheet_id: 1 ...>

>> ts2.billable_weeks.create(start_date: 1.week.ago, client: client)
=> #<BillableWeek id: 2, timesheet_id: 2 ...>

>> obie.billable_weeks.to_a
=> [#<BillableWeek id: 1, timesheet_id: 1 ...>, #<BillableWeek id: 2,
timesheet_id: 2 ...>]
```

Just for fun, let's see what happens if we try to create a `BillableWeek` with a `User` instance:

```
>> w = obie.billable_weeks.create(start_date: 3.weeks.ago, client: client)
=> #<BillableWeek id: nil, client_id: 2...
```

That nil `id` tells us that while a record was returned, it was not saved to the database. What do you think was wrong with it?

```
>> w.errors.messages
=> {:timesheet=>["must exist"]}
```

Logically, it isn't possible to create a billable week instance without a timesheet specified. But what if we specify a timesheet in the arguments to the billable week constructor? After all, that is the attribute that is missing.

```
>> obie.billable_weeks.create(timesheet: ts1, ...)
```

```
ActiveRecord::HasManyThroughCantAssociateThroughHasOneOrManyReflection:
  Cannot modify association 'User#billable_weeks' because the source
  reflection class 'BillableWeek' is associated to 'Timesheet' via
  :has_many.
```

Nope. Even though it seems like it should be possible, Rails doesn't want you to write it this way.

7.5.2.4   Usage Considerations and Examples

You can use non-aggregating `has_many` `:through` associations in almost the same ways as any other `has_many` associations. For instance, appending an object to a `has_many` `:through` collection will save the object as expected:

```
>> c = Client.create(name: "Trotter's Tomahawks", code: "ttom")
=> #<Client id: 5 ...>
```

```
>> c.timesheets << Timesheet.new(user: employee, ...)
=> #<ActiveRecord::Associations::CollectionProxy [#<Timesheet id: 2 ...>]>
```

The main benefit of `has_many` `:through` is that Active Record takes care of managing the instances of the join model for you. If we call `billable_weeks` on the client object, we'll see that there was a billable week object with default values created for us:

```
>> c.billable_weeks
BillableWeek Load (0.2ms) SELECT "billable_weeks".* FROM "billable_...
=> #<ActiveRecord::Associations::CollectionProxy [#<BillableWeek id: 2,
client_id: 2, billing_code_id: nil, timesheet_id: 7 ...>]>
```

As you can tell by the values of `client_id` and `timesheet_id`, the billable week object that was automatically created is properly associated with both the client and the timesheet. There are also other attributes (like billing code and the hours columns) that were not populated.

If we want to set those all in one operation, we could `create` the join model directly and include a new `Timesheet` object as one of the supplied properties.

```
>> bw = c.billable_weeks.create(billing_code: code,
                                timesheet: Timesheet.new(...))
```

This sort of operation would be impossible with `has_and_belongs_to_many` because it doesn't have an abstraction for the *join model*.

Unfortunately our example code is starting to get a little farfetched for this particular domain. I'm not sure why you would want to create a billable week instance without having a timesheet first.

7.5.2.5 Join Models and Validations

When you append to a non-aggregating `has_many :through` association with `<<`, Active Record will always create a new join model, even if one already exists for the two records being joined. We haven't reached the topic of validations in the book yet, but I do want to mention here that you can add `validates_unique-ness_of` constraints on the join model to keep duplicate joins from happening.

This is what such a constraint might look like on our `BillableWeek` join model.

```
validates_uniqueness_of :client_id, scope: :timesheet_id
```

That says, in effect: "There should only be one of each client per timesheet."

If your join model has additional attributes with their own validation logic, then there's another important consideration to keep in mind. Adding records directly to a `has_many :through` association causes a new join model to be automatically created with a blank set of attributes. Validations on additional columns of the join model will fail unless they have default values at the database level or are using the Attributes API. Speaking from experience, lots of times you'll need to add new records by creating join model objects directly and associating them appropriately.

7.5.3 Options

The options for `has_many :through` are the same as the options for `has_many`—remember that `:through` itself is just an option on `has_many`! However, some of `has_many`'s options change or become more significant when `:through` is used.

Active Record

First of all, the `:class_name` and `:foreign_key` options are no longer valid, since they are implied from the target association on the join model. The following are the rest of the options that have special significance together with `has_many` `:through`.

7.5.3.1 **source**

The `:source` option specifies which association to use on the associated class. This option is not mandatory because normally Active Record assumes that the target association is the singular (or plural) version of the `has_many` association name. If your association names don't match up, then you have to set `:source` explicitly.

For example, the following code will use the `BillableWeek`'s sheet association to populate `timesheets`.

```
has_many :timesheets, through: :billable_weeks, source: :sheet
```

7.5.3.2 **source_type**

The `:source_type` option is needed when you establish a `has_many` `:through` to a polymorphic `belongs_to` association on the join model. Consider the following example concerning clients and contacts:

```
class Client < ActiveRecord::Base
  has_many :client_contacts
  has_many :contacts, through: :client_contacts
end

class ClientContact < ActiveRecord::Base
  belongs_to :client
  belongs_to :contact, polymorphic: true
end
```

In this somewhat contrived example, the most important fact is that a `Client` has many `contacts`, through their polymorphic relationship to the join model, `ClientContact`. There isn't a `Contact` class; we just want to be able to refer to contacts in a polymorphic sense, meaning either a `Person` or a `Business`.

```
class Person < ActiveRecord::Base
  has_many :client_contacts, as: :contact
end

class Business < ActiveRecord::Base
  has_many :client_contacts, as: :contact
end
```

Now take a moment to consider the backflips that Active Record would have to perform in order to figure out which tables to query for a client's contacts. Remember that there isn't a contacts table!

```
>> Client.first.contacts
```

Active Record would theoretically need to be aware of every model class that is linked to the other end of the contacts polymorphic association. In fact, it cannot do those kinds of backflips, which is probably a good thing as far as performance is concerned:

```
>> Client.first.contacts
ActiveRecord::HasManyThroughAssociationPolymorphicSourceError: Cannot have a
has_many :through association 'Client#contacts' on the polymorphic object
'Contact#contact' without 'source_type'.
```

The only way to make this scenario work (somewhat) is to give Active Record some help by specifying which table it should search when you ask for the `contacts` collection, and you do that with the `source_type` option naming the target class, symbolized, like this:

```
class Client < ActiveRecord::Base
  has_many :client_contacts
  has_many :people, through: :client_contacts,
           source: :contact, source_type: :person

  has_many :businesses, through: :client_contacts,
           source: :contact, source_type: :business
end
```

Meh. Kind of loses the polymorphic goodness this way, doesn't it?

After the `:source_type` is specified, the association will work as expected, but we don't get a general purpose `contacts` collection.

```
>> Client.first.people.create!
=> [#<Person id: 1>]
```

If you're upset that you cannot associate `people` and `business` together in a contacts association, you could try writing your own accessor method for a client's contacts:

```
class Client < ActiveRecord::Base
  def contacts
```

```
     people_contacts + business_contacts
  end
end
```

Of course, you should be aware that calling that `contacts` method will result in at least two database requests and will return an `Array`, without the association proxy methods that you might expect it to have.

7.5.4   Unique Association Objects

The `distinct` scope method tells the association to include only unique objects. It is especially useful when using `has_many` `:through` since two different join model objects could easily reference the same related object. That's hard to explain without an example.

In our recurring example code, clients are connected to timesheets via billable weeks. If we query in that direction, and there is more than one billable week on a timesheet for the same client, then we get the same timesheet returned more than once.

```
>> Client.first.timesheets.reload.to_a
[#<Timesheet id: 1...>, #<Timesheet id: 1...>]
```

It's not extraordinary for two distinct model instances of the same database record to be in memory at the same time—it's just not usually desirable.

Here's how we fix it, by scoping the association.

```
class Client < ActiveRecord::Base
  has_many :timesheets, -> { distinct }, through: :billable_weeks
end
```

After adding the `distinct` scope to the `has_many` `:through` association, only one instance per record is returned.

```
>> Client.first.timesheets.reload.to_a
=> [#<Timesheet id: 1...>]
```

7.6   One-to-One Relationships

One of the most basic relationship types in object-oriented programming is a one-to-one object relationship. In Active Record we declare a one-to-one relationships using the `has_one` and `belongs_to` methods together. As in the case of a `has_many` relationship, you call `belongs_to` on the model whose database table contains the foreign key column linking the two records together.

7.6.1 `has_one`

Conceptually, `has_one` works almost exactly like `has_many` does, except that when the database query is executed to retrieve the related object, a `LIMIT 1` clause is added to the generated SQL so that only one row is returned.

The name of a `has_one` relationship should be singular, which will make it read naturally, for example: `has_one :last_timesheet`, `has_one :primary_account`, `has_one :profile_photo`, and so on.

Let's take a look at `has_one` in action by adding avatars for our users.

```
class Avatar < ActiveRecord::Base
  belongs_to :user
end

class User < ActiveRecord::Base
  has_one :avatar
  ...
end
```

That's simple enough. Firing this up in `rails console`, we can look at some of the new methods that `has_one` adds to `User`.

```
>> u = User.first
>> u.avatar
=> nil

>> u.build_avatar(url: '/avatars/smiling')
=> #<Avatar id: nil, url: "/avatars/smiling", user_id: 1>

>> u.avatar.save
=> true
```

As you can see, we can use `build_avatar` to build a new avatar object and associate it with the user. While it's great that `has_one` will associate an avatar with the user, it isn't really anything that `has_many` doesn't already do. So let's take a look at what happens when we assign a new avatar to the user.

```
>> u = User.first
>> u.avatar
=> #<Avatar id: 1, url: "/avatars/smiling", user_id: 1>

>> u.create_avatar(url: '/avatars/frowning')
=> #<Avatar id: 2, url: "/avatars/4567", user_id: 1>
```

```
>> Avatar.all.to_a
=> [#<Avatar id: 1, url: "/avatars/smiling", user_id: nil>, #<Avatar id: 2, url:
"/avatars/4567", user_id: 1>]
```

The last line from that console session is the most interesting because it shows that our initial avatar is now no longer associated with the user. Of course, the previous avatar was not removed from the database, which is something that we want in this scenario. So, we'll use the `dependent: :destroy` option to force avatars to be destroyed when they are no longer associated with a user.

```
class User < ActiveRecord::Base
  has_one :avatar, dependent: :destroy
end
```

With some additional fiddling around in the console, we can verify that it works as intended. In doing so, you might notice that Rails only destroys the avatar that was just removed from the user, so bad data that was in your database from before will still remain. Keep this in mind when you decide to add `dependent: :destroy` to your code, and remember to manually clear orphaned data that might otherwise remain.

This is definitely a case where not null and foreign-key constraints can help keep your database in order.

7.6.2 Using **has_one** together with **has_many**

As I alluded to earlier, `has_one` is sometimes used to single out one record of significance alongside an already established `has_many` relationship. For instance, let's say we want to easily be able to access the last timesheet a user was working on:

```
class User < ActiveRecord::Base
  has_many :timesheets

  has_one  :latest_sheet,
    -> { order('created_at desc') },
    class_name: 'Timesheet'
end
```

I had to specify a `:class_name` so that Active Record knows what kind of object we're associating. (It can't figure it out based on the name of the association, `:latest_sheet`.)

When adding a has_one relationship to a model that already has a has_many defined to the same related model, it is not necessary to add another belongs_to method call to the target object, just for the new has_one. That might seem a little counterintuitive at first, but if you think about it, the same foreign key value is being used to read the data from the database.

7.6.3   Options
The options for has_one associations are similar to the ones for has_many. For your convenience, we briefly cover the most relevant ones here.

7.6.3.1   **as**
Allows you to set up a polymorphic association, covered in Chapter 9, "Advanced Active Record."

7.6.3.2   **class_name**
Allows you to specify the class this association uses. Normally, this option is inferred by Rails from the name of the association, but it is especially common to need it with has_one.

7.6.3.3   **dependent**
The :dependent option specifies how Active Record should treat associated objects when the parent object is deleted. In the case of has_one, it's not so much deletion as de-association that triggers this option.

The default behavior is to do nothing with associated objects, which in certain situations will leave orphaned records in your database.

There are a few different values that you can pass and they work just like the :dependent option of has_many.

:**destroy** Destroys the associated object when it is no longer associated with the primary object.

:**delete** Deletes the object in the database without invoking callbacks.

:**restrict_with_exception** Raises exception if you try to replace an existing relationship.

:**restrict_with_error** Similar to _with_exception but adds an error to the owner object, which should cause its validations to fail before saving.

:**nullify** (Default) Sets the foreign key values to `nil` so that the relationship is broken.

7.6.4 Scopes

The scopes for `has_one` associations are similar to the ones for `has_many`. We briefly cover the most relevant ones here.

7.6.4.1 `where(*conditions)`

Enables you to specify conditions that the object must meet to be included in the association.

```
class User < ActiveRecord::Base
  has_one :manager, -> ( where(type: 'manager')),
    class_name: 'Person'
```

Here `manager` is specified as a person object that has `type = 'manager'`. I almost always use `where` conditions in conjunction with `has_one`. When Active Record loads the association, it's grabbing one of potentially many rows that have the right foreign key. That means that absent some explicit conditions (or perhaps an order scope), you're leaving it in the hands of the database to pick a row.

7.6.4.2 `order(*clauses)`

Enables you to specify a SQL fragment that will be used to order the results. This is an especially useful option with `has_one` when trying to associate the latest of something or another.

```
class User < ActiveRecord::Base
  has_one :latest_timesheet,
          -> { order('created_at desc') },
          class_name: 'Timesheet'
end
```

7.6.4.3 `readonly`

Sets the record in the association to read-only mode, which prevents saving it.

7.7 Working with Unsaved Objects and Associations

You can manipulate objects and associations before they are saved to the database, but there is some special behavior you should be aware of, mostly involving the saving of associated objects. Whether an object is considered unsaved is based on the result of calling `new_record?`.

7.7.1   One-to-One Associations

Assigning a new object to a `belongs_to` association does not save the parent or the associated object.

Assigning an object to a `has_one` association automatically saves that object (and potentially the object being replaced, if there is one) so that their foreign key fields are updated. The exception to this behavior is if the parent object is unsaved, since that would mean that there is no foreign key value to set.

When saves fail for any of the objects being updated (due to one of them being invalid) the assignment operation returns `false` and the assignment is cancelled. That behavior makes sense (if you think about it), but it can be the cause of much confusion when you're not aware of it. If you have an association that doesn't seem to work, check the validation rules of the related objects.

7.7.2   Collections

Adding a new object to `has_many` and `has_and_belongs_to_many` collections automatically saves it, unless the owner of the collection is not yet stored in the database (since there would be no foreign key value to save).

If objects being added to a collection (via << or similar means) fail to save properly, then the operation will return `false`. If you want your code to be a little more explicit, or you want to add an object to a collection without automatically saving it, then you can use the collection's `build` method. It's exactly like `create`, except that it doesn't `save`.

Members of a collection with changes are only automatically saved or updated when their parent is saved or updated if the `autosave` option is set to `true` on the parent. (The default is `false`.)

ⓘ Note that the `accepts_nested_attributes_for` method results in the associated collection's `autosave` option being turned on.

7.7.3   Deletion

Associations that are set with auto-saving turned on are also afforded the capability to have their records deleted when an inverse record is saved. This is to enable the records from both sides of the association to get persisted within the same transaction and is handled through the `mark_for_destruction` method.

Consider our `User` and `Timesheet` models again:

```
class User < ActiveRecord::Base
  has_many :timesheets, autosave: true
end
```

If I would like to have a particular set of `Timesheet` instances destroyed when the `User` is saved, this is how to mark them for destruction.

```
user = User.where(name: "Durran")
user.timesheets.closed.each(&:mark_for_destruction)
user.save # => closed timesheets get automatically deleted
```

Since both kinds of changes are persisted in the same transaction, if the operation were to fail the database would not be in an inconsistent state. Do note though, that even if a marked child record did not get deleted, the mark doesn't reset, so it would *still* be marked for destruction, and any later attempts to save its parent would once again attempt to delete it. You can use `reload` to clear the flag if necessary.

7.8 Association Extensions

The proxy objects that handle access to associations can be extended with your own application code. You can add your own custom finders and factory methods to be used specifically with a particular association.

For example, let's say you wanted a concise way to refer to an account's people by name. You may create an extension on the association like that shown in Listing 7.3.

Listing 7.3 An association extension on a people collection

```
class Account < ActiveRecord::Base
  has_many :people do
    def named(full_name)
      first_name, last_name = full_name.split(" ", 2)
        where(first_name: first_name, last_name: last_name).first_or_create
    end
  end
end
```

Now we have a `named` method available to use on the `people` collection.

```
account = Account.first
person = account.people.named("David Heinemeier Hansson")
person.first_name # => "David"
person.last_name # => "Heinemeier Hansson"
```

If you need to share the same set of extensions between many associations, you can specify an extension module, instead of a block with method definitions. Here is the same feature shown in Listing 7.3, except broken out into its own Ruby module:

```ruby
module ByNameExtension
  def named(full_name)
    first_name, last_name = full_name.split(" ", 2)
    where(first_name: first_name, last_name: last_name).first_or_create
  end
end
```

Now we can use it to extend many different relationships, as long as they're compatible. (Our contract in the example consists of a model with columns first_name and last_name.)

```ruby
class Account < ActiveRecord::Base
  has_many :people, -> { extending(ByNameExtension) }
end

class Company < ActiveRecord::Base
  has_many :people, -> { extending(ByNameExtension) }
end
```

If you need to use multiple named extension modules, you can pass an array of modules to the extending query method instead of a single module, like this:

```ruby
has_many :people, -> { extending(ByNameExtension, ByRecentExtension) }
```

In the case of name conflicts, methods contained in modules added later in the array supercede those earlier in the array.

Consider a Class Method Instead

Unless you have a valid reason to reuse the extension logic with more than one type of model, you're probably better off leveraging the fact that class methods are automatically available on has_many associations.

```ruby
class Person < ActiveRecord::Base
  belongs_to :account

  def self.named(full_name)
    first_name, last_name = full_name.split(" ", 2)
    where(first_name: first_name, last_name: last_name).first_or_create
  end
end
```

7.9   The `CollectionProxy` Class

`CollectionProxy`, the parent of all association proxies, contributes a handful of useful methods that apply to most kinds of associations and can come into play when you're writing association extensions.

7.9.1   Owner, Reflection, and Target

The object that holds the association is known as the `@owner`. The associated object (or array of objects) is known as the `@target`. Metadata about the association itself is available in `@reflection`, which is an instance of the class `ActiveRecord::Reflection::AssociationReflection`.

```
class Blog < ActiveRecord::Base
  has_many :posts
end

blog = Blog.first
```

The association proxy `blog.posts` is an instance of `CollectionProxy`. It has a reference to the blog object as `@owner` and the collection of its posts as `@target`.

The proxy delegates unknown methods to `@target` via Ruby's built-in `method_missing` hook. (This is, for instance, the reason that a `has_many` association proxy has all the same methods as `Array`.)

The `@target` object is not loaded until it is needed. For example, `blog.posts.count` is computed directly through SQL and does not trigger by itself the loading of post records into `@target`.

The `@reflection` object is an instance of `ActiveRecord::Reflection::AssociationReflection` and contains all of the configuration options for the association. That includes both default settings and those that were explicitly passed to the association method when it was declared.

It might not appear sane to expose these attributes publicly and allow their manipulation. However, without access to them it would be much more difficult to write advanced association extensions. The `loaded?`, `loaded`, `target`, and `target=` methods are public for similar reasons.

The following code sample demonstrates the use of `owner` within a `published_prior_to` extension method, originally contributed by Wilson Bilkovich:

```
class ArticleCategory < ActiveRecord::Base
  has_ancestry

  has_many :articles do
    def published_prior_to(date, options = {})
      if owner.is_root?
        Article.where('published_at < ? and category_id = ?', date, proxy_owner)
      else
        # self is the 'articles' association here so we inherit its scope
        self.all(options)
      end
    end
  end
end
```

> Ancestry (formerly acts_as_tree) is a gem/plugin that enables the records of a Ruby on Rails Active Record model to be organised as a tree structure (or hierarchy). It uses a single, intuitively formatted database column, using a variation on the materialised path pattern. It exposes all the standard tree structure relations (ancestors, parent, root, children, siblings, descendants), and all of them can be fetched in a single SQL query. Additional features are STI support, scopes, depth caching, depth constraints, easy migration from older plugins/gems, integrity checking, integrity restoration, arrangement of (sub)tree into hashes and different strategies for dealing with orphaned records.[2]

As you can see, the owner reference is used to check whether the parent of this association is a "top-level" node in the tree.

7.9.2 reload and reset

The reset method puts the association proxy back in its initial state, which is unloaded (cached association objects are cleared). The reload method invokes reset and then loads associated objects from the database.

7.10   Conclusion

The capability to model associations is what makes Active Record more than just a data-access layer. The ease and elegance with which you can declare those associations are what make Active Record more than your ordinary object-relational mapper.

---

2. https://github.com/stefankroes/ancestry

We have just covered the fundamentals of how Active Record associations work and ended on an advanced note by taking a quick look at `CollectionProxy`. I hope that the options and methods guide for each type of association provides a valuable reference guide for your day-to-day development activities.

Now lets formally dive into a subject that has begun to crop up here and there already: Validations.

CHAPTER 8

Validations

I have bought this wonderful machine—a computer. Now I am rather an authority on gods, so I identified the machine—it seems to me to be an Old Testament god with a lot of rules and no mercy.

—Joseph Campbell

The Validations API in Active Model, along with its supplementary functionality in Active Record allows you to declaratively define valid states for your model objects. The validation methods hook into the life cycle of an Active Record model object and are able to inspect the object to determine whether certain attributes are set, have values in a given range, or pass any other logical hurdles that you specify.

In this chapter, we'll describe the validation methods available and how to use them effectively. We'll also explore how those validation methods interact with your model's attributes and how the built-in error-messaging system messages can be used effectively in your application's user interface to provide descriptive feedback.

Finally, we'll cover how to use Active Model's validation functionality in your own, non-Active Record classes.

8.1 Finding Errors

Validation problems are also known as (drumroll please . . .) errors! Every Active Record model object contains a collection of errors, accessible (unsurprisingly) as the `errors` attribute.

When a model object is valid, the `errors` collection is empty. In fact, when you call `valid?` on a model object, a series of steps to find errors is taken as follows (slightly simplified):

1. Clear the `errors` collection.

2. Run validations.

3. Return whether the model's `errors` collection is now empty or not.

If the `errors` collection ends up empty, the object is valid. In cases where you have to write actual validation logic yourself, you mark an object invalid by adding items to the `errors` collection using its `add` methods. Simple as that.

We'll cover the methods of the `Errors` class in some more detail later on. It makes more sense to look at the validation methods themselves first.

8.2   The Simple Declarative Validations

Whenever possible, you should set validations for your models declaratively by using one or more of the following class methods available to all Active Record classes (listed alphabetically).

ℹ️ Unless otherwise noted, all of the `validates` methods accept a variable number of attributes, plus options. There are some options for these validation methods that are common to all of them, and we'll cover them at the end of the section.

8.2.1   `validates_absence_of`

The `validates_absence_of` method ensures specified attributes are blank. It uses the `blank?` method, defined on `Object`, which returns `true` for values that are `nil` or a blank string `""`. It is the polar opposite of the commonly used `validates_presence_of` validation method, covered later in this section.

```
class Account < ActiveRecord::Base
  validates_absence_of :spambot_honeypot_field
end
```

When the `validates_absence_of` validation fails, an error message is stored in the model object reading *"attribute must be blank."*

8.2.2 `validates_acceptance_of`

Many web applications have screens in which the user is prompted to agree to terms of service or some similar concept, usually involving a check box. No actual database column matching the attribute declared in the validation is required. When you call this method, it will create virtual attributes automatically for each named attribute you specify. I see this validation as a type of syntax sugar since it is so specific to web application programming.

```
class Account < ActiveRecord::Base
  validates_acceptance_of :privacy_policy, :terms_of_service
end
```

Note that you can use this validation with or without a boolean column on the table backing your model. A transient attribute will be created if necessary.

The fact that this validation defaults to creating transient attributes gives you an indication of how little your average web developer cares about things like terms of service and privacy policies. On the other hand, most users don't ever read them either!

Choose to store the value in the database only if you need to keep track of whether the user accepted the term, for auditing or other reasons.

When the `validates_acceptance_of` validation fails, an error message is stored in the model object reading *"attribute must be accepted."*

The `:accept` option makes it easy to change the value considered acceptance. The default value is `"1"`, which matches the value supplied by check boxes generated using Rails helper methods. Sometimes a little more attention is required from the user than just checking a box.

```
class Cancellation < ActiveRecord::Base
  validates_acceptance_of :account_cancellation, accept: 'YES'
end
```

If you use the preceding example in conjunction with a text field connected to the `account_cancellation` attribute, the user would have to type the word *YES* in order for the cancellation object to be valid.

Active Record

8.2.3 `validates_associated`

Used to ensure that *all* associated objects are valid on save. Works with any kind of association and is specific to Active Record (not Active Model.) We emphasize all because the default behavior of `has_many` associations is to ensure the validity of *only their new child records* on save.

> ⚠️ You probably don't need to use this particular validation nowadays since `has_many` associations default to `validate: true`. But realize that setting `validate: true` carelessly on a `belongs_to` association can now cause infinite loops.

A `validates_associated` on `belongs_to` will not fail if the association is `nil`. If you want to make sure that the association is populated and valid, you have to use `validates_associated` in conjunction with `validates_presence_of`.

> 💬 Tim says . . .
>
> It's possible to get similar behavior by using a combination of the `:autosave` and `:validate` options on a `has_many`.

8.2.4 `validates_confirmation_of`

The `validates_confirmation_of` method is another case of syntactic sugar for web applications, since it is so common to include dual-entry text fields to make sure that the user entered critical data such as passwords and email address correctly. This validation will create a virtual attribute for the confirmation value and compare the two attributes to make sure they match in order for the model to be valid.

Here's an example, using our fictional `Account` model again:

```
class Account < ActiveRecord::Base
  validates_confirmation_of :password
end
```

The user interface used to set values for the `Account` model would need to include extra text fields named with a `_confirmation` suffix, and when submitted, the value of those fields would have to match in order for this validation to pass. A simplified example of matching view code is provided.

```
= form_for account do |f|
  = f.label :login
  = f.text_field :login
```

```
= f.label :password
= f.password_field :password
= f.label :password_confirmation
= f.password_field :password_confirmation
= f.submit
```

I'm pretty sure the ubiquitous nature of this validation on user objects has wasted millions of developer hours in the Rails terminal!

8.2.5 `validates_each`

The `validates_each` method is a little more free-form than its companions in the validation family in that it doesn't have a predefined validation function. Instead, you give it an array of attribute names to check and supply a Ruby block to be used in checking each attribute's validity.

Sorry, I realize that was a mouthful. Perhaps an example would help.

```
class Invoice < ActiveRecord::Base
  validates_each :supplier_id, :purchase_order do |record, attr, value|
    record.errors.add(attr) unless PurchasingSystem.validate(attr, value)
  end
end
```

Notice that parameters for the model instance (`record`), the name of the attribute as a symbol, and the value to check are passed as parameters to the block. As per usual practice, the model object is marked valid or not by merit whether anything has been added to its `errors` object. The return value of the block is ignored.

There aren't too many situations where this method is necessary, but one plausible example is when interacting with external services for validation. You might wrap the external validation in a facade specific to your application and then call it using a `validates_each` block.

8.2.6 `validates_format_of`

To use `validates_format_of`, you'll have to know how to use Ruby regular expressions.[1] Pass the method one or more attributes to check and a regular expression as the (required) `:with` option.

A good example, as shown in the Rails docs, is checking for a valid email address format:

---

1. Check out the excellent http://rubular.com if you need help composing Ruby regular expressions.

```
class Person < ActiveRecord::Base
  validates_format_of :email,
    with: /\A([^@\s]+)@((?:[-a-z0-9]+\.)+[a-z]{2,})\z/
end
```

By the way, that example is totally not an RFC-compliant email address format
checker. If you need to validate email addresses try the plugin at https://github
.com/spectator/validates_email.

💬 Courtenay says . . .

Regular expressions are awesome but can get very complex, particularly
when validating domain names or email addresses. You can use #{} inside
regular expressions, so split up your regex into chunks like this:

```
validates_format_of :name, with:
/\A((localhost)|#{DOMAIN}|#{NUMERIC_IP})#{PORT}\z/
```

That expression is pretty straightforward and easy to understand. The
constants themselves are not so easy to understand but easier than if they
were all jumbled in together:

```
PORT = /((:]\d+)?)/
DOMAIN = /([a-z0-9\-]+\.?)*([a-z0-9]{2,})\.[a-z]{2,}/
NUMERIC_IP = /(?>(?:1?\d?\d|2[0-4]\d|25[0-5])\.){3}
(?:1?\d?\d|2[0-4]\d|25[0-5])(?:\/(?:[12]?\d|3[012])|-(?>(?:1?\d?\d|
2[0-4]\d|25[0-5])\.){3}(?:1?\d?\d|2[0-4]\d|25[0-5]))?/
```

💬 Lark says . . .

I'll take your readability Courtenay and raise you test isolation. Your regular
expression should itself be in a constant so you can test it.

8.2.7 `validates_inclusion_of` and `validates_exclusion_of`

These twin methods take a variable number of attribute names and an :in option.
When they run, they check to make sure that the value of the attribute is included (or
excluded, respectively) in the enumerable object passed as the :in option.

The politically incorrect examples in the Rails docs are probably some of the best
illustrations of their use, so I'll take inspiration from them:

```
class Person < ActiveRecord::Base
  validates_inclusion_of :gender, in: %w( m f ), message: '- O RLY?'
    . . .
```

```
class Account < ActiveRecord::Base
  validates_exclusion_of :username, in: %w( admin superuser ),
                              message: ', huh? Borat says "Naughty, naughty!"'
  ...
```

Notice that in the last example I introduced usage of the :message option, common to all validation methods, to customize the error message constructed and added to the errors object when the validation fails. We'll cover the default error messages and how to effectively customize them a little further along in the chapter.

8.2.8 `validates_length_of`

The `validates_length_of` method takes a variety of different options to let you concisely specify length constraints for a given attribute of your model.

```
class Account < ActiveRecord::Base
  validates_length_of :login, minimum: 5
end
```

If you're ever modeling a webapp that you think I might enjoy using, give me an early heads up and please remember to make the minimum length of the username 4 characters. Thanks!

8.2.8.1 Constraint Options

The :minimum and :maximum options work as expected, but don't use them together. To specify a range, use the :within option and pass it a Ruby range, as in the following example:

```
class Account < ActiveRecord::Base
  validates_length_of :username, within: 5..20
end
```

To specify an exact length of an attribute, use the :is option:

```
class Account < ActiveRecord::Base
  validates_length_of :account_number, is: 16
end
```

8.2.8.2 Error Message Options

Rails gives you the capability to generate detailed error messages for `validates_length_of` via the :too_long, :too_short, and :wrong_length options. Use %{count} in your custom error message as a placeholder for the number corresponding to the constraint.

```
class Account < ActiveRecord::Base
  validates_length_of :account_number, is: 16,
                      wrong_length: "should be %{count} characters long"
end
```

8.2.9 `validates_numericality_of`

The somewhat clumsily named `validates_numericality_of` method is used to ensure that an attribute can only hold a numeric value.

The `:only_integer` option lets you further specify that the value should only be an integer value and defaults to `false`.

```
class Account < ActiveRecord::Base
  validates_numericality_of :account_number, only_integer: true
end
```

The `:even` and `:odd` options do what you would expect and are useful for things like, I don't know, checking electron valences. (Actually, I'm not creative enough to think of what you would use this validation for, but there you go.)

The following comparison options are also available:

- `:equal_to`
- `:greater_than`
- `:greater_than_or_equal_to`
- `:less_than`
- `:less_than_or_equal_to`
- `:other_than`

8.2.9.1   Infinity and Other Special Float Values

Interestingly, Ruby has the concept of infinity built-in. If you haven't seen infinity before, try the following in a console:

```
>> (1.0/0.0)
=> Infinity
```

Infinity is considered a number by `validates_numericality_of`. Databases (like PostgreSQL) with support for the IEEE 754 standard should allow special float values like `Infinity` to be stored. The other special values are positive infinity (+INF), negative infinity (-INF), and not-a-number (NaN). IEEE 754 also distinguishes between positive zero (+0) and negative zero (-0). NaN is used to represent results of operations that are undefined.

8.2.10 `validates_presence_of`

One of the more common validation methods, `validates_presence_of`, is used to denote mandatory attributes. This method checks whether the attribute is blank using the `blank?` method, defined on `Object`, which returns `true` for values that are `nil` or a blank string `""`.

```
class Account < ActiveRecord::Base
  validates_presence_of :username, :email, :account_number
end
```

A common mistake is to use `validates_presence_of` with a boolean attribute, like the backing field for a check box. If you want to make sure that the attribute is true, use `validates_acceptance_of` instead.

The boolean value `false` is considered blank, so if you want to make sure that only `true` or `false` values are set on your model, use the following pattern:

```
validates_inclusion_of :protected, in: [true, false]
```

8.2.10.1 Validating the Presence and/or Existence of Associated Objects

When you're trying to ensure that an association is present, pass `validates_presence_of` its foreign key attribute, not the association variable itself. Note that the validation will fail in cases when both the parent and child object are unsaved (since the foreign key will be blank).

Many developers try to use this validation with the intention of ensuring that associated objects actually exist in the database. Personally, I think that would be a valid use case for an actual foreign-key constraint in the database, but if you want to do the check in your Rails code then emulate the following example:

```
class Timesheet < ActiveRecord::Base
  belongs_to :user
  validates_presence_of :user_id
  validate :user_exists

  protected

  def user_exists
    errors.add(:user_id, "doesn't exist") unless User.exists?(user_id)
  end
end
```

Without a validation, if your application violates a database foreign key constraint, you will get an Active Record exception.

8.2.11 `validates_uniqueness_of`

The `validates_uniqueness_of` method is Active Record-specific and ensures that the value of an attribute is unique for all models of the same type. *This validation does not work by adding a uniqueness constraint at the database level.* It does work by constructing and executing a query looking for a matching record in the database at validation time. If any record is returned when this method does its query, the validation fails.

```
class Account < ActiveRecord::Base
  validates_uniqueness_of :username
end
```

By specifying a `:scope` option, additional attributes can be used to determine uniqueness. You may pass `:scope` one or more attribute names as symbols (putting multiple symbols in an array).

```
class Address < ActiveRecord::Base
  validates_uniqueness_of :line_two, scope: [:line_one, :city, :zip]
end
```

It's also possible to specify whether to make the uniqueness constraint case-sensitive or not, via the `:case_sensitive` option (ignored for nontextual attributes).

With the addition of support for PostgreSQL array columns in Rails 4, the `validates_uniqueness_of` method can be used to validate that all items in the array are unique.

🗨 Tim says . . .

This validation is not foolproof due to a potential race condition between the `SELECT` query that checks for duplicates and the `INSERT` or `UPDATE` which persists the record. An Active Record exception could be generated as a result, so be prepared to handle that failure in your controller. I recommend that you use a unique index constraint in the database if you absolutely must make sure that a column value is unique.

8.2.11.1 Enforcing Uniqueness of Join Models

In the course of using join models (with `has_many :through`), it seems pretty common to need to make the relationship unique. Consider an application that models students, courses, and registrations with the following code:

```
class Student < ActiveRecord::Base
  has_many :registrations
  has_many :courses, through: :registrations
end

class Registration < ActiveRecord::Base
  belongs_to :student
  belongs_to :course
end

class Course < ActiveRecord::Base
  has_many :registrations
  has_many :students, through: :registrations
end
```

How do you make sure that a student is not registered more than once for a particular course? The most concise way is to use `validates_uniqueness_of` with a `:scope` constraint. The important thing to remember with this technique is to reference the foreign keys, not the names of the associations themselves:

```
class Registration < ActiveRecord::Base
  belongs_to :student
  belongs_to :course

  validates_uniqueness_of :student_id, scope: :course_id,
                          message: "can only register once per course"
end
```

Notice that since the default error message generated when this validation fails would not make sense, I've provided a custom error message that will result in the expression: "Student can only register once per course."

● Tim says . . .

Astute readers will notice that the validation was on `student_id` but the error message references "Student." Rails special cases this to do what you mean.

8.2.11.2 Limit Constraint Lookup

As of Rails 4, you can specify criteria that constrains a uniqueness validation against a set of records by setting the `:conditions` option.

To illustrate, let's assume we have an article that requires titles to be unique against all published articles in the database. We can achieve this using `validates_unique-ness_of` by doing the following:

```
class Article < ActiveRecord::Base
  validates_uniqueness_of :title,
    conditions: -> { where.not(published_at: nil) }
  ...
end
```

When the model is saved, Active Record will query for `title` against all articles in the database that are published. If no results are returned, the model is valid.

8.2.12 `validates_with`

All of the validation methods we've covered so far are essentially local to the class in which they are used. If you want to develop a suite of custom, reusable validation classes, then you need a way to apply them to your models, and that is exactly what the `validates_with` method enables you to do.

To implement a custom validator, extend `ActiveRecord::Validator` and implement the `validate` method. The record being validated is available as `record`, and you manipulate its `errors` hash to log validation errors.

The following examples, from Ryan Daigle's excellent post[2] on this feature, demonstrate a reusable email field validator:

```
class EmailValidator < ActiveRecord::Validator
  def validate()
    record.errors[:email] << "is not valid" unless
      record.email =~ /\A([^@\s]+)@((?:[-a-z0-9]+\.)+[a-z]{2,})\z/
  end
end

class Account < ActiveRecord::Base
  validates_with EmailValidator
end
```

The example assumes the existence of an email attribute on the record. If you need to make your reusable validator more flexible, you can access validation options at runtime via the `options` hash, like this:

```
class EmailValidator < ActiveRecord::Validator
  def validate()
    email_field = options[:attr]
    record.errors[email_field] << "is not valid" unless
      record.send(email_field) =~ /\A([^@\s]+)@((?:[-a-z0-9]+\.)+[a-z]{2,})\z/
  end
```

---

2. http://ryandaigle.com/articles/2009/8/11/what-s-new-in-edge-rails-independent-model-validators

```
end

class Account < ActiveRecord::Base
  validates_with EmailValidator, attr: :email
end
```

8.2.13 `RecordInvalid`

Whenever you do so-called bang operations (such as `save!`) and a validation fails, you should be prepared to rescue `ActiveRecord::RecordInvalid`. Validation failures will cause `RecordInvalid` to be raised, and its message will contain a description of the failures.

Here's a quick example from one of my applications that has pretty restrictive validations on its User model:

```
>> u = User.new
=> #<User ...>
>> u.save!
ActiveRecord::RecordInvalid: Validation failed: Name can't be blank,
Password confirmation can't be blank, Password is too short (minimum
is 5 characters), Email can't be blank, Email address format is bad
```

8.3   Common Validation Options

The following options apply to all of the validation methods.

8.3.1 `allow_blank` and `allow_nil`

In some cases, you only want to trigger a validation if a value is present; in other words, the attribute is optional. There are two options that provide this functionality.

The :`allow_blank` option skips validation if the value is blank according to the `blank?` method. Similarly, the :`allow_nil` option skips the validation if the value of the attribute is `nil`; it only checks for `nil`, and empty strings `""` are not considered nil, but they are considered blank.

8.3.2 `if` and `unless`

The :`if` and :`unless` options are covered in the next section, "Conditional Validation."

8.3.3 `message`

As we've discussed earlier in the chapter, the way that the validation process registers failures is by adding items to the `errors` object of the model object being checked.

Part of the error item is a specific message describing the validation failure. All of the validation methods accept a `:message` option so that you can override the default error message format.

```ruby
class Account < ActiveRecord::Base
  validates_uniqueness_of :username, message: "is already taken"
end
```

The default English locale file in Active Model defines most of the standard error message templates.

```
inclusion: "is not included in the list"
exclusion: "is reserved"
invalid: "is invalid"
confirmation: "doesn't match %{attribute}"
accepted: "must be accepted"
empty: "can't be empty"
blank: "can't be blank"
present: "must be blank"
too_long: "is too long (maximum is %{count} characters)"
too_short: "is too short (minimum is %{count} characters)"
wrong_length: "is the wrong length (should be %{count} characters)"
not_a_number: "is not a number"
not_an_integer: "must be an integer"
greater_than: "must be greater than %{count}"
greater_than_or_equal_to: "must be greater than or equal to %{count}"
equal_to: "must be equal to %{count}"
less_than: "must be less than %{count}"
less_than_or_equal_to: "must be less than or equal to %{count}"
other_than: "must be other than %{count}"
odd: "must be odd"
even: "must be even"
```

The default messages only use the count variable for interpolation, where appropriate, but `model`, `attribute`, and `value` are always available.

```
validates_uniqueness_of username, message: "%{value} is already registered"
```

8.3.4 on

By default, validations are run on save (both create and update operations). If you need to do so, you can limit a given validation to just one of those operations by passing the `:on` option either `:create` or `:update`.

Assuming that your application does not support changing emails, one good use for `on:  :create` might be in conjunction with `validates_uniqueness_of`, since checking uniqueness with a query on large datasets can be time-consuming.

```
class Account < ActiveRecord::Base
  validates_uniqueness_of :email, on: :create
end
```

8.3.5 `strict`

Rails 4 introduced a `:strict` validation option that defaults to `false`. Turning it on causes an exception `ActiveModel::StrictValidationFailed` to be raised when a model is invalid.

```
class Account < ActiveRecord::Base
  validates :email, presence: { strict: true }
end
```

To override the type of exception raised on error, pass the custom exception to the `:strict` option.

```
class Account < ActiveRecord::Base
  validates :email, presence: { strict: EmailRequiredException }
end
```

8.4   Conditional Validation

Since validation methods are based on the Active Model Callback API, they all accept `:if` and `:unless` options to determine at runtime (not during class definition) whether the validation needs to be run or not.

The following three types of arguments can be supplied as parameters:

Symbol The name of a method to invoke as a symbol. This is probably the most common option and offers the best performance.

String A snippet of Ruby code to `eval` might be useful when the condition is really short, but keep in mind that `eval`ing statements is relatively slow.

Proc A block of code to be `instance_evaled`, so that `self` is the current record. Perhaps the most elegant choice for one-line conditionals.

```
validates_presence_of :approver, if: -> { approved? && !legacy? }
```

8.4.1 Usage and Considerations

A primary use case for conditional validation is *when an object can be validly persisted in more than one state*. A very common example involves the `User` (or `Person`) model, used for login and authentication.

```
validates_presence_of :password, if: :password_required?
```

```
validates_presence_of :password_confirmation, if: :password_required?
validates_length_of :password, within: 4..40, if: :password_required?
validates_confirmation_of :password, if: :password_required?
```

This code is not DRY (meaning that it is repetitive). You can refactor it to make it a little dryer using the `with_options` method that Active Support mixes into `Object`.

```
with_options if: :password_required? do |user|
  user.validates_presence_of :password
  user.validates_presence_of :password_confirmation
  user.validates_length_of :password, within: 4..40
  user.validates_confirmation_of :password
end
```

The example validations check for the two cases when a (plaintext) password field should be required in order for the model to be valid.

```
def password_required?
  encrypted_password.blank? || !password.blank?
end
```

The first case is if the `encrypted_password` attribute is blank, because that means we are dealing with a new `User` instance that has not been given a password yet. The other case is when the `password` attribute itself is not blank; perhaps this is happening during an update operation when the user is attempting to reset a password.

8.4.2   Validation Contexts

Another way to accomplish conditional validation leverages support for *validation contexts*. Declare a validation and pass the name of an application-specific validation context as the value of the `:on` option. That validation will now only be checked when explicitly invoked using `record.valid?(context_name)`.

Consider the following example involving a report generation app. Saving a report without a name is fine, but publishing one without a name is not.

```
class Report < ActiveRecord::Base
  validates_presence_of :name, on: :publish
end

class ReportsController < ApplicationController
  expose(:report)

  # POST /reports/1/publish
```

```
    def publish
      if report.valid? :publish
        redirect_to report, notice: "Report published"
      else
        flash.now.alert = "Can't publish unnamed reports!"
        render :show
      end
    end
end
```

I can't let this example go without mentioning that it might be better (and definitely more RESTful) to create a Publication model to represent the publishing of a report and contain related validation logic, instead of mixing it up in `Report`.

8.5 Short-Form Validation

The `validates` method identifies an attribute and accepts options that correspond to the validators we've already covered in the chapter. It lets you group all the validations that apply to a single field together and can tighten up your model code nicely as well as make it more readable.

```
validates :username, presence: true,
  format: { with: /[A-Za-z0-9]+/ },
  length: { minimum: 3 },
  uniqueness: true
```

The following options are available for use with the `validates` method.

absence: true Alias for `validates_absence_of`. Supply additional options by replacing `true` with a hash.

```
validates :unwanted, absence: { message: "should not have been set" }
```

acceptance: true Alias for `validates_acceptance_of`, typically used with check boxes that indicate acceptance of terms. Supply additional options by replacing `true` with a hash.

```
validates :terms, acceptance: { message: 'must be accepted' }
```

confirmation: true Alias for `validates_confirmation_of`, typically used to ensure that email and password confirmation fields match up correctly. Supply additional options by replacing `true` with a hash.

```
validates :email, confirmation: { message: 'is required' }
```

exclusion: { in: [1,2,3] } Alias for `validates_exclusion_of`. If your only option is the array to exclude against, you can shorten the syntax further by supplying an array as the value.

```
validates :username, exclusion: %w(admin superuser)
```

format: { with: /.*/ } Alias for `validates_format_of`. If your only option is the regular expression, you can shorten the syntax further by making it the value like:

```
format: /[A-Za-z0-9]+/
```

inclusion: { in: [1,2,3] } Alias for `validates_inclusion_of`. If your only option is the inclusion array, you can shorten the syntax further by making the array the value.

```
validates :gender, inclusion: %w(male female)
```

length: { minimum: 0, maximum: 1000 } Alias for `validates_length_of`. If your only options are minimum and maximum lengths, you can shorten the syntax further by supplying a Ruby range as the value.

```
validates :username, length: 3..20
```

numericality: true Alias for `validates_numericality_of`. Supply additional options by replacing `true` with a hash.

```
validates :quantity, numericality: { message: 'should be a number' }
```

presence: true Alias for `validates_presence_of`. Supply additional options by replacing `true` with a hash.

```
validates :username, presence: { message: 'is missing (How do
          you expect to login without it?)' }
```

uniqueness: true Alias for `validates_uniqueness_of`. Supply additional options by replacing `true` with a hash.

```
validates :screenname, uniqueness: { message: "was nabbed by
          someone else first" }
```

8.6 Custom Validation Techniques

When declarative validation doesn't meet your needs, Rails gives you a few custom techniques.

8.6.1 Custom Validation Macros

Rails has the capability to add custom validation macros (available to all your model classes) by extending `ActiveModel::EachValidator`.

The following example is silly but demonstrates the functionality.

```
class ReportLikeValidator < ActiveModel::EachValidator
  def validate_each(record, attribute, value)
    unless value["Report"]
      record.errors.add(attribute, 'does not appear to be a Report')
    end
  end
end
```

If you have more than one custom validation class, you'd probably be best off giving them their own directory like `app/models/validations`.

Now that your custom validator exists, it is available to use with the `validates` macro in your model.

```
class Report < ActiveRecord::Base
  validates :name, report_like: true
end
```

The class name `ReportLikeValidator` is inferred from the symbol provided (`:report_like`).

You can receive options via the `validates` method by adding an `initializer` method to your custom validator class. For example, let's make `ReportLikeValidator` more generic.

```
class LikeValidator < ActiveModel::EachValidator
  def initialize(options)
    @with = options[:with]
    super
  end

  def validate_each(record, attribute, value)
    unless value[@with]
      record.errors.add(attribute, "does not appear to be like #{@with}")
    end
  end
end
```

Active Record

Our model code would change to

```
class Report < ActiveRecord::Base
  validates :name, like: { with: "Report" }
end
```

8.6.2   Create a Custom Validator Class

This technique involves inheriting from `ActiveModel::Validator` and implementing a `validate` method that takes the record to validate.

I'll demonstrate with a really wicked example.

```
class RandomlyValidator < ActiveModel::Validator
  def validate(record)
    record.errors[:base] << "FAIL #1" unless first_hurdle(record)
    record.errors[:base] << "FAIL #2" unless second_hurdle(record)
    record.errors[:base] << "FAIL #3" unless third_hurdle(record)
  end

  private
  def first_hurdle(record)
    rand > 0.3
  end

  def second_hurdle(record)
    rand > 0.6
  end

  def third_hurdle(record)
    rand > 0.9
  end
end
```

Use your new custom validator in a model with the `validates_with` macro.

```
class Report < ActiveRecord::Base
  validates_with RandomlyValidator
end
```

8.6.3   Add a **validate** Method to Your Model

Giving your model class a `validate` instance method might be the way to go if
you want to check the state of your object holistically and keep the code for doing
so inside of the model class itself.

> The `validate` method is an older technique that I can't fully endorse because it unnecessarily adds complexity to the model class as compared to how easy it is to create custom validators that are testable in isolation.

For example, assume that you are dealing with a model object with a set of three integer attributes (`:attr1`, `:attr2`, and `:attr3`) and a precalculated total attribute (`:total`). The total must always equal the sum of the three attributes:

```
class CompletelyLameTotalExample < ActiveRecord::Base
  def validate
    if total != (attr1 + attr2 + attr3)
      errors[:total] << "doesn't add up"
    end
  end
end
```

You can alternatively add an error message to the whole object instead of just a particular attribute, using the `:base` key, like this:

```
errors[:base] << "The total doesn't add up!"
```

One of the subtleties of writing validations in Rails is that when you are adding errors to a particular attribute, you use a sentence *fragment,* versus when you are adding to `:base`, you use an entire sentence. That's because at some point, you'll want to expose error messages to the user. The method used to do that for an attribute is `full_messages_for`, which takes the name of the attribute plus whatever errors have been added to an attribute and strings it all together into a whole sentence using Active Support's `to_sentence` method.

> ⚘ Remember: The way to mark an object as invalid is to add to its `Errors` object. The return value of a custom validation method is not used.

8.7 Skipping Validations

The methods `update_attribute` and `update_column` don't invoke validations, yet their companion method `update` does. Whoever wrote the related Rails API docs believes that this behavior is "especially useful for Boolean flags on existing records."

I don't know if that is entirely true or not, but I do know that it is the source of ongoing contention in the community. Unfortunately, I don't have much more to add other than some simple commonsense advice: Be very careful using the `update_attribute` or `update_column` methods. It can easily persist your model objects in invalid states.

8.8   Working with the Errors Hash

Some methods are provided to enable you to add validation errors to the collection manually and alter the state of the `Errors` object.

errors[:base] = msg Adds an error message related to the overall object state itself and not the value of any particular attribute. Make your error messages complete sentences, because Rails does not do any additional processing of them to make them readable.

errors[:attribute] = msg Adds an error message related to a particular attribute. The message should be a sentence fragment that reads naturally when prepended with the capitalized name of the attribute.

clear As you might expect, the `clear` method clears the state of the `Errors` object.

8.8.1   Checking for Errors

It's also possible to check the `Errors` object for validation failures on specific attributes with a couple of methods, just using square brackets notation. An array is always returned; it's an empty one when there aren't any validation errors for the attribute specified.

```
>> user.errors[:login]
=> ["zed is already registered"]
>> user.errors[:password]
=> []
```

Alternatively, you could also access full error messages for a specific attribute using the `full_messages_for` method. Just like accessing validation failures for attributes using bracket notation, an array is always returned.

```
>> user.errors.full_messages_for(:email)
=> ["Email can't be blank"]
```

8.9   Testing Validations with Shoulda

Even though validations are declarative code, if you're doing TDD then you'll want to specify them before writing them. Luckily, Thoughtbot's Shoulda Matchers library[3] contains a number of matchers designed to easily test validations.

---

3. https://github.com/thoughtbot/shoulda-matchers

```
describe Post do
  it { should validate_uniqueness_of(:title) }
  it { should validate_presence_of(:body).with_message(/wtf/) }
  it { should validate_presence_of(:title) }
  it { should validate_numericality_of(:user_id) }
end

describe User do
  it { should_not allow_value("blah").for(:email) }
  it { should_not allow_value("b lah").for(:email) }
  it { should allow_value("a@b.com").for(:email) }
  it { should allow_value("asdf@asdf.com").for(:email) }
  it { should ensure_length_of(:email).is_at_least(1).is_at_most(100) }
  it { should ensure_inclusion_of(:age).in_range(1..100) }
end
```

8.10   Conclusion

In this (relatively speaking) short chapter, we covered the Active Record Validations API in-depth. One of the most appealing aspects of Rails is how we can declaratively specify the criteria for determining the validity of model objects.

Active
Record

CHAPTER 9

Advanced Active Record

Respectful debate, honesty, passion, and working systems created an environment that not even the most die-hard enterprise architect could ignore, no matter how buried in Java design patterns. Those who placed technical excellence and pragmaticism above religious attachment and vendor cronyism were easily convinced of the benefits that broadening their definition of acceptable technologies could bring.[1]

—Ryan Tomayko (March 2006)

Active Record is a simple object-relational mapping (ORM) framework compared to other popular ORM frameworks, such as Hibernate in the Java world. Don't let that fool you, though: Under its modest exterior, Active Record has some pretty advanced features. To really get the most effectiveness out of Rails development, you need to have more than a basic understanding of Active Record—things like knowing when to break out of the one-table/one-class pattern or how to leverage Ruby modules to keep your code clean and free of duplication.

In this chapter, we wrap up this book's comprehensive coverage of Active Record by reviewing scopes, callbacks, single-table inheritance (STI), polymorphic models and other advanced features of the library. We also provide a cursory review of metaprogramming and Ruby domain-specific languages (DSLs) as they relate to Active Record.

---

1. http://lesscode.org/2006/03/12/someone-tell-gosling/

9.1   Scopes

Scopes (or "named scopes" if you're old school) enable you to define and chain query criteria in a declarative and reusable manner.

```
class Timesheet < ActiveRecord::Base
  scope :submitted, -> { where(submitted: true) }
  scope :underutilized, -> { where('total_hours < 40') }
```

To declare a scope, use the `scope` class method, passing it a name as a symbol and a callable object that includes a query criterion within. You can simply use Arel criteria methods such as `where`, `order`, and `limit` to construct the definition as shown in the example. The queries defined in a scope are only evaluated whenever the scope is invoked.

```
class User < ActiveRecord::Base
  scope :delinquent, -> { where('timesheets_updated_at < ?', 1.week.ago) }
```

Invoke scopes as you would class methods.

```
>> User.delinquent
=> [#<User id: 2, timesheets_updated_at: "2013-04-20 20:02:13"...>]
```

Note that instead of using the `scope` macro-style method, you can simply define a class method on an Active Record model, which returns a scoped method such as `where`. To illustrate, the following class method is equivalent to the `delinquent` scope defined in the previous example.

```
def self.delinquent
  where('timesheets_updated_at < ?', 1.week.ago)
end
```

9.1.1   Scope Parameters

You can pass arguments to scope invocations by adding parameters to the proc you use to define the scope query.

```
class BillableWeek < ActiveRecord::Base
  scope :newer_than, ->(date) { where('start_date > ?', date) }
```

Then pass the argument to the scope as you would normally.

```
BillableWeek.newer_than(Date.today)
```

9.1.2 Chaining Scopes

One of the benefits of scopes is that you can chain them together to create complex queries from simple ones:

```
>> Timesheet.underutilized.submitted.to_a
=> [#<Timesheet id: 3, submitted: true, total_hours: 37 ...
```

Scopes can be chained together for reuse within scope definitions themselves. For instance, let's say that we always want to constrain the result set of underutilized to submitted timesheets:

```
class Timesheet < ActiveRecord::Base
  scope :submitted, -> { where(submitted: true) }
  scope :underutilized, -> { submitted.where('total_hours < 40') }
```

9.1.3 Scopes and `has_many`

In addition to being available at the class context, scopes are available automatically on `has_many` association attributes.

```
>> u = User.find(2)
=> #<User id: 2, username: "obie"...>
>> u.timesheets.size
=> 3
>> u.timesheets.underutilized.size
=> 1
```

9.1.4 Scopes and Joins

You can use Arel's `join` method to create cross-model scopes. For instance, if we gave our recurring example `Timesheet` a `submitted_at` date attribute instead of just a boolean, we could add a scope to `User` enabling us to see who is late on their timesheet submission.

```
scope :tardy, -> {
  joins(:timesheets).
  where("timesheets.submitted_at <= ?", 7.days.ago).
  group("users.id")
}
```

Arel's `to_sql` method is useful for debugging scope definitions and usage.

```
>> User.tardy.to_sql
=> "SELECT "users".* FROM "users"
  INNER JOIN "timesheets" ON "timesheets"."user_id" = "users"."id"
  WHERE (timesheets.submitted_at <= '2013-04-13 18:16:15.203293')
  GROUP BY users.id" # query formatted nicely for the book
```

Note that as demonstrated in the example, it's a good idea to use unambiguous column references (including table name) in cross-model scope definitions so that Arel doesn't get confused.

9.1.5   Scope Combinations

Our example of a cross-model scope violates good object-oriented design principles: it contains the logic for determining whether or not a `Timesheet` is submitted, which is code that properly belongs in the `Timesheet` class. Luckily we can use Arel's merge method to fix it. First we put the late logic where it belongs, in `Timesheet`:

```
scope :late, -> { where("timesheet.submitted_at <= ?", 7.days.ago) }
```

Then we use our new late scope in tardy:

```
scope :tardy, -> {
  joins(:timesheets).group("users.id").merge(Timesheet.late)
}
```

If you have trouble with this technique, make absolutely sure that your scopes' clauses refer to fully qualified column names. (In other words, don't forget to prefix column names with tables.) The console and `to_sql` method are your friends for debugging.

9.1.6   Default Scopes

There may arise use cases where you want certain conditions applied to the finders for your model. Consider that our timesheet application has a default view of open timesheets—we can use a default scope to simplify our general queries.

```
class Timesheet < ActiveRecord::Base
  default_scope { where(status: "open") }
end
```

Now when we query for our `Timesheets`, by default the open condition will be applied:

```
>> Timesheet.pluck(:status)
=> ["open", "open", "open"]
```

Default scopes also get applied to your models when building or creating them which can be a great convenience or a nuisance if you are not careful. In our previous example all new `Timesheets` will be created with a status of "open."

```
>> Timesheet.new
=> #<Timesheet id: nil, status: "open">
>> Timesheet.create
=> #<Timesheet id: 1, status: "open">
```

You can override this behavior by providing your own conditions or scope to override the default setting of the attributes.

```
>> Timesheet.where(status: "new").new
=> #<Timesheet id: nil, status: "new">
>> Timesheet.where(status: "new").create
=> #<Timesheet id: 1, status: "new">
```

There may be cases where at runtime you want to create a scope and pass it around as a first class object leveraging your default scope. In this case Active Record provides the `all` method.

```
>> timesheets = Timesheet.all.order("submitted_at DESC")
=> #<ActiveRecord::Relation [#<Timesheet id: 1, status: "open"]>
>> timesheets.where(name: "Durran Jordan").to_a
=> []
```

There's another approach to scopes that provides a sleeker syntax, `scoping`, which enables the chaining of scopes via nesting within a block.

```
>> Timesheet.order("submitted_at DESC").scoping do
>> Timesheet.first
>> end
=> #<Timesheet id: 1, status: "open">
```

That's pretty nice, but what if we *don't* want our default scope to be included in our queries? In this case Active Record takes care of us through the `unscoped` method.

```
>> Timesheet.unscoped.order("submitted_at DESC").to_a
=> [#<Timesheet id: 2, status: "submitted">]
```

Similar to overriding our default scope with a relation when creating new objects, we can supply `unscoped` as well to remove the default attributes.

```
>> Timesheet.unscoped.new
=> #<Timesheet id: nil, status: nil>
```

Active Record

9.1.7   Using Scopes for CRUD

You have a wide range of Active Record's CRUD methods available on scopes, which gives you some powerful capabilities. For instance, let's give all our underutilized timesheets some extra hours.

```
>> u.timesheets.underutilized.pluck(:total_hours)
=> [37, 38]

>> u.timesheets.underutilized.update_all("total_hours = total_hours + 2")
=> 2

>> u.timesheets.underutilized.pluck(:total_hours)
=> [39]
```

Scopes including a `where` clause using hashed conditions will populate attributes of objects built off of them with those attributes as default values. Admittedly it's a bit difficult to think of a plausible use case for this feature, but we'll show it in an example. First, we add the following scope to `Timesheet`:

```
scope :perfect, -> { submitted.where(total_hours: 40) }
```

Now, building an object on the `perfect` scope should give us a submitted timesheet with 40 hours.

```
> Timesheet.perfect.build
=> #<Timesheet id: nil, submitted: true, user_id: nil, total_hours: 40 ...>
```

As you've probably realized by now, the Arel underpinnings of Active Record are tremendously powerful and truly elevate the Rails platform.

9.2   Callbacks

This advanced feature of Active Record enables the savvy developer to attach behavior at a variety of different points along a model's life cycle, such as after initialization, before database records are inserted, updated or removed, and so on.

Callbacks can do a variety of tasks, ranging from simple things such as logging and massaging of attribute values prior to validation to complex calculations. Callbacks can halt the execution of the life-cycle process taking place. Some callbacks can even modify the behavior of the model class on the fly. We'll cover all of those scenarios in this section, but first let's get a taste of what a callback looks like. Check out the following silly example:

```
class Beethoven < ActiveRecord::Base
  before_destroy :last_words
```

```
  protected

  def last_words
    logger.info "Friends applaud, the comedy is over"
  end
end
```

So prior to dying (ehrm, being `destroyed`), the last words of the `Beethoven` class will always be logged for posterity. As we'll see soon, there are 14 different opportunities to add behavior to your model in this fashion. Before we get to that list, let's cover the mechanics of registering a callback.

9.2.1   One-Liners

Now, if (and only if) your callback routine is really short,[2] you can add it by passing a block to the callback macro. We're talking one-liners!

```
class Napoleon < ActiveRecord::Base
  before_destroy { logger.info "Josephine..." }
  ...
end
```

Since Rails 3, the block passed to a callback is executed via `instance_eval` so that its scope is the record itself (versus needing to act on a passed in record variable). The following example implements "paranoid" model behavior, covered later in the chapter.

```
class Account < ActiveRecord::Base
  before_destroy { self.update_attribute(:deleted_at, Time.now); false }
  ...
```

9.2.2   Protected or Private

Except when you're using a block, the access level for callback methods should always be protected or private. It should never be public, since callbacks should never be called from code outside the model.

Believe it or not, there are even more ways to implement callbacks, but we'll cover those techniques further along in the chapter. For now, let's look at the lists of callback hooks available.

---

2. If you are browsing old Rails source code, you might come across callback macros receiving a short string of Ruby code to be eval'd in the binding of the model object. That way of adding callbacks was deprecated in Rails 1.2 because you're always better off using a block in those situations.

9.2.3   Matched **before/after** Callbacks

In total, there are 19 types of callbacks you can register on your models! Thirteen of them are matching before/after callback pairs, such as before_validation and after_validation. Four of them are around callbacks, such as around_save. (The other two, after_initialize and after_find, are special, and we'll discuss them later in this section.)

9.2.3.1   List of Callbacks

This is the list of callback hooks available during a save operation. (The list varies slightly depending on whether you're saving a new or existing record.)

- before_validation
- after_validation
- before_save
- around_save
- before_create (for new records) and before_update (for existing records)
- around_create (for new records) and around_update (for existing records)
- after_create (for new records) and after_update (for existing records)
- after_save

Delete operations have their own callbacks:

- before_destroy
- around_destroy executes a DELETE database statement on yield
- after_destroy is called after record has been removed from the database and all attributes have been frozen (read-only)

Callbacks may be limited to specific Active Record life cycles (:create, :update, :destroy), by explicitly defining which ones can trigger it, using the :on option. The :on option may accept a single lifecycle (like on: :create) or an array of life cycles on: [:create, :update].

```
# Run only on create
before_validation :some_callback, on: :create
```

Additionally, transactions have callbacks as well, for when you want actions to occur after the database is guaranteed to be in a permanent state. Note that only "after" callbacks exist here due to the nature of transactions—it's a bad idea to be able to interfere with the actual operation itself.

- `after_commit`

- `after_rollback`

- `after_touch`

---

❶ Skipping Callback Execution

The following Active Record methods, when executed, do not run any callbacks:

- `decrement`
- `decrement_counter`
- `delete`
- `delete_all`
- `increment`
- `increment_counter`
- `toggle`
- `update_column`
- `update_columns`
- `update_all`
- `update_counters`

9.2.4   Halting Execution

In earlier versions of Rails, it was easy to accidentally halt Active Record callbacks by returning `false`, and that behavior was blamed for scores of subtle bugs.

Rails 5 forces you to `throw(:abort)` explicitly in order to halt execution of the filter chain.

If you halt the chain then no further callbacks are executed. If there was a save underway, it will return `false`, while `save!` will raise a `RecordNotSaved` error.

The following configuration setting in `config/initializers/new_frame-work_defaults.rb` enables reverting to the old behavior.

```
# Do not halt callback chains when a callback returns false.
# Previous versions had true.
ActiveSupport.halt_callback_chains_on_return_false = false
```

If you are working with an older version of Rails or have changed the setting mentioned, please keep the following advice in mind: since the last expression of a Ruby method is returned implicitly, it is pretty common to write a callback that halts execution unintentionally. If you have an object with callbacks that mysteriously fails to save, make sure you aren't returning `false` or `nil` by mistake.

9.2.5 Callback Usages

Of course, the callback you should use for a given situation depends on what you're trying to accomplish. The best I can do is to serve up some examples to inspire you with your own code.

9.2.5.1 Cleaning Up Attribute Formatting with **before_validation** on Create

The most common examples of using `before_validation` callbacks have to do with cleaning up user-entered attributes. For example, the following `CreditCard` class cleans up its `number` attribute so that false negatives don't occur on validation:

```ruby
class CreditCard < ActiveRecord::Base
  before_validation on: :create do
    # Strip everything in the number except digits
    self.number = number.gsub(/[^0-9]/, "")
  end
end
```

9.2.5.2 Geocoding with **before_save**

Assume that you have an application that tracks addresses and has mapping features. Addresses should always be geocoded before saving, so that they can be displayed rapidly on a map later.[3]

As is often the case, the wording of the requirement itself points you in the direction of the `before_save` callback:

```ruby
class Address < ActiveRecord::Base

  before_save :geocode
  validates_presence_of :street, :city, :state, :country
  ...
```

---

3. I recommend the excellent Geocoder gem available at http://www.rubygeocoder.com/.

```
def to_s
  [street, city, state, country].compact.join(', ')
end

protected

def geocode
  result = Geocoder.coordinates(to_s)
  self.latitude = result.first
  self.longitude = result.last
end
end
```

ⓘ Note

For the sake of this example, we will not be using Geocoder's Active Record
extensions.

Before we move on, there are a couple of additional considerations. The preceding
code works great if the geocoding succeeds, but what if it doesn't? Do we still want
to allow the record to be saved? If not, we should halt the execution chain:

```
def geolocate
  result = Geocoder.coordinates(to_s)
  return false if result.empty? # halt execution

  self.latitude = result.first
  self.longitude = result.last
end
```

The only problem remaining is that we give the rest of our code (and by extension,
the end user) no indication of why the chain was halted. Even though we're not in a
validation routine, I think we can put the `errors` collection to good use here:

```
def geolocate
  result = Geocoder.coordinates(to_s)
  if result.present?
    self.latitude = result.first
    self.longitude = result.last
  else
    errors[:base] << "Geocoding failed. Please check address."
    throw(:abort)
  end
end
```

If the geocoding fails, we add a base error message (for the whole object) and halt
execution, so that the record is not saved.

9.2.5.3   Exercise Your Paranoia with `before_destroy`

What if your application has to handle important kinds of data that, once entered, should never be deleted? Perhaps it would make sense to hook into Active Record's destroy mechanism and somehow mark the record as deleted instead?

The following example depends on the `accounts` table having a `deleted_at` datetime column.

```
class Account < ActiveRecord::Base
  before_destroy do
    self.update_attribute(:deleted_at, Time.current)
    throw(:abort)
  end

  ...
end
```

After the `deleted_at` column is populated with the current time, we return `throw(:abort)` in the callback to halt execution. This ensures that the underlying record is not actually deleted from the database.[4]

It's probably worth mentioning that there are ways that Rails enables you to unintentionally circumvent `before_destroy` callbacks:

- The `delete` and `delete_all` class methods of `ActiveRecord::Base` are almost identical. They remove rows directly from the database without instantiating the corresponding model instances, which means no callbacks will occur.

- Model objects in associations defined with the option `dependent::delete_all` will be deleted directly from the database when removed from the collection using the association's `clear` or `delete` methods.

9.2.5.4   Cleaning Up Associated Files with `after_destroy`

Model objects that have files associated with them, such as attachment records and uploaded images, can clean up after themselves when deleted using the

---

4. Real-life implementation of the example would also need to modify all finders to include `deleted_at` is NULL conditions; otherwise, the records marked deleted would continue to show up in the application. That's not a trivial undertaking, and luckily you don't need to do it yourself. There's a Rails plugin named `destroyed_at` created by Dockyard that does exactly that, and you can find it at https://github.com/dockyard/destroyed_at.

`after_destroy` callback. The following method from thoughtbot's Paperclip[5] gem is a good example:

```
# Destroys the file. Called in an after_destroy callback
def destroy_attached_files
  Paperclip.log("Deleting attachments.")
  each_attachment do |name, attachment|
    attachment.send(:flush_deletes)
  end
end
```

9.2.6   Special Callbacks: `after_initialize` and `after_find`

The `after_initialize` callback is invoked whenever a new Active Record model is instantiated (either from scratch or from the database). Having it available prevents you from having to muck around with overriding the actual `initialize` method.

The `after_find` callback is invoked whenever Active Record loads a model object from the database, and is actually called before `after_initialize`, if both are implemented. Because `after_find` and `after_initialize` are called for each object found and instantiated by finders, performance constraints dictate that they can only be added as methods, and not via the callback macros.

What if you want to run some code only the first time that a model is ever instantiated and not after each database load? There is no native callback for that scenario, but you can do it using the `after_initialize` callback. Just add a condition that checks to see whether it is a new record:

```
after_initialize do
  if new_record?
    ...
  end
end
```

In a number of Rails apps that I've written, I've found it useful to capture user preferences in a serialized hash associated with the `User` object. The `serialize` feature of Active Record models makes this possible, since it transparently persists Ruby object graphs to a text column in the database. Unfortunately, you can't pass it a default value, so I have to set one myself:

```
class User < ActiveRecord::Base
  serialize :preferences # defaults to nil
```

---

5. Get Paperclip at https://github.com/thoughtbot/paperclip.

```
  . . .

  protected

  def after_initialize
    self.preferences ||= Hash.new
  end
end
```

Using the `after_initialize` callback, I can automatically populate the `preferences` attribute of my user model with an empty hash, so that I never have to worry about it being `nil` when I access it with code such as `user.preferences[:show_help_text] = false`.

💬 **Kevin says . . .**

You could change the preceding example to not use callbacks by using the Active Record `store`, a wrapper around serialize that is used exclusively for storing hashes in a database column.

```
class User < ActiveRecord::Base
  serialize :preferences # defaults to nil
  store :preferences, accessors: [:show_help_text]
  . . .
end
```

By default, the `preferences` attribute would be populated with an empty hash. Another added benefit is the capability to explicitly define accessors, removing the need to interact with the underlying hash directly. To illustrate, let's set the `show_help_text` preference to `true`:

```
>> user = User.new
=> #<User id: nil, properties: {}, ...>
>> user.show_help_text = true
=> true
>> user.properties
=> {"show_help_text" => true}
```

Ruby's metaprogramming capabilities, combined with the capability to run code whenever a model is loaded using the `after_find` callback, are a powerful mix. Since we're not done learning about callbacks yet, we'll come back to uses of `after_find` later on in the chapter, in the section "Modifying Active Record Classes at Runtime."

9.2.7 Callback Classes

It is common enough to want to reuse callback code for more than one object that
Rails gives you a way to write callback classes. All you have to do is pass a given callback queue an object that responds to the name of the callback and takes the model
object as a parameter.

Here's our paranoid example from the previous section as a callback class:

```
class MarkDeleted
  def self.before_destroy(model)
    model.update_attribute(:deleted_at, Time.current)
    false
  end
end
```

The behavior of `MarkDeleted` is stateless, so I added the callback as a class method.
Now you don't have to instantiate `MarkDeleted` objects for no good reason. All
you do is pass the class to the callback queue for whichever models you want to have
the mark-deleted behavior:

```
class Account < ActiveRecord::Base
  before_destroy MarkDeleted
  ...
end

class Invoice < ActiveRecord::Base
  before_destroy MarkDeleted
  ...
end
```

9.2.7.1 Multiple Callback Methods in One Class

There's no rule that says you can't have more than one callback method in a callback
class. For example, you might have special audit log requirements to implement:

```
class Auditor
  def initialize(audit_log)
    @audit_log = audit_log
  end

  def after_create(model)
    @audit_log.created(model.inspect)
  end

  def after_update(model)
    @audit_log.updated(model.inspect)
  end
```

```
  def after_destroy(model)
    @audit_log.destroyed(model.inspect)
  end
end
```

To add audit logging to an Active Record class, you would do the following:

```
class Account < ActiveRecord::Base
  after_create Auditor.new(DEFAULT_AUDIT_LOG)
  after_update Auditor.new(DEFAULT_AUDIT_LOG)
  after_destroy Auditor.new(DEFAULT_AUDIT_LOG)
  ....
end
```

Wow, that's ugly, having to add three `Auditors` on three lines. We could extract a local variable called `auditor`, but it would still be repetitive. This might be an opportunity to take advantage of Ruby's open classes, the fact that you can modify classes that aren't part of your application.

Wouldn't it be better to simply say `acts_as_audited` at the top of the model that needs auditing? We can quickly add it to the `ActiveRecord::Base` class, so that it's available for all our models.

On my projects, the file where "quick and dirty" code like the method in Listing 9.1 would reside is `lib/core_ext/active_record_base.rb`, but you can put it anywhere you want. You could even make it a plugin.

Listing 9.1   A quick-and-dirty 'acts as audited' method
```
class ActiveRecord::Base
  def self.acts_as_audited(audit_log=DEFAULT_AUDIT_LOG)
    auditor = Auditor.new(audit_log)
    after_create auditor
    after_update auditor
    after_destroy auditor
  end
end
```

Now, the top of `Account` is a lot less cluttered:

```
class Account < ActiveRecord::Base
  acts_as_audited
```

9.2.7.2   Testability
When you add callback methods to a model class, you pretty much have to test that they're functioning correctly in conjunction with the model to which they are added.

That may or may not be a problem. In contrast, callback classes are super-easy to test in isolation.

```
describe '#after_create' do
  let(:auditable) { double() }
  let(:log) { double() }
  let(:content) { 'foo' }

  it 'audits a model was created' do
    expect(auditable).to receive(:inspect).and_return(content)
    expect(log).to receive(:created).and_return(content)
    Auditor.new(log).after_create(auditable)
  end
end
```

9.3 Attributes API

The new Rails 5 Attributes API enables developers to declare a specific type for a given attribute of their model, along with an optional default value. It is not strict type validation in the technical sense but provides standardized hooks for casting and coercion logic in and out of your database.

Explicitly declaring an attribute overrides Active Record's standard type casting behavior and for the first time gives Rails developers a standardized way of specifying custom types, via classes that control how values are converted to and from SQL when assigned to a model. The primary impact should be less need for the use of `attr_accessor` and related methods in your model code.

Let's demonstrate use of the API with a simple `Event` class.

```
> rails g scaffold Event starts_at:date
```

In addition to the starting date, we want the user to be able to specify recurrence when they create a new event, all in the same form. So we add a few extra attributes to the event model.

```
class Event < ApplicationRecord
  attr_accessor :repeats
  attr_accessor :repeats_end
```

The intention is that based on the user input, we'll have our controller code create additional `Event` instances. (I'm not implying this is good or bad application design; I am just trying to keep the example understandable.)

The view, with those additional fields, looks something like this:

Active
Record

```
= form_for event do |f|
  - if event.errors.any?
    #error_explanation
      %h2= "#{pluralize(event.errors.count, "error")} prohibited this event from being saved:"
      %ul
        - event.errors.full_messages.each do |msg|
          %li= msg

  .field
    = f.label :starts_at
    = f.date_select :starts_at
  .field
    = f.label :repeats
    = f.check_box :repeats
  .field
    = f.label :repeats_end
    = f.date_select :repeats_end
  .actions
    = f.submit 'Save'
```

The form looks like this in the browser.

New event

Starts at

2016 ◊ November ◊ 23 ◊

Repeats

☐

Repeats end

2016 ◊ November ◊ 23 ◊

Save

Back

New Event form

Here's the related controller (with actions other than `create` hidden).

```
class EventsController < ApplicationController
  expose :events, -> { Event.all }
  expose :event

  def create
    byebug
    if event.save
```

```
      redirect_to event, notice: 'Event was successfully created.'
    else
      render :new
    end
  end

  private

  def event_params
    params.require(:event).permit(:starts_at, :repeats, :repeats_end)
  end
end
```

Notice I added a `byebug` on line 6. When I submit a form, I'll get a debugging console in my terminal.

```
Started POST "/events" for ::1 at 2016-11-23 12:25:43 -0500
Processing by EventsController#create as HTML
Parameters: {"utf8"=>"âœ"", "authenticity_token"=>"xizidXXPRLuTU7trrZpeIb7plNPTU0SyaNQiX\
bWlVvHKMQU96ODqaPUig1126phyKdEttAIGrCp8keaNOVP9TQ==", "event"=>{"starts_at(1i)"=>"2016", "\
starts_at(2i)"=>"11", "starts_at(3i)"=>"23", "repeats"=>"1", "repeats_end(1i)"=>"2017", "r\
epeats_end(2i)"=>"11", "repeats_end(3i)"=>"23"}, "commit"=>"Save"}


[2, 11] in ./auction/app/controllers/events_controller.rb
   2:   expose :events, ->{ Event.all }
   3:   expose :event
   4:
   5:   def create
   6:     byebug
=> 7:     if event.save
```

Rails gets incoming date data as a hash.

```
"repeats_end(1i)"=>"2017", "repeats_end(2i)"=>"11", "repeats_end(3i)"=>"23"
```

. . . and it gets check-box values as an integer.

```
"repeats"=>"1"
```

Let's check how those were set in our event model.

```
(byebug) event.repeats
"1"
(byebug) event.repeats_end
{1=>2016, 2=>11, 3=>25}
```

Not exactly useful yet. We need some type coercion.

9.3.1   Type Coercion

One of the most common kinds of model code in Rails is type coercion, that is, taking form-inputted values from the user and transforming them into representations
that are more useful to our code.

Continuing with the example from the last section, we had a couple of attributes that
need coercion: `event.repeats` and `event.repeats_end`. We'll accomplish it
the old way first, by transforming the incoming values on assignment.

```
class Event < ApplicationRecord
  attr_reader :repeats
  attr_reader :repeats_end

  def repeats=(val)
    @repeats = (val == "1")
  end

  def repeats_end=(val)
    @repeats_end = Date.new(*val.values)
  end
```

Now when we submit new event data, our `event` object has attributes of the right
type.

```
(byebug) event
#<Event id: nil, starts_at: "2016-11-23", created_at: nil, updated_at: nil>
(byebug) event.repeats
true
(byebug) event.repeats_end
Thu, 23 Nov 2017
```

Note that even though that seems to be working, our implementation leaves a lot to
be desired. For instance, check out the following bug.

```
>> e = Event.new(repeats: true)
=> #<Event id: nil, starts_at: nil, created_at: nil, updated_at: nil>
>> e.repeats
>> false
```

D'oh. As I hope you can imagine, even based on this simple example, accounting for
all edge cases in type conversion is tedious and error-prone.

What the new Attributes API gives you is the capability to declaratively tell Active
Record how to do type coercion, even for fields like our example's `repeats` and
`repeats_end` fields, which are not backed by columns in the database. Since it

leverages Rails' battle tested built-in type conversion, you can be more confident using it than reinventing the wheel in your application code.

Let's refactor `Event` to take advantage of the new API.

```
class Event < ApplicationRecord
  attribute :repeats, :boolean, default: false
  attribute :repeats_end, :date
end
```

And if we submit the new event form again:

```
(byebug) event
#<Event id: nil, starts_at: "2016-11-23", created_at: nil,
updated_at: nil>
(byebug) event.repeats
true
(byebug) event.repeats_end
Thu, 23 Nov 2017
(byebug)
```

There we go, exactly the same as last time, in less than half the code. It's worth pointing out that the attributes still don't show up in the the console's `inspect` representation of the object, but the type coercion worked exactly as intended.

While we're on the subject, you might be wondering how Active Record's type coercion logic works. Here's the relevant Rails source code for a boolean cast.

```
# activerecord/lib/active_model/type/boolean.rb
module ActiveModel
  module Type
    class Boolean < Value
      FALSE_VALUES =
        [false, 0, "0", "f", "F", "false", "FALSE", "off",
         "OFF"].to_set

      def type
        :boolean
      end

      private
        def cast_value(value)
          if value == ""
            nil
          else
            !FALSE_VALUES.include?(value)
          end
        end
```

```
      end
    end
end
```

In the remainder of the section, we'll get into more detail about how the Attributes API works, and how you can write your own type implementations.

9.3.2   The `attribute` Method

The `attribute` method takes at minimum a `name` and `cast_type` parameter.

Active Record comes with a slew of built-in cast types, taken from Active Model. You can examine them yourself at https://github.com/rails/rails/tree/master/activemodel/lib/active_model/type.

Cast Type	Type Class
`:big_integer`	`ActiveModel::Type::BigInteger`
`:binary`	`ActiveModel::Type::Binary`
`:boolean`	`ActiveModel::Type::Boolean`
`:date`	`ActiveModel::Type::Date`
`:date_time`	`ActiveModel::Type::DateTime`
`:decimal`	`ActiveModel::Type::Decimal`
`:float`	`ActiveModel::Type::Float`
`:integer`	`ActiveModel::Type::Integer`
`:string`	`ActiveModel::Type::String`
`:text`	`ActiveModel::Type::Text`
`:time`	`ActiveModel::Type::Time`

The `attribute` method also accepts the following options:

default   The default value to use when no value is provided. Overrides default set via database, if any. Otherwise, default will be `nil`.

array   If using PostgreSQL, set `array: true` to specify that the type should be an array of `cast_type`.

range   If using PostgreSQL, this option specifies that the type should be a range. Supply a Ruby range object with the desired valid range of values.

```
class Issue
    attribute :priority, :integer, range: [0..5]
```

Stuck on an old version of Rails that's missing the `attribute` declaration?
Try Virtus https://github.com/solnic/virtus.

9.3.3   Custom Types

Since there's only so many fundamental kinds of data (string, boolean, date, etc.) that
you can put into a database column, you normally start defining your own custom
type by extending one of the built-in cast types.

Logan Serman has a clever example in his blog at http://blog.metova.com/rails-
5-attributes-api. He extends the built in string type to give it `StringInquirer`
behavior. This nifty little Active Support class is what lets you ask strings if they
equal a certain value with Ruby-style boolean notation.

```
Rails.env.development?
```

Even though it's a little pointless, I'll apply the pattern to our `Event` class for illustrative purposes.

```
class Inquiry < ActiveRecord::Type::String
  def type
    :inquiry
  end

  def cast(value)
    super.inquiry
  end
end

class Event < ApplicationRecord
  attribute :repeats, Inquiry.new
  attribute :repeats_end, :date
end
```

By default, `cast` is invoked on both setting and getting values from the database.
If you only want to affect setting behavior, then override `deserialize` for the
getting and leave `cast` for setting only. (The default behavior is for `deserialize`
to call `cast`.)

When we check our event in the console, we see the new behavior.

```
=> 7:     if event.save
   8:       redirect_to event, notice: 'Event was successfully created.'
   9:     else
  10:       render :new
  11:     end
```

```
(byebug) event.repeats?
true
```

Of course, we lost the typecasting to boolean, which is why I called this particular example silly.

```
(byebug) event.repeats
"1"
```

If you implement `serialize` in a custom type, then it'll be invoked as part of generating SQL queries.

9.3.4   Registering New Attribute Types

If you're going to reuse a custom type throughout your application (or are providing it as part of a gem), then you probably want to register it globally in an initializer.

```
# config/initializers/custom_attribute_types.rb
ActiveRecord::Type.register :inquiry, Inquiry.new
```

The `register` method adds a new type to Active Record's registry, enabling it to be referenced by symbol in the call to `attribute`. If your custom type is only meant to be used with a specific database adapter, you can define that by passing an option `adapter:  :adapter_name`. If your type has the same name as a native type for the current adapter, an exception will be raised unless you specify `override:  true`.

Working with Money

The Money-Rails gem is essential for dealing with money and currency. Check it out at https://github.com/RubyMoney/money-rails

Lots of sample code out there related to the Attributes API (including the Rails source code itself) uses `to_f` to deal with money conversion. I'll show you why that's unsuitable for production use in just a few lines of playing around on the console:

```
>> 19.99 * 100.to_f
=> 1998.999999999998
>> (19.99 * 100.0).to_i
=> 1998
```

Floating numbers are by their very nature *imprecise*, which makes them highly unsuitable for use in money calculations. Hacker exploits based on the kinds of bugs that can be introduced by using floats to calculate monetary values are referred to as *salami slicing* or *penny slicing*, and have played a key role in the plots of films such as *Superman III* and *Office Space*.

9.4 Serialized Attributes

Active Record lets you mark an attribute backed by a text column in the database as being serialized. Whatever object (more accurately, graph of objects) you assign to that attribute will be stored in the database as YAML, Ruby's native serialization format.

💬 Sebastian says . . .

TEXT columns usually have a maximum size of 64K, and if your serialized attributes exceed the size constraints, you'll run into a lot of errors. On the other hand, if your serialized attributes are that big, you might want to rethink what you're doing. At least move them into a separate table and use a larger column type if your server allows it.

One of the first things that new Rails developers do when they discover the `serialize` declaration is to use it to store a hash of arbitrary objects related to user preferences. Why bother with the complexity of a separate preferences table if you can denormalize that data into the users table instead?

```
class User < ActiveRecord::Base
  # NOTE: Bad example, see the next section
  serialize :preferences, Hash
end
```

The optional second parameter (used in the example) takes a class that limits the type of object that can be stored. The serialized object must be of that class on retrieval or `SerializationTypeMismatch` will be raised.

The `serialize` method does not give us an easy way to set a default value. That's unfortunate, because it would be nice to be able to assume that our preferences attribute is already initialized when we want to use it.

For various reasons, the `serialize` method feels dated and useless compared to newer, related features. Read on to learn more about alternatives.

9.4.1 `ActiveRecord::Store`

Rails 3.2 introduced a `store` declaration, which uses `serialize` behind the scenes to declare a single-column key/value store.

```
class User < ApplicationRecord
  store :settings
end
```

An added benefit of using `store` is that its assigned serialized attribute is set to an empty `HashWithIndifferentAccess` by default, saving you from the kind of acrobatics we described in older editions of this book and giving you the capability to use either string or symbolic keys.

```
>> u = User.new(settings: {promos_ok: true})
>> u.settings
=> {'promos_ok' => true}
>> u.settings[:promos_ok]
=> true
```

9.4.1.1 Marshalling

Serializing and de-serializing data to get it in and out of the text column in your database is referred to as *marshalling*. You can use the default (YAML) or specify a different option using `:coder`, like this:

```
class User < ApplicationRecord
  store :settings, coder: JSON
end
```

The `:coder` option works with any object that responds to `load` and `dump`, so it's easy to roll your own implementation.

```
module B64Coder
  extend self

  def load(data)
    return {} unless data
    Marshal.load(Base64.decode64(data))
  end

  def dump(data)
    Base64.encode64(Marshal.dump(data || {}))
  end

end
```

9.4.1.2 Accessing Stored Data

Writing to a store accessor method will create a key/value pair within the serialized hash attribute, as shown in the following example:

```
>> user = User.new
=> #<User id: nil, preferences: {}, ...>
>> user.inline_help = false
=> false
```

```
>> user.preferences
=> {"inline_help"=>false}
```

Alternatively, you can use the `store_accessor` declaration to declare read/write accessors for a serialized attribute.

```
store_accessor :inline_help
```

If you only have a few accessors, you might want to just declare them inline as options to the `store` declaration:

```
class User < ApplicationRecord
  store :settings, accessors: [:inline_help, :promos_ok]
end
```

9.4.1.3   Overwriting Default Accessors

It's possible to do type coercion and other kinds of manipulation of the data being read and written from the store by overriding the generated reader and writer methods.

In the following example, `volume_adjustment` is automatically converted to/from an integer in the model code.

```
class Song < ApplicationRecord
  store :settings, accessors: [:volume_adjustment]

  def volume_adjustment
    super.to_i
  end

  def volume_adjustment=(decibels)
    super(decibels.to_s)
  end
end
```

Note that in our example, overwriting `volume_adjustment=` is not actually necessary; any value passed in will be coerced to a string on its way into the database.

9.4.1.4   Validations

If you define accessors, then you can also specify validations (with the exception of uniqueness, since it relies on database queries). Going back to the song example, let's apply a range constraint to the volume adjustment.

```
class Song < ApplicationRecord
  store :settings, accessors: [:volume_adjustment]

  validates_inclusion_of :volume_adjustment, :in => 1..10
```

9.4.1.5 Limitations

Unfortunately, Rails gives you one level of accessor syntax sugar and that's it. In other words, there's no built-in support for accessing *nested* hash values. The other big limitation is that it isn't possible to include data in serialized stores as part of SQL queries, which limits the use of `store` primarily to things such as user preferences and other kinds of data strictly bound in use to a particular object instance.

Don't despair, though. Backing a serialized attribute with a full-fledged object graph, including queries, is not only possible, it opens up some pretty amazing possibilities. Read on for more details.

9.4.2 Native Database Support for Serialized Attributes

Rails 4 offered huge improvements in how we can include non-relational data inside of relational tables by including support for PostgreSQL native Hstore (https://www.postgresql.org/docs/9.4/static/hstore.html), JSON, and JSONb type columns.

Now you can back serialized attributes with those more advanced column types instead of just a plain `text` field, and you gain the capability to query those fields via SQL expressions. Supposedly, the performance of these fields can rival dedicated NoSQL stores such as MongoDB, giving you the best of both worlds.

Note that there are significant differences between the column types:

`hstore` Stores values as strings. Single-level key/value store, no nesting allowed. May require type coercion on both database and application levels.

`json` Keeps exact copy of input provided, meaning that any and all operations involve re-parsing. Requires explicit indexing for querying. Preserves key ordering on output.

`jsonb` Keeps a binary representation in order to avoid re-parsing. Automatically indexed, meaning it's possible to query any path without a specific index. Does not preserve key ordering.

Don't bother using Hstore. Support for it is buggy and it has too many limitations when it comes to typecasting.

Both JSON types support automatic type conversion of arrays, numerics, booleans and nulls, as well as nesting. The PostgreSQL section has more detailed information about these types.

⚠ If you're setting a default value, like an empty hash, for any of these column types, make sure to pass the migration default value a Ruby hash { } and not a string (aka JSON) representation of a hash.

Querying JSON fields involves non-standard functions and operators (https://www .postgresql.org/docs/current/static/functions-json.html). It also may require quite a bit of attention paid to having the right indexes in place. Nando Vieira provides a lengthy and detailed explanation of the topic, including performance benchmarks at http://nandovieira.com/using-postgresql-and-jsonb-with-ruby-on-rails.

🔍 Note that if you're in a controller and you store params (the whole object or a subset) in a serialized field, under the covers Rails will invoke `to_unsafe_h` in order to transform the params into a hash for storage. Therefore, a side effect to take into consideration is that potentially un-permitted attributes will make it into storage.

9.5   Enums

One of the newest significant additions to Active Record (introduced in Rails 4.1) is the capability to set an attribute as an enumerable. Once an attribute has been set as an enumerable, Active Record will restrict the assignment of the attribute to a collection of predefined values.

🔍 Before you read any further, go check out this blog post[6] by the fine folks at Foraker Labs. It describes how to use the Enumerated Type[7] gem with Active Record, which I think has considerable advantages over Rails' own implementation.

To declare an enumerable attribute, use the `enum` macro-style class method, passing it an attribute name and an array of status values that the attribute can be set to.

```
class Post < ApplicationRecord
  enum status: %i(draft published archived)
  ...
end
```

----

6. https://www.foraker.com/blog/enumerated-types-in-activerecord
7. https://github.com/rafer/enumerated_type

Active Record implicitly maps each predefined value of an enum attribute to an integer, therefore the column type of the enum attribute must be an integer as well. By default, an enum attribute will be set to nil. To set an initial state, you can set a default value in a migration. It's recommended to set this value to the first declared status, which would map to 0.

```
class CreatePosts < ActiveRecord::Migration
  def change
    create_table :posts do |t|
      t.integer :status, default: 0
    end
  end
end
```

For instance, given our example, the default status of a Post model would be "draft":

```
>> Post.new.status
=> "draft"
```

You should never have to work with the underlying integer data type of an enum attribute, as Active Record creates both predicate and bang methods for each status value.

```
post.draft!
post.draft?        # => true
post.published?    # => false
post.status        # => "draft"

post.published!
post.published?    # => true
post.draft?        # => false
post.status        # => "published"

post.status = nil
post.status.nil?   # => true
post.status        # => nil
```

Active Record also provides scope methods for each status value. Invoking one of these scopes will return all records with that given status.

```
Post.draft
# Post Load (0.1ms)  SELECT "posts".* FROM "posts"
  WHERE "posts"."status" = 0
```

9.5.1   Prefixes and Suffixes

You probably shouldn't have more than one enum in a single class. But if for some reason you do, it's fairly easy to run into a name-collision problem with your statuses.

```
class Issue < ActiveRecord::Base
  enum :state, [:open, :closed]
  enum :other_state, [:something, :closed]
end
```

In the preceding example, the generated methods closed, closed?, and closed! for :other_state would collide and raise an error. Solve the problem by introducing either a :prefix or suffix parameter.

```
enum :state, [:open, :closed]
enum :other_state, [:something, :closed], prefix: 'other_state' end
```

9.5.2   Reflection

Active Record creates a class method with a pluralized name of the defined enum on the model that returns a hash with the key and value of each status. In our preceding example, the Post model would have a class method named statuses.

```
>> Post.statuses
=> {"draft"=>0, "published"=>1, "archived"=>2}
>> Post.statuses[:published]
=> 1
```

You should only need to access this class method when you need to know the underlying ordinal value of an enum.

9.5.3   State Machine

The enum feature provides Active Record with simple state machine functionality out of the box. If your application requires advanced state machine features such as declarative event definitions, status transition callbacks and conditional state transitions, try https://github.com/pluginaweek/state_machine.

9.6   Generating Secure Tokens

It's pretty common for Active Record models to need unique random tokens. Traditionally, you could create one like this.

```
class User < ActiveRecord::Base
  before_create :generate_token

  private
```

```
def generate_token
  self.token = loop do
    t = SecureRandom.hex(16)
    break t unless User.where(token: t).exists?
  end
end
```

Rails 5 introduces a useful macro-style class method called `has_secure_token` that wraps this functionality up into a one-liner.

```
class User < ApplicationRecord
  has_secure_token
```

User instances will automatically get a unique `token`.

```
>> user = User.create
=> #<User id: ...

>> user.token
=> "njHcvhKSwX9toZKEe9YETA8C"
```

The `has_secure_token` method takes an optional name parameter. Pass it a symbol matching the name of your database field.

```
class User < ApplicationRecord
  has_secure_token :auth_token
```

    ⚷ Stuck on an older version of Rails? There's an exact backport of this functionality for Rails 3 and 4 available at https://github.com/robertomiranda/has_secure_token.

9.6.1   Migrations

Under the covers, Rails uses `SecureRandom.base58(24)`, and collisions are very highly unlikely. However, it is still advisable to put a unique constraint on the database column just in case. Along those lines, if you declare the type of your column as `token` in a migration, then Rails will automatically add it as a string with a unique index.

9.6.2   Regenerating a Token

If for some reason you need to expire or otherwise reset your token, just call `regenerate_<name_of_token>`:

```
>> user.regenerate_token
```

```
   (0.1ms) begin transaction
 User Exists (0.1ms) SELECT 1 AS one FROM "users"...
 SQL (0.2ms) UPDATE "users" SET "updated_at" = ?, "token" = ? WHERE
 "users"."id" = ?  [["updated_at", 2016-11-21 22:20:33 UTC], ["token",
 "YDSNntcYiVKm8ueYy2zAXhqq"], ["id", 2]]
   (8.1ms) commit transaction
=> true

>> u.token
=> "YDSNntcYiVKm8ueYy2zAXhqq"
```

9.7   Calculation Methods

All Active Record classes have a `calculate` method that provides easy access to aggregate function queries in the database. Methods for `count`, `sum`, `average`, `minimum`, and `maximum` have been added as convenient shortcuts.

Calculation methods can be used in combination with Active Record relation methods to customize the query. Since calculation methods do not return an `ActiveRecord::Relation`, they must be the last method in a scope chain.

There are two basic forms of output:

Single aggregate value The single value is type cast to `Fixnum` for COUNT, `Float` for AVG, and the given column's type for everything else.

Grouped values This returns an ordered hash of the values and groups them by the `:group` option. It takes either a column name or the name of a `belongs_to` association.

The following examples illustrate the usage of various calculation methods.

```
Person.calculate(:count, :all) # The same as Person.count

# SELECT AVG(age) FROM people
Person.average(:age)

# Selects the minimum age for everyone with a last name other than 'Drake'
Person.where.not(last_name: 'Drake').minimum(:age)

# Selects the minimum age for any family without any minors
Person.having('min(age) > 17').group(:last_name).minimum(:age)
```

9.7.1   `average(column_name, *options)`

Calculates the average value on a given column. The first parameter should be a symbol identifying the column to be averaged.

9.7.2 `count(column_name, *options)`

Count operates using three different approaches. Count without parameters will return a count of all the rows for the model. Count with a `column_name` will return a count of all the rows for the model with the supplied column present.

9.7.3 `ids`

Return all the IDs for a relation based on its table's primary key.

```
User.ids # SELECT id FROM "users"
```

9.7.4 `maximum(column_name, *options)`

Calculates the maximum value on a given column. The first parameter should be a symbol identifying the column to be calculated.

9.7.5 `minimum(column_name, *options)`

Calculates the minimum value on a given column. The first parameter should be a symbol identifying the column to be calculated.

9.7.6 `pluck(*column_names)`

The `pluck` method queries the database for one or more columns of the underlying table of a model.

```
>> User.pluck(:id, :name)
=> [[1, 'Obie']]
>> User.pluck(:name)
=> ['Obie']
```

It returns an array of values of the specified columns with the corresponding data type.

9.7.7 `sum(column_name, *options)`

Calculates a summed value in the database using SQL. The first parameter should be a symbol identifying the column to be summed.

9.8 Batch Operations

Even though Active Record doesn't have too much in the way of optimizations for batch operations, that kind of work is sufficiently common as to deserve some explanation.

In this section, we cover the basics of CRUD operations on large datasets.

9.8.1   Creating Many Records

Imagine that we need to import a lot of records into a database, records that are stored in a CSV file. A naive, Rails-based approach to this challenge might be to simply load the CSV content using Ruby's standard CSV API and then iterate over each row, doing an Active Record `create!` for each:

```
CSV.foreach("path/to/import/items.csv") do |row|
  Item.create! legacy_id: row[0], name: row[1], etc...
end
```

When executed, that code would result in many `INSERT INTO 'items'...` kind of SQL statements being generated and run in the dataset. It would work and is easy to understand. But since inserts are relatively slow operations, the naive approach could take a very long time to execute given a large dataset.

A better approach would be to leverage the database's capabilities for doing bulk imports. However, since that functionality is not natively supported in Active Record, we'll need to drop down an abstraction level and execute custom SQL directly on the database connection.

Postgres, MySQL and the other dominant relational databases can all do at least two different types of bulk import operations. The first is simply to provide more than one list to the `VALUES` clause of the `INSERT INTO table_name` statement, aka a "multi-insert."

In the following example, we first take the effort of batching the input data, so we don't blow memory consumption out of control. It'll still chew up a bunch of memory on the Ruby side of the equation to build up the array, but the database side will be at least an order of magnitude faster.

```
CSV.foreach("path/to/import/items.csv") do |row|
  items << "('#{row[0]}','#{row[1]}'...)"
end

BATCH_SIZE = 1000

while items.any?
  next_batch = items.shift(BATCH_SIZE)
  sql = "INSERT INTO items(legacy_id, name, ...)
                VALUES " + next_batch.join(", ")
  ActiveRecord::Base.connection.execute(sql)
end
```

The value of BATCH_SIZE in the example is arbitrary. If you are faced with a situation requiring a lot of data importation on a regular basis, it'll probably be worthwhile to experiment with your batch size to find a value that is optimal for performance based on the shape of the input data and the configuration of your network and database hardware.

Multi-inserts can be quite tedious if you have a lot of columns because the columns names and values from the array must line up perfectly. It's also worth mentioning that with this and any other approach that puts incoming data directly into the database without going through Active Record, you had better make sure that incoming data is sanitized.

9.8.1.1 Bulk Insert Considerations

The two approaches have tradeoffs. The first is slow but enables you to rely on validations, security, and other logic present in the Active Record models. The first approach also makes it easy to create association instances based on denormalized input data. Since you're doing discrete create operations, you'd just add additional ones for dependent objects.

The multi-insert approach is faster, possibly *way faster*, but you lose validations, easy associations, and security protections (like sanitization). You also may need to worry about key constraints, what to do with duplicate data, and other kinds of error conditions. If not done in Ruby, that logic will need to be implemented on the database side (https://www.postgresql.org/docs/current/static/sql-insert.html), else you'll need to write additional programs that do post-import cleanup duties.

You should also put some thought into *transactions*, which affect both performance and program logic. A simple optimization for the first approach would be to wrap the individual create statements into a single large transaction like this:

```
Item.transaction do
  CSV.foreach("path/to/import/items.csv") do |row|
    Item.create! legacy_id: row[0], name: row[1], etc...
end
```

Without that call to Item.transaction, the default behavior for Active Record is to wrap each operation in its own transaction, and that is slow. However, you need to keep in mind the meaning of transaction—if there is any failure, none of the data will be inserted. Depending on your requirements, that could be a great or a terrible thing.

ACTIVE RECORD IMPORT GEM

There's a RubyGem called `activerecord-import` that is specifically made for simplifying multi-insert code in Rails. Not only does it provide a useful abstraction for simplifying your code, it also understands Active Record associations and can generate complex relationship inserts, while optimizing for the minimum number of statements needed and automatically avoiding N+1 insert problems.

The gem adds an `import` class method to Active Record. Here's a simple refactoring of our first example.

```
items = []
CSV.foreach("path/to/import/items.csv") do |row|
  item = Item.new legacy_id: row[0], name: row[1], etc...
end
Item.import items
```

In this case, we actually instantiated `Item` objects, but the library can also accept representations as arrays of data (and works faster that way).

```
items = []
CSV.foreach("path/to/import/items.csv") do |row|
  items << [row[0], row[1], etc...]
end
Item.import items, validate: false
```

The `import` method take options such as `validate`. Using raw data and turning off validation yields the fastest performance. Just as with its native SQL counterpart, each child array represents an individual record, and its list of values must appear in the same order as the columns appear in the database.

The other significant option to the `import` method is `batch_size`, so that you can tune performance.

This essential gem has a lot to offer, more than we can completely cover in this book. Learn more at https://github.com/zdennis/activerecord-import.

9.8.1.2 Using COPY to Import Millions of Rows

The INSERT based approaches we've covered so far do not really scale to the importation of millions of rows of data. To do that (assuming we have access to CSV formatted data that is sufficiently pre-processed) we can take advantage of bulk file import functionality that is usually built into the database itself. The example we present is based on Postgres' COPY FROM extension to the SQL standard[8] and uses functionality provided by the pg RubyGem (https://bitbucket.org/ged/ruby-pg/wiki/Home).

⚠ Caveat Importer: Whether you can use operations like COPY FROM may also be affected by whether you have access to the database server file system and many other factors.

```
# Setup raw connection
conn = ActiveRecord::Base.connection.raw_connection
conn.exec("COPY items (legacy_id, name, ...) FROM STDIN WITH CSV")

file = File.open('path/to/import/items.csv', 'r')
while !file.eof?
  # Add row to copy data
  conn.put_copy_data(file.readline)
end

# When finished with the import, call put_copy_end
# method provided by Ruby's PG driver
conn.put_copy_end

# check the result for errors and print them
while res = conn.get_result
  if err = res.error_message
    p err
  end
end
```

9.8.2   Reading Many Records at Once

Now that we've discussed putting a lot of data into the database at once, let's turn around and analyze how to get a lot of data out of the database all at once. This is yet another area where naive approaches have huge negative performance implications.

Let's say we want to generate a large CSV call list based on person data. We write a Rake task featuring a query and a loop over the results. Then we puts the fields we want to capture.

```
namespace :export do
  task :call-list do
    puts "name,phone"
```

---

8. https://www.postgresql.org/docs/current/static/sql-copy.html

```
Contact.where(...).each do |contact|
  puts "#{contact.name},#{contact.phone}"
end
```

Hopefully, this code is fairly self-explanatory. For simplicity's sake, the output is piped to an output file via the command line.

```
$ bundle exec rake export:call-list > new-call-list.csv
```

The biggest problem with this approach is that it costs a lot of memory. If the query returns a bunch of results, Active Record is going to instantiate objects for *all of them* before it starts writing anything to the output. There is no automatic use of cursors or anything of the sort.

⚓ Generating CSV output the way we do it in these examples can get tedious and error-prone. If you want to generate CSV output, you should definitely use the classic FasterCSV gem available at http://fastercsv.rubyforge .org/.

9.8.2.1 Optimizing Large Reads with `find_each`

For a job like this one, it wouldn't hurt to just break the processing of results into more digestible chunks. As long as those chunks fit into Ruby's working memory (heap) it shouldn't slow down too much. The code is not too much different either because batched queries are built into the Active Record API.

```
namespace :export do
  task :call-list do
    puts "name,phone"
    Contact.where(...).find_each do |contact|
      puts "#{contact.name},#{contact.phone}"
    end
```

The `find_each` method executes in batches of 1000 records by default. To use a different batch size, just pass it as an option.

`:batch_size` Specifies the size of the batch. Defaults to 1000.

`:begin_at` Specifies the primary key value to start from, inclusive of the value.

`:finish` Specifies the primary key value to end at, inclusive of the value.

`:error_on_ignore` Raises an error if the order and limit have to be ignored due to batching.

⚲ Using the full suite of `find_each` options, you can break big read jobs into work shared by multiple workers operating on the same processing queue. For example, you could give the first worker all the records with ids between 0 and 1000 and have worker 2 handle from 1001 to 2000, etc.

The sort order for `find_each` queries is automatically set to ascending on the primary key (`id ASC`) in order to make the batch ordering work. You can't set a query limit either, because that parameter is used to control the batch sizes.

⚲ Note that in the example provided, we are (presumably) only using some data that maps directly to database columns, not anything that actually requires behavior coded in the Active Record object. That means that a far more efficient and faster way to accomplish the same job is to use `pluck` since it yields arrays and avoids Active Record instantiation altogether.

9.8.2.2   Reading Groups of Records at a Time Using `find_in_batches`

In contrast to its sister method `find_each` (that yields once for each record in the entire result set) the `find_in_batches` method yields groups of records as an array. Pass it a block that takes the group as an argument, or chain it together with other enumerable methods.

```
namespace :export do
  task :call-list do
    puts "batch_num,name,phone"
    Contact.where(...).find_in_batches.with_index do |contacts, n|
      contacts.each do
        puts "#{n},#{contact.name},#{contact.phone}"
    end
```

9.8.2.3   Operating on Groups of Records Using `in_batches`

The third sister in this trifecta is `in_batches`, which (as you might guess) is very similar to `find_in_batches`. The difference is that instead of executing the find query itself, it yields an `ActiveRecord::Relation` object representing the batch. You can then use that relation to do operations other than loading an Active Record instance.

For example, you can use `in_batches` to efficiently clean up old data without thrashing your DB.

```
namespace :clean do
  task :notifications do
```

```
q = ['created_at < ?', 1.year.ago]
Notification.where(q).in_batches do |rel|
  rel.delete_all
  sleep(10) # throttle
end
```

Or you could make all of your users awesome!

```
User.in_batches.update_all(awesome: true)
```

The `in_batches` method yields groups of 1000 records by default. Its options are very similar to its sisters with the following two exceptions.

`:of` Specifies the size of the batch.

`:load` Specifies whether the relation should be loaded. Defaults to `false` because otherwise this method would behave almost exactly like `find_in_batches`.

9.8.3   Updating Many Records at Once

We already covered the use of `update_all` in Chapter 5, "Working with Active Record." As a reminder, this method creates a single SQL UPDATE statement. Active Record objects are not instantiated, and all matching rows are updated at once in a single transaction. Since individual objects are not involved, no callbacks or other Active Record logic gets executed.

Active Record actually has two very similar `update_all` methods, one on `ActiveRecord::Base` and the other on `ActiveRecord::Relation`. I consider the first to be supremely dangerous for use in production code because it indiscriminately updates all rows in a given table.

```
>> Event.update_all starts_at: Date.today
  SQL (8.4ms) UPDATE "events" SET "starts_at" = '2016-11-28'
=> 1
>> Event.where(id: 1).update_all starts_at: Date.today
  SQL (0.1ms) UPDATE "events" SET "starts_at" = '2016-11-28' WHERE "events"."id" = ? [["id", 1]]
=> 0
```

If the resulting N+1 query doesn't scare you off, and you need to trigger validations, then instead of using `update_all`, you can use plain ole `update`, a method that's been part of Active Record's base class since the beginning. Additionally, Rails 5 provides `ActiveRecord::Relation` its own `update` method. Both *respect validation*, but failure of any particular row update *does not cause the entire operation to fail*.

9.8.4   Bulk Deletion

Deleting more than one record at a time, especially through Active Record associations, can be tricky. Let's discuss some considerations to keep in mind using a hypothetical account registration system represented by the following Active Record models:

```
class Account
  has_many :registrations
  has_many :persons, through: :registrations

class Registration
  belongs_to :account
  belongs_to :person

class Person
  has_many :registrations
  has_many :accounts, through: :registrations
```

First of all, let's talk about what happens when dependency parameters are ommitted from the relationship declarations.

```
Person.where(criteria).delete_all
```

This bit of Ruby results in the following SQL mass deletion:

```
DELETE FROM `persons` where ...
```

Notice that no registrations are deleted.

Calling `destroy_all` has a lot more complex behavior, but also does not automatically remove any associated registration records.

```
Person.destroy_all
```

This code destroys data by instantiating each record and calling its #destroy method. Callbacks are executed, and the collection of objects that were destroyed will be returned. Each will be frozen, to reflect that no changes should be made (since they can't be persisted).

Instantiation, callback execution, and deletion of each record can be time consuming when you're removing many records at once. It generates at least one `SQL DELETE` query per record (or possibly more, to enforce your callbacks).

```
DELETE FROM `persons` where id `persons`.`id` = 1
DELETE FROM `persons` where id `persons`.`id` = 2
DELETE FROM `persons` where id `persons`.`id` = 3
-- and so on...
```

Basically, if you want to delete many rows quickly, without concern for their associations or callbacks, use `delete_all`.

9.8.4.1   Deletion of Dependent Data

If the relationships are defined with dependent behavior, then associated records can be automatically deleted.

```
class Account
  has_many :registrations, dependent: :destroy
  has_many :persons, through: :registrations

class Registration
  belongs_to :account
  belongs_to :person

class Person
  has_many :registrations, dependent: :destroy
  has_many :accounts, through: :registrations
```

In contrast to the previous example, now deleting an instance of either an account or a person will bulk delete associated registration records.

9.8.4.2   Deleting via Associations

It's preferable in most cases to rely on the machinery of Active Record's dependent logic to bulk delete associated records. Why? Because like we stated at the opening of the chapter, things can get tricky. For example, what if (in the name of being explicit) we chose to do person deletion in two steps, first deleting registrations.

```
person.registrations.destroy
```

If there is no `:dependent` option set on `has_many :registrations`, then the associations are *nullified*, that is, the registration's `person_id` foreign key will be set to null, and you'd have *orphaned* registration records dirtying your database. That may or may not be what you wanted to happen. Probably not.

What if the `:dependent` option is set?

```
class Person
  has_many :registrations, dependent: :destroy
  has_many :accounts, through: :registrations
```

Then even calling `delete_all` on the association like this

```
person.registrations.delete_all
```

does not do exactly what you might expect. The resulting SQL will look something like this (join ommitted for clarity):

```
DELETE FROM registrations WHERE registrations.person_id = 1 AND
registrations.id IN (1, 2, 3...)
```

Depending on whether the `:dependent` option is set to `destroy`, Active Record may also go ahead and query the data so that it can return frozen objects.

In this case, it's probably better to just be a bit more explicit rather than use the association.

```
Registration.where(person_id: person.id).delete_all
```

results in

```
DELETE FROM registrations WHERE registrations.person_id = 1
```

That's signficantly cleaner and faster.

9.9   Single-Table Inheritance (STI)

A lot of applications start out with a `User` model of some sort. Over time, as different kinds of users emerge, it might make sense to make a greater distinction between them. `Admin` and `Guest` classes are introduced, as subclasses of `User`. Now, the shared behavior can reside in `User`, and subtype behavior can be pushed down to subclasses. However, all user data can still reside in the `users` table—all you need to do is introduce a `type` column that will hold the name of the class to be instantiated for a given row.

To delve into the topic of single-table inheritance, let's turn back to our example of a recurring `Timesheet` class. We need to know how many `billable_hours` are outstanding for a given user. The calculation can be implemented in various ways, but in this case we've chosen to write a pair of class and instance methods on the `Timesheet` class:

```
class Timesheet < ActiveRecord::Base
  ...

  def billable_hours_outstanding
    if submitted?
      billable_weeks.map(&:total_hours).sum
    else
      0
    end
  end
```

```
def self.billable_hours_outstanding_for(user)
  user.timesheets.map(&:billable_hours_outstanding).sum
end
```

I'm not suggesting that this is great code. It works, but it's inefficient, and that `if/else` condition is a little fishy. Its shortcomings become apparent once requirements emerge related to marking a `Timesheet` as paid. The requirements force us to modify `Timesheet`'s `billable_hours_outstanding` method even though it is unrelated code:

```
def billable_hours_outstanding
  if submitted? && not paid?
    billable_weeks.map(&:total_hours).sum
  else
    0
  end
end
```

That latest change is a clear violation of the *open-closed principle*, which urges you to write code that is open for extension, but closed for modification. We know that we violated the principle, because we were forced to change the `billable_hours_outstanding` method to accommodate the new `Timesheet` status. Though it may not seem like a large problem in our simple example, consider the amount of conditional code that will end up in the `Timesheet` class once we start having to implement functionality such as `paid_hours` and `unsubmitted_hours`.[9]

So what's the answer to this messy question of the constantly changing conditional? Given that you're reading the section of the book about single-table inheritance, it's probably no big surprise that we think one good answer is to use object-oriented inheritance. To do so, let's break our original `Timesheet` class into four classes.

```
class Timesheet < ActiveRecord::Base
  ...

  def self.billable_hours_outstanding_for(user)
    user.timesheets.map(&:billable_hours_outstanding).sum
  end
end

class DraftTimesheet < Timesheet
  def billable_hours_outstanding
    0
  end
end
```

---

9. http://en.wikipedia.org/wiki/Open/closed_principle has a good summary.

```
class SubmittedTimesheet < Timesheet
  def billable_hours_outstanding
    billable_weeks.map(&:total_hours).sum
  end
end
```

Now when the requirements demand the capability to calculate partially paid timesheets, we need only add some behavior to a `PaidTimesheet` class. No messy conditional statements in sight!

```
class PaidTimesheet < Timesheet
  def billable_hours_outstanding
    billable_weeks.map(&:total_hours).sum - paid_hours
  end
end
```

9.9.1 Mapping Inheritance to the Database

Mapping object inheritance effectively to a relational database is not one of those problems with a definitive solution. We're only going to deep dive into the one mapping strategy that Rails supports natively, which is single-table inheritance, called STI for short.

In STI, you establish one table in the database to hold all of the records for any sub-type of object in a given inheritance hierarchy. In Active Record STI, that one table is named after the top parent class of the hierarchy. In the example we've been considering, that table would be named `timesheets`.

Hey, that's what it was called before, right? Yes, but to enable STI we have to add a `type` column. It will contain a string representing the type of the stored object. The following migration would properly set up the database for our example:

```
class AddTypeToTimesheet < ActiveRecord::Migration
  def change
    add_column :timesheets, :type, :string
  end
end
```

No default value is needed. Once the type column is added to an Active Record model, Rails will automatically take care of keeping it populated with the right value. Using the console, we can see this behavior in action:

```
>> d = DraftTimesheet.create
>> d.type
=> 'DraftTimesheet'
```

When you try to find an object using the query methods of a base STI class, Rails will automatically instantiate objects using the appropriate subclass.

This is especially useful in polymorphic situations, such as the timesheet example we've been describing, where we retrieve all the records for a particular user and then call methods that behave differently depending on the object's class.

```
>> Timesheet.first
=> #<DraftTimesheet:0x2212354...>
```

9.9.2   STI Considerations

Although Rails makes it extremely simple to use single-table inheritance, there are a few caveats that you should keep in mind.

To begin with, you cannot have an attribute on two different subclasses with the same name but a different type. Since Rails uses one table to store all subclasses, these attributes with the same name occupy the same column in the table. Frankly, there's not much of a reason why that should be a problem unless you've made some pretty bad data-modeling decisions.

More importantly, you need to have one column per attribute on any subclass, and any attribute that is not shared by all the subclasses must accept `nil` values. In the recurring example, `PaidTimesheet` has a `paid_hours` column that is not used by any of the other subclasses. `DraftTimesheet` and `SubmittedTimesheet` will not use the `paid_hours` column and leave it null in the database. In order to validate data for columns not shared by all subclasses, you must use Active Record validations and not the database.

Third, it is not a good idea to have subclasses with too many unique attributes. If you do, you will have one database table with many null values in it. Normally, a tree of subclasses with a large number of unique attributes suggests that something is wrong with your application design and that you should refactor. So if you have an STI table that is getting out of hand, it is time to reconsider your decision to use inheritance to solve your particular problem. Perhaps your base class is too abstract?

As an STI table gets wider and wider, full of nullable columns, it begins to resemble a schemaless document store like MongoDB. If you designed your application with an STI table as a main/primary data repository, maybe you should not be using a relational database in the first place? You might even be in for a world of hurt in the future[10] as the application gets more complicated and you want to stop using STI.

---

10. https://about.futurelearn.com/blog/refactoring-rails-sti/

Finally, legacy database constraints may require a different name in the database for the `type` column. In this case, you can set the new column name using the class setter method `inheritance_column` in the base class. For the `Timesheet` example, we could do the following:

```
class Timesheet < ActiveRecord::Base
  self.inheritance_column = 'object_type'
end
```

Now Rails will automatically populate the `object_type` column with the object's type.

9.9.3   STI and Associations

It seems pretty common for applications, particularly data-management ones, to have models that are very similar in terms of their data payload, mostly varying in their behavior and associations to each other. If you used object-oriented languages prior to Rails, you're probably already accustomed to breaking down problem domains into hierarchical structures.

Take, for instance, a Rails application that deals with the population of states, counties, cities, and neighborhoods. All of these are places, which might lead you to define an STI class named `Place` as shown in Listing 9.2. I've also included the database schema for clarity[11]:

Listing 9.2   The places database schema and the place class

```
# == Schema Information
#
# Table name: places
#
# id :integer(11) not null, primary key
# region_id :integer(11)
# type :string(255)
# name :string(255)
# description :string(255)
# latitude :decimal(20, 1)
# longitude :decimal(20, 1)
# population :integer(11)
# created_at :datetime
# updated_at :datetime
class Place < ActiveRecord::Base
end
```

---

11. For autogenerated schema information added to the top of your model classes, try the annotate gem at https://github.com/ctran/annotate_models

`Place` is, in essence, an abstract class. It should not be instantiated, but there is no foolproof way to enforce that in Ruby. (No big deal, this isn't Java!) Now let's go ahead and define concrete subclasses of `Place`:

```
class State < Place
  has_many :counties, foreign_key: 'region_id'
end

class County < Place
  belongs_to :state, foreign_key: 'region_id'
  has_many :cities, foreign_key: 'region_id'
end

class City < Place
  belongs_to :county, foreign_key: 'region_id'
end
```

You might be tempted to try adding a `cities` association to `State`, knowing that `has_many :through` works with both `belongs_to` and `has_many` target associations. It would make the `State` class look something like this:

```
class State < Place
  has_many :counties, foreign_key: 'region_id'
  has_many :cities, through: :counties
end
```

That would certainly be cool, if it worked. Unfortunately, in this particular case, since there's only one underlying table that we're querying, there simply isn't a way to distinguish among the different kinds of objects in the query:

```
Mysql::Error: Not unique table/alias: 'places': SELECT places.* FROM
places INNER JOIN places ON places.region_id = places.id WHERE
((places.region_id = 187912) AND ((places.type = 'County'))) AND
((places.`type` = 'City' ))
```

What would we have to do to make it work? Well, the most realistic would be to use specific foreign keys, instead of trying to overload the meaning of `region_id` for all the subclasses. For starters, the `places` table would look like the example in Listing 9.3.

Listing 9.3   The places database schema revised
```
# == Schema Information
#
# Table name: places
#
```

```
# id :integer(11) not null, primary key
# state_id :integer(11)
# county_id :integer(11)
# type :string(255)
# name :string(255)
# description :string(255)
# latitude :decimal(20, 1)
# longitude :decimal(20, 1)
# population :integer(11)
# created_at :datetime
# updated_at :datetime
```

The subclasses would be simpler without the `:foreign_key` options on the associations. Plus you could use a regular `has_many` relationship from `State` to `City`, instead of the more complicated `has_many :through`.

```
class State < Place
  has_many :counties
  has_many :cities
end

class County < Place
  belongs_to :state
  has_many :cities
end

class City < Place
  belongs_to :county
end
```

Of course, all those null columns in the places table won't win you any friends with relational database purists. That's nothing, though. Just a little bit later in this chapter we'll take a second, more in-depth look at polymorphic `has_many` relationships, which will make the purists positively hate you.

✎ Interested in trying *Multiple Table Inheritance*? The technique, dubbed MTI for short, lets you define Active Record objects that persist their attributes across more than one table. MTI is not built in to Rails proper, but you can get it via a battle-tested RubyGem called `ActiveRecord::ActsAs`. We don't want to get into the details of how to use it in this book, but you can check it out at https://github.com/hzamani/active_record-acts_as. It seems to be especially suited to tackling design of ecommerce applications.

9.10   Abstract Base Model Classes

In contrast to single-table inheritance, it is possible for Active Record models to share common code via inheritance and still be persisted to different database tables. In fact, every Rails developer uses an abstract model in their code whether they realize it or not: `ActiveRecord::Base`.

The `Base` class has tons of behavior in it, but you can't instantiate one and save it in your database. It must be subclassed to be useful.

Using this technique in your own code involves creating an abstract base model class that persistent subclasses will extend. It's actually one of the simpler techniques that we broach in this chapter.

Let's take the `Place` class from the previous section (refer to Listing 9.3) and revise it to be an abstract base class in Listing 9.4. It's simple really—we just have to add one line of code:

Listing 9.4   The abstract place class

```
class Place < ActiveRecord::Base
  self.abstract_class = true
end
```

Marking an Active Record model abstract is essentially the opposite of making it an STI class with a type column. You're telling Rails: "Hey, I don't want you to assume that there is a table named `places`."

For this refactoring to work, we would next have to establish individual tables for states, counties, and cities. A side effect is that we would no longer be able to query across subtypes with code like `Place.all`.

Both class and instance methods are shared down the inheritance hierarchy of Active Record models. So are constants and other class members brought in through module inclusion. That means we can put all sorts of code inside `Place` that will be useful to its subclasses.

Even after 10+ years, use of abstract classes in Rails does not come with a bunch of hard-and-fast rules to guide you—previous experience with object-oriented techniques and experimentation is really helpful.

9.11 Polymorphic `has_many` Relationships

Rails gives you the capability to make one class belong_to more than one type of another class, as eloquently stated by blogger Mike Bayer:

> The "polymorphic association," on the other hand, while it bears some resemblance to the regular polymorphic union of a class hierarchy, is not really the same since you're only dealing with a particular association to a single target class from any number of source classes, source classes which don't have anything else to do with each other; i.e., they aren't in any particular inheritance relationship and probably are all persisted in completely different tables. In this way, the polymorphic association has a lot less to do with object inheritance and a lot more to do with aspect-oriented programming (AOP); a particular concept needs to be applied to a divergent set of entities which otherwise are not directly related. Such a concept is referred to as a cross-cutting concern, such as, all the entities in your domain need to support a history log of all changes to a common logging table. In the AR example, an Order and a User object are illustrated to both require links to an Address object.[12]

In other words, this is not polymorphism in the typical object-oriented sense of the word; rather, it is something unique to Rails.

9.11.1 Modeling User Comments

In our recurring Time and Expenses example, let's assume that we want both `BillableWeek` and `Timesheet` to have many comments (a shared `Comment` class). A naive way to solve this problem might be to have the `Comment` class belong to both the `BillableWeek` and `Timesheet` classes and have `billable_week_id` and `timesheet_id` as columns in its database table.

```
class Comment < ActiveRecord::Base
  belongs_to :timesheet
  belongs_to :expense_report
end
```

I call that approach naive because it would be difficult to work with and hard to extend. Among other things, you would need to add code to the application to ensure that a `Comment` never belonged to both a `BillableWeek` and a `Timesheet` at the same time. The code to figure out what a given comment is attached to would be cumbersome to write. Even worse, every time you want to be able to add comments to another type of class, you'd have to add another nullable foreign key column to the comments table.

---

12. http://techspot.zzzeek.org/2007/05/29/polymorphic-associations-with-sqlalchemy/

Rails solves this problem in an elegant fashion, by enabling us to define what it terms polymorphic associations. We first mentioned the technique when we described the `polymorphic: true` option of the `belongs_to` association in Chapter 7, "Active Record Associations."

9.11.1.1 The Interface

Using a polymorphic association, we need define only a single `belongs_to` and add a pair of related columns to the underlying database table. From that moment on, any class in our system can have comments attached to it (which would make it commentable), without needing to alter the database schema or the `Comment` model itself.

```
class Comment < ActiveRecord::Base
  belongs_to :commentable, polymorphic: true
end
```

There isn't a `Commentable` class (or module) in our application. We named the association `:commentable` because it accurately describes the interface of objects that will be associated in this way. The name `:commentable` will turn up again on the other side of the association:

```
class Timesheet < ActiveRecord::Base
  has_many :comments, as: :commentable
end

class BillableWeek < ActiveRecord::Base
  has_many :comments, as: :commentable
end
```

Here we have the friendly `has_many` association enhanced with an `:as` parameter. The `:as` marks this association as polymorphic and specifies which interface we are using on the other side of the association. While we're on the subject, the other end of a polymorphic `belongs_to` can be either a `has_many` or a `has_one` and work identically.

9.11.1.2 The Database Columns

Here's a migration that will create the `comments` table:

```
class CreateComments < ActiveRecord::Migration
  def change
    create_table :comments do |t|
      t.text :body
      t.integer :commentable t.string :commentable_type
```

```
      end
    end
  end
```

As you can see, there is a column called `commentable_type` that stores the class name of the associated object. The Migrations API actually gives you a one-line shortcut with the `references` method, which takes a `polymorphic` option:

```
create_table :comments do |t|
  t.text :body
  t.references :commentable, polymorphic: true
end
```

We can see how it comes together using the Rails console (some lines ommitted for brevity):

```
>> c = Comment.create(body: 'I could be commenting anything.')
>> t = TimeSheet.create
>> b = BillableWeek.create
>> c.update_attribute(:commentable, t)
=> true
>> "#{c.commentable_type}: #{c.commentable_id}"
=> "Timesheet: 1"
>> c.update_attribute(:commentable, b)
=> true
>> "#{c.commentable_type}: #{c.commentable_id}"
=> "BillableWeek: 1"
```

As you can tell, both the `Timesheet` and the `BillableWeek` that we played with in the console had the same id (1). Thanks to the `commentable_type` attribute, stored as a string, Rails can figure out which is the correct related object.

9.11.1.3 `has_many` `:through` and Polymorphics

There are some logical limitations that come into play with polymorphic associations. For instance, since it is impossible for Rails to know the tables necessary to join through a polymorphic association, the following hypothetical code, which tries to find everything that the user has commented on, will not work.

```
class Comment < ActiveRecord::Base
  belongs_to :user # author of the comment
  belongs_to :commentable, polymorphic: true
end

class User < ActiveRecord::Base
  has_many :comments
```

```
    has_many :commentables, through: :comments
end
```

```
>> User.first.commentables
          ActiveRecord::HasManyThroughAssociationPolymorphicSourceError:
  Cannot have a has_many :through association 'User#commentables'
  on the polymorphic object
```

If you really want to do so, it's possible to use has_many :through with poly-morphic associations but only by specifying exactly what type of polymorphic asso-ciations you want via the :source_type option. In most cases, you will also need to use the :source option, since the association name will not match the interface name used for the polymorphic association:

```
class User < ActiveRecord::Base
  has_many :comments
  has_many :commented_timesheets, through: :comments,
          source: :commentable, source_type: 'Timesheet'
  has_many :commented_billable_weeks, through: :comments,
          source: :commentable, source_type: 'BillableWeek'
end
```

It's verbose, and the whole scheme loses its elegance if you go this route, but it works:

```
>> User.first.commented_timesheets.to_a
=> [#<Timesheet ...>]
```

9.12   Foreign-Key Constraints

Referential integrity is a relational database concept. It refers to the enforcement of otherwise implied relationships among data and is accomplished using foreign key constraints. Referential integrity ensures that the relationship between rows in two related tables remains synchronized during database operations.

We haven't really mentioned foreign-key constraints so far, even though we're near-ing the end of our Active Record coverage. That's mainly because historically, DHH took a hard line against the use of foreign-key constraints in Rails applications (http://stackoverflow.com/a/7805719/626048), to the extent that some described his view of databases as a "giant hash."

However, the years have worn down this particular Rails opinion, to the extent that Rails 4.2 shipped with built-in support for declaring foreign key constraints in migrations. The feature was championed by Yves Senn and largely made possible due to the work of Rails hero Matthew Higgins, maintainer of the hugely popular Foreigner[13] gem.

Consider the following example based on our recurring online auction system sample code.

```
class User < ActiveRecord::Base
  has_many :auctions
  validates :name, presence: true
end

class Auction < ActiveRecord::Base
  belongs_to :user
  validates :user, presence: true
end
```

Our online auction system has become very popular and soon we are beset by spammers, creating auctions merely for their own nefarious purposes. Not only do they create an auction, but they slam it with bids in a way that makes them show up on our homepage.

The abuse is obvious, so we give the site administrators functionality for deleting users when they notice abuse. We want associated data to get cleaned up, so we make some enhancements to our model.

```
class User < ActiveRecord::Base
  has_many :auctions, dependent: :destroy
  validates :name, presence: true
end

class Auction < ActiveRecord::Base
  belongs_to :user
  validates :user, presence: true

  has_many :bids, dependent: :destroy
end
```

Months later, we're called back in to help diagnose error reports related to the site homepage blowing up with errors when it tries to render the of list popular auctions.

The error we find in the logs is

```
undefined method 'name' for nil:NilClass
```

---

13. https://github.com/matthuhiggins/foreigner

Upon investigation, it appears that some spammy auctions are still in the database, even though they do not have an associated user. Rendering fails when the view tries to output the name of who posted the auction. In the database, their `user_id` field is set to `null`.

But why? Hadn't we set the `:dependent` option to protect ourselves?

Turns out that battling spammers is a cat'n'mouse affair. After awhile, the site administrators got tired of their reactive approach to fighting them. So they hired a data scientist to write software capable of figuring out which users were in the early process of engaging in spammy behavior. The data scientist's nightly job outputs a CSV file.

Manually deleting users based on a CSV file sucks, so our crafty site administrator whipped up a cron job and Rake task to take the data scientist's CSV file and automatically delete users based on it every night.

The first version of his script looked something like this:

```
user_ids = CSV.read(csv_path).flatten
User.destroy(user_ids)
```

This job seemed to work fine, sometimes. If the list of users to delete was particularly long, it timed out. So after skimming some StackOverflow posts, our site administrator changed his Rake task to look like this instead:

```
user_ids = CSV.read(csv_path).flatten
User.where(id: user_ids).delete_all
```

Uh-oh. If you remember our coverage of bulk deletion earlier in this chapter, you realize that the `delete_all` method doesn't instantiate the objects it is deleting, and therefore no `after_destroy` callbacks are fired, which makes our `:dependent` declaration useless.

As we start writing a clean-up script to look for orphaned auctions, it occurs to us that this mess is our own fault for not using foreign key constraints to maintain referential integrity in the first place.

Shaking our heads, we go ahead and add a migration to link auctions and users *at the database level.*

```
def change
  add_foreign_key :auctions, :users
end
```

Active Record

Now the site admin's nightly cron job will fail if it tries to delete a user with auctions. The problem is that all the spammy users have auctions, so we have basically broken the nightly script altogether.

After some analysis, the solution we choose is to let the database *and not our Rails code* handle the entire cleanup job. We do that by specifying a *cascading delete* operation on our foreign key.

```
def change
  add_foreign_key :auctions, :users, on_delete: :cascade
end
```

The `:cascade` option says that we want rows deleted in the child table when corresponding rows are deleted in the parent table.

If we had designed these tables with foreign keys, indexes, and cascading deletes from the start, our migration might have looked like this:

```
create_table :auctions do |t|
  t.references :user, index: true, foreign_key: {on_delete:
      :cascade}
...
```

There might be circumstances wher you want to create a *composite foreign key*, meaning one that references more than one column, which is something that is not natively supported in the migration API. Or you might want to leverage some behavior specific to your particular database version, not natively supported by Rails. In those cases you'll need to execute SQL DDL statements using Active Record's `connection.execute` functionality. If you go down that road, remember to change your schema dumping to `:sql` so that your migration changes are preserved when the database is rebuilt.

9.12.1 Foreign Key Names and Indexes

Foreign key declarations are made like this

```
def change
  add_foreign_key :auctions, :users
end
```

will reference the id column of the users table. If the column names can not be derived from the table names, the migrations API gives you `:column` and `:primary_key` options to let you get more explicit.

Rails will generate a name for every foreign key starting with `fk_rails_` followed by 10 characters that are deterministically generated from the tables and columns involved. The `add_foreign_key` method also has a `:name` option in case you need to specify explicitly use of a different index name for some reason.

9.12.2   Removing Foreign Keys

There are three different ways to remove foreign keys using the Migrations API:

```
# let Active Record figure out the column name
remove_foreign_key :accounts, :branches

# remove foreign key for a specific column
remove_foreign_key :accounts, column: :owner_id

# remove foreign key by name
remove_foreign_key :accounts, name: :special_fk_name
```

9.13   Modules for Reusing Common Behavior

In this section, we'll talk about one strategy for breaking out functionality that is shared between disparate model classes. Instead of using inheritance, we'll put the shared code into modules.

In the section "Polymorphic `has_many` Relationships," we described how to add a commenting feature to our recurring sample Time and Expenses application. We'll continue fleshing out that example, since it lends itself to factoring out into modules.

The requirements we'll implement are as follows: Both users and approvers should be able to add their comments to a `Timesheet` or `ExpenseReport`. Also, since comments are indicators that a timesheet or expense report requires extra scrutiny or processing time, administrators of the application should be able to easily view a list of recent comments. Human nature being what it is, administrators occasionally gloss over the comments without actually reading them, so the requirements specify that a mechanism should be provided for marking comments as "OK" first by the approver, then by the administrator.

Again, here is the polymorphic `has_many :comments, as: :commentable` that we used as the foundation for this functionality:

```
class Timesheet < ActiveRecord::Base
  has_many :comments, as: :commentable
end

class ExpenseReport < ActiveRecord::Base
  has_many :comments, as: :commentable
```

```
end

class Comment < ActiveRecord::Base
  belongs_to :commentable, polymorphic: true
end
```

Next, we enable the controller and action for the administrator that list the 10 most recent comments with links to the item to which they are attached.

```
class Comment < ActiveRecord::Base
  scope :recent, -> { order('created_at desc').limit(10) }
end

class CommentsController < ApplicationController
  before_action :require_admin, only: :recent
  expose(:recent_comments) { Comment.recent }
end
```

Here's some of the simple view template used to display the recent comments.

```
%ul.recent.comments
  - recent_comments.each do |comment|
    %li.comment
      %h4= comment.created_at
      = comment.text
      .meta
        Comment on:
        = link_to comment.commentable.title, comment.commentable
        # Yes, this would result in N+1 selects.
```

So far, so good. The polymorphic association makes it easy to access all types of comments in one listing. In order to find all of the unreviewed comments for an item, we can use a named scope on the `Comment` class together with the comments association.

```
class Comment < ActiveRecord::Base
  scope :unreviewed, -> { where(reviewed: false) }
end

>> timesheet.comments.unreviewed
```

Both `Timesheet` and `ExpenseReport` currently have identical `has_many` methods for comments. Essentially, they both share a common interface. They're commentable!

To minimize duplication, we could specify common interfaces that share code in Ruby by including a module in each of those classes where the module contains the code common to all implementations of the common interface. So, mostly for the sake of example, let's go ahead and define a `Commentable` module to do just that and include it in our model classes:

```
module Commentable
  has_many :comments, as: :commentable
end

class Timesheet < ActiveRecord::Base
  include Commentable
end

class ExpenseReport < ActiveRecord::Base
  include Commentable
end
```

Whoops, this code doesn't work! To fix it, we need to understand an essential aspect of the way that Ruby interprets our code dealing with open classes.

9.13.1   A Review of Class Scope and Contexts

In many other interpreted, OO programming languages, you have two phases of execution—one in which the interpreter loads the class definitions and says "this is the definition of what I have to work with," followed by the phase in which it executes the code. This makes it difficult (though not necessarily impossible) to add new methods to a class dynamically during execution.

In contrast, Ruby lets you add methods to a class at any time. In Ruby, when you type `class MyClass`, you're doing more than simply telling the interpreter to define a class; you're telling it to "execute the following code in the scope of this class."

Let's say you have the following Ruby script:

```
class Foo < ActiveRecord::Base
  has_many :bars
end
class Foo < ActiveRecord::Base
  belongs_to :spam
end
```

When the interpreter gets to line 1, you are telling it to execute the following code (up to the matching end) in the context of the `Foo` class object. Because the `Foo` class object doesn't exist yet, it goes ahead and creates the class. At line 2, we execute the statement `has_many :bars` in the context of the `Foo` class object. Whatever the `has_many` method does, it does right now.

When we again say class Foo at line 4, we are once again telling the interpreter to execute the following code in the context of the Foo class object, but this time, the interpreter already knows about class Foo; it doesn't actually create another class. Therefore, on line 5, we are simply telling the interpreter to execute the belongs_ to :spam statement in the context of that same Foo class object.

In order to execute the has_many and belongs_to statements, those methods need to exist in the context in which they are executed. Because these are defined as class methods in ActiveRecord::Base, and we have previously defined class Foo as extending ActiveRecord::Base, the code will execute without a problem.

However, when we define our Commentable module like this

```
module Commentable
  has_many :comments, as: :commentable
end
```

we get an error when it tries to execute the has_many statement. That's because the has_many method is not defined in the context of the Commentable module object.

Given what we now know about how Ruby is interpreting the code, we now realize that what we really want is for that has_many statement to be executed in the context of the including class.

9.13.2 The `included` Callback

Luckily, Ruby's Module class defines a handy callback that we can use to do just that. If a Module object defines the method included, it gets run whenever that module is included in another module or class. The argument passed to this method is the module/class object into which this module is being included.

We can define an included method on our Commentable module object so that it executes the has_many statement in the context of the including class (Timesheet, ExpenseReport, and so on):

```
module Commentable
  def self.included(base)
    base.class_eval do
      has_many :comments, as: :commentable
    end
  end
end
```

Now, when we include the `Commentable` module in our model classes, it will execute the `has_many` statement just as if we had typed it into each of those classes' bodies.

The technique is common enough, within Rails and gems, that it was added as a first-class concept in the Active Support API as of Rails 3. The preceding example becomes shorter and easier to read as a result:

```
# app/models/concerns/commentable.rb
module Commentable
  extend ActiveSupport::Concern
  included do
    has_many :comments, as: :commentable
  end
end
```

Whatever is inside of the `included` block will get executed in the class context of the class where the module is included.

As of version 4.0, Rails includes the directory `app/models/concerns` as the place to keep all your application's model *concerns*. Any file found within this directory will automatically be part of the application load path.

💬 Courtenay says . . .

There's a fine balance to strike here. Magic like `include Commentable` certainly saves on typing and makes your model look less complex, but it can also mean that your association code is doing things you don't know about. This can lead to confusion and hours of head-scratching while you track down code in a separate module. My personal preference is to leave all associations in the model and extend them with a module. That way you can quickly get a list of all associations just by looking at the code.

9.14 Value Objects

In Domain Driven Design[14] (DDD) there is a distinction between Entity Objects and Value Objects. All model objects that inherit from `ActiveRecord::Base` would be considered *Entity Objects* in DDD.

An Entity object cares about identity, since each one is unique, regardless of similarities between attribute values. In Active Record, uniqueness is derived from the

---

14. http://www.domaindrivendesign.org/

primary key. Comparing two different Entity Objects for equality should always return false, even if all of its attributes (other than the primary key) are equivalent.

Here is an example comparing two hypothetical Active Record address objects:

```
>> home = Address.create(city: "Brooklyn", state: "NY")
>> office = Address.create(city: "Brooklyn", state: "NY")
>> home == office
=> false
```

In this case, you are actually creating two new Address records and persisting them to the database, therefore they have different primary key values. They are different *entities*.

In contrast, *Value Objects* are generally immutable, and they are considered equal if their attributes are equal. When creating Value Objects for use with Active Record you do not inherit from ActiveRecord::Base but instead simply define a standard Ruby object. This form of composition is called an Aggregate in DDD.

The attributes of a Value Object are stored in the database alongside the columns of its parent object.

A simple example is that of a Person with a single Address. To model this using composition, first we need a Person model with corresponding address fields for the Address object. We create it with the following migration:

```
class CreatePeople < ActiveRecord::Migration[5.0]
  def change
    create_table :people do |t|
      t.string :name
      t.string :address_street
      t.string :address_city
      t.string :address_state
    end
  end
end
```

The Person model looks like this:

```
class Person < ActiveRecord::Base
  def address
    @address ||= Address.new(address_city, address_state)
  end

  def address=(address)
    self[:address_city] = address.city
    self[:address_state] = address.state

    @address = address
```

```
    end
end
```

Now we need a corresponding `AddressType` object, which looks like this:

```
class Address
  attr_reader :city, :state

  def initialize(city, state)
    @city, @state = city, state
  end

  def ==(other_address)
    city == other_address.city && state == other_address.state
  end
end
```

Note that this is just a standard Ruby object that does not inherit from `ActiveRecord::Base`. We have defined reader methods for our attributes and are assigning them upon initialization. We also have to define our own == method for use in comparisons. Wrapping this all up we get the following usage:

```
>> gary = Person.create(name: "Gary")
>> gary.address_city = "Brooklyn"
>> gary.address_state = "NY"
>> gary.address
=> #<Address:0x007fcbfcce0188 @city="Brooklyn", @state="NY">
```

Note that we don't use Active Record's Attributes API to define the attributes of `Address`. The core team has hinted that the Attributes API is destined for migration into Active Model in a future version of Rails, but until that happens, you can only use it with Active Record objects.

Alternately you can instantiate the address directly and assign it using the address accessor:

```
>> gary.address = Address.new("Brooklyn", "NY")
>> gary.address
=> #<Address:0x007fcbfa3b2e78 @city="Brooklyn", @state="NY">
```

9.14.1   Immutability

It's also important to treat Value Objects as immutable. Don't allow them to be changed after creation. Instead, create a new object instance with the new value instead. Active Record will not persist Value Objects that have been changed through means other than the writer method on the parent object.

9.14.1.1   The Money Gem

A common approach to using Value Objects is in conjunction with the money gem.[15]

```
class Expense < ActiveRecord::Base
  def cost
    @cost ||= Money.new(cents || 0, currency || Money.default_currency)
  end

  def cost=(cost)
    self[:cents] = cost.cents
    self[:currency] = cost.currency.to_s

    cost
  end
end
```

Remember to add a migration with the two columns, the integer `cents`, and the string `currency` that money needs.

```
class CreateExpenses < ActiveRecord::Migration
  def change
    create_table :expenses do |t|
        t.integer :cents
        t.string :currency
    end
  end
end
```

Now asking for or setting the cost of an item would use a `Money` instance.

```
>> expense = Expense.create(cost: Money.new(1000, "USD"))
>> cost = expense.cost
>> cost.cents
=> 1000
>> expense.currency
=> "USD"
```

9.15   Non-persisted Models

In Rails 3, if you wanted to use a standard Ruby object with Action View helpers, such as `form_for`, the object had to *"act"* like an Active Record instance. This involved including/extending various Active Model module mixins and implementing the method `persisted?`. At a minimum, `ActiveModel::Conversion`

---

15. https://github.com/RubyMoney/money

should be included and `ActiveModel::Naming` extended. These two modules alone provide the object all the methods it needs for Rails to determine partial paths, routes, and naming. Optionally, extending `ActiveModel::Translation` adds internationalization support to your object, while including `ActiveModel::Validations` enables validations to be defined. All modules are covered in detail in the Active Model API Reference.

To illustrate, let's assume we have a `Contact` class that has attributes for `name`, `email`, and `message`. However, the data for contacts in our application is stored in a proprietary third-party API, not our relational database.

The following implementation of `Contact` in Action Pack and Action View works in all modern versions of Rails:

```
class Contact
  extend ActiveModel::Naming
  extend ActiveModel::Translation
  include ActiveModel::Conversion
  include ActiveModel::Validations

  attr_accessor :name, :email, :message

  validates :name, presence: true
  validates :email,
    format: { with: /\A([^@\s]+)@((?:[-a-z0-9]+\.)+[a-z]{2,})\z/ },
    presence: true
  validates :message, length: {maximum: 1000}, presence: true

  def initialize(attributes = {})
    attributes.each do |name, value|
      send("#{name}=", value)
    end
  end

  def persisted?
    false
  end
end
```

Rails 4 introduced `ActiveModel::Model`, a module mixin that removes the drudgery of manually having to implement a compatible interface and dramatically simplifies the code above.

Active Record

Model takes care of including/extending the modules mentioned above, defines an initializer to set all attributes on initialization, and sets persisted? to false by default. Using it, the Contact class can be implemented as follows:

```
class Contact
  include ActiveModel::Model

  attr_accessor :name, :email, :message

  validates :name, presence: true
  validates :email,
    format: { with: /\A([^@\s]+)@((?:[-a-z0-9]+\.)+[a-z]{2,})\z/ },
    presence: true
  validates :message, length: {maximum: 1000}, presence: true
end
```

9.16 Modifying Active Record Classes at Runtime

The metaprogramming capabilities of Ruby, combined with the after_find callback, open the door to some interesting possibilities, especially if you're willing to blur your perception of the difference between code and data. I'm talking about modifying the behavior of model classes on the fly, as they're loaded into your application.

Listing 9.5 is a drastically simplified example of the technique, which assumes the presence of a config column on your model. During the after_find callback, we get a handle to the unique singleton class[16] of the model instance being loaded. Then we execute the contents of the config attribute belonging to this particular Account instance, using Ruby's class_eval method. Since we're doing this using the singleton class for this instance, rather than the global Account class, other account instances in the system are completely unaffected.

Listing 9.5 Runtime metaprogramming with after_find
```
class Account < ActiveRecord::Base
  ...

  Protected

  def after_find

    singleton = class << self; self; end
```

---

16. I don't expect this to make sense to you unless you are familiar with Ruby's singleton classes and the capability to evaluate arbitrary strings of Ruby code at runtime. A good place to start is http://yehudakatz.com/2009/11/15/metaprogramming-in-ruby-its-all-about-the-self/.

```
      singleton.class_eval(config)
   end
end
```

I used powerful techniques like this one in a supply chain application that I wrote for a large industrial client. "Lot" is a generic term in the industry used to describe a shipment of product. Depending on the vendor and product involved, the attributes and business logic for a given lot vary quite a bit. Since the set of vendors and products being handled changed on a weekly (sometimes daily) basis, the system needed to be reconfigurable without requiring a production deployment.

Without getting into too much detail, the application allowed the maintenance programmers to easily customize the behavior of the system by manipulating. Ruby code stored in the database, associated with whatever product the lot contained.

For example, one of the business rules associated with lots of butter being shipped for Acme Dairy Co. might dictate a strictly integral product code, exactly 10 digits in length. The code, stored in the database and associated with the product entry for Acme Dairy's butter product, would therefore contain the following two lines:

```
validates_numericality_of :product_code, only_integer: true
validates_length_of :product_code, is: 10
```

9.16.1   Considerations

A relatively complete description of everything you can do with Ruby metaprogramming, and how to do it correctly, would fill its own book. For instance, you might realize that doing things like executing arbitrary Ruby code straight out of the database is inherently dangerous. That's why I emphasize again that the examples shown here are very simplified. All I want to do is give you a taste of the possibilities.

If you do decide to begin leveraging these kinds of techniques in real-world applications, you'll have to consider security and approval workflow and a host of other important concerns. Instead of allowing arbitrary Ruby code to be executed, you might feel compelled to limit it to a small subset related to the problem at hand. You might design a compact API, or even delve into authoring a domain-specific language (DSL), crafted specifically for expressing the business rules and behaviors that should be loaded dynamically. Proceeding down the rabbit hole, you might write custom parsers for your DSL that could execute it in different contexts—some for error detection and others for reporting. It's one of those areas where the possibilities are quite limitless.

9.16.2   Ruby and Domain-Specific Languages

My former colleague Jay Fields and I pioneered the mix of Ruby metaprogramming, Rails, and internal[17] domain-specific languages while doing Rails application development for clients. I still occasionally speak at conferences and blog about writing DSLs in Ruby.

Jay has also written and delivered talks about his evolution of Ruby DSL techniques, which he calls Business Natural Languages (or BNL for short[18]).

When developing BNLs, you craft a domain-specific language that is not necessarily valid Ruby syntax but is close enough to be transformed easily into Ruby and executed at runtime, as shown in Listing 9.6.

Listing 9.6   Example of business natural language
```
employee John Doe
compensate 500 dollars for each deal closed in the past 30 days
compensate 100 dollars for each active deal that closed more than
365 days ago
compensate 5 percent of gross profits if gross profits are greater than
1,000,000 dollars
compensate 3 percent of gross profits if gross profits are greater than
2,000,000 dollars
compensate 1 percent of gross profits if gross profits are greater than
3,000,000 dollars
```

The capability to leverage advanced techniques such as DSLs is yet another powerful tool in the hands of experienced Rails developers.

💬 Courtenay says . . .

DSLs suck! Except the ones written by Obie, of course. The only people who can read and write most DSLs are their original authors. As a developer taking over a project, it's often quicker to just reimplement instead of learning the quirks and exactly which words you're allowed to use in an existing DSL. In fact, a lot of Ruby metaprogramming sucks too. It's common for people gifted with these new tools to go a bit overboard. I consider metaprogramming, `self.included`, `class_eval`, and friends to be a bit of

---

17. The qualifier internal is used to differentiate a domain-specific language hosted entirely inside of a general-purpose language, such as Ruby, from one that is completely custom and requires its own parser implementation.

18. Googling BNL will give you tons of links to the Toronto-based band Barenaked Ladies, so you're better off going directly to the source at http://blog.jayfields.com/2006/07/business-natural-language -material.html.

a code smell on most projects. If you're making a web application, future developers and maintainers of the project will appreciate your using simple, direct, granular, and well-tested methods, rather than monkeypatching into existing classes or hiding associations in modules. That said, if you can pull it off—your code will become more powerful than you can possibly imagine.

9.17   PostgreSQL

Out of all the databases supported by Active Record, PostgreSQL always seems to get the most attention and coolest features. In this section, we present a handful of features that are only available using PostgreSQL.

9.17.1   Array Type

This `array` column type allows us to conveniently store a list of values, such as strings, within a single database row.

For instance, assuming we had an `Article` model, we could store all the article's tags in an array attribute named `tags`. Since the tags are not stored in another table, when Active Record retrieves an article from the database, it does so in a single query.

To declare a column as an array, pass `true` to the `:array` option for a column type such as `string`:

```
class AddTagsToArticles < ActiveRecord::Migration
  def change
    change_table :articles do |t|
      t.string :tags, array: true
    end
  end
end
# ALTER TABLE "articles" ADD COLUMN "tags" character varying(255)[]
```

The array column type will also accept the option `:length` to limit the number of items allowed in the array.

```
t.string :tags, array: true, length: 10
```

To set a default value for an array column, you must use the PostgreSQL array notation (`{value}`). Setting the `default` option to `{}` ensures that every row in the database will default to an empty array.

```
t.string :tags, array: true, default: '{rails,ruby}'
```

The migration in the preceding code sample would create an array of strings that defaults every row in the database to have an array containing strings "rails" and "ruby".

```
>> article = Article.create
   (0.1ms) BEGIN
   SQL (66.2ms) INSERT INTO "articles" ("created_at", "updated_at") VALUES
   ($1, $2) RETURNING "id" [["created_at", Wed, 23 Oct 2013 15:03:12

>> article.tags
=> ["rails", "ruby"]
```

If the PgArrayParser gem[19] is included in the application Gemfile, Rails will use it when parsing PostgreSQL's array representation. The gem includes a native C extention and JRuby support.

9.17.1.1   Querying

If you wish to query an array column using Active Record, you can use the ANY and ALL functions. To demonstrate, given our previous example, using the ANY method we could query for any articles that have the tag "rails":

```
Article.where("? = ANY(tags)", "rails")
```

Alternatively, the ALL function searches for arrays where all values in the array equal the value specified. (Not useful for tagging.)

If you are doing queries on large tables with array column type, the column should probably be indexed with either GiST or GIN.

```
add_index :articles, :tags, using: 'gin'
```

9.17.2   Network Address Types

PostgreSQL comes with column types exclusively for IPv4, IPv6, and MAC addresses. IPv4 or IPv6 host address are represented with Active Record data types inet and cidr, where the former accepts values with nonzero bits to the right of the netmask. When Active Record retrieves inet/cidr data types from the database, it converts the values to IPAddr objects. MAC addresses are represented with the macaddr data type, which are represented as a string in Ruby.

---

19. https://github.com/DockYard/pg_array_parser

To set a column as a network address in an Active Record migration, set the data type of the column to `inet`, `cidr`, or `macaddr`:

```
class CreateNetworkAddresses < ActiveRecord::Migration
  def change
    create_table :network_addresses do |t|
      t.inet :inet_address
      t.cidr :cidr_address
      t.macaddr :mac_address
    end
  end
end
```

Setting an `inet` or `cidr` type to an invalid network address will result in an `IPAddr::InvalidAddressError` exception being raised. If an invalid MAC address is set, an error will occur at the database level resulting in an `ActiveRecord::StatementInvalid: PG::InvalidTextRepresentation` exception being raised.

```
>> address = NetworkAddress.new
=> #<NetworkAddress id: nil, inet_address: nil, ...>

>> address.inet_address = 'abc'
IPAddr::InvalidAddressError: invalid address

>> address.inet_address = "127.0.0.1"
=> "127.0.0.1"

>> address.inet_address
=> #<IPAddr: IPv4:127.0.0.1/255.255.255.255>

>> address.save && address.reload
=> #<NetworkAddress id: 1,
     inet_address: #<IPAddr: IPv4:127.0.0.1/255.255.255.255>, ...>
```

9.17.3   UUID Type

The `uuid` column type represents a Universally Unique IDentifier (UUID), a 128-bit value that is generated by an algorithm that makes it highly unlikely that the same value can be generated twice.

To set a column as a UUID in an Active Record migration, set the type of the column to `uuid`:

```
add_column :table_name, :unique_identifier, :uuid
```

When reading and writing to a UUID attribute, you will always be dealing with a Ruby string:

```
record.unique_identifier = 'a0eebc99-9c0b-4ef8-bb6d-6bb9bd380a11'
```

If an invalid UUID is set, an error will occur at the database level resulting in an `ActiveRecord::StatementInvalid:  PG::InvalidTextRepresentation` exception being raised.

9.17.4   Range Types

If you have ever needed to store a range of values, Active Record now supports PostgreSQL range types. These ranges can be created with both inclusive and exclusive bounds. The following range types are natively supported:

- `daterange`

- `int4range`

- `int8range`

- `numrange`

- `tsrange`

- `tstzrange`

To illustrate, consider a scheduling application that stores a date range representing the availability of a room.

```
class CreateRooms < ActiveRecord::Migration
  def change
    create_table :rooms do |t|
      t.daterange :availability
    end
  end
end

room = Room.create(availability: Date.today..Float::INFINITY)
room.reload
room.availability # Tue, 22 Oct 2013...Infinity
room.availability.class # Range
```

Note that the `Range` class does not support exclusive lower bound. For more detailed information about the PostgreSQL range types, consult the official documentation (http://www.postgresql.org/docs/9.3/static/rangetypes.html).

9.17.5 JSON Type

Introduced in PostgreSQL 9.2, the `json` column type adds the capability for Post-greSQL to store JSON structured data directly in the database. When an Active Record object has an attribute with the type of `json`, the encoding/decoding of the JSON itself is handled behind the scenes by `ActiveSupport::JSON`. This enables you to set the attribute to a hash or already encoded JSON string. If you attempt to set the JSON attribute to a string that cannot be decoded, a `JSON::ParserError` will be raised.

To set a column as JSON in an Active Record migration, set the data type of the column to `json`:

```
add_column :users, :preferences, :json
```

To demonstrate, let's play with a `preferences` attribute. To begin, I'll create a user with the color preference of blue.

```
>> user = User.create(preferences: { color: "blue"} )
  (0.2ms) BEGIN
  SQL (1.1ms) INSERT INTO "users" ("preferences") VALUES ($1) RETURNING
  "id" [["preferences", {:color=>"blue"}]]
  (0.4ms) COMMIT
=> #<User id: 1, preferences: {:color=>"blue"}>
```

Next up, let's verify that when we retrieve the user from the database the `preferences` attribute doesn't return a JSON string but a hash representation instead.

```
>> user.reload
  User Load (10.7ms) SELECT "users".* FROM "users" WHERE "users"."id" = $1
  LIMIT 1 [["id", 1]]
=> #<User id: 1, preferences: {"color"=>"blue"}>

>> user.preferences.class
=> Hash
```

9.17.6 Index Types

PostgreSQL provides several index types: B-tree, Hash, GiST, SP-GiST, GIN and BRIN. Each index type uses a different algorithm that is best suited to different types of queries. By default, the `CREATE INDEX` command creates B-tree indexes, which fit the most common situations.

If you are doing any queries on columns with textual content such as hstore and json types, be sure to add the appropriate index,[20] which is probably GIN or GiST. The distinguishing factor between the two index types is that GIN index lookups are three times faster than GiST indexes. However, they also take three times longer to build.

You can define a non-default index using Active Record migrations by setting the index option :using to :gin or :gist, respectively.

```
add_index :photos, :properties, using: :gin
add_index :photos, :properties, using: :gist # alternate
```

GIN and GiST indexes support queries with @>, ?, ?&, and ?| operators that we used in the hstore and json example code.

9.18   Conclusion

With this chapter we conclude our comprehensive coverage of Active Record. Among other things, we examined how callbacks let us factor our code in a clean and object-oriented fashion. We also expanded our modeling options by considering single-table inheritance, abstract classes, and Active Record's distinctive polymorphic relationships.

At this point in the book, we've covered two parts of the MVC pattern: the model and the controller. It's now time to delve into the third and final part: the view.

---

20. https://www.postgresql.org/docs/9.6/static/indexes-types.html

CHAPTER 10

Action View

> The very powerful and the very stupid have one thing in common. Instead of altering their views to fit the facts, they alter the facts to fit their views . . . which can be very uncomfortable if you happen to be one of the facts that needs altering.
>
> —Doctor Who

If controllers are the skeleton and musculature of your Rails application, then models form the heart and mind, and your view templates (based on Action View, the third major component of Rails) are your application's skin and fashion accessories—the part that is visible to the outside world.

Action View is the Rails API for putting together the visual component of your application, namely the HTML and associated content that will be rendered in a web browser whenever someone uses your Rails application. In this brave new world of REST resources, Action View is involved in generating almost any sort of output you generate, not just HTML.

ERb versus Haml

Action View contains a full-featured templating system based on a Ruby library named ERb. It takes data prepared by the controller layer and interleaves it with view code to create a presentation layer for the end user. It's also one of the first things you learn about Rails and part of the standard Ruby library. While ERb is the Rails standard, I much prefer a templating solution named Haml (http://haml-lang.com/) and as such, have used it all over the book for examples. I think Haml is such a superior choice over ERb that, other than mentioning it here, this edition does not cover ERb at all. Haml, on the other hand, get its own full chapter.

In this chapter, we cover the fundamentals of the Action View framework, from effective use of partials, to the significant performance boosts possible via caching.

10.1   Layouts and Templates

Rails has easy conventions for template usage, related to the location of templates with the Rails project directories.

The `app/views` directory contains subdirectories corresponding to the name of controllers in your application. Within each controller's view subdirectory, you place a template named to match its corresponding action.

The special `app/views/layout` directory holds layout templates, intended to be reusable containers for your views. Again, naming conventions are used to determine which templates to render, except that this time it is the name of the controller that is used for matching.

10.1.1   Template Filename Conventions

The filename of a template in Rails carries a lot of significance. Its parts, delimited with periods, correspond to the following information:

- name (usually maps to action)
- locale (optional)
- content type
- templating engine(s)
- variant (optional, new in Rails 4.1)

We'll get into specifics about this naming scheme a little further along in the chapter.

10.1.2   Layouts

A layout is an HTML document container meant to be reused by many controller's actions. Simple applications may have one layout shared by all actions, while more complex applications may have many layouts, even one or more per controller.

Action View decides which layout to render based on the inheritance hierarchy of controllers being executed. Most Rails applications have an `application.html.haml` file in their layout directory, because it's part of the files generated by the `rails new` bootstrapping script. The base layout shares its name with the `ApplicationController`, which is typically extended by all the other controllers in an application; therefore it is picked up as the default layout for all views.

It is picked up, unless of course, a more specific layout template is in place, but quite often it makes sense to use just one application-wide template, such as the simple one shown in Listing 10.1.

Listing 10.1   A simple general-purpose application.html.haml layout template

```
!!! 5
%html
  %head
    %meta{ charset: 'utf-8' }
    %title TR4W Time and Expenses Sample Application
    = csrf_meta_tag
    = stylesheet_link_tag 'application', media: 'all'
    = javascript_include_tag 'application'
  %body
    = yield
```

10.1.3   Yielding Content

The Ruby language's built-in `yield` keyword is put to good use in making layout and action templates collaborate. Notice the use of `yield` at the end of the layout template:

```
%body
  = yield
```

In this case, `yield` by itself is a special message to the rendering system. It marks where to insert the output of the action's rendered output, which is usually the template corresponding to that action.

You can add extra places in your layout where you want to be able to yield content by including additional `yield` invocations—just make sure to pass a unique identifier as the argument. A good example is a layout that has left and right sidebar content (simplified, of course):

```
%body
  .left.sidebar
    = yield :left
  content
    = yield
  right.sidebar
    = yield :right
```

The `.content` div receives the main template markup generated. But how do you give Rails content for the left and right sidebars? Easy—just use the `content_for` method anywhere in your template code. I usually stick it at the top of the template so that it's obvious.

```
- content_for :left do
  %h2 Navigation
  %ul
    %li ...

- content_for :right do
  %h2 Help
  %p Lorem ipsum dolor sit amet, consectetur adipisicing elit...

%h1 Page Heading
%p ...
```

Besides sidebars and other types of visible content blocks, I suggest you yield for additional content to be added to the HEAD element of your page, as shown in Listing 10.2.

Listing 10.2   Yielding additional head content
```
!!! 5
%html
  %head
    %meta{ charset: 'utf-8' }
    %title TR4W Time and Expenses Sample Application
    = csrf_meta_tag
    = stylesheet_link_tag 'application', media: 'all'
    = javascript_include_tag 'application'
    = yield :head
  %body
    = yield
```

🗨 Kevin says . . .

Yielding in the HEAD element is also a great technique to include page specific meta tags, such as those required for Facebook Open Graph.

10.1.4   Conditional Output

One of the most common idioms you'll use when coding Rails views is to conditionally output content to the view. The most elementary way to control conditional output is to use if statements.

```
- if show_subtitle?
  %h2= article.subtitle
```

A lot of times you can use inline `if` conditions and shorten your code, since the `=` outputter doesn't break if you feed it a nil value. Just add a postfix `if` condition to the statement:

```
%h2= article.subtitle if show_subtitle?
```

Of course, there's a problem with the preceding example. The `if` statement on a separate line will eliminate the `<h2>` tags entirely, but the one-liner second example does not.

There are a couple of ways to deal with the problem and keep it a one-liner. First, there's the butt-ugly solution that I've occasionally seen in some Rails applications, which is the only reason why I'm mentioning it here!

```
= "<h2>#{h(article.subtitle)}</h2>".html_safe if show_subtitle?
```

A more elegant solution involves Rails' `content_tag` helper method, but admittedly a one-liner is probably not superior to its two-line equivalent in this case.

```
= content_tag('h2', article.subtitle) if show_subtitle?
```

Helper methods, both the ones included in Rails like `content_tag` and the ones that you'll write on your own, are your main tool for building elegant view templates. Helpers are covered extensively in Chapter 11, "All about Helpers."

10.1.5   Decent Exposure

We've seen how layouts and yielding content blocks work, but other than that, how should data get from the controller layer to the view? During preparation of the template, instance variables set during execution of the controller action will be copied over as instance variables of the template context. Even though it's the standard way exposed by Rails documentation, sharing state via instance variables in controllers promotes close coupling with views.

Hashrocket's Decent Exposure gem (https://github.com/hashrocket/decent_exposure) provides a declarative manner of exposing an interface to the state that controllers contain, thereby decreasing coupling and improving your testability and overall design.

When invoked, Decent Exposure's `expose` macro creates a method with the given name, evaluates the provided block and memoizes the result. This method is then declared as a `helper_method`, so that views may have access to it, and is made

Action
View

unroutable as an action. When no block is given, `expose` attempts to intuit which resource you want to acquire:

```
expose :timesheet
```

Does something kind of like this, just more concisely:

```
Timesheet.find(params[:timesheet_id] || params[:id])
```

The symbol passed to `expose` is used to guess the class name of the object you want to find and related parameters—useful since almost every controller in a normal Rails application uses this kind of code in the show, edit, update and destroy actions.

In a slightly more complicated scenario, you might need to find an instance of an object using something other than a simple `find` method on its Active Record class. Decent Exposure provides an array of options for customizing default behavior, including `:scope`:

```
expose :client
expose :timesheet, scope: -> { client.timesheets }
```

The example says, "search for timesheets in the client's association instead of the `Timesheet` class." And note that exposures can refer to each other.

In the RESTful controller paradigm, with its nesting of resources, you'll find yourself using this particular idiom again and again.

Exposing completely custom code is just a matter of passing a block

```
expose :client
expose :timesheet, scope: -> { client.timesheets }
expose :timesheet_approval_presenter do
  TimesheetApprovalPresenter.new(timesheet, current_user)
end
```

or a symbol

```
expose :client
expose :timesheet, scope: -> { client.timesheets }
expose :timesheet_approval_presenter, :setup_presenter
...

private
```

```
def setup_presenter
  ...
  TimesheetApprovalPresenter.new(timesheet, current_user)
end
```

The last couple of examples also demonstrate how `expose` declarations can depend on each other. In fact, proper use of `expose` should eliminate most model-lookup code from your actual controller actions.

At Hashrocket, use of Decent Exposure has proven so beneficial that it completely replaced direct use of instance variables in controllers and views. The helper methods created by the `expose` macro are just referred to directly in the view.

10.1.6   Standard Instance Variables

More than just instance variables from the controller are copied over to the template.

10.1.6.1   `assigns`

Want to see everything that comes across the controller-view boundary? Throw = `debug(assigns)` into your template and take a look at the output. The `assigns` attribute is essentially internal to Rails, and you should not use it directly in your production code.

10.1.6.2   `base_path`

Local filesystem path pointing to the base directory of your application where templates are kept.

10.1.6.3   `controller`

The current controller instance is made available via `controller`, before it goes out of scope at the end of request processing. You can take advantage of the controller's knowledge of its name (via the `controller_name` attribute) and the action that was just performed (via the `action_name` attribute), in order to structure your CSS more effectively.

```
%body{ class: "#{controller.controller_name} #{controller.action_name}" }
```

That would result in a BODY tag looking something like this, depending on the action executed:

```
<body class="timesheets index">
```

Action View

ℹ Note

You could also replicate the functionality in the previous example by using
the Haml helper method `page_class`.

```
%body{ class: page_class }
```

Hopefully you already know that the C in CSS stands for cascading, which refers to
the fact that class names cascade down the tree of elements in your markup code and
are available for creation of rules. The trick is to automatically include the controller
and action name as classnames of your `body` element, so that you can use them to
customize the look and feel of the page very flexibly later on in the development
cycle. For example, here's how you would use the technique to vary the background
of header elements depending on the controller path in SCSS:

```scss
body {
  .timesheets .header {
      background: image_url(timesheet-bg.png) no-repeat left top;
  }
  .expense_reports .header {
      background: image_url(expense-reports-bg.png) no-repeat left top;
  }
}
```

10.1.6.4 `cookies`

The `cookies` variable is a hash containing the user's cookies. There might be situations where it'd be okay to pull values out to affect rendering, but most of the time
you'll be using cookies in your controller, not the view.

10.1.6.5 `flash`

The `flash` has popped up in larger code samples throughout the book so far,
whenever you want to send the user a message from the controller layer but only for
the duration of the next request.

```ruby
def create
  if user.try(:authorize, params[:user][:password])
    redirect_to home_url, notice: "Welcome, #{user.first_name}!"
  else
    redirect_to :new, alert: "Login invalid."
  end
end
```

A common Rails practice is to use `flash[:notice]` to hold benign notice messages, and `flash[:alert]` for communication of a more serious nature.

ⓘ Note

It's so common to set `flash` notice and `alert` messages on redirects that Rails enables you to set them in the `redirect_to` method as optional parameters.

```
def create
  if user.try(:authorize, params[:user][:password])
    redirect_to home_url, notice: "Welcome, #{user.first_name}!"
  else
    redirect_to home_url, alert: "Bad login"
  end
end
```

Special accessors for notices and alerts are included as helper methods on the flash object itself, since their use is so common.

```
def create
  if user.try(:authorize, params[:user][:password])
    redirect_to home_url, notice: "Welcome, #{user.first_name}!"
  else
    redirect_to action: "new", alert: "Login invalid."
  end
end
```

10.1.7 Displaying `flash` Messages

Personally, I like to conditionally output both `notice` and `alert` messages in `div` elements, right at the top of my layout, and use CSS to style them as shown in Listing 10.3:

Listing 10.3   Standardized flash notice and error placement in application.html.haml

```
%html
  ...
  %body
    - if flash.notice
      .notice= flash.notice
    - if flash.alert
      .notice.alert= flash.alert

    = yield
```

The CSS for `.notice` defines most of the style for the element, and `.alert` overrides just the aspects that are different for alerts.

⚲ A modern way to display flash notices is within a *toast* (aka *snackbar*) widget at the bottom of the screen (http://www.w3schools.com/howto/howto_js_snackbar.asp).

10.1.7.1 `flash.now`

Sometimes you want to give the user a flash message but only for the current request. In fact, a common newbie Rails programming mistake is to set a flash notice and *not* redirect, thereby incorrectly showing a flash message on the following request.

It is possible to make flash cooperate with a render by using the `flash.now` method.

```
class ReportController < ActionController::Base
  def create
    if report.save
      redirect_to report_path(report), notice: "#{report.title} has been created."
    else
      flash.now.alert = "#{report.title} could not be created."
      render :new
    end
  end
end
```

The `flash.now` object also has `notice` and `alert` accessors, like its traditional counterpart.

10.1.7.2 `logger`

Have something to record for posterity in the logs while you're rendering the view? Use the `logger` method to get the view's `Logger` instance, the same as `Rails.logger`, unless you've changed it.

10.1.7.3 `params`

This is the same `params` hash that is available in your controller. It's very dangerous from a security perspective to put unfiltered parameter data into the output stream of your template.

10.1.7.4 `request` and `response`

The HTTP `request` and `response` objects are exposed to the view, but other than for debugging purposes, I can't think of any reason why you would want to use them directly from your template.

10.1.7.5 `session`

The `session` variable is the user's session hash. There might be situations where it'd be okay to pull values out to affect rendering, but I shudder to think that you might try to set values in the session from the view layer. Use with care, and primarily for debugging, just like `request` and `response`.

10.2 Partials

A partial is a fragment of template code. The *Rails Way* is to use partials to factor view code into modular chunks that can be assembled in layouts with as little repetition as possible.

In older versions of Rails, the syntax for including a partial within a template started with `render :partial`, but now passing a string to `render` within your view will get interpreted to mean you want to render a partial. Partial template names must begin with an underscore, which serves to set them apart visually within a given view template directory. However, you leave the underscore out when you refer to them.

```
%h1 Details
= render 'details'
```

10.2.1 Simple Use Cases

The simplest partial use case is simply to extract a portion of template code. Some developers divide their templates into logical parts by using partial extraction. Sometimes it is easier to understand the structure of a screen if the significant parts are factored out of it.

For instance, Listing 10.4 is a simple user registration screen that has its parts factored out into partials.

Listing 10.4 Simple user registration form with partials
```
%h1 User Registration
= error_messages_for :user
= form_for :user, url: users_path do
  .registration
    .details.demographics
      = render 'details'
      = render 'demographics'
    .location
      = render 'location'
    .opt_in
      = render 'opt_in'
    .terms
      = render 'terms'
  %p= submit_tag 'Register'
```

While we're at it, let me pop open one of those partials. To conserve space, we'll take a look at one of the smaller ones, the partial containing the opt-in check boxes of this particular app. The source is in Listing 10.5; notice that its name begins with an underscore.

Listing 10.5   The opt-in partial in the file app/views/users/_opt_in.html.haml

```
%fieldset#opt_in
  %legend Spam Opt In
  %p
    = check_box :user, :send_event_updates
    Send me updates about events!
    %br
    = check_box :user, :send_site_updates
    Notify me about new services
```

Personally, I like partials to be entirely contained inside a semantically significant markup container. In the case of the opt-in partial in Listing 10.5, both check-box controls are contained inside a single `fieldset` element, which I've given an `id` attribute. Following that rule, more as a loose guideline than anything else, helps me to mentally identify how the contents of this partial are going to fit inside the parent template. If we were dealing with other markup, perhaps outside of a form, I might choose to wrap the partial markup inside a well-identified `div` container, instead of a `fieldset`.

10.2.2   Reuse of Partials

Since the registration form is neatly factored out into its component parts, it is easy to create a simple edit form using some of its partials, as in Listing 10.6.

Listing 10.6   Simple user edit form reusing some of the same partials

```
%h1 Edit User
= form_for :user, url: user_path(@user), method: :put do
  .settings
    .details
      = render 'details'
    .demographics
      = render 'demographics'
    .opt_in
      = render 'opt_in'
    %p= submit_tag 'Save Settings'
```

If you compare Listings 10.4 and 10.6, you'll notice that markup skeleton changed and the page has less content than the registration form. Perhaps the user's location is handled in greater detail on another screen, and certainly you don't want to require agreement of terms every time the user changes her settings.

10.2.3 Shared Partials

Until now we've been considering the use of partials that reside in the same directory as their parent template. However, you can easily refer to partials that are in other directories, just by prefixing the directory name. You still leave off the underscore, which has always felt a little weird.

Let's add a `captcha` partial to the bottom of the registration form from Listing 10.4, to help prevent spammers from invading our web application:

```
...
  .terms
    = render 'terms'
  .captcha
    = render 'shared/captcha'
%p= submit_tag 'Register'
```

Since the `captcha` partial is used in various different parts of the application, it makes sense to let it reside in a shared folder rather than any particular view folder. However, you do have to be a little bit careful when you move existing template code into a shared partial. It's quite possible to inadvertently craft a partial that depends implicitly on where it's rendered.

For example, take the case of the Rails-talk mailing list member with a troublesome partial defined in `login/_login.html.haml`:

```
= form_tag do
  %fieldset
    %label
      Username:
      = text_field_tag :username, params[:username]
    %br
    %label
      Password:
      = password_field_tag :password, params[:password]
    %br
    = submit_tag "Login"
```

The login form submission worked when he rendered this partial as part of the login controller's `login` action ("the login page"), but not when it was included as part of the view for any other section of his website. The problem is that `form_tag` (covered in the next chapter) takes an optional action parameter telling it where to post its information. If you leave out the action, the form will post back to its current URL, which will vary for shared partials, depending on where they're being used from.

An alternate, perhaps more important lesson here is: give forms embedded in shared partials explicit URL targets.

10.2.4   Passing Variables to Partials

Partials inherit the variables and methods exposed to their parent templates implicitly. That's why the form helpers used in the partials of Listings 10.4 and 10.6 work: They rely implicitly on an `user` method to be in scope. I feel it's fine to use this implicit sharing in some cases, particularly when the partials are tightly bound to their parent templates. It would be especially true in cases where the only reason you broke out a partial in the first place was to reduce the size and complexity of a particularly large template.

However, once you get into the practice of breaking out partial templates for reuse, depending on implicit context gets a lot more dicey. That's why Rails supports the passing of locally scoped variables to partial templates, as in the following snippet:

```
= render 'shared/address', form: form
```

The values of the optional hash are converted into locally scoped variables (no @) in the partial.

Listing 10.7 is a variation on the registration template. This time we're using the version of `form_for` that yields a block parameter representing the form to its form helper methods. We'll pass that form parameter on, too.

Listing 10.7   Simple user registration template passing form as local variable
```
%h1 User Registration
= form_for :user, url: users_path do |form|
  .registration
    .details.address.demographics
      = render 'details', form: form
      = render 'shared/address', form: form
  %p= form.submit 'Register'
```

And finally, in Listing 10.8 we have the shared address form.

Listing 10.8   A simple shared address partial using local variable

```
%fieldset.address
  %legend Address
  %p
    %label Street
    %br
    = form.text_area :street, rows: 2, cols: 40
  %p
    %label City
    %br
    = form.text_field :city
  %p
    %label State
    %br
    = form.text_field :state, size: 2
  %p
    %label Zip
    %br
    = form.text_field :zip, size: 15
```

The form helper methods, which we'll cover in Chapter 11, "All about Helpers," have a variation in which they are called on the `form` variable yielded by the `form_for` method. That is exactly what we passed on to these partials.

10.2.4.1   The `local_assigns` Hash

If you need to check for the presence of a certain local variable in a partial, you can do it by checking the `local_assigns` hash that is part of every template. Using the Ruby idiom `defined? variable` won't work due to limitations of the rendering system.

```
- if local_assigns.has_key? :special
  = special
```

10.2.5   Rendering an Object

The `render` method also provides a shorthand syntax for rendering an object into a partial, which strictly depends on Rails naming conventions.

```
= render entry
```

   Rails magic alert!

The partial corresponding to the last code snippet is named `_entry.html.haml` and gets a local variable named `entry`. This is equivalent to the following:

Action
View

```
= render partial: 'entry', object: entry
```

To set a different local variable name other than the name of the partial, you could use the `locals` hash as seen earlier in the chapter or specify the desired name through the `:as` option.

```
= render partial: 'entry', object: some_entry, as: :item
```

10.2.6   Rendering Collections

One of the best uses of partials is to render collections. Once you get into the habit of rendering collections with partials, you won't want to go back to the relative ugliness of cluttering your templates with `for` loops and `each`.

When the `render` method gets an `Enumerable` as its first argument, it assumes that you want to render a collection of partials.

```
= render entries
```

This is simple and precise yet very dependent on naming conventions. The objects being rendered are exposed to the partial template as a local variable named the same as the partial template itself. In turn the template should be named according to the class of the objects being rendered.

The partial corresponding to the last code snippet is named `_entry.html.haml` and gets a local variable named `entry`.

```
= div_for(entry) do
  = entry.description
  #{distance_of_time_in_words_to_now entry.created_at} ago
```

💬 **Kevin says . . .**

If the collection passed into the `render` method is empty, `nil` is returned. Using this knowledge, you can write code such as

```
= render(entries) || "No entires exist"
```

to provide fallback content.

Since the partial template used is based on the class of each item, you can easily render a heterogeneous collection of objects. This technique is particularly useful in conjunction with collections of STI subclasses.

If you want to override that behavior, then revert to the older partial syntax and specify the `:partial` and `:collection` options explicitly like this:

```
= render partial: 'entry', collection: @entries
```

10.2.6.1 The `partial_counter` Variable

There's another variable set for collection-rendered partials that doesn't get much attention. It's a 0-indexed counter variable that tracks the number of times a partial has been rendered. It's useful for rendering numbered lists of things. The name of the variable is the name of the partial, plus `_counter`.

```
= div_for(entry) do
  "#{entry_counter}:#{entry.description}
  #{distance_of_time_in_words_to_now entry.created_at} ago"
```

10.2.6.1 Sharing Collection Partials

If you wanted to use the same partial that you use with a collection, except with a single entry object, you'd have to pass it that single instance via the locals hash described in the preceding section, like this:

```
= render 'entry', entry: some_entry
```

10.2.7 Logging

If you take a look at your development log, you'll notice that it shows which partials have been rendered and how long they took.

```
Rendering template within layouts/application
Rendering listings/index
Rendered listings/_listing 0.6ms
Rendered listings/_listing 0.3ms
Rendered listings/_listing 0.2ms
Rendered listings/_listing 0.2ms
Rendered listings/_listing 0.2ms
Rendered layouts/_login 2.4ms
Rendered layouts/_header 3.3ms
Rendered layouts/_footer 0.1ms
```

10.3 Conclusion

In this chapter, we've covered the Action View framework with an explanation of templating and how the Rails rendering system works. We've also covered the use of partials in-depth, since their use is essential for effective Rails programming.

Now it's time to cover the mechanism whereby you can inject a whole bunch of smarts into your view layer without cluttering up your templates: Helpers.

CHAPTER 11

All about Helpers

Thank you for helping Helpers Helping the Helpless. Your help was very . . . helpful!

—Mrs. Duong in the movie *The Weekenders*

Throughout the book so far, we've mentioned some of the varied helper methods provided by Rails to help you assemble the user interface of your web application. This chapter lists and explains all of the helper modules and their methods, followed by instructions on effectively creating your own helpers.

---

❶ Note

This chapter is essentially reference material. Although every effort has been made to make it readable straight through, you will notice that coverage of Action View's helper modules is arranged alphabetically, starting with `Active-ModelHelper` and ending with `UrlHelper`. Within each module's section, the methods are broken up into logical groups whenever appropriate.

11.1 `ActiveModelHelper`

Older editions of the book documented the `ActiveModelHelper` module, which contained helper methods for dynamically generating HTML forms from Active Model-backed objects. That code was removed from Rails and is essentially abandoned.

If you are looking for similar functionality that works with Rails 5, then check out the hugely popular Formtastic gem at https://github.com/justinfrench/formtastic.

395

11.2 `AssetTagHelper`

This module provides methods for generating HTML that links views to assets such as images, JavaScripts, stylesheets, and feeds. These methods do not verify that assets exist before linking to them, they simply create link tags.

The `AssetTagHelper` module includes some methods that you will use on a daily basis during active Rails development, particularly `image_tag`.

11.2.1 Head Helpers

Some of the helper methods in this module help you add content to the `head` element of your HTML document.

11.2.1.1 `auto_discovery_link_tag(type = :rss, url_options = {}, tag_options = {})`

Returns a link tag that browsers and news readers can use to autodetect an RSS or ATOM feed. The type can either be `:rss` (default) or `:atom`. Control the link options in `url_for` format using the `url_options`.

You can modify the `link` tag itself using the `tag_options` parameter:

`:rel` Specify the relation of this link; defaults to `"alternate"`.

`:type` Override MIME type (such as `"application/atom+xml"`) that Rails would otherwise generate automatically for you.

`:title` Specify the title of the link; defaults to a capitalized type.

```
auto_discovery_link_tag
# => <link rel="alternate" type="application/rss+xml" title="RSS"
#       href="http://www.currenthost.com/controller/action" />

auto_discovery_link_tag(:atom)
# => <link rel="alternate" type="application/atom+xml" title="ATOM"
#       href="http://www.currenthost.com/controller/action" />

auto_discovery_link_tag(:rss, {action: "feed"})
# => <link rel="alternate" type="application/rss+xml" title="RSS"
#       href="http://www.currenthost.com/controller/feed" />

auto_discovery_link_tag(:rss, {action: "feed"}, {title: "My RSS"})
# => <link rel="alternate" type="application/rss+xml" title="My RSS"
#       href="http://www.currenthost.com/controller/feed" />
```

11.2.1.2   `favicon_link_tag(source='favicon.ico', options={})`

Returns a link loading a favicon file. By default, Rails will set the icon to `favicon.ico`. You may specify a different file in the first argument.

The `favicon_link_tag` helper accepts an optional options hash that accepts the following:

`:rel` Specify the relation of this link; defaults to `'shortcut icon'`

`:type` Override the auto-generated MIME type; defaults to `'image/vnd.microsoft.icon'`

```
favicon_link_tag '/myicon.ico'
# => <link href="/assets/favicon.ico" rel="shortcut icon"
#        type="image/vnd.microsoft.icon" />
```

11.2.1.3   `javascript_include_tag(*sources)`

Returns a `script` tag for each of the sources provided. You can pass in the filename (the `.js` extension is optional) of JavaScript files that exist in your `app/assets/javascripts` directory for inclusion into the current page, or you can pass their full path, relative to your document root.

```
javascript_include_tag "xmlhr"
# => <script src="/assets/xmlhr.js?1284139606"></script>

javascript_include_tag "common", "/elsewhere/cools"
# => <script src="/assets/common.js?1284139606"></script>
# <script src="/elsewhere/cools.js?1423139606"></script>
```

When the Asset Pipeline is enabled, passing the name of the manifest file as a source will include all JavaScript or CoffeeScript files that are specified within the manifest.

```
javascript_include_tag "application"
```

By default, not including the `.js` extension to a JavaScript source will result in `.js` being suffixed to the filename. However, this does not play well with JavaScript templating languages, as they have extensions of their own. To rectify this, as of Rails 4.1, setting the option `:extname` to `false` will tell the `javascript_include_tag` helper to not append `.js` to the supplied source.

```
javascript_include_tag 'templates.jst', extname: false
# => <script src="/javascripts/templates.jst"></script>
```

Helpers

You can modify the HTML attributes of the script tag by passing a hash as the last argument.

11.2.1.4 `stylesheet_link_tag(*sources)`

Returns a stylesheet `link` tag for the sources specified as arguments. If you don't specify an extension, `.css` will be appended automatically. Just like other helper methods that take a variable number of arguments plus options, you can pass a hash of options as the last argument and they will be added as attributes to the tag.

```
stylesheet_link_tag "style"
# => <link href="/stylesheets/style.css" media="screen"
#       rel="Stylesheet" type="text/css" />

stylesheet_link_tag "style", media: "all"
# => <link href="/stylesheets/style.css" media="all"
#       rel="Stylesheet" type="text/css" />

stylesheet_link_tag "random.styles", "/css/stylish"
# => <link href="/stylesheets/random.styles" media="screen"
#       rel="Stylesheet" type="text/css" />
##   <link href="/css/stylish.css" media="screen"
#       rel="Stylesheet" type="text/css" />
```

You can modify the HTML attributes of the script tag by passing a hash as the last argument.

11.2.2 Asset Helpers

This module also contains a series of helper methods that generate asset-related markup. It's important to generate asset tags dynamically because often assets are either packaged together or served up from a different server source than your regular content. Asset helper methods also timestamp your asset source URLs to prevent browser caching problems.

11.2.2.1 `audio_tag(source, options = {})`

Returns an HTML 5 audio tag based on the `source` argument.

```
audio_tag("sound")
# => <audio src="/audios/sound" />

audio_tag("sound.wav")
# => <audio src="/audios/sound.wav" />

audio_tag("sound.wav", autoplay: true, controls: true)
# => <audio autoplay="autoplay" controls="controls" src="/audios/sound.wav" />
```

11.2.2.2 `image_tag(source, options = {})`

Returns an `img` tag for use in a template. The `source` parameter can be a full path or a file that exists in your images directory. You can add additional arbitrary attributes to the `img` tag using the options parameter. The following two options are treated specially:

`:alt` If no alternate text is given, the filename part of the source is used, after being capitalized and stripped of the extension.

`:size` Supplied as `widthxheight` so `"30x45"` becomes the attributes `width="30"` and `height="45"`. The `:size` option will fail silently if the value is not in the correct format.

```
image_tag("icon.png")
# => <img src="/assets/icon.png" alt="Icon" />

image_tag("icon.png", size: "16x10", alt: "Edit Entry")
# => <img src="/assets/icon.png" width="16" height="10" alt="Edit Entry" />

image_tag("/photos/dog.jpg", class: 'icon')
# => <img src="/photos/icon.gif" alt="Dog" class="icon"/>
```

11.2.2.3 `video_tag(sources, options = {})`

Returns an HTML 5 `video` tag for the `sources`. If `sources` is a string, a single video tag will be returned. If `sources` is an array, a `video` tag with nested `source` tags for each source will be returned. The `sources` can be full paths or files that exists in your public videos directory.

You can add normal HTML video element attributes using the `options` hash. The `options` supports two additional keys for convenience and conformance:

`:poster` Set an image (like a screenshot) to be shown before the video loads. The path is calculated using `image_path`.

`:size` Supplied as `widthxheight` in the same manner as `image_tag`. The `:size` option can also accept a stringified number, which sets both `width` and `height` to the supplied value.

```
video_tag("trailer")
# => <video src="/videos/trailer" />

video_tag("trailer.ogg")
# => <video src="/videos/trailer.ogg" />

video_tag("trail.ogg", controls: true, autobuffer: true)
```

```
# => <video autobuffer="autobuffer" controls="controls"
#       src="/videos/trail.ogg" />

video_tag("trail.m4v", size: "16x10", poster: "screenshot.png")
# => <video src="/videos/trailer.m4v" width="16" height="10"
#       poster="/images/screenshot.png" />

video_tag(["trailer.ogg", "trailer.flv"])
# => <video>
#       <source src="trailer.ogg"/>
#       <source src="trailer.flv"/>
#    </video>
```

11.2.3   For Plugins Only

A handful of class methods in `AssetTagHelper` relate to configuration and are intended for use in plugins.

- `register_javascript_expansion`
- `register_stylesheet_expansion`

11.3   `AssetUrlHelper`

This module provides methods for generating asset paths and URLs and contains some of the most commonly used helpers in Rails. All have `_path` and `_url` variants, which produce relative and absolute URL strings, accordingly:

```
image_path("rails.png")
# => "/assets/rails.png"

image_url("rails.png")
# => "http://www.example.com/assets/rails.png"
```

🔑 Note that all of these methods are aliased so that you have a workaround in case of name conflict with your own application's resources names such as assets, images, etc.

11.3.1   `asset_path(source, options = {})`

Computes the path to asset in public directory. If `:type` options is set, a file extension will be appended and scoped to the corresponding public directory.

All other asset `*_path` helpers delegate through this method.

```
asset_path "application.js"
# => /assets/application.js
```

```
asset_path "application", type: :javascript
# => /assets/application.js
asset_path "application", type: :stylesheet
# => /assets/application.css
```

Also aliased as `path_to_asset`.

11.3.2 `asset_url(source, options = {})`

Computes the full URL to an asset in the public directory. This will use `asset_path` internally, so they behave the same way. If the `:host` option is set, it overrides the global `config.action_controller.asset_host` setting normally set in `config/environments/production.rb`.

```
asset_url "application.js", host: "http://cdn.example.com"
# => http://cdn.example.com/assets/application.js
```

Also aliased as `url_to_asset`.

11.3.3 `audio_path(source, options = {})`

Computes the path to an audio asset in the public audios directory. Full paths from the document root will be passed through. Used internally by `audio_tag` to build the audio path.

```
audio_path("horse")
# => /audios/horse
audio_path("horse.wav")
# => /audios/horse.wav
audio_path("sounds/horse.wav")
# => /audios/sounds/horse.wav
audio_path("/sounds/horse.wav")
# => /sounds/horse.wav
audio_path("http://www.example.com/sounds/horse.wav")
# => http://www.example.com/sounds/horse.wav
```

Also aliased as `path_to_audio`.

11.3.4 `audio_url(source, options = {})`

Computes the full URL to an audio asset in the public audios directory. This will use `audio_path` internally. Since `audio_url` is based on `asset_url` you can set `:host` options.

Also aliased as `url_to_audio`.

Helpers

11.3.5 `font_path(source, options = {})`

Computes the path to a font asset in the `app/assets/fonts` directory, which you would have to add yourself to your Rails project since it's not generated by default.

Full paths from the document root (beginning with a "/") will be passed through.

```
font_path("font.ttf")
# => /assets/font.ttf
font_path("dir/font.ttf")
# => /assets/dir/font.ttf
font_path("/dir/font.ttf")
# => /dir/font.ttf
```

Also aliased as `path_to_font`.

11.3.6 `font_url(source, options = {})`

Computes the full URL to a font asset. Uses `font_path` internally, so most of their behaviors will be the same. Since `font_url` is based on `asset_url` method you can set `:host` options.

Also aliased as `url_to_font`.

11.3.7 `image_path(source)`

Computes the path to an image asset in the `app/assets/images` directory. Full paths from the document root (beginning with a "/") will be passed through. This method is used internally by `image_tag` to build the image path.

```
image_path("edit.png")
# => /assets/edit.png
image_path("icons/edit.png")
# => /images/icons/edit.png
image_path("/icons/edit.png")
# => /icons/edit.png
```

If you have images as application resources this method may conflict with their named routes. The alias `path_to_image` is provided to avoid that. Rails uses the alias internally, and plugin authors are encouraged to do so.

Also aliased as `path_to_image`

11.3.8 `image_url(source, options = {})`

Computes the full URL to an image asset. This will use `image_path` internally, so most of their behaviors will be the same. Since `image_url` is based on `asset_url` you can set `:host` options.

Also aliased as `url_to_image`.

11.3.9 `javascript_path(source, options = {})`

Computes the path to a JavaScript asset in the public javascripts directory. If the source filename has no extension, .js will be appended (except for explicit URIs) Full paths from the document root will be passed through. Used internally by `javascript_include_tag` to build the script path.

```
javascript_path "xmlhr"
# => /assets/xmlhr.js
javascript_path "dir/xmlhr.js"
# => /assets/dir/xmlhr.js
javascript_path "/dir/xmlhr"
# => /dir/xmlhr.js
javascript_path "http://www.example.com/js/xmlhr"
# => http://www.example.com/js/xmlhr
javascript_path "http://www.example.com/js/xmlhr.js"
# => http://www.example.com/js/xmlhr.js
```

Also aliased as `path_to_javascript`.

11.3.10 `javascript_url(source, options = {})`

Computes the full URL to a JavaScript asset in the public javascripts directory. This will use `javascript_path` internally, so most of their behaviors will be the same. Since `javascript_url` is based on `asset_url` you can set `:host` options.

Also aliased as `url_to_javascript`

11.3.11 `stylesheet_path(source, options = {})`

Computes the path to a stylesheet asset in the public stylesheets directory. If the source filename has no extension, `.css` will be appended (except for explicit URIs). Full paths from the document root will be passed through. Used internally by `stylesheet_link_tag` helper method to build the stylesheet path.

```
stylesheet_path "style"
# => /assets/style.css
stylesheet_path "dir/style.css"
# => /assets/dir/style.css
```

Helpers

```
stylesheet_path "/dir/style.css"
# => /dir/style.css
stylesheet_path "http://www.example.com/css/style"
# => http://www.example.com/css/style
stylesheet_path "http://www.example.com/css/style.css"
# => http://www.example.com/css/style.css
```

Also aliased as `path_to_stylesheet`.

11.3.12 `stylesheet_url(source, options = {})`

Computes the full URL to a stylesheet asset in the public stylesheets directory. This will use `stylesheet_path` internally, so most of their behaviors will be the same. Since `stylesheet_url` is based on `asset_url` you can set `:host` options.

Also aliased as `url_to_stylesheet`.

11.3.13 `video_path`

Computes the path to a video asset in the `public/videos` directory, which you would have to add yourself to your Rails project since it's not generated by default. Full paths from the document root will be passed through. Used internally by `video_tag` to build the video `src` path.

```
video_path("hd")
# => /videos/hd
video_path("hd.avi")
# => /videos/hd.avi
video_path("trailers/hd.avi")
# => /videos/trailers/hd.avi
video_path("/trailers/hd.avi")
# => /trailers/hd.avi

video_path("http://www.example.com/vid/hd.avi")
# => http://www.example.com/vid/hd.avi
```

Also aliased as `path_to_video`.

11.3.14 `video_url(source, options = {})`

Computes the full URL to a video asset in the public videos directory. This will use `video_path` internally, so most of their behaviors will be the same. Since `video_url` is based on `asset_url` method you can set `:host` options.

Also aliased as `url_to_video`.

11.3.15   Using Asset Hosts

By default, Rails links to these assets on the current host in the public folder, but you can direct Rails to link to assets from a dedicated asset server by setting `Action-Controller::Base.asset_host` in the application configuration, typically in `config/environments/production.rb`.

For example, you'd define `assets.example.com` to be your asset host this way, inside the configure block of your environment-specific configuration files:

```
config.action_controller.asset_host = "assets.example.com"
```

This module's helpers automatically take the asset host setting into account:

```
image_tag("rails.png")
# => <img alt="Rails" src="http://assets.example.com/assets/rails.png" />
stylesheet_link_tag("application")
# => <link href="http://assets.example.com/assets/application.css" media=
        "screen" rel="stylesheet" />
```

Why serve your assets from a different host name? Browsers open a limited number of simultaneous connections to a single host. The exact number varies by browser and version. This limit may cause some asset downloads to wait for previous assets to finish before they can begin.

You can use the `%d` wildcard in the `asset_host` setting to distribute the requests over four hosts. For example, `assets%d.example.com` will spread the asset requests over `assets0.example.com`, `assets0.example.com`, etc.

This may improve the asset loading performance of your application. It is also possible the combination of additional connection overhead (DNS, SSL) and the overall browser connection limits may result in this solution being slower. You should be sure to measure your actual performance across targeted browsers both before and after this change.

To implement the corresponding hosts you can either set up four actual hosts or use wildcard DNS to CNAME the wildcard to a single asset host.

If needed for some reason, you can exert more control over the asset host by setting `asset_host` to a proc, and it will get executed on demand. The proc is passed a `source` parameter with the absolute path of the asset (for example "/assets/rails. png") to work with. The second parameter is the http `request`, letting you inspect different aspects of the incoming request, such as whether it is secure.

Helpers

```
config.action_controller.asset_host = Proc.new { |source, request|
  if request && request.ssl?
    "#{request.protocol}#{request.host_with_port}"
  else
    "#{rest.protocol}assets.example.com"
  end
}
```

Note that the `request` parameter might not be supplied, the prime example being when assets are precompiled via a Rake task. Make sure to use a `Proc` instead of a lambda, since a `Proc` allows missing parameters and sets them to nil.

As with other parts of Rails that take procs, an alternative that accomodates more complex logic is implementing a custom asset host object that responds to `call` and takes either one or two parameters just like the proc.

```
config.action_controller.asset_host = AssetHostingConfig.new
```

11.4 `AtomFeedHelper`

Provides an `atom_feed` helper to aid in generating Atom feeds in Builder templates.

```
atom_feed do |feed|
  feed.title("My great blog!)
  feed.updated(@posts.first.created_at)

  @posts.each do |post|
    feed.entry(post) do |entry|
      entry.title(post.title)
      entry.content(post.body, type: 'html')

      entry.author do |author|
        author.name("DHH")
      end
    end
  end
end
```

The options for `atom_feed` are:

language Defaults to "en-US".

root_url The HTML alternative that this feed is doubling for. Defaults to "/" on the current host.

url The URL for this feed. Defaults to the current URL.

id The id for this feed. Defaults to `tag:#{request.host},#{options}:`
`#{request.fullpath.spl`.

schema_date The date at which the tag scheme for the feed was first used. A
good default is the year you created the feed. See http://feedvalidator.org/
docs/error/InvalidTAG.html for more information. If not specified, 2005 is
used by default.

instruct Hash of XML processing instructions in the form `{target =>`
`{attribute => value, ...}}` or `{target => [{attribute =>`
`value, ...}, ]}`.

Other namespaces can be added to the root element:

```
atom_feed(
  'xmlns:app' => 'http://www.w3.org/2007/app',
  'xmlns:openSearch' => 'http://a9.com/-/spec/opensearch/1.1/'
) do |feed|
  feed.title("My great blog!")
  feed.updated((@posts.first.created_at))
  feed.tag!(openSearch:totalResults, 10)

  @posts.each do |post|
    feed.entry(post) do |entry|
      entry.title(post.title)
      entry.content(post.body, type: 'html')
      entry.tag!('app:edited', Time.now)

      entry.author do |author|
        author.name("DHH")
      end
    end
  end
end
```

The Atom spec defines five elements that may directly contain xhtml content if
`type: 'xhtml'` is specified as an attribute:

- `content`
- `rights`
- `title`
- `subtitle`
- `summary`

Helpers

If any of these elements contain xhtml content, this helper will take care of the needed enclosing div and an xhtml namespace declaration.

```
entry.summary type: 'xhtml' do |xhtml|
  xhtml.p pluralize(order.line_items.count, "line item")
  xhtml.p "Shipped to #{order.address}"
  xhtml.p "Paid by #{order.pay_type}"
end
```

The `atom_feed` method yields an `AtomFeedBuilder` instance. Nested elements also yield `AtomBuilder` instances.

11.5 `CacheHelper`

This module contains helper methods related to caching fragments of a view. Fragment caching is useful when certain elements of an action change frequently or depend on complicated state, while other parts rarely change or can be shared among multiple parties. The boundaries of a fragment to be cached are defined within a view template using the `cache` helper method.

This topic and its helper method are covered in detail in the caching section of Chapter 17, "Caching and Performance."

11.6 `CaptureHelper`

One of the great features of Rails views is that you are not limited to rendering a single *flow* of content. Along the way, you can define blocks of template code that should be inserted into other parts of the page during rendering using `yield`, as described in Chapter 10's section about yielding content.

The technique is accomplished via a pair of methods from the `CaptureHelper` module.

11.6.1 `capture(&block)`

The `capture` method lets you capture part of a template's output (inside a block) and assign it to an instance variable. The value of that variable can subsequently be used anywhere else on the template.

```
- message_html = capture do
  %div
    This is a message
```

I don't think that the `capture` method is that useful on its own in a template. It's a lot more useful when you use it in your own custom helper methods. It gives you the capability to write your own helpers that grab template content wrapped using a block. We cover that technique later on in this chapter in the section "Writing Your Own View Helpers."

11.6.2 `content_for(name, &block)`

This helper helps you to designate a part of your template as content for another part of the page. It works similarly to its sister method `capture` (in fact, it uses `capture` itself). Instead of returning the contents of the block provided to it, it stores the content to be retrieved using `yield` elsewhere in the template (or most commonly, in the surrounding layout).

A common example is to insert *sidebar* content into a layout. In the following example, the link will not appear in the *flow* of the view template. It will appear elsewhere in the template, wherever `yield :navigation_sidebar` appears.

```
- content_for :navigation_sidebar do
  = link_to 'Detail Page', item_detail_path(item)
```

By default, the `content_for` helper concatenates whatever blocks it is given with the same identifier.

Take the following example of a navigation scheme. First we add a link to home:

```
- content_for :navigation do
  = link_to 'Home', root_path
```

And in another place in the view templates, we add a link for the login:

```
- content_for :navigation do
  = link_to 'Login', login_path
```

Then, in another template or layout, the following code would render both links in order:

```
= yield :navigation
```

If the `flush` parameter is `true`, then `content_for` replaces previous content instead of concatenating.

Simple content can be passed as a parameter, like this:

```
- content_for :page_script, javascript_include_tag('page-specific')
```

Helpers

⚠ Due to inherent limitations, the `content_for` helper is ignored in caches. So you shouldn't use it in markup that is destined to be fragment cached.

11.6.3 `content_for?(name)`

Using this method, you can check whether the template will ultimately yield any content under a particular name using the `content_for` helper method so that you can make layout decisions earlier in the template. The following example clearly illustrates usage of this method, by altering the CSS class of the `body` element dynamically:

```
%body{class: content_for?(:right_col) ? 'one-column' : 'two-column'}
  = yield
  = yield :right_col
```

11.6.4 `provide(name, content = nil, &block)`

The `provide` helper method works the same way as `content_for`, except for when used with streaming. When streaming, `provide` flushes the current buffer straight back to the layout and stops looking for more contents.

If you want to concatenate multiple times to the same buffer when rendering a given template you should use `content_for` instead.

11.7 **ControllerHelper**

This undocumented module provides all methods and behavior that delegate to the view's associated controller. That includes methods such as `flash`, `action_name`, and `controller_name`, etc.

11.8 **CsrfHelper**

The `CsrfHelper` module only contains one method, named `csrf_meta_tags`. Including it in the <head> section of your template will output meta tags "csrf-param" and "csrf-token" with the name of the cross-site request forgery protection parameter and token, respectively.

```
%head
= csrf_meta_tags
```

The meta tags "csrf-param" and "csrf-token" are used by Rails to generate dynamic forms that implement non-remote links with `:method`. You don't need to use these tags for regular forms as they generate their own hidden fields containing the same data.

For AJAX requests other than GETs, extract the `csrf-token` from the meta-tag and send as the `"X-CSRF-Token"` HTTP header. If you are using jQuery with `jquery-rails`, this happens automatically.

11.9 **DateHelper**

The `DateHelper` module is used primarily to create HTML `select` tags for different kinds of calendar data. It also features one of the longest-named helper methods, a beast peculiar to Rails, called `distance_of_time_in_words_to_now`.

💬 Lark says . . .

I guess that helper method name was too much of a mouthful, since at some point it was aliased to `time_ago_in_words`.

11.9.1 The Date and Time Selection Helpers

The following methods help you create form field input tags dealing with date and time data. All of them are prepared for multi-parameter assignment to an Active Record object. That's a fancy way of saying that even though they appear in the HTML form as separate input fields, when they are posted back to the server, it is understood that they refer to a single attribute of the model. That's some Rails magic for you!

🔑 Using the traditional Rails date input fields should be a crime. Use an HTML5 text input field with `type=date` instead, to get a native calendar widget for free.

11.9.1.1 `date_select(object_name, method, options = {}, html_options = {})`

Returns a matched set of three `select` tags (one each for year, month, and day) preselected for accessing a specified date-based attribute (identified by the `method` parameter) on an object assigned to the template (identified by `object_name`).

It's possible to tailor the selects through the options hash, which accepts all the keys that each of the individual select builders do (such as `:use_month_-numbers` for `select_month`).

The `date_select` method also takes `:discard_year`, `:discard_month`, and `:discard_day` options, which drop the corresponding `select` tag from the set of three. Common sense dictates that discarding the month select will also automatically discard the day select. If the day is omitted, but not the month, Rails will assume that the day should be the first of the month.

It's also possible to explicitly set the order of the tags using the `:order` option with an array of symbols `:year`, `:month`, and `:day` in the desired order. Symbols may be omitted, and the respective `select` tag is not included.

Passing `disabled: true` as part of the options will make elements inaccessible for change.

```
date_select(:post, "written_on")
date_select(:post, "written_on", start_year: 1995,
                                 use_month_numbers: true,
                                 discard_day: true,
                                 include_blank: true)
date_select(:post, "written_on", order: [:day, :month, :year])
date_select(:user, "birthday", order: [:month, :day])
```

If anything is passed in the `html_options` hash it will be applied to every select tag in the set.

11.9.1.2 `datetime_select(object_name, method, options = {}, html_options = {})`

Works exactly like `date_select`, except for the addition of hour and minute `select` tags. Seconds may be added with the option `:include_seconds`. Along with the addition of time information come additional discarding options: `:discard_hour`, `:discard_minute`, and `:discard_seconds`.

Setting the `ampm` option to `true` returns hours in the AM/PM format.

```
datetime_select("post", "written_on")
datetime_select("post", "written_on", ampm: true)
```

11.9.1.3 `time_select(object_name, method, options = {}, html_options = {})`

Returns a set of `select` tags (one for hour, minute, and optionally second) preselected for accessing a specified time-based attribute (identified by `method`) on an object assigned to the template (identified by `object_name`). You can include the seconds by setting the `:include_seconds` option to `true`.

As with `datetime_select`, setting `ampm: true` will result in hours displayed in the AM/PM format.

```
time_select("post", "sunrise")
time_select("post", "written_on", include_seconds: true)
time_select("game", "written_on", ampm: true)
```

11.9.2   The Individual Date and Time Select Helpers

Sometimes you need just a particular element of a date or time, and Rails obliges you with a comprehensive set of individual date and time select helpers. In contrast to the date and time helpers that we just looked at, the following helpers are not bound to an instance variable on the page. Instead, they all take a date or time Ruby object as their first parameter. (All of these methods have a set of common options, covered in the following subsection.)

11.9.2.1   `select_date(date = Date.current, options = {}, html_options = {})`

Returns a set of `select` tags (one each for year, month, and day) pre-selected with the date provided (or the current date). It's possible to explicitly set the order of the tags using the `:order` option with an array of symbols `:year`, `:month`, and `:day` in the desired order.

```
select_date(started_at, order: [:year, :month, :day])
```

11.9.2.2   `select_datetime(datetime = Time.current, options = {}, html_options = {})`

Returns a set of `select` tags (one each for year, month, day, hour, and minute) pre-selected with the datetime. Optionally, setting the `include_seconds: true` option adds a seconds field. It's also possible to explicitly set the order of the tags using the `:order` option with an array of symbols `:year`, `:month`, and `:day`, `:hour`, `:minute`, and `:seconds` in the desired order. You can also add character values for the `:date_separator` and `:time_separator` options to control visual display of the elements (they default to `"/"` and `":"`).

11.9.2.3   `select_day(date, options = {}, html_options = {})`

Returns a `select` tag with options for each of the days 1 through 31 with the current day selected. The date can also be substituted for a day value ranging from 1 to 31. If displaying days with a leading zero is your preference, setting the option `use_two_digit_numbers` to `true` will accomplish this.

```
select_day(started_at)
select_day(10)
select_day(5, use_two_digit_numbers: true)
```

Helpers

By default, the field name defaults to `day` but can be overridden using the `:field_name` option.

11.9.2.4 `select_hour(datetime, options = {}, html_options = {})`

Returns a `select` tag with options for each of the hours 0 through 23 with the current hour selected. The `datetime` parameter can be substituted with an hour number from 0 to 23. Setting the `ampm` option to `true` will result in hours displayed in the AM/PM format. By default, the field name defaults to `hour` but can be overridden using the `:field_name` option.

11.9.2.5 `select_minute(datetime, options = {}, html_options = {})`

Returns a `select` tag with options for each of the minutes 0 through 59 with the current minute selected. Also can return a `select` tag with options by `minute_step` from 0 through 59 with the 00 minute selected. The `datetime` parameter can be substituted by a seconds value of 0 to 59. By default, the field name defaults to `minute` but can be overridden using the `:field_name` option.

11.9.2.6 `select_month(date, options = {}, html_options = {})`

Returns a `select` tag with options for each of the months January through December with the current month selected. By default, the month names are presented as user options in the drop-down selection, and the month numbers (1 through 12) are used as values submitted to the server.

It's also possible to use month numbers for the presentation instead of names by setting `use_month_numbers: true`. To display month numbers with a leading zero, set option `:use_two_digit_numbers` to `true`. If you happen to want both numbers and names, set `add_month_numbers: true`. If you would prefer to show month names as abbreviations, set the `:use_short_month` option to `true`. Finally, if you want to use your own month names, set the value of the `:use_month_names` key in your options to an array of 12 month names.

```
# Will use keys like "January", "March"
select_month(Date.today)

# Will use keys like "1", "3"
select_month(Date.today, use_month_numbers: true)

# Will use keys like "1 - January", "3 - March"
```

```
select_month(Date.today, add_month_numbers: true)

# Will use keys like "Jan", "Mar"
select_month(Date.today, use_short_month: true)

# Will use keys like "Januar", "Marts"
select_month(Date.today, use_month_names: %w(Januar Februar Marts ...))
```

By default, the field name defaults to `month` but can be overridden using the `:field_name` option.

11.9.2.7 select_second(datetime, options = {}, html _options = {})

Returns a `select` tag with options for each of the seconds 0 through 59 with the current second selected. The `datetime` parameter can either be a `DateTime` object or a second given as a number. By default, the field name defaults to `second` but can be overridden using the `:field_name` option.

11.9.2.8 select_time(datetime = Time.current, options = {}, html_options = {})

Returns a set of HTML `select` tags (one for hour and minute). You can set the `:time_separator` option to format the output. It's possible to take an input for sections by setting option `:include_seconds` to `true`.

```
select_time(some_time, time_separator: ':', include_seconds: true)
```

11.9.2.9 select_year(date, options = {}, html_options = {})

Returns a `select` tag with options for each of the five years on each side of the current year selected. The five-year radius can be changed using the `:start_year` and `:end_year` options. Both ascending and descending year lists are supported by making `:start_year` less than or greater than `:end_year`. The date parameter can either be a `Date` object or a year given as a number.

```
# ascending year values
select_year(Date.today, start_year: 1992, end_year: 2007)

# descending year values
select_year(Date.today, start_year: 2005, end_year: 1900)
```

By default, the field name defaults to `year`, but can be overridden using the `:field_name` option.

Helpers

11.9.3   Common Options for Date Selection Helpers

All of the select-type methods share a number of common options that are as follows:

:discard_type Set to `true` if you want to discard the type part of the select name. If set to `true`, the `select_month` method would use simply `date` (which can be overwritten using `:prefix`) instead of `date[month]`.

:field_name Enables you to override the natural name of a `select` tag (from day, minute, and so on).

:include_blank Set to `true` if it should be possible to set an empty date.

:prefix Overwrites the default prefix of `date` used for the names of the `select` tags. Specifying `birthday` would result in a name of `birthday[month]` instead of `date[month]` when passed to the `select_month` method.

:use_hidden Set to `true` to embed the value of the datetime into the page as an HTML hidden input, instead of a `select` tag.

:disabled Set to `true` if you want show the select fields as disabled.

:prompt Set to `true` (for a generic prompt), a prompt string or a hash of prompt strings for `:year`, `:month`, `:day`, `:hour`, `:minute`, and `:second`.

11.9.4   **distance_in_time** Methods with Complex Descriptive Names

Some `distance_in_time` methods have really long, complex descriptive names that nobody can ever remember without looking them up. Well, at least for the first dozen times or so you might not remember.

I find the following methods to be a perfect example of the Rails way when it comes to API design. Instead of going with a shorter and necessarily more cryptic alternative, the framework author decided to keep the name long and descriptive. It's one of those cases where a nonprogrammer can look at your code and understand what it's doing. Well, probably.

I also find these methods remarkable in that they are part of why people sometimes consider Rails part of the Web 2.0 phenomenon (circa 2008). What other web framework would include ways to humanize the display of timestamps?

11.9.4.1 `distance_of_time_in_words(from_time, to_time = 0, include_seconds_or_options = {}, options = {}))`

Reports the approximate distance in time between two `Time`, `DateTime`, or `Date` objects or integers as seconds. Set the `include_seconds` parameter to `true` if you want more detailed approximations when the distance is less than 1 minute. The easiest way to show what this method does is via examples:

```
>> from_time = Time.current

>> helper.distance_of_time_in_words(from_time, from_time + 50.minutes)
=> about 1 hour

>> helper.distance_of_time_in_words(from_time, from_time + 15.seconds)
=> less than a minute

>> helper.distance_of_time_in_words(from_time, from_time + 15.seconds,
    include_seconds: true)
=> less than 20 seconds

>> helper.distance_of_time_in_words(from_time, 3.years.from_now)
=> about 3 years
```

The Rails API docs ask you to note that Rails calculates 1 year as 365.25 days.

11.9.4.2 `distance_of_time_in_words_to_now(from_time, include_seconds_or_options = {})`

Works exactly like `distance_of_time_in_words` except that the `to_time` is hard-coded to the current time. Usually invoked on `created_at` or `updated_at` attributes of your model, followed by the string `ago` in your template, as in the following example:

```
%strong= comment.user.name
%br
%small= "#{distance_of_time_in_words_to_now(review.created_at)} ago"
```

Note that this method is aliased to `time_ago_in_words` for those who prefer shorter method names.

11.9.5 `time_tag(date_or_time, *args, &block)`

Introduced in Rails 3.1, the `time_tag` returns an HTML5 time element for a given date or time. Using the semantic `time_tag` helper ensures that your date or times within your markup are in a machine-readable format. Setting the option `pubdate`

Helpers

to `true` will add the attribute to the tag, indicating that the date or time is a publishing date. The following examples show the output you can expect when using it:

```
time_tag(Date.current)
# => <time datetime="2013-08-13">August 13, 2013</time>

time_tag(Time.current)
# => <time datetime="2013-08-13T14:58:29Z">August 13, 2013 14:58</time>

time_tag(Time.current, pubdate: true)
# => <time datetime="2013-08-13T15:02:56Z"
        pubdate="pubdate">August 13, 2013 15:02</time>

= time_tag(Date.current) do
%strong Once upon a time
# => <time datetime="2013-08-13"><strong>Once upon a time</strong></time>
```

11.10 `DebugHelper`

The `DebugHelper` module only contains one method, named `debug`. Output it in your template, passing it an object that you want dumped to YAML and displayed in the browser inside PRE tags. Useful for debugging during development, but not much else.

11.11 `FormHelper`

The `FormHelper` module provides a set of methods for working with HTML forms, especially as they relate to Active Record model objects assigned to the template. Its methods correspond to each type of HTML input fields (such as text, password, select, and so on) available. When the form is submitted, the value of the input fields are bundled into the `params` that is passed to the controller.

There are two types of form helper methods. The types found in this module are meant to work specifically with Active Record model attributes, and the similarly named versions in the `FormTagHelper` module are not.

 Note

The form helper methods in this section can also be used with non Active Record models, as long as the model passes the Active Model Lint tests found in the module `ActiveModel::Lint::Tests`. The easiest way to do this is to include the module mixin `ActiveModel::Model` to your class.

11.11.1   Creating Forms for Models

The core method of this helper is `form_for`, and we mentioned it in Chapter 3, "REST, Resources, and Rails."

The `form_for` helper method creates an HTML form that allows the user to create or update the attributes of a specific model object and potentially associated objects. The method takes a block and yields a `form` object, on which you can invoke input helper methods. When you call input helper methods on the `form` object, you omit their first `object_name` parameter, since it can be inferred from the form.

The `form_for` method can be used in several slightly different ways, depending on how much you wish to rely on Rails to infer automatically from the model how the form should be constructed. For a generic model object, a form can be created by passing `form_for` a string or symbol naming an object:

```
= form_for :person do |f|
  .field
    First name:
    = f.text_field :first_name
  .field
    Last name:
    = f.text_field :last_name
  .field
    Bio:
    = f.text_area :bio
  .field
    Admin?
    = f.check_box :admin
  .actions
    = f.submit
```

In the example above, the variable f yielded to the block is a `FormBuilder` object that incorporates the knowledge about the model object represented by `:person` passed to `form_for`. Methods defined on the `FormBuilder` are used to generate fields bound to this model.

Thus, for example

```
f.text_field :first_name
```

will get expanded to

```
text_field :person, :first_name
```

which results in an HTML <input> tag, the name attribute of which is person [first_name]. This means that when the form is submitted, the value entered by the user will be available in the controller as params[:person][:first_name].

If :person also happens to be the name of an instance variable @person, then the default value of the fields shown when the form is initially displayed will be the value of the corresponding attributes of @person.

11.11.1.1   Use with Model Object Instances

While our examples so far have passed form_for a symbol as its first argument, it's entirely possible to pass a live object instance instead. This behaves in almost the same way as outlined previously, with a couple of small exceptions. First, the prefix used to name the input elements within the form (and their prefix in the params hash) is derived from the object's class. If the object is an instance of Post you'll get attributes submitted as params[:post].

A second, important effect is that the default values used to fill the form's inputs will be taken from the model object instance.

Third, if the model object passed in is configured as a RESTful resource, Rails will try to infer the URL and HTTP method that the form should use automatically, instead of requiring explicit options to be set.

Assume that post in the following example is an existing resource to be edited by the user.

```
form_for post do |f|
```

is *syntax sugar* for

```
form_for post, as: :post, url: post_path(post), method: :patch,
               html: { class: "edit_post", id: "edit_post_45" } do |f|
}
```

The form_for method also recognizes new records, by calling new? on the object you pass to it, and would result in the following options:

```
url: posts_path, html: { class: "new_post", id: "new_post" }
```

11.11.1.2   **form_for** Options

In any of its variants, the rightmost argument to form_for is an optional hash of options:

as If you want the resulting params hash posted to your controller to be named based on something other than the class name of the object you pass to `form_for`, you can pass an arbitrary symbol to the `:as` option:

```
form_for person, as: :client do |f|
```

In that case, the following call to `text_field`

```
f.text_field :first_name
```

would get expanded to

```
text_field :client, :first_name, object: person
```

and submitted to the controller as `params[:client][:first_name]`.

authenticity_token Authenticity token to use in the form. Use only if you need to pass a custom authenticity token string or not at all (by passing `false`).

✎ If your app only uses remote forms, you may remove the automatic embedded authenticity tokens by setting `config.action_view.embed_authenticity_token_in_remote_forms = false`. This is really helpful when you're fragment-caching the form. Remote forms get their authenticity token from a `meta` tag in the page head, so embedding one inside the form is unnecessary.

---

builder Optional form builder class (instead of `ActionView::Helpers::FormBuilder`).

enforce_utf8 Set to `false` to disable the hidden input with name utf8. Having trouble with incoming data that is not UTF-8 encoded? Take a look at https://github.com/singlebrook/utf8-cleaner.

html Optional HTML attributes for the generated HTML `form` tag.

method The HTTP method to use when submitting the form. This option defaults to POST. For browser compatibility reasons, if PATCH, PUT, DELETE or another verb is used, a hidden input with name _method is added to the form in order to simulate the verb, and Rails will pick it up automatically. (POST will still be used as the underlying transport method.)

namespace A namespace that will be prefixed with an underscore on the generated HTML id of the form.

remote If set to `true`, Rails UJS code will control the submit behavior (as opposed to a normal HTML submit action.) More on this topic in Chapter 20, "Ajax on Rails."

Helpers

url The URL to which the form is submitted. It takes the same fields you pass to `url_for` or `link_to`. In particular, you may pass a named route directly here as well. Defaults to the current action.

11.11.1.3   Resource-Oriented Style

The preferred way to use `form_for` is to rely on automated resource identification, which will use the conventions and named routes of that approach, instead of manually configuring the `:url` option.

For example, if `post` is an existing record to be edited, then the resource-oriented style:

```
= form_for post do |f|
```

is equivalent to

```
= form_for post, as: :post, url: post_path(post),
    method: :patch, html: { class: "edit_post",
    id: "edit_post_45" } do |f|
```

The `form_for` method also recognizes new records, by calling `new?` on the object you pass to it.

```
= form_for(Post.new) do |f|
```

expands to

```
= form_for post, as: :post, url: posts_path, html: { class: "new_post",
    id: "new_post" } do |f|
```

The individual conventions can be overridden by supplying an object argument plus `:url`, `:method`, and/or `:html` options.

```
= form_for(post, url: super_post_path(post)) do |f|
```

You can create forms with namespaced routes by passing an array as the first argument, as in the following example, which would map to `admin_post_url`:

```
= form_for([:admin, post]) do |f|
```

The following example is the equivalent (old-school) version of `form_tag`, which doesn't use a yielded form object and explicitly names the object being used in the input fields:

```
= form_tag people_path do
  .field
    = label :person, :first_name
```

```
      = text_field :person, :first_name
    .field
      = label :person, :last_name
      = text_field :person, :last_name
    .buttons
      = submit_tag 'Create'
```

The first version has slightly less repetition (remember your DRY principle) and is almost always going to be more convenient as long as you're rendering Active Record objects.

11.11.1.4   Variables Are Optional

If you explicitly specify the object name parameter for input fields rather than letting them be supplied by the form, keep in mind that it doesn't have to match a *live* object instance in scope for the template. Rails won't complain if the object is not there. It will simply put blank values in the resulting form.

11.11.1.5   Rails-Generated Form Conventions

The HTML generated by the `form_for` invocations in the preceding example is characteristic of Rails forms and follows specific naming conventions.

In case you're wondering, the `authenticity_token` hidden field with gibberish up near the top of the form has to do with protection against malicious Cross-Site Request Forgery (CSRF) attacks.

```html
<form accept-charset="UTF-8" action="/people" method="post">
  <div style="margin:0;padding:0;display:inline">
    <input name="utf8" type="hidden" value="&#x2713;" />
    <input name="authenticity_token" type="hidden"
           value="afl+6u3J/2meoHtve69q+tD9gPc3/QUsHCqPh85Z4WU=" /></div>
  <div class='field'>
    <label for="person_first_name">First name</label>
    <input id="person_first_name" name="person[first_name]" type="text" />
  </div>
  <div class='field'>
    <label for="person_last_name">Last name</label>
    <input id="person_last_name" name="person[last_name]" type="text" />
  </div>
  <div class='buttons'>
  <input name="commit" type="submit" value="Create" />
  </div>
</form>
```

When this form is submitted, the `params` hash will look like the following example (using the format reflected in your development log for every request):

Helpers

```
Parameters: {"utf8"=>"✓",
"authenticity_token"=>"afl+6u3J/2meoHtve69q+tD9gPc3/QUsHCqPh85Z4WU=",
"person"=>{"first_name"=>"William", "last_name"=>"Smith"},
"commit"=>"Create"}
```

ℹ The parameters contain utf8=✓ to force the client to use UTF-8 encoding in its request. It works because the key-value-pair (which is ignored by the server) contains a unicode-only character. This workaround/hack is primarily necessary because old versions of Microsoft Internet Explorer tried to send everything in Latin-1 encoding.

As you can see, the params hash has a nested "person" value, which is accessed using params[:person] in the controller. That's pretty fundamental Rails knowledge, and I'd be surprised if you didn't know it already. I promise we won't rehash much more basic knowledge after the following section.

11.11.1.6 Displaying Existing Values

If you were editing an existing instance of Person, that object's attribute values would have been filled into the form. That's also pretty fundamental Rails knowledge. What about if you want to edit a new model object instance, pre-populated with certain values? Do you have to pass the values as options to the input helper methods? No. Since the form helpers display the values of the model's attributes, it would simply be a matter of initializing the object with the desired values in the controller, as follows:

```
expose :person, build: -> {
  # Set default values that you want to appear in the form
  Person.new(first_name: 'First', last_name: 'Last')
}
```

We covered the Decent Exposure gem and its expose method in the last chapter.

Since you're only using new, no record is persisted to the database, and your default values magically appear in the input fields.

MIXING INPUT HELPERS

Note that form_for doesn't create an exclusive scope. It's possible to use both the stand-alone FormHelper methods along with methods from FormTagHelper.

For example:

```
= form_for :person do |f|
  %label First name
  = f.text_field :first_name
  %label Last name
  = f.text_field :last_name
  = check_box_tag "person[admin]", "1", @person.company.admin?
  Admin?
  = f.submit
```

This also works for the methods in `FormOptionHelper` and `DateHelper` that are designed to work with an object as base, like `collection_select` and `datetime_select`.

11.11.2 How Form Helpers Get Their Values

A rather important lesson to learn about Rails form helper methods is that the value they display comes directly from the database prior to *meddling* by the developer. Unless you know what you're doing, you may get some unexpected results if you try to override the values to be displayed in a form.

Let's illustrate with a simple `LineItem` model, which has a decimal `rate` attribute (by merit of a `rate` column in its database table). We'll override its implicit rate accessor with one of our own:

```
class LineItem < ActiveRecord::Base
  def rate
    "A RATE"
  end
end
```

In normal situations, the overridden accessor is hiding access to the real rate attribute, as we can illustrate using the console:

```
>> li = LineItem.new
=> #<LineItem ...>
>> li.rate
=> "A RATE"
```

However, suppose you were to compose a form to edit line items using form helpers:

```
= form_for line_item do |f|
  = f.text_field :rate
```

You would find that it works normally, as if that overridden `rate` accessor doesn't exist. The fact is that Rails form helpers use special methods named `attribute_before_type_cast` (which are covered in Chapter 5, "Working with Active

Record"). The preceding example would use the method `rate_before_type_cast` and bypass the overriding method we defined.

11.11.3   Integrating Additional Objects in One Form

The `fields_for` helper method creates a scope around a specific model object like `form_for` but doesn't create the form tags themselves. Neither does it have an actual HTML representation as a `div` or `fieldset`. The `fields_for` method is suitable for specifying additional model objects in the same form, particularly associations of the main object being represented in the form.

11.11.3.1   Generic Examples

The following simple example represents a person and its associated permissions.

```
= form_for person do |f| %>
  First name:
  = f.text_field :first_name
  Last name:
  = f.text_field :last_name
  .permissions
    = fields_for person.permission do |permission_fields|
      Admin?:
      = permission_fields.check_box :admin
```

11.11.3.2   Nested Attributes Examples

When the object belonging to the current scope has a nested attribute writer for a certain attribute, `fields_for` will yield a new scope for that attribute. This enables you to create forms that set or change the attributes of a parent object and its associations in one go.

Nested attribute writers are normal setter methods named after an association. The most common way of defining these writers is either by declaring `accepts_nested_attributes_for` in a model definition or by defining a method with the proper name. For example, the attribute writer for the association `:address` is called `address_attributes=`.

Whether a one-to-one or one-to-many style form builder will be yielded depends on whether the normal reader method returns a single object or an array of objects. Consider a simple Ruby `Person` class that returns a single `Address` from its `address` reader method and responds to the `address_attributes=` writer method:

```
class Person
```

```
  def address
    @address
  end

  def address_attributes=(attributes)
    # Process the attributes hash
  end
end
```

This model can now be used with a nested `fields_for`, like:

```
= form_for person do |f|
  = f.fields_for :address do |address_fields|
    Street:
    = address_fields.text_field :street
    Zip code:
    = address_fields.text_field :zip_code
```

When address is already an association on a Person you can use `accepts_nested_attributes_for` to define the writer method for you, like this:

```
class Person < ActiveRecord::Base
  has_one :address
  accepts_nested_attributes_for :address
end
```

> The `:autosave` option is automatically enabled on every association for which `accepts_nested_attributes_for` is used.

If you want to destroy the associated model through the form, you have to enable it first using the `:allow_destroy` option for `accepts_nested_attributes_for` like this:

```
class Person < ActiveRecord::Base
  has_one :address
  accepts_nested_attributes_for :address, allow_destroy: true
end
```

Now, when you use a check box form element specially named _destroy, with a value that evaluates to `true`, the logic generated by `accepts_nested_attribute_for` will destroy the associated model. (This is a super useful technique for list screens that enable deletion of multiple records at once using check boxes.)

```
= form_for person do |f|
  = f.fields_for :address do |address_fields|
```

```
Delete this address:
= address_fields.check_box :_destroy
```

11.11.3.3 `fields_for` with One-to-Many Associations

Consider a Person class that returns an array of Project instances from the projects reader method and responds to the projects_attributes= writer method:

```
class Person < ActiveRecord::Base
  def projects
    [@project1, @project2]
  end

  def projects_attributes=(attributes)
    # Process the attributes hash
  end
end
```

This model can now be used with a nested fields_for helper method in a form. The block given to the nested fields_for call will be repeated for each instance in the collection automatically:

```
= form_for person do |f|
  = f.fields_for :projects do |project_fields|
    .project
      Name:
      = project_fields.text_field :name
```

It's also possible to specify the instance to be used by doing the iteration yourself. The symbol passed to fields_for refers to the reader method of the parent object of the form, but the second argument contains the actual object to be used for fields:

```
= form_for person do |f|
  - person.projects.select(&:active?).each do |project|
    = f.fields_for :projects, project do |project_fields|
      .project
        Name:
        = project_fields.text_field :name
```

Since fields_for also understands a collection as its second argument in that situation, you can shrink that last example to the following code. Just inline the projects collection:

```
= form_for person do |f|
  = f.fields_for :projects, projects.select(&:active?) do |project_fields|
```

```
.project
  Name:
  = project_fields.text_field :name
```

If in our example Person was an Active Record model and projects was one of its has_many associations, then you could use `accepts_nested_attributes_for` to define the writer method for you:

```
class Person < ActiveRecord::Base
  has_many :projects
  accepts_nested_attributes_for :projects
```

If the hash submitted contains an `id` key that matches an already associated record, the matching record will be modified. If `id` is missing, a new record instance will be appended to the association.

As with using `accepts_nested_attributes_for` with a `belongs_to` association, if you want to destroy any of the associated models through the form, you have to enable it first using the `:allow_destroy` option:

```
class Person < ActiveRecord::Base
  has_many :projects
  accepts_nested_attributes_for :projects, allow_destroy: true
```

This will make it possible for you to specify which models to destroy in the attributes hash by adding a boolean form element named `_destroy`

```
= form_for person do |form|
  = form.fields_for :projects do |project_fields|
    Delete this project
     = project_fields.check_box :_destroy
```

You may also set a `:reject_if` proc to silently ignore any new record hashes if they fail to pass your criteria.

```
class Person < ActiveRecord::Base
  has_many :projects
  accepts_nested_attributes_for :projects, reject_if: proc { |attr|
  attr['name'].blank? }
```

 ⚲ The reason `reject_if` is useful is because it's quite common in situations where you have multiple lines of form inputs for child records for the UI to purposely leave a line or two blank at the end of the list as placeholders for new records.

11.11.3.4   Saving Nested Attributes

Nested records are updated on save, even when the intermediate parent record is unchanged. For example, consider the following model code:

```
class Project < ActiveRecord::Base
  has_many :tasks
  accepts_nested_attributes_for :tasks
end

class Task < ActiveRecord::Base
  belongs_to :project
  has_many :assignments
  accepts_nested_attributes_for :assignments
end

class Assignment < ActiveRecord::Base
  belongs_to :task
end
```

The following spec snippet illustrates nested saving:

```
# setup project, task and assignment objects...
project.update(name: project.name,
               tasks_attributes: [{
                                    id: task.id,
                                    name: task.name,
                                    assignments_attributes: [
                                      {
                                        id: assignment.id
                                        name: 'Paul'
                                    }]
               }]

assignment.reload
expect(assignment.name).to eq('Paul')
```

11.11.4   Customized Form Builders

Under the covers, the `form_for` and `fields_for` methods use a class named `ActionView::Helpers::FormBuilder`. An instance of it is yielded to the form block. Conveniently, you can subclass it in your application to override existing or define additional form helpers.

For example, let's say you made a builder class to automatically add labels to form inputs when `text_field` is called. You'd enable it with the `:builder` option like:

```
= form_for person, builder: LabelingFormBuilder do |f|
```

The `FormBuilder` object can be thought of as serving as a proxy for the methods in the `FormHelper` module. This class, however, allows you to call methods with the model object you are building the form for.

The standard set of helper methods for form building are located in the `field_helpers` class attribute of `ActionView::Helpers::FormBuilder`, and we're about to cover them individually in the next section.

If needed, you can create your own custom `FormBuilder` templates by subclassing `ActionView::Helpers::FormBuilder` and adding your own helper methods, like this one:

```
class MyFormBuilder < ActionView::Helpers::FormBuilder
  def div_radio_button(method, tag_value, options = {})
    @template.content_tag(:div,
      @template.radio_button(
        @object_name, method, tag_value, objectify_options(options)
      )
    )
  end
end
```

The preceding code creates a new method `div_radio_button` that wraps a `div` around a new radio button.

⚡ Note that when options are passed in, you must call `objectify_options` in order for the model object to get correctly passed to the method. If `objectify_options` is not called, then the newly created helper will not be linked back to the model.

The `div_radio_button` code from above can now be used as follows:

```
= form_for @person, :builder => MyFormBuilder do |f|
  I am a child:
  = f.div_radio_button(:admin, "child")
  I am an adult:
  = f.div_radio_button(:admin, "adult")
```

Detailed instructions about making custom form builder classes would fill its own chapter, but you could view the source of some popular Rails form builders such as SimpleForm[1] and formtastic[2] to learn more.

---

1. https://github.com/plataformatec/simple_form
2. https://github.com/justinfrench/formtastic

If you invest in making your custom form builder and like it so much that you want to use it by default across your whole app, it's possible to replace Rails' built-in form builder. Just override the value of `ActionView::Base.default_form_builder` in an initializer.

```
ActionView::Base.default_form_builder = MySuperSpecialFormBuilder
```

11.11.5 Form Inputs

For each of these methods, there is a similarly named form builder method that omits the `object_name` parameter, referencing instead the object that was passed in to `form_for` or `fields_for`.

11.11.5.1 `button(value = nil, options = {}, &block)`

Adds a button to a form.

```
f.button("Create post")
# => <button name='button' type='submit'>Create post</button>
```

When no `value` is given, it checks whether the object is a new resource or not in order to automatically generate an appropriate label:

```
= form_for post do |f|
  = f.button %>
```

In the preceding example, if `post` is a new record, it will use "Create Post" as its button label, otherwise, it uses "Update Post". Default labels for buttons can be customized using I18n, under the `helpers.submit` key (the same as submit helper) and accept the `%{model}` as an interpolation variable:

```
en:
  helpers:
    submit:
      create: "Create a %{model}"
      update: "Confirm changes to %{model}"
```

Rails also searches for a key specific to the provided object, in case you want to further customize the button values for a specific model:

```
en:
  helpers:
    submit:
      post:
```

```
create: "Add %{model}"
```

Since buttons can contain additional markup, passing a block to the button method instead of a value lets you wrap more than just a simple string value.

```
f.button do
  content_tag(:strong, 'Ask me!')
end

# => <button name='button' type='submit'>
#      <strong>Ask me!</strong>
#    </button>
```

11.11.5.2 `check_box(object_name, method, options = {}, checked_value = "1", unchecked_value = "0")`

Returns a check box tag tailored for accessing a specified attribute (identified by `method`) on an object encapsulated in the form builder or identified by the optional `object_name`. The model attribute should return an integer; if that integer is above zero, then the check box is checked. Additional options on the input tag can be passed in as `options`. The `checked_value` defaults to 1 while the default `unchecked_value` is set to 0, which will naturally typecast to boolean values.

Note that this helper generates an extra hidden input field to ensure that a `false` value is passed even if the check box is unchecked. Ordinarily, if it was unchecked it would simply be missing from the request parameters.

```
check_box('timesheet', 'approved')
# => <input name="timesheet[approved]" type="hidden" value="0"/>
#    <input checked="checked" type="checkbox" id="timesheet_approved"
#      name="timesheet[approved]" value="1" />
```

This way, the client either sends only the hidden field (representing the check box is unchecked), or both fields. Since the HTML specification says key/value pairs have to be sent in the same order they appear in the form, and parameters extraction gets the last occurrence of any repeated key in the query string, this little hack works for ordinary forms.

Unfortunately the hack fails for check boxes within array-like nested form fields, as in the following example.

```
= fields_for "project[invoice_attributes][]", invoice, index: nil do |form|
  = form.check_box :paid
```

In this situation, for each item with a checked check box you will end up with an extra ghost item for that attribute, assigned to "0". A potential workaround is to lose some of the magic by working with `check_box_tag`.

11.11.5.3 `color_field(object_name, method, options = {})`

Creates an HTML5-style color input field that enables setting of a color via hex values (as a string). The default value of a `color_field` is set to `"#000000"` if the underlying attribute is `nil`.

```
color_field(:car, :paint_color)
# => <input id="car_paint_color" name="car[paint_color]" type="color"
#       value="#000000" />"
```

To override the default value, pass a string in the format `"#RRGGBB"` to the option `:value`. This method is otherwise identical to `text_field`.

11.11.5.4 `date_field(object_name, method, options = {})`

Creates an HTML5-style date input field.

```
date_field(:person, :birthday)
# => <input id="person_birthday" name="person[birthday]" type="date" />
```

The default value is generated by trying to call `strftime` with `"%Y-%m-%d"` on the object's value, which makes it behave as expected for instances of `DateTime` and `ActiveSupport::TimeWithZone`. You can override the default by setting the `:value` option explicitly with a string in the format YYYY-MM-DD (ISO8601).

```
user.born_on = Date.new(1984, 1, 27)
...
date_field(:user, :born_on, value: "1984-05-12")
# => <input id="user_born_on" name="user[born_on]" type="date"
#     value="1984-05-12" />
```

The `:min` and `:max` options accept instances of `Date` or `Time`, or a string in the format YYYY-MM-DD (ISO8601).

```
date_field(:user, "born_on", min: Date.today)
# => <input id="user_born_on" name="user[born_on]" type="date"
#             min="2014-05-20" />

date_field(:user, "born_on", min: "2014-05-20")
# => <input id="user_born_on" name="user[born_on]" type="date"
#             min="2014-05-20" />
```

11.11.5.5 `datetime_field(object_name, method, options = {})`

Creates an HTML5-style datetype input field that accepts time entry in UTC. If a `DateTime` or `ActiveSupport::TimeWithZone` instance is provided to the helper by the underlying attribute, it calls `strftime` with "%Y-%m-%dT%T.%L%z" on the value to attempt setting a default value.

To override the default value, pass a string in the format "%Y-%m-%dT%T.%L%z" to the option `:value`. This method is otherwise identical to `date_field`.

11.11.5.6 `datetime_local_field(object_name, method, options = {})`

Creates an HTML5-style datetime-local input field. This method is otherwise identical to `datetime_field`, except that the value used is local over UTC.

11.11.5.7 `email_field(object_name, method, options = {})`

Creates an HTML5-style email input field. This method is otherwise identical to `text_field`.

```
email_field(:user, :email)
# => <input id="user_email" name="user[email]" type="email" />
```

11.11.5.8 `file_field(object_name, method, options = {})`

Creates a file upload field and automatically adds `multipart: true` to the enclosing form. See `file_field_tag` for more details.

11.11.5.9 `hidden_field(object_name, method, options = {})`

Creates a hidden field, with parameters and options similar to `text_field`.

11.11.5.10 `label(object_name, method, content_or_options = nil, options = nil, &block)`

Creates a label tag with the `for` attribute pointed at the specified input field.

```
label('timesheet', 'approved')
# => <label for="timesheet_approved">Approved</label>
label('timesheet', 'approved', 'Approved?')
# => <label for="timesheet_approved">Approved?</label>
```

Many of us like to link labels to input fields by nesting. (Many would say that's the correct usage of labels.) As of Rails 3 the `label` helper accepts a block so that nesting is possible and works as would be expected.

Helpers

```
= f.label :terms do
  = f.check_box :accept_terms
  %span Accept #{link_to "Terms", terms_path}
```

11.11.5.11 `month_field(object_name, method, options = {})`

Creates an HTML5-style month input field. A month value is represented by four digits for the year, followed by a dash, and ending with two digits representing the month (ex.2013-08).

If a `DateTime` or `ActiveSupport::TimeWithZone` instance is provided to the helper, it calls `strftime` with "%Y-%m" on the object's value to attempt setting a default value.

```
month_field(:user, :born_on)
# => <input id="user_born_on" name="user[born_on]" type="month" />
```

To override the default value, pass a string in the format "%Y-%m" to the option `:value`. This method is otherwise identical to `datetime_field`.

11.11.5.12 `number_field(object_name, method, options = {})`

Creates an HTML5-style number input field. This method is otherwise identical to `text_field` with the following additional options:

:min The minimum acceptable value.

:max The maximum acceptable value.

:in A range specifying the `:min` and `:max` values.

:step The acceptable value granularity.

11.11.5.13 `password_field(object_name, method, options = {})`

Creates a traditional password input field. This method is otherwise identical to `text_field` but renders empty by default for security reasons. If you want to pre-populate the user's password you can do something like

```
password_field(:user, :password, value: user.password)
```

🔑 You should never have a reason to pre-populate a password field with a password, because you should never store a user password in plaintext.

11.11.5.14   `radio_button(object_name, method, tag_value, options = {})`
Creates a traditional HTML radio button input field.

```
= radio_button(:post, :category, "rails")
= radio_button(:post, :category, "ruby")
```

11.11.5.15   `range_field(object_name, method, options = {})`
Creates an HTML5-style range input field. This method is otherwise identical to `number_field`.

11.11.5.16   `search_field(object_name, method, options = {})`
Creates an HTML5-style search input field. This method is otherwise identical to `text_field`.

Inputs of type "search" may be styled differently by some browsers, often with rounded corners.

11.11.5.17   `telephone_field(object_name, method, options = {})`
Creates an HTML5-style telephone input field. This method is otherwise identical to `text_field` and is aliased as `phone_field`.

11.11.5.18   `text_area(object_name, method, options = {})`
Creates a traditional HTML multiline text input field (the `textarea` tag). The `:size` option lets you easily specify the dimensions of the text area, instead of having to resort to explicit `:rows` and `:cols` options.

```
text_area(:comment, :body, size: "25x10")
# => <textarea name="comment[body]" id="comment_body" cols="25" rows="10">
#    </textarea>
```

11.11.5.19   `text_field(object_name, method, options = {})`
Creates a standard HTML text input field.

11.11.5.20   `time_field(object_name, method, options = {})`
Creates an HTML5-style input field of type "time". If a `DateTime` or `Active-Support::TimeWithZone` instance is provided to the helper, it calls `strftime` with "%T.%L" on the object's value to attempt setting a default value.

Helpers

```
time_field(:task, :started_at)
# => <input id="task_started_at" name="task[started_at]" type="time" />
```

To override the default value, pass a string in the format "%T.%L" to the option `:value`. This method is otherwise identical to `datetime_field`.

11.11.5.21 url_field(object_name, method, options = {})
Creates an HTML5-style input field of type "url". This method is otherwise identical to `text_field`.

11.11.5.22 week_field(object_name, method, options = {})
Creates an HTML5-style input field of type "week". If a `DateTime` or `Active-Support::TimeWithZone` instance is provided to the helper, it calls `strftime` with "%YW%W" on the object's value to attempt setting a default value.

```
week_field(:task, :started_at)
# => <input id="task_started_at" name="task[started_at]" type="week" />
```

To override the default value, pass a string in the format "%Y-W%W" to the option `:value`. This method is otherwise identical to `datetime_field`.

11.12 FormOptionsHelper
The methods in the `FormOptionsHelper` module are all about helping you to work with HTML `select` elements, by giving you ways to turn collections of objects into `option` tags.

11.12.1 Select Helpers
The following methods help you to create `select` tags based on a pair of `object` and `attribute` identifiers.

11.12.1.1 collection_select(object, method, collection, value_method, text_method, options = {}, html_options = {})
Returns both `select` and `option` tags for the given `object` and `method` using the `value_method` and `text_method` symbols provided to construct a list of `option` tags from the `collection` parameter.

11.12.1.2   `grouped_collection_select(object, method, collection, group_method, group_label_method, option_key_method, option_value_method, options = {}, html_options = {})`

Returns select, optgroup, and option tags for the given object and method using option_groups_from_collection_for_select (covered later in this chapter).

11.12.1.3   `select(object, method, collection, options = {}, html_options = {})`

Creates a select tag and a series of contained option tags for the provided object and attribute. The value of the attribute currently held by the object (if any) will be selected, provided that the object is available (not nil). See options_for_ select section for the required format of the choices parameter.

Here's a small example where the value of @post.person_id is 1:

```
= select(:post, :person_id,
  Person.all.collect { |p| [ p.name, p.id ] },
  { include_blank: true })
```

Executing that helper code would generate the following HTML output:

```
<select id="post_person_id" name="post[person_id]">
  <option value=""></option>
  <option value="1" selected="selected">David</option>
  <option value="2">Sam</option>
  <option value="3">Tobias</option>
</select>
```

If necessary, specify selected: value to explicitly set the selection or select- ed: nil to leave all options unselected. The include_blank: true option inserts a blank option tag at the beginning of the list, so that there is no preselected value. Also, you can disable specific values by setting a single value or an array of values to the :disabled option.

11.12.1.4   `time_zone_select(object, method, priority_zones = nil, options = {}, html_options = {})`

Returns select and option tags for the given object and method, using time_ zone_options_for_select to generate the list of option tags.

Helpers

In addition to the `:include_blank` option documented in the preceding section, this method also supports a `:model` option, which defaults to `ActiveSupport::TimeZone`. This may be used by users to specify a different `timezone` model object.

Additionally, setting the `priority_zones` parameter with an array of `ActiveSupport::TimeZone` objects will list any specified priority time zones above any other.

```
time_zone_select(:user, :time_zone, [
  ActiveSupport::TimeZone['Eastern Time (US & Canada)'],
  ActiveSupport::TimeZone['Pacific Time (US & Canada)']
])
# => <select id="user_time_zone" name="user[time_zone]">
#      <option value="Eastern Time (US &amp; Canada)">
#        (GMT-05:00) Eastern Time (US &amp; Canada)
#      </option>
#      <option value="Pacific Time (US &amp; Canada)">
#        (GMT-08:00) Pacific Time (US &amp; Canada)
#      </option>
#      <option disabled="disabled" value="">-------------</option>
#      <option value="American Samoa">(GMT-11:00) American Samoa</option>
#      ...
```

Finally, setting the option `:default` to an instance of `ActiveSupport::TimeZone`, sets the default selected value if none was set.

11.12.2   Checkbox/Radio Helpers

The following methods create `input` tags of type "check box" or "radio" based on a collection.

11.12.2.1   `collection_check_boxes(object, method, collection, value_method, text_method, options = {}, html_options = {}, &block)`

The form helper `collection_check_boxes` creates a collection of check boxes and associated labels based on a collection.

To illustrate, assuming we have a `Post` model that has multiple categories, using the `collection_check_boxes` helper, we can add the capability to set the `category_ids` of the post:

```
collection_check_boxes(:post, :category_ids, Category.all, :id, :name)
# => <input id="post_category_ids_1" name="post[category_ids][]"
#      type="checkbox" value="1" />
#    <label for="post_category_ids_1">Ruby on Rails</label>
```

```
#     <input id="post_category_ids_2" name="post[category_ids][]"
#       type="checkbox" value="2" />
#     <label for="post_category_ids_2">Ruby</label>
#     ...
```

If you wanted to change the way the labels and check boxes are rendered, passing a block will yield a builder:

```
collection_check_boxes(:post, :category_ids, Category.all,
  :id, :name) do |item|
  item.label(class: 'check-box') { item.check_box(class: 'check-box') }
end
```

The builder also has access to methods `object`, `text`, and `value` of the current item being rendered.

11.12.2.2 `collection_radio_buttons(object, method, collection, value_method, text_method, options = {}, html_options = {}, &block)`

The form helper `collection_radio_buttons` creates a collection of radio buttons and associated labels based on a collection. It is predominately used to set an individual value, such as a `belongs_to` relationship on a model.

💬 Kevin says . . . .

Use `collection_radio_buttons` with a collection that only has a handful of items unless you want your page to be polluted with radio buttons. Fall back to a `collection_select` for a large collection.

```
collection_radio_buttons(:post, :author_id, Author.all, :id, :name)
# => <input id="post_author_1" name="post[author_id][]"
#       type="radio" value="1" />
#     <label for="post_author_1">Obie</label>
#     <input id="post_author_2" name="post[author_id][]"
#       type="radio" value="2" />
#     <label for="post_author_2">Kevin</label>
#     ...
```

Similar to the `collection_check_boxes` helper, if you wanted to change the way the labels and radio buttons are rendered, passing a block yields a builder:

```
collection_radio_buttons(:post, :author_id,
  Author.all, :id, :name) do |item|
  item.label(class: 'radio-button') {
    item.radio_button(class: 'radio-button')
```

Helpers

```
}
end
```

The builder also has access to the methods `object`, `text`, and `value` of the current item being rendered.

11.12.3   Option Helpers

For all of the following methods, only `option` tags are returned, so you have to invoke them from within a select helper or otherwise wrap them in a `select` tag.

11.12.3.1   `grouped_options_for_select(grouped_options, selected_key = nil, options = {})`

Returns a string of `option` tags, such as `options_for_select`, but surrounds them with `optgroup` tags.

11.12.3.2   `option_groups_from_collection_for_select (collection, group_method, group_label_method, option_key_method, option_value_method, selected_key = nil)`

Returns a string of `option` tags, like `options_from_collection_for_select` but surrounds them with `optgroup` tags. The `collection` should return a subarray of items when calling `group_method` on it. Each group in the `collection` should return its own name when calling `group_label_method`. The `option_key_method` and `option_value_method` parameters are used to calculate `option` tag attributes.

It's probably much easier to show in an example than to explain in words.

```
option_groups_from_collection_for_select(@continents, :countries,
  :continent_name, :country_id, :country_name, @selected_country.id)
```

This example could output the following HTML:

```
<optgroup label="Africa">
  <option value="1">Egypt</option>
  <option value="4">Rwanda</option>
  ...
</optgroup>
  <optgroup label="Asia">
  <option value="3" selected="selected">China</option>
  <option value="12">India</option>
  <option value="5">Japan</option>
  ...
```

```
</optgroup>
```

For the sake of clarity, here are the model classes reflected in the example:

```
class Continent
  def initialize(name, countries)
    @continent_name = name; @countries = countries
  end

  def continent_name
    @continent_name
  end

  def countries
    @countries
  end
end

class Country
  def initialize(id, name)
    @id, @name = id, name
  end

  def country_id
    @id
  end

  def country_name
    @name
  end
end
```

11.12.3.3 `options_for_select(container, selected = nil)`

Accepts a container (hash, array, or anything else enumerable) and returns a string of `option` tags. Given a container where the elements respond to first and last (such as a two-element array), the "lasts" serve as option values and the "firsts" as option text. It's not too hard to put together an expression that constructs a two-element array using the `map` and `collect` iterators.

For example, assume you have a collection of businesses to display, and you're using a select field to enable the user to filter based on the category of the businesses. The category is not a simple string; in this example, it's a proper model related to the business via a `belongs_to` association:

```
class Business < ActiveRecord::Base
  belongs_to :category
```

```
end

class Category < ActiveRecord::Base
  has_many :businesses

  def <=>(other)
    ...
  end
end
```

A simplified version of the template code for displaying that collection of businesses might look like the following:

```
- opts = businesses.map(&:category).collect { |c| [c.name, c.id] }
= select_tag(:filter, options_for_select(opts, selected_filter))
```

The first line puts together the `container` expected by `options_for_select` by first aggregating the `category` attributes of the `businesses` collection using map and the nifty `&:method` syntax. The second line generates the `select` tag using those options (covered later in the chapter). Realistically, you want to massage that category list a little more, so that it is ordered correctly and does not contain duplicates:

```
... businesses.map(&:category).uniq.sort.collect {...
```

Particularly with smaller sets of data, it's perfectly acceptable to do this level of data manipulation in Ruby code. And of course, you probably don't want to ever shove hundreds or especially thousands of rows in a `select` tag, making this technique quite useful. Remember to implement the spaceship method in your model if you need it to be sortable by the `sort` method.

Also, it's worthwhile to experiment with eager loading in these cases, so you don't end up with an individual database query for each of the objects represented in the `select` tag. In the case of our example, the controller would populate the businesses collection using code like this:

```
expose(:businesses) do
  Business.where(...).includes(:category)
end
```

Hashes are turned into a form acceptable to `options_for_select` automatically—the keys become firsts and values become lasts.

If the `selected` parameter is specified (with either a value or array of values for multiple selections), the matching *last* or element will get the selected attribute:

```
options_for_select([["Dollar", "$"], ["Kroner", "DKK"]])
# => <option value="$">Dollar</option>
#    <option value="DKK">Kroner</option>

options_for_select([ "VISA", "MasterCard" ], "MasterCard")
# => <option>VISA</option>
#    <option selected="selected">MasterCard</option>

options_for_select({ "Basic" => "$20", "Plus" => "$40" }, "$40")
# => <option value="$20">Basic</option>
#    <option value="$40" selected="selected">Plus</option>

>> options_for_select([ "VISA", "MasterCard", "Discover" ],
                       ["VISA", "Discover"])
# => <option selected="selected">VISA</option>
#    <option>MasterCard</option>
#    <option selected="selected">Discover</option>
```

A lot of people have trouble getting this method to correctly display their selected item. Make sure that the value you pass to `selected` matches the type contained in the object collection of the `select`; otherwise, it won't work. In the following example, assuming `price` is a numeric value, without the `to_s`, selection would be broken, since the values passed as options are all strings:

```
options_for_select({ "Basic" => "20", "Plus" => "40" }, price.to_s)
# => <option value="20">Basic</option>
#    <option value="40" selected="selected">Plus</option>
```

11.12.3.4 `options_from_collection_for_select(collection, value_method, text_method, selected=nil)`

Returns a string of `option` tags that have been compiled by iterating over the collection and assigning the result of a call to the `value_method` as the option value and the `text_method` as the option text. If selected is specified, the element returning a match on `value_method` will get preselected.

```
options_from_collection_for_select(Person.all, :id, :name)
# => <option value="1">David</option>
     <option value="2">Sam</option>
     . . .
```

11.12.3.5 `time_zone_options_for_select(selected = nil, priority_zones = nil, model = ::ActiveSupport::TimeZone)`

Returns a string of `option` tags for pretty much any timezone in the world. Supply an `ActiveSupport::TimeZone` name as selected to have it preselected. You can also supply an array of `ActiveSupport::TimeZone` objects as `priority _zones`, so that they will be listed above the rest of the (long) list. `TimeZone. us_zones` is a convenience method that gives you a list of the U.S. timezones only.

The `selected` parameter must be either `nil` or a string that names an `Active-Support::TimeZone` (covered in Appendix B, "Active Support API Reference").

11.13 FormTagHelper

The following helper methods generate HTML form and input tags based on explicit naming and values, contrary to the similar methods present in `FormHelper`, which require association to an Active Record model instance. All of these helper methods take an `options` hash, which may contain special options or simply additional attribute values that should be added to the HTML tag being generated.

11.13.1 `button_tag(content_or_options = nil, options = nil, &block)`

Creates a button element that can be used to define a submit, reset, or generic button to be used with JavaScript.

```
button_tag('Submit')
# => <button name="button" type="submit">Submit</button>

button_tag('Some call to action',type: 'button')
# => <button name="button" type="button">Some call to action</button>
```

11.13.2 `check_box_tag(name, value = "1", checked = false, options = {})`

Creates a check box input field. Unlike its fancier cousin, `check_box` in `Form-Helper`, this helper does not give you an extra hidden input field to ensure that a `false` value is passed even if the check box is unchecked.

```
check_box_tag('remember_me')
# => <input id="remember_me" name="remember_me" type="checkbox" value="1"/>

check_box_tag('remember_me', 1, true)
# => <input checked="checked" id="remember_me" name="remember_me"
#        type="checkbox" value="1" />
```

11.13.3 `color_field_tag(name, value = nil, options = {})`

Creates a color input field that enables setting of a color via hex values. This method is otherwise identical to `text_field_tag`.

11.13.4 `date_field_tag(name, value = nil, options = {})`

Creates a date input field. This method is otherwise identical to `text_field_tag`.

11.13.5 `datetime_field_tag(name, value = nil, options = {})`

Creates a datetime input field, which accepts time in UTC. This method is otherwise identical to `text_field_tag` with the following additional options:

`:min` The minimum acceptable value.

`:max` The maximum acceptable value.

`:step` The acceptable value granularity.

11.13.6 `datetime_local_field_tag(name, value = nil, options = {})`

Creates an input field of type "datetime-local". This method is otherwise identical to `datetime_field_tag`, except that the value is not in UTC.

11.13.7 `email_field_tag(name, value = nil, options = {})`

Creates an email input field. This method is otherwise identical to `text_field_tag`.

11.13.8 `field_set_tag(legend = nil, options = nil, &block)`

Wrap the contents of the given block in a `fieldset` tag and optionally give it a `legend` tag.

11.13.9 `file_field_tag(name, options = {})`

Creates a file upload field. If you're using this helper (rather than `file_field`) remember to set your HTML form to multipart or file uploads will mysteriously not work:

```
= form_tag '/upload', multipart: true do
```

Helpers

```
= label_tag :file, 'File to Upload'
= file_field_tag :file
= submit_tag
```

This input field has a couple of unique options.

:multiple Most modern browser will allow the user to select multiple files if this option is set to `true`.

:accept Set to one or more MIME-types to filter the kinds of files that the user will be able to select in the Select File dialog.

When a form containing this input is submitted, the controller action will receive a `File` object pointing to the uploaded file as it exists in a `tempfile` on your system. Processing of an uploaded file is beyond the scope of this book.

🔑 If you're smart, you'll use Jonas Nicklas' excellent CarrierWave gem instead of reinventing the wheel. Check it out at https://github.com/carrierwaveuploader/carrierwave.

11.13.10 `form_tag(url_for_options = {}, options = {}, &block)`

Starts a `form` tag, with its action attribute set to the URL passed as the `url_for_options` parameter.

The `:method` option defaults to POST. Browsers handle HTTP GET and POST natively; if you specify "patch," "delete," or any other HTTP verb is used, a hidden input field will be inserted with the name `_method` and a value corresponding to the `method` supplied. The Rails request dispatcher understands the `_method` parameter, which is the basis for the RESTful techniques you learned in Chapter 3, "REST, Resources, and Rails."

The `:multipart` option enables you to specify that you will be including file-upload fields in the form submission and the server should be ready to handle those files accordingly.

The `:authenticity_token` option is used only if you need to pass a custom authenticity token string or for indicating not to include one at all by setting the option to `false`.

Setting the option `:remote` to `true` will enable the unobtrusive JavaScript drivers to take control of the submit behavior (covered in Chapter 20).

```
form_tag('/posts')
# => <form action="/posts" method="post">

>> form_tag('/posts/1', method: :patch)
# => <form action="/posts/1" method="post">
#       <input name="_method" type="hidden" value="patch" />
#       ...

form_tag('/upload', multipart: true)
# => <form action="/upload" method="post" enctype="multipart/form-data">
```

You might note that all parameters to `form_tag` are optional. If you leave them off, you'll get a form that posts back to the URL that it came from—a quick and dirty solution that I use quite often when prototyping or experimenting. To quickly set up a controller action that handles post-backs, just include an `if/else` condition that checks the request method, something like the following:

```
def add
  if request.post?
    # handle the posted params
    redirect_back(fallback_location: root_path)
  end
end
```

Notice that if the request is a post, I handle the form `params` and then redirect back to the original URL (using `redirect_back`). Otherwise, execution simply falls through and would render whatever template is associated with the action.

11.13.11 `hidden_field_tag(name, value = nil, options = {})`
Creates a hidden field, with parameters similar to `text_field_tag`.

11.13.12 `image_submit_tag(source, options = {})`
Displays an image that, when clicked, will submit the form. The interface for this method is the same as its cousin `image_tag` in the `AssetTagHelper` module.

Image input tags are popular replacements for standard submit tags, because they make an application look fancier. They are also used to detect the location of the mouse cursor on click—the `params` hash will include x and y data.

11.13.13 `label_tag(name = nil, content_or_options = nil, options = nil, &block)`
Creates a label tag with the `for` attribute set to `name`.

Helpers

11.13.14 month_field_tag(name, value = nil, options = {})

Creates an input field of type "month". This method is otherwise identical to `text_field_tag` with the following additional options:

:min The minimum acceptable value.

:max The maximum acceptable value.

:step The acceptable value granularity.

11.13.15 number_field_tag(name, value = nil, options = {})

Creates a number input field. This method is otherwise identical to `text_field_tag` with the following additional options:

:min The minimum acceptable value.

:max The maximum acceptable value.

:in A range specifying the :min and :max values

:step The acceptable value granularity.

11.13.16 password_field_tag(name = "password", value = nil, options = {})

Creates a password input field. This method is otherwise identical to `text_field_tag`.

11.13.17 radio_button_tag(name, value, checked = false, options = {})

Creates a radio button input field. Make sure to give all of your radio button options the same name so that the browser will consider them linked.

11.13.18 range_field_tag(name, value = nil, options = {})

Creates a range input field. This method is otherwise identical to `number_field_tag`.

11.13.19 `search_field_tag(name, value = nil, options = {})`

Creates a search input field. This method is otherwise identical to `text_field_tag`.

11.13.20 `select_tag(name, option_tags = nil, options = {})`

Creates a drop-down selection box, or if the `:multiple` option is set to `true`, a multiple-choice selection box. The `option_tags` parameter is an actual string of `option` tags to put inside the `select` tag. You should not have to generate that string explicitly yourself. Instead, use the helpers in `FormOptions` (covered in the previous section of this chapter), which can be used to create common select boxes such as countries, time zones, or associated records.

11.13.21 `submit_tag(value = "Save changes", options = {})`

Creates a submit button with the text value as the caption. In conjunction with the unobtrusive JavaScript driver, one can set a `:data` attribute named `:disable_with` that can be used to provide a name for disabled versions of the submit button.

```
submit_tag('Save article', data: { disable_with: 'Please wait...' })
# => <input data-disable-with="Please wait..."
#      name="commit" type="submit" value="Save article" />
```

11.13.22 `telephone_field_tag(name, value = nil, options = {})`

Creates a telephone input field. This method is otherwise identical to `text_field_tag` and is aliased as `phone_field_tag`.

11.13.23 `text_area_tag(name, content = nil, options = {})`

Creates a multiline text input field (the `textarea` tag). The `:size` option lets you easily specify the dimensions of the text area, instead of having to resort to explicit `:rows` and `:cols` options.

```
text_area_tag(:body, nil, size: "25x10")
# => <textarea name="body" id="body" cols="25" rows="10"></textarea>
```

Helpers

11.13.24 `text_field_tag(name, value = nil,`
`options = {})`

Creates a standard text input field.

11.13.25 `time_field_tag(name, value = nil,`
`options = {})`

Creates an input field of type "time". This method is otherwise identical to `text_field_tag` with the following additional options:

`:min` The minimum acceptable value.

`:max` The maximum acceptable value.

`:step` The acceptable value granularity.

11.13.26 `url_field_tag(name, value = nil,`
`options = {})`

Creates an input field of type "url". This method is otherwise identical to `text_field_tag`.

11.13.27 `utf8_enforcer_tag()`

Creates the hidden UTF8 enforcer tag.

```
utf8_enforcer_tag
# => <input name="utf8" type="hidden" value="&#x2713;" />
```

11.13.28 `week_field_tag(name, value = nil,`
`options = {})`

Creates an input field of type "week". This method is otherwise identical to `text_field_tag` with the following additional options:

`:min` The minimum acceptable value.

`:max` The maximum acceptable value.

`:step` The acceptable value granularity.

11.14 `JavaScriptHelper`

Provides helper methods to facilitate inclusion of JavaScript code in your templates. Not terribly useful if you're using Haml and `:javascript` filters.

11.14.1 `escape_javascript(javascript)`

Escapes line breaks, single and double quotes for JavaScript segments. It's also aliased as `j`.

11.14.2 `javascript_tag(content_or_options_with_block = nil, html_options = {}, &block)`

Outputs a `script` tag with the content inside. The `html_options` are added as tag attributes.

11.15 NumberHelper

This module provides assistance in converting numeric data to formatted strings suitable for displaying in your view. Methods are provided for phone numbers, currency, percentage, precision, positional notation, and file size.

11.15.1 `number_to_currency(number, options = {})`

Formats a number into a currency string. You can customize the format in the options hash.

`:locale` Sets the locale to be used for formatting, defaults to current locale.

`:precision` Sets the level of precision, defaults to 2.

`:unit` Sets the denomination of the currency, defaults to `"$"`.

`:separator` Sets the separator between the units, defaults to `"."`.

`:delimiter` Sets the thousands delimiter, defaults to `","`.

`:format` Sets the format for non-negative numbers, defaults to `"%u%n"`.

`:negative_format` Sets the format for negative numbers, defaults to prepending a hyphen to the formatted number.

`:raise` Setting to `true` raises `InvalidNumberError` when the number is invalid.

```
number_to_currency(1234567890.50)
# => $1,234,567,890.50

number_to_currency(1234567890.506)
# => $1,234,567,890.51

number_to_currency(1234567890.506, precision: 3)
# => $1,234,567,890.506
```

```
number_to_currency(1234567890.50, unit: "&pound;", separator: ",", delimiter: "")
# => &pound;1234567890,50
```

11.15.2 `number_to_human_size(number, options = {})`

Formats a number that is more readable to humans. Useful for numbers that are extremely large, like 1200000000, which would become "1.2 Billion". You can customize the format in the options hash.

:locale Sets the locale to be used for formatting, defaults to current locale.

:precision Sets the level of precision, defaults to 3.

:significant If `true`, precision will be the number of significant digits, otherwise the number of fractional digits are used. Defaults to `true`.

:separator Sets the separator between fractional and integer digits, defaults to `"."`.

:delimiter Sets the thousands delimiter, defaults to `""`.

:strip_insignificant_zeros Setting to `true` removes insignificant zeros after the decimal separator, defaults to `true`.

:units A hash of unit quantifier names or a string containing an I18n scope where to find this hash. It might have the following keys:

- integers: `:unit`, `:ten`, `*:hundred`, `:thousand`, `:million`, `*:billion`, `:trillion`, `*:quadrillion`

- fractionals: `:deci`, `:centi`, `*:mili`, `:micro`, `:nano`, `*:pico`, `:femto`

:format Sets the format for non-negative numbers, defaults to `"%n %u"`. The field types are:

- `%u`: The quantifier

- `%n`: The number

```
number_to_human(123)                    # => "123"
number_to_human(1234)                   # => "1.23 Thousand"
number_to_human(1234567)                # => "1.23 Million"
number_to_human(489939, precision: 4)   # => "489.9 Thousand"
```

💬 **Kevin says . . .**

Rails provides the capability to set your own custom unit qualifier by setting the `:units` option.

```
number_to_human(10000, units: {unit: "m", thousand: "km"}) # => "10 km"
```

11.15.3 `number_to_human_size(number, options = {})`

Formats the bytes in size into a more understandable representation. Useful for reporting file sizes to users. You can customize the format in the options hash.

`:locale` Sets the locale to be used for formatting, defaults to current locale.

`:precision` Sets the level of precision, defaults to 3.

`:significant` If `true`, precision will be the number of significant digits, otherwise the number of fractional digits are used. Defaults to `true`.

`:separator` Sets the separator between fractional and integer digits, defaults to `"."`.

`:delimiter` Sets the thousands delimiter, defaults to `""`.

`:strip_insignificant_zeros` Setting to `true` removes insignificant zeros after the decimal separator, defaults to `true`.

`:format` Sets the format for non-negative numbers, defaults to `"%u%n"`.

`:prefix` Setting to `:si` formats the number using the SI prefix, defaults to `:binary`.

`:raise` Setting to `true` raises `InvalidNumberError` when the number is invalid.

```
number_to_human_size(123)               => 123 Bytes
number_to_human_size(1234)              => 1.21 KB
number_to_human_size(12345)             => 12.1 KB
number_to_human_size(1234567)           => 1.18 MB
number_to_human_size(1234567890)        => 1.15 GB
number_to_human_size(1234567890123)     => 1.12 TB
number_to_human_size(1234567, precision: 2) => 1.2 MB
```

11.15.4 `number_to_percentage(number, options = {})`

Formats a number as a percentage string. You can customize the format in the options hash.

`:locale` Sets the locale to be used for formatting, defaults to current locale.

`:precision` Sets the level of precision, defaults to 3

`:significant` If `true`, precision will be the number of significant digits, otherwise the number of fractional digits are used. Defaults to `false`.

`:separator` Sets the separator between the units, defaults to `"."`

`:delimiter` Sets the thousands delimiter, defaults to `""`.

Helpers

:strip_insignificant_zeros Setting to `true` removes insignificant zeros after the decimal separator, defaults to `false`.

:format Sets the format of the percentage string, defaults to `"%n%"`.

:raise Setting to `true` raises `InvalidNumberError` when the number is invalid.

```
number_to_percentage(100)                    => 100.000%
number_to_percentage(100, precision: 0)      => 100%
number_to_percentage(302.0574, precision: 2) => 302.06%
```

11.15.5 number_to_phone(number, options = {})

Formats a number (either integer or string) as a U.S. phone number. You can customize the format in the options hash.

:area_code Adds parentheses around the area code.

:delimiter Specifies the delimiter to use, defaults to `"-"`.

:extension Specifies an extension to add to the end of the generated number.

:country_code Sets the country code for the phone number.

:raise Setting to `true` raises `InvalidNumberError` when the number is invalid.

```
number_to_phone(1235551234)                  # => "123-555-1234"
number_to_phone("1235551234", area_code: true) # => "(123) 555-1234"
number_to_phone("1235551234", delimiter: " ") # => "123 555 1234"
```

11.15.6 number_with_delimiter(number, options = {})

Formats a number with grouped thousands using a delimiter. You can customize the format in the options hash.

:locale Sets the locale to be used for formatting, defaults to current locale.

:delimiter Sets the thousands delimiter, defaults to `","`.

:separator Sets the separator between the units, defaults to `"."`.

:raise Setting to `true` raises `InvalidNumberError` when the number is invalid.

```
number_with_delimiter(12345678)                  # => "12,345,678"
number_with_delimiter(12345678.05)               # => "12,345,678.05"
number_with_delimiter(12345678, delimiter: ".")  # => "12.345.678"
```

11.15.7 `number_with_precision(number, options = {})`

Formats a number with the specified level of precision. You can customize the format in the options hash.

`:locale` Sets the locale to be used for formatting, defaults to current locale.

`:precision` Sets the level of precision, defaults to 3

`:significant` If `true`, precision will be the number of significant digits, otherwise the number of fractional digits are used. Defaults to `false`.

`:separator` Sets the separator between the units, defaults to `"."`

`:delimiter` Sets the thousands delimiter, defaults to `""`.

`:strip_insignificant_zeros` Setting to `true` removes insignificant zeros after the decimal separator, defaults to `false`.

`:raise` Setting to `true` raises `InvalidNumberError` when the number is invalid.

```
number_with_precision(111.2345)              # => "111.235"
number_with_precision(111.2345, precision: 2) # => "111.23"
```

11.16 OutputSafetyHelper

This is an extremely simple helper module.

11.16.1 `raw(stringish)`

Bypasses HTML sanitization by calling `to_s`, then `html_safe` on the argument passed to it. Since escaping tags happens by default, this helper method can be used when you don't want Rails to automatically escape template content. This is not recommended if the data being rendered comes from the user's input.

11.16.2 `safe_join(array, sep=$,)`

Syntax sugar! Returns an HTML safe string by first escaping all array items and joining them by calling `Array#join` using the supplied separator. The returned string is also called with `html_safe` for good measure.

```
safe_join(["<p>foo</p>".html_safe, "<p>bar</p>"], "<br />")
# => "<p>foo</p>&lt;br /&gt;&lt;p&gt;bar&lt;/p&gt;"
```

Helpers

11.16.3 `to_sentence(array, options = {})`

Converts an array to a comma-separated sentence where the last element is joined by the connector word. This simply wraps Active Support's `Array#to_sentence` method together with `html_safe` escaping.

11.17 RecordTagHelper

This module assists in creation of HTML markup code that follows good, clean naming conventions.

11.17.1 `content_tag_for(tag_name, single_or_multiple _records, prefix = nil, options = nil, &block)`

This helper method creates an HTML element with `id` and `class` parameters that relate to the specified Active Record object. For instance, assuming `@person` is an instance of a `Person` class with an `id` value of `123`, then the following template code

```
= content_tag_for(:tr, @person) do
  %td= @person.first_name
  %td= @person.last_name
```

will produce the following HTML

```
<tr id="person_123" class="person">
  ...
</tr>
```

If you require the HTML `id` attribute to have a prefix, you can specify it as a third argument:

```
content_tag_for(:tr, @person, :foo) do ...
# => "<tr id="foo_person_123" class="person">..."
```

The `content_tag_for` helper also accepts a hash of options, which will be converted to additional HTML attributes on the tag. If you specify a `:class` value, it will be combined with the default class name for your object instead of replacing it (since replacing it would defeat the purpose of the method!).

```
content_tag_for(:tr, @person, :foo, class: 'highlight') do ...
# => "<tr id="foo_person_123" class="person highlight">..."
```

11.17.2 `div_for(record, *args, &block)`

Produces a wrapper `div` element with `id` and `class` parameters that relate to the specified Active Record object. This method is exactly like `content_tag_for` except that it's hard-coded to output `div` elements.

11.18 RenderingHelper

This module contains helper methods related to rendering from a view context, to be used with an `ActionView::Renderer` object. Development of an Action View renderer is outside the scope of this book, but for those who are interested, investigating the source code for `ActionView::TemplateRenderer` and `ActionView::PartialRenderer` would be a good starting point.[3]

11.19 SanitizeHelper

The `SanitizeHelper` module provides a set of methods for scrubbing text of undesired HTML elements. Rails sanitizes and escapes `html` content by default, so this helper is really intended to assist with the inclusion of dynamic content into your views, especially content coming from rich-edit controls like TinyMCE, Quill and others.

11.19.1 `sanitize(html, options = {})`

Encodes all tags and strips all attributes (not specifically allowed) from the `html` string passed to it. Also strips `href` and `src` tags with invalid protocols, particularly in an effort to prevent abuse of `javascript` attribute values.

```
= sanitize @article.body
```

With its default settings, the `sanitize` method does its best to counter known hacker tricks such as using unicode/ascii/hex values to get past the JavaScript filters.

You can customize the behavior of `sanitize` by adding or removing allowable tags and attributes using the `:attributes` or `:tags` options.

```
= sanitize @article.body, tags: %w(table tr td),
    attributes: %w(id class style)
```

Helpers

---

3. https://github.com/rails/rails/tree/4-0-stable/actionpack/lib/action_view/renderer

It's possible to add tags to the default allowed tags in your application by altering the value of `config.action_view.sanitized_allowed_tags` in an initializer. For instance, the following code adds support for basic HTML tables:

```
class Application < Rails::Application
  config.action_view.sanitized_allowed_tags = 'table', 'tr', 'td'
end
```

You can also remove some of the tags that are allowed by default.

```
class Application < Rails::Application
  config.after_initialize do
    ActionView::Base.sanitized_allowed_tags.delete 'div'
  end
end
```

Or change them altogether.

```
class Application < Rails::Application
  config.action_view.sanitized_allowed_attributes = 'id', 'class', 'style'
end
```

Sanitizing user-provided text does not guarantee that the resulting markup will be valid (conforming to a document type) or even well-formed. The output may still contain unescaped <, >, & characters that confuse browsers and adversely affect rendering.

11.19.2 `sanitize_css(style)`

Sanitizes a block of CSS code. Used by `sanitize` when it comes across a style attribute in HTML being sanitized.

11.19.3 `strip_links(html)`

Strips all link tags from text, leaving just the link text.

```
strip_links('<a href="http://www.rubyonrails.org">Ruby on Rails</a>')
# => Ruby on Rails

strip_links('Please email me at <a href="mailto:me@email.com">me@email.com</a>.')
# => Please email me at me@email.com.

strip_links('Blog: <a href="http://www.myblog.com/" class="nav">Visit</a>.')
# => Blog: Visit
```

11.19.4   `strip_tags(html)`

Strips all tags from the supplied HTML string, including comments. Its HTML parsing capability is limited by that of the html-scanner tokenizer built into Rails.[4]

```
strip_tags("Strip <i>these</i> tags!")
# => Strip these tags!

strip_tags("<b>Bold</b> no more!    <a href='more.html'>See more here</a>...")
# => Bold no more!    See more here...

strip_tags("<div id='top-bar'>Welcome to my website!</div>")
# => Welcome to my website!
```

11.20   TagHelper

This module provides helper methods for generating HTML tags programmatically.

11.20.1   `cdata_section(content)`

Returns a CDATA section wrapping the given `content`.

🔍 Use the `:cdata` filter in Haml to accomplish the same thing more elegantly.

CDATA sections are used to escape blocks of text containing characters that would otherwise be recognized as markup. CDATA sections begin with the string `<![CDATA[` and end with (and may not contain) the string `]]>`.

11.20.2   `content_tag(name, content_or_options_with_ block = nil, options = nil, escape = true, &block)`

Returns an HTML block tag of type `name` surrounding the content. Add HTML attributes by passing an attributes hash as `options`. Instead of passing the content as an argument, you can also use a block to hold additional markup (and/or additional calls to `content_tag`), in which case you pass your `options` as the second parameter. Set `escape` to `false` to disable attribute value escaping.

Here are some simple examples of using `content_tag` without a block:

```
content_tag(:p, "Hello world!")
# => <p>Hello world!</p>
```

---

4. You can examine the source code of the html-scanner yourself by opening up https://github.com/rails/rails/blob/4-0-stable/actionpack/lib/action_view/vendor/html-scanner/html/sanitizer.rb.

```
content_tag(:div, content_tag(:p, "Hello!"), class: "message")
# => <div class="message"><p>Hello!</p></div>

content_tag("select", options, multiple: true)
# => <select multiple="multiple">...options...</select>
```

Here it is with content in a block (shown as template code rather than in the console):

```
= content_tag :div, class: "strong" do
  Hello world!
```

The preceding code produces the following HTML:

```
<div class="strong">Hello world!</div>
```

11.20.3 `escape_once(html)`

Returns an escaped version of HTML without affecting existing escaped entities.

```
escape_once("1 > 2 &amp; 3")
# => "1 &lt; 2 &amp; 3"

escape_once("&lt;&lt; Accept & Checkout")
# => "&lt;&lt; Accept &amp; Checkout"
```

11.20.4 `tag(name, options = nil, open = false, escape = true)`

Returns an empty HTML tag of type name, which by default is XHTML compliant. Setting open to `true` will create an open tag compatible with HTML 4.0 and below. Add HTML attributes by passing an attributes hash to options. Set escape to `false` to disable attribute value escaping.

The options hash is used with attributes with no value like (`disabled` and `readonly`), which you can give a value of `true` in the options hash. You can use symbols or strings for the attribute names.

```
tag("br")
# => <br />

tag("br", nil, true)
# => <br>

tag("input", type: 'text', disabled: true)
# => <input type="text" disabled="disabled" />

tag("img", src: "open.png")
# => <img src="open.png" />
```

11.21   TextHelper

The methods in this module provide filtering, formatting, and string transformation capabilities.

11.21.1   `concat(string)`

The preferred method of outputting text in your views is to use the `= expression` in Haml syntax, or the `<%= expression %>` in eRuby syntax. The regular puts and print methods do not operate as expected in an eRuby code block—that is, if you expected them to output to the browser. If you absolutely must output text within a non-output code block like `- expression` in Haml, or `<% expression %>` in eRuby, you can use the `concat` method. I've found that this method can be especially useful when combined with `capture` in your own custom helper method implementations.

The following example code defines a helper method that wraps its block content in a div with a particular CSS class.

```
def wrap(&block)
  concat(content_tag(:div, capture(&block), class: "wrapped_content"))
end
```

You would use it in your template as follows:

```
- wrap do
  My wrapped content
```

11.21.2   `current_cycle(name = "default")`

Returns the current cycle string after a cycle has been started. Useful for complex table highlighting or any other design need that requires the current cycle string in more than one place.

```
- # Alternate background colors with coordinating text color
- [1,2,3,4].each do |item|
  %div(style="background-color:#{cycle('red', 'green', 'blue')}")
    %span(style="color:dark#{current_cycle}")= item
```

> ✎ Reset the cycle by calling `reset_cycle`.

11.21.3   `cycle(first_value, *values)`

Creates a `Cycle` object whose `to_s` method cycles through elements of the array of values passed to it, every time it is called. This can be used, for example, to

Helpers

alternate classes for table rows. Here's an example that alternates CSS classes for even and odd numbers, assuming that the `@items` variable holds an array with 1 through 4:

```
%table
  - @items.each do |item|
    %tr{ class: cycle('even', 'odd') }
      %td= item
```

As you can tell from the example, you don't have to store the reference to the cycle in a local variable or anything like that; you just call the `cycle` method repeatedly. That's convenient, but it means that nested cycles need an identifier. The solution is to pass cycle a `name: cycle_name` option as its last parameter. Also, you can manually reset a cycle by calling `reset_cycle` and passing it the name of the cycle to reset. For example, here is some data to iterate over:

```
# Cycle CSS classes for rows, and text colors for values within each row
@items = [{first: 'Robert', middle: 'Daniel', last: 'James'},
          {first: 'Emily', last: 'Hicks'},
          {first: 'June', middle: 'Dae', last: 'Jones'}]
```

And here is the template code. Since the number of cells rendered varies, we want to make sure to reset the colors cycle before looping:

```
- @items.each do |item|
  %tr{ class: cycle('even', 'odd', name: 'row_class') }
    - item.values.each do |value|
      %td{ class: cycle('red', 'green', name: 'colors') }
        = value
    - reset_cycle 'colors'
```

11.21.4 `xcerpt(text, phrase, options = {})`

Extracts an excerpt from text that matches the first instance of `phrase`. The `:radius` option expands the excerpt on each side of the first occurrence of `phrase` by the number of characters defined in `:radius` (which defaults to 100). If the excerpt radius overflows the beginning or end of the text, the `:omission` option will be prepended/appended accordingly. Use the `:separator` option to set the delimitation.

If the phrase isn't found, nil is returned. Let's look at some examples.

```
excerpt('This is an example', 'an', radius: 5)
# => "...s is an examp..."
```

```
excerpt('This is an example', 'is', radius: 5)
# => "This is an..."

excerpt('This is an example', 'is')
# => "This is an example"

excerpt('This next thing is an example', 'ex', radius: 2)
# => "...next..."

excerpt('This is also an example', 'an', radius: 8, omission: '<chop> ')
# => "<chop> is also an example"
```

11.21.5 `highlight(text, phrases, options = {})`

Highlights one or more phrases everywhere in text by inserting into a highlighter template. The highlighter can be specialized by passing the option `:highlighter` as a single-quoted string with `\1` where the phrase is to be inserted.

```
highlight('You searched for: rails', 'rails')
# => You searched for: <mark>rails</mark>

highlight('You searched for: ruby, rails, dhh', 'actionpack')
# => You searched for: ruby, rails, dhh

highlight('You searched for: rails', ['for', 'rails'],
  highlighter: '<em>\1</em>')
# => You searched <em>for</em>: <em>rails</em>

highlight('You searched for: rails', 'rails',
  highlighter: '<a href="search?q=\1">\1</a>')
# => You searched for: <a href="search?q=rails">rails</a>
```

Note that as of Rails 4, the `highlight` helper now uses the HTML5 `mark` tag by default.

11.21.6 `pluralize(count, singular, plural = nil)`

Super useful for creating highly polished apps. This helper attempts to pluralize the singular word unless count is 1. If the plural is supplied, it will use that when count is > 1. If the `ActiveSupport Inflector` is loaded, it will use the `Inflector` to determine the plural form; otherwise, it will just add an "s" to the singular word.

```
pluralize(1, 'person')
# => 1 person
```

Helpers

```
pluralize(2, 'person')
# => 2 people

pluralize(3, 'person', 'users')
# => 3 users

pluralize(0, 'person')
# => 0 people
```

11.21.7 `reset_cycle(name = "default")`

Resets a cycle (see the `cycle` method in this section) so that it starts cycling from its first element the next time it is called. Pass in a `name` to reset a named cycle.

11.21.8 `simple_format(text, html_options = {}, options = {})`

Returns text transformed into HTML using simple formatting rules. Two or more consecutive newlines (\n\n) are considered to denote a paragraph and thus are wrapped in p tags. One newline (\n) is considered to be a line break, and a `br` tag is appended. This method does not remove the newlines from the text.

Any attributes set in `html_options` will be added to all outputted paragraphs. The following options are also available:

`:sanitize` Setting this option to `false` will not sanitize any text.

`:wrapper_tag` A string representing the wrapper tag, defaults to `"p"`.

11.21.9 `truncate(text, options = {}, &block)`

If `text` is longer than the `:length` option (defaults to 30), `text` will be truncated to the length specified, and the last three characters will be replaced with the `:omission` (defaults to `"..."`). The `:separator` option enables defining the delimitation. Finally, to not escape the output, set `:escape` to `false`.

```
truncate("Once upon a time in a world far far away", length: 7)
=> "Once..."

truncate("Once upon a time in a world far far away")
# => "Once upon a time in a world..."

truncate("And they found that many people were sleeping better.",
  length: 25, omission: '... (continued)')
# => "And they f... (continued)"
```

11.21.10 `word_wrap(text, options = {})`

Wraps the text into lines no longer than the `:line_width` option. This method breaks on the first whitespace character that does not exceed `:line_width` (which is 80 by default).

```
word_wrap('Once upon a time')
# => Once upon a time

word_wrap('Once upon a time', line_width: 8)
# => Once\nupon a\ntime

word_wrap('Once upon a time', line_width: 1)
# => Once\nupon\na\ntime
```

11.22 TranslationHelper and the I18n API

I18n stands for *internationalization*, and the I18n gem that ships with Rails makes it easy to support multiple languages other than English in your Rails applications. When you internationalize your app, you do a sweep of all the textual content in your models and views that needs to be translated, as well as demarking data like currency and dates, which should be subject to localization.[5]

Rails provides an easy-to-use and extensible framework for translating your application to a single custom language other than English or for providing multi-language support in your application.

The process of *internationalization* in Rails involves the abstraction of strings and other locale-specific parts of your application (such as dates and currency formats) out of the codebase and into a locale file.

The process of *localization* means to provide translations and localized formats for the abstractions created during internationalization. In the process of *localizing* your application you'll probably want to do the following three things:

- Replace or add to Rails' default locale.
- Abstract strings used in your application into keyed dictionaries—e.g., flash messages, static text in your views, etc.
- Store the resulting dictionaries somewhere.

---

5. This section is an authorized remix of the complete guide to using I18n in Rails, by Sven Fuchs and Karel Minarik, available at http://guides.rubyonrails.org/I18n.html.

Helpers

Internationalization is a complex problem. Natural languages differ in so many ways (e.g., in pluralization rules) that it is hard to provide tools for solving all problems at once. For that reason the Rails I18n API focuses on the following:

- Providing support for English and similar languages by default.

- Making it easy to customize and extend everything for other languages.

As part of this solution, every static string in the Rails framework—e.g., Active Record validation messages, time and date formats—has been internationalized, so *localization* of a Rails application means *overriding* Rails defaults.

11.22.1   Localized Views

Before diving into the more complicated localization techniques, let's briefly cover a simple way to translate views that is useful for content-heavy pages. Assume you have a `BooksController` in your application. Your `index` action renders content in `app/views/books/index.html.haml` template. When you put a *localized variant* of that template such as `index.es.html.haml` in the same directory, Rails will recognize it as the appropriate template to use when the locale is set to `:es`. If the locale is set to the default, the generic `index.html.haml` view will be used normally.

You can make use of this feature when working with a large amount of static content that would be clumsy to maintain inside locale dictionaries. Just bear in mind that any changes to a template must be kept in sync with all of its translations.

11.22.2   `TranslationHelper` Methods

The following two methods are provided for use in your views and assume that I18n support is set up in your application.

11.22.2.1   `localize(*args)` Aliased to `l`

Delegates to Active Support's `I18n#translate` method with no additional functionality. Normally you want to use `translate` instead.

11.22.2.2   `translate(key, options = {})` Aliased to `t`

Delegates to Active Support's `I18n#translate` method, while performing three additional functions. First, it'll catch `MissingTranslationData` exceptions and turn them into inline spans that contain the missing key, such that you can see within your views when keys are missing.

Second, it'll automatically scope the key provided by the current partial if the key starts with a period. So if you call `translate(".foo")` from the `people/index.html.haml` template, you'll be calling `I18n.translate("people.index.foo")`. This makes it less repetitive to translate many keys within the same partials and gives you a simple framework for scoping them consistently. If you don't prepend the key with a period, nothing is converted.

Third, it'll mark the translation as safe HTML if the key has the suffix "_html" or the last element of the key is the word "html". For example, calling `translate("header.html")` will return a safe HTML string that won't be escaped.

11.22.3   I18n Setup

There are just a few simple steps to get up and running with I18n support for your application.

Following the *convention over configuration* philosophy, Rails will set up your application with reasonable defaults. If you need different settings, you can overwrite them easily.

Rails adds all `.rb` and `.yml` files from the `config/locales` directory to your translations load path, automatically.[6] The default `en.yml` locale in this directory contains a sample pair of translation strings:

```
en:
  hello: "Hello world"
```

This means, that in the `:en` locale, the key `hello` will map to the "Hello world" string.[7]

You can use YAML or standard Ruby hashes to store translations in the default (`Simple`) backend.

Unless you change it, the I18n library will use English (`:en`) as its default locale for looking up translations. Change the default in using code similar to:

```
config.i18n.default_locale = :de
```

---

6. The translations load path is just an array of paths to your translation files that will be loaded automatically and available in your application. You can pick whatever directory and translation file naming scheme makes sense for you.

7. Every string inside Rails is internationalized in this way, see for instance Active Record validation messages in the file or time and date formats in the file.

Helpers

ℹ Note

The I18n library takes a **pragmatic approach** to locale keys (after some discussion[8]), including only the locale ("language") part, like :en, :pl, not the region part, like :en-US or :en-UK, which are traditionally used for separating "languages" and "regional setting" or "dialects". Many international applications use only the "language" element of a locale such as :cz, :th, or :es (for Czech, Thai and Spanish). However, there are also regional differences within different language groups that may be important. For instance, in the :en-US locale you would have $ as a currency symbol, while in :en-UK, you would have £. Nothing stops you from separating regional and other settings in this way: you just have to provide full "English – United Kingdom" locale in a :en-UK dictionary. Rails I18n plugins such as Globalize3[9] may help you implement it.

11.22.4   Setting and Passing the Locale

If you want to translate your Rails application to a single language other than English, you can just set default_locale to your locale in application.rb as shown earlier, and it will persist through the requests. However, you probably want to provide support for more locales in your application, depending on the user's preference. In such case, you need to set and pass the locale between requests.

⚠ Warning

You may be tempted to store the chosen locale in a session or a cookie. Do not do so. The locale should be transparent and a part of the URL. This way you don't break people's basic assumptions about the web itself: if you send a URL of some page to a friend, she should see the same page, same content.

You can set the locale in a before_action in your ApplicationController like this:

```
before_action :set_locale

def set_locale
  # if params[:locale] is nil then I18n.default_locale will be used
  I18n.locale = params[:locale]
end
```

---

8. https://groups.google.com/forum/?hl=en#!topic/rails-I18n/FN7eLH2-lHA
9. https://github.com/svenfuchs/globalize3

This approach requires you to pass the locale as a URL query parameter as in `http://example.com/books?locale=pt`. (This is, for example, Google's approach.)

Getting the locale from `params` and setting it accordingly is not the hard part of this technique. Including the locale parameter in every URL generated by your application *is* the hard part. To include an explicit option in every URL

```
= link_to books_url(locale: I18n.locale)
```

would be tedious at best and impossible to maintain at worst.

A `default_url_options` method in `ApplicationController` is useful precisely in this scenario. It enables us to set defaults for `url_for` and helper methods dependent on it.

```
def default_url_options(options={})
  logger.debug "default_url_options is passed options: #{options.inspect}\n"
  { locale: I18n.locale }
end
```

Every helper method dependent on `url_for` (e.g., helpers for named routes like `root_path` or `root_url`, resource routes like `books_path` or `books_url`, etc.) will now automatically include the locale in the query string, like

```
http://localhost:3000/?locale=ja
```

Having the locale hang at the end of every path in your application can negatively impact readability of your URLs. Moreover, from an architectural standpoint, locales are a concept that live above other parts of your application domain, and your URLs should probably reflect that.

You might want your URLs to look more like `www.example.com/en/books` (which loads the English locale) and `www.example.com/nl/books` (which loads the Netherlands locale). This is achievable with the same `default_url_options` strategy we just reviewed. You just have to set up your routes with a `scope` option in this way:

```
# config/routes.rb
scope "/:locale" do
  resources :books
end
```

Helpers

Even with this approach, you still need to take special care of the root URL of your application. A URL like http://localhost:3000/nl will not work automatically because the `root "books#index"` declaration in your `routes.rb` doesn't take locale into account. After all, there should only be one "root" of your website.

A possible solution is to map a URL like the following:

```
# config/routes.rb
get '/:locale' => "dashboard#index"
```

Do take special care about the order of your routes, so this route declaration does not break other ones. It would be most wise to add it directly before the `root` declaration at the end of your routes file.

⚠ Warning

This solution has currently one rather big **downside**. Due to the `default_url_options` implementation, you have to pass the `:id` option explicitly, like `link_to 'Show', book_url(id: book)` and not depend on Rails' magic in code like `link_to 'Show', book`. If this should be a problem, have a look at Sven Fuchs's routing_filter[10] plugin which simplifies working with routes in this way.

11.22.4.1   Setting the Locale from the Domain Name

Another option you have is to set the locale from the domain name where your application runs. For example, we want `www.example.com` to load the English (or default) locale and `www.example.es` to load the Spanish locale. Thus the *top-level domain name* is used for locale setting. This has several advantages:

- The locale is a very *obvious* part of the URL.

- People intuitively grasp in which language the content will be displayed.

- It is very trivial to implement in Rails.

- Search engines seem to like that content in different languages lives at different, inter-linked domains.

You can implement it like this in your `ApplicationController`:

```
before_action :set_locale
```

---

10. https://github.com/svenfuchs/routing-filter

```
def set_locale
  I18n.locale = extract_locale_from_uri
end

# Get locale from top-level domain or return nil
def extract_locale_from_tld
  parsed_locale = request.host.split('.').last
  (available_locales.include? parsed_locale) ? parsed_locale  : nil
end
```

Try adding localhost aliases to your file to test this technique.

```
127.0.0.1 application.com

127.0.0.1 application.it

127.0.0.1 application.pl
```

11.22.4.2   Setting the Locale from the Host Name

We can also set the locale from the subdomain in a very similar way inside of `ApplicationController`.

```
before_action :set_locale

def set_locale
  I18n.locale = extract_locale_from_uri
end

def extract_locale_from_subdomain
  parsed_locale = request.subdomains.first
  (available_locales.include? parsed_locale) ? parsed_locale : nil
end
```

11.22.4.3   Setting Locale from Client Supplied Information

In specific cases, it would make sense to set the locale from client-supplied information, i.e., not from the URL. This information may come, for example, from the users' preferred language (set in their browser), can be based on the users' geographical location inferred from their IP, or users can provide it simply by choosing the locale in your application interface and saving it to their profile. This approach is more suitable for web-based applications or services, not for websites. See the sidebar about *sessions*, *cookies*, and RESTful architecture.

Helpers

USING **Accept-Language**

One source of client supplied information would be an `Accept-Language` HTTP header. People may set this in their browser[11] or other clients (such as `curl`).

A trivial implementation of setting locale based on the `Accept-Language` header in `ApplicationController` might be:

```
before_action :set_locale

def set_locale
  I18n.locale = extract_locale_from_accept_language_header
  logger.debug "* Locale set to '#{I18n.locale}'"
end

private

def extract_locale_from_accept_language_header
  request.env['HTTP_ACCEPT_LANGUAGE'].scan(/^[a-z]{2}/).first
end
```

In real production environments you should use much more robust code than the example above. Try plugins such as Iain Hecker's http_accept_language[12] or even Rack middleware such as locale.[13]

USING GEOIP (OR SIMILAR) DATABASE

Yet another way of choosing the locale from client information would be to use a database for mapping the client IP to the region, such as GeoIP Lite Country.[14] The mechanics of the code would be very similar to the preceding code—you would need to query the database for the user's IP and look up your preferred locale for the country/region/city returned.

USER PROFILE

You can also provide users of your application with means to set (and possibly override) the locale in your application interface as well. Again, mechanics for this approach would be very similar to the code above—you'd probably let users choose a locale from a dropdown list and save it to their profile in the database. Then you'd set the locale to this value using a `before_action` in `ApplicationController`.

---

11. http://www.w3.org/International/questions/qa-lang-priorities
12. https://github.com/iain/http_accept_language
13. https://github.com/rack/rack-contrib/blob/master/lib/rack/contrib/locale.rb
14. http://dev.maxmind.com/geoip/legacy/geolite/

11.22.5   Internationalizing Your Application

After you've set up I18n support for your Ruby on Rails application and told it which locale to use and how to preserve it between requests, you're ready for the really interesting part of the process: actually internationalizing your application.

⚠ Premature *internationalization* is as bad, and possibly worse, than premature *optimization*. Features under active development are likely to get refactored, changed or eliminated, and if you have already invested in translation, you might be in for a world of pain trying to figure out which keys are still in use. Internationalization usually comes relatively late in the timeline of a project. Work on it when you feel confident that no more major changes will be happening.

11.22.5.1   The Public I18n API

First of all, you should be acquainted with the I18n API. The two most important methods of the I18n API are

```
translate # Lookup text translations
localize # Localize Date and Time objects to local formats
```

These have the aliases #t and #l, so you can use them like

```
I18n.t 'store.title'
I18n.l Time.now
```

11.22.5.2   The Process

I18n and localization take place primarily in certain parts of your Rails application with user-facing strings:

- Views
- Mailers
- Forms
- Models

Controllers shouldn't contain much in the way of strings subject to I18n, with the exception of alerts and notice messages. Helpers probably shouldn't contain much text either.

Take the following basic pieces of a simple Rails application as an example for describing the process.

Helpers

```
# config/routes.rb
Rails.application.routes.draw do
  root "home#index"
end

# app/controllers/home_controller.rb
class HomeController < ApplicationController
  def index
    flash[:notice] = "Welcome"
  end
end

# app/views/home/index.html.haml
%h1 Hello world!
%p.notice= flash[:notice]
```

The example has two strings that are currently hard-coded in English. To internationalize this code, we must replace those strings with calls to Rails' #t helper with a key that makes sense for the translation.

```
# app/controllers/home_controller.rb
class HomeController < ApplicationController
  def index
    flash[:notice] = t(:welcome_flash)
  end
end

# app/views/home/index.html.haml
%h1= t(:hello_world)
%p.notice= flash[:notice]
```

Now when you render this view, it will show an error message that tells you that the translations for the keys :hello_world and :welcome_flash are missing.

Rails adds a t (translate) helper method to your views so that you do not need to spell out I18n.t all the time. Additionally, this helper will catch missing translations and wrap the resulting error message into a <span class= "translation_missing">.

To make the example work you would add the missing translations into the dictionary files (thereby doing the localization part of the work):

```
# config/locale/en.yml
en:
  hello_world: Hello World
  welcome_flash: Welcome

# config/locale/pirate.yml
```

```
pirate:
  hello_world: Ahoy World
  welcome_flash: All aboard!
```

 Note

You need to restart the server when you add or edit locale files.

You may use YAML (`.yml`) or plain Ruby (`.rb`) files for storing your translations. YAML is the preferred option among Rails developers. However, it has one big disadvantage. YAML is very sensitive to whitespace and special characters, so the application may not load your dictionary properly. Ruby files will crash your application on first request, so you may easily find what's wrong. (If you encounter any "weird issues" with YAML dictionaries, try putting the relevant portion of your dictionary into a Ruby file.)

For a completely different, and potentially much easier (albeit pricey), solution to internationalizing your application, check out PhraseApp.[15] They have a product called the In-Context-Editor, that makes the actual web UI of your application editable by teams of translators. It's the way to go for large I18n jobs.

11.22.5.3   Adding Date/Time Formats

Okay! Now let's add a timestamp to the view, so we can demo the date/time localization feature as well. To localize the time format you pass the Time object to `I18n.l` or use Rails' `#l` helper method in your views.

```
# app/views/home/index.html.haml
%h1= t(:hello_world)
%p.notice= flash[:notice]
%p= l(Time.now, format: :short)
```

And in our pirate translations file let's add a time format (it's already there in Rails' defaults for English):

```
# config/locale/pirate.yml
pirate:
  time:
    formats:
      short: "arrrround %H'ish"
```

15. http://phraseapp.com

Helpers

The `rails-i18n` repository

There's a great chance that somebody has already done much of the hard work of translating Rails' defaults for your locale. See the `rails-i18n` repository at GitHub[16] for an archive of various locale files. When you put such file(s) in `config/locale/` directory, they will automatically be ready for use.

11.22.6   Organization of Locale Files

Putting translations for all parts of your application in one file per locale could be hard to manage. You can store these files in a hierarchy that makes sense to you.

For example, your `config/locale` directory could look like this:

```
|-defaults
|---es.rb
|---en.rb
|-models
|---book
|-----es.rb
|-----en.rb
|-views
|---defaults
|-----es.rb
|-----en.rb
|---books
|-----es.rb
|-----en.rb
|---users
|-----es.rb
|-----en.rb
|---navigation
|-----es.rb
|-----en.rb
```

This way, you can separate model and model attribute names from text inside views, and all of this from the "defaults" (e.g., date and time formats). Other stores for the I18n library could provide different means of such separation.

---

16. https://github.com/svenfuchs/rails-I18n

ⓘ Note

The default locale loading mechanism in Rails does not load locale files in nested dictionaries, like we have here. So, for this to work, we must explicitly tell Rails to look further through settings in

```
# config/application.rb
config.i18n.load_path += Dir[File.join(Rails.root, 'config',
  'locales', '**', '*.{rb,yml}')]
```

11.22.7   Looking Up Translations

11.22.7.1   Basic Lookup, Scopes, and Nested Keys

Translations are looked up by keys, which can be either Symbols or Strings, so these calls are equivalent:

```
I18n.t :message
I18n.t 'message'
```

The `translate` method also takes a `:scope` option, which can contain one or more additional keys that will be used to specify a "namespace" or scope for a translation key:

```
I18n.t :invalid, scope: [:activerecord, :errors, :messages]
```

This looks up the `:invalid` message in the Active Record error messages.

Additionally, both the key and scopes can be specified as dot-separated keys as in the following:

```
I18n.translate :"activerecord.errors.messages.invalid"
```

Thus the following four calls are equivalent:

```
I18n.t 'activerecord.errors.messages.invalid'
I18n.t 'errors.messages.invalid', scope: :activerecord
I18n.t :invalid, scope: 'activerecord.errors.messages'
I18n.t :invalid, scope: [:activerecord, :errors, :messages]
```

Context matters, especially in translation work. Therefore, in anything but the most basic circumstances, forget about using symbols and scopes as identifiers. Just use explicit dot notation across the board, and create prefix schemes that match the organization of your resources. It's a lot easier to understand and maintain. PhraseApp has a great writeup on the subject of

Helpers

translation key naming at https://phraseapp.com/blog/posts/ruby-lessons-learned-naming-and-managing-rails-I18n-keys/.

11.22.7.2 Default Values

When a `:default` option is given, its value will be returned if the translation is missing:

```
I18n.t :missing, default: 'Not here'
# => 'Not here'
```

If the `:default` value is a Symbol, it will be used as a key and translated. You can provide multiple values as default. The first one that results in a value will be returned.

For example, the following first tries to translate the key `:missing` and then the key `:also_missing`. As both do not yield a result, the string "Not here" will be returned:

```
I18n.t :missing, default: [:also_missing, 'Not here']
# => 'Not here'
```

11.22.7.3 Bulk and Namespace Lookup

To look up multiple translations at once, an array of keys can be passed:

```
I18n.t [:odd, :even], scope: 'activerecord.errors.messages'
# => ["must be odd", "must be even"]
```

Also, a key can translate to a (potentially nested) hash of grouped translations. For instance, you can receive *all* Active Record error messages as a Hash with

```
I18n.t 'activerecord.errors.messages'
# => { inclusion: "is not included in the list", exclusion: ... }
```

11.22.7.4 View Scoped Keys

Rails implements a convenient way to reference keys inside of views. Assume you have the following local file:

```
es:
  books:
    index:
      title: "Título"
```

You can reference the value of `books.index.title` inside of the `app/views/books/index.html.haml` template by prefixing the key name with a dot. Rails will automatically fill in the scope based on the identity of the view.

```
= t '.title'
```

> ⚠ The experts at PhraseApp advise strongly against using scoped keys, and we agree with them. Once you begin having similar keys in different contexts, it becomes way too difficult to maintain. Even though it'll cost some more keystrokes, for the sake of maintainability explicit key identifiers should be globally unique in the context of your whole application.

11.22.7.5   Interpolation

In many cases you want to abstract your translations in such a way that variables can be interpolated into the translation. For this reason the I18n API provides an interpolation feature.

All options besides `:default` and `:scope` that are passed to `translate` will be interpolated to the translation:

```
I18n.backend.store_translations :en, thanks: 'Thanks %{name}!
I18n.translate :thanks, name: 'Jeremy'
# => 'Thanks Jeremy!'
```

If a translation uses `:default` or `:scope` as an interpolation variable, an `I18n::ReservedInterpolationKey` exception is raised. If a translation expects an interpolation variable, but this has not been passed to `translate`, an `I18n::MissingInterpolationArgument` exception is raised.

11.22.7.6   Pluralization

In English there are only one singular and one plural form for a given string, e.g., "1 message" and "2 messages," but other languages have different grammars with additional or fewer plural forms.[17] Thus, the I18n API provides a flexible pluralization feature.

The `:count` interpolation variable has a special role in that it both is interpolated to the translation and used to pick a pluralization from the translations according to the pluralization rules defined by Unicode:

---

17. http://www.unicode.org/cldr/charts/supplemental/language_plural_rules.html

Helpers

```
I18n.backend.store_translations :en, inbox: {
  one: '1 message',
  other: '%{count} messages'
}

I18n.translate :inbox, count: 2
# => '2 messages'

I18n.translate :inbox, count: 1
# => 'one message'
```

The algorithm for pluralizations in :en is as simple as

```
entry[count == 1 ? 0 : 1]
```

The translation denoted as :one is regarded as singular, versus any other value regarded as plural (including the count being zero).

If the lookup for the key does not return a Hash suitable for pluralization, an I18n:: InvalidPluralizationData exception is raised.

11.22.8   How to Store Your Custom Translations

The Simple backend shipped with Active Support enables you to store translations in both plain Ruby and YAML format. A Ruby hash locale file would look like the following:

```
{
  pt:: {
    foo:: {
      bar:: "baz"
    }
  }
}
```

The equivalent YAML file would look like this:

```
pt:
  foo:
    bar: baz
```

In both cases the top level key is the locale. :foo is a namespace key and :bar is the key for the translation "baz".

Here is a real example from the Active Support en.yml translations YAML file:

```
en:
  date:
```

```
formats:
  default: "%Y-%m-%d"
  short: "%b %d"
  long: "%B %d, %Y"
```

So, all of the following equivalent lookups will return the `:short` date format
`"%B %d"`:

```
I18n.t 'date.formats.short'
I18n.t 'formats.short', scope: :date
I18n.t :short, scope: 'date.formats'
I18n.t :short, scope: [:date, :formats]
```

Generally, we recommend using YAML as a format for storing translations.

11.22.8.1 Translations for Active Record Models

You can use the methods `Model.human_name` and `Model.human_attri-
bute_name`(attribute) to transparently look up translations for your model and
attribute names.

For example, when you add the following translations:

```
en:
  activerecord:
    models:
      user: Dude
    attributes:
      user:
        login: "Handle"
        # will translate User attribute "login" as "Handle"
```

`User.human_name` will return "Dude" and `User.human_attribute_name`
(`:login`) will return "Handle."

11.22.8.2 Error Message Scopes

Active Record validation error messages can also be translated easily. Active Record
gives you a couple of namespaces where you can place your message translations in
order to provide different messages and translation for certain models, attributes,
and/or validations. It also transparently takes single-table inheritance into account.

This gives you quite powerful means to flexibly adjust your messages to your application's needs.

Consider a User model with a `validates_presence_of` validation for the name
attribute like

Helpers

```
class User < ActiveRecord::Base
  validates_presence_of :name
end
```

The key for the error message in this case is `:blank`. Active Record will look up this key in the namespaces:

```
activerecord.errors.models.[model_name].attributes.[attribute_name]
activerecord.errors.models.[model_name]
activerecord.errors.messages
```

Thus, in our example it will try the following keys in this order and return the first result:

```
activerecord.errors.models.user.attributes.name.blank
activerecord.errors.models.user.blank
activerecord.errors.messages.blank
```

When your models are additionally using inheritance then the messages are looked up in the inheritance chain.

For example, you might have an Admin model inheriting from User:

```
class Admin < User
  validates_presence_of :name
end
```

Then Active Record will look for messages in this order:

```
activerecord.errors.models.admin.attributes.title.blank
activerecord.errors.models.admin.blank
activerecord.errors.models.user.attributes.title.blank
activerecord.errors.models.user.blank
activerecord.errors.messages.blank
```

This way you can provide special translations for various error messages at different points in your model's inheritance chain and in the attributes, models, or default scopes.

11.22.8.3   Error Message Interpolation

The translated model name, translated attribute name, and value are always available for interpolation.

So, for example, instead of the default error message `"can not be blank"` you could use the attribute name like `"Please fill in your %{attribute}"`.

Validation Interpolation	With Option	Message	Interpolation
validates_confirmation_of	–	:confirmation	–
validates_acceptance_of	–	:accepted	–
validates_presence_of	–	:blank	–
validates_length_of	:within, :in	:too_short	count
validates_length_of	:within, :in	:too_long	count
validates_length_of	:is	:wrong_length	count
validates_length_of	:minimum	:too_short	count
validates_length_of	:maximum	:too_long	count
validates_format_of	–	:taken	–
validates_uniqueness_of	–	:invalid	–
validates_inclusion_of	–	:inclusion	–
validates_exclusion_of	–	:exclusion	–
validates_associated	–	:invalid	–
validates_numericality_of	–	:not_a_number	–
validates_numericality_of	:greater_than	:greater_than	count
validates_numericality_of	:greater_than_ or_equal_to	:greater_than_ or_equal_to	count
validates_numericality_of	:equal_to	:equal_to	count
validates_numericality_of	:less_than_ or_equal_to	:less_than_or_ equal_to	count
validates_numericality_of	:odd	:odd	–
validates_numericality_of	:even	:even	–

11.22.9   Overview of Other Built-In Methods That Provide I18n Support

Rails uses fixed strings and other localizations, such as format strings and other format information in a couple of helpers. Here's a brief overview.

11.22.9.1   Action View Helper Methods

- distance_of_time_in_words translates and pluralizes its result and interpolates the number of seconds, minutes, hours, and so on. See datetime .distance_in_words[18] translations.

---

18. https://github.com/rails/rails/blob/4-0-stable/actionpack/lib/action_view/locale/en.yml#L4

Helpers

- `datetime_select` and `select_month` use translated month names for populating the resulting select tag. See `date.month_names`[19] for translations. `datetime_select` also looks up the order option from `date.order`[20] (unless you pass the option explicitly). All date selection helpers translate the prompt using the translations in the `datetime.prompts`[21] scope if applicable.

- The `number_to_currency`, `number_with_precision`, `number_to_percentage`, `number_with_delimiter`, and `number_to_human_size` helpers use the number format settings located in the `number`[22] scope.

11.22.9.2 Active Record Methods

- `human_name` and `human_attribute_name` use translations for model names and attribute names if available in the `activerecord.models`[23] scope. They also support translations for inherited class names (e.g., for use with STI) as explained in the section "Error Message Scopes."

- `ActiveRecord::Errors#generate_message` (which is used by Active Record validations but may also be used manually) uses `human_name` and `human_attribute_name`. It also translates the error message and supports translations for inherited class names as explained in the section "Error Message Scopes."

- `ActiveRecord::Errors#full_messages` prepends the attribute name to the error message using a separator that will be looked up from `activerecord.errors.format` (and which defaults to `"%{attribute} %{message}"`).

11.22.9.3 Active Support Methods

- `Array#to_sentence` uses format settings as given in the `support.array` scope.

11.22.10 Exception Handling

In some contexts you might want to change I18n's default exception handling behavior. For instance, the default exception handling does not enable catching of missing translations during automated tests easily. For this purpose a different exception

---

19. https://github.com/rails/rails/blob/4-0-stable/activesupport/lib/active_support/locale/en.yml#L155
20. https://github.com/rails/rails/blob/4-0-stable/activesupport/lib/active_support/locale/en.yml#L18
21. https://github.com/rails/rails/blob/4-0-stable/actionpack/lib/action_view/locale/en.yml#L39
22. https://github.com/rails/rails/blob/4-0-stable/activesupport/lib/active_support/locale/en.yml#L37
23. https://github.com/rails/rails/blob/4-0-stable/activerecord/lib/active_record/locale/en.yml#L37

handler can be specified. The specified exception handler must be a method on the
I18n module. You would add code similar to the following to your file or other kind
of initializer.

```
module I18n
  def just_raise_that_exception(*args)
    raise args.first
  end
end

I18n.exception_handler = :just_raise_that_exception
```

This would re-raise all caught exceptions including `MissingTranslationData`.

11.23   UrlHelper

This module provides a set of methods for making links and getting URLs that
depend on the routing subsystem, covered extensively in Chapter 2, "Routing," and
Chapter 3, "REST, Resources, and Rails," of this book.

11.23.1   button_to(name = nil, options = nil, html_options = nil, &block)

Generates a form containing a single button that submits to the URL created by the
set of options. This is the safest method to ensure that links that cause changes to
your data are not triggered by search bots or accelerators. If the HTML button does
not work with your layout, you can also consider using the `link_to` method (also
in this module) with the `:method` modifier.

The options hash accepts the same options as the `url_for` method.

The generated form element has a class name of `button-to` to enable styling
of the form itself and its children. This class name can be overridden by setting
`:form_class` in `:html_options`. The `:method` option works just like the
`link_to` helper. If no `:method` modifier is given, it defaults to performing a
POST operation.

```
button_to("New", action: "new")
# => "<form method="post" action="/controller/new" class="button-to">
#        <div><input value="New" type="submit" /></div>
#      </form>"

button_to "Delete Image", { action: "delete", id: @image.id },
    method: :delete, data: { confirm: "Are you sure?" }
# => "<form method="post" action="/images/delete/1" class="button_to">
```

Helpers

```
#        <div>
#          <input type="hidden" name="_method" value="delete" />
#          <input data-confirm='Are you sure?'
#            value="Delete Image" type="submit" />
#          <input name="authenticity_token" type="hidden"
#            value="10f2163b45388899..."/>
#        </div>
#      </form>"
```

11.23.2 current_page?(options)

Returns true if the current request URI was generated by the given options. For example, let's assume that we're currently rendering the /shop/checkout action:

```
current_page?(action: 'process')
# => false

current_page?(action: 'checkout')  # controller is implied
# => true

current_page?(controller: 'shop', action: 'checkout')
# => true
```

11.23.3 link_to(name = nil, options = nil, html_ options = nil, &block)

One of the fundamental helper methods. Creates a link tag of the given name using a URL created by the set of options. The valid options are covered in the description of this module's url_for method. It's also possible to pass a string instead of an options hash to get a link tag that uses the value of the string as the href for the link. If nil is passed as a name, the link itself will become the name.

:data Adds custom data attributes.

method: symbol Specifies an alternative HTTP verb for this request (other than GET). This modifier will dynamically create an HTML form and immediately submit the form for processing using the HTTP verb specified (:post, :patch, or :delete).

remote: true Enables the unobtrusive JavaScript driver to make an Ajax request to the URL instead of following the link.

The following data attributes work alongside the unobtrusive JavaScript driver:

confirm: 'question?' The unobtrusive JavaScript driver will display a Java-Script confirmation prompt with the question specified. If the user accepts, the link is processed normally; otherwise, no action is taken.

:disable_with Used by the unobtrusive JavaScript driver to provide a name for disabled versions.

Generally speaking, GET requests should be idempotent, that is, they do not modify the state of any resource on the server and can be called one or many times without a problem. Requests that modify server-side resources or trigger dangerous actions like deleting a record should not usually be linked with a normal hyperlink, since search bots and so-called browser accelerators can follow those links while spidering your site, leaving a trail of chaos.

⚠ If the user has JavaScript disabled, the request will always fall back to us-ing GET, no matter what `:method` you have specified. This is accomplished by including a valid `href` attribute. If you are relying on the POST be-havior, your controller code should check for it using the `post?`, `de-lete?`, or `patch?` methods of `request`.

As usual, the `html_options` will accept a hash of HTML attributes for the link tag.

```
= link_to "Help", help_widgets_path

= link_to "Rails", "http://rubyonrails.org/",
    data: { confirm: "Are you sure?" }

= link_to "Delete", widget_path(@widget), method: :delete,
    data: { confirm: "Are you sure?" }

[Renders in the browser as...]

<a href="/widgets/help">Help</a>

<a href="http://rubyonrails.org/" data-confirm="Are you sure?">Rails</a>

<a href="/widgets/42" rel="nofollow" data-method="delete"
  data-confirm="Are you sure?">View</a>
```

Helpers

11.23.4 `link_to_if(condition, name, options = {}, html_options = {}, &block)`

Syntax sugar. Creates a link tag using the same options as `link_to` if the condition is `true`; otherwise, only the `name` is output (or `block` is evaluated for an alternative value, if one is supplied).

11.23.5 `link_to_unless(condition, name, options = {}, html_options = {}, &block)`

Syntax sugar. Creates a link tag using the same options as `link_to` unless the condition is `true`, in which case only the `name` is output (or block is evaluated for an alternative value, if one is supplied).

11.23.6 `link_to_unless_current(name, options = {}, html_options = {}, &block)`

Creates a link tag using the same options as `link_to` unless the condition is `true`, in which case only the `name` is output (or `block` is evaluated for an alternative value, if one is supplied).

Although it might seem silly at first, this method is pretty useful sometimes. Remember that the block given to `link_to_unless_current` is evaluated if the current action is the action given. So, if we had a comments page (that shared its template with the associated blog post) and we wanted to render a "Go Back" link instead of a link to the comments page when the user is in the process of commenting, we could do something like

```
link_to_unless_current("Comment", { controller: 'comments', action: 'new'}) do
  link_to("Go back", posts_path)
end
```

Despite the given example, this helper is most often used for creating navigation menus.

11.23.7 `mail_to(email_address, name = nil, html_options = {}, &block)`

Creates a `mailto` link tag to the specified `email_address`, which is also used as the name of the link unless `name` is specified. Additional HTML attributes for the link can be passed in `html_options`.

The `mail_to` helper has several methods for customizing the email address itself by passing special keys to `html_options`:

:subject The subject line of the email.

:body The body of the email.

:cc Add cc recipients to the email.

:bcc Add bcc recipients to the email.

Here are some examples of usages:

```
mail_to "me@domain.com"
# => <a href="mailto:me@domain.com">me@domain.com</a>

mail_to "me@domain.com", "My email"
# => <a href="mailto:me@domain.com">My email</a>

mail_to "me@domain.com", "My email", cc: "ccaddress@domain.com",
  subject: "This is an email"
# => <a href="mailto:me@domain.com?cc=ccaddress@domain.com&
    subject=This%20is%20an%20email">My email</a>
```

ⓘ Note

In previous versions of Rails, the `mail_to` helper provided options for encoding the email address to hinder email harvesters. If your application is still dependent on these options, add the `actionview-encoded_mail_to` gem to your `Gemfile`.

11.23.7.1 Redirecting Back

If you pass the magic symbol `:back` to any method that uses `url_for` under the covers (`redirect_to`, etc.) the contents of the `HTTP_REFERER` request header will be returned. (If a referer is not set for the current request, it will return `java-script:history.back()` to try to make the browser go back one page.)

```
url_for(:back)
# => "javascript:history.back()"
```

As of Rails 5, don't pass `:back` to `redirect_to`. Use the new `redirect_back` method instead, and pass it a fallback location explicitly.

```
redirect_back(fallback_location: root_path)
```

Helpers

11.24   Writing Your Own View Helpers

As you develop an application in Rails, you should be on the lookout for opportunities to refactor duplicated view code into your own helper methods. As you think of these helpers, you add them to one of the helper modules defined in the app/helpers folder of your application.

There is an art to effectively writing helper methods, similar in nature to what it takes to write effective APIs. Helper methods are basically a custom, application-level API for your view code. It is difficult to teach API design in a book form. It's the sort of knowledge that you gain by apprenticing with more experienced programmers and lots of trial and error. Nevertheless, in this section, we'll review some varied use cases and implementation styles that we hope will inspire you in your own application design.

11.24.1   Small Optimizations: The `title` Helper

Here is a simple helper method that has been of use to me on many projects now. It's called h1_title, and it combines two simple functions essential to a good HTML document:

- Setting the title of the page in the document's head.

- Setting the content of the page's h1 element.

This helper assumes that you want the title and h1 elements of the page to be the same and has a dependency in your application layout (or whatever partial contains the contents of your <head> element.

The code for the helper is in Listing 11.1 and would be added to app/helpers/application_helper.rb since it is applicable to all views.

Listing 11.1   The h1_title helper
```
def h1_title(name)
  content_for(:title) { name }
  content_tag("h1", name)
end
```

First it sets content to be yielded in the layout as :title, and then it outputs an h1 element containing the same text. I could have used string interpolation on the second line, such as "<h1>#{name}</h1>", but it would have been sloppier than using the built-in Rails helper method content_tag.

My application template is now written to `yield :title` so that it gets the page title.

```
%html
  %head
    %title= yield :title
```

As is hopefully obvious, you call the `h1_title` method in your view template where you want to have an `h1` element:

```
- h1_title "New User"
= form_for(user) do |f|
  ...
```

11.24.2   Encapsulating View Logic: The `photo_for` Helper

Here's another relatively simple helper. This time, instead of simply outputting data, we are encapsulating some view logic that decides whether to display a user's profile photo or a placeholder image. It's logic that you would otherwise have to repeat over and over again throughout your application.

The dependency (or contract) for this particular helper is that the user object being passed in has a `profile_photo` associated to it, which is an attachment model based on Rick Olson's old attachment_fu Rails plugin. The code in Listing 11.2 should be easy enough to understand without delving into the details of `attachment_fu`. Since this is an example, I broke out the logic for setting `src` into an `if/else` structure; otherwise, this would be a perfect place to use Ruby's ternary operator.

Listing 11.2   The `photo_for` helper encapsulating common view logic
```
def photo_for(user, size=:thumb)
  if user.profile_photo
    src = user.profile_photo.public_filename(size)
  else
    src = 'user_placeholder.png'
  end
  link_to(image_tag(src), user_path(user))
end
```

Helpers

🗨 Tim says . . .

Luckily, the latest generation of attachment plugins such as Paperclip and CarrierWave use a NullObject pattern to alleviate the need for you to do this sort of thing.

11.24.3   Smart View: The **breadcrumbs** Helper

Lots of web applications feature user-interface concepts called breadcrumbs. They are made by creating a list of links, positioned near the top of the page, displaying how far the user has navigated into a hierarchically organized application. I think it makes sense to extract breadcrumb logic into its own helper method instead of leaving it in a layout template.

The trick to our example implementation (shown in Listing 11.3) is to use the presence of helper methods exposed by the controller, on a convention specific to your application, to determine whether to add elements to an array of breadcrumb links.

Listing 11.3   breadcrumbs helper method for a corporate directory application

```
1  def breadcrumbs
2    return if controller.controller_name == 'home'
3
4    html = [link_to('Home', root_path)]
5
6    # first level
7    html << link_to(company.name, company) if respond_to? :company
8
9    # second level
10   html << link_to(department.name, department) if respond_to? :department
11
12   # third and final level
13   html << link_to(employee.name, employee) if respond_to? :employee
14
15   html.join(' &gt; ').html_safe
16 end
```

Here's the line-by-line explanation of the code, noting where certain application-design assumptions are made.

On line 2, we abort execution if we're in the context of the application's homepage controller, since its pages don't ever need breadcrumbs. A simple return with no value implicitly returns nil, which is fine for our purposes. Nothing will be output to the layout template.

On line 4 we are starting to build an array of HTML links, held in the html local variable, which will ultimately hold the contents of our breadcrumb trail.

The first link of the breadcrumb trail always points to the home page of the application, which of course will vary, but since it's always there we use it to initialize the array. In this example, it uses a named route called root_path.

After the `html` array is initialized, all we have to do is check for the presence of the methods returning objects that make up the hierarchy (lines 7 to 13). It is assumed that if a department is being displayed, its parent company will also be in scope. If an employee is being displayed, both department and company will be in scope as well. This is not just an arbitrary design choice. It is a common pattern in Rails applications that are modelled on REST principles and using nested resource routes.

Finally, on line 15, the array of HTML links is joined with the > character, to give the entire string the traditional breadcrumb appearance. The call to `html_safe` tells the rendering system that this is HTML code and we're cool with that—don't sanitize it!

11.25   Wrapping and Generalizing Partials

I don't think that partials (by themselves) lead to particularly elegant or concise template code. Whenever there's a shared partial template that gets used over and over again in my application, I will take the time to wrap it up in a custom helper method that conveys its purpose and formalizes its parameters. If appropriate, I might even generalize its implementation to make it more of a lightweight, reusable component.

11.25.1   A `tiles` Helper

Let's trace the steps to writing a helper method that wraps what I consider to be a general-purpose partial. Listing 11.4 contains code for a partial for a piece of a user interface that is common to many applications and generally referred to as a tile. It pairs a small thumbnail photo of something on the left side of the widget with a linked name and description on the right.

Tiles can also represent other models in your application, such as users and files. As I mentioned, tiles are a very common construct in modern user interfaces and operating systems. So let's take the cities tiles partial and transform it into something that can be used to display other types of data.

ⓘ Note

I realize that it has become passé to use HTML tables and I happen to agree that `div`-based layouts plus CSS are a lot more fun and flexible to work with. However, for the sake of simplicity in this example, and since the UI structure we're describing is tabular, I've decided to structure it using a table.

Listing 11.4 A `tiles` partial prior to wrapping and generalization

```
1   %table.cities.tiles
2     - cities.in_groups_of(columns) do |row|
3       %tr
4         - row.each do |city|
5           %td[city]
6             .left
7               = image_tag(city.photo.url(:thumb))
8             .right
9               .title
10                = city.name
11              .description
12                = city.description
```

11.25.1.1 Explanation of the Tiles Partial Code

Since we're going to transform this city-specific partial into a generalized UI component, I want to make sure that the code we start with makes absolute sense to you first. Before proceeding, I'm going through the implementation line by line and explaining what everything in Listing 11.4 does.

Line 1 opens up the partial with a table element and gives it semantically significant CSS classes so that the table and its contents can be properly styled.

Line 2 leverages a useful `Array` extension method provided by Active Support, called `in_groups_of`. It uses both of the local variables: `cities` and `columns`. Both will need to be passed into this partial using the `:locals` option of the `render :partial` method. The `cities` variable will hold the list of cities to be displayed, and `columns` is an integer representing how many city tiles each row should contain. A loop iterates over the number of rows that will be displayed in this table.

Line 3 begins a table row using the `tr` element.

Line 4 begins a loop over the tiles for each row to be displayed, yielding a `city` for each.

Line 5 opens a `td` element and uses Haml's *object reference* notation to auto-generate a `dom_id` attribute for the table cell in the style of `city_98`, `city_99`, and so on.

Line 6 opens a `div` element for the left side of the tile and has the CSS class name needed so that it can be styled properly.

Line 7 calls the `image_tag` helper to insert a thumbnail photo of the city.

Skipping along, lines 9–10 insert the content for the `.title div` element, in this case, the name and state of the city.

Line 12 directly invokes the `description` method.

11.25.1.2 Calling the Tiles Partial Code

In order to use this partial, we have to call `render :partial` with the two required parameters specified in the `:locals` hash:

```
= render "cities/tiles", cities: @user.cities, columns: 3
```

I'm guessing that most experienced Rails developers have written some partial code similar to this and tried to figure out a way to include default values for some of the parameters. In this case, it would be really nice to not have to specify `:columns` all the time, since in most cases we want there to be three.

The problem is that since the parameters are passed via the `:locals` hash and become local variables, there isn't an easy way to insert a default value in the partial itself. If you left off the `columns: n` part of your partial call, Rails would bomb with an exception about `columns` not being a local variable or method. It's not the same as an instance variable, which defaults to `nil` and can be used willy nilly.

Experienced Rubyists probably know that you can use the `defined?` method to figure out whether a local variable is in scope or not, but the resulting code would be very ugly. The following code might be considered elegant, but it doesn't work![24]

```
columns = 3 unless defined? columns
```

Instead of teaching you how to jump through annoying Ruby idiom hoops, I'll show you how to tackle this challenge the Rails way, and that is where we can start discussing the helper wrapping technique.

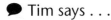 **Tim says . . .**

Obie might not want to make you jump through Ruby idiom hoops, but I don't mind . . .

11.25.1.3 Write the Helper Method

First, I'll add a new helper method to the `CitiesHelper` module of my application, like in Listing 11.5. It's going to be fairly simple at first. In thinking about the name of the method, it occurs to me that I like the way that `tiled(cities)` will read instead of `tiles(cities)`, so I name it that way.

---

24. If you want to know why it doesn't work, you'll have to buy the first book in this series: *The Ruby Way*, ISBN: 0672328844.

Helpers

Listing 11.5   The `CitiesHelper` tiled method

```
module CitiesHelper
  def tiled(cities, columns=3)
    render "cities/tiles", cities: cities, columns: columns
  end
end
```

Right from the start I can take care of that default `columns` parameter by giving the helper method parameter for columns a default value. That's just a normal feature of Ruby. Now instead of specifying the `render :partial` call in my view template, I can simply write `= tiled(cities)`, which is considerably more elegant and terse. It also serves to decouple the implementation of the tiled city table from the view. If I need to change the way that the tiled table is rendered in the future, I just have to do it in one place: the helper method.

11.25.2   Generalizing Partials

Now that we've set the stage, the fun can begin. The first thing we'll do is move the helper method to the `ApplicationHelper` module so that it's available to all view templates. We'll also move the partial template file to `app/views/shared/_tiled_table.html.haml` to denote that it isn't associated with a particular kind of view and to more accurately convey its use. As a matter of good code style, I also do a sweep through the implementation and generalize the identifiers appropriately. The reference to `cities` on line 2 becomes `collection`. The block variable `city` on line 4 becomes `item`. Listing 11.6 has the new partial code.

Listing 11.6   Tiles partial code with revised naming

```
%table.tiles
  - collection.in_groups_of(columns) do |row|
    %tr
      - row.each do |item|
        %td[item]
          .left
            = image_tag(item.photo.public_filename(:thumb))
          .right
            .title
              = item.name
            .description
              = item.description
```

There's still the matter of a contract between this partial code and the objects that it is rendering. Namely, they must respond to the following messages: `photo`, `name`, and `description`. A survey of other models in my application reveals that I need more flexibility. Some things have names, but others have titles. Sometimes I want the description to appear under the name of the object represented, but other times I want to be able to insert additional data about the object plus some links.

11.25.2.1 Lambda: The Ultimate Flexibility

Ruby enables you to store references to anonymous methods (also known as *procs* or *lambdas*) and call them at will whenever you want.[25] Knowing this capability is there, what becomes possible? For starters, we can use lambdas to pass in blocks of code that will fill in parts of our partial dynamically.

For example, the current code for showing the thumbnail is a big problem. Since the code varies greatly depending on the object being handled, I want to be able to pass in instructions for how to get a thumbnail image without having to resort to big `if`/ `else` statements or putting view logic in my model classes. Please take a moment to understand the problem I'm describing, and then take a look at how we solve it in Listing 11.7. Hint: The `thumbnail`, `link`, `title`, and `description` variables hold lambdas!

Listing 11.7   Tiles partial code refactored to use lambdas

```
.left
  = link_to thumbnail.call(item), link.call(item)
.right
  .title
    = link_to title.call(item), link.call(item)
  .description
    = description.call(item)
```

Notice that in Listing 11.7, the contents of the left and right `div` elements come from variables containing lambdas. On line 2 we make a call to `link_to` and both of its arguments are dynamic. A similar construct on line 5 takes care of generating the title link. In both cases, the first lambda should return the output of a call to `image_tag`, and the second should return a URL. In all of these lambda usages, the `item` currently being rendered is passed to the lambdas as a block variable.

---

25. If you're familiar with Ruby already, you might know that Proc.new is an alternate way to create anonymous blocks of code. I prefer lambda, at least in Ruby 1.9, because of subtle behavior differences. Lambda blocks check the arity of the argument list passed to them when call is invoked, and explicitly calling return in a lambda block works correctly.

Helpers

💬 Wilson says . . .

Things like `link.call(item)` could potentially look even sassier as `link[item]`, except that you'll shoot your eye out doing it. (`Proc#[]` is an alias for `Proc#call`.)

11.25.2.2   The New Tiled Helper Method

If you now direct your attention to Listing 11.8, you'll notice that the `tiled` method is changed considerably. In order to keep my positional argument list down to a manageable size, I've switched over to taking a hash of options as the last parameter to the `tiled` method. This approach is useful, and it mimics the way that almost all helper methods take options in Rails.

Default values are provided for all parameters, and they are all passed along to the partial via the `:locals` hash given to `render`.

Listing 11.8 The tiled collection helper method with lambda parameters

```
module ApplicationHelper

  def tiled(collection, opts={})
    opts[:columns] ||= 3

    opts[:thumbnail] ||= lambda do |item|
      image_tag(item.photo.url(:thumb))
    end

    opts[:title] ||= lambda { |item| item.to_s }

    opts[:description] ||= lambda { |item| item.description }

    opts[:link] ||= lambda { |item| item }

    render "shared/tiled_table",
      collection: collection,
      columns: opts[:columns],
      link: opts[:link],
      thumbnail: opts[:thumbnail],
      title: opts[:title],
      description: opts[:description]
  end
end
```

Finally, to wrap up this example, here's a snippet showing how to invoke our new `tiled` helper method from a template, overriding the default behavior for links:

```
tiled(cities, link: lambda { |city| showcase_city_path(city) })
```

The `showcase_city_path` method is available to the lambda block, since it is a closure, meaning that it inherits the execution context in which it is created.

11.26 Conclusion

This very long chapter served as a thorough reference for helper methods, both those provided by Rails and ideas for ones that you will write yourself. Effective use of helper methods leads to more elegant and maintainable view templates. At this point you should also have a good overview of how I18n support in Ruby on Rails works and are ready to start translating your project.

Before we fully conclude our coverage of Action View, we'll jump into the world of Ajax and JavaScript. Arguably, one of the main reasons for Rails's continued popularity is its support for those two crucial technologies of Web 2.0.

This chapter is published under the Creative Commons Attribution-ShareAlike 4.0 license, http://creativecommons.org/licenses/by-sa/4.0/.

Helpers

CHAPTER 12

Haml

> HAML gave us a great take on how views can also be done. It looks a little cryptic at first, but don't let that shake you off. Once you internalize the meaning of %, #, and . it should be all good (and you already know most just from CSS). [. . .] Additionally, I can't help but have respect for a Canadian who manages to swear more than I did during my vendoritis rant and drink beer at the same time. A perfect example of the diversity in the Rails community. Very much part of what makes us special.[1]
>
> —David (talking about Haml and Hampton Catlin in September 2006)

Haml (http://haml.info) is a "whitespace-sensitive" HTML templating engine that uses indentation to determine the hierarchy of an HTML document. Haml was created because its creator, Hampton Catlin, was tired of having to type markup and wanted all of his output code to be beautifully formatted. What he invented was a new templating engine that removed a lot of noisy boilerplate, such as angle brackets (from ERb) and did away with the need to close blocks and HTML tags.

We love Haml because it's truly minimal, enabling a developer to focus simply on the structure of the page and not on the content. Today it's common to keep view logic out of your templates, but that directive has been a guiding principle of Haml since its beginning. According to the 2012 Ruby Survey,[2] 36.96% of Rubyists prefer Haml over ERb, and 15.84% demand it in their projects. Haml is also the standard templating engine at various professional Ruby agencies, such as Hashrocket, Envy Labs, Remarkable Labs, and Astrails.

Haml

---

1. http://david.heinemeierhansson.com/arc/2006_09.html
2. http://survey.hamptoncatlin.com/survey/stats

In this chapter, we'll cover the fundamentals of Haml, from creating HTML elements, to using filters to create other kinds of textual content embedded in your document.

12.1   Getting Started

To start using the Haml template language over ERb in your project, first add the `haml-rails` gem to your `Gemfile` and run `bundle install`.

```
# Gemfile
gem 'haml-rails'
```

The benefit of using `haml-rails` over simply the `haml` gem is it adds support for Rails specific features. For instance, when you use a controller or scaffold generator, `haml-rails` will generate Haml views instead of using the Rails default of ERb. The `haml-rails` gem also configures Haml templates to work with cache digests out of the box.

12.2   The Basics

In this section, we'll cover how to create HTML elements and attributes using Haml.

12.2.1   Creating an Element

To create an HTML element in Haml, you simply need to prefix the percent character `%` to an element name. The element name can be any string, enabling you to use elements introduced in HTML5, such as `header`.

Haml
```
%header content
```

HTML
```
<header>content</header>
```

Haml will automatically handle generating opening and closing tags for the element on compilation. Not only does this make templates more concise and clean, it also eliminates common errors such forgetting to not close HTML tags.

12.2.2   Attributes

Attributes in Haml are defined using two styles. The first style involves defining attributes between curly braces ({ }). These attribute "brackets" are really just Ruby hashes and are evaluated as such. Because of this, local variables and Ruby logic can be used when defining attributes.

```
%a{ title: @article.title, href: article_path(@article) } Title
```

⚿ Multiline Attributes

Attribute hashes can be separated on multiple lines for readability. All new-lines must be placed right after the comma:

```
%a{ title: @article.title,
    href: article_path(@article) } Title
```

The second style follows the more traditional way of defining HTML attributes using equal signs. Note that attributes are separated by white space, not commas.

```
%a(title=@article.title href=article_path(@article)) Title
```

⚿ In both styles, the right-hand value of each attribute must be a valid Ruby expression.

12.2.2.1   Data Attributes

Introduced with HTML 5, data attributes enable custom data to be embedded in any HTML element by prefixing an attribute with `data-`. Instead of littering the attribute hash with multiple attribute keys prefixed with `data-`, you can define all their data attributes in a nested hash associated with the key `:data`, like this:

Haml
```
%article{ data: { author_id: 1 } } Lorem Ipsum...
```

HTML
```
<article data-author-id='123'>Lorem Ipsum...</article>
```

Note that underscores are automatically replaced with a hyphen. Not that you'd want to, but you can change this behavior by setting the Haml configuration option `hyphenate_data_attrs` to `false`. (Haml configuration options are covered in detail later in this chapter.)

It's also possible to nest data hashes more than one level, to reduce verbosity when attributes share common roots.

Haml
```
%article{ data: { author: {id: 1, name: "Kevin Wu" } } Lorem Ipsum...
```

HTML
```
<article data-author-id='123' data-author-name='Kevin Wu'>Lorem
    Ipsum...</article>
```

Haml

12.2.2.2 Boolean Attributes

In HTML, there exist certain attributes that do not have a value associated with them, such as `required`.

```
<input type="text" required>
```

These are referred to as *boolean* attributes in Haml, since their value does not matter, only that they're present. To represent these attributes in using the hash-style attribute syntax, set the value of the attribute to `true`.

```
%input{ type: 'text', required: true }
```

Otherwise, if you're using the HTML attribute style syntax, a boolean value doesn't have to be set at all.

```
%input(type="text" required)
```

XHTML

If the format of Haml is set to `:xhtml`, boolean attributes will be set to their name. To illustrate, given the preceding example, Haml would render the following HTML:

```
<input type="text" required="required" />
```

12.2.3 Classes and IDs

Haml was designed to promote the DRY principle (not repeating code unnecessarily.) As such, it provides a shorthand syntax for adding id and class attributes to an element. The syntax is borrowed from CSS, where ids are represented by a pound (#) and classes by a period (.). Both of these signs must be placed immediately after the element and before an attributes hash.

Haml
```
#content
  .entry.featured
    %h3.title Haml
    %p.body Lorem Ipsum...
```

HTML
```
<div id='content'>
  <div class='entry featured'>
    <h3 class='title'>Haml</h3>
    <p class='body'>Lorem Ipsum...</p>
  </div>
</div>
```

As the preceding example shows, multiple class names can be specified in the same way as CSS, by chaining the class names together with periods. In a slightly more complicated scenario, the shortcut CSS style class and id syntax can be combined with long-hand attributes. Both values are merged together when compiled down to HTML.

Haml
```
%article.featured{ class: @article.visibility }
```

HTML
```
<article class='feature visible'>...</article>
```

Haml has some serious tricks up its sleeves for dealing with complex id and class attributes. For instance, an array of class names will automatically be joined with a space.

Haml
```
%article{ class: [@article.visibility, @article.category] }
```

HTML
```
<article class='visible breakingnews'>...</article>
```

Arrays of id values will be joined with an underscore.

Haml
```
%article{ id: [@article.category, :article, @article.id] }
```

HTML
```
<article id='sports_article_1234'>...</article>
```

Note that the array is flattened and any elements that evaluate to `false` or `nil` will be dropped automatically. This lets you do some pretty clever tricks at the expense of readability and maintainability.

```
%article{ class: [@article.visibility,
  @article.published_at < 4.hours.ago && 'breakingnews'] }
```

In the example, if the article was published less than four hours ago, then `break-ingnews` will be added as one of the CSS classes of the element.

While we're on the subject, remember that it is advisable to migrate this kind of logic into your Ruby classes. In this particular example, we might give the `Article` class (or one of its presenters or decorator classes) a `breakingnews?` method and use it instead of inlining the business logic.

```
def breaking?
  published_at < 4.hours.ago
```

Haml

```
end
```

```
%article{ class: [@article.visibility, @article.breaking? && 'breakingnews'] }
```

If `breaking?` returns `false`, then the Ruby expression short circuits to `false`, and Haml ignores that particular class name.

12.2.4   Implicit Divs

The default elements of Haml are divs. Since they are used so often in markup, you can simply define a div with a class or id using `.` or `#`, respectively.

Haml
```
#container
  .content Lorem Ipsum...
```

HTML
```
<div id="container">
  <div class="content">
    Lorem Ipsum...
  </div>
</div>
```

Implicit Div Creation

Not having to specify div tags explicitly helps your markup to be more semantic from the start, placing focus on the intention of the div instead of treating it as just another markup container. It's also one of the main reasons that we recommend Haml over ERb. We believe that Haml templates lessen mental burden by communicating the structure of your DOM in a way that maps cleanly to the CSS that will be applied to the document.

12.2.5   Empty Tags

In HTML, there are certain elements that don't require a closing tag, such as `br`. By default, Haml will not add a closing tag for the following tags:

- `area`
- `base`
- `br`
- `col`
- `hr`

- img

- input

- link

- meta

- param

To illustrate, consider the following example:

```
%hr
```

would render HTML

```
<hr>
```

or XHTML

```
<hr />
```

Adding a forward slash character (/) at the end of a tag definition causes Haml to treat it as being an empty element. The list of empty tags Haml uses can be overridden using the `autoclose` configuration setting. Haml configuration options are covered in detail later in this chapter.

12.3   Doctype

A doctype must be the first item in any HTML document. By including the characters !!! at the beginning of a template, Haml will automatically generate a doctype based on the configuration option `:format`, set to `:html5` by default. Adding !!! to a template would result in the following HTML:

```
<!DOCTYPE html>
```

Haml also enables the specifying of a specific doctype after !!!. A complete listing of supported doctypes can be found on Haml's reference website.[3]

12.4   Comments

There are two types of comments in Haml, those that appear in rendered HTML and those that don't.

---

3. http://haml.info/docs/yardoc/file.REFERENCE.html#doctype_

12.4.1   HTML Comments

To leave a comment that will be rendered by Haml, place a forward slash (/) at the beginning of the line you want commented. Anything nested under that line will also be commented out.

Haml
```
/ Some comment
```

HTML
```
<!-- Some comment -->
```

You can use this feature to produce Internet Explorer conditional comments by suffixing the condition in square brackets like this:

```
/[if lt IE 9]
```

12.4.2   Haml Comments

Besides conditional comments for targeting Internet Explorer, comments left in your markup are meant to communicate a message to other developers working with the template. These messages should not be rendered to the browser as they are specific to your team. In Haml, starting a line with -# ensures any text following the pound sign isn't rendered at all.

Haml
```
-# Some important comment...
%h1 The Rails 5 Way
```

HTML
```
<h1>The Rails 5 Way</h1>
```

If any text is nested beneath this kind of *silent comment,* it will also be ommitted from the resulting output.

12.5   Evaluating Ruby Code

Somewhat similar to ERb, using = results in Haml evaluating Ruby code following the equals character and outputting the result into the document.

Haml
```
%p= %w(foo bar).join(' ')
```

HTML
```
<p>foo bar</p>
```

Alternatively, using the hyphen character – evaluates Ruby code but doesn't insert its output into the resulting document. This is commonly used in combination with if/ else statements and loops.

```
- if flash.notice
  .notice= flash.notice
```

Note that Ruby blocks don't need to be explicitly closed in Haml. As seen in the previous example, any indentation beneath a Ruby evaluation command indicates a block.

💬 Kevin says . . .

Do not use – to set variables. If you find yourself doing so, this is an indication that you need to create some form of view object, such as a presenter or decorator.

Lines of Ruby code can be broken up over multiple lines as long as each line but the last ends with a comma.

```
= image_tag post.mage_url,
    class: 'featured-image'
```

12.5.1 Interpolation

Ruby code can can be interpolated in two ways in Haml, inline with plain text using #{}, or using string interpolation in combination with =. To illustrate, the following two lines of Haml code samples are equivalent:

```
%p By: #{post.author_name}
```

```
%p= "By: #{post.author_name}"
```

Both are valid. The first is considered much better form, because it's more concise.

12.5.2 Escaping/Unescaping HTML

To match the default Rails XSS protection scheme, Haml will sanitize any HTML sensitive characters from the output of =. This results in any = call to behave like &=.

Haml
```
&= "Cookies & Cream"
```

HTML
```
Cookies &amp; Cream
```

Haml

Alternatively, to unescape HTML with Haml, simply use != instead of =. If the Haml configuration option `escape_html` is set to `false`, then any call to = will behave like !=. (You probably will never want to do that.)

Haml
```
!= "Remember the awful <blink> tag?"
```

HTML
```
Remember the awful <blink> tag?
```

12.5.3   Escaping the First Character of a Line

On rare occasion, you might want to start a line of your template with a character such as = that would normally be interpreted. You may escape the first character of a line using a backslash.

Haml
```
%p
  \= equality for all =
```

HTML
```
<p>
  = equality for all =
</p>
```

12.5.4   Multiline Declarations

Haml is meant to be used for layout and design. Although you can technically write multiline declarations within a template, the creators of Haml made this intentionally awkward to discourage people from doing so.

If you do for some reason need declarations that span multiple lines in a Haml template, you can do so by adding the multiline operator | to the end of each line.

```
#content
  %p= h( |
    "While possible to write" +               |
    "multiline Ruby code, " +                 |
    "it is not the Haml way" +                |
    "as you should eliminate as much Ruby" + |
    "in your views as possible")              |
```

We highly recommend extracting multi-line Ruby code into helpers, decorators, or presenters.

12.6 Helpers

Haml provides a variety of helpers that are useful for day-to-day development, such as creating list items for each item in a collection and setting CSS ids and classes based on a model or controller.

12.6.1 Object Reference []

Given an object, such as an Active Record instance, Haml can output an HTML element with the id and class attributes set by that object via the [] operator. For instance, assuming @post is an instance of a Post class, with an id value of 1 then the following template code

```
%li[@post]
  %h4= @post.title
  = @post.excerpt
```

renders

```
<li class='post' id='post_1'>...</li>
```

This is similar to using Rails helpers div_for and content_tag_for, covered in Chapter 11, "All about Helpers."

12.6.2 `page_class`

Returns the name of the current controller and action to be used with the class attribute of an HTML element. This is commonly used with the body element, to enable easy style targeting based on a particular controller or action. To illustrate, assuming the current controller is PostsController and action index

```
%body{ class: page_class }
```

renders

```
<body class='posts index'>
```

> ⚠ Using this technique is incompatible with Turbolinks, which changes the contents of the body without altering the body attributes. Don't say I didn't warn you.

12.6.3 `list_of(enum, opts = {}) { |item| ... }`

Given an Enumerable object and a block, the list_of method will iterate and yield the results of the block into sequential <li> elements.

Haml

Haml
```
%ul
  = list_of [1, 2, 3] do |item|
    Number #{item}
```

HTML
```
<ul>
    <li>Number 1</li>
    <li>Number 2</li>
    <li>Number 3</li>
</ul>
```

12.7 Filters

Haml ships with a collection of filters that enable you to pass arbitrary blocks of text content as input to another processor, with the resulting output inserted into the document. The syntax for using a filter is a colon followed by the name of the filter. For example, to use the markdown filter

```
:markdown
  # The Rails 5 Way

  Some even more awesome **Rails** related content.
```

renders

```
<h1>The Rails 5 Way</h1>

<p>Some even more awesome <strong>Rails</strong> related content.</p>
```

Here is a table of all the filters that Haml supports by default:

`:cdata`	Surrounds the filtered text with CDATA tags.
`:coffee` or `coffeescript`	Compiles filtered text into JavaScript using CoffeeScript.
`:css`	Surrounds the filtered text with `style` tags.
`:erb`	Parses the filtered text with ERb. All Embedded Ruby code is evaluated in the same context as the Haml template.
`:escaped`	HTML-escapes filtered text.
`:javascript`	Surrounds the filtered text with `script` tag.
`:less`	Compiles filtered text into CSS using Less.
`:markdown`	Parses the filtered text with Markdown.
`:plain`	Does not parse filtered text. Can be used to insert chunks of HTML that will be inserted as is without going through Haml.

:preserve	Inserts filtered text with whitespace preserved.
:ruby	Parses the filtered text with the Ruby interpreter. Ruby code is evaluated in the same context as the Haml template.
:sass	Compiles filtered text into CSS using Sass, enclosed in a `<style>` tag.
:scss	Same as the `:sass` filter, except it uses the SCSS syntax to produce the CSS output.

Some filters require external gems to be added to your `Gemfile` in order to work. For instance, the `:markdown` filter requires a markdown gem, such as `redcarpet`. To use a specific library when there is more than one choice, tell Tilt which one to pick:

```
Tilt.prefer Tilt::RedCarpetTemplate
```

> ⚠ Note that `#{}` interpolation within filters is never HTML-escaped automatically, the way it is in normal template code.

12.8   Haml and Content

In Chris Eppstein's blog post "Haml Sucks for Content,"[4] he stated his opinions on why one shouldn't use Haml to build content:

> Haml's use of CSS syntax for IDs and class names should make it very clear: The markup you write in Haml is intended to be styled by your stylesheets. Conversely, content does not usually have specific styling—it is styled by tags.

Essentially what Chris was trying to convey is to not use native Haml syntax for creating anything other than skeletal (or structural) HTML markup. Use filters to inline reader content, such as in this example using the `:markdown` filter.

```
%p
  Do
  %strong not
  use
  %a{ href: "http://haml.info" } Haml
  for content
```

is equivalent to the following markdown within a filter

```
:markdown
  Do **not* use [Haml](http://haml.info) for content
```

---

4. http://chriseppstein.github.io/blog/2010/02/08/haml-sucks-for-content

We like the idea, but admit that your mileage may vary. It really depends on the type of project you're working on and the capabilities of the person that will be maintaining the Haml template source files.

12.9 Configuration Options

Haml provides various configuration options to control exactly how markup is rendered. Options can be set by setting the `Haml::Template.options` hash in a Rails initializer.

```
# config/initializers/haml.rb
Haml::Template.options[:format] = :html5
```

12.9.1 `autoclose`

The `autoclose` option accepts an array of all tags that Haml should self-close if no content is present. Defaults to `[meta, img, link, br, hr, input, area, param, col, base]`.

12.9.2 `cdata`

Determines whether Haml will include CDATA sections around JavaScript and CSS blocks when using the `:javascript` and `:css` filters, respectively.

When `format` is set to `html`, defaults to `false`. If the `format` is `xhtml`, `cdata` will always be set to `true` and cannot be overridden.

This option also affects the following filters: * `:sass` * `:scss` * `:less` * `:coffeescript`

12.9.3 `compiler_class`

The compiler class to use when compiling Haml to HTML. Defaults to `Haml::Compiler`.

12.9.4 `encoding`

The default encoding for HTML output is `Encoding.default_internal`. If that is not set, the default is the encoding of the Haml template. The encoding option can be set to either a string or an `Encoding` object.

12.9.5 `escape_attrs`

If set to `true` (default), will escape all HTML-sensitive characters in attributes.

12.9.6 `escape_html`

When Haml is used with a Rails project, the `escape_html` option is automatically set to `true` to match Rails' XSS protection scheme. This causes = to behave like &= in Haml templates.

12.9.7 `format`

Specifies the output format of a Haml template. By default, it's set to `:html5`. Other options include:

- `:html4`

- `:xhtml`: Will cause Haml to automatically generate self-closing tags and wrap the output of JavaScript and CSS filters inside CDATA.

12.9.8 `hyphenate_data_attrs`

Haml converts underscores in all data attributes to use hyphens by default. To disable this functionality, set `hyphenate_data_attrs` to `false`.

12.9.9 `mime_type`

The MIME type that rendered Haml templates are served with. If this is set to `text/xml` then the format will be overridden to `:xhtml` even if it has been set to `:html4` or `:html5`.

12.9.10 `parser_class`

The parser class to use. Defaults to `Haml::Parser`.

12.9.11 `preserve`

The `preserve` option accepts an array of all tags that should have their newlines preserved using the `preserve` helper. Defaults to `['textarea', 'pre']`.

12.9.12 `remove_whitespace`

Setting to `true` causes all tags to be treated as if whitespace removal Haml operators are present. Defaults to `false`.

12.9.13 `ugly`

Haml does not attempt to format or indent the output HTML of a rendered template. By default, `ugly` is set to `false` in every Rails environment except `production`. This enables you to view the rendered HTML in a pleasing format when you're in development but yields higher performance in production.

Haml

12.10   Conclusion

In this chapter, we learned how Haml helps developers create clear, well-indented markup in your Rails applications. In the following chapter we will cover how to manage sessions with Active Record, memcached, and cookies.

CHAPTER 13

Session Management

I'd hate to wake up some morning and find out that you weren't you!

—Dr. Miles J. Binnell (Kevin McCarthy) in *Invasion of the Body Snatchers* (Allied Artists, 1956)

HTTP is a stateless protocol. Without the concept of a session (not unique to Rails), there'd be no way to know that any HTTP request was related to another one. You'd never have an easy way to know who is accessing your application! Identification of your user (and presumably, authentication) would have to happen on each and every request handled by the server.[1]

Luckily, whenever a new user accesses our Rails application, a new session is automatically created. Using the session, we can maintain just enough server-side state to make our lives as web programmers significantly easier.

We use the word *session* to refer both to the time that a user is actively using the application, as well as to refer to the persistent hash data structure that we keep around for that user. That data structure takes the form of a hash, identified by a unique session id, a 32-character string of random hex numbers. When a new session is created, Rails automatically sends a cookie to the browser containing the session id, for future reference. From that point on, each request from the browser sends the session id back to the server, and continuity can be maintained.

The Rails way to design web applications dictates minimal use of the session for storage of stateful data. In keeping with the *share nothing* philosophy embraced by

---

1. If you are really new to web programming and want a very thorough explanation of how web-based session management works, you may want to read the information available at http://www.technicalinfo.net/papers/WebBasedSessionManagement.html.

519

Rails, the proper place for persistent storage of data is the database, period (or some other cached repository).

The bottom line is that the longer you keep objects in the user's session hash, the more problems you create for yourself in trying to keep those objects from becoming stale (in other words, out of date in relation to the database).

This chapter deals with matters related to session use, starting with the question of what to put in the session.

13.1   What to Store in the Session

Deciding what to store in the session hash does not have to be super-difficult if you simply commit to storing as little as possible in it. Generally speaking, integers (for key values) and short string messages are okay. **Objects are not.**

13.1.1   The Current User

There is one important integer that most Rails applications store in the session, and that is the `current_user_id`—not the current user object but its id. Even if you roll your own login and authentication code (which you shouldn't do), don't store the entire User (or Person) in the session while the user is logged in. (See Chapter 14, "Authentication and Authorization," for more information about keeping track of the current user.)

The authentication system should take care of loading the user instance from the database prior to each request and making it available in a consistent fashion, via a method on your `ApplicationController`. In particular, following this advice will ensure that you are able to disable access to given users without having to wait for their session to expire.

13.1.2   Session Use Guidelines

Here are some more general guidelines on storing objects in the session:

- They must be serializable by Ruby's Marshal API, which excludes certain types of objects such as a database connection and other types of I/O objects.

- Large object graphs may exceed the size available for session storage. Whether this limitation is in effect for you depends on the session store chosen and is covered later in the chapter. (It's 4KB when storing the session in browser cookies.)

- Critical data should not be stored in the session, since it can be suddenly lost by the user (by closing the browser or clearing cookies).

- Objects with attributes that change often should not be kept in the session.

- Modifying the structure of an object and keeping old versions of it stored in the session is a recipe for disaster. Deployment scripts should clear old sessions to prevent this sort of problem from occurring, but with certain types of session stores, such as the cookie store, this problem is hard to mitigate. The simple answer (again) is to just not keep anything, except for the occasional id, in the session and especially not full objects.

ℹ You used to be able to turn off the session, but since Rails 2.3, applications that don't need sessions don't have to worry about them. Sessions are lazy-loaded, which means unless you access the session in a controller action, there is no performance implication.

13.2 Storage Mechanisms

The mechanisms through which sessions are persisted can vary. Rails' default behavior is to store session data as cookies in the browser, which is fine for almost all applications. If you need to exceed the 4KB storage limit inherent in using cookies, then you can opt for an alternative session store. But of course, you shouldn't be exceeding that limit, because you shouldn't be keeping much other than an id or two in the session. Have I said that enough?

There are potential security concerns related to *session-replay attacks* involving cookies, which might push you in the direction of using an alternative form of session storage.

13.2.1 Active Record Session Store

In previous version of Rails, the capability to switch over to storing sessions in the database was built into framework itself. However as of version 4.0, the Active Record session store has been extracted into its own gem. Read about it at https://github.com/rails/activerecord-session_store.

🔍 The reason it's been extracted is that using it is considered a bad idea. If your application receives a large amount of traffic, the sessions database table is continuously bombarded with read/write operations. And why are you putting more than 4KB in the session, anyway?

Session

13.2.2   Memcached Session Storage

If you are running a high-traffic Rails deployment, you're probably already leveraging memcached in some way or another. The `memcached` server daemon is a remote-process memory cache that helps power some of the most highly trafficked sites on the Internet.

The memcached session storage option lets you use your `memcached` server as the repository for session data and is blazing fast. It's also nice because it has built-in expiration, meaning you don't have to expire old sessions yourself.

To use memcached, the first step is to add the dalli gem to your `Gemfile` and run `bundle`:

```
# Gemfile
gem 'dalli'
```

Next, set up your Rails environment to use memcached as its cache store. At a minimum, you can set the configuration setting `cache_store` to `:mem_cache_store`:

```
# config/environments/production.rb
config.cache_store = :mem_cache_store
```

ℹ️ Note

Since Rails 4, when defining a `cache_store` using option `:mem_cache_store` the dalli[2] gem is used behind the scenes instead of the `memcache-client` gem. Besides being threadsafe, which Rails 4 is by default, here are some of the reasons why Dalli is the new default memcached client:

- It is approximately 20% faster than the `memcache-client` gem.
- Dalli has the capability to handle failover with recovery and adjustable timeouts.
- Dalli uses the newer memcached binary protocol.

  For more details, see the Cache Storage section in Chapter 17, "Caching and Performance."

Next, modify Rails' default session store setting in `config/initializers/session_store.rb`. At minimum, replace the contents of the file with the following:

```
Rails.application.config
  session_store ActionDispatch::Session::CacheStore
```

---

2. https://github.com/mperham/dalli

This will tell Rails to use the `cache_store` of the application as the underlying session store as well. Additionally, you could explicitly set the number of seconds a session is available for by setting the `:expire_after` option.

```
Rails.application.config.
  session_store ActionDispatch::Session::CacheStore,
    expires_after: 20.minutes
```

13.2.3 The Controversial `CookieStore`

In February 2007, core-team member Jeremy Kemper made a pretty bold commit to Rails. He changed the default session storage mechanism from the venerable `PStore` to a new system based on a `CookieStore`. His commit message summed it up well:

> Introduce a cookie-based session store as the Rails default. Sessions typically contain at most a user_id and flash message; both fit within the 4K cookie size limit. A secure hash is included with the cookie to ensure data integrity (a user cannot alter his user_id without knowing the secret key included in the hash). If you have more than 4K of session data or don't want your data to be visible to the user, pick another session store. Cookie-based sessions are dramatically faster than the alternatives.

I describe the `CookieStore` as controversial because of the fallout over making it the default session storage mechanism. For one, it imposes a very strict size limit, only 4KB. A significant size constraint like that is fine if you're following the Rails way and not storing anything other than integers and short strings in the session. If you're bucking the guidelines, well, you might have an issue with it.

13.2.3.1 Encrypted Cookies

Lots of people have complained about the inherent insecurity of storing session information, including the current user information on the user's browser. In Rails 3, cookies were only digitally signed, which verified that they were generated by your application and were difficult to alter. However, the contents of the cookie could still be easily read by the user. As of Rails 4, all cookies are encrypted by default, making them not only hard to alter but hard to read too.

13.2.3.2 Replay Attacks

Another problem with cookie-based session storage is its vulnerability to replay attacks, which generated an enormous message thread on the railscore mailing list. S. Robert James kicked off the thread[3] by describing a replay attack:

---

3. If you want to read the whole thread (all 83 messages of it), simply search Google for "Replay attacks with cookie session." The results should include a link to the topic on the Ruby on Rails: Core Google Group.

Session

Example:
1. User receives credits, stored in his session.
2. User buys something.
3. User gets his new, lower credits stored in his session.
4. Evil hacker takes his saved cookie from step 1 and pastes it back in his browser's cookie jar. Now he's gotten his credits back.

This is normally solved using something called *nonce*. Each signing includes a once-only code, and the signer keeps track of all of the codes and rejects any message with the code repeated. But that's very hard to do here, since there may be several app servers serving up the same application.

Of course, we could store the nonce in the DB, but that defeats the entire purpose!

The short answer is: Do not store sensitive data in the session. Ever. The longer answer is that coordination of nonces across multiple servers would require remote process interaction on a per-request basis, which negates the benefits of using the cookie session storage to begin with.

13.3   Cookies

This section is about using cookies, not the cookie session store. The cookie container, as it's known, looks like a hash, and is available via the `cookies` method in the scope of controllers. Lots of Rails developers use cookies to store user preferences and other small nonsensitive bits of data. Be careful not to store sensitive data in `cookies`, since they can be read by users. The cookies container is also available by default in view templates and helpers.

13.3.1   Reading and Writing Cookies

The cookie container is filled with cookies received, along with the request, and sends out any cookies that you write to it with the response. Note that cookies are read by value, so you won't get the cookie object itself back, just the value it holds as a string (or as an array of strings if it holds multiple values).

To create or update cookies, you simply assign values using the brackets operator. You may assign either a single string value or a hash containing options, such as `:expires`, which takes a number of seconds before which the cookie should be deleted by the browser. Remember that Rails convenience methods for time are useful here:

```
# writing a simple session cookie
cookies[:list_mode] = "false"
```

```
# specifying options, curly brackets are needed to avoid syntax error
cookies[:recheck] = { value: "false", expires: 5.minutes.from_now }
```

I find the :path options useful in enabling you to set options specific to particular sections or even particular records of your application. The :path option is set to '1', the root of your application, by default.

The :domain option enables you to specify a domain, which is most often used when you are serving up your application from a particular host but want to set cookies for the whole domain.

```
cookies[:login] = {
  value: @user.security_token,
  domain: '.domain.com',
  expires:Time.now.next_year
}
```

Cookies can also be written using the :secure option, and Rails will only ever transmit them over a secure HTTPS connection:

```
# writing a simple session cookie
cookies[:account_number] = { value: @account.number, secure: true }
```

Finally, you can delete cookies using the delete method:

```
cookies.delete :list_mode
```

13.3.1.1 Accessing Cookies from JavaScript

The :httponly option tells Rails whether cookies can be accessible via scripting or only HTTP. It defaults to true as a security precaution. You can change it on a per-use basis like the other cookie options or change the default behavior for the whole app in config/initializers/session_store.rb.

```
# Be sure to restart your server when you modify this file.

Rails.application.config.session_store :cookie_store, key:
      "_my_application_session", http only: false
```

13.3.1.2 Permanent Cookies

Here's some Rails magic. Writing cookies to the response via the cookies.per-manent hash automatically gives them an expiration date 20 years in the future.

```
cookies.permanent[:remember_me] = current_user.id
```

Session

13.4   Conclusion

Deciding how to use the session is one of the more challenging tasks that faces a web application developer. That's why we put a couple of sections about it right in the beginning of this chapter. We also covered the various options available for configuring sessions, including storage mechanisms and methods for timing out sessions and the session lifecycle. We also covered use of a closely related topic, browser cookies.

CHAPTER 14

Authentication and Authorization

> Thanks goodness [sic], there's only about a billion of these because DHH doesn't think auth/auth [sic] belongs in the core.
>
> —George Hotelling at http://del.icio.us/revgeorge/authentication

If you're building a web application, more often than not you will need some form of user security. User security can be broken up into two categories, *authentication*, which verifies the identity of a user, and *authorization*, which verifies what they are able to do in your application.

In version 3.1, Rails introduced `has_secure_password`, which adds methods to set and authenticate against a BCrypt password. Although this functionality now exists in the framework, it is only a small part of a robust authentication solution. We still need to write our own authentication code, or we have to look outside of Rails core for a suitable solution.

In this chapter, we'll cover authentication with Warden and Devise, writing your own authentication code with `has_secure_password`, and an authorization library called Pundit.

14.1 Warden

As we mentioned in Chapter 1, "Rails Configuration and Environments," the foundation of Rails and all other signficant Ruby-based web frameworks is a simple HTTP adapter library called Rack. Warden provides a mechanism for authentication in Rack-based Ruby applications. It's made to support multiple applications sharing the same Rack instance.

Warden is designed to be lazy. That is, if you don't use it, it doesn't do anything, but when you do use it, it will spring into action and provide an underlying mechanism to enable authentication in any Rack-based application.

Warden enables all downstream middlewares and endpoints to share a common authentication mechanism, whilst still enabling the overall application to manage it. Each application can access the authenticated user, or request authentication in the same way, using the same logic throughout the Rack graph. Each application can layer whatever sugary API on top, and the underlying system will still work.

We don't use Warden directly but rather through a higher-level authentication library such as Devise. However, it's still worthwhile understanding how Warden works in case you want to step outside normal conventions.

14.1.1   Middleware

Warden sits in the Rack stack, after the session middleware (that stores a session, hash-like object in `env['rack.session']`).

Warden injects a lazy object into the Rack environment at `env['warden']`. This lazy object allows you to interact with it to ask if it's authenticated or to force authentication to occur in any downstream piece of Rack machinery.

```
# Ask whether a request has been authenticated already
env['warden'].authenticated?
# Ask if a request is authenticated for a particular scope (:foo)
env['warden'].authenticated?(:foo)
# Try to authenticate via the :password strategy
env['warden'].authenticate(:password)
# Try to authenticate and raise exception on failure
env['warden'].authenticate!(:password)
```

After authentication is performed, if successful, it will provide access to a `user` object.

```
env['warden'].authenticate(:password)
env['warden'].user # the user object
```

By placing the authentication process directly after the session middleware, all downstream middleware and applications gain access to the authentication object. This enables all Rack middlewares and endpoints to use the same underlying authentication system as the rest of your application.

14.1.2   Strategies

A *strategy* is the place where the logic of authentication is actually run. Warden uses the concept of cascading strategies to determine whether a request should be authenticated. It will try strategies one after another until

- A strategy succeeds
- No strategies are found relevant
- A strategy fails

Conceptually, a strategy is where you put the logic for authenticating a request. Practically, it's a descendent of `Warden::Strategies::Base`.

Let's take a look at defining a Warden strategy that authenticates a user with username and password attributes:

```
Warden::Strategies.add(:password) do
  def valid?
    params['username'] || params['password']
  end

  def authenticate!
    u = User.authenticate(params['username'], params['password'])
    u.nil? ? fail!("Could not log in") : success!(u)
  end
end
```

The example code declares a strategy called `:password`. The optional `valid?` method acts as a guard for the strategy, if needed. If you declare it, the strategy will only be tried if it returns `true`.

The strategy above is reasoning that if there's either a `username` or a `password` param, then the user is trying to login. If there's only one of them, then the `User.authenticate` call will fail, but it was still the desired (valid) strategy.

The `authenticate!` method is where the work of actually authenticating the request happens.

You have a number of request related methods available.

request   The `Rack::Request` object.

session   The session object for the request.

params   The parameters of the request.

env   The Rack env object.

There are also a number of actions you can take in your strategy.

halt!   Stops cascading of strategies and makes this one the last one processed.

pass   Ignore this strategy.

success   Pass a user object to *log in* a user. Causes a `halt!`.

fail!   Sets the strategy to fail. Causes a `halt!`.

redirect   Redirect to another URL. You can supply it with params to be encoded and also options. Causes a `halt!`.

custom   Enables you to optionally introduce new middleware by returning a custom Rack array to be handed back untouched. Causes a `halt!`.

There are a couple more miscellaneous methods to be aware of too.

headers   Sets headers to respond with relevance to the strategy.

errors   Provides access to an errors object where you can add errors relating to authentication.

14.1.3   Scopes

Warden scopes provide a mechanism for allowing multiple authenticated users to share a single session.

The most common example is `:admin` and `:user`. The `:user` scope is used for normal users to gain access to the application. The `:admin` scope is used to log in users who are admins and have elevated privileges.

Whether or not to use this technique (multiple users in a single session) has more to do with how you want to design your application's user experience than technical limitations.

For instance, how would we implement *impersonation* with this technique? Imagine that the `:admin` is logged in and wants to view your site as a particular `:user`. We can log both users into the same session to enable the admin to impersonate the user.

Note that multiple scopes are well-supported by Devise (covered later in the chapter). We only present this functionality in Warden as a useful example of how scopes work.

```
class ImpersonationController < AdminController
  expose(:user)
```

```
  def create
    warden = request.env['warden']
    if warden.authenticated?(:admin)
      # sign out existing user
      warden.authenticated?(:user) && warden.logout(:user)
      # sign in user to impersonate
      warden.set_user(user, scope: :user)

      redirect_to root_path, notice: "Now impersonating  #{user.name}"
    end
  end
end
```

How do we stop impersonating?

```
class ImpersonationController < AdminController

  ...

  def destroy
    warden = env['warden']
    # activate both sessions
    warden.authenticated?(:admin) && warden.authenticated?(:user)
    # log out only the user session and only the user session data is cleared
    warden.logout(:user)

    redirect_to "/admin"
end
```

When you log out the user in the example above, the user is removed from the overall session (they're logged out), but their scoped session data is also cleared. The admin's scoped session data is, however, left intact.

Warden is fairly complex. A full explanation is found in its wiki at https://github.com/hassox/warden/wiki.

14.2 Devise

Devise[1] is a highly modular Rack-based authentication framework that sits on top of Warden. It has a robust feature set and leverages the use of Rails generators. Its flexibility means that you get to pick and choose which parts of it are most suitable for your application.

---

1. https://github.com/plataformatec/devise

Devise is a huge topic, and due to space and scope constraints, we only scrape the surface of it in this book. As of the latest edition, the Devise Wiki's "How-to" section has 99 articles and counting (https://github.com/plataformatec/devise/wiki/How-Tos).

14.2.1 Getting Started

Add the devise gem to your project's `Gemfile` and `bundle install`. Then you can generate the Devise configuration by running

```
$ rails generate devise:install
```

This will create the initializer for Devise and an English version I18n YAML for Devise's messages. Devise will also alert you at this step to remember to do some mandatory Rails configuration if you have not done so already. This includes setting your default host for Action Mailer, setting up your root route, and making sure your flash messages will render in the application's default layout.

14.2.2 Modules

Adding authentication functionality to your models using Devise is based on the concept of adding different modules to your class, based on only what you need. The available modules for you to use are:

confirmable Adds the capability to require email confirmation of user accounts.

database-authenticatable Handles authentication of a user, as well as password encryption.

lockable Can lock an account after *n* number of failed login attempts.

omniauthable Adds support for Oauth authentication via Omniauth (https://github.com/:intridea/omniauth).

recoverable Provides password reset functionality.

registerable Alters user sign up to be handled in a registration process, along with account management.

rememberable Provides *remember me* functionality.

timeoutable Enables sessions to be expired in a configurable time frame.

trackable Stores login counts, timestamps, and IP addresses.

validatable Adds customizable validations to email and password.

Knowing which modules you wish to include in your model is important for setting up your models, migrations, and configuration options later on.

14.2.3 Models

To set up authentication in a model, run the Devise generator for that model and then edit it. For the purpose of our examples, we will use the ever-so-exciting `User` model.

```
$ rails generate devise User
```

This will create your model, a database migration, and route for your shiny new model. Devise will have given you some default modules to use, which you will need to alter in your migration and model if you want to use different modules. In our example we only use a subset of what is offered.

Our resulting database migration looks like

```ruby
class DeviseCreateUsers < ActiveRecord::Migration
  def change
    create_table(:users) do |t|
      ## Database authenticatable
      t.string :email,              null: false, default: ""
      t.string :encrypted_password, null: false, default: ""

      ## Recoverable
      t.string   :reset_password_token
      t.datetime :reset_password_sent_at

      ## Rememberable
      t.datetime :remember_created_at

      ## Trackable
      t.integer  :sign_in_count, default: 0
      t.datetime :current_sign_in_at
      t.datetime :last_sign_in_at
      t.string   :current_sign_in_ip
      t.string   :last_sign_in_ip
      ## Confirmable
      # t.string   :confirmation_token
      # t.datetime :confirmed_at
      # t.datetime :confirmation_sent_at
      # t.string   :unconfirmed_email # Only if using reconfirmable

      ## Lockable
      # t.integer  :failed_attempts, default: 0 # Only if lock strategy
      #   is :failed_attempts
```

```
    # t.string    :unlock_token # Only if unlock strategy is :email or :both
    # t.datetime :locked_at

    t.timestamps
  end

  add_index :users, :email,                   unique: true
  add_index :users, :reset_password_token, unique: true
  # add_index :users, :confirmation_token,     unique: true
  # add_index :users, :unlock_token,           unique: true
  end
end
```

We then modify our `User` model to mirror the modules we included in our migration.

```
class User < ActiveRecord::Base
  # Include default devise modules. Others available are:
  # :confirmable, :lockable, :timeoutable and :omniauthable
  devise :database_authenticatable, :registerable,
         :recoverable, :rememberable, :trackable, :validatable
end
```

Now we're ready to `rake db:migrate` and let the magic happen.

Remember to restart your server after installing Devise, otherwise you'll get all sorts of weird errors.

14.2.4   Mappings / Scopes

Devise refers to its models as mappings because they map to underlying Warden scopes (as discussed in the previous section). Most web applications have a single Devise mapping/scope, but of those that have more, the most common pair is probably `:user` and `:admin`.

Designing an application with separate scopes (and sessions) for admins and users is a decision that has to be made with an eye towards security and UX concerns. Splitting the scopes adds complexity in some regards but might result in an overall cleaner and easier to maintain codebase. (Not having to sprinkle `user.admin?` conditionals all over the place sounds like a good choice.)

14.2.5   Controllers

Devise generates handy helper methods that can be used in your controllers to authenticate your model or get access to the currently signed in person. For example, if you want to restrict access in a controller you may use one of the helpers as a `before_action`.

```
class MeatProcessorController < ApplicationController
  before_action :authenticate_user!
end
```

🔍 For Rails 5, note that the boilerplate `protect_from_forgery` is no longer prepended to the `before_action` chain, so if you have called `authenticate_user!` in your `ApplicationController` class before `protect_from_forgery`, some requests will error out with a "Can't verify CSRF token authenticity" exception. To resolve the problem, either change the order in which you call them or use `protect_from_forgery prepend: true`.

You can also access the currently signed in user via the `current_user` helper method or the current session via the `user_session` method. Use `user_signed_in?` if you want to check whether the user had logged in without using the `before_action`.

💬 Thais says . . .

The helper methods are generated dynamically, so in the case where your authenticated models are named differently use the model name instead of user in the examples. An instance of this could be with an Admin model—your helpers would be `current_admin`, `admin_signed_in?`, and `admin_session`.

Here is the full list of helper methods generated by Devise for each of your authenticated models (which Devise refers to as mappings):

- `authenticate_#{mapping}!`
- `#{mapping}_signed_in?`
- `current_#{mapping}`
- `#{mapping}_session`

If you have defined groups, each group gets the same set of helper methods, with the addition of a `current_#{group_name.to_s.pluralize}` method that returns all currently authenticated mappings.

Auth

14.2.5.1   Additional Controller Helpers

Devise adds a slew of helper methods to its controllers. The most common are

devise_controller? Returns `true` if called on a Devise controller, `false` otherwise. Useful if you want to apply a before filter to all controllers related to authentication.

devise_parameter_sanitizer Override this method in your application controller to use your own parameter sanitizer.

14.2.6   Routing

Devise's main directive is its entry in your `config/routes.rb` file, accomplished with the `devise_for` method.

```
devise_for :users
```

Absent additional configuration, this declaration will use the controllers and views built into Devise to provide you with auto-magical functionality.

Assuming that you create a custom scoped controller for admins

```
rails generate devise:controllers admins
```

then Devise will generate new controller templates in `app/controllers/admins`, and the sessions controller within that folder will look like this:

```
class Admins::SessionsController < Devise::SessionsController
  # GET /admins/sign_in
  # def new
  #   super
  # end
  ...
end
```

In that case, you'd tell the router to use that controller:

```
devise_for :admins, controllers: { sessions: "admin/sessions" }
```

14.2.6.1   Overriding Defaults

The `devise_for` is responsible for generating all needed routes for Devise, based on what modules you have defined in your model.

Let's say you have a `User` model configured to use the `authenticatable`, `confirmable`, and `recoverable` modules.

Declaring `devise_for :users` in your routes will look inside your `User` model to determine the modules used and create their associated routes:

```
> rails routes | grep 'devise'

    new_user_session GET    /users/sign_in
        {controller:"devise/sessions", action:"new"}
        user_session POST    /users/sign_in
        {controller:"devise/sessions", action:"create"}
destroy_user_session DELETE /users/sign_out
        {controller:"devise/sessions", action:"destroy"}

   new_user_password GET    /users/password/new(.:format)
        {controller:"devise/passwords", action:"new"}

  edit_user_password GET    /users/password/edit(.:format)
        {controller:"devise/passwords", action:"edit"}
        user_password PUT    /users/password(.:format)
        {controller:"devise/passwords", action:"update"}
                     POST    /users/password(.:format)
        {controller:"devise/passwords", action:"create"}

new_user_confirmation GET   /users/confirmation/new(.:format)
        {controller:"devise/confirmations", action:"new"}
    user_confirmation GET    /users/confirmation(.:format)
        {controller:"devise/confirmations", action:"show"}
                     POST    /users/confirmation(.:format)
        {controller:"devise/confirmations", action:"create"}
```

If you need to customize the routes generated by Devise, you can pass it options such as `:class_name`, `:path_prefix`, and so on, including the possibility to change `path_names` for I18n translation lookups:

```
devise_for :users,
           path: "auth",
           path_names: {
             sign_in: 'login',
             sign_out: 'logout',
             password: 'secret',
             confirmation: 'verification',
             unlock: 'unblock',
             registration: 'register',
             sign_up: 'cmon_let_me_in' }
```

14.2.6.2 Namespaces

The `devise_for` integrates nicely with namespaces in your application. Calling it inside of a namespace like this

```
namespace :publisher do
  devise_for :account
end
```

results in many changes from the standard behavior. The example provided will use `publisher/sessions` controller instead of `devise/sessions`. You can revert this change or configure it directly by passing the `:module` option described below to `devise_for`. All the helpers and methods for controllers and views are affected as well. The example provided will provide you with the following methods: `current_publisher_account`, `authenticate_publisher_account!`, `publisher_account_signed_in?`, etc.

14.2.6.3   Options

The primary `devise_for` option not affected by namespace is the model name. It can be explicitly set via the `:class_name` option.

Options for `devise_for` method include the following:

class_name Sets up a different class to be looked up by Devise, if it cannot be deduced automatically by the route name.

```
devise_for :users, class_name: 'Account'
```

path Enables you to set up a path name that will be used instead of the default. The following route configuration would set up your authentication route as `/accounts` instead of `/users`:

```
devise_for :users, path: 'accounts'
```

singular Overrides the generated singular name for a given resource. This is used as the helper methods names in controller (`authenticate_#{singular}!`, `#{singular}_signed_in?"`, `current_#{singular}`, and `#{singular}_session`), as the scope name in routes, and as the scope given to warden.

```
devise_for :admins, singular: :manager
class ManagerController < ApplicationController
  before_filter authenticate_manager!

  def show
    @manager = current_manager
    ...
  end
end
```

Don't do stuff like this unless absolutely necessary.

---

path_names Override default I18n lookup keys.

```
devise_for :users, path_names: {
  sign_in: 'login', sign_out: 'logout',
  password: 'secret', confirmation: 'verification',
  Registration: 'register', edit: 'edit/profile'
}
```

controllers Explicitly override specified default controllers in order to implement custom behavior.

```
devise_for :users, controllers: { sessions: "users/sessions" }
```

failure_app A Rack app to be invoked on authentication failure.

sign_out_via The HTTP method(s) accepted for the `sign_out` action (defaults to `:get`). If you wish to restrict this to accept only `:post` or `:delete` requests, you should do:

```
devise_for :users, sign_out_via: [:post, :delete]
```

module The namespace where to find controllers (defaults to "devise", thus referencing `devise/sessions`, `devise/registrations`, etc.). This option lets you change them all at once.

```
devise_for :users, module: "users"
```

skip Specify routes to *not* be generated. Accepts `:all` as an option, meaning it will not generate any routes at all.

```
devise_for :users, skip: :sessions
```

only The opposite of `:skip`

skip_helpers Skip generating URL helpers like `new_session_path(user)`. Occasionally useful for avoiding conflicts with previous routes.

format Whether to include (`.:format`) in the generated routes. Set to `true` by default, set to `false` to disable.

constraints Same as any other routing constraints.

defaults Same as any other routing defaults.

⚲ For a full description of routing functionality, check the Devise source code http://www.rubydoc.info/github/plataformatec/devise/ActionDispatch/Routing/Mapper#devise_for-instance_method.

14.2.6.4   Adding Custom Actions to Override Controllers

The `devise_for` method has a sister named `devise_scope` that gives you the capability to add arbitrary routes to Devise's default list of known actions. This is

Auth

important if you add a custom action to a controller that overrides an out of the box Devise controller.

```
class RegistrationsController < Devise::RegistrationsController
  def update
    # do something different here
  end

  def deactivate
    # not a standard action
    # deactivate code here
  end
end
```

In order to get Devise to recognize the deactivate action, your devise_scope entry should look like this:

```
devise_scope :owner do
 post "deactivate", to: "registrations#deactivate", as: "deactivate_registration"
end
```

14.2.6.5 Post Sign-in Options

You can control where a newly authenticated user gets routed via naming convention in routes.rb. Devise will look for a route named #{mapping}_root_path.

For example, if you had a Devise mapping for user, you could define it in one of the following two ways:

```
get '/users' => 'users#index', as: :user_root # creates user_root_path

namespace :user do
  root 'users#index' # creates user_root_path
end
```

If a mapping-specific root path is not found, Devise will redirect to the main root_path of the application.

To override this behavior with more complicated logic of your own, override the after_sign_in_path_for(resource) method in your Application-Controller. It is passed the authenticated object as resource so that you can use its attributes as part of your routing logic. For example, you could redirect to the user's own dashboard, profile, or something along those lines.

```
def after_sign_in_path_for(resource)
  stored_location_for(resource) ||
    if resource.is_a?(User)
```

```
    user_dashboard_url(resource)
  else
    super
  end
end
```

The `stored_location_for` method returns and deletes a URL stored in the session for the given resource. This makes it possible to automatically take the user to the page they were trying to access before being prompted to log in.

Devise also gives you a similar `after_sign_out_path_for(resource_or_scope)` in case you want to send users to a location other than `root_path` after signing out.

14.2.7 Views

Devise is built as a Rails Engine, and comes with views for all of your included modules. All you need to do is write some CSS, and you're off to the races. However, there may be some situations where you want to customize them, and Devise provides a nifty script to copy all of the internal views into your application.

```
rails generate devise:views
```

If you are authenticating more than one model and don't want to use the same views for both, just set the following option in your `config/initializers/devise.rb`:

```
config.scoped_views = true
```

ERb to Haml

The views extracted from the Devise Rails Engine are ERb templates. If your preference is to use Haml for templates, you can convert the Devise ERb templates via the `html2haml` gem.

After the gem is installed, run the following command from the root of your Rails project:

```
$ for file in app/views/devise/**/*.erb; do html2haml -e $file
    ${file%erb}haml && rm $file; done
```

14.2.8 Configuration

When you first set up Devise using `rails generate devise:install`, a `devise.rb` was tossed into your `config/initializers` directory. This initializer is where all the configuration for Devise is set, and it is already packed full

of commented-out goodies for all configuration options with excellent descriptions
for each option.

🗨 **Durran says . . .**

Using MongoDB as your main database? Under the general configuration
section in the initializer, switch the requirement of `active---record` to
`mongoid` for pure awesomeness.

Devise comes with internationalization support out of the box and ships with
English message definitions located in `config/locales/devise.en.yml`.
(You'll see this was created after you ran the install generator at setup.) This file can
be used as the template for Devise's messages in any other language by staying with
the same naming convention for each file.

Create a Chilean Spanish translation in `config/locales/devise.cl`
`.yml` weon!

14.2.9   Strong Parameters

With the addition of Strong Parameters to Rails 4, Devise has followed suit and
moved the concern of mass-assignment to the controller. In Devise, mass-assignment
parameter sanitation occurs in the following three actions:

sign_in Corresponding to controller action `Devise::SessionsController-`
`#new`, only authentication keys, such as `email`, are permitted.

sign_up Corresponding to controller action `Devise::RegistrationsCon-`
`troller#create`, permits authentication keys, `password`, and `password`
`_confirmation`.

account_update Corresponding to controller action `Devise::Registra-`
`tionsController#update`, permits authentication keys, `password`,
`password_confirmation`, and `current_password`.

If you require additional parameters to be permitted by Devise, the simplest way
to do so is through a `before_action` callback in `ApplicationController`.

```
class ApplicationController < ActionController::Base
  before_action :devise_permitted_parameters, if: :devise_controller?

  protected
```

```
    def devise_permitted_parameters
      devise_parameter_sanitizer.for(:sign_up) << :phone_number
    end
end
```

Additionally, you can completely change the Devise defaults by passing a block to `devise_parameter_sanitizer`.

```
class ApplicationController < ActionController::Base
  before_action :devise_permitted_parameters, if: :devise_controller?

  protected

  def devise_permitted_parameters
    devise_parameter_sanitizer.
      for (:sign_in) { |user| user.permit(:email, :password, :remember_me,
        :username) }
  end
end
```

For more details on Strong Parameters, see Chapter 15, "Security."

14.2.10 Extensions

There are plenty of third party extensions out there for Devise for all sorts of uses. Here are some our favorites:

cas_authenticatable Enables single sign on using CAS.

devise_campaignable Have your users automatically added to a mail campaign tool of your choice. Currently supports MailChimp, but it is easy to adapt for CampaignMonitor and other email service providers.

devise_uid Adds support for UUID primary keys.

invitable Adds support for sending account invitations by email.

ldap_authenticatable Authenticate users using LDAP.

two_factor_authentication Provides a foundation for implementing two-factor authentication, for enhanced security.

A complete list of extensions, including many external authentication integrations, can be found at: https://github.com/plataformatec/devise/wiki/Extensions.

14.2.11   Testing with Devise

To enable Devise test helpers in controller specs, create the spec support file `devise.rb` in the `spec/support` folder.

```
# spec/support/devise.rb
RSpec.configure do |config|
  config.include Devise::TestHelpers, type: :controller
end
```

This will add helper methods `sign_in` and `sign_out` that enable creating and destroying a session for a controller spec, respectively. Both methods accept an instance of a Devise model.

```
require 'spec_helper'

describe AuthenticatedController do
  let(:user) { FactoryGirl.create(:user) }

  before do
    sign_in user
  end

  ...
end
```

14.2.12   Summary

Devise is an excellent solution if you want a large number of standard features out of the box while writing almost no code at all. It has a clean and easy to understand API and can be used with little to no ramp up time on any application.

14.3   `has_secure_password`

Prior to version 3.1, Rails did not include any sort of standard authentication mechanism. That changed with the introduction of `has_secure_password`, an Active Model mechanism that adds methods to set and authenticate against a BCrypt password.[2] However, `has_secure_password` is only a small piece to a complete authentication solution. Unlike other solutions like Devise, one still needs to implement a few extra items in order to get `has_secure_password` running properly.

---

2. A BCrypt password is based on the Blowfish cipher, incorporating a salt and is resistant to brute-force attacks. For more information, see the Wikipedia article on the subject (https://en.wikipedia .org/wiki/Bcrypt).

14.3.1   Getting Started

To use Active Model's `has_secure_password`, uncomment the required gem dependency `bcrypt` in your `Gemfile` and run `bundle install`.

```
gem 'bcrypt', '~> 3.1.7'
```

14.3.2   Creating the Models

To add authentication to a model, it must have an attribute named `password_digest`. For the purpose of our example, let's generate a new User model that will authenticate with an email and password.

```
$ rails generate model User email:string password_digest:string
```

Then edit the `CreateUsers` migration to add the columns your application needs to satisfy its authentication requirements.

```
class CreateUsers < ActiveRecord::Migration
  def change
    create_table :users do |t|
      t.string :email
      t.string :password_digest t.timestamps
      t.index(:email, unique: true)
    end
  end
end
```

Next, set up your `User` model, by adding the macro-style method `has_secure_password`. We've added a uniqueness validation for `email` to ensure we can only have one email per user.

```
class User < ActiveRecord::Base
  has_secure_password

  validates :email, presence: true, uniqueness: { case_sensitive: false }
end
```

A virtual attribute `password` is automatically added to the model, which when set, automatically copies its encrypted value to `password_digest`. Validations on create for the presence and confirmation of `password` are also automatically added.

To illustrate, let's create and authenticate a user in the console:

```
>> user = User.create(email: 'user@example.com')
=> #<User id: nil, email: "user@example.com", password_digest: nil,
```

```
    created_at: nil, updated_at: nil>

>> user.valid?
=> false

>> user.errors.full_messages
=> ["Password can't be blank"]

>> user = User.create(email: 'user@example.com',
      password: 'therails4way', password_confirmation: 'therails4way')
=> #<User id: 1, email: "user@example.com", password_digest:
    "$2a$10$RZfWUZiGze9Bk13PFOYB5eWKZuJUMAnqU/90rpcywGja...",
    created_at: "2013-10-01 15:26:55", updated_at: "2013-10-01 15:26:55">

>> user.authenticate('abcdefgh')
=> false

>> user.authenticate('therails4way')
=> #<User id: 1, email: "user@example.com", password_digest:
   "$2a$10$RZfWUZiGze9Bk13PFOYB5eWKZuJUMAnqU/90rpcywGja...",
   created_at: "2013-10-01 15:26:55", updated_at: "2013-10-01 15:26:55">
```

14.3.3   Setting Up the Controllers

Once the User model has been set up, we need to create a sessions controller to manage the session for your authenticated model. A resourceful controller for "users" is also required, but its implementation will depend on your own application's requirements.

To create the controllers, run the following in the terminal:

```
$ rails generate controller sessions
$ rails generate controller users
```

In your ApplicationController you will need to provide access to the current user so that all of your controllers can access this information easily.

```
class ApplicationController < ActionController::Base
  protect_from_forgery with: :exception

  helper_method :current_user

  protected

  def current_user
    @current_user ||= User.find(session[:user_id]) if session[:user_id]
  end
end
```

The `SessionsController` should respond to `new`, `create`, and `destroy` in order to leverage all basic sign-in/out functionality.

```ruby
class SessionsController < ApplicationController
  def new
  end

  def create
    user = User.where(email: params[:email]).first

    if user && user.authenticate(params[:password])
      session[:user_id] = user.id
      redirect_to root_url, notice: 'Signed in successfully.'
    else
      flash.now.alert = 'Invalid email or password.'
      render :new
    end
  end

  def destroy
    session[:user_id] = nil
    redirect_to root_url, notice: 'Signed out successfully.'
  end
end
```

Make sure you've added the routes for the new controllers.

```ruby
Rails.application.routes.draw do
    resource :session, only: [:new, :create, :destroy]
    resources :users
    ...
end
```

Finally, create a view `app/views/sessions/new.html.haml` containing a sign-in form to enable users to create a session within your application:

```haml
%h1 Sign in

- if flash.alert
  .alert= flash.alert

= form_tag session_path do
  .field
    = label_tag :email
    = email_field_tag :email, params[:email],
        placeholder: 'Enter your email address', required: true

  .field
    = label_tag :password
```

```
  = password_field_tag :password, params[:password],
      placeholder: 'Enter your password', required: true

= submit_tag 'Sign in'
```

14.3.4   Controller, Limiting Access to Actions

Now that you are authenticating, you will want to control access to specific controller actions. A common pattern for handling this is through the use of action callbacks in your controllers, where the authentication checks reside in your `ApplicationController`.

```
class ApplicationController < ActionController::Base
  ...

  protected

  def authenticate
    unless current_user
      redirect_to new_session_url,
        alert: 'You need to sign in or sign up before continuing.'
    end
  end
end

class DashboardController < ApplicationController
  before_action :authenticate
end
```

14.3.5   Summary

We've only scratched the surface of implementing a full blown authentication solution using `has_secure_password`. Although the implementation is simple, it leaves a bit to be desired. Some things to consider when creating your own authentication framework from scratch include "remember me" functionality, the capability for a user to reset a password, token authentication, and so on.

Realistically, there's little reason to write your own "full-blown" authentication framework instead of using a mature solution like Devise or its lighter-weight alternative, Authem (https://github.com/paulelliott/authem).

14.4 Pundit

Authorization is the process of specifying access rights to resources,[3] such as models. Once a user has been authenticated within an application, using authorization, you can limit a user from performing certain actions, for instance updating a record. Besides actions, one could even limit what is visible to a user based on their role. For example, if we created a blog application, a normal user should only be able to view published posts, while an administrator should be able to view all posts within the application.

Pundit[4] is a minimal authorization library created by the folks at Elabs that is focused around a notion of policy classes. A policy is a class that has the same name as a model class, suffixed with the word "Policy". It accepts both a user and model instance that are used to determine whether the provided user has permissions to perform certain actions.

The Can Can gem is a much more popular option for authorization, but I have found through experience that its design quickly leads to unmaintainable code in larger applications (https://github.com/ryanb/cancan).

14.4.1 Getting Started

Add the `pundit` gem to your project's `Gemfile` and `bundle install`. Then you can install Pundit by running the `pundit:install` generator:

```
$ rails generate pundit:install
```

This will create an application policy in `app/policies` for Pundit. Although optional, inheriting from `ApplicationPolicy` for each of your policy files is recommended, as it ensures by default no resourceful action is authorized.

```
# app/policies/application_policy.rb
class ApplicationPolicy
  attr_reader :user, :record

  def initialize(user, record)
    @user = user
    @record = record
  end

  def index?
```

---

3. http://en.wikipedia.org/wiki/Authorization
4. https://github.com/elabs/pundit

```
      false
    end

  def show?
    scope.where(id: record.id).exists?
  end

  def create?
    false
  end

  def new?
    create?
  end

  def update?
    false
  end

  def edit?
    update?
  end

  def destroy?
    false
  end

  def scope
    Pundit.policy_scope!(user, record.class)
  end
end
```

Next, to include the Pundit methods within a controller, include `Pundit` in your `ApplicationController`:

```
class ApplicationController < ActionController::Base
  include Pundit
end
```

14.4.2   Creating a Policy

To create a policy for a model, run the Pundit generator for that model and then edit it. To illustrate, we will use the `Post` model from the preceding example of a blog application.

```
$ rails generate pundit:policy post
```

The generator creates the following `PostPolicy` in the `app/policies` folder:

```
class PostPolicy < ApplicationPolicy
  class Scope < Struct.new(:user, :scope)
    def resolve
      scope
    end
  end
end
```

In the case of our example, let's guard against non-administrator users from creating a blog post by implementing the `create?` predicate method.

```
class PostPolicy < ApplicationPolicy
  def create?
    user.admin?
  end
  ...
end
```

Besides checking against a role, you can add permission conditions based on the record itself. For example, in this blogging application, an administrator can only delete a post if it hasn't been published.

```
class PostPolicy < ApplicationPolicy
  def destroy?
    user.admin? && !record.published?
  end
  ...
end
```

14.4.3   Controller Integration

Pundit provides various helper methods to be used in controllers to authorize a user to perform an action against a record. For example, the `authorize` method will automatically infer the policy file based on the passed in record instance.

💬 Kevin Says . . .

The second argument to a Pundit policy check can be any object, not necessarily just an Active Record instance.

To illustrate, let's check whether the current user can create a post within the `PostsController`:

```
class PostsController < ApplicationController
  expose(:post)

  def create
```

```
    authorize post
    post.save
    respond_with(post)
  end

  ...
end
```

The above call to `authorize` is equivalent to `PostPolicy.new(current_user, @post).create?`. If the user is not authorized, Pundit will raise a `NotAuthorizedError` exception.

---

❶ Note

The `authorize` method will gain access to the currently logged in user by calling the `current_user` method. This can be overridden by implementing a method called `pundit_user` in your controller.

If you want to ensure authorization is always executed within your controllers, Pundit also provides a method `verify_authorized` that raises an exception if `authorize` hasn't been called. This method should be run within an `after_action` callback.

```
class ApplicationController < ActionController::Base
  after_filter :verify_authorized, except: :index
end
```

14.4.4   Policy Scopes

Using Pundit, we can define a scope within a policy to limit what records are returned based on a user role. For example, in our recurring blogging application example, an administrator should be able to view all posts, whereas a user should only be able to view posts that have been published. This is achieved by implementing a nested class named `Scope` under the policy class. The instances of the scope must respond to the method `resolve`, which should return an `ActiveRecord::Relation`.

```
class PostPolicy < ApplicationPolicy
  class Scope < Struct.new(:user, :scope)
    def resolve
      if user.admin?
        scope
      else
        scope.where(published: true)
      end
    end
```

```
  end
  ...
end
```

Pundit provides a helper method, `policy_scope`, that infers the policy file based on the class passed into it and returns the scope specific to the current user's permissions.

```
def index
  @posts = policy_scope(Post)
end
```

which is equivalent to

```
def index
  @posts = PostPolicy::Scope.new(current_user, Post).resolve
end
```

To ensure policy scopes are always called for specific controller actions, run `verify_policy_scoped` in an `after_action` callback. If `policy_scope` is not called, an exception will be raised.

```
class ApplicationController < ActionController::Base
  after_filter :verify_policy_scoped, only: :index
end
```

14.4.5   Strong Parameters

Pundit also makes it possible to explicitly set what attributes are allowed to be mass-assigned with strong parameters based on a user role.

```
# app/policies/assignment_policy.rb
class AssignmentPolicy < ApplicationPolicy
  def permitted_attributes
    if user.admin?
      [:title, :question, :answer, :status]
    else
      [:answer]
    end
  end
end
```

```
# app/controllers/assignments_controller.rb
class AssignmentsController < ApplicationController
  expose(:assignment, attributes: :assignment_params)

  def update
```

```
    assignment.save
    respond_with(assignment)
  end

  private

  def assignment_params
    params.require(:assignment).
      permit(policy(assignment).permitted_attributes)
  end
end
```

14.4.6   Testing Policies

Although Pundit comes with its own RSpec matchers for testing, our preference is to use an RSpec matcher created by the team at Thunderbolt Labs[5] as it provides better readability.

To get started, add the following into a file under spec/support:

```
# spec/support/matchers/permit_matcher.rb
RSpec::Matchers.define :permit do |action|
  match do |policy|
    policy.public_send("#{action}?")
  end

  failure_message do |policy|
    "#{policy.class} does not permit #{action} on #{policy.record}  for
      #{policy.user.inspect}."
  end

  failure_message_when_negated do |policy|
    "#{policy.class} does not forbid #{action} on #{policy.record} for
      #{policy.user.inspect}."
  end
end
```

Using the above RSpec matcher, you can test policies that look like

```
# spec/policies/post_policy.rb
require 'spec_helper'

describe PostPolicy do
  subject(:policy) { PostPolicy.new(user, post) }

  let(:post) { FactoryGirl.build_stubbed(:post) }
```

---

5. http://thunderboltlabs.com/blog/2013/03/27/testing-pundit-policies-with-rspec

```
  context "for a visitor" do
    let(:user) { nil }

    it { is_expected.to permit(:show) }
    it { is_expected.to_not permit(:create) }
    it { is_expected.to_not permit(:new) }
    it { is_expected.to_not permit(:update) }
    it { is_expected.to_not permit(:edit) }
    it { is_expected.to_not permit(:destroy) }
  end

  context "for an administrator" do
    let(:user) { FactoryGirl.create(:administrator) }

    it { is_expected.to permit(:show)}
    it { is_expected.to permit(:create) }
    it { is_expected.to permit(:new) }
    it { is_expected.to permit(:update) }
    it { is_expected.to permit(:edit) }
    it { is_expected.to permit(:destroy) }
  end
end
```

14.5   Conclusion

In addition to a tour of Warden, the authentication middleware underlying all major Rails authentication frameworks, we covered our favorite auth frameworks: Devise and Pundit. Keep in mind that there are plenty more options out there to examine if those are not well-suited for your application. Also, you were able to see how easy it is to roll your own simple authentication solution using has_secure_password.

CHAPTER 15

Security

Ruby on Rails security sucks lolz amirite? No. Well, no to the nuance. Software security does, in general, suck. Virtually every production system has security bugs in it. When you bring pen testers in to audit your app, to a first approximation, your app will lose. While Ruby on Rails cherishes its Cool-Kid-Not-Lame-Enterprise-Consultingware image, software which is absolutely Big Freaking Enterprise consultingware, like say the J2EE framework or Spring, have seen similar vulnerabilities in the past.[1]

—Patrick McKenzie

Security is a very broad topic, one that we can't possibly cover in a single book chapter. Still there are things that every competent web developer using Rails should know.

Unlike many other software engineering topics, security is not something that you can solve by investing more hours to fix bugs or inefficient algorithms. Nor is it something you can do by trial and error. You have to know most common attack vectors and how to avoid vulnerabilities.

We will look into common web application security problems and the ways that Rails deals with them, as well as general security guidelines and practices. Along the way we will discuss management of passwords and other private information, log masking, mass-assignment attributes protection, SQL Injection, Cross-Site Scripting (XSS), Cross-Site Request Forgery (XSRF) and more.

---

1. http://www.kalzumeus.com/2013/01/31/what-the-rails-security-issue-means-for-your-startup/

15.1   Password Management

We can safely say leaking your customer's plain text passwords is probably one of the most embarrassing security problems to have. Especially as the "do not store plain text passwords" mantra is widely known, and doing the right thing is really not that hard. Quite easy actually. It usually boils down to using one of the many libraries available. It's also not something that you need to pay constant attention to. You do it once, and you are done.

> The biggest problem with storing plain text passwords is that many people use the same password on multiple sites, and so in an event of a leak, you do not only expose user's accounts in your application but potentially also put a lot of other people's accounts at risk.

The solution is simple and well known: securely hash all passwords. Secure hashing is not the same as encryption, as encryption assumes the ability to decrypt, while secure hashing is a one-way function. Once you store a password, there is no way to get it back in the original form.

Popular hash functions include MD5 and SHA1. MD5 is considered insecure and is no longer used for password security,[2] but you'll occasionally see it used to hash values that are not under attack.

"How do you check a hashed password?" you might ask. It's simple, actually—when we need to test a password given to a login form, we just pass it through the same one-way hash function and compare the results.

The actual low level details are a bit more complicated, as we also want to protect against what is known as dictionary rainbow table attack. An attacker might get access to a database of hashed user passwords and compare the hashes to a table of hashes of dictionary words. Statistically, if you have enough users, a significant number of them will use dictionary words for their passwords. This allows an attacker to find out their password from the rainbow table and, using other information you have stored (like user email), try to gain access to those user's accounts on other services.

You prevent rainbow table attacks by using a *salt*, a random string that is generated for every user during account creation and which is used together with the user's password when calculating the hashed password that we store in the database.

---

2. Carnegie Mellon's Software Engineering Institute says that MD5 "should be considered cryptographically broken and unsuitable for further use." http://www.kb.cert.org/vuls/id/836068

Since the salt is random for every user there is no way to prepare a dictionary table of every dictionary word with every possible salt. So the attacker is left with the brute force attack, actually trying to pick passwords one by one, by trying every possible password combination with the user's salt.

To make it even harder on the attacker, most "serious" password storage libraries use a secure hashing algorithm that was intentionally made very "expensive" to compute, usually by doing a lot of rounds of hash function computation in a sequence.

We've delved into the gory details, and you might wonder if it involves a lot of work to implement this stuff in Rails. It does not. All the popular authentication libraries like Authlogic and Devise implement salted-hashing of passwords right out of the box.

15.1.1   BCrypt

Even if you're not using a third-party authentication gem for some reason, Rails itself has straightforward support for secure password storage with the help of the popular BCrypt library.

To add secure hashed passwords to an ActiveModel class you just need to call the `has_secure_password` class method: {#has_secure_password}.

The usage is very simple:

```
class User
  has_secure_password
end
```

From the Rails documentation:

> This mechanism requires you to have a `password_digest` attribute.
>
> Validations for presence of password on create, confirmation of password (using a `password_confirmation` attribute) are automatically added. If you wish to turn off validations, pass `validations: false` as an argument. You can add more validations by hand if need be.
>
> If you don't need the confirmation validation, just don't set any value to the `password_confirmation` attribute and the validation will not be triggered.
>
> You need to add bcrypt-ruby (~> 3.0.0) to Gemfile to use #has_secure _password:
>
> ```
> gem 'bcrypt-ruby', '~> 3.0.0'
> ```

To actually validate the password during authentication you can use the `authenticate` method:

```
User.find_by(email: "john@doe.com").try(:authenticate, params[:password])
```

The method will return the object itself if the password matches or `nil` otherwise.

Security

15.2   Log Masking

Great, we are no longer storing the passwords in the database. We are not done though. We might still be leaking the passwords and other sensitive information into the application logs. For every request, Rails logs the request parameters into the log file unless the parameter name includes one of the "filtered" strings. For a "filtered" parameter Rails will replace the value by [FILTERED] before the logging:

```
Started POST
  "/users?name=john&password=[FILTERED]&password_confirmation=[FILTERED]"
  for 127.0.0.1 at 2013-02-24 22:29:59 +0000
Processing by UsersController#create as */*
  Parameters: {"name"=>"john", "password"=>"[FILTERED]",
  "password_confirmation"=>"[FILTERED]"}
```

Rails protects any parameter that includes password in its name by default, so both password and password_confirmation are already covered. If your password is using a differently named parameter, or if you want to protect other information (for example credit card numbers), you should add those parameter names to the special Rails configuration variable filter_parameters.

By default, standard Rails projects include config/initializers/filter_parameter_logging.rb with the following line:

```
Rails.application.config.filter_parameters += [:password]
```

To protect another parameter, simply add it to the array, e.g.:

```
Rails.application.config.filter_parameters += [:password, :cc, :ccv]
```

15.3   SSL (Secure Sockets Layer)

So now our apps are secure, right? We properly encrypted our passwords in the database and we filtered sensitive data from being recorded in our logs. Well, we're not quite finished with security yet. The password (and other potentially sensitive data) is still vulnerable to eavesdropping while in-transit from the user's browser to your web server.

To completely secure the information you need to use SSL (Secure Sockets Layer). Configuring and managing SSL for your web server is out of the scope of this book, but there are things to be done on the Rails side, which we will cover now.

First, set `config.force_ssl = true` in your configuration file to force all access to the application over SSL. Then specify use of Strict-Transport-Security HTTP header[3] and secure cookies.

The `force_ssl` setting works by redirecting to an HTTPS URL with same parameters if you try to access the application via plain HTTP.

🔎 Trying to access a non-GET HTTP action with HTTP might not actually work as you can not redirect to a POST request. The way to go is to use `force_ssl` on the GET request that renders the form. In which case standard form helpers will keep the HTTPS format for the form submit action.

If you want fine-grained control over the forcing of SSL connections, you can supply parameters to a controller's `force_ssl` class method. It accepts the same kind of options as a `before_action`, as well as `:host` and `:port` options in case you need to specify a domain.

```
class UsersController < ApplicationController
    force_ssl only: [:new, :edit], host: "www.foobar.com"
```

If class-level options are not suitable for your application, you can always roll your own logic inside an action method. The `ssl?` method of a request option returns `true` if the request was received over an HTTPS connection.

15.4 Model Mass-Assignment Attributes Protection

Since its origins, Rails has featured a convenient mass-assignment feature enabling assignment of multiple model attributes by passing a hash of values. As such, it's common to create a model using `User.create(params[:user])` and to update it later using `User.update(params[:user])`.

Without protection, direct mass-assignment access to all model attributes would be easy to exploit. For example, if you happen to define an `is_admin` boolean field in the "users" table, an attacker could give themselves admin privileges by sneaking in an `is_admin=true` on an otherwise innocent registration form.

In the previous Rails versions, mass-assignment protection was implemented on the model level using `attr_accessible` and `attr_protected` class level methods.

---

3. http://tools.ietf.org/html/draft-hodges-strict-transport-sec-02?

Security

In a nutshell, you could call `attr_accessible` with a list of model attributes to indicate that those attributes are safe to mass-update. `attr_protected` would do the opposite, disabling access to passed attributes. This is referred to as whitelisting and blacklisting, respectively.

There were several practical problems with the former approach:

- It was too cumbersome to use, as it restricted mass-assignment globally, including tests and access from other models. In those cases you usually know very well what attributes you are assigning and having to jump through hoops to do so. The result wasn't very pleasant.

- Simple whitelisting and blacklisting didn't allow for special cases where access to attributes depend on other attributes or other records, for example, user roles and permissions.

- Models don't feel like the right place to define these kinds of restrictions, since most of the time we only need restrictions on mass-assignment when passing unfiltered parameters to models inside a controller action method.

Rails 4 introduced a new and improved way of controlling mass-assignment attributes. The functionality was made available and proven in earlier Rails versions with the `strong_parameters` gem. The new approach forbids mass-assignment of a model attribute from a controller unless that attribute was white-listed.

Whitelisting is configured using two simple methods (`permit` and `require`) that are exposed on a controller's `params` object. Calls to those methods can be chained to validate nested `params` hashes.

Calling `require` will validate that the parameter is actually present and throw an `ActionController::ParameterMissing` exception if it is not. It will also return the "extracted" value of the parameter.

```
params.require(:user)
```

An `ActionController::ParameterMissing` exception, unless unhandled, will bubble up to the Rails dispatcher and result in an HTTP 400 Bad Request response.

Calling `permit` with a list of attributes will enable those attributes to "pass through" to the model during mass-assignment but only if the value is one of the supported "scalar" types: `String,  Symbol,  NilClass,  Numeric,  TrueClass,`

`FalseClass, Date, Time, DateTime, StringIO, IO, ActionDispatch ::Http::UploadedFile` or `Rack::Test::UploadedFile`. This restriction disables evil injection of arrays, hashes or any other objects.

```
params.require(:user).permit(
  :name, :email, :password, :password_confirmation)
```

Another option is to pass a hash. This will enable you to declare that one of the attributes can contain an array of scalar values:

```
params.permit(ids: [])
```

To whitelist all the attributes in a given hash call `permit!` method on it:

```
params.require(:log_entry).permit!
```

Using a combination of `permit` and `require`, it's relatively easy to implement different parameter filtering options for creating new records and updating existing records or any other "complicated" logic required:

Listing 15.1   A typical `UsersController` with param filtering

```
class UsersController < ApplicationController

  def create
    user = User.create!(create_params)
    redirect_to user
  end

  def update
    user = User.find(params[:id])
    user.update!(update_params)
    redirect_to user
  end

private

  def create_params
    params.require(:user).permit(:name, :email, :password,
      :password_confirmation)
  end

  def update_params
    params.require(:user).permit(name: true, email: true, tags: [])
  end
end
```

Security

There is an uncommon edge case that could trip up experienced Rails developers new to Rails 5. It crops up when slicing values from `params` for later use. In Rails 5, `params` was changed to be an instance of `ActionController::Parameters` that *behaves a lot like a hash* but *always enforces security constraints*. Line 2 in the following example does not return a hash.

```
def do_something_with_params
  params.slice(:param, :other_param)
end
```

Unless you call `permit` first, the results of that `slice` operation will return an empty object. The following code *does* work the way intended.

```
def do_something_with_params
  params.permit([:param, :other_param]).to_h
end
```

If you know the parameters you're trying to store are not originating in the wild and are guaranteed to be safe, you can choose to use `to_unsafe_hash` and skip the permit calls.

```
def do_something_with_params
  params.to_unsafe_h.slice(:param, :other_param)
end
```

The `controller` and `action` parameters are always allowed by default. There is a configuration option in `application.rb` that enables other parameters to be marked as always safe and available.

```
config.always_permitted_parameters = %w(controller action param other_param)
```

15.5   SQL Injection

SQL injection attacks were very popular when people wrote SQL code for their applications by hand. But even today, if you're not careful, you can introduce code that is susceptible to this kind of attack.

15.5.1   What Is a SQL Injection?

SQL injection is a catch-all description for attacks on SQL database-driven applications. The attacker includes malicious fragments of SQL code in otherwise legitimate input provided to the application, in the hopes that the application "messes up" and sends those fragments along to the database to be executed.

Let's see how this can happen. Suppose that we implemented product search functionality in our application using the following piece of code:

```
class ProductsController < ApplicationController
  def search
    @products = Product.where("name LIKE '%#{params[:search_terms]}%'")
  end
end
```

For a search string "test," this code will execute the following SQL query:

```
SELECT * FROM products WHERE name LIKE '%test%';
```

Okay so far. But what if the user submits `search_terms` with a value of `'; DELETE FROM users;?` In this case, the resulting SQL code sent to the database is:

```
SELECT * FROM products WHERE name LIKE '%';DELETE FROM users;%';
```

That second statement will wipe out the entire 'users' table in the database.

Using variations on the same theme, an attacker could modify the users table to reset an administrator's password or retrieve data that he shouldn't have access to.

To protect ourseleves from this attack we could start escaping all the user input ourselves, but fortunately we don't have to do that, as Active Record already does it for us. We just need to know how to use it correctly.

The first rule to remember is to never directly inject user's input into any string that will be used as a part of a SQL query. Instead we should use the variable substitution facility provided by Active Record (and other object-mapping software—they all have it):

```
@products = Product.where('name LIKE ?', "%#{params[:query]}%")
```

The '?' character in the query fragment serves as a variable placeholder. You can have more than one in any given query, just make sure to pass the right number of variables to interpolate.

You can read more about this behavior in Chapter 5, "Working with Active Record."

15.6   Cross-Site Scripting (XSS)

Cross-Site Scripting is one of the most common security vulnerabilities, but that doesn't make it any less severe. When successfully exploited it can give an attacker a bypass around application authorization and authentication mechanisms and leak personal information.

The attack works by injecting client-side executable code into the application pages. An example of such code can be JavaScript that "leaks" cookies to a remote server, which would allow the attacker to "clone" any affected session. So if the attacker is able to lay his hands on the administrator session he would be able to impersonate an administrator without actually passing the required authentication procedures, just by using an already authenticated session.

There are several ways attack code can "leak" the information. One of the simplest ones is to insert an image tag into the DOM with image reference to the attacker's server and image path including the leaked information. The attacker's server access logs will capture the information where it can be retrieved later.

All recent versions of Rails make it relatively easy to avoid this kind of attack. In this section we will discuss the key elements provided by Rails to defend against XSS attacks and point out things to watch out for.

The most common mistake leading to an XSS vulnerability is failing to escape user input when rendering HTML. There are several possible vectors of attack for exploiting this mistake.

Attack code can be first saved into the database (like, for example, injecting it into a post title, or comment body, etc.), in which case such a database record becomes infected. Anyone visiting a page with infected data will run the malicious JavaScript code embedded in the record, allowing the attacker to access the visiting user's session and do whatever they're allowed to do.

Another vector involves passing attack code as a URL parameter that is directly rendered into the page, causing the victim to visit an "infected" URL.

In both cases the victim's browser is exposed to the attack code, which will execute in the browser's context. The solution is to always "escape" or "sanitize" unsafe HTML content.

In this context, "escaping" means replacing some of the string characters by an HTML escape sequences that will remove the special meaning from the text and cause it to render as regular text. Sanitizing, on the other hand, means validating the HTML content to ensure only "good" HTML tags and attributes are used.

Note that sanitizing is inherently less secure than escaping, and should only be used where rendered content must contain HTML markup. An example would be a WYSIWYG HTML editor on a text area that manages code that is later rendered on a page.

15.6.1   HTML Escaping

In previous versions of Rails you had to think hard about escaping and utilize the h view helper method to escape potentially unsafe content. Rails core fielded a lot of criticism for making our code "unsafe by default." Having to think about escaping turns out to be very error-prone, and many developers forgot to do it properly. Recent versions of Rails (starting with 3.0) do a much better job. Every string is tagged as either safe or unsafe. All unsafe strings are automatically escaped by default. You only need to think about explicitly managing the "safeness" of strings when you're writing helpers that output HTML into your template.

For obvious reasons, all Rails HTML helpers will output "safe" strings that can be directly rendered on a page. Otherwise you would have to call `html_safe` on the output of a helper.

For example, let's look at the following view fragment:

```
%li= link_to @user.name, user_path(@user), class: user_class(@user)
```

The user's name will be escaped and so will the return value of the `user_class` view helper method, (assuming it wasn't tagged as safe). The result of `user_path(@user)` is an unsafe string, so it will be escaped as well.

The net result of those changes in later versions of Rails is that it becomes easy to ensure proper HTML escaping. The "right thing" will be done in most cases, and Rails will play it safe by default. Occasionally Rails feels like it escapes "too much" when you forget to use `html_safe` on the return value of a custom view helper method. But the error is usually easy to spot.

Even though Rails is safe by default, you should still be very careful when you call `html_safe` though. Calling it on unsafe input without validation will absolutely create an XSS vulnerability in your application.

🔍 The most common source of confusion about needing `html_safe` in view helper methods happens when manipulating literal strings.

```
def paragraphize(text)
  text.split("\r\n\r\n").map do |paragraph|
    content_tag(:p, paragraph)
  end.join.html_safe
end
```

The call to `content_tag` on line 3 will properly escape its input, so we don't have to manually escape `paragraph`. It is itself a view helper method, so it will tag its return value as `html_safe`. However, `join` will join the safe strings from `content_tag` with an unsafe `""` which is used as the default join string. You'll scratch your head and wonder what's going on, before adding the final `html_safe` in a state of confusion.

15.6.2   HTML Sanitization

In contrast to escaping, sanitization leaves some HTML intact. The idea is to only leave "safe" html tags that we want and to remove all the rest. As usual with filtering problems, there are 2 approaches: blacklisting and whitelisting.

Blacklisting involves trying to detect and remove "bad" HTML fragments, like Java-Script tags or script content in links. Whitelisting only allows HTML elements that are explicitly allowed, and escapes anything else.

Blacklisting is not a secure solution, since new hacks are being devised all the time, and there's no way we'd be able to be 100% sure that our blacklist is complete at all times. Therefore, we *must* use the whitelisting approach.

Rails has a `SanitizeHelper` module for "scrubbing text of undesired HTML elements." It includes several methods for our disposal that we already covered in Chapter 11, "All about Helpers," so we won't repeat them here.

15.6.3   Input versus Output Escaping

One more thing to discuss about HTML escaping is timing. When should we do it? On input of user data or during rendering (output)?

The rule of thumb is to escape on output, the rationale being that we might want to render the content in different formats and each has its own escaping requirements. For example, escaping HTML on input will not help us if the output format is JSON, which requires escaping of quote characters and not HTML tags.

Sanitization also mostly makes sense on output, as it will allow us to change the rules without re-applying them on all the data already stored.

⚮ Especially cautious application developers might decide to escape and sanitize on both input and output, but we find that it usually isn't necessary.

15.7   XSRF (Cross-Site Request Forgery)

Cross-Site Request Forgery (usually abbreviated as CSRF or XSRF) is a type of web application vulnerability that allows an attacker to modify application state on behalf of a user that is logged into the application by luring the user to click on a carefully crafted link, visit a page, or even just open an email with malicious embedded images.

Assume that an intern named Frank at a banking institution implemented account fund transfer functionality as an HTTP GET method, like so:

```
GET /transfers?from_account_id=123&to_account_id=456&amount=1000
```

Note that you would NEVER do something like this in real life. This example is for illustrative purposes only. In fact, if you're following proper RESTful practices, a GET would not make any modifications to server state. We're about to see why . . .

Of course everyone, even interns, knows you should authenticate banking transfers. So Frank does some research on Rails security and properly authenticates and authorizes the request.

You see the problem yet? No? Assume an end-user logs into his online banking, leaves it logged in and flips over to check his email in another browser tab. Even a relatively unsophisticated attacker could send him an HTML email with the following image:

```
<img src="http://banking-domain/transfers?from_account_id=<users_account_id>
&to_account_id=<attacker_account_id>&amount=1000">
```

It's a long shot, but if this image is opened by the victim's browser while it is authenticated and authorized, the transfer will get executed because the session cookie from the bank is still valid.

Fortunately for the bank, Frank's code was reviewed, and the reviewer pointed out the problem. So Frank *fixed* the problem by modifying his transfer action to use a POST instead of GET.

Security

Are the bank's customers safe yet? Not quite. An attacker can still "lure" victims to an innocent-looking site hosting JavaScript that will post to the fund transfer URL from within the victim's browser.

So how do we protect ourselves against this chicanery?

15.7.1   Restricting HTTP Method for Actions with Side-Effects

First we must only allow side effects on non-GET requests (e.g., POST, DELETE, PATCH). This is actually specified by HTTP protocol guidelines, and there are several ways to accomplish the restriction in Rails.

First, we can restrict the request methods at the routing level:

```
post 'transfers' => 'transfers#create'

resources :users do
  post :activate, on: :member
end
```

Rails' standard `resources` routing helper exhibits the correct behavior by default. It will require POST to access `create`, PATCH to access `update`, and DELETE to access `destroy`. You need to be careful when you define your own non-resource routes, especially if you use `:action` segment routes.

The truly paranoid among us can use a controller class method called `verify` to make sure that proper methods are used for controller actions with side-effects:

```
class UsersController < ApplicationController
  verify method: [:post, :put, :delete], only: [:activate, :create,
    :update], redirect_to: '/'
```

15.7.2   Require Security Token for Protected Requests

Using the proper HTTP request method is not enough. We need to ensure that the requests originate form our application. You could check the referrer of HTTP requests, but the proper way to do it is to include a security token as a parameter or header on protected requests and validate the token on the server side.

Rails has built-in facilities to handle exactly this kind of security check. The boilerplate implementation of ApplicationController generated for new apps includes the following code:

```
class ApplicationController
  # Prevent CSRF attacks by raising an exception.
```

```
  # For APIs, you may want to use :null_session instead.
  protect_from_forgery with: :exception
end
```

This code adds a `verify_authenticity_token` before action callback to all requests in your application. The `protect_from_forgery` method takes `:if`/`:except` parameters just like a normal `before_action` declaration.

Additionally, the `with` parameter accepts one of the supported protection strategies: `:exception`, `:null_session`, or `:reset_session`.

`:exception` Raises `ActionController::InvalidAuthenticityToken` exception.

`:reset_session` Resets the user's session.

`:null_session` (default) Executes the request as if no session exists. Used by default if no `with` parameter is supplied.

The difference between `:reset_session` and `:null_session` is that `:null_session` doesn't actually change the session, only substitutes an empty one for the current requests, while `:reset_session` will leave it empty for subsequent requests as well.

15.7.3 Client-Side Security Token Handling

Now that we are requiring a security token on the server side we need to pass it from the client side. Standard Rails form helpers (e.g., `form_for`) will include the token as a hidden parameter.

The same goes for the Rails link helpers that generate non-GET Ajax requests (e.g., `link_to` with `method: :post`). Note that the actual handling of security tokens is done in the UJS JavaScript library.

To function properly the browser needs access to the security token from the server. It is provided with a call to `csrf_meta_tags` in your application layout header section:

```
%head
  ....
  = csrf_meta_tags
```

This will render two meta tags:

```
<meta content="authenticity_token" name="csrf-param" />
<meta content="...." name="csrf-token" />
```

The actual token is stored in the session. It is generated for the first time when it is needed and preserved for the duration of the session. The call to `csrf_meta_tags` is included in the boilerplate application template of a fresh Rails app.

15.8   Session Fixation Attacks

A session fixation attack is something to be aware of if you implement your own session management. The Rails cookies session store is immune from these types of attacks.

Many session security implementations depend on the session id being a secret. If the attacker is successfully able to force a user to use their session id and login into the system, the attacker can get access to the authenticated session by using that id.

Session fixation attacks are only possible when hackers are able to force the setting of a third session id in the user's browser through a URL or other means. For example, in some configurations of PHP, you can allow a session id to be passed as a URL parameter called `_my_app_session_id`. The attacker can send victims to the malicious link, which then redirects back to the target system including a session id that they generated.

Defending against this hack is pretty simple. Whenever you elevate a user's privileges, call the `reset_session` helper, which ensures that their session id is changed. Attackers are left with an old unauthenticated session.

ℹ️ Any decent Rails authentication system, like Devise, already protects you from session fixation attacks. So you don't usually need to worry about it unless you are doing something unusual.

15.9   Keeping Secrets

As a general rule, you should not store secret things in your source code. This includes passwords, security tokens, API keys, etc. Assume that a determined attacker will gain access to your source code and use it to their advantage, if they can.

So where do you store secret parts of your application's configuration, including API keys and tokens for external services? The recommended way is to get those from your process environment.

For example, let's say you need to configure a Pubnub service. The following code will enable you to configure Pubnub using five environment variables. (Put it in `config/initializers/pubnub.rb`.)

```
PUBNUB = Pubnub.new(
    ENV["PUBNUB_PUBLISH_KEY"],
    ENV["PUBNUB_SUBSCRIBE_KEY"],
    ENV["PUBNUB_SECRET_KEY"],
    ENV["PUBNUB_CYPHER"] || "",
    ENV["PUBNUB_SSL"] == "true")
```

If you deploy to Heroku you can easily configure environment variables using the Heroku command-line tool:

```
$ heroku config:add PUBNUB_PUBLISH_KEY=.... PUBNUB_SUBSCRIBE_KEY=... ...
```

Other deployment options should enable you to define environment variables easily since it's a common need.

Even if you have no easy way to control the environment directly, you almost always have a way to add extra files to the deployment directory. You can load such a file into your environment like this (add this code to the top of your `config/application.rb`):

```
# change this path according to your needs
ENV_PATH = File.expand_path('../env.rb',  FILE )
require ENV_PATH if File.exists?(ENV_PATH)
```

The `env.rb` file can assign environment variables as needed:

```
ENV["PUBNUB_PUBLISH_KEY"] = "..."
```

IMPORTANT: Rails, by default, stores a very important secret in the source code. Take a look at `config/secrets.yml`:

```
Rails.application.secrets.secret_key_base = '...'
```

Change this to the following:

```
# config/secrets.yml

...
production:
  secret_key_base: <%= ENV["SECRET_KEY_BASE"] %>
```

This token is used to sign the session cookie, and it allows anyone that has it to modify the session to their liking, bypassing most security measures.

15.10   Conclusion

Security is a topic that should never be taken lightly, especially when developing business-critical applications. Since exploits are always being discovered, it's very important to keep up-to-date on new developments. We recommend that you check out http://guides.rubyonrails.org/security.html[4] and http://railssecurity.com[5] for the latest information available.

✎ You should consider using Code Climate[6] to automatically analyze and audit your Rails code after every git push. Tell Bryan and Noah that *The Rails Way* sent you.

---

4. http://guides.rubyonrails.org/security.html
5. http://railssecurity.com
6. http://codeclimate.com

CHAPTER 16

Action Mailer

It's a cool way to send emails without tons of code.

—Jake Scruggs

Integration with email is a crucial part of most modern web application projects. Whether it's sign-up confirmations, password recovery, or letting users control their accounts via email, you'll be happy to hear that Rails offers great support for both sending and receiving email, thanks to its Action Mailer framework.

In this chapter, we'll cover what's needed to set up your deployment to be able to send and receive mail with the Action Mailer framework and by writing mailer models, the entities in Rails that encapsulate code having to do with email handling.

16.1 Mailer Models

A mailer model is a class that encapsulates code for a particular class of automated emails in your application. A small application might only have one mailer, and larger ones might have many. There could be a correlation between mailer classes and other parts of your domain or not. It all depends.

Let's go ahead and create a mailer model that will contain code pertaining to sending notices in our time and expenses sample app. Rails provides a generator to get us started rapidly. This mailer will send out notices to users of our sample application who are late in entering their time.

```
$ rails generate mailer NoticesMailer
    create  app/mailers/notices_mailer.rb
    invoke  haml
    create    app/views/notices_mailer
```

575

```
identical    app/views/layouts/mailer.text.haml
identical    app/views/layouts/mailer.html.haml
   invoke  rspec
   create    spec/mailers/notices_mailer_spec.rb
   create    spec/mailers/previews/notices_mailer_preview.rb
```

A view folder for the mailer is created at app/views/notices_mailer, and the
mailer itself is stubbed out at app/mailers/notices_mailer.rb:

```
class NoticesMailer < ApplicationMailer
end
```

Kind of like a default Active Record subclass, there's not much there at the start.
The generated class inherits from ApplicationMailer, which was created at the
time that the application was newly bootstrapped, in app/mailers/applica-
tion_mailer.rb

```
class ApplicationMailer < ActionMailer::Base
  default from: "system@timeandexpenses.com"
  layout 'mailer'
end
```

This class, which inherits from ActionMailer::Base, follows what should
already be a familiar pattern in Rails. It gives you a place to set property and code
behavior that is shared across all mailers.

16.1.1   Preparing Outbound Email Messages

You work with Action Mailer classes by defining public mailer methods that correspond to types of emails that you want to send. Inside the public method, you assign
instance variables needed to render the message template(s) and then call the mail
method, which is conceptually similar to the render method used in controllers.

Continuing with our example, let's flesh out a late_timesheet mailer action in
the NoticesMailer class that takes recipient and week_of parameters.

Listing 16.1   Adding a mailer method
```
class NoticesMailer < ActionMailer::Base
    def late_timesheet(recipient:, week_of:)
      @recipient = recipient
      @week_of = week_of
      mail to: recipient.email,
           subject: "[T&E] Your timesheet is late!!!"
    end
  end
```

To keep things simple, we're passing the objects needed directly from parameters to the template, as instance variables. Then we call `mail` to send the message.

16.1.2   Decent Exposure

For the sake of system robustness, some claim that it's better for parameters to async processes (like mailer actions) to be simple integers and strings rather than complex objects.[1]

If you follow that advice, the first part of your mailer action method will contain essentially boilerplate code that uses ids to look up Active Record objects and assign them to instance variables. We can significantly cut down on that boilerplate, plus eliminate the use of icky instance variables by using Decent Exposure, just like we do in our controller actions.

```
class PostMailer < ApplicationMailer
  expose(:posts, -> { Post.last_week.popular.take(10) })
  expose(:post)

  def top_ten_posts_for_last_week
    mail to: User.active.pluck(:email)
  end

  def featured_post(id:)
    @greeting = "Featured Post"
    mail to: "to@example.org"
  end
end
```

In the example, both `posts` and `post` are exposed as helper methods to your mailer template.

Note that in order for this technique to work, you must use Ruby 2-style named parameters for your action methods. The mailer's instance methods are not called directly but rather through the mailer class, which gives the Decent Exposure library a chance to hook into the execution chain and do its magic.

16.1.2.1   Action Instance Methods

The following methods are available inside of a mailer action.

---

1. Marshalling versus extra database lookups: determining the tradeoffs are left as an exercise for the reader.

attachments Enables you to add normal and inline file attachments to your message.

```
attachments["myfile.zip"] = File.read("/myfile.zip")
attachments.inline["logo.png"] = File.read("/logo.png")
```

headers Enables you to supply a hash of arbitrary custom email headers.

```
headers("X-Author" => "Obie Fernandez")
```

mail Generates an email message to be sent. It takes an optional hash of parameters and headers passed to the `Mail::Message` initializer and an optional block. If no block is specified, mailer templates will be used to construct the email with the same name as the method in the mailer. If a block is specified these can be customized.

16.1.2.2 `mail` Method Parameters

The following parameters can be passed to the `mail` method:

subject Required. A subject line for the message.

to Required. The recipient addresses for the message, either as a string (for a single address) or an array (for multiple addresses). Remember that this method expects actual address strings, not your application's user objects.

```
def missing_timesheets_for_last_week
  mail to: User.missing_timesheets_for_last_week.pluck(:email),
       subject: "[T&E] Your timesheet is late!!!"
end
```

from Required. Specifies the from address for the message as a string.

cc Specifies carbon-copy recipient (Cc:) addresses for the message, either as a string (for a single address) or an array for multiple addresses.

bcc Specifies blind recipient (Bcc:) addresses for the message, either as a string (for a single address) or an array for multiple addresses.

reply_to Sets the email for the reply-to header.

date An optional explicit sent on date for the message, usually passed `Time.now`. Will be automatically set by the delivery mechanism if you don't supply a value, and cannot be set using the default macro.

content_type MIME type for the message.

body Lets you provide the message body yourself and overrides template rendering behavior. Rails defaults to `text/plain` unless you tell it otherwise using `content_type`.

dynamic_delivery_options Lets you override the default delivery options (e.g., SMTP credentials) per mailer action. Rarely needed.

Here's a useful mailer that I have in almost every production Rails app I've ever worked on:

```
class UtilityMailer < ApplicationMailer
  def notify_support(subject:, message:)
    mail to: ENV['SUPPORT_EMAIL'],
         subject: subject,
         body: message
  end
end
```

16.1.2.3   `mail` Method Formats
The `mail` method takes an optional block letting you provide custom formats similar to Rails routes.

```
mail(to: "user@example.com") do |format|
  format.text
  format.html
end
```

16.1.3   Mailer Views
The body of the email is created by using a view template (regular Haml or ERb) that has the instance variables in the mailer available as instance variables in the template. So the corresponding text template for the mailer method in Listing 16.1 could look like this:

```
Dear <%= @recipient.name =%>,

Your timesheet for the week of <%= @week_of.strftime("%m/%d") %>
        is late. You should feel ashamed.

Sincerely,
T&E System
```

⚡ Don't use Haml for plain text email templates. ERb is actually a little easier and doesn't lose line breaks. Try it and see.

If the recipient was Aslak, the email generated would look like this:

```
From: system@timeandexpenses.com
To: aslak@tw.com
```

```
Subject: [T&E] Your timesheet is late!!!

Dear Aslak,

Your timesheet for the week of Aug 15th is late. Shame on you!
```

Mailer views are located in the `app/views/name_of_mailer_class` directory. The specific mailer view is known to the class because its name is the same as the mailer method. In our example from above, our mailer view for the `late_timesheet` method will be in `app/views/late_notice_mailer/late_notice.html` `.haml` for the HTML version and `app/views/late_notice_mailer/` `late_notice.text.erb` for the plain text version.

⚠ Note that plain text email templates have a text extension, not `txt`! That tripped me up pretty badly once.

16.1.4   HTML Email Messages

To send mail as HTML, make sure your view template generates HTML and that the corresponding template name corresponds to the email method name. You can also override this template name in the block in the formatter, although I'd be hard pressed to imagine why you would need to do so.

```
mail(to: "user@example.com") do |format|
  format.text
  format.html { render "another_template" }
end
```

16.1.5   The **render** Method

The `render` method inside a mailer formatter block is very similar to its Action View counterpart. It understands parameters such as `text` or `nothing` to override template rendering. It also understands `layout`, in case you want to specify a different layout for a particular mailer action.

16.1.6   Multipart Messages

If a plain text and HTML template are present for a specific mailer action, the text template and the HTML template will both get sent by default as a multipart message. The HTML part will be flagged as alternative content for those email clients that support it.

16.1.6.1   Implicit Multipart Messages

As mentioned earlier in the chapter, multipart messages can also be used implicitly, without passing a block of formatters to the `mail` method, because Action Mailer will automatically detect and use multipart templates, where each template is named after the name of the action, followed by the content type. Each such detected template will be added as a separate part to the message.

For example, if the following templates existed, each would be rendered and added as a separate part to the message, with the corresponding content type. The same body hash is passed to each template.

- `signup_notification.text.haml`

- `signup_notification.text.html.haml`

- `signup_notification.text.xml.builder`

- `signup_notification.text.yaml.erb`

16.1.7   Attachments

Including attachments in emails is relatively simple; just use the `attachments` method in your class.

```
class NoticesMailer < ActionMailer::Base
  def late_timesheet(recipient:, week_of:)
    @recipient = recipient
    @week_of = week_of
    attachments["handbook.pdf"] = File.read("/docs/employee/handbook.pdf")
    mail to: recipient.email,
      from: "test@myapp.com",
      subject: "[T&E] Your timesheet is late!!!"
  end
end
```

If you wanted to use the image inline in the HTML template just use `attachments.inline` like this:

```
attachments.inline["shame.jpg"] = File.read("app/assets/images/shame.jpg")
```

> Notice that `File.read` works with a relative path at the root of your Rails application.

You can access this attachment in the template via the `attachments` hash, calling the `url` method to get the image's relative content id path. (The content id path, or `cid` for short, is like a URL pointing to a specific part of a multipart message.)

```
-# app/views/notices_mailer/late_notice.html.haml

%p Dear #{@recipient.name},

%p Your timesheet for the week of #{@week_of.strftime("%m/%d")}
        is late. Here's a photo depicting how you should feel
        about it.

%p= image_tag attachments['shame.jpg'].url, alt: "Shame on you"

%p Sincerely,

%p T&E System
```

16.1.7.1   Attachment Parameters and Alternate Encodings

Rails automatically Base64 encodes attachments. If you want something different, encode your content yourself and pass in the encoded `content` and `encoding` information in a hash to the `attachments` method. Pass the file name and specify headers and content and Action Mailer, and Mail will use the settings you pass in.

```
control, encoded_content = PGP.crypt(message)

attachments['control'] = {
  mime_type: 'application/pgp-encrypted',
  encoding: 'PGP',
  content: encoded_content
}
attachments['encoded_content'] = {
  mime_type: 'application/octet-stream',
  encoding: 'PGP',
  content: encoded_content
}
```

 The example is just illustrative pseudo-code. If you're interested in learning how to use PGP in your Rails application, check out the Mail:GPG Gem https://github.com/jkraemer/mail-gpg.

Once you specify an encoding, Mail will assume that your content is already encoded and not try to Base64 encode it.

16.1.8 Generating URLs

Generating application URLs is handled through named routes or using the `url_for` helper. Since mail does not have request context like controllers do, the host configuration option needs to be set. The best practice for this is to define them in the corresponding environment configuration, although it can be defined on a per mailer basis or even per method call.

```
# config/environments/production.rb
config.action_mailer.default_url_options = { host: 'accounting.com' }
```

In your mailer you can now generate your URL. It is important to note that you cannot use the `_path` variation for your named routes since email readers don't have the concept of a current URL from which to derive a hostname.

16.1.9 Mailer Layouts

Mailer layouts behave just like controller layouts. To be automatically recognized they need to have the same name as the mailer itself. In our ongoing example code in this chapter, a template would automatically be used for our HTML emails.

Just like with normal views, you can also add custom layouts if your heart desires, either at the class level or as an optional parameter to the `render` method.

```
class LateNotice < ApplicationMailer
  layout "alternative"

  def late_timesheet(user, week_of)
    mail(to: user.email) do |format|
      format.html { render layout: "another" }
    end
  end
end
```

We've now talked extensively about preparing email messages for sending, but what about actually sending them to the recipients?

16.1.10 Sending an Email

Sending emails involves calling the mailer action at the *class level* of your mailer class. That's unintuitive, because mailer actions are implemented as *instance methods*, but that's the way it works.

```
aslak = User.find_by(email: "aslak@thoughtworks.com")
LateNotice.late_timesheet(recipient: aslak,
  week_of: 1.week.ago).deliver_later
```

Mailer class methods return an `ActionMailer::MessageDelivery` object, which can be told to `deliver_now` or `deliver_later` to send itself out.

`ActionMailer::MessageDelivery` is just a wrapper object around a `Mail::Message`. If you want to inspect, alter, or do anything else with the `Mail::Message` object, you can access it via the `message` method on the delivery object.

16.1.11   Asynchronous Delivery

Active Job integrates with Action Mailer to easily enable sending of emails without holding up request processing. Just use `deliver_later` instead of `deliver_now`.

Newly created jobs are placed in a queue named `mailers`. That behavior can be customized in an initializer or environment script using the following setting:

```
config.action_mailer.deliver_later_queue_name = 'default'
```

16.1.12   Callbacks

As of Rails 4, the capability to define action callbacks for a mailer was added. Like their Action Controller counterparts, you can specify `before_action`, `after_action`, and `around_action` callbacks to run shared pre- and post-processing code within a mailer.

Callbacks accept one or more symbols, representing a matching method in the mailer class:

```
before_action :set_headers
```

Or you can pass the callback a block to execute, like this:

```
before_action { logger.info "Sending out an email!" }
```

A common example of why you would use a callback in a mailer is to set inline attachments, such as images, that are used within the email template.

```
class NoticesMailer < ActionMailer::Base
  before_action :set_inline_attachments

  def late_timesheet(user, week_of)
    @recipient = user.name
    mail(
      to: recipient.email,
      from: "test@myapp.com",
```

```
      subject: "[Time and Expenses] Timesheet notice"
    )
  end

  protected

  def set_inline_attachments
    attachments["logo.png"] = File.read("/images/logo.png")
  end
end
```

Action callbacks are covered in detail in Chapter 4, "Working with Controllers," in the "Action Callbacks" section.

16.1.13   Interceptors

There are situations, particularly in staging environments, when you want to intercept emails prior to delivery. Action Mailer provides this functionality via *Interceptors*. You can register them to make modifications to mail messages right before they are processed for delivery.

```
class SandboxEmailInterceptor
  def self.delivering_email(message)
    message.to = ['sandbox@example.com']
  end
end
```

For an interceptor to be active, you need to register it. Do that in an initializer file or within the environment script where you want the interceptor to be active.

```
ActionMailer::Base.register_interceptor(SandboxEmailInterceptor)
```

16.2   Previews

By default in Rails, all email messages sent in development via Action Mailer are set to test mode. This means if you send an email from your application, the output of that message would display in your development log. While this can show you if the output is correct, it does not indicate whether the email message is rendered correctly. A way around this would be to connect your development environment to an actual SMTP server. Even though this would enable you to view the email in your mail client of choice, it's also a very bad idea—combined with realistic sample user data, you could accidentally email real people.

Rails 4.1 introduced Action Mailer previews, which give us a means of rendering plain text and HTML mail templates in the browser without having to deliver them. It's super useful.

When we generated our `LateNotice` mailer in the beginning of the chapter, an action mailer preview class was generated and placed in `spec/mailers/previews/late_notice_preview.rb`.

It's empty by default, so let's flesh it out with some code that pulls up a user created in our `db/seeds.rb`

```ruby
# Preview all emails at http://localhost:3000/rails/mailers/notices_mailer
class NoticesMailerPreview < ActionMailer::Preview
  def late_timesheet
    user = User.find_by!(email: "obie@trxw.com")
    NoticesMailer.late_timesheet(recipient: user, week_of: 1.week.ago)
  end
end
```

🔑 You might be tempted to use fixtures or `FactoryGirl` to create test data for your mailer previews. The problem with that approach is that since you're not in a test environment, the data you create in the preview code is not cleaned up automatically. I prefer using seed data because then I don't have to worry about object lifecycles.

By default, all previews are located in the `test/mailers/previews` directory. However, this directory path can be overridden using the `preview_path` configuration option.

```ruby
# For those using RSpec
config.action_mailer.preview_path = "#{Rails.root}/spec/mailers/previews"
```

To obtain a listing of all Action Mailer previews available within your application, navigate to `http://localhost:3000/rails/mailers/` while running a local development server instance.

I pull up my own list of mailer preview instances and select the link for Notices Mailer, `late_timesheet`.

From:	
To:	obie@trxw.com
Date:	Fri, 23 Dec 2016 22:11:38 +0000
Subject:	**[T&E] Your timesheet is late!!!**
Attachments:	shame.jpg

View as HTML email ⌄

Dear Obie,

Your timesheet for the week of 12/16 is late, here's a photo depicting how you should feel about it.

Sincerely,

T&E System

A Mailer Preview

16.3   Receiving Emails

Third-party email service providers all provide some sort of inbound email processing capability, and they all work the same way. I strongly recommend using them instead of Rails' own inbound email capabilities.

For instance, let's say you're using the excellent Postmark service for sending email. Postmark can be configured[2] to accept and parse any emails sent to your server's unique inbound email address and/or all emails sent to a forwarding domain that you set up for that purpose. Postmark will POST incoming email messages as JSON to a URL you specify. This enables you to treat incoming email as a data source just like you would JSON being posted from a web client or mobile app.

---

2. http://developer.postmarkapp.com/developer-process-email.html

16.3.1   The `receive` Method

If you're on a really tight budget or have some other reason preventing you from using a third-party email service provider, then you can try setting up your server to receive emails using Rails itself. The first step is to add a public method named `receive` to one of your application's `ActionMailer::Base` subclasses. It will take a `Mail::Message`[3] object instance as its single parameter.

When there is incoming email to handle, the raw email string is converted into a `Mail::Message` object automatically, and your `receive` method is invoked for further processing. You don't have to implement the `receive` class method yourself; it is inherited from `ActionMailer::Base`.[4]

That's all pretty confusing to explain, but simple in practice.

Listing 16.2   A simple `MessageArchiver` mailer class with a receive method

```
class MessageArchiver < ActionMailer::Base

    def receive(email)
      person = Person.where(email: email.to.first).first!
      person.emails.create(
        subject: email.subject,
        body: email.body
      )
    end
  end
```

The `receive` class method can be the target for a Postfix recipe or any other mail-handler process that can pipe the contents of the email to another process. The `rails runner` command makes it easy to handle incoming mail:

```
$ /path/to/app/bin/rails runner 'MessageArchiver.receive(STDIN.read)'
```

That way, when a message is received, the `receive` class method would be fed the raw string content of the incoming email via `STDIN`.

16.3.2   Handling Incoming Attachments

Processing files attached to incoming email messages is just a matter of using the `attachments` attribute of `Mail::Message`, as in Listing 16.3. This example

---

3. https://github.com/mikel/mail

4. If you are using a third-party email service, such as Sendgrid, be sure to checkout the Griddler gem by thoughtbot (https://github.com/thoughtbot/griddler). It's a Rails engine that hands off pre-processed email objects to a class solely responsible for processing the incoming email.

assumes that you have a `Person` class, with a `has_many` association `photos`, that contains a Carrierwave attachment.[5]

```
class PhotoByEmail < ApplicationMailer

  def receive(email)
    person = Person.where(email: email.from.first).first!
    if email.has_attachments?
      email.attachments.each do |file|
        person.photos.create(asset: file)
      end
    end
  end
end
```

There's not much more to it than that, except of course to wrestle with the configuration of your mail-processor (outside of Rails) since they are notoriously difficult to configure.[6] After you have your mail-processor calling the `rails runner` command correctly, add a `crontab` so that incoming mail is handled about every five minutes or so, depending on the needs of your application.

16.4   Testing Email Content

Ben Mabey's `email_spec`[7] gem provides a nice way to test your mailers using RSpec. Add it to your Gemfile, and then first make the following additions to your `spec/spec_helper.rb`.

```
RSpec.configure do |config|
  config.include(EmailSpec::Helpers)
  config.include(EmailSpec::Matchers)
end
```

Mailer specs reside in `spec/mailers`, and `email_spec` provides convenience matchers for asserting that the mailer contains the right attributes.

reply_to Checks the reply-to value.

deliver_to Verifies the recipient.

deliver_from Assertion for the sender.

bcc_to Verifies the Bcc.

---

5. Carrierwave, created by Jonas Nicklas, can be found at https://github.com/jnicklas/carrierwave.

6. Rob Orsini, author of O'Reilly's *Rails Cookbook* recommends getmail, which you can get from http://pyropus.ca/software/getmail

7. https://github.com/bmabey/email-spec

cc_to Verifies the Cc.

have_subject Performs matching of the subject text.

include_email_with_subject Performs matching of the subject text in
   multiple emails.

have_body_text Matches for text in the body.

have_header Checks for a matching email header.

These matchers can then be used to assert that the generated email has the correct
content included in it.

```
require "spec_helper"

describe InvoiceMailer do
  let(:invoice) { Invoice.new(name: "Acme", email: "joe@example.com") }

  describe "#create_late" do
    subject(:email) { InvoiceMailer.create_late(invoice) }

    it "delivers to the invoice email" do
      expect(email).to deliver_to("joe@example.com")
    end

    it "contains the invoice name" do
      expect(email).to have_body_text(/Acme/)
    end

    it "has a late invoice subject" do
      expect(email).to have_subject(/Late Invoice/)
    end
  end
end
```

If you're attempting to test whether or not the mailer gets called and sends the email,
it is recommended to simply check via a mock that the deliver method got executed.

16.5   Sending via API

In addition to SMTP, the major email service vendors all provide the capability to
send *transactional* email via API. For example, sending single emails through Postmark
is as simple as sending an HTTP POST request to their /e-mail endpoint with a
JSON message (http://developer.postmarkapp.com/developer-send-api.html).

```
{
  "From": "sender@example.com",
  "To": "receiver@example.com",
  "Cc": "copied@example.com",
  "Bcc": "blank-copied@example.com",
  "Subject": "Test",
  "Tag": "Invitation",
  "HtmlBody": "<b>Hello</b>",
  "TextBody": "Hello",
  "ReplyTo": "reply@example.com",
  "Headers": [
    {
      "Name": "CUSTOM-HEADER",
      "Value": "value"
    }
  ],
  "TrackOpens": true,
  "TrackLinks": "HtmlOnly"
}
```

> ✿ As you can tell from the example code, using third-party email service providers also gives you value-added features like tagging and tracking of opens and link click-throughs.

Realistically, there's little reason to use third-party APIs directly in this way, because they all have well-supported libraries that integrate with Action Mailer. To use Postmark, just add the `postmark-rails` gem and configure accordingly.

```
config.action_mailer.delivery_method = :postmark
config.action_mailer.postmark_settings = { api_key: ENV['POSTMARK_KEY'] }
```

16.6 Configuration

If your production server has `sendmail` installed, then Action Mailer will happily use it to send emails. If you don't, and you don't want to use a third-party email service, then you can try setting up Rails to send email directly via SMTP.

Lacking sendmail, Rails will try to send email via SMTP (port 25) of localhost. If you happen to be running Rails on a host that has an SMTP daemon running and it accepts SMTP email locally, you don't have to do anything else in order to send mail. If you don't have SMTP available on localhost, you have to decide how your system will send email.

Mail

The `ActionMailer::Base` class has a hash named `smtp_settings` that holds configuration information. The settings here will vary depending on the SMTP server that you use.

The sample code (shown in Listing 16.3) demonstrates the SMTP server settings that are available (and their default values). Perhaps you'll want to add similar code to your production environment:

Listing 16.3   SMTP settings for ActionMailer

```
ActionMailer::Base.smtp_settings = {
    address: 'smtp.yourserver.com', # default: localhost
    port: 25,# default: 25
    domain: 'yourserver.com', # default: localhost.localdomain
    user_name: 'user', # no default
    password: 'password', # no default
    authentication: :plain # :plain, :login or :cram_md5
}
```

Q. The vast majority of Rails applications rely on third-party SMTP services that specialize in delivering automated email, avoiding user spam filters and blacklists. The most popular email service providers in the world are Sendgrid, Postmark, and Mailgun. If you're already using Mailchimp (and you probably are, judging by their popularity) then their transactional email add-on, formerly named Mandrill, is another potential option.

16.7   Conclusion

In this chapter, we learned how Rails makes sending and receiving email easy. With relatively little code, you can set up your application to send out email, even HTML email with inline graphics attachments. Receiving email is even easier, except perhaps for setting up mail-processing scripts and cron jobs. We also briefly covered the configuration settings that go in your application's environment specific configuration related to mail.

CHAPTER 17

Caching and Performance

Watch me lean then watch me rock.

—Soulja Boy

Historically, Rails suffered from unfair criticisms over perceived weaknesses in scalability. The continued success of Rails in ultra high traffic usage at companies such as Groupon has made liars of the critics. It turns out that the raw CPU efficiency missing from Ruby is just not too much of a factor in IO-bound web applications. It is entirely possible to make your Rails application responsive and scalable with ease. Those mechanisms used to squeeze maximum performance out of your Rails apps are the subject of this chapter.

Much of that performance comes from view caching, letting you specify that anything from entire pages down to fragments of the page should be captured to disk as HTML files and sent along by your web server on future requests with minimal involvement from Rails itself. ETag support means that, in best-case scenarios, it's not even necessary to send any content at all back to the browser, beyond a couple of HTTP headers.

17.1 View Caching

Active View's templating system is both flexible and powerful. However, it is relatively slow, even in the best case scenarios. Sometimes, just rendering a page can consume 80% of the average request processing time.[1] Therefore, once you get the

---

1. http://www.appneta.com/blog/russian-doll-caching/

basic functionality of your app coded, it's worth doing a pass over your views and figuring out how to cache their content to achieve maximum performance.

Historically, there have been three types of view caching in Rails. As of Rails 4, two of those types, action and page caching, were extracted into officially supported, but separate, gems. Even though a consensus is emerging that "Russian-Doll" caching using fragment caching is enough, we briefly cover the other two methods here for the sake of completeness:

Page caching The output of an entire controller action is cached to disk, with no further involvement by the Rails dispatcher.

Action caching The output of an entire controller action is cached, but the Rails dispatcher is still involved in subsequent requests, and controller filters are executed.

Fragment caching Arbitrary reusable bits and pieces of your page's output are cached to prevent having to render them again in the future.

Knowing that your application will eventually require caching should influence your design decisions. Projects with optional authentication often have controller actions that are impossible to page or action-cache because they handle both login states internally.

Most of the time, you won't have too many pages with completely static content that can be cached using `caches_page` or `caches_action`, and that's where fragment caching comes into play. It's also the main reason that these two pieces of functionality were extracted out of core Rails.

🔍 For scalability reasons, you might be tempted to page cache skeleton markup or content that is common to all users, then use Ajax to subsequently modify the page. It works, but I can tell you from experience that it's difficult to develop and maintain and probably not worth the effort for most applications.

17.1.1   Page Caching

The simplest form of caching is page caching, triggered by use of the `caches_page` macro-style method in a controller. It tells Rails to capture the entire output of the request to disk so that it is served up directly by the web server on subsequent requests without the involvement of the dispatcher. On subsequent requests, nothing will be logged to the Rails log, nor will controller filters be triggered—absolutely nothing to do with Rails will happen, just like the static HTML that happens with files served from your project's `public` directory.

```
class HomepageController < ApplicationController
  caches_page :index

  def index
    ...
```

Beginning in Rails 4, if you want to use page caching then you need to add its gem to your Gemfile:

```
gem 'actionpack-page_caching'
```

Next, include the module and specify the folder in which to store cached pages in `ApplicationController`:

```
class ApplicationController < ActionController::Base
  include ActionController::Caching::Pages
  self.page_cache_directory = "#{Rails.root.to_s}/public/cache/pages"
end
```

For classic Rails behavior, you may set the `page_cache_directory` to the public root, but if you don't, then ensure that your webserver knows where to find cached versions.[2]

Sample Nginx/Puma configuration file with page caching enabled
```
upstream puma_server_domain_tld {
  server unix:/path/to/the/puma/socket;
}
server {
  listen 80;
  server_name domain.tld;
  root /path/to/the/app;
  location / {
    proxy_set_header X-Forwarded-For $proxy_add_x_forwarded_for;
    proxy_set_header Host $http_host;
    proxy_redirect off;
    # try the $uri, then the uri inside the cache folder, then the puma socket
    try_files $uri /page_cache/$uri /page_cache/$uri.html @puma;
  }
  location @puma{
    proxy_pass http://puma_server_domain_tld;
    break;
```

Caching

2. http://www.rubytutorial.io/page-caching-with-rails-4

```
  }
}
```

17.1.2   Action Caching

By definition, if there's anything that has to change on every request or specific to an end user's view of that page, page caching is not an option. On the other hand, if all we need to do is run some filters that check conditions before displaying the page requested, the `caches_action` method will work. It's almost like page caching, except that controller filters are executed prior to serving the cached HTML file. That gives you the option to do some extra processing, redirect, or even blow away the existing action cache and re-render if necessary.

As with page caching, this functionality has been extracted from Rails 4 and above, so you need to add the official action caching gem to your Gemfile in order to use it:

```
gem 'actionpack-action_caching'
```

Action caching is implemented with fragment caching (covered later in this chapter) and an `around_action` controller callback. The output of the cached action is keyed based on the current host and the path, which means that it will still work even with Rails applications serving multiple subdomains using a DNS wildcard. Also, different representations of the same resource, such as HTML and XML, are treated like separate requests and cached separately.

Listing 17.1 (like most of the listings in this chapter) is taken from a dead-simple blog application with public and private entries. On default requests, we run a filter that figures out whether the visitor is logged in and redirects them to the `public` action if not.

Listing 17.1   A controller that uses page and action caching
```
class EntriesController < ApplicationController
  before_action :check_logged_in, only: [:index]

  caches_page :public
  caches_action :index

  def public
    @entries = Entry.where(private: false).limit(10)
    render :index
  end

  def index
    @entries = Entry.limit(10)
  end
```

```
private

def check_logged_in
  redirect_to action: 'public' unless logged_in?
end

end
```

The `public` action displays only the public entries and is visible to anyone, which is what makes it a candidate for page caching. However, since it doesn't require its own template, we just call `render :index` explicitly at the end of the public action.

---

❶ Caching in Development Mode?

I wanted to mention up front that caching is disabled in development mode. If you want to play with caching during development for testing purposes, you can toggle it at the command line:

```
$ rails dev:cache Development mode is now being cached.
```

Additional information about this topic is available in Chapter 1's section about configuring cache settings.

17.1.3   Fragment Caching

Users are accustomed to all sorts of dynamic content on the page, and your application layout will be filled with things like welcome messages and notification counts. Fragment caching enables us to capture parts of the rendered page and serve them up on subsequent requests without needing to render their content again. The performance improvement is not quite as dramatic as with page or action caching, since the Rails dispatcher is still involved in serving the request, and often the database is still hit with requests. However, automatic key expiration means that "sweeping" old cached content is significantly easier than with page or action caching. And actually, the best way to use fragment caching is on top of a cache store like Memcached that'll automatically kick out old entries, meaning there's little to no sweeping required.[3]

17.1.3.1   The `cache` Method

Fragment caching is, by its very nature, something that you specify in your view template rather than at the controller level. You do so using the cache view helper method of the `ActionView::Helpers::CacheHelper` module. In addition

---

3. It's also possible to do the same with Redis. See http://antirez.com/post/redis-as-LRU-cache.html

to its optional parameters, the method takes a block, which enables you to easily wrap content that should be cached.

Once we log in to the sample application reflected in Listing 17.1, the header section should probably display information about the user, so action-caching the index page is out of the question. We'll remove the `caches_action` directive from the `EntriesController` but leave `cache_page` in place for the public action. Then we'll go into the `entries/index.html.haml` template and add fragment caching, as shown in Listing 17.2.

Listing 17.2   The index template with cache directive
```
%h1 #{@user.name}'s Journal
%ul.entries
  - cache do
    = render partial: 'entry', collection: @entries
```

Just like that, the HTML that renders the collection of entries is stored as a cached fragment associated with the entries page. Future requests will not need to re-render the entries. Here's what it looks like when Rails checks to see whether the content is already in the cache:

```
"get" "views/localhost:3000/entries/d57823a936b2ee781687c74c44e056a0"
```

The cache was not *warm* on the first request, so Rails renders the content and sets it into the cache for future use:

```
"setex" "views/localhost:3000/entries/d57823a936b2ee781687c74c44e056a0"
"5400" "\x04\bo: ActiveSupport::Cache::Entry\b:\x0b@valueI\"\x02\xbbf
<li class="entry">...
```

If you analyze the structure of the keys being sent to the cache (in this case Redis) you'll notice that they are composed of several distinct parts.

views/ Indicates that we are doing some view caching.

hostname/ The host and port serving up the content. Note that this doesn't break with virtual hostnames since the name of the server itself is used.

type/ In the case of our example it's `entries`, but that spot in the key would contain some indicator of the type of data being rendered. If you do not provide a specific key name, it will be set to the name of the controller serving up the content.

digest/ The remaining hexadecimal string is an MD5 hash of the template content, so that changing the content of the template *busts* the cache. This functionality (available in Rails 4 and beyond) eliminates the need for homebrewed template versioning schemes. Most template dependencies can be derived from calls to render in the template itself.[4]

⚠ Despite the nifty cache-busting behavior of adding template digests to your cache keys automatically, there are some situations where changes to the way you're generating markup will not bust the cache correctly. The primary case is when you have markup generated in a helper method, and you change the body of that helper method. The digest hash generated for templates that use that helper method will not change; they have no way of knowing to do so. There is no super elegant solution to this problem. Rails core suggests adding a comment to the template where the helper is used and modifying it whenever the behavior of the helper changes.[5]

17.1.3.2   Fragment Cache Keys

The cache method takes an optional name parameter that we left blank in Listing 17.2. That's an acceptable solution when there is only one cached fragment on a page. Usually there'll be more than one. Therefore, it's a good practice to identify the fragment in a way that will prevent collisions with other fragments whether they are on the same page or not. Listing 17.3 is an enhanced version of the entries page. Since this blog handles content for multiple users, we're keying the list of entries off the user object itself.

Listing 17.3   Enhanced version of the entries page

```
%h1 #{@user.name}'s Journal

- cache @user do
  %ul.entries
    = render partial: 'entry', collection: @entries

- content_for :sidebar do
  - cache [@user, :recent_comments] do
    = render partial: 'comment', collection: @recent_comments
```

Notice that we've also added recent comments in the sidebar and named those fragment cache accordingly to show how to namespace cache keys. Also note the use

---

4. https://github.com/rails/cache_digests#implicit-dependencies
5. https://github.com/rails/cache_digests#explicit-dependencies

of an array in place of a name or single object for those declarations, to create a *compound key*.

After the code in Listing 17.3 is rendered, there will be at least two fragments in the cache, keyed as follows:

```
views/users/1-20131126171127/1e4adb3067d5a7598ea1d0fd0f7b7ff1
views/users/1-20131126171127/recent_comments/1f440155af81f1358d8f97a099395802
```

Note that the recent comments are correctly identified with a suffix. We'll also add a suffix to the cache of entries, to make sure that we don't have future conflicts.

```
- cache [@user, :entries] do
  %ul.entries
    = render partial: 'entry', collection: @entries
  ...
```

17.1.3.3   Accounting for URL Parameters

Earlier versions of Rails transparently used elements of the page's URL to key fragments in the cache. It was an elegant solution to a somewhat difficult problem of caching pages that take parameters. Consider, for instance, what would happen if you added pagination, filtering, or sorting to your list of blog entries in our sample app: the cache directive would ignore the parameters because it's keying strictly on the identity of the user object. Therefore, we need to add any other relevant parameters to a compound key for that page content.

For example, let's expand our compound key for user entries by adding the page number requested:

```
- cache [@user, :entries, page: params[:page]] do
  %ul.entries
    = render partial: 'entry', collection: @entries
```

The key mechanism understands hashes as part of the compound key and adds their content using a slash delimiter.

```
views/users/1-20131126171127/entries/page/1/1e4adb3067d5a7598ea1d0fd0f7b7ff1
views/users/1-20131126171127/entries/page/2/1e4adb3067d5a7598ea1d0fd0f7b7ff1
views/users/1-20131126171127/entries/page/3/1e4adb3067d5a7598ea1d0fd0f7b7ff1
etc...
```

If your site is localized, you probably want to include the user's locale in the compound key so that you don't serve up the wrong languages to visitors from different places.

```
- cache [@user, :entries, locale: @user.locale, page: params[:page]] do
  %ul.entries
    = render partial: 'entry', collection: @entries
```

As you can tell, construction of cache keys can get complicated, and that's a lot of logic to be carrying around in our view templates. DRY up your code if necessary by extracting into a view helper and/or overriding the key object's cache_key method.

```
class User
  def cache_key
    [super, locale].join '-'
  end
```

---

❶ Object Keys

As you've seen in our examples so far, the cache method accepts objects, whether by themselves or in an array as its name parameter. When you do that, it'll call cache_key or to_param on the object provided to get a name for the fragment. By default, Active Record and Mongoid objects respond to cache_key with a dashed combination of their id and updated_at timestamp (if available).

17.1.3.4   Global Fragments

Sometimes, you'll want to fragment-cache content that is not specific to a single part of your application. To add globally keyed fragments to the cache, simply use the name parameter of the cache helper method, but give it a string identifier instead of an object or array.

In Listing 17.4, we cache the site stats partial for every user, using simply :site_stats as the key.

Listing 17.4   Caching the stats partial across the site
```
%h1 #{@user.name}'s Journal

- cache [@user, :entries, page: params[:page]] do
  %ul.entries
    = render partial: 'entry', collection: @entries

- content_for :sidebar do
  - cache(:site_stats) do
    = render partial: 'site_stats'
  ...
```

Caching

Now, requesting the page results in the following key being added to the cache:

```
views/site_stats/1e4adb3067d5a7598ea1d0fd0f7b7ff1
```

17.1.3.5   Relation Cache Keys

As of Rails 5, you have a new option for caching data originating with Active Record queries: `ActiveRecord::Relation` now has a `cache_key` method. Assume that our `Auction` class has a `live` scope, and use it as the object that we pass to the `cache` method. When `cache_key` is invoked on it, this is what the resulting key will look like:

```
>> Auction.live.all.cache_key
=> "auctions/query-c4b1ec1948b8f67ed32b36805-27-20160116111659084027"
```

auctions Identifies the table supplying the data.

query-\<hex-digest\> An MD5 hexadecimal digest of the SQL used to query the database.

27 The number of results returned from the database.

20160116111659084027 Timestamp of the newest record in the result set (based on the value of `:created_at` attribute).

While this technique is promising, there are some sharp edge-cases to take into account. First of all, because of the reliance on counting the number of results items, it doesn't work on relations that include a `limit` clause. Secondly, modifying one of the records doesn't necessarily invalidate the cache. For an in-depth discussion of the pitfalls and possible alternatives, as well as insight into how this particular cache key implementation will be fixed in future versions of Rails, see the discussion thread at https://github.com/rails/rails/pull/21503.

17.1.4   Russian-Doll Caching

If you nest calls to the `cache` method and provide objects as key names, you get a strategy referred to as "Russian-Doll" caching by David[6] and others.[7]

To take advantage of this strategy, let's update our example code, assuming that a user has many entries (and remembering that this is a simple blog application).

---

6. http://signalvnoise.com/posts/3113-how-key-based-cache-expiration-works

7. http://blog.remarkablelabs.com/2012/12/russian-doll-caching-cache-digests-rails-4-countdown-to-2013

Listing 17.5   Russian-doll nesting

```
%h1 #{@user.name}'s Journal

- cache [@user, :entries, page: params[:page]] do
  %ul.entries
    = render partial: 'entry', collection: @entries

- content_for :sidebar do
  - cache(:site_stats) do
    = render partial: 'site_stats'

# entries/_entry.html.haml

- cache entry do
  %li[entry]
    %p.content= entry.content
    ...
```

Now we retain fast performance even if the top-level cache is busted. For instance, adding a new entry would update the timestamp of the @user, but only the new entry has to be rendered. The rest of the content already exists as smaller fragments that are not invalid and can get reused.

Listing 17.6   Example of using touch to invalidate a parent record's cache key

```
class User < ActiveRecord::Base
  has_many :entries
end

class Entry < ActiveRecord::Base
  belongs_to: user, touch: true
end
```

For this to work correctly, there has to be a way for the parent object (@user in the case of the example) to be updated automatically when one of its dependent objects changes. That's where the touch functionality of Active Record and other object mapper libraries comes in, as demonstrated in Listing 17.6.

Outside of the Rails world, the Russian-Doll strategy is also known as *generational caching*.

> I have found that using this strategy can dramatically improve application performance and lessen database load considerably.
>
> It can save tons of expensive table scans from happening in the database. By sparing the database of these requests, other queries that do hit the database can be completed more quickly.

Caching

In order to maintain cache consistency this strategy is conservative in nature, this results in keys being expired that don't necessarily need to be expired. For example if you update a post in a particular category, this strategy will expire all the keys for all the categories. While this may seem somewhat inefficient and ripe for optimization, I've often found that most applications are so read-heavy that these types of optimization don't make a noticeable overall performance difference. Plus, the code to implement those optimizations then become application or model specific, and more difficult to maintain.

. . . in this strategy nothing is ever explicitly deleted from the cache. This has some implications with respect to the caching tool and eviction policy that you use. This strategy was designed to be used with caches that employ a Least Recently Used (LRU) eviction policy (like Memcached). An LRU policy will result in keys with the old generations being evicted first, which is precisely what you want. Other eviction policies can be used (e.g. FIFO) although they may not be as effective.[8]

Later in the chapter, we discuss how to configure Memcached as your application's cache.

David details an extreme form of Russian-Doll caching in his seminal blog post "How Basecamp Next got to be so damn fast without using much client-side UI" (http://signalvnoise.com/posts/3112-how-basecamp-next-got-to-be-so-damn-fast-without-using-much-client-side-ui). The level of detail he goes into is too much for this book, but we recommend his strategy of aggressively cached reuse of identical bits of markup in many different contexts of his app. CSS modifies the display of the underlying markup to fit its context properly.

17.1.5 Collection Caching

Starting with Rails 5, if you know ahead of time that you will be rendering a collection of objects that contain cached fragments, then you can explicitly tell Rails to grab all the data at once using `read_multi` instead of one at a time. You do that by adding `cached: true` to your collection rendering.

```
= render partial: 'entry', collection: @entries
```

Using this technique can speed up rendering significantly by avoiding what's known as an "N+1 select problem" in the database world. Some claim speed improvements of up to 76%.[9]

---

8. Jonathan Kupferman discussing web application caching strategies: http://www.regexprn.com/2011/06/web-application-caching-strategies_05.html

9. https://ninjasandrobots.com/rails-faster-partial-rendering-and-caching

You'll see this behavior reflected in the logs like this.

```
Rendered collection of entries/_entry.html.erb [20 / 20 cache hits] (219.5ms)
```

17.1.6   Conditional Caching

Rails provides `cache_if` and `cache_unless` convenience helpers that wrap the `cache` method and add a boolean parameter.

```
- cache_unless current_user.admin?, @expensive_stats_to_calculate do
  ...
```

17.1.7   Expiration of Cached Content

Whenever you use caching, you need to consider any and all situations that will cause the cache to become stale (out of date). As we've seen, so-called *generational caching* attempts to solve cache expiry by tying the keys to information about the versions of the underlying objects. But if you don't use generational caching, then you need to write code that manually sweeps away old cached content or makes it time-out, so that new content can be cached in its place.

17.1.7.1   Time-Based Expiry

The simplest strategy for cache invalidation is simply time-based, that is, tell the cache to automatically invalidate content after a set time period. All of the Rails cache providers (Memcached, Redis, etc.) accept an option for time-based expiry. Just add `:expires_in` to your fragment cache directive:

```
- cache @entry, expire_in: 2.hours do
  = render @post
```

We can tell you from experience that this kind of cache invalidation is only good for a narrow set of circumstances. Most of the time, you only want to invalidate when underlying data changes state.

17.1.7.2   Expiring Pages and Actions

The `expire_page` and `expire_action` controller methods let you explicitly delete content from the cache in your action, so that it is regenerated on the next request. There are various ways to identify the content to expire, but one of them is by passing a hash with `url_for` conventions used elsewhere in Rails. Given the esoteric nature of this topic, we leave it as a research exercise for the motivated reader.

17.1.7.3   Expiring Fragments

The sample blogging app we've been playing with has globally cached content to clear out, for which we'll be using the `expire_fragment` method.

```
def create
  @entry = @user.entries.build(params[:entry])
  if @entry.save
    expire_fragment(:site_stats)
    redirect_to entries_path(@entry)
  else
    render action: 'new'
  end
end
```

This isn't the greatest or most current Rails code in the world. All it's doing is showing you basic use of `expire_fragment`. Remember that the key you provide to `expire_fragment` needs to match the key you used to set the cache in the first place. The difficulty in maintaining this kind of code is the reason that key invalidation is considered one of the hardest problems in computer science!

Occasionally, you might want to blow away any cached content that references a particular bit of data. Luckily, the `expire_fragment` method also understands regular expressions. In the following example, we invalidate anything related to a particular user:

```
expire_fragment(%r{@user.cache_key})
```

> ⚠ The big gotcha with regular expressions and `expire_fragment` is that it is not supported for use with Memcached. However, in recent years more and more developers are choosing Redis as their cache store, since it's also used for queuing asynchronous jobs and other reasons. Redis does support regular expressions for expiration.

17.1.8   Automatic Cache Expiry with Sweepers

Since caching is a unique concern, it tends to feel like something that should be applied in an aspect-oriented fashion instead of procedurally.

A `Sweeper` class is kind of like an old-school Active Record `Observer` object, except that it's specialized for use in expiring cached content. When you write a sweeper, you tell it which of your models to observe for changes, just as you would with callback classes and observers.

> ℹ️ Remember that observers are no longer included in Rails by default, so if you need sweepers, you'll have to add the official observers gem to your Gemfile.

```
gem 'rails-observers'
```

Listing 17.7   Moving expiry logic out of controller into a Sweeper class
```
class EntrySweeper < ActionController::Caching::Sweeper
  observe Entry

  def expire_cached_content(entry)
    expire_page controller: 'entries', action: 'public'
    expire_fragment(:site_stats)
  end

  alias_method :after_commit, :expire_cached_content
  alias_method :after_destroy, :expire_cached_content

end
```

Once you have a `Sweeper` class written, you still have to tell your controller to use that sweeper in conjunction with its actions. Here's the top of the revised entries controller:

```
class EntriesController < ApplicationController
  caches_page :public
  cache_sweeper :entry_sweeper, only: [:create, :update, :destroy]
  ...
```

Like many other controller macros, the `cache_sweeper` method takes `:only` and `:except` options. There's no need to bother the sweeper for actions that can't modify the state of the application, so we do indeed include the `:only` option in our example.

17.1.9   Avoiding Extra Database Activity

Once you have fragments of your view cached, you might think to yourself that it no longer makes sense to do the database queries that supply those fragments with their data. After all, the results of those database queries will not be used again until the cached fragments are expired. The `fragment_exist?` method lets you check for the existence of cached content and takes the same parameters that you used with the associated `cache` method.

Here's how we would modify the index action accordingly:

```
def index
  unless fragment_exist? [@user, :entries, page: params[:page]]
    @entries = Entry.all.limit(10)
  end
end
```

Now the finder method will only get executed if the cache needs to be refreshed. However, as Tim pointed out in previous editions of this book, the whole issue is moot if you use Decent Exposure[10] to make data available to your views via methods, not instance variables. Because Decent Exposure method invocations are inside the templates instead of your controllers, inside the blocks passed to the `cache` method, the problem solves itself.

We actually disputed whether to even include this section in the current edition. Since view rendering is so much slower than database access, avoidance of database calls represents a minor additional optimization on top of the usual fragment caching. Meaning you should only have to worry about this if you're trying to squeeze every last bit of performance out of your application, and even then, we advise you to really think about it.

17.1.10   Cache Logging

If you've turned on caching during development, you can monitor the Rails console or development log for messages about caching and expiration.

```
Write fragment views/pages/52781671756e6bd2fa060000-20131110153647/
stats/1f440155af81f1358d8f97a099395802 (1.4ms)
Cache digest for pages/_page.html: 1f440155af81f1358d8f97a099395802
Read fragment views/pages/52781604756e6bd2fa050000-20131104214748/
stats/1f440155af81f1358d8f97a099395802 (0.3ms)
```

17.1.11   Cache Storage

You can set up your application's default cache store by calling `config.cache_store=` in the Application definition inside your `config/application.rb` file or in an environment specific configuration file. The first argument will be the cache store to use, and the rest of the argument will be passed as arguments to the cache store constructor.

---

10. https://github.com/voxdolo/decent_exposure

By default, Rails gives you three different options for storage of action and fragment cache data. Other options require installation of third-party gems.[11]

ActiveSupport::Cache::FileStore Keeps the fragments on disk in the `cache_path`, which works well for all types of environments (except Heroku) and shares the fragments for all the web server processes running off the same application directory.

ActiveSupport::Cache::MemoryStore Keeps fragments in process memory, in a threadsafe fashion. This store can potentially consume an unacceptable amount of memory if you do not limit it and implement a good expiration strategy. The cache store has a bounded size specified by the `:size` options to the initializer (default is `32.megabytes`). When the cache exceeds the allotted size, a cleanup will occur and the least recently used entries will be removed. Note that only small Rails applications that are deployed on a single process will ever benefit from this configuration.

ActiveSupport::Cache::MemCacheStore Keeps the fragments in a separate process using a proven cache server named `memcached`.

See Appendix B, "Active Support API Reference," "`Cache::Store`," for full documentation of caching methods included in Active Support.

17.1.11.1 Redis-Based Caching

The `redis-rails` gem provides a full set of stores (*Cache, Session, HTTP Cache*), but it's not a default part of Rails. To install, add the following to your Gemfile:

```
gem 'redis-rails'
```

Then configure the cache store to use `:redis_store` in an initializer or environment script.

```
config.cache_store = :redis_store, "redis://localhost:6379/0/cache",
        { expires_in: 90.minutes }
```

It's also possible to provide a hash instead of a URL.

```
config.cache_store = :redis_store, {
  host: "localhost",
  port: 6379,
  db: 0,
```

---

11. See http://edgeguides.rubyonrails.org/caching_with_rails.html#cache-stores for a full list of support cache providers, including Terracotta's Ehcache.

```
  password: "mysecret",
  namespace: "cache"
}
```

17.1.11.2   Configuration Examples

The `:memory_store` option is enabled by default. Unlike session data, which is limited in size, fragment-cached data can grow to be quite large, which means you almost certainly don't want to use this default option in production.

```
config.cache_store = :memory_store, expire_in: 1.minute, compress: true
config.cache_store = :file_store, "/path/to/cache/directory"
```

All cache stores take the following hash options as their last parameter:

expires_in Supply a time for items to be expired from the cache.

compress Specify whether to use compression or not.

compress_threshold Specify the threshold at which to compress, with the default being 16K.

namespace If your application shares a cache with others, this option can be used to create a namespace for it.

race_condition_ttl This option is used in conjunction with the `:expires_in` option on content that is accessed and updated heavily. It prevents multiple processes from trying to simultaneously repopulate the same key. The value of the option sets the number of seconds that an expired entry can be reused (be *stale*) while a new value is being regenerated.

17.1.11.3   Limitations of File-Based Storage

As long as you're hosting your Rails application on a single server, setting up caching is fairly straightforward and easy to implement (of course, coding it is a different story).

If you think about the implications of running a cached application on a cluster of distinct physical servers, you might realize that cache invalidation is going to be painful. Unless you set up the file storage to point at a shared filesystem such as NFS or GFS, it won't work.

17.2   Data Caching

Each of the caching mechanisms described in the previous section is actually using an implementation of an `ActiveSupport::Cache::Store`, covered in detail inside Appendix B, "Active Support API Reference."

Rails actually always exposes its default cache store via the `Rails.cache` method, and you can use it anywhere in your application or from the console:

```
>> Rails.cache.write(:color, :red)
=> true
>> Rails.cache.read :color
=> :red
```

17.2.1 Eliminating Extra Database Lookups

One of the most common patterns of simple cache usage is to eliminate database lookups for commonly accessed data, using the cache's `fetch` method. For the following example, assume that your application's user objects are queried very often by id. The `fetch` method takes a block that is executed and used to populate the cache when the lookup *misses*, that is, a value is not already present.

Listing 17.8   The fetch method
```
class User < ActiveRecord::Base
  def self.fetch(id)
    Rails.cache.fetch("user_#{id}") { User.find(id) }
  end

  def after_commit
    Rails.cache.write("user_#{id}", self)
  end

  def after_destroy
    Rails.cache.delete("city_#{id}")
  end
end
```

With relatively little effort, you could convert the code in Listing 17.8 into a `Concern` and include it wherever needed.

17.2.2 Initializing New Caches

We can also initialize a new cache directly or through `ActiveSupport::Cache.lookup_store` if we want to use different caches for different reasons. (Not that we recommend doing that.) Either one of these methods of creating a new cache takes the same expiration and compression options as mentioned previously, and the same three stores exist as for fragment caching: `FileStore`, `MemoryStore`, and `MemCacheStore`.

```
ActiveSupport::Cache::MemCacheStore.new(
  expire_in: 5.seconds
```

```
)
ActiveSupport::Cache.lookup_store(
  :mem_cache_store, compress: true
)
```

Once you have your cache object, you can read and write to it via its very simple API and any Ruby object that can be serialized can be cached, including nils.

```
cache = ActiveSupport::Cache::MemoryStore.new
cache.write(:name, "John Doe")
cache.fetch(:name) # => "John Doe"
```

17.2.3 **fetch** Options
There are several now-familiar options that can be passed to fetch in order to provide different types of behavior for each of the different stores. Options in addition to those listed here are available based on the individual cache implementations.

:compress Use compression for this request.

:expire_in Tell an individual key in the cache to expire in *n* seconds.

:force If set to true will force the cache to delete the supplied key.

:race_condition_ttl Supply seconds as an integer and a block. When an item in the cache is expired for less than the number of seconds, its time gets updated and its value is set to the result of the block.

There are other available functions on caches, and additional options can be passed depending on the specific cache store implementation.

delete(name, options) Delete a value for the key.

exist?(name, options) Will return true if a value exists for the provided key.

read(name,options) Get a value for the supplied key or return nil if none found.

read_multi(*names) Return the values for the supplied keys as a hash of key/value pairs.

write(name, value, options) Write a value to the cache.

17.3 Control of Web Caching
Action Controller offers a pair of methods for easily setting HTTP 1.1 Cache-Control headers. Their default behavior is to issue a *private* instruction, so that intermediate caches (web proxies) must not cache the response. In this context, *private* only controls where the response may be cached and not the privacy of the message content.

The `public` setting indicates that the response may be cached by any cache or proxy and should never be used in conjunction with data served up for *a particular end user.*

Using `curl --head` we can examine the way that these methods affect HTTP responses. For reference, let's examine the output of a normal index action.

```
$ curl --head localhost:3000/reports
HTTP/1.1 200 OK
Etag: "070a386229cd857a15b2f5cb2089b987"
Connection: Keep-Alive
Content-Type: text/html; charset=utf-8
Date: Wed, 15 Sep 2010 04:01:30 GMT
Server: WEBrick/1.3.1 (Ruby/1.8.7/2009-06-12)
X-Runtime: 0.032448
Content-Length: 0
Cache-Control: max-age=0, private, must-revalidate
Set-Cookie: ...124cc92; path=/; HttpOnly
```

Don't get confused by the content length being zero. That's only because `curl--head` issues a HEAD request. If you're experimenting with your own Rails app, try `curl -v localhost:3000` to see all the HTTP headers plus the body content.

17.3.1 `expires_in(seconds, options = )`
This method will overwrite an existing `Cache-Control` header.[12]

Examples include

```
expires_in 20.minutes
expires_in 3.hours, public: true
expires_in 3.hours, 'max-stale' => 5.hours, public: true
```

Setting expiration to 20 minutes alters our reference output as follows:

```
Cache-Control: max-age=1200, private
```

17.3.2 `expires_now`
Sets an HTTP 1.1 Cache-Control header of the response to `no-cache`, informing web proxies and browsers that they should not cache the response for subsequent requests.

---

12. See http://http://www.w3.org/Protocols/rfc2616/rfc2616-sec14.html#sec14.9 for more information.

17.4 ETags

The bulk of this chapter deals with caching content so that the server does less work than it would have to do otherwise but still incurs the cost of transporting page data to the browser. The *ETags* scheme, where E stands for *entity*, enables you to avoid sending any content to the browser at all if nothing has changed on the server since the last time a particular resource was requested. A properly implemented ETags scheme is one of the most significant performance improvements that can be implemented on a high traffic website.[13]

Rendering automatically inserts the Etag header on *200 OK* responses, calculated as an MD5 hash of the response body. If a subsequent request comes in that has a matching `Etag`,[14] the response will be changed to a *304 Not Modified*, and the response body will be set to an empty string.

The key to performance gains is to short circuit the controller action and prevent rendering if you know that the resulting `Etag` is going to be the same as the one associated with the current request. I believe you're actually being a good Internet citizen by paying attention to proper use of ETags in your application. According to RFC 2616,[15] "the preferred behavior for an HTTP/1.1 origin server is to send both a strong entity tag and a Last-Modified value."

Rails does not set a `Last-Modified` response header by default, so it's up to you to do so using one of the following methods.

17.4.1 `fresh_when(options)`

Sets `ETag` and/or `Last-Modified` headers and renders a `304 Not Modified` response if the request is already *fresh*. Freshness is calculated using the `cache_key` method of the object (or array of objects) passed as the `:etag` option.

For example, the following controller action shows a public article:

```
expose(:article)

def show
  fresh_when(etag: article,
             last_modified: article.created_at.utc,
             public: true)
end
```

---

13. Tim Bray wrote a now-classic blog post on the topic at http://www.tbray.org/ongoing/When/200x/2008/08/14/Rails-ETags.

14. http://www.w3.org/Protocols/rfc2616/rfc2616-sec14.html#sec14.19

15. http://www.w3.org/Protocols/rfc2616/rfc2616-sec13.html#sec13.3.4

This code will only render the show template when necessary. As you can tell, this is superior even to view caching because there is no need to check the server's cache, and data payload delivered to the brower is almost completely eliminated.

17.4.2 `stale?(options)`

Sets the ETag and/or Last-Modified headers on the response and checks them against the client request (using fresh_when). If the request doesn't match the options provided, the request is considered stale and should be generated from scratch.

You want to use this method instead of fresh_when if there is additional logic needed at the controller level in order to render your view.

```
expose(:article)

expose(:statistics) do
  article.really_expensive_operation_to_calculate_stats
end

def show
  if stale?(etag: article,
            last_modified: article.created_at.utc,
            public: true)
    # decent_exposure memoizes the result, later used by the view
    statistics()

    respond_to do |format|
      ...
    end
  end
end
```

The normal rendering workflow is only triggered inside of the stale? conditional if needed.

17.5   Conclusion

We've just covered a fairly complicated subject: caching. Knowing how to use caching will really save your bacon when you work on Rails applications that need to scale. Indeed, developers of high-traffic Rails websites tend to see Rails as a fancy HTML generation platform with which to create content ripe for caching.

CHAPTER 18

Background Processing

People count up the faults of those who keep them waiting.

—French Proverb

Users of modern websites have lofty expectations when it comes to application responsiveness—most likely they will expect behavior and speed similar to that of desktop applications. Proper user experience guidelines would dictate that no HTTP request/response cycle should take more than a second to execute. However, there will be actions that arise that simply cannot achieve this time constraint.

Tasks of this nature can range from simple, long running tasks due to network latency to more complex tasks that require heavy processing on the server. Examples of these actions could be sending an email or processing video, respectively. In these situations it is best to have the actions execute asynchronously, so that the responsiveness of the application remains swift while the procedures run.

In this chapter these types of tasks are referred to as background jobs. They include any execution that is handled in a separate process from the Rails application serving up responses to web requests.

Rails provides a framework for declaring jobs and making them run on a variety of queuing backends. It is called *Active Job*.

18.1 Active Job

The main point of the Active Job framework is to ensure that all Rails apps have a consistent job infrastructure in place. That way other Rails features and third-party gems have a standardized foundation to build upon, without worrying about API

617

differences between job runners implementations such as Delayed Job and Resque. (That was exactly the situation prior to the introduction of Active Job in Rails 4.2, and it was painful.)

Active Job works "out of the box" with a simple in-process thread pool. The main problem with it is that jobs in the queue will be dropped if the server is restarted. For more bulletproof operation, you'll want to use one of the background processing libraries covered later in the chapter. We'll be discussing the strengths and weaknesses of each one so that you can determine what is appropriate for your application. However, since the introduction of Active Job in Rails 4.2, this decision is more of an operational concern than anything else.

18.1.1   Creating a Job

This section describes how to create a job and place it in a queue for processing. Active Job objects can be defined by creating a class that inherits from the `Active-Job::Base class`. The only necessary method to implement is the `perform` method. However, most of the time you use a Rails generator to start from a boilerplate class.

18.1.2   Job Generator

Let's use that generator to create a job in `app/jobs`, along with a corresponding spec. The job of the job (ha!) will be to remove auctions that have ended more than an hour ago:

```
$ rails g job auctions_cleanup
  invoke rspec
  create spec/jobs/auctions_cleanup_job_spec.rb
  create app/jobs/auctions_cleanup_job.rb
```

Incidentally, we could have told the generator that job will run on a specific queue with the `--queue` command-line parameter, like this:

```
$ rails g job auctions_cleanup --queue urgent
```

If you don't provide a queue name, it ends up in a queue called simply `default`. Let's look at the Ruby class generated.

```
class AuctionsCleanupJob < ApplicationJob
  queue_as :default

  def perform(*args)
    # Do something later
```

```
    end
end
```

The signature of the `perform` method is totally up to you as the developer. For our cleanup job, we'll take a cutoff time and pass it to a service object that takes care of the actual work involved.

```
class AuctionsCleanupJob < ApplicationJob
  queue_as :default
  def perform(cutoff)
    ArchiveAuctions.concluded_older_than(cutoff)
  end
end
```

    🔍 It's always a good idea to minimize the business logic contained in job classes. Instead, give that responsibility to a model or service class that can be well-tested in isolation from the background processing machinery.

18.1.3   Enqueueing a Job

Now somewhere else in the codebase, or perhaps in a crontab, you'll enqueue the job for processing by the background library.

```
# Enqueue a job to be performed as soon as the queuing system is
# free.
AuctionsCleanupJob.perform_later 2.hours.ago
```

For those of you that are new to asynchronous processing, it's worth mentioning that the work won't actually be performed unless the *worker* processes (or threads, whatever the case may be) belonging to the background processing library, are actually running. If they're not, the job will just sit in its *queue* awaiting execution.

18.1.4   Delayed Execution

Calling `perform_later` immediately queues the job for execution. But what if we want to delay execution, perhaps to a time when the server is less busy? Call `set` first, like this:

```
# Enqueue a job to be performed at midnight
AuctionsCleanupJob
      .set(wait_until: Date.tomorrow.midnight)
      .perform_later(2.hours.ago)
```

We inserted a `set` method in the call chain. It has a number of options besides `wait_until`, listed next:

:wait Enqueues the job after a specified delay period has elapsed.

:wait_until Enqueues the job at the time specified.

:queue Enqueues the job on a specified queue. Make sure your queuing backend "listens" to the queue name you specify here. For some backends, you need to specify which queues the workers process.

:priority Enqueues the job with the specified priority. This is the first time we're mentioning priority so far in the chapter. It's simply an integer value that can be used by the underlying queue system (if supported) to prioritize jobs relative to each other.

18.1.5 Immediate Execution

It is possible to call the `perform_now` class method on a job to bypass the queuing system and execute the job code immediately in the same process. I find it useful for command-line and admin tools that bypass normal application workflow.

Here's an example of the `AuctionsCleanupJob` called from a Rake task:

```
namespace :auctions do
  task :archive_completed do
    AuctionsCleanupJob.perform_now(2.hours.ago)
  end
end
```

18.1.6 Callbacks / Hooks

Active Job provides lifecycle callbacks/hooks that can be used to add behavior to jobs and catch exceptions raised during execution. An example would be the automatic retrying of a failed job.

An example job that needs to retry itself automatically on failure and log some information before it started processing would appear as follows:

```
class NotificationJob < Application Job
  before_enqueue do |job|
    Logger.info "Starting Notification Job #{job.id}"
  end

  def perform(user_id)
    user = User.find(user_id)
    Notifier.send_notification_to(user)
  end
```

```
    rescue_from(ActiveRecord::RecordNotFound) do |exceptxion|
      # Do something with the exception
    end
end
```

18.1.7   Declarative Error Handling

You can declaratively handle error conditions using the `retry_on` and `discard_on` class methods of `ActiveJob::Base`.

```
class RemoteServiceJob < ActiveJob::Base
  retry_on CustomAppException # defaults to 3s wait, 5 attempts
  retry_on AnotherCustomAppException, wait: ->(executions) {executions *2 }
  retry_on ActiveRecord::Deadlocked, wait: 5.seconds, attempts: 3
  retry_on Net::OpenTimeout, wait: :exponentially_longer, attempts: 10
  discard_on ActiveJob::DeserializationError

  def perform(*args)
    # Might raise CustomAppException or AnotherCustomAppException
    # for something domain specific
    # Might raise ActiveRecord::Deadlocked when a local db
    # deadlock is detected
    # Might raise Net::OpenTimeout when the remote service is down
  end
end
```

18.1.7.1   `retry_on(ExceptionClass, wait: 5.seconds, attempts: 3)`

Declare that a particular exception should cause the job to retry automatically. Defaults to 3 attempts, 5 seconds apart. The values passed to the options can be lambdas or a symbol pointing to a private method, as in the preceding example.

18.1.7.2   `discard_on(ExceptionClass)`

Tells Active Job to not retry a job if a paticular exception is raised.

18.1.8   Integration with Action Mailer

One of the most common jobs in a modern web application is sending emails outside of the request-response cycle, so the user doesn't have to wait on it. Active Job is integrated with Action Mailer so you can easily send emails asynchronously:

```
# If you want to send the email now use #deliver_now
UserMailer.welcome(@user).deliver_now

# If you want to send the email through Active Job use #deliver_later
UserMailer.welcome(@user).deliver_later
```

18.1.9   GlobalID

Active Job supports GlobalID[1] for parameters. This makes it possible to pass model objects to your job instead of class/id pairs, which you then have to manually deserialize.

Before GlobalID jobs would look like this:

```
class TrashableCleanupJob < ApplicationJob
  def perform(trashable_class, trashable_id, depth)
    trashable = trashable_class.constantize.find(trashable_id)
    trashable.cleanup(depth)
  end
end
```

Ugh. Now you can simply do:

```
class TrashableCleanupJob < ApplicationJob
  def perform(trashable, depth)
    trashable.cleanup(depth)
  end
end
```

This technique works with any class that mixes in `GlobalID::Identification`, which is the case with Active Record models since Rails 4.2.

⚠ If a passed record is deleted after the job is enqueued but before the `perform` method is called, then Active Job will raise an `ActiveJob::DeserializationError`.

18.2   Queueing Backends

At the time of publication, Active Job has adapters for nearly a dozen queueing backend systems. We provide descriptions for a few of them in this chapter. An up-to-date list and feature comparison table should always be available online at http://api.rubyonrails.org/classes/ActiveJob/QueueAdapters.html.

18.2.1   Sucker Punch

Sucker Punch is a single-process Ruby asynchronous processing library, and it represents a step up from Rails' in-memory store. The fact that it shares the main server process reduces hosting costs on a service like Heroku.

---

1. https://github.com/rails/globalid

Sucker Punch is built on top of `concurrent-ruby`, which means it will only work with Ruby web servers designed to be concurrent. Nowadays, the most popular concurrent Ruby web server is [Puma].[2]

When using Sucker Punch, each job type gets its own queue (pool) with individual workers working to clear pending jobs. Unlike most other background processing libraries, Sucker Punch's jobs are stored in memory. The benefit is that there is no additional infrastructure requirement (i.e., database, redis, etc.). However, if the web processes are restarted with jobs remaining in the queue, those will be lost. Therefore, Sucker Punch is generally recommended for jobs that are fast and non-mission critical.

To use Sucker Punch, simply add it to your Gemfile:

```
gem 'sucker_punch'
```

Then configure the backend to use it in an initializer:

```
config.active_job.queue_adapter = :sucker_punch
```

That's literally all there is to it, which makes it the least complicated of the background processing libraries we describe in this chapter.

18.2.2 Sidekiq

Sidekiq (http://sidekiq.org) is a full-featured background processing library. Like Resque (covered later in this chapter), Sidekiq uses Redis for its storage engine, minimizing the overhead involved in job processing compared to other options.

Sidekiq is probably the best performing and memory efficient background processing library in the Ruby ecosystem. In fact over the last few years it has broken out into mainstream use even by developers working in Python, JavaScript and other worlds. It is also backed by a company that provides paid, enterprise-level support and a Pro version with advanced features.

Among its benefits, the primary one is that Sidekiq is natively multithreaded, which enables it to process jobs in parallel without the overhead of having to run multiple processes. It also means Sidekiq can process jobs with a much smaller memory footprint compared to other background processing libraries, such as Delayed Job or Resque.

⚠ Since Sidekiq is multithreaded, all code executed by Sidekiq should be threadsafe.

---

2. http://puma.io

To use Sidekiq, add it to your Gemfile:

```
gem 'sidekiq'
```

Then configure the backend to use it in an initializer:

```
config.active_job.queue_adapter = :sidekiq
```

Sidekiq depends on Redis and will assume by default that a Redis server can be found at `localhost:6379`. That's the usual situation in development and test modes, and even in smaller production deployments.

In larger production deployments, you're probably going to be running Redis on a different server. To override the location, add an initializer script that configures redis in both `Sidekiq.configure_server` and `Sidekiq.configure_client` code blocks.

```
# config/environments/production.rb

Sidekiq.configure_server do |config|
  config.redis = {
    url: 'redis://redis.example.com:6379/10',
    namespace: 'tr5w'
  }
end

Sidekiq.configure_client do |config|
  config.redis = {
    url: 'redis://redis.example.com:6379/10',
    namespace: 'tr5w'
  }
end
```

Note that setting the `:namespace` option is completely optional but highly recommended if Sidekiq is sharing access to a Redis database.

🗩 Juanito says . . .

Keep in mind that Sidekiq requires Redis 2.4 or greater.

18.2.2.1 Running Sidekiq Workers

To start up Sidekiq workers, run the `sidekiq` command from the root of your Rails application.

```
$ bundle exec sidekiq
```

This allows for starting a Sidekiq process that begins processing against the "default" queue. To use multiple queues, you can pass the name of a queue and and optional weight to the `sidekiq` command.

```
$ bundle exec sidekiq -q default -q critical,2
```

Queues have a weight of 1 by default. If a queue has a higher weight, it will be checked that many more times than a queue with a weight of 1. For instance, in the example above, the *critical* queue is checked twice as often as *default*.

Stopping jobs involves sending signals to the *sidekiq* process, which then takes the appropriate action on all processors:

TERM Signals that Sidekiq should shut down within the `-t` timeout option. Any jobs that are not completed within the timeout period are pushed back into Redis. These jobs are executed again once Sidekiq restarts. By default, the timeout period is 8 seconds.

USR1 Continues working on current jobs but stops accepting any new ones.

18.2.2.2   Concurrency

By default, Sidekiq starts up 25 concurrent processors. To explicitly set the number of processors for Sidekiq to use, pass the `-c` option to the `sidekiq` command.

```
$ bundle exec sidekiq -c 100
```

> ### ❶ Active Record Database Connections
> When using Sidekiq alongside Active Record, ensure that the Active Record connection pool setting `pool` is close or equal to the number of Sidekiq processors.
>
> ```
> production:
>   adapter: postgresql
>   database: example_production
>   pool: 25
> ```

18.2.2.3   `sidekiq.yml`

If you find yourself having to specify different options to the `sidekiq` command for multiple environments, you configure Sidekiq using a YAML file.

```
# config/sidekiq.yml
---
:concurrency:   10
```

```
:queues:
  - [default,  1]
  - [critical,  5]
staging:
  :concurrency:  25
production:
  :concurrency:  100
```

Now, when starting the `sidekiq` command, pass the path of `sidekiq.yml` to the `-C` option.

```
$ bundle exec sidekiq -e $RAILS_ENV -C config/sidekiq.yml
```

18.2.2.4   Error Handling

Sidekiq ships with support to notify the following exception notification services if an error occurs within a worker during processing:

- Airbrake

- Honeybadger

Other services, such as Sentry and New Relic, implement their own Sidekiq middleware that handles the reporting of errors. Installation usually involves adding a single `require` statement to a Rails initializer.

```
# config/initializers/sentry.rb
require 'raven/sidekiq'
```

18.2.2.5   Job ID

Active Job has its own Job ID, which means nothing to Sidekiq. In Rails 5 and later, you can get Sidekiq's JID by calling `provider_job_id` on a job instance, like this:

```
job = SomeJob.perform_later
jid = job.provider_job_id
```

18.2.2.6   Monitoring

When Resque was released, it set a precedent for Ruby background processing libraries by shipping with a web interface to monitor your queues and jobs. Sidekiq follows suit and also comes with a Sinatra application that can be run stand-alone or be mounted with your Rails application.

To run the web interface stand-alone, create a `config.ru` file and boot it with any Rack server:

```
require 'sidekiq'

Sidekiq.configure_client do |config|
  config.redis = { size: 1 }
end

require 'sidekiq/web'
run Sidekiq::Web
```

If you prefer to access the web interface within your Rails application, explicitly mount `Sidekiq::Web` to a path in your `config/routes.rb` file.

```
require 'sidekiq/web'

Rails.application.routes.draw do
  mount Sidekiq::Web => '/sidekiq'
  ...
end
```

Since the web interface is a Sinatra application, you will need to add the `sinatra` gem to your `Gemfile`.

```
# Gemfile
gem 'sinatra', '>= 1.3.0', require: nil
```

18.2.2.7   Summary

Sidekiq is highly recommended for any Rails application that has a large number of jobs. It's the fastest and most efficient background processing library available due to it being multithreaded.

With a Redis backend, Sidekiq does not suffer from the potential database locking issues that can arise when using Delayed Job and has significantly better performance with respect to queue management over both Delayed Job and Resque.

Note that Redis stores all of its data in memory, so if you are expecting a large number of jobs but do not have a significant amount of RAM to spare, you may need to look at a different framework.

18.2.3   Resque

Resque (https://github.com/resque/resque) is a background processing framework that supports multiple queues and, like Sidekiq, uses Redis for its persistent storage. Rather than threads, Resque uses a parent/child forking architecture, which

Background

makes its resource consumption predictable and easily managed. Resque also comes with a Sinatra web application to monitor the queues and jobs.

We recommend the use of Resque where a large number of jobs are in play at the same time and your code is not threadsafe. It does not support priority queueing but does support multiple queues, which is advantageous when jobs can be categorized together and given pools of workers to run them.

To use Resque, add it to your Gemfile:

```
gem 'resque'
```

Then add a `config/resque.yml` pointing to the location of your Redis instances:

```
development: localhost:6379
staging:     localhost:6379
production:  localhost:6379
```

Then configure the backend to use it in `config/initializers/resque.rb`:

```
config.active_job.queue_adapter = :resque

rails_env = ENV['RAILS_ENV'] || 'development'
config = YAML.load_file(Rails.root.join 'config','resque.yml')
Resque.redis = config[rails_env]
```

18.2.3.1 Worker Hooks

Because Resque is multi-process, it provides a number of worker hooks that you define in an initializer script. They are `before_first_fork`, `before_fork`, and `after_fork`. Before hooks are executed in the parent process, while after hooks execute in child processes. This is important to note since changes in the parent process will be permanent for the life of the worker, whereas changes in the child process will be lost when the job completes.

```
# Before the worker's first fork
Resque.before_first_fork do
  puts "Creating worker"
end

# Before every worker fork
Resque.before_fork do |job|
  puts "Forking worker"
end

# After every worker fork
Resque.after_fork do |job|
```

```
  puts "Child forked"
end
```

Worker hooks are primarily used for setting up shared resources. Those can include external connection pools, as well as mutexes, for operating on jobs that must be serialized.

18.2.3.2   Running Workers

Resque comes with two rake tasks that can be used to run workers, one to run a single worker for one or more queues, the second to run multiple workers. Configuration options are supplied as environment variables when running the tasks and enable defining the queue for the workers to monitor, logging verbosity, and the number of workers to start.

```
# Start 1 worker for the communications queue
$ QUEUE=communications rake environment resque:work

# Start 6 workers for the communications queue
$ QUEUE=communications COUNT=6 rake resque:workers

# Start 2 workers for all queues
$ QUEUE=* COUNT=2 rake resque:workers
```

Stopping jobs involves sending signals to the parent Resque workers, which then take the appropriate action on the child and themselves:

QUIT Waits for the forked child to finish processing, then exits.

TERM/INT Immediately kills the child process and exits.

USR1 Immediately kills the child process but leaves the parent worker running.

USR2 Finishes processing the child action, then waits for CONT before spawning another.

CONT Continues to start jobs again if it was halted by a USR2.

18.2.3.3   Monitoring

Just like Sidekiq, one of the really nice features of Resque is the web interface that it ships with for monitoring your queues and jobs. It can run stand-alone or be mounted with your Rails application.

To run stand-alone, simply run `resque-web` from the command line. If you prefer to access the web interface within your Rails application, explicitly mount an instance of `Resque::Server.new` to a path in your `config/routes.rb` file.

```
require "resque/server"

Rails.application.routes.draw do
  mount Resque::Server.new => '/resque'
  ...
end
```

18.2.3.4   Plugins

Resque has a strong plugin ecosystem to provide it with additional useful features. Most plugins are modules that are included in your job classes, only to be used on specific jobs that need the extra functionality. Plugins of note are listed next, and a complete list can be found at https://github.com/resque/ resque/wiki/plugins.

resque-scheduler A job scheduler built on top of Resque.

resque-throttle Restricts the frequency with which jobs are run.

resque-retry Adds configurable retry and exponential backoff behavior for failed jobs.

18.2.4   Que

Our favorite newcomer to the background processing arena is called Que. It claims to protect _your jobs with the same ACID guarantees as the rest of your data, which it accomplishes by putting its own data inside of Postgres along with the rest of your application data. I consider it a modern spiritual successor to the venerable Delayed Job, described later in the chapter.

Que uses advisory locks,[3] which gives it several advantages over other RDBMS-backed queues:

- **Concurrency**—Workers don't block each other when trying to lock jobs, as often occurs with "SELECT FOR UPDATE"–style locking. This allows for very high throughput with a large number of workers.

- **Efficiency**—Locks are held in memory, so locking a job doesn't incur a disk write. These first two points are what limit performance with other queues—all workers trying to lock jobs have to wait behind one that's persisting its UPDATE on a locked_at column to disk (and the disks of however many other servers your database is synchronously replicating to). Under heavy load, Que's bottleneck is CPU, not I/O.

---

3. http://www.postgresql.org/docs/current/static/explicit-locking.html#ADVISORY-LOCKS

- **Safety**—If a Ruby process dies, the jobs it's working won't be lost, or left in a locked or ambiguous state—they immediately become available for any other worker to pick up.

Additionally, there are the general benefits of storing jobs in Postgres, alongside the rest of your data, rather than in Redis or a dedicated queue:

- **Transactional Control**—Queue a job along with other changes to your database, and it'll commit or rollback with everything else. If you're using Active Record or Sequel, Que can piggyback on their connections, so setup is simple and jobs are protected by the transactions you're already using.

- **Atomic Backups**—Your jobs and data can be backed up together and restored as a snapshot. If your jobs relate to your data (and they usually do), there's no risk of jobs falling through the cracks during a recovery.

- **Fewer Dependencies**—If you're already using Postgres (and you probably should be), a separate queue is another moving part that can break.

- **Security**—Postgres' support for SSL connections keeps your data safe in transport, for added protection when you're running workers on cloud platforms that you can't completely control.

Que's primary goal is reliability. You should be able to leave your application running indefinitely without worrying about jobs being lost due to a lack of transactional support or left in limbo due to a crashing process. Que does everything it can to ensure that jobs you queue are performed exactly once (though the occasional repetition of a job can be impossible to avoid—see the Que docs on how to write a reliable job[4]).

Que's secondary goal is performance. It won't be able to match the speed or throughput of a dedicated queue, or maybe even a Redis-backed queue, but it should be fast enough for most use cases. In benchmarks of RDBMS queues[5] using PostgreSQL 9.3 on an AWS c3.8xlarge instance, Que approaches 10,000 jobs per second or about twenty times the throughput of DelayedJob.

Que also includes a worker pool, so that multiple threads can process jobs in the same process. It can even do this in the background of your web process—if you're running on Heroku, for example, you don't need to run a separate worker dyno.

Background

---

4. https://github.com/chanks/que/blob/master/docs/writing_reliable_jobs.md
5. https://github.com/chanks/queue-shootout

To install, add Que to your Gemfile:

```
gem 'que'
```

Bundle install, then generate and run a migration for the job table.

```
$ rails g que:install
$ rails db:migrate
```

⚠ If you're using Active Record to dump your database's schema, set your `schema_format` to `:sql` so that Que's table structure is managed correctly.

18.2.4.1 Related Projects

- que-web[6] is a Sinatra-based UI for inspecting your job queue.

- que-testing[7] enables making assertions on enqueued jobs.

- que-go[8] is a port of Que for the Go programming language. It uses the same table structure so that you can use the same job queue from Ruby and Go applications.

- wisper-que[9] adds support for Que to wisper (https://github.com/krisleech/wisper).

18.2.4.2 Caveats

Que's job table undergoes a lot of churn when it is under high load, and like any heavily written table, is susceptible to bloat and slowness if Postgres isn't able to clean it up. The most common cause of this is long-running transactions, so it's recommended to try to keep all transactions against the database housing Que's job table as short as possible. This is good advice to remember for any high-activity database but bears emphasizing when using tables that undergo a lot of writes.

18.2.5 Delayed Job

Delayed Job is a robust background processing library, extracted from Shopify.com back in 2008. It still works well in situations where the total number of jobs is low and the tasks they execute are not long running or consume large amounts of memory.

---

6. https://github.com/statianzo/que-web
7. https://github.com/statianzo/que-testing
8. https://github.com/bgentry/que-go
9. https://github.com/joevandyk/wisper-que

In contrast to `Sidekiq` and `Resque`, Delayed Job keeps its queues in a database along with the rest of your application data. Therefore, along with adding `delayed_job` to your Gemfile, you also need to add one of the following backend gems:

`delayed_job_active_record` Use the same database as Active Record.

`delayed_job_mongoid` Use Mongoid (to connect to MongoDB).

The Delayed Job wiki has a full list[10] of supported backends.

18.2.5.1   Getting Started

Run the Delayed Job generator to create your execution and migration scripts.

```
$ rails generate delayed_job:active_record
```

This will create a database migration that will need to be run to set up the `delayed_jobs` table in the database, as well as a command-line script to run Delayed Job workers.

To change the default settings for Delayed Job, first add a `delayed_job.rb` in your `config/initializers` directory. Options then can be configured by calling various methods on `Delayed::Worker`, which include settings for changing the behavior of the queue with respect to tries, timeouts, maximum run times, sleep delays, and other options.

```
Delayed::Worker.destroy_failed_jobs = false
Delayed::Worker.sleep_delay = 30
Delayed::Worker.max_attempts = 5
Delayed::Worker.max_run_time = 1.hour
Delayed::Worker.max_priority = 10
```

18.2.5.2   Running Workers

To start up Delayed Job workers, use the `delayed_job` command created by the generator. This enables starting a single worker or multiple workers on their own processes and also provides the capability to stop all workers.

```
# Start a single worker
RAILS_ENV=staging bin/delayed_job start

# Start multiple workers, each in a separate process
RAILS_ENV=production bin/delayed_job -n 4 start
```

Background

---

10. https://github.com/collectiveidea/delayed_job/wiki/Backends

```
# Stop all workers
RAILS_ENV=staging bin/delayed_job stop
```

💬 Durran says . . .

Delayed Job workers generally have a lifecycle that is equivalent to an application deployment. Because of this, their memory consumption grows over time and may eventually have high swap usage, causing workers to become unresponsive. A good practice is to have a monitoring tool like God or monit watching jobs and restarting them when their memory usage hits a certain point.

18.2.5.3 Caveats

Do note that if you are using Delayed Job with a relational database backend and have a large number of jobs, performance issues may arise due to the table locking the framework employs. Since jobs may have a long lifecycle, be wary of resource consumption due to workers not releasing memory once jobs are finished executing. Also where job execution can take a long period of time, higher priority jobs will still wait for the other jobs to complete before being processed. In these cases, using a non-relational backend, such as MongoDB or potentially another library such as Sidekiq, may be advisable.

18.3   Rails Runner

Rails comes with a built-in tool for running tasks independent of the web cycle. The `rails runner` command simply loads the default Rails environment and then executes some specified Ruby code. Popular uses include the following:

- Importing "batch" external data
- Executing any (class) method in your models
- Running intensive calculations, delivering emails in batches, or executing scheduled tasks

Usages involving `rails runner` that you should avoid at all costs are the following:

- Processing incoming email
- Tasks that take longer to run as your database grows

18.3.1   Getting Started

For example, let us suppose that you have a model called "Report." The Report
model has a class method called `generate_rankings`, which you can call from
the command line using

```
$ rails runner 'Report.generate_rankings'
```

Since we have access to all of Rails, we can even use the Active Record finder methods to extract data from our application.[11]

```
$ rails runner 'User.pluck(:email).each { |e| puts e }'
charles.quinn@highgroove.com
me@seebq.com
bill.gates@microsoft.com
obie@obiefernandez.com
```

This example demonstrates that we have access to the User model and are able to
execute arbitrary Rails code. In this case, we've collected some email addresses that
we can now spam to our heart's content. (Just kidding!)

18.3.2   Usage Notes

There are some things to remember when using `rails runner`. You must specify
the production environment using the `-e` option; otherwise, it defaults to development. The `rails runner` help option tells us:

```
$ rails runner -h

Usage: rails runner [options] ('Some.ruby(code)' or a filename)
    -e, --environment=name   Specifies the environment for the runner to
                             operate under (test/development/production).
                             Default: development
```

Using `rails runner`, we can easily script any batch operations that need to run
using cron or another system scheduler. For example, you might calculate the most
popular or highest-ranking product in your e-commerce application every few minutes or nightly, rather than make an expensive query on every request:

```
$ rails runner â€"e production 'Product.calculate_top_ranking'
```

A sample `crontab` to run that script might look like

```
0 */5 * * * root  /usr/local/bin/ruby \
/apps/exampledotcom/current/script/rails runner -e production \
'Product.calculate_top_ranking'
```

---

11. Be careful to escape any characters that have specific meaning to your shell.

The script will run every five hours to update the `Product` model's top rankings.

18.3.3   Considerations

On the positive side: It doesn't get any easier and there are no additional libraries to install. That's about it. As for negatives: The `rails runner` process loads the entire Rails environment. For some tasks, particularly short-lived ones, that can be quite wasteful of resources. Also, nothing prevents multiple copies of the same script from running simultaneously, which can be catastrophically bad, depending on the contents of the script.

● Wilson says . . .

Do not process incoming email with `rails runner`. It's a Denial of Service attack waiting to happen.

18.3.4   Summary

The Rails Runner is useful for short tasks that need to run infrequently, but jobs that require more heavy lifting, reporting, and robust failover mechanisms are best handled by other libraries.

18.4   Conclusion

Most web applications today will need to incorporate some form of asynchronous behavior, and we've covered some of the important libraries available when needing to implement background processing. There are many other frameworks and techniques available for handling this, so choose the solution that is right for your needs—just remember to never make your users wait.

CHAPTER 19

Asset Pipeline

It's not enough to solve the problem, we have to have the pleasure.

—DHH, RailsConf 2011 keynote

The Asset Pipeline is one of those Rails *magic* features that makes a developer's life so easy that once you master it you will never want to go back. It also significantly improves perceived performance of your application and reduces burdens on your application server. It's a huge win for Rails overall that nonetheless might make you want to tear your hair out and switch to (shudder) Django until you understand how it works. Persevere! We promise it's worth the learning curve. According to David, the Asset Pipeline was by far his favorite element of the Rails 3.1 release.

"Wait," you might ask, "what is an asset"?

It's simple—by "assets" we mean images, Javscript, CSS, and other static files that we need in order to properly render our pages.

Web applications built with early versions of Rails shared common problems with managing static assets. Before the Asset Pipeline, you just dumped all your JavaScript files into the `public/javascripts` directory, all your CSS files into `public/stylesheets` and your image files into `public/images` without any structure. Afterward, you could load all your Javscript files within your templates using the helper `<%= javascript_include_tag :all %>`. It completely ignored files in subdirectories of `public/javascripts`, so that if you wanted to organize your assets into subdirectories you had to manually load them into your layout. What a mess!

There were other inconveniences as well. For instance, if you wanted to load the files in a certain order, you had to replace the :all directive with a manually maintained list of "includes" in the exact order that you needed. When you wanted to use a library that came with JavaScript and CSS files (e.g., twitter bootstrap) you had to copy those files into your public directory and keep it under source control so that they will be available for the running application. Worse, you had to read the README files carefully to figure out just exactly what files you needed to copy and in which exact order you had to load them. Not fun.

19.1   Introduction to Asset Management

The major goal of the Asset Pipeline is to make management of static assets easy, even trivial. In this chapter, we discuss organization of assets, how can they be packaged into neat external gem dependencies, available asset pre-processors and compressors, helpers that assist us with the Asset Pipeline, and more.

Incidentally, automated asset management is not a new concept. It has existed since before the Rails era, and plugins to add this critical functionality to Rails began appearing many years ago. The most successful one is Sprockets, written primarily by Sam Stephenson of 37signals and Rails core team fame. Sprockets was eventually incorporated into Rails itself and is at the core of the Rails Asset Pipeline implementation.

✎ In Rails 4, the whole Asset Pipeline was extracted into a separate gem, "sprockets-rails," and can be removed from your application Gemfile to disable it.

Which features of asset management solutions would be most useful to us in building a Rails application?

For starters, we could **organize** the asset files into a sensible directory tree instead of "junk drawer" directories filled haphazardly.

We might also want to **compress** all our assets, so that they can be served faster to web browsers and eat up less bandwidth.

We could also **consolidate** multiple source files of the same kind (JavaScript or CSS) into single files, reducing the number of HTTP requests made by the browser and significantly improving page load times.

On the other hand, compressing and consolidating all those source files could make **debugging** during development a nightmare, so our wish list would also include the capability to turn those features off, except for production environments.

What else? To speed up page loading times even more, we might "pre-shrink" our asset files with the **maximum compression level**, so that our web server doesn't waste CPU cycles zipping up the same files over and over again on each request.

We would also want to include **cache-busting** features, giving us the capability to force expiration of stale assets from all cache layers (HTTP proxies, browsers, etc.) when their content changes.

Furthermore, we might want the capability totransparently **compile** languages such as CoffeeScript for JavaScript assets and Sass and Less for CSS stylesheets.

All the highlighted features in our wish list and more are part of the Asset Pipeline, making this aspect of Rails programming a lot more enjoyable than in earlier versions.

We could try to describe how the entire Asset Pipeline works at the high level now, but it would require too many forward references to stuff we haven't yet explained. Therefore we are going to build out our understanding from the bottom up. Keep in mind the overall goal: concatenating and serving asset files and "bundles" composed of multiple files, which can possibly be pre- and post-processed or compiled from different formats.

Now let's dive in.

19.2   Organization. Where Does Everything Go?

Asset Pipeline continues with the Rails tradition of separate directories for images, stylesheets and scripts but adds an additional dimension of organization. There are now three locations where you can store assets in your project directory. Those are `app/assets`, `lib/assets`, and `vendor/assets`.

This small change already gives us a much better way to organize the project files. Files specific to the current project go into `app/assets`, external libraries go into `vendor/assets`, and assets for your own libraries can go into `lib/assets`.

ℹ️ You can still put files into the `public` directory, and Rails will serve them same as before, with no processing.

Pipeline

You no longer need to copy the static assets bundled with your gems into your project directory. The Asset Pipeline will find them automatically and make them available for your application (more on this later).

19.3 Manifest Files

The organizational structure doesn't just involve new directories. If you look into the app/assets directory of a freshly generated Rails application, you'll notice a couple of files with include directives in them: app/assets/javascripts/application.js and app/assets/stylesheets/application.css. Those are called asset manifest files, and they specify instructions on where the pipeline processor can find other assets and in which order to load them. The loaded files are concatenated into a single "bundle" file named after the manifest.

Let's take a look at application.js:

```
// This is a manifest file that'll be compiled into application.js,
// which will include all the files listed below.
//
// Any JavaScript/Coffee file within this directory, lib/assets/
// javascripts, or any plugin's vendor/assets/javascripts
// directory can be referenced here using a relative path.
//
// It's not advisable to add code directly here, but if you do,
// it'll appear at the bottom of the compiled file. JavaScript code
// in this file should be added after the last require_* statement.
//
// Read Sprockets README (https://github.com/rails/
// sprockets#sprockets-directives) for details about supporteddirectives.
//
//= require rails-ujs
//= require turbolinks
//= require_tree
```

Let's also take a look at application.css:

```
/*
 * This is amanifest file that'll becompiled into application.css,
 * which will include all the files listed below.
 *
 *Any CSS and SCSS file within this directory, lib/assets/stylesheets,
 * vendor/assets/stylesheets, or vendor/assets/stylesheets of plugins,
 * if any,can be referenced here using a relative path.
 *
 * You're free to add application-wide styles to this file and they'll
 * appear at the top of the compiled file, but it's generally better
 * to create a new file per style scope.
```

```
 *
 *= require_self
 *= require_tree .
 */
```

A manifest is just a JavaScript or CSS file with a commented block at the beginning of the file that includes special directives in it that specify other files of the same format to concatenate in the exact order. Several comment formats are supported:

```
// This is a single line comment (JavaScript, SCSS)
//= require foo
```

```
/* This is a multi-line comment (CSS, SCSS, JavaScript)
 *= require foo
 */
```

```
# This is a single line comment too (CoffeeScript)
#= require foo
```

> ⚠ Note the equal signs at the beginning of the lines. If you skip those the directives won't work.

Make as many manifest files as you need. For example, the `admin.css` and `admin.js` manifest could contain the JS and CSS files that are used for the admin section of an application.

19.3.1   Manifest Directives

There are several manifest directives available:

require The most basic one. It concatenates the content of the referenced file you specify into the final packaged asset "bundle." It will only do it once, even if the same filename appears multiple times in the manifest, either directly or as a part of `require_tree` (see below).

include Just like `require` but will insert the file again if it appears in the manifest more than once.

require_self Inserts the content of the file itself (after the directives). This is often useful when you want to make sure that JavaScript code from a manifest comes before any other code that is loaded with `require_tree`. We see an example of that in the default `application.css`.

require_directory Will load all the files of the same format in the specified directory in an alphabetical order. It will skip files that were already loaded.

require_tree Just like `require_directory`, but it will also recursively load all the files in subdirectories as well. It will skip files that were already loaded as well.

depend_on Declares a dependency on a file without actually loading it into the "bundle." It can be useful to force Rails to recompile cached asset bundle in response to the change in this file, even if it is not concatenated into the bundle directly.

Directives are processed in the order they are read in the file, but when you use `require_tree` there is no guarantee of the order in which files will be included. If for dependency reasons you need to make sure of a certain order, just require those files explicitly.

19.3.2   Search Path

When you require an asset from a manifest file Rails searches for it in all directories in its search path. You do not need to specify file extensions. The processor assumes you are looking for files that match the type of the manifest file itself.

The search path includes all the directories that are **directly** under the default assets locations `app/assets`, `lib/assets`, and `vendor/assets` by default, meaning you can easily add other directories for new asset types to the list by creating them under any of the standard asset locations, e.g., `app/assets/fonts`.

Files in subdirectories can be accessed by using a relative path:

```
// this will load the app/assets/javascripts/library/foo.js
//= require 'library/foo'
```

The directories are traversed in the order that they appear in the search path. The first file with the required name "wins."

Note that all the directories in the search path are "equal," and can store files of any format. It means you can put your JavaScript files in `app/assets/stylesheets` and CSS files in `app/assets/javascripts`, and Rails will work just the same. But your fellow developers will probably stop talking to you.

19.3.3   Gemified Assets

As mentioned before, gems can contain assets, and there are gems that exist with the sole purpose of packaging asset files for Asset Pipeline.

To make gem assets available to an application the gem has to define an "engine" i.e., a class that inherits from `Rails::Engine`. Once "required" it will add `app/assets`, `lib/assets`, and `vendor/assets` directories from the gem to the search path.

Let's see the example from jquery-rails. You can find its engine in the `lib/jquery/ui/rails/engine.rb` file of the gem's source code:

```
module Jquery
  module Ui
    module Rails
      class Engine < ::Rails::Engine
      end
    end
  end
end
```

This Ruby file is loaded when you include this Gem into your application and as a result all the subdirectories of gem's `vendor/assets` directory are added to the search path.

19.3.4   Index Files

Index files make inclusion of "bundles" of files easy. If, for example, your Foobar library has a directory `lib/assets/foobar` with `index.js` file inside, Rails will recognize this file as a manifest and let you include the whole "bundle" with a single directive:

```
//= require 'foobar'
```

As with your Rails project, manifest files can encapsulate all the gem asset files and ensure proper load order without any additional effort on your part.

19.3.5   Format Handlers

Asset Pipeline is not called a pipeline for nothing. Source files go into one end, get processed and compiled (if necessary), concatenated and compressed, then come out of the other end of the pipeline as bundles. There are multiple stages that the source files go through while traversing the pipeline.

There are many format handlers available with Rails, with more available as third party gems. Some of them are compilers, like CoffeeScript, that compile one format into another. Others are more simple pre-processors like "Interpolated Strings" engine that performs Ruby substitution, e.g., #{...} regardless of the underlying format of the file so that it can process a CoffeeScript file before it will be compiled into JavaScript.

Before we continue with individual handlers, we should discuss the file naming scheme, because the file extensions used on an asset determine which handlers are invoked. Asset files that are intended for compilation/pre-processing can have more than one extension, concatenated one after the other.

When asked to serve products in a manifest, either explicitly or as part of a compound require directive, the Asset Pipeline constructs the output by iteratively processing the file from one format into the next. It starts with the processing corresponding to the rightmost file extension and continues until the requested leftmost extension format is obtained.

For example, let's dissect the processing of an asset source file named `products.css.sass.erb.str`.

The pipeline will first pass this file through an Interpolated Strings engine, then the ERb template engine, after which the result is treated as a Sass file. Sass files get compiled into normal CSS, which is in turn served to the browser as the final result.[1]

In case it wasn't obvious, the order in which you specify the file extensions is important. If you were to name a file foo.css.erb.sass, the first processor to get the file would be the Sass compiler, and it would blow up when it encountered ERb tags.

Naturally, for this entire scheme to work, pre-processors and/or compilers should be available for all the relevant formats. A wide swath of pre-processing power is provided to Rails by a gem named Tilt, a generic interface to multiple Ruby template engines.[2] The following table outlines the Tilt engines, file extensions, and required libraries.

Engine	File Extensions	Required Libraries
Asciidoctor	.ad, .adoc, .asciidoc	asciidoctor (>= 0.1.0)
ERb	erb, .rhtml	none (included ruby stdlib)
Interpolated String	.str	none (included ruby core)
Erubis	.erb, .rhtml, .erubis	erubis

---

1. We are ignoring post-processing for a moment.

2. For an up-to-date list of supported formats please refer to Tilt's README file. https://github.com/rtomayko/tilt

Engine	File Extensions	Required Libraries
Haml	.haml	haml
Sass	.sass	haml (< 3.1) or sass (>= 3.1)
Scss	.scss	haml (< 3.1) or sass (>= 3.1)
Less CSS	.less	less
Builder	.builder	builder
Liquid	.liquid	liquid
RDiscount	.markdown, .mkd, .md	rdiscount
Redcarpet	.markdown, .mkd, .md	redcarpet
BlueCloth	.markdown, .mkd, .md	bluecloth
Kramdown	.markdown, .mkd, .md	kramdown
Maruku	.markdown, .mkd, .md	maruku
RedCloth	.textile	redcloth
RDoc	.rdoc	rdoc
Radius	.radius	radius
Markaby	.mab	markaby
Nokogiri	.nokogiri	nokogiri
CoffeeScript	.coffee	coffee-script (+ javascript)
Creole (Wiki markup)	.wiki, .creole	creole
WikiCloth (Wiki markup)	.wiki, .mediawiki, .mw	wikicloth
Yajl	.yajl	yajl-ruby
CSV	.rcsv	none (Ruby >= 1.9), fastercsv (Ruby < 1.9)

🔍 Note that quite a few of the extensions recognized by Tilt have dependencies on gems that don't automatically come with Rails.

19.4 Custom Format Handlers

Even though Tilt provides quite a few formats, you might need to implement your own. Template handler classes have a simple interface. They define a class attribute named `default_handler` containing the desired MIME-type of the content and a class method with the signature call(template) that receives the template content and returns the processed result.

For example, here is the handler class from the Rabl[3] gem, used to generate JSON using templates.

```
module ActionView
    module Template::Handlers
      classRabl
        class_attribute :default_format
        self.default_format = Mime::JSON

        def self.call(template)
          # ommitted for clarity...
        end
      end
    end
  end
```

Note that by convention, template handlers are defined in the `ActionView::Template::Handle` module. Once your custom code is available to your application in the `lib` folder or as a gem, register it using the `register_template_handler` method, providing the extension to match, and the handler class:

```
ActionView::Template.register_template_handler :rabl,
        ActionView::Template::Handlers::Rabl
```

19.5   Post-Processing

In addition to pre-processing various formats into JavaScripts and stylesheets, the Asset Pipeline can also post-process the results. By default post-processing compressors are available for both stylesheets and JavaScripts.

19.5.1   Stylesheets

By default stylesheets are compressed using the YUI Compressor,[4] which is the only stylesheets compressor available out of the box with Rails.

You can control it by changing the `config.assets.css_compressor` configuration option, that is set to `yui` by default.

When using Sass in a Rails project, you could set the CSS compressor to use Sass' standard compressor with the `config.assets.css_compressor = :sass` option.

---

3. https://github.com/nesquena/rabl
4. http://yui.github.io/yuicompressor/css.html

19.5.2 JavaScripts

There are several JavaScript compression options available: `:closure`, `:uglifier`, and `:yui`, provided by `closure-compiler`, `uglifier`, or `yui-compressor` gems, respectively.

The `:uglifier` option is the default, but you can control it by changing the `config.assets.js_compressor` configuration option.

19.5.3 Custom Compressor

You can use a custom post-processor by defining a class with a `compress` method that accepts a string and assigning an instance of it to one of the configuration options above, like this:

```
class MyProcessor
  def compress(string)
    # dosomething
  end
end

config.assets.css_compressor = MyProcessor.new
```

19.6 Helpers

To link assets into your Rails templates, you use the same old helpers as always, `javascript_include_tag` and `stylesheet_link_tag`. Call these helpers in the `<head>` of your layout template, passing them the name of your manifest files.

```
<%=stylesheet_link_tag "application" %>
<%=javascript_include_tag "application" %>
```

One of the common frustrations of the Asset Pipeline learning curve is figuring out that you don't need to explicitly link to every asset file in your layout template anymore. Unless you break off large portions of assets for different parts of your app (most commonly, for admin sections) you'll just need one each for the `application.js` and `application.css` files. If you try to explicitly include or link to assets that are bundled up, your app will work in development mode where it's possible to serve up assets dynamically. However, it will break in production where assets must be precompiled. The bundled-up assets will simply not exist.

You'll know that you're running into this problem when you get the following error:

```
ActionView::Template::Error (foo.js isn't precompiled)
```

Pipeline

To fix this problem, make sure that `foo.js` is required in one of your manifest files, and get rid of the call to `javascript_include_tag "foo"`.

By default, Rails only seeks to precompile assets named "application." If you have a good reason to break off additional bundles of assets, like for the admin section of your app, tell the pipeline to precompile those bundles by adding the names of the manifest files to the `config.assets.precompile` array in `config/initializers/assets.rb`.

```
# Precompile additional assets.
# application.js, application.css, and all non-JS/CSS in app/assets
# folder are already added.
# Rails.application.config.assets.precompile += %w(search.js )
```

19.6.1   Images

The venerable `image_tag` helper knows to search the `asset/images` directory tree and not just the public folder. It will also search through the paths specified in the `config.assets.paths` setting in `config/initializers/assets.rb` and any additional paths added by gems.

```
# Add additional assets to the asset load path
# Rails.application.config.assets.paths << Emoji.images_path
```

     ✎ If you're passing user-supplied data to the `image_tag` helper, note that a blank or non-existent path will raise a server exception during processing of the template.

19.6.2   Getting the URL of an Asset File

The `asset_path` and `asset_url` helpers can be used if you need to generate the URL of an asset. But you'd need to make sure to include the `.erb` file extension at the rightmost position. For example, consider the following snippet of JavaScript taken from a file named `transitions.js.erb` which contains the line:

```
this.loadImage('<%= asset_path "noise.jpg" %>');
```

The Asset Pipeline runs the source through ERb processing first and interpolates in the correct path to the desired JPG file.

19.6.3   Built-in Sass Asset Path Helpers

Similarly, in a Sass stylesheet named `layout.css.scss.erb` you might have the following code, but you wouldn't for reasons that we'll explain momentarily:

```
header {
    background-image: url("<%= asset_path "header-photo-vert.jpg" %>");
}
```

Because this is such a common construct, Rails' Sass processing has built-in helpers, useful for referencing image, font, video, audio, and other stylesheet assets.

```
header {
    background-image: image-url("header-photo-vert.jpg");
}
```

Reusing a familiar pattern, `image-url("rails.png")` becomes `url(/assets/rails.png)` and `image-path("rails.png")` becomes `"/assets/rails.png"`. The more generic form can also be used, but the asset path and class must both be specified: `asset-url("rails.png", image)` becomes `url(/assets/rails.png)` and `asset-path("rails.png", image)` becomes `"/assets/rails.png"`.

19.6.4 Data URLs

You can easily embed the source of an image directly into a CSS file using the Data URL scheme[5] with the `asset_data_uri` method like this:

```
icon {
    background: url(<%= asset_data_uri 'icon.png' %>)
}
```

Many different kinds of content can be inlined using data URLs, although a full explanation of each is outside the scope of this book. Generally speaking, you want to keep the size of inlined data small to avoid blowing up the size of your CSS file.

19.7 Fingerprinting

In the past, Rails encoded and appended an asset's file timestamp to all asset paths like this:

```
<link href="/assets/foo.css?1385926153" media="screen" rel="stylesheet" />
```

This simple scheme enabled you to set a cache-expiration date for the asset far into the future, but still instantly invalidate it by updating the file. The updated timestamp changed the resulting URL, which busted the cache.

Pipeline

---

5. http://tools.ietf.org/html/rfc2397

Note that in order for this scheme to work correctly, all your application servers had to return the same timestamps. In other words, they needed to have their clocks synchronized. If one of them drifted out of sync, you would see different timestamps at random and the caching wouldn't work properly.

Another problem with the old approach was that it appended the timestamps as a query parameter. Not all cache implementations treat query parameters as parts of their cache key, leading to stale cache hits or no caching at all.

Yet another problem was that with many deployment methods, file timestamps would change on each deployment. This led to unnecessary cache invalidations after each production deploy.

The new Asset Pipeline drops the time stamping scheme and uses content fingerprinting instead. Fingerprinting makes the file name dependent on the files' content so that the filename only ever changes when the actual file content is changed.

It's worth knowing that these two lines

```
<%= javascript_include_tag "application" %>
<%= stylesheet_link_tag "application" %>
```

will look like this in production:

```
<script src="/assets/application-908e25f4bf641868d8683022a5b62f54.js">
</script>
<link
  href="/assets/application-4dd5b109ee3439da54f5bdfd78a80473.css"
  media="screen" rel="stylesheet"></link>
```

In the rare case that you want to invalidate all your assets at the same time, you can take advantage of the fact that Rails uses a version identifier as part of the configuration of its fingerprinting algorithm. The version string is stored in `config/initializers/assets.rb`.

```
#Version of your assets, change this if you want to expire all your
        assets. Rails.application.config.assets.version = '1.0'
```

19.8   Serving the Files

To take full advantage of asset fingerprinting provided by the Asset Pipeline, you should configure your web server to set headers on your precompiled assets to a far-future expiration date. With cache headers in place, a client will only request an asset once until either the filename changes or the cache has expired.

Here's an example for Apache:

```
# The Expires* directives requires the Apache module `mod_expires` to be enabled.
<Location /assets/>
  # Use of ETag is discouraged when Last-Modified is present
  Header unset ETag
  FileETag None
  # RFC says only cache for 1 year
  ExpiresActive On
  ExpiresDefault "access plus 1 year"
</Location>
```

And here's one for Nginx:

```
location ~ ^/assets/ {
  expires 1y;
  add_header Cache-Control public;
  add_header  Last-Modified "";
  add_header ETag "";
  break;
}
```

The fingerprinting feature is controlled by the `config.assets.digest` Rails setting. By default it is only set in the "production" environment.

> Note that the Asset Pipeline always makes copies of non-fingerprinted asset files available in the same `/assets` directory.

19.8.1 Configuration Settings

Default configuration of your Asset Pipeline settings lives in a boilerplate-generated script in `config/initializers/assets.rb`.

The first standard setting `assets.version` enables you to expire cached assets associated with the frontend of your application, all at once, in one fell swoop. It consists of a version number used as a salt in the fingerprinting of your project's asset URLs.

```
# Version of your assets, change this if you want to expire all your assets.
Rails.application.config.assets.version = '1.0'
```

It's rare to need to change this setting but very useful if you do.

The next setting is the `asset.paths` array.

```
# Add additional assets to the asset load path
# Rails.application.config.assets.paths << Emoji.images_path
```

Pipeline

It is an array of directory names that serve as the search path for asset helper methods. By modifying it you can add your own paths to the list.

```
config.assets.paths << Rails.root.join("app", "react", "assets")
```

Finally, there is a setting for adding additional asset configurations beyond the default `application`. This is theoretically useful in scenarios where you want to create deployable packages of assets that are either a subset or completely apart from your primary application bundle.

```
# Precompileadditional assets.
# application.js, application.css, and all non-JS/CSS in app/assets
# folder are already added.
# Rails.application.config.assets.precompile += %w(search.js )
```

19.8.2   Who Delivers the Assets?

In development mode, assets are served through a middleware called Sprockets. That's not necessarily the case in production since many Rails deployments live behind a reverse HTTP proxy server such as Nginx or Apache. Those servers both serve as load balancers for pools of Rails application server instances and serve static files directly. In other words, when Nginx sees a request for an asset such as `/assets/rails.png` it will grab it from disk at `/public/assets/rails.png` and serve it directly. The Rails server will never see these requests.

The configuration settings that control that behavior exist in `config/environments/production.rb`.

```
# Disable serving static files from the `/public` folder by default since
# Apache or NGINX already handles this.
config.public_file_server.enabled = ENV['RAILS_SERVE_STATIC_FILES'].present?

# Specifies the header that your server uses for sending files.
# config.action_dispatch.x_sendfile_header = "X-Sendfile" # for apache
# config.action_dispatch.x_sendfile_header = 'X-Accel-Redirect' # for nginx
```

As you can see, whether or not Rails serves static files is determined by the `RAILS_SERVE_STATIC_FILES` environment variable.

A modern approach to hosting Rails applications adheres to something called the twelve-factor app standard.[6] One of its tenets is to minimize the divergence between development and production environments. Heroku is perfect for twelve-factor apps in this regard, because it handles load-balancing requests to your Rails application at

---

6. https://12factor.net

its own HTTP-level routing layer, separate from your application. That means a production Rails application on Heroku can just handle requests for static assets directly. The same goes for Rails applications that live behind an edge caching CDN (Content Delivery Network) such as CloudFlare. Doing so is generally recommended, especially for consumer-facing applications.

19.8.3   GZip Compression

If you've been poking around the files generated by the Asset Pipeline, you may have noticed that it also generates full-compression gzipped versions of its output files. (Alongside `/assets/application.css`, there is also `/assets/application.css.gz`.) The benefit of doing it during the pre-compilation process and not on-the-fly is that it only happens once, enabling the use of the maximum compression level to minimize file size and minimizing CPU load on the server.

That said, it takes some configuration on the web server to enable serving up those pre-compressed files.

As an example, for Nginx you should add `gzip_static on;` to the configuration:

```
location ~ ^/assets/ {
  expires      1y;
  add_header   Cache-Control public;
  add_header   Last-Modified "";
  add_header   ETag "";
  gzip_static on;
  break;
}
```

19.9   Rake Tasks

Rails production mode expects all manifests and asset files to be precompiled on disk and available to be served up out of the location specified in `config.assets.prefix` setting, which defaults to `public/assets`.

   ⚲ Compiled asset files should never be versioned in source control, and the default `.gitignore` file for Rails includes a line for `public/assets/*`.

As part of deploying your application to production, you'll call the following rake task to create compiled versions of your assets directly on the server:

```
$ RAILS_ENV=production bundle exec rake assets:precompile
```

Pipeline

Note that cloud-platforms such as Heroku automatically do this step for you in such a way that is compatible with their otherwise read-only file system. However, Heroku also prevents your Rails application from being initialized as part of asset pre-compilation, and certain references to objects or methods will not be available, causing the compile process to fail. To catch these errors, pre-compile assets on your development machine and note any issues that crop up. Just be aware that local pre-compilation will result in the creation of a bunch of asset files in your `/public/assets` directory. Those can and will be served up instead of the Asset Pipeline being invoked, even in development mode. If you're scratching your head wondering why changes to your JavaScript and CSS files are not being reflected in your browser, then you probably need to delete pre-compiled assets. Use the `rake assets:clobber` task to get rid of them easily.

> The official Asset Pipeline guide[7] goes into great detail about using pre-compiled assets with development mode or even setting up Rails to compile assets on the fly. It's rare that you would want or need to do either.

19.10 Yarn

We've talked a lot in this chapter about how assets are served up from the server to the browser, but we neglected to mention anything about how you procure those assets in the first place. That's because until now, including JavaScript libraries as part of your application has been an exercise in patience and unclear decision making. Sometimes you copied files into the `/vendor/assets/javascripts` directory tree. Other times you declared a `gemified` version in your Gemfile. The uncertainty goes away in Rails 5.1 with the introduction of Yarn.[8]

As a Rubyist, it would be fair for you to think of Yarn as *Bundler for JavaScript*. (In fact, Yehuda Katz, the creator of Bundler, is part of the Yarn team.) In contrast to its older, more popular cousin NPM, Yarn uses a detailed lock file format and deterministic algorithm for installs to guarantee that an install that worked on one system will work exactly the same way on any other system.

Yarn has a lot of features, but the main one we care about in Rails is using it to download and lock JavaScript library packages. Most packages will be installed from then npm registry and referred to by simply their package name. For example, `yarn add react` will install the react package from then npm registry.

---

7. http://guides.rubyonrails.org/asset_pipeline.html#local-precompilation
8. https://yarnpkg.com

If you're using Yarn for the first time, you'll need to install its executable first.

```
$ brew install yarn
```

Note that Yarn requires and will install Node as a dependency, which can take quite a bit of time (10-20 minutes or longer).

As an example, I'll use it to grab a copy of Bootstrap for my Choons Click project:

```
$ yarn add bootstrap@4.0.0-alpha.6
yarn add v0.24.6
[1/4] ðŸ"◇  Resolving packages...
[2/4] ðŸšš  Fetching packages...
[3/4] ðŸ"—  Linking dependencies...
[4/4] ðŸ"ƒ  Building fresh packages...
success Saved lockfile.
success Saved 3 new dependencies.
â"œâ"€  bootstrap@4.0.0-alpha.6
â"œâ"€  jquery@3.2.1
â""â"€  tether@1.4.0
âœ¨      Done in 1.75s.
```

Note that a specific version of a package can be requested using the @ symbol.

After adding a package using Yarn, your Rails project will contain a `/node_modules` directory. If you're trying to use Yarn on a version of Rails older than 5.1, you'll have to add that directory to the asset load path yourself. The directive goes in `config/initializers/assets.rb`:

```
# Add Yarn node_modules folder to the asset load path.
Rails.application.config.assets.paths << Rails.root.join('node_modules')
```

Now, what's left is to reference our freshly downloaded bootstrap package in the Asset Pipeline.

```
# In app/assets/stylesheets/application.css:
*= require bootstrap/dist/css/bootstrap
```

```
# In app/assets/javascripts/application.js:
//= require bootstrap/dist/js/bootstrap
```

When I try to use some Bootstrap functionality in my app, I spot the following error message in my browser console.

```
Uncaught Error: Bootstrap's JavaScript requires jQuery. jQuery
        must be included before Bootstrap's JavaScript.
```

> Isn't jQuery included in Rails? It used to be, but was dropped in Rails 5.1 when UJS was reimplemented using *vanilla JavaScript*.

I'll fix the error with additional lines in the Asset Pipeline manifests

```{lang=ruby,linenos=off}
# In app/assets/stylesheets/application.css:
*= require bootstrap/dist/css/bootstrap
*= require tether/dist/css/tether

# In app/assets/javascripts/application.js:
//= require tether/dist/js/tether
//= require jquery/dist/jquery
//= require bootstrap/dist/js/bootstrap
```

19.11 Webpack

What we didn't cover at all in this chapter (on purpose, because it is a complex topic), are viable alternatives to the Asset Pipeline, of which there are at least a few. I felt like it would be negligent at this point in Rails history to neglect mentioning that the primary competitor to the Asset Pipeline is a wonderful piece of JavaScript software called Webpack.[9]

As opposed to declaring dependencies in external manifest files, Webpack enables you to declare dependencies inside of each component. This style is closer to what we would associate with normal general-purpose computing in languages such as Ruby. Webpack is able to understand `require` statements inside of your JavaScript and CSS files and figure out dependency graphs in order to create deployable asset bundles. This functionality is extremely useful for applications that have rich-client front ends and want to treat JavaScript as a first-class citizen in their project.

For a comical and extremely long detailed write up on the subject, check out this blog post by the incomparable Giles Bowkett: http://gilesbowkett.blogspot .com/2016/10/let-asset-pipeline-die.html.

In Rails 5.1 it is easy to use Webpack *together with* the Asset Pipeline, via the web-packer gem,[10] officially supported and maintained by Rails core team.

---

9. http://webpack.github.io/
10. https://github.com/rails/webpacker

You can either add Webpacker during setup of a new Rails 5.1+ application using new --webpack option:

```
# Available Rails 5.1+
rails newmyapp --webpack
```

Or you can add it to your Gemfile, run bundle and rails webpacker:install, which is what I'll do right now with my Choons Click project.

```
# Gemfile
gem 'webpacker', '~> 2.0'
```

If you're following along with your own project, get ready for a lot of console action.

```
$ rails webpacker:install
      create  config/webpacker.yml
Copying webpack core config and loaders
      create  config/webpack
      create  config/webpack/configuration.js
      create  config/webpack/development.js
      create  config/webpack/production.js
      create  config/webpack/shared.js
      create  config/webpack/test.js
      create  config/webpack/loaders
      create  config/webpack/loaders/assets.js
      create  config/webpack/loaders/babel.js
      create  config/webpack/loaders/coffee.js
      create  config/webpack/loaders/erb.js
      create  config/webpack/loaders/sass.js
Copying .postcssrc.yml to app root directory
      create  .postcssrc.yml
Copying .babelrc to app root directory
      create  .babelrc
Creating javascript app source directory
      create  app/javascript
      create  app/javascript/packs/application.js
Copying binstubs
       exist  bin
      create  bin/webpack-dev-server
      create  bin/webpack
      append  .gitignore
Installing all JavaScript dependencies
         run  yarn add webpack webpack-merge js-yaml path-
      complete-extname webpack-manifest-plugin babel-loader@7.x
      coffee-loader coffee-script babel-core babel-preset-env
```

```
            babel-polyfill compression-webpack-plugin rails-
            erb-loader glob extract-text-webpack-plugin node-
            sass file-loader sass-loader css-loader style-loader
            postcss-loader autoprefixer postcss-smart-import precss
            resolve-url-loader babel-plugin-syntax-dynamic-import
            babel-plugin-transform-class-properties from "."
yarn add v0.24.6
[1/4] ðŸ”◈}  Resolving packages...
warning precss > postcss-partial-import > fs-promise@0.3.1: Use
            mz or fs-extra^3.0 with Promise Support
[2/4] ðŸšš  Fetching packages...
[3/4] ðŸ"─  Linking dependencies...
warning "rails-erb-loader@5.0.2" has incorrect peer dependency "webpack@2".
warning "extract-text-webpack-plugin@2.1.2" has incorrect peer
            dependency "webpack@^2.2.0".
[4/4] ðŸ"ƒ  Building fresh packages...
success Saved lockfile.
success Saved 605 new dependencies.
â"œâ"€ abbrev@1.1.0
[... over 600 dependencies snipped for brevity]
â""â"€ yargs@6.6.0
âœ¨  Done in 52.03s.
Installing dev server for live reloading
            run  yarn add --dev webpack-dev-server from "."
yarn add v0.24.6
[1/4] ðŸ"◈  Resolving packages...
[2/4] ðŸšš  Fetching packages...
[3/4] ðŸ"─  Linking dependencies...
warning "extract-text-webpack-plugin@2.1.2" has incorrect peer
            dependency "webpack@^2.2.0".
warning "rails-erb-loader@5.0.2" has incorrect peer dependency
            "webpack@2".
warning "webpack-dev-server@2.5.0" has incorrect peer dependency
            "webpack@^2.2.0".
[4/4] ðŸ"ƒ  Building fresh packages...
success Saved lockfile.
success Saved 104 new dependencies.
â"œâ"€ accepts@1.3.3
[... over 100 dependencies snipped for brevity]
â""â"€ websocket-extensions@0.1.1
âœ¨   Done in 10.77s.
Webpacker successfully installed ðŸŽ‰ ðŸ◈°
```

The /node_modules directory tree will end up with hundreds of JavaScript source package directories in it, which bloats your project size and makes it a little more annoying to search for stuff (unless you exclude node_modules, the search space grows an order of magnitude or two larger than usual).

19.11.1   Webpack executables

Webpacker ships with two binstubs: `./bin/webpack` and `./bin/webpack -dev-server`. Both are thin wrappers around the standard webpack executables to ensure that the right configuration file and environment variables are loaded based on your environment.

In development, you'll need to run `webpack-dev-server` in a separate terminal from `rails server` to have your `app/javascript/packs/*.js` files compiled as you make changes.

The `webpack-dev-server` executable launches the Webpack Dev Server, which serves your pack files on `http://localhost:8080/` by default and supports live code reloading in the development environment.

My recommendation is to run the two processes together in one terminal using Foreman. Just add the webpacker process to your `Procfile` like this:

```
# Procfile
web: bundle exec rails s
webpacker: ./bin/webpack-dev-server
```

Remember that Foreman runs your Rails server on port 5000 instead of 3000.

19.11.2   Linking to Webpack Processed Files in Your Application

The `webpacker` gem introduces a view helper called `javascript_pack_tag`, which you can use similarly to `javascript_include_tag` in your layout:

```
!!!
%html
  %head
    %meta{:content => "text/html; charset=UTF-8", "http-equiv" =>
        "Content-Type"}/
    %title ChoonsClick
    = csrf_meta_tags
    = stylesheet_link_tag    'application', media: 'all', 'data
        -turbolinks-track': 'reload'
    = javascript_include_tag 'application', 'data-turbolinks-track': 'reload'
    = javascript_pack_tag 'application'
  %body
    = yield
```

Pipeline

Webpack also extracts all the referenced CSS stylesheets within your app and compiles them into separate [pack_name].css bundles so that in your views you can use a `stylesheet_pack_tag` helper method to link them.

```
= stylesheet_pack_tag 'hello_react'
```

In similar fashion, you can link to images, fonts, and any other asset you want to link to in your views from `app/javascript` using `asset_pack_path` helper method.

> Detailing everything you can do with Webpack in Rails would take at least a chapter, probably a small book, and this book is big enough already. Your first stop on the journey to learning how to use this exciting new technology in Rails should be the Webpacker gem readme at https://github.com/rails/webpacker.

19.12 Conclusion

The Asset Pipeline is an important part of making Ruby on Rails a productive web framework. In this chapter, we've covered the major aspects of working with the Asset Pipeline and how to configure it for production. We've also introduced you to Yarn and Webpack, two technologies that are keeping Rails current in a world that is increasingly dependent on large JavaScript components.

CHAPTER 20

Ajax on Rails

Ajax isn't a technology. It's really several technologies, each flourishing in its own right, coming together in powerful new ways.

—Jesse J. Garrett, who coined the name AJAX

Ajax is an acronym that stands for Asynchronous JavaScript and XML. It encompasses techniques that enable us to liven up web pages with behaviors that happen outside the normal HTTP request life-cycle (without a page refresh).

Some example use-cases for Ajax techniques are

- "Type ahead" input suggestion, as in Google search.
- Sending form data asynchronously.
- Seamless navigation of web-presented maps, as in Google Maps.
- Dynamically updated lists and tables, as in Gmail and other web-based email services.
- Web-based spreadsheets.
- Forms that allow in-place editing.
- Live preview of formatted writing alongside a text input.

Ajax is made possible by the `XMLHttpRequestObject` (or XHR for short), an API that is available in all modern browsers. It enables JavaScript code on the browser to exchange data with the server and use it to change the user interface of your application on the fly, without needing a page refresh.

661

Incidentally, Ajax, especially in Rails, has very little to do with XML, despite its presence there at the end of the acronym. By default Rails does not even include XML parsing capabilities. The payload of asynchronous requests can be anything. Often they are simply form parameters exchanged for snippets of HTML, dynamically inserted into the page's DOM. Most common these days is for the client and server to talk to each other using data encoded in a simple variant of JavaScript called JSON.

It's outside the scope of this book to teach you the fundamentals of JavaScript and/or Ajax. It's also outside of our scope to dive into the design considerations of adding Ajax to your application, elements of which are lengthy and occasionally controversial. Proper coverage of those subjects would require a whole book and there are many such books to choose from in the marketplace. Therefore, the rest of the chapter will assume that you understand what Ajax is and why you would use it in your applications. It also assumes that you have a basic understanding of JavaScript programming.

CoffeeScript

CoffeeScript is a Rubyesque language that compiles into JavaScript. Because DHH and many Rails developers are fans of CoffeeScript, support for using it (including the compiler) is natively included in Rails itself. This book assumes that the reader is familiar with CoffeeScript syntax.

20.1 Unobtrusive JavaScript

So-called *unobtrusive JavaScript* is a technique that attaches rich behavior to DOM elements based on CSS-style selectors, instead of having to declare event handlers as element attributes. Prior to version 3.0, trying to write rich browser functionality into your Rails apps was *obstrusive*, and generated markup was coupled to your JavaScript library of choice. For example, one of the most dramatic changes caused by the move to UJS was in the way that delete links were generated.

Prior to UJS, your HTML would look something like this:

```
<a href="/users/1" onclick="if (confirm('Sure?')) { var f=
  document.createElement('form'); f.style.display = 'none';
  this.parentNode.appendChild(f); f.method = 'POST'; f.action =
  this.href;var m = document.createElement('input'); m.setAttribute('type',
  'hidden'); m.setAttribute('name', '_method'); m.setAttribute('value',
  'delete'); f.appendChild(m);f.submit(); };return false;">Delete</a>
```

This is the same functionality in modern Rails code:

```
= link_to 'Delete', user_path(1), method: :delete,
    data: { confirm: "Are you sure?" }
```

Note that Rails uses the HTML5 data attributes as a means to attach custom events to DOM elements.

Rails UJS support requires the csrf_meta_tag, which must be placed in the head of the document and adds the csrf-param and csrf-token meta tags used in dynamic form generation.

```
%head
  = csrf_meta_tag
```

CSRF stands for cross-site request forgery and the csrf_meta_tag is one method of helping to prevent the attack from happening. CSRF protection is covered in detail in Chapter 15, "Security."

20.1.1   Helpers

As covered in Chapter 11, "All about Helpers," Rails ships with view helper methods to generate markup for common HTML elements. The following is a listing of Action View helpers that have hooks to enable Ajax behavior via the unobtrusive JavaScript driver.

20.1.1.1   `button_to`

The button_to helper generates a form containing a single button that submits to the URL created by the set of options. Setting the :remote option to true, enables the unobtrusive JavaScript driver to make an Ajax request in the background to the URL.

To illustrate, the following markup

```
= button_to("New User", new_user_path, remote: true)
```

generates

```
<form action="/users/new" class="button_to" data-remote="true"
  method="post">
  <div>
    <input type="submit" value="New User">
    <input name="authenticity_token" type="hidden"
      value="HDVQ/5AHK+f5ChqN8qaah8Pd0gZzkoa21vqbvbayHBY=">
  </div>
</form>
```

Ajax

To display a JavaScript confirmation prompt with a question specified, supply data attribute `:confirm` with a question. If accepted, the button will be submitted normally; otherwise, no action is taken.

```
= button_to("Deactivate", user, data: { confirm: 'Are you sure?' })
```

The unobtrusive JavaScript driver also enables the disabling of the button when clicked via the `:disable_with` data attribute. This prevents duplicate requests from hitting the server from subsequent button clicks by a user. If used in combination with `remote: true`, once the request is complete, the unobtrusive JavaScript driver will re-enable the button and reset the text to its original value.

```
= button_to("Deactivate", user, data: { disable_with: 'Deactivating...' })
```

20.1.1.2 `form_for`

The `form_for` helper is used to create forms with an Active Model instance. To enable the submission of a form via Ajax, set the `:remote` option to `true`. For instance, assuming we had a form to create a new user, the following

```
= form_for(user, remote: true) do |f|
  ...
```

would generate

```
<form accept-charset="UTF-8" action="/users" class="new_user"
  data-remote="true" id="new_user" method="post">
  ...
</form>
```

20.1.1.3 `form_tag`

Like `form_for`, the `form_tag` accepts the `:remote` option to enable Ajax form submission. For detailed information on `form_tag`, see Chapter 11, "All about Helpers."

20.1.1.4 `link_to`

The `link_to` helper creates a link tag of the given name using a URL created by the set of options. Setting the option `:remote` to `true`, allows the unobtrusive JavaScript driver to make an Ajax request to the URL instead of the following the link.

```
= link_to "User", user, remote: true
```

By default, all links will always perform an HTTP GET request. To specify an alternative HTTP verb, such as DELETE, you can set the :method option with the desired HTTP verb (:post, :patch, or :delete).

```
= link_to "Delete User", user, method: :delete
```

If the user has JavaScript disabled, the request will always fall back to using GET, no matter what :method you have specified.

The link_to helper also accepts data attributes :confirm and :disable_ with, covered earlier in the button_to section.

20.1.2   UJS Custom Events

When a form, link, or button is marked with the data-remote attribute, the UJS driver fires the following custom events:

Event Name	Parameters	Occurrence
ajax:before	event	Ajax event is started, aborts if stopped.
ajax:beforeSend	event, xhr, settings	Before request is sent, aborts if stopped.
ajax:send	event, xhr	Request is sent.
ajax:success	event, data, status, xhr	Request completed, and HTTP response was a success.
ajax:error	event, xhr, status, error	Request completed, and HTTP response returned an error.
ajax:complete	event, xhr, status	After request completed, regardless of outcome.
ajax:aborted: required	event, elements	When there exists blank required field in a form. Continues with submission if stopped.
ajax:aborted: file	event, elements	When there exists a populated file field in the form. Aborts if stopped.

This enables you, for instance, to handle the success/failure of Ajax submissions. To illustrate, let's bind to both the ajax:success and ajax:error events in the following CoffeeScript:

Ajax

```
$(document).ready ->
  $("#new_user")
    .on "ajax:success", (event, data, status, xhr) ->
      $(@).append xhr.responseText
    .on "ajax:error", (event, xhr, status, error) ->
      $(@).append "Something bad happened"
```

20.2   Ajax and JSON

JavaScript Object Notation (JSON) is a simple way to encode JavaScript objects. It is also considered a language-independent data format, making it a compact, human-readable, and versatile interchange format. This is the preferred method of interchanging data between the web application code running on the server and any code running in the browser, particularly for Ajax requests.

Rails provides a to_json on every object, using a sensible mechanism to do so for every type. For example, BigDecimal objects, although numbers, are serialized to JSON as strings, since that is the best way to represent a BigDecimal in a language-independent manner. You can always customize the to_json method of any of your classes if you wish, but it should not be necessary to do so.

20.2.1   Ajax `link_to`

To illustrate an Ajax request, let's enable our sample app's Client controller to respond to JSON and provide a method to supply the number of draft timesheets outstanding for each client:

```
respond_to :html, :xml, :json
...
# GET /clients/counts
# GET /clients/counts.json
def counts
  respond_with(Client.all_with_counts) do |format|
    format.html { redirect_to clients_path }
  end
end
```

Sample code not working? Make sure you have the Responders gem (https://github.com/plataformatec/responders).

This uses the Client class method `all_with_counts`, which returns an array of hashmaps:

```
def self.all_with_counts
```

```
all.map do |client|
  { id: client.id, draft_timesheets_count: client.timesheets.draft.count }
end
end
```

When GET /clients/counts is requested and the content type is JSON, the
response is the following:

```
[{"draft_timesheets_count":0,  "id":20},
 {"draft_timesheets_count":1,  "id":21}]
```

You will note in the code example that HTML and XML are also supported content
types for the response, so it's up to the client to decide which format works best for
them. We'll look at formats other than JSON in the next few sections.

In this case, our Client index view requests a response in JSON format:

```
- content_for :head do
  = javascript_include_tag 'clients.js'
...
%table#clients_list
...
  - @clients.each do |client|
    %tr[client]
      %td= client.name
      %td= client.code
      %td.draft_timesheets_count= client.timesheets.draft.count
...
= link_to 'Update draft timesheets count', counts_clients_path,
    remote: true, data: { type: :json }, id: 'update_draft_timesheets'
```

To complete the asynchronous part of this Ajax-enabled feature, we also need to
add an event-handler to the UJS ajax:success event, fired when the Ajax call on
the update_draft_timesheets element completes successfully. Here, jQuery
is used to bind a JavaScript function to the event once the page has loaded. This is
defined in clients.js:

```
$(function() {
  $("#update_draft_timesheets").on("ajax:success", function(event, data) {
    $(data).each(function() {
      var td = $('#client_' + this.id + ' .draft_timesheets_count')
      td.html(this.draft_timesheets_count);
    });
  });
});
```

In each row of the `clients` listing, the respective `td` with a class of `draft_timesheets_count` is updated in place with the values from the JSON response. There is no need for a page refresh, and user experience is improved.

20.3　Ajax and HTML

The Ruby classes in your Rails application will normally contain the bulk of that application's logic and state. Ajax-heavy applications can leverage that logic and state by transferring HTML, rather than JSON, to manipulate the DOM.

A web application may respond to an Ajax request with a HTML fragment, used to insert or replace an existing part of the page. This is most usually done when the transformation relies on complex business rules and perhaps complex state that would be inefficient to duplicate in JavaScript.

Let's say your application needs to display clients in some sort of priority order, and that order is highly variable and dependent on the current context. There could be a bunch of rules dictating what order they are shown in. Perhaps it's that whenever a client has more than a certain number of draft timesheets, we want to flag that in the page.

```
%td.draft_timesheets_count
  - if client.timesheets.draft.count > 3
    %span.drafts-overlimit WARNING!
    %br
  = client.timesheets.draft.count
```

Along with that, let's say on a Friday or Saturday we need to group clients by their *hottest spending day* so we can make ourselves an action plan for the beginning of the following week.

These are just two business rules that, when combined, are a bit of a handful to implement both in Rails and in JavaScript. Applications tend to have many more than just two rules combining, and it quickly becomes prohibitive to implement those rules in JavaScript to transform JSON into DOM changes. That's particularly `true` when the page making the Ajax call is external and not one we've written.

We can opt to transfer HTML in the Ajax call and use JavaScript to update a section of the page with that HTML. Under one context, the snippet of HTML returned could look like

```
<tr id="client_22" class="client"></tr>
<tr>
  <td></td><td>Aardworkers</td><td>AARD</td><td>$4321</td>
  <td class="draft_timesheets_count">0</td>
```

```
</tr>
<tr id="client_23" class="client"></tr>
<tr>
  <td></td><td>Zorganization</td><td>ZORG</td><td>$9999</td>
  <td class="draft_timesheets_count">1</td>
</tr>
```

Whereas, in another context, it could look like

```
<tr>
  <td>Friday</td>
</tr>
<tr>
  <td>Saturday</td>
</tr>
<tr id="client_24" class="client"></tr>
<tr>
  <td></td><td>Hashrocket</td><td>HR</td><td>$12000</td>
  <td class="draft_timesheets_count">
   <span class="drafts-overlimit">WARNING!</span>
   5
  </td>
</tr>
<tr id="client_22" class="client"></tr>
<tr>
  <td></td><td>Aardworkers</td><td>AARD</td><td>$4321</td>
  <td class="draft_timesheets_count">0</td>
</tr>
```

The JavaScript event handler for the Ajax response then just needs to update the
innerHTML of a particular HTML element to alter the page, without having to
know anything about the business rules used to determine what the resulting HTML
should be.

The counterargument to this technique is that it tightly couples your presentation layer to server-side logic. Larger teams, with specialized roles such as
frontend engineers, may find it preferable to maintain much looser coupling
between tiers.

20.4   JSONP Requests

JSONP *pads*, or wraps, JSON data in a call to a JavaScript function that exists on your
page. You specify the name of that function in a callback query string parameter.
Note that some public APIs may use something other than callback, but it has
become the convention in Rails and most JSONP applications.

💬 **Xavier says . . .**

Although the Wikipedia entry[1] for Ajax does not specifically mention JSONP and the request is not XHR by Rails' definition, we'd like to think of it as Ajax anyways—it is, after all, asynchronous JavaScript.

JSONP is one alternative for obtaining cross-domain data, avoiding the browser's *same-origin policy*. This introduces a pile of safety and security issues that are beyond the scope of this book. However, if you need to use JSONP, the Rails stack provides an easy way to handle JSONP requests (with `Rack::JSONP`) or make JSONP requests (with UJS and jQuery).

To respond to JSONP requests, activate the Rack JSONP module from the `rack-contrib` RubyGem in your `environment.rb` file:

```
class Application < Rails::Application
  require 'rack/contrib'
  config.middleware.use 'Rack::JSONP'
  ...
```

Then, just use UJS to tell jQuery it's a JSONP call by altering the `data-type` to `jsonp`:

```
= link_to 'Update draft timesheets count', counts_clients_path,
    remote: true, data: { type: :jsonp }, id: 'update_draft_timesheets'
```

jQuery automatically adds the `?callback=` and random function name to the query string of the request URI. In addition to this it also adds the necessary `script` tags to our document to bypass the same-origin policy. Our existing event handler is bound to `ajax:success` so it is called with the data just like before. Now, though, it can receive that data from another web application.

jQuery also makes the request as if it is for JavaScript, so our Rails controller needs to `respond_to :js`. Unfortunately, the Rails automatic rendering for JavaScript responses isn't there yet, so we add a special handler for JavaScript in our controller:

```
respond_to :html, :js
...

def counts
  respond_with(Client.all_with_counts) do |format|
    format.html { redirect_to clients_path }
```

1. http://en.wikipedia.org/wiki/Ajax_(programming)

```
      format.js { render json: Client.all_with_counts.to_json }
   end
end
```

We still convert our data to JSON. The `Rack::JSONP` module then *pads* that JSON data in a call to the JavaScript function specified in the query string of the request. The response looks like this:

```
jsonp123456789([{"id":1,"draft_timesheets_count":0},
{"id":2,"draft_timesheets_count":1}])
```

When the Ajax response is complete, your Ajax event handler is called and the JSON data is passed to it as a parameter.

20.5   Conclusion

Rails' baked-in support for Ajax is often credited as a big factor in its initial surge in popularity. However, in recent times developers are choosing more and more to break out browser clients into stand-alone "single-page apps" (SPAs) that don't even reside in the same source repository as their backend Rails code. Still, going the SPA route introduces a boatload of potentially unnecessary complexity. DHH has been an unrelenting proponent of the "majestic monolith" style,[2] made possible by the Ajax functionality described in this chapter.

Ajax

---

2. https://m.signalvnoise.com/the-majestic-monolith-29166d022228

CHAPTER 21
Turbolinks

Turbolinks is a JavaScript library that, when enabled, attaches a click handler to all links of an HTML page. When a link is clicked, Turbolinks will execute an Ajax request, and replace the contents of the current page with the response's <body> tag.

When Turbolinks is activated, it uses the HTML5 History API to dynamically change the address of the current page, enabling users to bookmark a specific page and use the back button as they normally would.

The biggest advantage of Turbolinks is that it enables the user's browser to only fetch the required stylesheets, JavaScripts, and even images once to render the page. Turbolinks effectively makes your site appear faster and more responsive.

Turbolinks is automatically included in new Rails 5 projects. To integrate Turbolinks into an existing Rails application that doesn't have it yet, include the turbolinks gem in your Gemfile and run bundle install.

```
# Gemfile
gem 'turbolinks'
```

Next, add "require turbolinks" in your JavaScript manifest file.

```
// app/assets/javascripts/application.js
//= require jquery
//= require jquery_ujs
//= require turbolinks
```

Despite the example above, Turbolinks does not depend on any particular JavaScript framework, such as jQuery. Its creators have attempted to make using it as unobtrusive as possible.

673

21.1   Turbolinks Usage

Turbolinks intercepts all clicks on <a href> links to the same domain. When you click an eligible link, Turbolinks prevents the browser from following it. Instead, Turbolinks changes the browser's URL using the History API (https://developer .mozilla.org/en-US/docs/Web/API/History), requests the new page using XML-HttpRequest (https://developer.mozilla.org/en-US/docs/Web/API/XMLH), and then renders the HTML response.

During rendering, Turbolinks replaces the current <body> element outright and merges the contents of the <head> element. The JavaScript window and document objects, and the HTML <html> element, persist from one rendering to the next.

21.1.1   Each Navigation Is a Visit

Turbolinks models navigation as a *visit* to a *location* (URL) with an *action*. Understanding this abstraction is vital to understanding how Turbolinks works overall.

Visits represent the entire navigation lifecycle from click to render. That includes changing browser history, issuing the network request, restoring a copy of the page from cache, rendering the final response, and updating the scroll position.

There are two types of visit: an *application visit*, which has an action of *advance* or *replace*, and a *restoration visit*, which has an action of *restore*.

21.1.2   Application Visits

Application visits are initiated by clicking a Turbolinks-enabled link or programmatically by calling Turbolinks.visit(location).

An application visit always issues a network request. When the response arrives, Turbolinks renders its HTML and completes the visit.

If possible, Turbolinks will render a preview of the page from a local cache immediately after the visit starts. This improves the perceived speed of frequent navigation between the same pages.

If the visit's location includes an anchor, Turbolinks will attempt to scroll to the anchored element. Otherwise, it will scroll to the top of the page.

Application visits result in a change to the browser's history; the visit's *action* determines how. The default visit action is *advance*. During an advance visit, Turbolinks pushes a new entry onto the browser's history stack using `history.pushState` (https://developer.mozilla.org/en-US/docs/Web/API/History/pushState).

You may wish to visit a location without pushing a new history entry onto the stack. The *replace* visit action uses `history.replaceState`[1] to discard the topmost history entry and replace it with the new location. To specify that following a link should trigger a replace visit, annotate the link with `data-turbolinks-action="replace"`:

```
<a href="/edit" data-turbolinks-action="replace">Edit</a>
```

To programmatically visit a location with the replace action, pass the `action: "replace"` option to `Turbolinks.visit` like this:

```
Turbolinks.visit("/edit", { action: "replace" })
```

21.1.3   Restoration Visits

Turbolinks automatically initiates a restoration visit when you navigate with the browser's back or forward buttons. If possible, it will render a copy of the page from local cache without making a request. Otherwise, it will retrieve a fresh copy of the page over the network. See the section "Understanding Turbolinks Caching" for more details.

Turbolinks saves the scroll position of each page before navigating away and automatically returns to this saved position on restoration visits.

Restoration visits have an action of *restore*, and Turbolinks reserves them for internal use. You should not attempt to annotate links or invoke `Turbolinks.visit` with an action of `restore`.

21.1.4   Canceling Visits Before They Start

Application visits can be canceled before they start, regardless of whether they were initiated by a link click or a call to `Turbolinks.visit`.

Listen for the `turbolinks:before-visit` event to be notified when a visit is about to start, and use `event.data.url` (or `$event.originalEvent.data.url` when using jQuery) to check the visit's location. Then cancel the visit by calling `event.preventDefault()`.

---

1. https://developer.mozilla.org/en-US/docs/Web/API/History/pushState

Turbolinks

Restoration visits cannot be canceled and do not fire `turbolinks:`
`before-visit`. Turbolinks issues restoration visits in response to history
navigation that has *already taken place,* typically via the browser's back or
forward buttons.

21.1.5   Disabling Turbolinks on Specific Links

Turbolinks can be disabled on a per-link basis by annotating a link *or any of its ancestors*
with `data-turbolinks="false"`.

```
<a href="/" data-turbolinks="false">Disabled</a>
<div data-turbolinks="false">
   <a href="/">Disabled</a>
</div>
```

To re-enable when an ancestor has opted out, use `data-turbolinks="true"`:

```
<div data-turbolinks="false"> <a href="/" data-turbolinks="true">Enabled</a>
</div>
```

Links with Turbolinks disabled will be handled normally by the browser.

21.2   Building Your Turbolinks Application

Turbolinks is fast because it doesn't reload the page when you follow a link. Instead,
your application becomes a persistent, long-running process in the browser. This
requires you to rethink the way you structure your JavaScript.

In particular, you can no longer depend on a full page load to reset your environment every time you navigate. The JavaScript `window` and `document` objects
retain their state across page changes, and any other objects you leave in memory
will stay in memory.

With awareness and a little extra care, you can design your application to gracefully
handle this constraint without tightly coupling it to Turbolinks.

21.2.1   Running JavaScript When a Page Loads

You may be used to installing JavaScript behavior in response to the `window.onload`,
`DOMContentLoaded`, or jQuery `ready` events. With Turbolinks, these events will fire
only in response to the initial page load—not after any subsequent page changes.

In many cases, you can simply adjust your code to listen for the `turbolinks:load`
event, which fires once on the initial page load and again after every Turbolinks visit.

```
document.addEventListener("turbolinks:load", function() {
  // ...
})
```

When possible, avoid using the `turbolinks:load` event to add event listeners directly to elements on the page body. Instead, consider using event delegation[2] to register event listeners once on `document` or `window`.

21.2.2   Working with Script Elements

Your browser automatically loads and evaluates any `<script>` elements present on the initial page load. When you navigate to a new page, Turbolinks looks for any `<script>` elements in the new page's `<head>` that aren't present on the current page. Then it appends them to the current `<head>` where they're loaded and evaluated by the browser. You can use this to load additional JavaScript files on-demand.

Turbolinks evaluates `<script>` elements in a page's `<body>` each time it renders the page. You can use inline body scripts to set up per-page JavaScript state or bootstrap client-side models. To install behavior, or to perform more complex operations when the page changes, avoid script elements and use the `turbolinks:load` event instead.

Annotate `<script>` elements with `data-turbolinks-eval="false"` if you do not want Turbolinks to evaluate them after rendering. Note that this annotation will not prevent your browser from evaluating scripts on the initial page load.

21.3   Understanding Turbolinks Caching

Turbolinks maintains a browser-based cache of recently visited pages. This cache serves two purposes: to display pages without accessing the network during restoration visits and to improve perceived performance by showing temporary previews during application visits.

When navigating by history (via Restoration Visits), Turbolinks will restore the page from cache without loading a fresh copy from the network, if possible.

Otherwise, during standard navigation (via Application Visits), Turbolinks will immediately restore the page from cache and display it as a preview while simultaneously loading a fresh copy from the network. This gives the illusion of instantaneous page loads for frequently accessed locations.

---

2. https://learn.jquery.com/events/event-delegation/

Turbolinks

Turbolinks saves a copy of the current page to its cache just before rendering a new page. Note that Turbolinks copies the page using `cloneNode(true)` (https:// developer.mozilla.org/en-US/docs/Web/API/Node/cloneNode), which means any attached event listeners and associated data are discarded.

21.3.1   Preparing the Page to Be Cached

Listen for the `turbolinks:before-cache` event if you need to prepare the document before Turbolinks caches it. You can use this event to reset forms, collapse expanded UI elements, or tear down any third-party widgets so the page is ready to be displayed again.

```
document.addEventListener("turbolinks:before-cache", function() {
  // ...
})
```

21.3.2   Detecting When a Preview Is Visible

Turbolinks adds a `data-turbolinks-preview` attribute to the `<html>` element when it displays a preview from cache. You can check for the presence of this attribute to selectively enable or disable behavior when a preview is visible. The same attribute can be used in your CSS to change the appearance of the page while it is inactive.

```
if (document.documentElement.hasAttribute("data-turbolinks-preview")) {
// Turbolinks is displaying a preview
}
```

21.3.3   Opting Out of Caching

You can control caching behavior on a per-page basis by including a `<meta name="turbolinks-cache-control">` element in your page's `<head>` and declaring a caching directive.

Use the `no-preview` directive to specify that a cached version of the page should not be shown as a preview during an application visit. Pages marked no-preview will only be used for restoration visits.

To specify that a page should not be cached at all, use the `no-cache` directive. Pages marked no-cache will always be fetched over the network, including during restoration visits.

```
<head>
  ...
```

```
  <meta name="turbolinks-cache-control" content="no-cache">
</head>
```

To completely disable caching in your application, ensure every page contains a no-cache directive.

21.4   Making Transformations Idempotent

Often you'll want to perform client-side transformations to HTML received from the server. For example, you might want to use the browser's knowledge of the user's current time zone to group a collection of elements by date.

Suppose you have annotated a set of elements with `data-timestamp` attributes indicating the elements' creation times in UTC. You have a JavaScript function that queries the document for all such elements, converts the timestamps to local time, and inserts date headers before each element that occurs on a new day.

Consider what happens if you've configured this function to run on `turbolinks:load`. When you navigate to the page, your function inserts date headers. Navigate away, and Turbolinks saves a copy of the transformed page to its cache. Now press the back button—Turbolinks restores the page, fires `turbolinks:load` again, and your function inserts a second set of date headers.

To avoid this problem, make your transformation function *idempotent*. An idempotent transformation is safe to apply multiple times without changing the result beyond its initial application.

One technique for making a transformation idempotent is to keep track of whether you've already performed it by setting a `data` attribute on each processed element. When Turbolinks restores your page from cache, these attributes will still be present. Detect these attributes in your transformation function to determine which elements have already been processed.

A more robust technique is simply to detect the transformation itself. In the date grouping example above, that means checking for the presence of a date divider before inserting a new one. This approach gracefully handles newly inserted elements that weren't processed by the original transformation.

21.5   Responding to Page Updates

Turbolinks may not be the only source of page updates in your application. New HTML can appear at any time from Ajax requests, WebSocket connections, or other

Turbolinks

client-side rendering operations, and this content will need to be initialized as if it came from a fresh page load.

You can handle all of these updates, including updates from Turbolinks page loads, in a single place with the precise lifecycle callbacks provided by `Mutation-Observer`[3] and Custom Elements (https://developer.mozilla.org/en-US/docs/Web/Web_Components/Custom_Elements).

In particular, these APIs give you callbacks when elements are attached to and removed from the document. You can use these callbacks to perform transformations and register or tear down behavior as soon as matching elements appear on the page, regardless of how they were added.

By taking advantage of `MutationObserver`, Custom Elements, and idempotent transformations, there's little need to couple your application to Turbolinks' events.

21.6   Persisting Elements across Page Loads

Turbolinks enables you to mark certain elements as *permanent*. Permanent elements persist across page loads so that any changes you make to those elements do not need to be reapplied after navigation.

Consider a Turbolinks application with a shopping cart. At the top of each page is an icon with the number of items currently in the cart. This counter is updated dynamically with JavaScript as items are added and removed.

Now imagine a user who has navigated to several pages in this application. She adds an item to her cart, then presses the back button in her browser. Upon navigation, Turbolinks restores the previous page's state from cache, and the cart item count erroneously changes from 1 to 0.

You can avoid this problem by marking the counter element as permanent. Designate permanent elements by giving them an HTML `id` and annotating them with `data-turbolinks-permanent`.

```
<div id="cart-counter" data-turbolinks-permanent>1 item</div>
```

Before each render, Turbolinks matches all permanent elements by `id` and transfers them from the original page to the new page, preserving their data and event listeners.

---

3. https://developer.mozilla.org/en-US/docs/Web/API/MutationObserver

21.7 Advanced Turbolinks

In addition to what we've already covered, there are a number of advanced Turbolinks techniques that you should know about.

21.7.1 Displaying Progress

During Turbolinks navigation, given its Ajax nature, the browser will not display a native progress indicator. The lack of feedback can be disorienting to the end user, so Turbolinks installs a CSS-based progress bar to provide feedback while it does its thing.

The progress bar is enabled by default and appears automatically for any page that takes longer than 500ms to load. It is implemented as a `<div>` element with the class name `turbolinks-progress-bar`. Its default styles appear first in the document and can be overridden by rules that come later.

For example, the following CSS will result in a thick green progress bar:

```
.turbolinks-progress-bar {
  height: 5px;
  background-color: green;
}
```

To disable the progress bar entirely, set its `visibility` style to `hidden`:

```
.turbolinks-progress-bar {
  visibility: hidden;
}
```

21.7.2 Reloading When Certain Things Change

Turbolinks can track the URLs of asset elements in `<head>` from one page to the next and automatically issue a full reload if they change. This ensures that users always have the latest versions of your application's scripts and styles.

Annotate asset elements with `data-turbolinks-track="reload"`, and include a version identifier in your asset URLs. The identifier could be a number, a last-modified timestamp, or better, a digest of the asset's contents, as in the following example:

```
<head>
  ...
  <link rel="stylesheet" href="/application-258e88d.css" data-turbolinks-track="reload">
  <script src="/application-cbd3cd4.js" data-turbolinks-track="reload"></script>
</head>
```

Turbolinks

You can actually use this asset tracking behavior with any HTML element in the head of the document, such as `<link>`, `<script>`, or even `<meta>`. An element annotated with `data-turbolinks-track="reload"` will trigger a full reload if it changes in any way, e.g., if its attributes are not identical, or if the element is present on one page but not on the next.

Note that Turbolinks will only consider tracked assets in `<head>` and not elsewhere on the page.

21.7.3 Setting a Root Location

By default, Turbolinks only loads URLs with the same origin—i.e., the same protocol, domain name, and port—as the current document. A visit to any other URL falls back to a full page load.

In some cases, you may want to further scope Turbolinks to a path on the same origin. For example, if your Turbolinks application lives at `/app`, and the non-Turbolinks help site lives at `/help`, links from the app to the help site shouldn't use Turbolinks.

Include a `<meta name="turbolinks-root">` element in your pages' `<head>` to scope Turbolinks to a particular root location. Turbolinks will only load same-origin URLs that are prefixed with this path.

```
<head>
  ...
  <meta name="turbolinks-root" content="/app">
</head>
```

21.7.4 Following Redirects

When you visit location `/one` and the server redirects you to location `/two`, you expect the browser's address bar to display the redirected URL.

However, Turbolinks makes requests using `XMLHttpRequest`, which transparently follows redirects. There's no way for Turbolinks to tell whether a request resulted in a redirect without additional cooperation from the server.

To work around this problem, Rails sends a `Turbolinks-Location` header in response to a visit that was redirected using `redirect_to`, and Turbolinks will replace the browser's topmost history entry with the value provided. If for some reason you are performing redirects manually (so-to-speak, without using the `redirect_to` helper method), then you'll have to take care of adding the header yourself.

21.7.5   Redirecting After a Form Submission

Submitting an HTML form to the server and redirecting in response is a common pattern in web applications. Standard form submission is similar to navigation, resulting in a full page load. Using Turbolinks you can improve the performance of form submission without complicating your server-side code.

Instead of submitting forms normally, submit them using XHR. In response to an XHR submit on the server, return JavaScript that performs a `Turbolinks.visit` to be evaluated by the browser.

If form submission results in a state change on the server that affects cached pages, consider first clearing Turbolinks' cache with `Turbolinks.clearCache()`. Rails actually performs this optimization automatically for non-GET XHR requests that redirect with the `redirect_to` helper.

21.7.6   Setting Custom HTTP Headers

You can observe the `turbolinks:request-start` event to set custom headers on Turbolinks requests. Access the request's XMLHttpRequest object via `event.data.xhr`, then call the `setRequestHeader`[4] method as many times as you wish.

For example, you might want to include a request ID with every Turbolinks link click and programmatic visit.

```
document.addEventListener("turbolinks:request-start", function(event) {
  var xhr = event.data.xhr
  xhr.setRequestHeader("X-Request-Id", "123...")
})
```

21.8   Turbolinks API Reference

The functions in the following sections are available for controlling Turbolinks in your JavaScript code.

21.8.1   `Turbolinks.visit`

Performs an Application Visit to the given *location* (a string containing a URL or path) with the specified *action* (a string, either `"advance"` or `"replace"`).

```
Turbolinks.visit(location)
Turbolinks.visit(location, { action: action })
```

---

4. https://developer.mozilla.org/en-US/docs/Web/API/XMLHttpRequest

Turbolinks

If *location* is a cross-origin URL or falls outside of the specified root (see "Setting a Root Location") or if the value of `Turbolinks.supported` is `false`, Turbolinks performs a full page load by setting `window.location`.

If *action* is unspecified, Turbolinks assumes a value of `"advance"`.

Before performing the visit, Turbolinks fires a `turbolinks:before-visit` event on document. Your application can listen for this event and cancel the visit with `event.preventDefault()` (see "Canceling Visits Before They Start").

21.8.2 `Turbolinks.clearCache`

Removes all entries from the Turbolinks page cache. Call this when state has changed on the server that may affect cached pages.

```
Turbolinks.clearCache()
```

21.8.3 `Turbolinks.supported`

Detects whether Turbolinks is supported in the current browser.

```
if (Turbolinks.supported) {
  // ...
}
```

21.9   Turbolinks Events

Turbolinks emits events that enable you to track the navigation lifecycle and respond to page loading. Except where noted, Turbolinks fires events on the browser's `document` object.

- `turbolinks:click` fires when you click a Turbolinks-enabled link. The clicked element is the event target. Access the requested location with `event.data.url`. Cancel this event to let the click fall through to the browser as normal navigation.

- `turbolinks:before-visit` fires before visiting a location, except when navigating by history. Access the requested location with `event.data.url`. Cancel this event to prevent navigation.

- `turbolinks:visit` fires immediately after a visit starts.

- `turbolinks:request-start` fires before Turbolinks issues a network request to fetch the page. Access the `XMLHttpRequest` object with `event.data.xhr`.

- `turbolinks:request-end` fires after the network request completes. Access the `XMLHttpRequest` object with `event.data.xhr`.

- `turbolinks:before-cache` fires before Turbolinks saves the current page to cache.

- `turbolinks:before-render` fires before rendering the page. Access the new `<body>` element with `event.data.newBody`.

- `turbolinks:render` fires after Turbolinks renders the page. This event fires twice during an application visit to a cached location: once after rendering the cached version and again after rendering the fresh version.

- `turbolinks:load` fires once after the initial page load and again after every Turbolinks visit. Access visit timing metrics with the `event.data.timing` object.

21.10   Conclusion

Rails' baked-in support for Ajax is often credited as a big factor in its initial surge in popularity. However, in recent times developers are choosing more and more to break out browser clients into stand-alone "single-page apps" (SPAs) that don't even reside in the same source repository as their backend Rails code. Still, going the SPA route introduces a boatload of potentially unnecessary complexity. DHH has been an unrelenting proponent of the "majestic monolith" style,[5] made possible by the Ajax functionality described in this chapter.

---

5. https://m.signalvnoise.com/the-majestic-monolith-29166d022228

CHAPTER 22

Action Cable

Action Cable provides an easy way to add real-time, low-latency communication between the browser and your Rails 5 server backend, using a technology called web sockets. It eliminates the need for Ajax polling, or old-school, brute-force methods like this classic webmaster technique:

```
<meta http-equiv="refresh" content="5" />
```

Most importantly, it is well integrated into the rest of Rails and follows its conventions in a way that feels natural. DHH formally introduced it in his 2015 Railsconf keynote, alongside Rails API mode—both innovations represent ways that Ruby on Rails is staying relevant in the face of competition from the likes of React, Angular, and Firebase.

22.1 Web Sockets

Web sockets provide "full-duplex" communications over a single, stateful HTTP connection between a web browser and a server. The protocol is general-purpose enough be used with most any kind of client/server application, but in this chapter we're talking about using web sockets to establish real-time communication between Java-Script code running in the browser and Ruby code running on your Rails backend.

The WebSocket protocol[1] was standardized by the IETF in 2011, and the WebSocket API implemented in modern browsers is standardized by the W3C; its documentation is maintained by the WHATWG community as part of the HTML Living Standard.[2]

---

1. https://tools.ietf.org/html/rfc6455
2. https://html.spec.whatwg.org/multipage/comms.html#network

Action Cable packages up client and server side handlers for web socket communications, along with an implementation of a Publish-Subscribe (PubSub) message
queue pattern based on Redis.

22.2 Publish-Subscribe Pattern

The Publish-Subscribe pattern is popular and well-documented, including extensive
explanations in books such as the modern classic Enterprise Integration Patterns.[3] It
models a way for applications to broadcast events to interested listeners.

22.3 Connections

Connections form the foundation of the client-server relationship. For every
WebSocket accepted by the server, a connection object is instantiated. This object
becomes the parent of all the channel subscriptions that are created from there
on. The connection itself does not deal with any specific application logic beyond
authentication and authorization, so you won't find yourself adding much code there.

The client of a WebSocket connection is called the *consumer*. An individual user will
create one *consumer-connection pair* per browser tab, window, or device they have open.

In Action Cable, connections are instances of `ApplicationCable::Connec-
tion`. In this class, you authorize the incoming connection and proceed to establish
it if the user can be identified.

```ruby
# app/channels/application_cable/connection.rb
module ApplicationCable
  class Connection < ActionCable::Connection::Base
    identified_by :current_user

    def connect
      self.current_user = find_verified_user
    end

    private

    def find_verified_user
      if current_user = User.find_by(id: cookies.signed[:user_id])
        current_user
      else
        reject_unauthorized_connection
      end
    end
  end
end
```

---

3. http://www.enterpriseintegrationpatterns.com/patterns/messaging/PublishSubscribeChannel.html

🔑 This example relies on the fact that you will already have handled authentication of the user somewhere else in your application and that a successful authentication sets a signed cookie with the user ID. Don't let the use of `current_user` fool you; this class has nothing to do with Devise.

The macro-style `identified_by` is used to declare what property of the connection instance will be used to find that particular connection instance later on when needed. In the case of the preceding example, we use the actual `current_user` instance. By identifying the connection by this same current user, you're also ensuring that you can later retrieve all open connections by a given user (and potentially disconnect them all if the user is deleted or unauthorized).

The preceding example also illustrates the fact that WebSocket connections are sent cookies upon initialization just like normal HTTP requests.

22.4   Channels

A channel class encapsulates a logical unit of work, similar to the role played by a controller in the familiar Model-View-Controller pattern.

The Rails generator script creates an abstract `ApplicationCable::Channel` class for encapsulating shared logic between your channels.

```
# app/channels/application_cable/channel.rb
module ApplicationCable
  class Channel < ActionCable::Channel::Base
  end
end
```

You extend this base class to create your own channel classes.

In this chapter we'll be using examples drawn from our Auction sample codebase. Auction pages automatically update in real-time when new bids are submitted.

```
class BidChannel < ApplicationCable::Channel
  def subscribed
    auction = Auction.find(params[:auction_id])
    stream_for auction
  end
end
```

Notice that (just like controllers), the subscribed method has access to a `params` hash, containing parameters set by the client.

22.5   Subscriptions

Consumers (in the browser) subscribe to channels over a WebSocket connection that is established using the following JavaScript, generated by the default Rails application generator:

```
// app/assets/javascripts/cable.js
//= require action_cable
//= require_self
//= require_tree ./channels

(function() {
  this.App || (this.App = {});

  App.cable = ActionCable.createConsumer();
}).call(this);
```

The first half of this file should look familiar; it's a manifest.

The preceding code will ready a consumer that'll connect to an endpoint on your server. (It connects to `/cable` by default.) Connection behavior *lazy*, it won't happen until you've also specified at least one subscription you're interested in having.

22.5.1   Subscribers

A consumer becomes a subscriber by creating a subscription to a given channel:

```
App.cable.subscriptions.create { channel: "BidChannel", auction_id: 1},
  connected: ->
    console.log("connected")

  received: (data) ->
    console.log(data)
    $("span#current_bid").html(data["price"])
```

A consumer can act as a subscriber to a given channel any number of times. For example, a consumer could subscribe to multiple chat rooms at the same time:

```
App.cable.subscriptions.create { channel: "ChatChannel" , room: "1st Room" }
App.cable.subscriptions.create { channel: "ChatChannel" , room: "2nd Room" }
```

22.6   Streams

Streams provide the mechanism by which channels route published content (broadcasts) to subscribers. You establish a connection to a stream in the `subscribed` handler of a channel using the `stream_for` method like this:

```
class BidChannel < ApplicationCable::Channel
  def subscribed
    auction = Auction.find(params[:auction_id])
    stream_for auction
  end
end
```

As you can see in the preceding example, if you have a stream that is related to a model, then the broadcasting subscription can be generated directly from an Active Record model instance.

22.6.1   Broadcasting

A broadcasting is a pub/sub link where anything transmitted by a publisher is routed directly to the channel subscribers who are streaming that named broadcasting. Each channel can be streaming zero or more broadcastings.

Broadcasting messages to a channel that has been configured in the way shown previously is as easy as:

```
BidChannel.broadcast_to(auction, bid)
```

Broadcastings are time-dependent and should not be confused with an event queue. If a particular consumer is not connected to a channel when a message is sent, they will not get it when they connect later.

22.7   Subscriptions Revisited (Browser-Side)

We briefly mentioned earlier that consumers can pass parameters from the client side to the server side when creating a subscription. An object passed as the first argument to `subscriptions.create` becomes the params hash in the cable channel. The keyword channel is required:

```
App.cable.subscriptions.create { channel: "BidChannel", auction_id: 1}
```

22.8   Rebroadcasting

A common use case for Action Cable, and the foundation of almost all Action Cable tutorials on the internet, is the rebroadcasting of a message sent by one client to any other connected clients (aka "a chatroom"). WebSocket connections are bi-directional—as we're about to see, the consumer can invert its role and send data to the server to consume. When that happens, the channel's `receive` method is invoked.

```
# app/channels/chat_channel.rb
class ChatChannel < ApplicationCable::Channel
  def subscribed
    stream_from "chat_#{params[:room]}"
  end

  def receive(data)
    ActionCable.server.broadcast("chat_#{params[:room]}", data)
  end
end
```

Notice that the subscription identifier string in the example code is `"chat_#{params[:room]}"`, rather than being an Active Record object.

```
# app/assets/javascripts/cable/subscriptions/chat.coffee
App.chatChannel = \
 App.cable.subscriptions.create { channel: "ChatChannel", room: 1 },
    received: (data) ->
      # data => { sent_by: "Paul", body: "This is a cool chat app." }

App.chatChannel.send({ sent_by: "Paul", body: "This is a cool chat app." })
```

The chat message sent using `App.chatChannel.send` will be received by all connected clients, including the client that sent the message.

22.9 Channel Actions

The following example presents a channel that tracks whether a user is online or not and what page they're currently visiting. (This is useful for creating presence features such as showing a green dot next to a user name if they're online).

```
# app/channels/appearance_channel.rb
class AppearanceChannel < ApplicationCable::Channel
  def subscribed
    current_user.appear
  end

  def unsubscribed
    current_user.disappear
  end

  def appear(data)
```

```
    current_user.appear(on: data['appearing_on'])
  end

  def away
    current_user.away
  end
end
```

When a subscription is initiated the `subscribed` callback gets fired, and we take that opportunity to say "the current user has indeed appeared." Remember that `current_user` has been set in `ApplicationCable::Channel` when the connection was established.

The appear/disappear API (exemplified as `current_user.appear`) could be backed by Redis or a database, but explaining that part is out of scope for this chapter.

Notice that there are two methods that we haven't seen before in this channel: `appear(data)` and `away`. These aren't part of Action Cable or anything, rather they are arbitrary actions designed in much the same way that you might add non-RESTful actions to a Rails controller class.

Here's how those methods are invoked in the browser:

```coffee
# app/assets/javascripts/cable/subscriptions/appearance.coffee
App.cable.subscriptions.create "AppearanceChannel",
  # Called when the subscription is ready for use on the server.
  connected: ->
    @install()
    @appear()

  # Called when the WebSocket connection is closed.
  disconnected: ->
    @uninstall()

  # Called when the subscription is rejected by the server.
  rejected: ->
    @uninstall()

  appear: ->
    # Calls `AppearanceChannel#appear(data)` on the server.
    @perform("appear", appearing_on: $("main").data("appearing-on"))

  away: ->
    # Calls `AppearanceChannel#away` on the server.
    @perform("away")

  buttonSelector = "[data-behavior~=appear_away]"
```

```
install: ->
  $(document).on "turbolinks:load.appearance", =>
    @appear()

  $(document).on "click.appearance", buttonSelector, =>
    @away()
    false

  $(buttonSelector).show()

uninstall: ->
  $(document).off(".appearance")
  $(buttonSelector).hide()
```

Notice how the @perform function is used, along with the name of the action and
parameters in order to invoke a method on the connection class.

22.10   Configuration

Action Cable has two required configurations: a subscription adapter and allowed
request origins.

22.10.1   Subscription Adapter

By default, Action Cable looks for a configuration file in config/cable.yml.
The file must specify an adapter for each Rails environment. See the Dependencies
section for additional information on adapters.

```
development:
  adapter: async

test:
  adapter: async

production:
  adapter: redis
  url: redis://10.10.3.153:6381
  channel_prefix: appname_production
```

The following sections present the subscription adapters available.

22.10.1.1   Async Adapter

The async adapter is intended for development/testing and should not be used in
production.

22.10.1.2 Redis Adapter

Action Cable contains two Redis adapters: "normal" Redis and Evented Redis. Both of the adapters require a URL pointing to the Redis server. Additionally, a `channel_prefix` variable may be provided to scope the connection and avoid channel name collisions when using the same Redis server for multiple applications.

22.10.1.3 PostgreSQL Adapter

The PostgreSQL adapter uses Active Record's connection pool, and thus the application's `config/database.yml` database configuration, for its connection.

22.10.2 Allowed Request Origins

Action Cable will only accept requests from specified origins, which are passed to the server config as an array. The origins can be instances of strings or regular expressions, against which a check for a match will be performed.

By default, Action Cable allows all requests from `localhost:3000` when running in the development environment.

```
config.action_cable.allowed_request_origins = ['http://example.com']
```

You probably shouldn't do this, but if you want to live dangerously you can disable forgery protection and allow requests from any origin:

```
config.action_cable.disable_request_forgery_protection = true
```

22.10.3 Consumer Configuration

The URL that the browser-side code of Action Cable will use to connect to your server is specified using a call to `action_cable_meta_tag` in your HTML layout HEAD. This uses a URL or path typically set via config.action_cable.url in the environment configuration files.

22.10.4 Worker Count

Your server configuration must provide at least the same number of database connections as you have Action Cable workers. The default worker pool size is set to four (4), so you have to make at least that many available. The number of data connections can be changed in `config/database.yml` through the `pool` attribute.

Cable

22.11   Running Stand-Alone Cable Servers

Action Cable can run alongside your Rails application instead of inside its same process. For example, to listen for WebSocket requests on `/websocket`, specify that
path to `config.action_cable.mount_path` in an initializer:

```
Rails.application.action_cable.mount_path = '/websocket'
```

You can use `App.cable = ActionCable.createConsumer()` to connect to
the cable server as long as `action_cable_meta_tag` is invoked in the layout.
Specify your custom path as the first argument to `createConsumer`.

```
App.cable = ActionCable.createConsumer("/websocket")
```

For every instance of your server you create and for every worker your server
spawns, you will also have a new instance of Action Cable, but the use of Redis
keeps messages synced across connections.

The cable servers can be separated from your normal application server. It's still a
Rack application, but it is its own Rack application.

Separating your cable servers means that, for instance, on Heroku, your cable
servers would have their own line in the `Procfile` and their own set of dynos.

The recommended basic setup is as follows:

```
# cable/config.ru
require_relative '../config/environment'
Rails.application.eager_load!

run ActionCable.server
```

Then you start the server using a binstub in bin/cable ala:

```
#!/bin/bash
bundle exec puma -p 28080 cable/config.ru
```

22.12   Generator

Rails provides a generator script for creating new channels.

```
$ rails g channel
Usage:
  rails generate channel NAME [method method] [options]
```

```
Options:
  [--skip-namespace], [--no-skip-namespace]  # Skip namespace (affects
                                             # only isolated applications)
  [--assets], [--no-assets]                  # Indicates when to generate
                                             # assets
                                             # Default: true

Runtime options:
  -f, [--force]              # Overwrite files that already exist
  -p, [--pretend], [--no-pretend]  # Run but do not make any changes
  -q, [--quiet], [--no-quiet]      # Suppress status output
  -s, [--skip], [--no-skip]        # Skip files that already exist

Description:
============
  Stubs out a new cable channel for the server (in Ruby) and client (in
  CoffeeScript). Pass the channel name, either CamelCased or under_scored,
  and an optional list of channel actions as arguments.

  Note: Turn on the cable connection in app/assets/javascript/cable.js
  after generating any channels.
Example:
========
    rails generate channel Chat speak

    creates a Chat channel class and CoffeeScript asset:
        Channel:    app/channels/chat_channel.rb
        Assets:     app/assets/javascript/channels/chat.coffee
```

22.13   Conclusion

This chapter provided you with a crash course in Action Cable and hopefully piqued your interest in using it the next time you need some real-time client-server communication in your project.

This chapter is licensed under a Creative Commons Attribution-ShareAlike 4.0 International[4] License.

Cable

CHAPTER 23

RSpec

> I do not think there is any thrill that can go through the human heart like that felt by the inventor as he sees some creation of the brain unfolding to success.
>
> —Nikola Tesla

RSpec is a Ruby domain-specific language for specifying the desired behavior of Ruby code. Its strongest appeal is that RSpec scripts (or simply *specs*) can achieve a remarkable degree of readability, letting developers communicate their intention with greater readability and expressiveness than is achievable using the standard Rails testing framework.

23.1 Introduction

Since RSpec scripts are so readable, I can't really think of a better way of introducing you to the framework than to show part of a real-world spec. The following code is excerpted and adapted from an old Hashrocket client project:

```
require 'rails_helper'

describe Timesheet, type: :model do
  let(:timesheet) { build(:timesheet) }

  describe "hours worked" do
    it "expects a number" do
      timesheet.hours_worked = 'abc'
      expect(timesheet.error_on(:hours_worked).size).to eq(1)
    end
  end

  context "when submitted" do
```

699

```
  it "sends an email notification to the manager" do
    expect(Notifier).to receive(:send_later).
      with(:deliver_timesheet_submitted, timesheet)
    timesheet.submit
  end
 end
end
```

Once you get adept at writing RSpec, the following lines of Ruby code

```
describe Timesheet do
  describe "when submitted" do
    it "sends an email notification to the manager" do
```

. . . should automatically coalesce in your mind into the statement: Timesheet when submitted sends an email notification to the manager.

RSpec is an example of a Ruby-based *Domain Specific Language*, which is one of the main reasons it feels like such a natural part of the *Rails Way* to me and others. The building blocks of the RSpec DSL are very simple. The `describe` method creates an `ExampleGroup` object, which is a shared context for a set of specification examples defined using the `it` method, which itself creates `Example` objects.

You should pass sentence fragments to `describe` and `it` that succinctly identify the context you're about to specify. The better you get at writing RSpec, the more your examples will read like natural language sentences.

🔧 RSpec's `describe` method is aliased as `context`. Use the former to describe things (like attributes) and the latter to describe situations.

23.2   Behavior-Driven Development

We can't talk about RSpec without mentioning *behavior-driven development* (or BDD for short), an offshoot of test-driven development (TDD). One of the prime directives of BDD is to describe software in a single notation which is directly accessible to domain experts, testers and developers, so as to improve communication (https://www.agilealliance.org/glossary/bdd/).

RSpec syntax is an implementation of that *single notation*, in Ruby. The intention is to make it easy to describe the desired behavior of a piece of software, *before* implementing it. Given its roots in TDD, if you add RSpec coverage after the fact, you're *doing it wrong*.

> ⚷ The suite of specs you end up with when practicing BDD serves to prevent regressions over time, but never forget that the main purpose of BDD is to foster clean application design and speed up implementation cycles.

Doing justice to the topic of BDD and RSpec would require a book, which is why my friends David Chelimsky, Aslak Hellesoy, Dave Astels, and Bryan Helmkamp wrote a great 400+ page reference bible for Pragmatic Programmers. In contrast, this chapter is purely an RSpec primer, with emphasis on how to use it effectively with Rails.

23.2.1   "Up and Down the Stack . . . "

You can use RSpec to specify and test every part of your Rails application, from models and controller classes, to view templates and routing configuration, all in isolation. An isolated spec is basically the same as a unit test, and serves the same purpose in a TDD sense.

If you add a gem called Capybara[1] to the equation, then RSpec can also be used to create integration tests that exercise the entire Rails stack from top to bottom, like this:

```
require 'rails_helper'

feature "Search Documents" do
  let(:user) { create(:user, name: 'Joe') }

  let(:published_doc) do
    create(:document, title: 'Global Equities 2016', status: 'published')
  end

  let(:private_doc) do
    create(:document, title: 'Global Equities 2017', status: 'draft')
  end

  background { login_as user }

  scenario "takes you to the search results page" do
    search_for("Global")
    expect(current_path).to include(search_results_path)
  end

  scenario "doesn't return draft docs" do
    search_for("Global")
    expect(page).to_not have_content(private_doc.title)
  end
```

---

1. https://github.com/jnicklas/capybara

```
  def search_for(term)
    visit search_path
    fill_in 'Search', with: term
    click_button 'Search'
  end
end
```

Use of methods such as `visit` and `fill_in`, as well the checking the contents of objects such as `page`, hint at what this spec is doing: exercising your entire Rails application from top to bottom.

But let's take a step back and cover some RSpec basics first.

23.3   Basic Syntax and API

This section contains a somewhat comprehensive, yet concise, rundown of RSpec's syntax and API methods. It assumes at least passing familiarity with automated testing concepts.

23.3.1   Contexts (aka Example Groups)

The `describe` method and its alias `context` are used to group together related examples of behavior and serve as factories for `ExampleGroup` objects. Capybara adds an additional `feature` alias that serves the same purpose. All of these methods take a string (or other object that can be cast to a string) as their first argument and a block that bounds their scope.

The first and outermost example group almost always gets the class/object under test as its argument, like this:

```
describe Timesheet, type: :model do
```

Immediately under that first example group declaration, you generally have one or more `let` statements. What are they?

23.3.2   Shared Variables

The `let` method simplifies the creation of memoized variables for use in your spec. (*Memoized* means that the code block associated with the `let` is executed once and stored for future invocations, increasing performance.)

The use of `let` eliminates the need for instance variables by creating a proper interface for declaring significant shared variables needed in the spec.

Why use the `let` method instead of instance variables? Let's step through a typical spec coding session to understand the motivation. Imagine that you're writing a spec, and it all starts simply enough with a local `blog_post` variable.

```
describe BlogPost do
  it "does something" do
    blog_post = BlogPost.new title: 'Hello'
    expect(blog_post).to ...
  end
end
```

You continue on, writing another similar example, and you start to see some duplication. The `blog_post` creation is being done twice.

```
describe BlogPost do
  it "does something" do
    blog_post = BlogPost.new title: 'Hello'
    expect(blog_post).to ....
  end

  it "does something else" do
    blog_post = BlogPost.new title: 'Hello'
    expect(blog_post).to ...
  end
end
```

So, you refactor the instance creation into a before block and start using an instance variable in the examples.

```
describe BlogPost do
  before do
    @blog_post = BlogPost.new title: 'Hello'
  end

  it "does something" do
    expect(@blog_post).to ...
  end

  it "does something else" do
    expect(@blog_post).to ...
  end
end
```

And here comes the punchline: you replace the instance variables with a *variable* described by a `let` expression.

```
describe BlogPost do
  let(:blog_post) { BlogPost.new title: 'Hello' }

  it "does something" do
    expect(blog_post).to ...
  end
```

```
  it "does something else" do
    expect(blog_post).to ...
  end
end
```

In case it's not obvious, the advantage of using `let` is mostly in the realm of readability. First of all, it gets rid of instance variables with their hideous ampersands. Second, it gets variable initialization out of the `before` block, which arguably has no business setting up a bunch of variables in the first place.

Finally, `let` shows you *who the players are* in your spec. A set of `let` declarations at the top of an example group reads like a cast of characters in a playbill. You can easily refer to it when you're deep in the code of an example.

Note that `let` declarations are lazy. Their blocks do not get executed until you refer to their objects elsewhere in your spec. That elsewhere can be another `let`, like in this code:

```
let(:org) { create(:organization_with_network_and_users) }
let(:network) { org.networks.first }
let(:user1) { org.users.first }
let(:user2) { org.users.second }
let!(:name) { expression }
```

Sometimes the lazy evaluation of a `let` is not good enough.

```
describe Article do
  let(:current_user) { create(:user) }
  let(:article) { create(:article) }
  let(:comment) { user.comment(article, 'first') }

  describe "#clear_comments" do
    it "removes all comments" do
      expect {
        article.clear_comments
      }.to change {
        article.comments.count
      }
```

Since `comment` is never invoked, this spec will fail. The article never got any comments, so the count didn't change. Using `let!` ensures the initial comment gets created and the spec passes:

```
let!(:comment) { user.comment(article, 'first') }
```

23.3.3 Examples

The `it` method takes a description plus a block, similar to `describe`. As mentioned already, the idea is to complete the thought that was started in the `describe` method so that it forms a complete sentence.

Assertions (aka expectations) will always happen within the context of an `it` block, and in most cases you should try to limit yourself to one expectation per `it` block.

```
context "when there are no search results" do
  before do
    email_search_for(user, '123')
  end

  it "shows the search form" do
    expect(current_url).to eq(colleagues_url)
  end

  it "renders an error message" do
    expect(page).to have_selector('.error',
      text: 'No matching email addresses found.')
  end
end
```

The most reasonable exception that I've seen to the *one expectation per example* guideline is when you're testing interfaces to remote systems. Repeatedly setting up and tearing down remote data can become time-consuming and weigh down the performance of your entire test suite.

⚷ If every spec begins with "should," then "should" is redundant everywhere and becomes noise. Use the should_not gem[2] if you need help remembering or enforcing this rule.

23.3.3.1 `specify`

The specify method is used to remove duplication and improve readability. Look at the following spec, which uses normal describe/it syntax:

---

2. https://github.com/should-not/should_not

```
describe BlogPost do
  let(:blog_post) { create(:blog_post) }

  it "to not be published" do
    expect(blog_post).to_not be_published
  end
end
```

Note how the example says "to not be published" in plain English, but the Ruby code within it says essentially the same thing: `expect(blog_post).to_not be_published`. If you squint, you'll realize that's a DRY violation—we are repeating ourselves.

Here's an alternative implementation of the same spec, this time using `specify`:

```
describe BlogPost do
  context "upon creation" do
    let(:blog_post) { create(:blog_post) }
    specify { expect(blog_post).to_not be_published }
  end
end
```

The English phrase has been removed, and the Ruby code has been moved into a block passed to the `specify` method. Since the Ruby block already reads like English, there's no need to repeat yourself, and we turned seven lines of code into four.

RSpec automatically generates English output by introspecting on the expectations created in the example blocks. Here's what the RSpec output looks like for the last spec:

```
BlogPost
  upon creation
    should not be published
```

🔍 To get this pretty output, run your spec with the documentation output formatter (`--format documentation`).

23.3.3.2 `pending`

When you leave the block off of an example, RSpec treats it as pending.

```
describe GeneralController do
  describe "GET to index" do
    it "will be implemented eventually"
  end
end
```

RSpec prints out pending examples at the end of its run output, which makes it potentially useful for tracking work in progress.

```
Pending:
  GeneralController on GET to index will be implemented eventually
    # Not yet implemented
    # ./spec/controllers/general_controller_spec.rb:6

Finished in 0.00024 seconds
1 example, 0 failures, 1 pending

Randomized with seed 31820
```

A quick and and easy way to mark existing examples as pending is to prepend the `it` method with an x, like so:

```
describe GeneralController do
  describe "on GET to index" do
    xit "should be successful" do
      get :index
      expect(response).to be_successful
    end
  end
end
```

This is especially useful for debugging and refactoring.

You can also explicitly create pending examples by inserting a call to the `pending` method anywhere inside of an example.

```
describe GeneralController do
  describe "on GET to index" do
    it "is successful" do
      pending("not implemented yet")
    end
  end
end
```

Interestingly, you can use `pending` with a block to keep broken code from failing your spec. However, if at some point in the future the broken code does execute without an error, the pending block will cause a failure.

```
describe BlogPost do
  it "defaults to rating of 3.0" do
    pending "implementation of new rating algorithm" do
      expect(BlogPost.new.rating).to eq(3.0)
    end
```

```
    end
end
```

✎ Pro-tip: You can make all examples in a group pending simply by calling `pending` once in the group's `before` block.

```
describe 'Veg-O-Matic' do
  before { pending }

  it 'slices' do
    # will not run, instead displays "slices (PENDING: TODO)"
  end

  it 'dices' do
    # will also be pending
  end

  it 'juliennes' do
    # will also be pending
  end
end
```

We've been talking a lot about how to set up examples, but now let's actually discuss how to set expectations that can pass or fail.

23.3.4   Expectations

The preferred way to define positive and negative expectations is to use `expect(...).to` and `expect(...).to_not`, respectively.

✎ RSpec expectations used to be done using `should` and `should_not` methods mixed into Ruby's `Object` method, but that syntax was deprecated in RSpec 3.

You pass a parameter or block that you want to create an expectation for to the `expect` method. Then you chain `to` or `to_not` to specify whether the expectation is to be positive or negative. Finally, you must pass a matcher to the `to` (or `to_not`) method, which is what makes the example pass or fail depending on the behavior of the matcher.

```
expect(page).to have_selector('.error',
  text: 'No matching email addresses found.')
```

In the preceding example, `have_selector` is the *matcher*. The full list of matchers available is dynamic and almost endless, covering all sorts of different attributes and behaviors of objects.

There are several ways to generate expectation matchers and pass them to `expect(...).to` (and `expect(...).to_not`):

```
expect(receiver).to eq(expected) # any value
# Passes if (receiver == expected)

expect(receiver).to eql(expected)
# Passes if (receiver.eql?(expected))

expect(receiver).to match(regexp)
# Passes if (receiver =~ regexp)

expect(user.network).to be(organization.networks.first)
# Passes if both references point to same exact object instance
```

Learning to write expectations is probably one of the meatier parts of the RSpec learning curve. The full list of built-in matchers is available at https://github.com/rspec/rspec-expectations.

23.3.4.1 Commonly Used Matchers

Besides the equality matchers mentioned already, here are some other commonly used matchers.

```
# Comparisons
expect(actual).to be > expected
expect(actual).to be_within(delta).of(expected)

# Types
expect(actual).to be_an_instance_of(Expected)
expect(actual).to be_a(ClassThatWasExpected) # alias
expect(actual).to be_an(ExpectedClass) # another alias
```

As you can hopefully tell from all these aliases, the authors of RSpec (and Rubyists in general) take code readability very seriously.

```
# Truthiness
expect(actual).to be_truthy   # truthy means not `nil` or `false`
expect(actual).to be true
expect(actual).to be_falsy
expect(actual).to be false
expect(actual).to be_nil
```

RSpec

```
expect(actual).to_not be_nil

# Errors
expect { ... }.to raise_error
expect { ... }.to raise_error(ErrorClass)
expect { ... }.to raise_error("message")
expect { ... }.to raise_error(ErrorClass, "message")

# Collection Membership
expect(actual).to include(expected)   # works for strings too
expect(actual).to start_with(expected)
expect(actual).to end_with(expected)
expect(actual).to contain_exactly(individual, items)

# Change
expect { expr }.to change(object, :method)
expect { expr }.to change { object.method }
```

23.3.4.2   Predicate Matchers

So-called *predicate matchers* are dynamic; that is, they operate based on naming conventions for methods on the expected object.

```
expect(actual).to be_xxx        # passes if actual.xxx?
expect(actual).to have_xxx(:arg) # passes if actual.has_xxx?(:arg)
```

In practice, this is what it looks like:

```
expect(3).to be_odd
expect(feed).to have_unread_notifications
expect({foo: "foo"}).to have_key(:foo)
expect({bar: "bar"}).to_not  have_key(:foo)
```

As an alternative to prefixing arbitrary predicate matchers with be_, you may choose from the indefinite article versions be_a_ and be_an_, making your specs read much more naturally:

```
expect("a string").to be_an_instance_of(String)
expect(3).to be_a_kind_of(Integer)
expect(3).to be_a_kind_of(Numeric)
expect(3).to be_an_instance_of(Fixnum)
expect(3).to_not be_instance_of(Numeric) #fails
```

23.3.4.3   Compound Matcher Expressions

You can create compound matcher expressions using and or or methods:

```
expect(alphabet).to start_with("a").and end_with("z")
expect(stoplight.color).to eq("red").or eq("green").or eq("yellow")
```

It's even more common than that to chain matcher expressions together to create richer expectations.

For example,

```
expect {
  BlogPost.create title: 'Hello'
}.to change(BlogPost, :count).by(1)
```

The by method refines the change matcher. In our example, we're making sure that the record was saved to the database, thus increasing the record count by 1.

There are a few different variations on the change syntax. Here's one more example, where we're more explicit about before and after values by further chaining from and to methods:

```
describe "#publish!" do
  let(:blog_post) { BlogPost.create title: 'Hello' }

  it "updates published_on date" do
    expect {
      blog_post.publish!
    }.to change {
      blog_post.published_on
    }.from(nil).to(Date.today)
  end
end
```

The published_on attribute is examined both before and after invocation of the expect block. This style of change assertion comes in handy when you want to ensure a precondition of the value. Asserting from guarantees a known starting point.

Besides expecting changes, the other common expectation has to do with code that should generate exceptions:

```
describe "#unpublish!" do
  context "when brand new" do
    let(:blog_post) { BlogPost.create title: 'Hello' }

    it "raises an exception" do
      expect {
        blog_post.unpublish!
      }.to raise_error(NotPublishedError, /not yet published/)
    end
  end
end
```

RSpec

In this example, we attempt to "unpublish" a brand new blog post that hasn't been published yet. Therefore, we expect an exception to be raised.

23.3.5   Metadata

Metadata is a somewhat esoteric topic, because it's not used in usual day-to-day Rails programming, but I wanted to at least touch on it before moving forward. Specs have what is referred to as *metadata*.

The class or string description passed to a context declaration is the simplest example and is accessed as `described_class`, like this:

```
RSpec.describe Fixnum do
  it "is available as described_class" do
    expect(described_class).to eq(Fixnum)
  end
end
```

Contexts and examples can also take optional arguments (called *user-defined metadata*). You simply enter symbols or a hash of options after the description string. Symbols must come first and are the same as putting them as keys in the hash, equal to `true`.

A super common example of metadata you'll see on a regular basis is the way that you tag different kinds of Rails specs.

```
RSpec.describe User, type: :model do
  ...
```

The `type: :model` portion of the context declaration in the preceding example is metadata.

Hooks, lets, and example blocks yield a variable called `example`, which can be used to read metadata explicitly.

```
RSpec.describe "a group with user-defined metadata", :basic, :foo => 17 do
  it 'has access to the metadata in the example' do |example|
    expect(example.metadata[:basic]).to be_true
    expect(example.metadata[:foo]).to eq(17)
  end
```

23.3.6   Hooks

The `before` and `after` hooks are akin to the `setup` and `teardown` methods of xUnit frameworks like `MiniTest`. They are used to set up the state as it should be prior to running an example, and if necessary, to clean up the state after the example has run.

> Even though I do not like the practice, I would be remiss to not mention
> that `before` hooks are often used to initialize instance variables. Instance
> variables defined in context hooks are available in their own contexts and
> also nested contexts.

A common use case for before hooks (that shows up elsewhere in this chapter) is
logging in a user.

```
before(:each) do
  sign_in(user)
end
```

Here is the entire list of hooks, in the order in which they are executed.

- `before` `:suite`

- `before` `:context` (aliased to `:all`)

- `around` (before `example.run` invoked)

- `before` `:example` (aliased to `:each`)

- `after` `:example` (aliased to `:each`)

- `around` (after `example.run` invoked)

- `after` `:context` (aliased to `:all`)

- `after` `:suite`

As you can see in the preceding list, RSpec also has an `around` hook. While the
other hooks are fairly self-explanatory, the `around` hook has some special charac-
teristics that bear mentioning.

First of all, one of the main reasons you might want to use the `around` hook, given
that its behavior is easy to replicate with `before` and `after`, is the way that it takes
its examples as `Proc` instances, which makes it trivial to pass examples to Ruby
methods that expect blocks.

An example, illustrated here in pseudo-code, is running an example inside of a
transaction:

```
class Database
  def self.transaction
    puts "open transaction"
    yield
    puts "close transaction"
```

RSpec

```
    end
end

RSpec.describe "around filter" do
  around(:example) do |example|
    Database.transaction(&example)
  end

  it "gets passed as a proc" do
    puts "run the example"
  end
end
```

Run the preceding code and you'll notice that the message "run the example" prints inside the open and close transaction messages.

If you're not passing the example block along to another method, you invoke it using the run method. Here's a real example, using the Database Cleaner gem:

```
config.around(:each) do |example|
  DatabaseCleaner.cleaning do
        example.run
    end
  end
```

23.3.6.1   Global Hooks

As you can see in the preceding example, the hook is invoked on the RSpec config object, rather than inside a particular spec file. Doing that defines behavior for all example groups and examples in the whole suite.

23.3.6.2   Hook Gotchas

Here are some things to be aware of with hooks:

- *Exceptions in before(:example)* are captured and reported as failures for their examples. Since before hooks serve as setup mechanisms, exceptions equal failure.

- *Exceptions raised in before(:context) are captured and reported as failures for their context and nested contexts too.* You should see failure messages for any examples in the group with the failing hook, as well as any examples in nested groups.

- *Around hooks don't share state the way that before and after hooks do.* If you try to set instance variables in an around hook, you'll find that they are not available elsewhere in your spec. State and expectations for mocking do not work in around hooks either.

- *Around hooks continue executing even if their nested examples raise an exception.* This behavior makes sense given their typical use case of ensuring that some particular cleanup behavior always happens.

- *All hooks execute in the order they are declared.* They won't overwrite each other if you declare multiples of the same type.

23.3.7 Implicit Subject

Whether you realize it or not, every RSpec example group has a *subject*. Think of it as *the thing being described*. If you pass Rspec a class, then it will try initializing it as its *implicit subject*.

Let's start with an easy example:

```
describe BlogPost do
  it { is_expected.to be_invalid }
end
```

By convention, the implicit subject here is a `BlogPost.new` instance. The `is_expected` call may look like it is being called *off of nothing*, but actually the call is delegated by the example to the implicit subject. It's just as if you'd written the expression:

```
expect(BlogPost.new).to be_invalid
```

23.3.8 Explicit Subject

If the implicit subject of the example group doesn't quite do the job for you, you can specify a subject explicitly. For example, maybe we need to tweak a couple of the blog post's attributes on instantiation:

```
describe BlogPost do
  subject { BlogPost.new(title: 'foo', body: 'bar') }
  it { is_expected.to be_valid }
end
```

Here we have the same delegation story as with implicit subject. The `is_expected.to be_valid` call is delegated to the subject.

You can also call methods on the `subject` directly. For example, you may need to invoke a method to change state before setting an expectation:

```
describe BlogPost do
  subject { BlogPost.new title: 'foo', body: 'bar' }

  it "sets published timestamp" do
```

```
    subject.publish!
    expect(subject).to be_published
  end
end
```

Here we call the `publish!` method off the subject. Mentioning `subject` directly is the way we get ahold of that `BlogPost` instance we set up. Finally, we assert that `published?` boolean is `true`.

💬 Kevin says . . .

Although you can explicitly call `subject` within your specs, it's not very intention revealing. An alternative is to use "named subjects," which enables a subject to be assigned an intention revealing name (using an alias for `let`).

To demonstrate, here is the preceding example using a "named subject":

```
describe BlogPost do
  subject(:blog_post) { BlogPost.new title: 'foo', body: 'bar' }

  it "sets published timestamp" do
    blog_post.publish!
    expect(blog_post).to be_published
  end
end
```

23.4   Custom Expectation Matchers

When you find that none of the stock expectation matchers provide a natural-feeling expectation, you can very easily write your own. All you need to do is write a Ruby class that implements the following two methods:

- `matches?(actual)`
- `failure_message`

The following methods are optional for your custom matcher class:

- `does_not_match?(actual)`
- `failure_message_when_negated`
- `description`

The example given in the RSpec API documentation is a game in which players can be in various zones on a virtual board. To specify that a player bob should be in zone 4, you could write a spec like

```
expect(bob.current_zone).to eq(Zone.new("4"))
```

However, it's more expressive to say one of the following, using the custom matcher in Listing 23.1.

Listing 23.1 BeInZone custom expectation matcher class

```
# expect(bob) to be_in_zone(4) and expect(bob).to_not be_in_zone(3)
class BeInZone
  def initialize(expected)
    @expected = expected
  end

  def matches?(actual)
    @actual = actual
    @actual.current_zone.eql?(Zone.new(@expected))
  end

  def failure_message
    "expected #{@actual.inspect} to be in Zone #{@expected}"
  end

  def failure_message_when_negated
    "expected #{@actual.inspect} not to be in Zone #{@expected}"
  end
end
```

In addition to the matcher class, you would need to write the following method so that it'd be in scope for your spec.

```
def be_in_zone(expected)
  BeInZone.new(expected)
end
```

This is normally done by including the method and the class in a module, which is then included in your spec.

```
describe "Player behaviour" do
  include CustomGameMatchers
  ...
end
```

Or you can include helpers globally in a `spec_helper.rb` file required from your spec file(s):

```
RSpec.configure do |config|
  config.include CustomGameMatchers
end
```

RSpec

23.4.1   Custom Matcher DSL

RSpec includes a DSL for easier definition of custom matchers. The DSL's directives match the methods you implement on custom matcher classes. Just add code
similar to the following example in a file within the spec/support directory.

```ruby
require 'nokogiri'

RSpec::Matchers.define :contain_text do |expected|
  match do |response_body|
    squished(response_body).include?(expected.to_s)
  end

  failure_message do |actual|
    "expected the following element's content to include
    #{expected.inspect}:\n\n#{response_text(actual)}"
  end

  failure_message_when_negated do |actual|
    "expected the following element's content to not include
    #{expected.inspect}:\n\n#{squished(actual)}"
  end

  def squished(response_body)
    Nokogiri::XML(response_body).text.squish
  end
end
```

23.4.2   Fluent Chaining

You can create matchers that obey a fluent interface using the chain method:

```ruby
RSpec::Matchers.define(:tip) do |expected_tip|
  chain(:on) do |tab|
    @tab = tab
  end

  match do |person|
    person.tip_for(@tab) == expected_tip
  end
end
```

This matcher can be used as follows:

```ruby
describe Customer do
  it { is_expected.to tip(10).on(50) }
end
```

In this way, you can begin to create your own fluent domain-specific languages for
testing your complex business logic in a very readable way.

23.5   Helper Methods

The `let` method is an example of a helper. You can define your own helper methods simply by defining methods using normal Ruby `def` syntax, inside of an example group. These helper methods will be available to examples in the group in which they are defined and groups nested within that group but not parent or sibling groups.

```
RSpec.describe "an example" do
  def help
    :available
  end

  it "has access to methods defined in its group" do
    expect(help).to be(:available)
  end
end
```

In the many years that I've been doing RSpec, I've never defined a helper method this way. However, I have defined helper methods in a module and included them using the `config.include` configuration option.

You would define these helper modules somewhere inside of the `spec/support` directory, probably in their own file.

```
# spec/support/helpers.rb
module Helpers
  def help
    :available
  end
end
```

You can include this module in all example groups like this:

```
RSpec.configure do |c|
  c.include Helpers
end

RSpec.describe "an example group" do
  it "has access to the helper methods defined in the module" do
    expect(help).to be(:available)
  end
end
```

Create *macro-style* helpers by mixing in your module using `config.extend` instead of `include`. The methods in the module will be available in the example groups themselves (but not in the actual examples).

```
RSpec.configure do |c|
```

```
  c.extend Helpers
end

RSpec.describe "an example group" do
  puts "Help is #{help}"
```

You can find a complete description of this topic in the official RSpec documentation at https://relishapp.com/rspec/rspec-core/v/3-5/docs/helper-methods/define-helper-methods-in-a-module.

23.6   Shared Behaviors

Often you'll want to specify similar behavior in multiple specs. It would be silly to type out the same code over and over. Fortunately, RSpec has a feature named shared behaviors that aren't run individually but, rather, are included into other behaviors; they are defined using shared_examples.

```
shared_examples "a phone field" do
  it "has 10 digits" do
    business = Business.new(phone_field: '8004567890')
    expect(business.errors_on(:phone_field)).to be_empty
  end
end

shared_examples "an optional phone field" do
  it "handles nil" do
    business = Business.new phone_field: nil
    expect(business.attributes[phone_field]).to be_nil
  end
end
```

You can invoke a shared example using the it_behaves_like method, in place of an it.

```
describe "phone" do
  let(:phone_field) { :phone }
  it_behaves_like "a phone field"
end

describe "fax" do
  let(:phone_field) { :fax }
  it_behaves_like "a phone field"
  it_behaves_like "an optional phone field"
end
```

You can put the code for shared examples almost anywhere, but the default convention is to create a file named spec/support/shared_examples.rb to hold them.

23.7   Shared Context

When used in combination, `shared_context` and `include_context` enable you to share before/after hooks, `subject` declarations, `let` declarations, and method definitions across example groups. This is useful in cases when several examples share some state. To define a shared context, supply a name and block of code to the `shared_context` macro-style method.

```
# spec/support/authenticated_user.rb
RSpec.shared_context 'authenticated user' do
  let(:current_user) { create(:user) }

  before do
    sign_in current_user
  end
end
```

To include a shared context in your examples, use the `include_context` macro-style method.

```
context "user is authenticated" do
  include_context 'authenticated user'
  ...
end
```

The recommended location to place `shared_context` definitions is in the spec/support directory.

23.8   Mocks and Stubs

RSpec has mocking and stubbing facilities that are almost the same and equally powerful as any competitors.

    Confused about the difference between mocks and stubs? Read Martin Fowler's explanation at https://www.martinfowler.com/articles/mocksArentStubs .html.

23.8.1   Test Doubles

A test double is an object that stands in for another in your system during a code example. To create a test double object, you simply call the `double` method anywhere in a spec and give it a name as an optional parameter.

⚲ Although it's not required, it's a good idea to give test double objects a name if you will be using more than one of them in your spec. If you use multiple anonymous test doubles, you'll probably have a hard time telling them apart if one fails.

```
echo = double('echo')
```

With a test double, you can set expectations about what messages are sent to your test double during the course of your spec (commonly known as a mock).

Mocks with message expectations will cause the spec to fail if its expectations are not met. To set an expectation on a test double, we use the `receive` matcher.

```
expect(echo).to receive(:sound)
```

The chained method `with` is used to define expected parameters. If we care about the return value, we chain `and_return` at the end of the expectation.

```
expect(echo).to receive(:sound).with("hey").and_return("hey")
```

ℹ Note

In older versions of RSpec, you would define mock and stub objects via the `mock` and `stub` methods, respectively. Although these methods are still available in RSpec 3.0, they are available only for backwards compatibility and may be removed in a future version.

23.8.2   Stubs

You can easily create a stub object in RSpec via the `double` factory method. You pass stub a name, along with default attributes, and the method returns values as a hash.

```
yodeler = double('yodeler', yodels?: true)
```

By the way, there's no rule that the name parameter of a mock or stub needs to be a string. It's pretty typical to pass `double` a class reference corresponding to the real type of object. However, that class is not used in any special way; it's just an identifier.

```
yodeler = double(Yodeler, yodels?: true)
```

23.8.3 Null Objects

Occasionally you just want an object for testing purposes that accepts any message passed to it—a pattern known as null object. It's possible to make one using the `as_null_object` method with a test double object.

```
null_object = double('null').as_null_object
```

23.8.4 Partial Mocking and Stubbing

You can install or replace methods on any object, not just doubles, with a technique called partial mocking and stubbing. Just use `allow` (instead of `expect`) plus the usual `receive` syntax but on a "real" object instead of a test double, like this:

```
allow(invoice).to receive(:billed_expenses).and_return(543.21)
```

Note that the underlying method is *not* invoked. If you try to stub a method on an object that doesn't respond to that method, then RSpec will try to help you out by raising an error. That precautionary measure can be turned on and off in `spec_helper.rb`:

```
# Prevents you from mocking or stubbing a method that does not exist on
# a real object. This is generally recommended, and will default to
# true in RSpec 4
mocks.verify_partial_doubles = true
```

23.8.5 `receive_message_chain`

It's really common to find yourself writing some gnarly code when you rely on `double` to spec behavior of nested method calls.[3] But, sometimes you need to stub methods *down a dot chain*, where one method is invoked on another method, which is itself invoked on another method, and so on. For example, you may need to stub out a set of recent, unpublished blog posts in chronological order, like `BlogPost.recent.unpublished.chronological`.

Try to figure out what's going on in the following example. I bet it takes you more than a few seconds!

```
allow(BlogPost).to receive(:recent).
  and_return(double(unpublished: double(chronological: [double,
    double, double])))
```

---

3. Active Record scopes are notoriously prone to causing this problem.

That example code can be factored to be more verbose, which makes it a little easier to understand but is still pretty bad.

```
chronological = [double, double, double]
unpublished = double(chronological: chronological)
recent = double(unpublished: unpublished)
allow(BlogPost).to receive(recent).and_return(recent)
```

Luckily, Rspec gives you the `receive_message_chain` method, which understands exactly what you're trying to do here and dramatically simplifies the code needed:

```
allow(BlogPost)
  .to receive_message_chain(:recent, :unpublished, :chronological)
  .and_return([double, double, double])
```

However, just because it's so easy to stub the chain, doesn't mean it's the right thing to do. The question to ask yourself is, "Why am I testing something related to methods so deep down a chain? Could I move my tests down to that lower level?" Demeter would be proud.

23.9   Running Specs

Specs are executable documents. Each example block is executed inside its own object instance, to ensure that the integrity of each is preserved (with regard to instance variables, etc.).

If I run a spec using the `rspec` command that should have been installed on my system by the RSpec gem, I'll get output similar to that of `Test::Unit`—familiar, comfortable, and passing. Just not too informative.

```
$ rspec spec/models/colleague_import_spec.rb
.........

Finished in 0.330223 seconds
9 examples, 0 failures
```

RSpec is capable of outputting results of a spec run in many formats. The traditional dots output that looks just like `Test::Unit` is called progress and, as we saw a moment ago, is the default. However, if we add the `-fd` command-line parameter to `rspec`, we can cause it to output the results of its run in a very different and much more interesting format, the documentation format.

```
$ rspec -fd spec/models/billing_code_spec.rb
BillingCode
```

```
    has a bidirectional habtm association
    removes bidirectional association on deletion

Finished in 0.066201 seconds
2 examples, 0 failures
```

Nice, huh? If this is the first time you're seeing this kind of output, I wouldn't be surprised if you drifted off in speculation about whether RSpec could help you deal with sadistic PHB-imposed[4] documentation requirements.

Having these sorts of self-documenting capabilities is one of the biggest wins you get in choosing RSpec. It compels many people to work toward better spec coverage of their project. I also know from experience that development managers tend to really appreciate RSpec's output, even to the extent of incorporating it into their project deliverables.

Besides the different formatting, there are all sorts of other command-line options available. Just type `rspec --help` to see them all.

23.9.1   Failing and Skipping Examples

You can make an example fail by calling `fail` in it. (I don't think this is particularly useful.)

You can also `skip` an example, which is similar to pending, covered earlier in the chapter, but with different semantics. I've never actually done that, but I have used a neat trick for temporarily skipping examples—prefix `it`, `specify`, or `example` with an `x`.

```
describe "accepting" do
  let(:scheduled_at) { 2.days.from_now }

  xit "a proposed time" do
    # skipped
```

🔍 Try the same trick, but with an `f` instead of an `x` and see what happens!

There are a huge number of ways to fail, make pending, and skip examples—they're all detailed in the official RSpec documentation at https://relishapp.com/rspec/rspec-core/v/3-5/docs/pending-and-skipped-examples.

---

4. Pointy-Haired Boss, as per Dilbert comic strips.

23.9.2   Filtering

Remember earlier in the chapter we covered metadata. One of the use cases for it is to constrain which examples are run via filters. The most common use case is to run a subset of examples belonging to a particular category. Remember, you specify metadata using only symbols, meaning you can treat them as tags.

For more information on filtering, refer to the official RSpec documentation at https://relishapp.com/rspec/rspec-core/v/3-5/docs/filtering.

23.10   Factory Girl

Throughout the examples in this chapter, we've been using a test data generator gem by Thoughtbot called Factory Girl. It replaces the need for Rails' built-in test fixtures functionality and gives you the capability to easily generate both saved and unsaved instances of Active Record objects. It also offers support for multiple factories for the same class (representing different roles and use cases), as well as factory inheritance. It's a powerful and extremely popular bit of software.

23.10.1   Setup

To use Factory Girl in Rails install the Rails-specific gem, not the core library.

```
gem 'factory_girl_rails'
```

Once the gem is installed, Rails generators will generate boilerplate Factory Girl factory definition files instead of fixtures.

Since we're using RSpec, we'll keep our factory definitions in `spec/factories`. You can put all your factory definitions into one big `factory.rb` file, or you can have one factory definion file per Active Record model class. I prefer to use one file on smaller projects.

Next, include Factory Girl's methods in your RSpec scopes by adding the following line to the configuration block in `rails_helper.rb`:

```
config.include FactoryGirl::Syntax::Methods
```

23.10.2   Factory Definitions

Factory Girl has its own DSL-like syntax for defining model factories. Each factory has a name and a set of attributes. The name is used to guess the class of the object by default, but it's possible to explicitly specify it:

```
FactoryGirl.define do
  factory :user do
```

```
    first_name "John"
    last_name "Doe"
    admin false
  end

  factory :admin, class: User do
    first_name "Admin"
    last_name "User"
    admin true
  end
end
```

It is highly recommended that you have one factory for each class that provides the simplest set of attributes necessary to create an instance of that class. If you're creating Active Record objects, that means that you should only provide attributes that are required through validations and that do not have defaults.

Other factories can be created through inheritance to cover common scenarios for each class. For instance, we could refactor the previous code example to be a little more concise using inheritance:

```
FactoryGirl.define do
  factory :user do
    name "John Doe"
    admin false

    factory :admin do
      name "Admin"
      admin true
    end
  end
end
```

🔍 Attempting to define multiple factories with the same name will raise an error.

Assuming that one of your helper files contains the line `FactoryGirl.find_ definitions` then factory definition files will be automatically loaded from the following locations:

```
test/factories.rb
spec/factories.rb
test/factories/*.rb
spec/factories/*.rb
```

RSpec

23.10.3   Usage

`factory_girl` supports several different build strategies: `build`, `create`, `attributes_for`, and `build_stubbed`:

```ruby
# Returns a User instance that's not saved
user = build(:user)

# Returns a saved User instance
user = create(:user)

# Returns a hash of attributes that can be used to build a User instance
attrs = attributes_for(:user)

# Returns an object with all defined attributes stubbed out
stub = build_stubbed(:user)

# Passing a block to any of the methods above will yield the return object
create(:user) do |user|
  user.posts.create(attributes_for(:post))
end
```

No matter which strategy is used, it's possible to override the defined attributes by passing a hash following the symbolized name of the factory:

```ruby
>> user = build(:user, first_name: "Joe")
>> user.first_name
=> "Joe"
```

23.10.4   Static versus Dynamic Attributes

Most factory attributes can be added using static values that are evaluated when the factory is defined, but some attributes (such as associations and other attributes that must be dynamically generated) will need values assigned each time an instance is generated. These "dynamic" attributes can be added by passing a block instead of a parameter:

```ruby
factory :user do
  first_name "John"
  last_name "Doe"
  activation_code { User.generate_activation_code }
  date_of_birth   { 21.years.ago }
end
```

Because of the block syntax in Ruby, defining hash attributes as Hashes (like for populating serialized or JSON columns) requires two sets of curly brackets:

```ruby
factory :user do
```

```
  preferences { { marketing_emails: false, sms_alerts: true } }
end
```

23.10.5   Aliases

You can define aliases to existing factories to make them easier to re-use as associations in other factories. This comes in handy when, for example, your Post object has an author attribute that actually refers to an instance of a User class.

```
factory :user, aliases: [:author, :commenter] do
  first_name "John"
  last_name "Doe"
  date_of_birth { 18.years.ago }
end

factory :post do
  author
  title "How to read a book effectively"
  body "There are five steps involved."
end

factory :comment do
  commenter
  body "Great article!"
end
```

23.10.6   Dependent Attributes

Attributes can be based on the values of other attributes using the evaluator that is yielded to dynamic attribute blocks:

```
factory :user do
  first_name "Joe"
  last_name "Blow"
  email { "#{first_name}.#{last_name}@example.com".downcase }
end
```

23.10.7   Associations

It's possible to set up associations within factories. As I've already shown you in previous examples, if the factory name is the same as the association name, the factory name can be left out.

```
factory :post do
  author
end
```

You can also specify a different factory or override attributes:

```
factory :post do
  association :author, factory: :user, last_name: "Writely"
end
```

The behavior of the association method varies depending on the build strategy used for the parent object.

```
# Builds and saves a User and a Post
post = create(:post)
post.new_record?        # => false
post.author.new_record? # => false
```

```
{lang=ruby}
# Builds and saves a User, and then builds but does not save a Post
post = build(:post)
post.new_record?        # => true
post.author.new_record? # => false
```

To not save the associated object, specify `strategy: :build` in the factory:

```
factory :post do
  # ...
  association :author, factory: :user, strategy: :build
end
```

```
# Builds a User, and then builds a Post, but does not save either
post = build(:post)
post.new_record?        # => true
post.author.new_record? # => true
```

🔑 Note that the `strategy: :build` option must be passed to an explicit call to association and cannot be used with implicit associations.

Generating data for a `has_many` relationship is a bit more involved, depending on the amount of flexibility desired.

```
FactoryGirl.define do
  # post factory with a `belongs_to` association for the user
  factory :post do
    title "Through the Looking Glass"
    user
  end

  # user factory without associated posts
  factory :user do
    name "John Doe"
```

```
factory :user_with_posts do
  # posts_count is declared as transient meaning it won't be
  # passed to the model as an attribute. However, it will be
  # available in the evaluator
  transient do
    posts_count 5
  end
```

The `after(:create)` callback yields the user instance itself and the evaluator, which stores all values from the factory (including transient attributes).

The `create_list` method takes a factory name, followed by the number of records to create and any attributes you want to override.

```
after(:create) do |user, evaluator|
  create_list(:post, evaluator.posts_count, user: user)
```

This enables us to do the following:

```
create(:user).posts.length # 0
create(:user_with_posts).posts.length # 5
create(:user_with_posts, posts_count: 15).posts.length # 15
```

23.10.8 Sequences

Unique values in a specific format (for example, e-mail addresses) can be generated using sequences. Sequences are defined by calling `sequence` in a definition block, and values in a sequence are generated by calling `generate`:

```
# Defines a new sequence
FactoryGirl.define do
  sequence :email do |n|
    "person#{n}@example.com"
  end
end

generate :email
# => "person1@example.com"

generate :email
# => "person2@example.com"
```

Sequences can be used in dynamic attributes:

```
factory :invite do
  invitee { generate(:email) }
end
```

Or (somewhat confusingly) as implicit attributes:

```
factory :user do
  email # Same as `email { generate(:email) }`
end
```

It's also possible to define an in-line sequence that is only used in a particular factory, which I also find somewhat confusing in practice:

```
factory :user do
  sequence(:email) { |n| "person#{n}@example.com" }
end
```

You can also override the initial value:

```
factory :user do
  sequence(:email, 1000) { |n| "person#{n}@example.com" }
end
```

Without a block, the value will increment itself, starting at its initial value (which defaults to 1):

```
factory :post do
  sequence(:position)
end
```

Sequences can also have aliases. The sequence aliases share the same counter but make it easier to reuse succinctly. It's the same design approach used for factory name aliases:

```
factory :user do
  sequence(:email, 1000, aliases: [:sender, :receiver]){ |n|
    "person#{n}@example.com"
  }
end
```

23.10.9 Traits

Traits enable you to group attributes together and then apply them to any factory. It's a more fine-grained way to control factory creation, in contrast to using separate factories or inheritance.

```
factory :story do
  title "My awesome story"
  author

  trait :published do
    published true
```

```
  end

  trait :unpublished do
    published false
  end

  trait :week_long_publishing do
    start_at { 1.week.ago }
    end_at { Time.now }
  end

  trait :month_long_publishing do
    start_at { 1.month.ago }
    end_at { Time.now }
  end

  factory :week_long_published_story,
    traits: [:published, :week_long_publishing]

  factory :month_long_published_story,
    traits: [:published, :month_long_publishing]

  factory :week_long_unpublished_story,
    traits: [:unpublished, :week_long_publishing]

  factory :month_long_unpublished_story,
    traits: [:unpublished, :month_long_publishing]
end
```

Traits can be used as attributes:

```
factory :week_long_published_story_with_title, parent: :story do
  published
  week_long_publishing
  title { "Publishing that was started at #{start_at}" }
end
```

> ⚷ Traits that define the same attributes won't raise `AttributeDefini-tionErrors`; the trait that defines the attribute last gets precedence.

You can also override individual attributes granted by a trait in subclasses.

```
factory :user do
  name "Friendly User"
  login { name }

  trait :male do
    name "John Doe"
```

```
    gender "Male"
    login { "#{name} (M)" }
  end

  factory :brandon do
    male
    name "Brandon"
  end
end
```

Traits can also be passed in as a list of symbols when you construct an instance from `factory_girl`.

```
# creates an admin user with gender "Male" and name "Jon Snow"
create(:user, :admin, :male, name: "Jon Snow")
```

This capability works with `build`, `build_stubbed`, `attributes_for`, and `create`. The `create_list` and `build_list` methods are supported as well. Just remember to pass the number of instances as the second parameter.

```
# creates 3 admin users with gender "Male" and name "Jon Snow"
create_list(:user, 3, :admin, :male, name: "Jon Snow")
```

Traits can be used with associations easily too:

```
factory :post do
  association :user, :admin, name: 'John Doe'
end
```

Traits can be used within other traits to mix in their attributes.

```
factory :order do
  trait :completed do
    completed_at { 3.days.ago }
  end

  trait :refunded do
    completed
    refunded_at { 1.day.ago }
  end
end
```

Finally, traits can accept transient attributes.

```
factory :invoice do
  trait :with_amount do
    transient do
      amount 1
    end
```

```
      after(:create) do |invoice, evaluator|
        create :line_item, invoice: invoice, amount: evaluator.amount
      end
    end
end
```

```
>> create :invoice, :with_amount, amount: 2
```

23.10.10 Callbacks

There are four distinct callbacks available when constructing objects with Factory Girl:

after(:build) Called after a factory is built (via `FactoryGirl.build`, `FactoryGirl.create`)

before(:create) Called before a factory is saved (via `FactoryGirl.create`)

after(:create) Called after a factory is saved (via `FactoryGirl.create`)

after(:stub) Called after a factory is stubbed (via `FactoryGirl.build_stubbed`)

The following example defines a factory that calls the `generate_hashed_password` method after it is built.

```
factory :user do
  after(:build) { |user| generate_hashed_password(user) }
end
```

Note that you'll have an instance of the `user` passed to the block, in case you need it. You can also define multiple types of callbacks on the same factory:

```
factory :user do
  after(:build) { |user| do_something_to(user) }
  after(:create) { |user| do_something_else_to(user) }
end
```

Factories can also define any number of the same kind of callback. These callbacks will be executed in the order they are specified:

```
factory :user do
  after(:create) { this_runs_first }
  after(:create) { then_this }
end
```

Calling `create` will invoke both `after_build` and `after_create` callbacks. Also, like standard attributes, child factories will inherit (and can also define) callbacks from their parent factory.

RSpec

Multiple callbacks can be assigned to run a block; this is useful when building various strategies that run the same code (since there are no callbacks that are shared across all strategies).

```
factory :user do
  callback(:after_stub, :before_create) { do_something }
  after(:stub, :create) { do_something_else }
  before(:create, :custom) { do_a_third_thing }
end
```

To override callbacks for all factories, define them within the `FactoryGirl` `.define` block:

```
FactoryGirl.define do
  after(:build) { |object| puts "Built #{object}" }
  after(:create) { |object| AuditLog.create(attrs: object.attributes)
      }
```

. . .

You can also write callbacks that rely on Symbol's `to_proc` behavior to invoke methods on the object instance being built, like this:

```
# app/models/user.rb
class User < ActiveRecord::Base
  def confirm!
    # confirm the user account
  end
end
```

```
# spec/factories.rb
FactoryGirl.define do
  factory :user do
    after :create, &:confirm!
  end
end
```

23.10.11   Building or Creating Multiple Records

Sometimes, you'll want to create or build multiple instances of a factory at once.

```
built_users = build_list(:user, 25)
created_users = create_list(:user, 25)
```

These methods will build or create a specific number of factories and return them as an array. To set the attributes for each of the factories, you can pass in a hash as you normally would to a normal factory.

```
twenty_year_olds = build_list(:user, 25, date_of_birth: 20.years.ago)
```

The `build_stubbed_list` method will give you fully stubbed out instances:

```
build_stubbed_list(:user, 25) # array of stubbed users
```

There's also a set of `*_pair` methods for creating two records at a time:

```
built_users = build_pair(:user) # array of two built users
created_users = create_pair(:user) # array of two created users
```

If for some reason you need multiple attribute hashes, `attributes_for_list` will generate them:

```
users_attrs = attributes_for_list(:user, 25) # array of attribute hashes
```

23.10.12 Factory Girl and Active Record

When you invoke a factory, your definitions are used to compile a list of attributes that should be assigned to the resulting instance, as well as any associated factories. Associations are saved first so that foreign keys can be properly set on dependent models. To create a new model instance, Factory Girl first calls `new` without any arguments and then assigns each attribute in the order it is defined in the factory definition (including associations). Finally, it calls `save!` (which means an exception will be raised if creation fails).

Note that Factory Girl doesn't do anything special to create Active Record model instances. It doesn't interact with the database directly or extend Active Record or your models in any way.

As an example, take these factory definitions:

```
FactoryGirl.define do
  sequence(:email) { |n| "person-#{n}@example.com" }

  factory :user do
    email
  end

  factory :post do
    user
    title "Hello"
  end
end
```

If you call

```
post = create(:post)
```

it is roughly equivalent to writing the following:

```
user = User.new
user.email = "person-1@example.com"
user.save!
post = Post.new
post.title = "Hello"
post.user = user
post.save!
```

If your model has a polymorphic association, then you need to specify which factory to use to satisfy the association:

```
factory :post do
  association :author, factory: :user
  title "Hello"
end
```

A comprehensive explanation of Factory Girl (yes there's more!) would take much more room than what we can afford to use up in this chapter. Your best place to find out about topics like using Factory Girl with non-Active Record classes and testing factories is https://github.com/thoughtbot/factory_girl/blob/master/GETTING_STARTED.md.

23.11   RSpec and Rails

Throughout this chapter, we've been using the RSpec Rails gem, a drop-in replacement for the Rails testing subsystem. It supplies verification, mocking, and stubbing features customized for use with Rails models, controllers, and views. To install it, add the `rspec-rails` gem to your Gemfile's development and test groups.

   🔑 The reason you add `rspec-rails` to both the development and test groups is so that it can be picked up by your generator scripts.

Here's what that area of the Gemfile looks like in one of my typical projects:

```
group :development do
  gem 'foreman'
  gem 'listen', '~> 3.0.5'
  gem 'web-console', '>= 3.3.0'
end
```

```
group :development, :test do
  # Call 'byebug' anywhere in the code to stop execution and get a debugger console
  gem 'byebug', platform: :mri
  gem 'figaro'
  gem 'pry-rails'
  gem 'rspec-rails', '~> 3.5'
end

group :test do
  gem 'capybara'
  gem 'database_cleaner'
  gem 'factory_girl_rails'
  gem 'launchy'
  gem 'rspec-activemodel-mocks'
  gem 'timecop'
  gem 'vcr'
  gem 'webmock'
end
```

After bundling, run `rails g rspec:install` to generate the necessary configuration files and `spec` directory.

```
$ rails g rspec:install
    create .rspec
    create spec
    create spec/spec_helper.rb
    create spec/rails_helper.rb
```

Note that the generated `.rspec` file contains `--require spec_helper`, which will cause it to always be loaded, without the need for an explicit require.

23.11.1   `spec_helper.rb`

The `spec_helper` script contains the basic configuration for an RSpec installation. It lets you tweak settings that affect how RSpec itself operates, from its syntax, to the way that it communicates the results of spec runs, to the ways that it lets you mock and stub dependent objects.

A lot of the more interesting RSpec options are commented by default in the generated boilerplate file. Definitely dive in there and play with them for a better experience. My favorite is the block of code that changes the result formatter to be more verbose when you're running a single spec.

```
# Many RSpec users commonly either run the entire suite or an individual
# file, and it's useful to allow more verbose output when running an
# individual spec file.
if config.files_to_run.one?
  # Use the documentation formatter for detailed output,
  # unless a formatter has already been configured
  # (e.g. via a command-line flag).
  config.default_formatter = 'doc'
end
```

23.11.2 `rails_helper.rb`

If you are specifying/testing "plain-old Ruby objects" that happen to live in your Rails application, then you don't need to drag in the entire Rails environment. However, that's the exception to the rule. Most of the time you will want to initialize the Rails environment, as well as RSpec Rails features, by requiring `rails_helper` at the top of your spec.

The top of this helper looks like the top of almost any other script that runs Rails:

```
ENV['RAILS_ENV'] ||= 'test'
require File.expand_path('../../config/environment', FILE )
```

The rest of the file is like a Rails-flavored layer of cake on top of what was defined in `spec_helper.rb`. It includes things like settings related to maintainance of test data in the database using fixtures and code to check for pending migrations. It also has the following option:

```
# RSpec Rails can automatically mix in different behaviours to your tests
# based on their file location, for example enabling you to call `get` and
# `post` in specs under `spec/controllers`.
#
# You can disable this behaviour by removing the line below, and instead
# explicitly tag your specs with their type, e.g.:
#
#     RSpec.describe UsersController, :type => :controller do
#       # ...
#     end
#
# The different available types are documented in the features, such as in
# https://relishapp.com/rspec/rspec-rails/docs
config.infer_spec_type_from_file_location!
```

Some people like to be explicit, some don't. I won't judge you either way.

The RSpec Rails gem provides four different contexts for specs, corresponding to the four major kinds of objects you write in Rails. Along with the API support you need to write Rails specs, it also provides code generators and a bundle of Rake tasks.

```
$ rails -T spec
rails spec # Run all specs in spec directory (excluding plugin specs)
rails spec:controllers # Run the code examples in spec/controllers
rails spec:helpers    # Run the code examples in spec/helpers
rails spec:models     # Run the code examples in spec/models
rails spec:views      # Run the code examples in spec/views
```

23.11.3 Model Specs

Model specs help you design and verify the domain model of your Rails application, both Active Record and your own classes. RSpec Rails doesn't provide too much special functionality for model specs because there's not really much needed beyond what's provided by the base library.

Let's generate a Schedule model and examine the default spec that is created along with it.

```
$ rails generate model Schedule name:string
    invoke active_record
    create    db/migrate/20131202160457_create_schedules.rb
    create    app/models/schedule.rb
    invoke    rspec
    create      spec/models/schedule_spec.rb
```

The boilerplate spec/models/schedule_spec.rb looks like

```
require 'spec_helper'

describe Schedule do
  pending "add some examples to (or delete) #{__FILE__}"
end
```

Assume, for example, that our Schedule class has a collection of day objects.

```
class Schedule < ActiveRecord::Base
  has_many :days
end
```

Let's specify that we should be able to get a roll-up total of hours from schedule objects. Instead of fixtures, we'll mock out the days dependency.

```
require 'spec_helper'

describe Schedule do
```

```
  let(:schedule) { Schedule.new }

  it "should calculate total hours" do
    days = double('days')
    expect(days).to receive(:sum).with(:hours).and_return(40)
    allow(schedule).to receive(:days).and_return(days)
    expect(schedule.total_hours).to eq(40)
  end
end
```

Here we've taken advantage of the fact that association proxies in Rails are rich objects. Active Record gives us several methods for running database aggregate functions. We set up an expectation that `days` should receive the `sum` method with one argument—`:hours`—and return `40`. We can satisfy this specification with a very simple implementation:

```
class Schedule
  has_many :days

  def total_hours
    days.sum :hours
  end
end
```

A potential benefit of mocking the `days` proxy is that we no longer rely on the database[5] in order to write our specifications and implement the `total_hours` method, which will make this particular spec execute lightning fast.

On the other hand, a valid criticism of this approach is that it makes our code harder to refactor. Our spec would fail if we changed the implementation of `total_hours` to use `Enumerable#inject`, even though the external behavior doesn't change. Specifications are not only describing the visible behavior of object but the interactions between an object and its associated objects as well. Mocking the association proxy in this case lets us clearly specify how a `Schedule` should interact with its `Days`.

Leading mock objects advocates see mock objects as a temporary design tool. You may have noticed that we haven't defined the `Day` class yet. So another benefit of using mock objects is that they enable us to specify behavior in true isolation and during design-time. There's no need to break our design rhythm by stopping to create the `Day` class and database table. This may not seem like a big deal for such a

---

5. Well, that's not quite true. Active Record still connects to the database to get the column information for Schedule.

simple example, but for more involved specifications it is really helpful to just focus on the design task at hand. After the database and real object models exist, you can go back and replace the mock `days` with calls to the real deal. This is a subtle, yet very powerful, message about mocks that is usually missed.

23.11.3.1 Mocking and Stubbing Active Record

Once you start using mocking and stubbing in Rails, you'll inevitably run into situations where Active Record pushes back due to *type mismatches*. The most common scenario is trying to assign a double to an association proxy.

```
>> Bid.create!(auction: double('auction'))

=> ActiveRecord::AssociationTypeMismatch:
     Auction expected, got RSpec::Mocks::Double
```

One solution is to always use real Active Record objects instead of doubles. Another is to use the `rspec-activemodel-mocks` gem. It provides two methods for creating fake Active Record objects, `mock_model` and `stub_model`.

The `mock_model` method creates a test double with the most common Active Model and Active Record methods already stubbed out. The first argument to `mock_model` is either the class that you're mocking or a string representing the name of a class. The second argument is a hash of attributes to stub out, exactly like `double`.

Mocks created with `mock_model` slot right in to associations.

```
>> Bid.create!(auction: mock_model(Auction))
=> #<Bid id: 12, user_id: 1004, auction_id: 1003, ...>
```

Notice that the values of `user_id` and `auction_id` are a little suspicious? They are fake.

⚡ You can even use `mock_model` to impersonate model classes that don't even exist yet, which makes it a great tool for real test-driven design.

The second method is `stub_model(ActiveRecordClass)`, and it does require a real Active Record class as its first parameter. It stubs out its own `to_param` method to return a generated value that is unique to each object. If you want to mimic a new record, chain the `as_new_record` method.

```
stub_model(Person)
stub_model(Person).as_new_record
```

RSpec

```
stub_model(Person) {|p| p.first_name = "David"}
```

As you can see in the third example provided, you can use an Active Record–style block to initialize stubbed attributes.

23.11.4 Routing Specs

One of Rails' central components is routing. The routing mechanism is the way Rails takes an incoming request URL and maps it to the correct controller and action. Given its importance, it is a good idea to specify the routes in your application. You can do this by providing specs in the `spec/routes` directory and have two matchers to use, `route_to` and `be_routable`.

```
context "Messages routing" do
  it "routes /messages/ to messages#show" do
    expect(get: "/messages").to route_to(
      controller: "articles",
      action: "index"
    )
  end

  it "does not route an update action" do
    expect(post: "/messages").to_not be_routable
  end
end
```

23.11.5 Controller Specs

RSpec gives you the capability to specify your controllers either in isolation from their associated views or together with them, as in regular Rails tests.

According to the API docs:

> Controller Specs support running specs for Controllers in two modes, which represent the tension between the more granular testing common in TDD and the more high-level testing built into Rails. BDD sits somewhere in between: we want to achieve a balance between specs that are close enough to the code to enable quick fault isolation and far enough away from the code to enable refactoring with minimal changes to the existing specs.

23.11.5.1 Setup

The controller class is passed to the `describe` method like this:

```
RSpec.describe MessagesController, type: :controller do
```

If your example requires an authenticated user, as is usually the case, you can sign one in inside of a `before` block.

```
let(:user) { create(:user) }

before(:each) do
  sign_in(user)
end
```

The `sign_in` helper method is provided by Devise via the following two lines in `rails_helper.rb`, which should have been added by the Devise installer script:

```
# Enable Devise mocking
config.include Devise::Test::ControllerHelpers, type: :controller
```

23.11.5.2 Writing Examples

I typically organize my controller examples by action and HTTP method. Depending on the application, I might have a high-level context entitled "happy path," where I avoid cluttering the examples with test for edge cases.

In the following example, I've written a basic spec for the `index` action. The most fundamental expectation is that the response should be successful, returning HTTP's `200 OK` response code.

I trigger execution of the controller action using a method matching the desired HTTP method, such as `get` or `post`. (The others are `patch`, `put`, `head`, and `delete`.)

```
it "is successful" do
  get :index
  expect(response.status).to eq(200)
end
```

If the action takes parameters, I supply them via a `params` hash option.

```
describe "accepting" do
  let(:scheduled_at) { 2.days.from_now }

  it "a proposed time" do
  post :accept, params: { id: call_request.id,
                          scheduled_at: scheduled_at.to_s }
```

Besides `params`, you can also pass `session`, `flash`, and `cookies` to set those values, respectively. You also have the capability to simulate request headers and CGI variables.

```
# setting an HTTP Header
get :index, headers: "Content-Type" => "text/plain"
```

```
# setting a CGI variable
get :index, headers: "HTTP_REFERER" => "http://example.com/home"
```

If you are trying to test an AJAX request, then you can set `xhr: true`.

```
post :decline, params: { id: call_request.id }, xhr: true
```

23.11.5.3 Expectations

If the controller action I'm testing is supposed to redirect, then I set an expectation for a 302 status code and assert on the redirect location.

```
expect(response.status).to eq(302)
expect(response.headers["Location"]).to include("upcoming")
```

Other basic expectations that apply to most controller actions include checking the template to be rendered and variable assignment.

```
it "renders the index template " do
  get :index
  expect(response).to render_template(:index)
end

it "assigns the found messages for the view" do
  get :index
  expect(assigns(:messages)).to include(@message)
end
```

You are given access to the controller instance under test via the method `con-troller`. This gives you the capability to stub out helper methods. For instance, let's say you were using something other than Devise for authentication. Then you might want to stub out `current_user` (or its equivalent) to return a user instance.

```
let(:user) { stub_model(User, name: "Quentin") }

before(:each) do
  allow(controller).to receive(:current_user).and_return(user)
end
```

23.11.5.4 Isolation and Integration Modes

By default, RSpec on Rails controller specs run in isolation mode, meaning that view templates are not involved. The benefit of this mode is that you can spec the controller in complete isolation from the view, hence the name.

> Maybe you can sucker someone else into maintaining the view specs? Just kidding, but view specs for complicated user interfaces are known to be a pain in the you-know-what. On the other hand, having separate view specs provides much better *fault isolation*, which is a fancy way of saying that you'll have an easier time figuring out what's wrong when something fails.

A section on View Specs is coming up soon, but if you prefer to exercise your views in conjunction with your controller logic inside the same controller specs, just as traditional Rails functional tests do, then you can tell RSpec on Rails to run in integration mode using the `render_views` macro. It's not an all-or-nothing decision—you can specify the option at whatever context level you want.

```
describe "Requesting /messages using GET" do
  render_views
```

23.11.5.5 Specifying Errors

Ordinarily, Rails rescues exceptions that occur during action processing, so that it can respond with a 501 error code and give you that great error page with the stack trace and request variables and so on. In order to directly specify that an action should raise an error, you bypass Rails' default handling of errors and those specified with `rescue_from` with RSpec method `bypass_rescue`.

To illustrate, assuming the `ApplicationController` invokes `rescue_from` for the exception `AccessDenied` and redirects to `401.html`

```
class ApplicationController < ActionController::Base
  rescue_from AccessDenied, with: :access_denied

  private

  def access_denied
    redirect_to "/401.html"
  end
end
```

then we could test that an error was raised for a controller action using `bypass_rescue`.

```
it "raises an error" do
  bypass_rescue
  expect { get :index }.to raise_error(AccessDenied)
end
```

If `bypass_rescue` was not included in the preceding example, the spec would have failed due to Rails rescuing the exception and redirecting to the page `401.html`.

23.11.6   View Specs

Controller specs let us integrate the view to make sure there are no errors with the view, but sometimes we can do even better by specifying the views themselves. RSpec will let us write a specification for a view, completely isolated from the underlying controller. We can specify that certain tags exist and that the right data is output in the user interface.

Assuming you have RSpec Rails installed and available to your development environment, then among the boilerplate files that you will get when you generate resources and/or controllers are view specs. This is what a default one looks like:

```
require 'rails_helper'

RSpec.describe "messages/show.html.haml", type: :view do
  pending "add some examples to (or delete) #{ FILE }"
end
```

The `type: :view` option tells RSpec to expect the example group (`describe` or `context`) to contain the path to a template.

Let's say we want to write a page that displays a private message sent between members of an internet forum. RSpec creates the `spec/views/messages` directory when we use the controller generator. The first thing we would do is create a file in that directory for the show view, naming it `show.html.haml_spec.rb`. Next we would set up the information to be displayed on the page.

```
describe "messages/show.html.haml" do
  before(:each) do
    @message = build(:message, subject: "RSpec rocks!")

    sender = build(:person, name: "Obie Fernandez")
    expect(@message).to receive(:sender).and_return(sender)

    recipient = build(:person, name: "Pat Maddox")
    expect(@message).to receive(:recipient).and_return(recipient)
```

If you want to be a little more concise at the cost of one really long line of code that you'll have to break up into multiple lines, you can create the mocks inline like this:

```
describe "messages/show.html.haml " do
```

```
before(:each) do
  @message = build_stubbed(:message,
    subject: "RSpec rocks!",
    sender: FactoryGirl.build_stubbed(:person, name: "Obie Fernandez"),
    recipient: FactoryGirl.build_stubbed(:person, name: "Pat Maddox"))
```

Either way, this is standard mock usage similar to what we've seen before. Again, mocking the objects used in the view enables us to completely isolate the specification.

23.11.6.1   Assigning Variables

We now need to assign the message to the view. The `rspec_rails` gem gives us a method named `assign` to do just that.

```
assign(:message, @message)
```

Fantastic! Now we are ready to begin specifying the view page.

23.11.6.2   Rendering

To trigger rendering, we'll use the `render` method, which picks up a path to a template from its example group description. The `render` method has the same underlying code as render in a controller context, so the usual options such as :`partial` and :`collection` will also work.)

The result of rendering the view template will be made available as rendered, which is the object on which we will set our expectation.

```
it "displays the message subject" do
  render
  expect(rendered).to contain('RSpec rocks!')
end
```

Let's get a little more specific and verify that the message subject is wrapped in an <h1> tag. We'll use Capybara's `have_selector`, which takes two arguments—a CSS-style selector and a hash of options such as :`text`.

```
it "displays the message subject as primary heading" do
  render
  expect(rendered).to have_selector('h1', text: 'RSpec rocks!')
end
```

23.11.7   Helper Specs

Helper specs are marked by :`type` => :`helper` or detected automatically based on their location in `spec/helpers` if you have set `config.infer_spec_type_from_file_location`!. They expose a helper object, which includes the helper module being specified, the `ApplicationHelper` module (if there is one) and all of the helpers built into Rails. They do not include the other helper modules in your app, only the one specified in the spec itself.

To access the methods you're specifying, simply call them directly on the `helper` object. Note that helper specs are for testing helper methods in isolation, helper methods defined in controllers are not included.

```
describe ProfileHelper, :type => :helper do
  describe "#profile_photo" do
    it "returns nil if user's photos is empty" do
      user = mock_model(User, photos: [])
      expect(helper.profile_photo(user)).to be_nil
    end
```

It's a bad practice, but if your helper method relies on a particular instance variable being set, you can use the `assign` method, just like you would in a view spec.

```
RSpec.describe ApplicationHelper, :type => :helper do
  describe "#page_title" do
   it "returns the instance variable" do
    assign(:title, "My Title")
    expect(helper.page_title).to eql("My Title")
  end
```

23.11.8   RSpec and Generators

RSpec ensures that other generators in your project are aware that it is your chosen test library. Subsequently, it will be used for command-line generation of models, controllers, etc.

```
$ rails generate model Invoice
      invoke       active_record
      create       db/migrate/20100304010121_create_invoices.rb
      create       app/models/invoice.rb
      invoke       rspec
      create       spec/models/invoice_spec.rb
```

23.11.9   RSpec Options

The `.rspec` file contains a list of default command-line options. The generated file looks like

```
--color
--format progress
```

You can change it to suit your preference. I like my spec output in color but usually prefer the more verbose output of `--format documentation`.

💬 Tim says . . .

I go back and forth between preferring the dots of the `progress` format and the verbose output of the `documentation` format. With the more verbose output and long spec suites, it's easy to miss whether something failed if you look away from your screen. Especially on terminals with short buffers.

Here are some additional options that you might want to set in your `.rspec`

```
--fail-fast        Tells RSpec to stop running the test suite on the
                   first failed test

-b, --backtrace    Enable full backtrace

-p, --profile      Enable profiling of examples w/output of top
                   10 slowest examples
```

23.11.10   Support Files

As mentioned already in the chapter, RSpec Rails has the notion of supporting files containing custom matchers and any other code that helps set up additional functionality for your spec suite, and you keep those files in the `spec/support` directory.

If you want to load support files automatically, kind of how Rails handles its initializers, find the following line in `spec/rails_helper.rb` and uncomment it.

```
Dir[Rails.root.join("spec/support/**/*.rb")].each  { |f| require f }
```

💬 Tim says . . .

Traditionally a lot of extra helper methods were put into the `spec_helper` file, hence its name. However, nowadays it's generally easier to organize your additions in `spec/support` files, for the same reasons `config/initializers` can be easier to manage than sticking everything in `config/environment.rb`.

While we're on the subject, keep in mind that any methods defined at the top level of a support file will become global methods available from all objects, which almost certainly is not what you want. Instead, create a module and mix it in, just like you'd do in any other part of your application.

```
module AuthenticationHelpers
  def sign_in_as(user)
    # ...
  end
end


Rspec.configure do |config|
  config.include AuthenticationHelpers
end
```

23.12   Feature Specs with Capybara

A well-written acceptance/integration test suite is an essential ingredient in the success of any complex software project, particularly those run on Agile principles and methodologies, such as Extreme Programming (aka "XP"). One of the best definitions for an acceptance test is from the XP official website:

> The customer specifies scenarios to test when a user story has been correctly
> implemented. A story can have one or many acceptance tests, what ever it
> takes to ensure the functionality works. http://www.extremeprogramming
> .org/rules/functionaltests.html

Acceptance tests let us know that we are done implementing a given feature, or user story, in XP lingo. Incidentally, Capybara adds a DSL to RSpec that enables defining examples using the same XP lingo we are used to. Instead of using the describe method to group together related examples of behavior, we use feature. Instead of before we can describe common setup tasks as background. And to specify a scenario for a given feature, we use the scenario method with a description instead of it. Although these methods are simply aliases for existing RSpec methods, they add a level of readability and provide a visual differentiator from isolated RSpec examples.

```
feature "Some Awesome Feature" do
  background do
    # Setup some common state for all scenarios
    # same as `before(:each)`
  end

  scenario "A feature scenario" do
    ...
  end
end
```

Feature specs should be kept in the spec/features directory.

23.12.1 Capybara DSL

Besides `feature`, `background`, and `scenario`, the Capybara gem provides a DSL that enables you to interact with your application as you would via a web browser.

```ruby
require 'rails_helper'

RSpec.feature 'Authentication' do
  let(:email) { 'bruce@wayneenterprises.com' }
  let(:password) { 'i4mb4tm4n!!!' }

  scenario "signs in with correct credentials" do
    create :user, email: email, password: password
    visit(new_user_session_path)
    fill_in 'Email', with: email
    fill_in 'Password', with: password
    click_on 'Sign in'
    expect(response.status).to eq(302)
    expect(current_path).to eq(dashboard_path)
    expect(page).to have_content('Signed in successfully')
  end
  ...
end
```

Navigating to a web page using Capybara is done via the `visit` method, which will perform a `GET` request on the supplied path.

```ruby
visit('/dashboard')
visit(new_user_session_path)
```

To interact with a web page, Capybara provides action methods that enable the clicking of buttons or links and the capability to fill-in forms. The following are a listing of action methods you can expect to find in a Capybara feature spec:

```ruby
attach_file('Image', '/path/to/image.jpg')
check('A Checkbox')
choose('A Radio Button')
click_link('Link Text')
click_button('Save')
click_on('Link Text') # a link or a button
fill_in('Name', with: 'Bruce')
select('Option', from: 'Select Box')
uncheck('A Checkbox')
```

For a full reference of each action method, see the Capybara official documentation at http://rubydoc.info/github/jnicklas/capybara/master/Capybara/Node/Actions.

Finally, Capybara provides various matchers to assert a page contains a CSS selector, an XPath, or content.

```
expect(page).to have_selector('header h1')
expect(page).to have_css('header h1')

expect(page).to have_selector(:xpath, '//header/h1')
expect(page).to have_xpath('//header/h1')

expect(page).to have_content('TR4W')
```

23.12.1.1   Capybara Drivers

By default, Capybara uses `Rack::Test` as a headless driver to interact with your web application. It is best suited for acceptance tests that don't require any outside interaction or JavaScript testing. You can also override the driver that Capybara uses through the `default_driver` configuration setting.

```
Capybara.default_driver = :selenium
```

If only some scenarios test JavaScript, you can keep `:rack_test` as the default driver and explicitly set a driver for JavaScript.

```
Capybara.javascript_driver = :poltergeist
```

For any scenarios that require the JavaScript driver, add `js: true` following the scenario description.

```
scenario "JavaScript dependent scenario", js: true do
...
end
```

These driver settings should be set in `spec/spec_helper.rb`

23.13   Working with Files in Your Specs

Rails 5 introduced a neat little helper method called `file_fixture`, and in RSpec it is configured by default to read files out of the `spec/fixtures/files` directory.

```
file_fixture("example.txt").read # get the file's content
file_fixture("example.mp3").size # get the file size
```

If you're using the excellent Carrierwave gem (or doing any sort of file manipulation in your app), then you might find yourself having to read files into Factory Girl factory definitions.

```
FactoryGirl.define do
  factory :star do
    name "Cat Wrangler"
    description "Excellence in project management of ADD people"
    image { file_fixture('stars/cat-wrangler.jpg') }
  end
end
```

Note that a side effect of using real files with Carrierwave in your specs is that they might be repeatedly uploaded to AWS, slowing things down significantly and spending money for no good reason. To avoid that situation, you must tell Fog (the gem that interfaces Carrierwave to AWS) to operate in mock mode.

```
# spec/support/mock_fog.rb
Fog.mock!
service = Fog::Storage.new({
  :provider               => 'AWS',
  :aws_access_key_id       => ENV.fetch('AWS_ACCESS_KEY_ID'),
  :aws_secret_access_key   => ENV.fetch('AWS_SECRET_ACCESS_KEY')
})
service.directories.create(:key => 'name_of_your_bucket')
```

23.14 RSpec Tools

There are several open-source projects that enhance RSpec's functionality and your productivity or can be used in conjunction with RSpec and other testing libraries.

23.14.1 Database Cleaner

The database_cleaner gem (https://github.com/DatabaseCleaner/database_cleaner) enhances your ability to maintain a pristine data environment for your RSpec examples. It has a set of strategies for cleaning the database on an ongoing basis during spec runs and works with all sorts of databases and mapping libraries, not just Active Record and relational databases.

A full explanation of how to use Database Cleaner is out of scope. However, it is worth mentioning a common configuration issue related to integration testing. When Capybara runs, it takes care of starting and stopping the HTTP server that will be used for testing the application *in its own process*. However, drivers such as Selenium and Poltergeist require a separate, *out-of-process* HTTP server. In those cases, you can't use the default RSpec strategy of running every example in a transaction and then rolling it back to maintain a clean, isolated context. Database transactions are not shared across threads (nevermind processes), which means if you were to run a Capybara driver like Poltergeist in a transaction, any data you set in RSpec for the

RSpec

scenario would not be visible. Changes provoked by the application code in Polter-geist would not be visible to your spec either.

With the right combination of before hooks, we can configure RSpec to use a trun-cation strategy just for those JavaScript dependent scenarios. Using truncation, the entire database is emptied out after each test instead of running in a transaction. The reason you don't just want to use it by default is because it is much, much slower than using transactions.

```
RSpec.configure do |config|
  config.before(:suite) do
    DatabaseCleaner.clean_with(:truncation)
  end
  config.before(:each) do
    DatabaseCleaner.strategy = :transaction
  end
  config.before(:each, js: true) do
    DatabaseCleaner.strategy = :truncation
  end
  config.before(:each) do
    DatabaseCleaner.start
  end
  config.after(:each) do
    DatabaseCleaner.clean
  end
end
```

23.14.2   Guard-RSpec

Guard-RSpec is an automated testing framework that automagically runs (parts of) your spec suite whenever spec files are modified. It can really supercharge your red-green-refactor cycle!

Get it at https://github.com/guard/guard-rspec

23.14.3   Spring

As your application grows, an automated test suite can start to slow down your workflow when writing specs at a frequent rate. This is due to the nature of Rails needing to load the environment for each spec run. Spring alleviates this problem by loading the Rails environment only once and having the remaining specs use the preloaded environment. Spring is included in Rails by default as of version 4.1.

Get it at https://github.com/rails/spring

23.14.4   Flatware

Flatware enables you to distribute the work of running a large spec suite over all of the processors in your computer.

> Long test suites plague the lives of many a Ruby on Rails developer. For any project of significant size a massive test suite is needed to verify the correctness of the system. This verification has an upside of course, but also a downside. Long test suites kill productivity.

Learn more at https://hashrocket.com/blog/posts/true-parallel-processing-for -ruby-tests-with-flatware.

23.14.5   Specjour

If you work in an office environment alongside many other developers using Apple workstations, Specjour can significantly reduce the run time of your entire spec suite by using your co-workers' spare CPU cycles. It distributes the work over a LAN via Bonjour, running the specs in parallel on however many number of workers it finds available.

Get it at https://github.com/sandro/specjour.

23.14.6   SimpleCov

SimpleCov is a code coverage tool for Ruby. You can run it on your specs to see how much of your production code is covered. It provides HTML output to easily tell what code is covered by specs and what isn't. The results are outputted into a directory named `coverage` and contain a set of HTML files that you can browse by opening `index.html`.

Get it at https://github.com/colszowka/simplecov.

23.14.7   Timecop

The Timecop gem provides "time travel" and "time freezing" capabilities, making it dead simple to test time-dependent code in your specs. In other words, it provides a unified method to mock `Time.now`, `Date.today`, and `DateTime.now`.

Get it at https://github.com/travisjeffery/timecop.

23.14.8   WebMock

WebMock is a library for stubbing and setting expectations on HTTP requests in Ruby.

Get it at https://github.com/bblimke/webmock

I consider WebMock a must-have for serious development projects because it shuts down access from your specs to the outside world. You absolutely want that restriction because having your specs interacting with third-party services during a test run introduces serious delays and unpredictability into what should be an absolutely deterministic process.

23.14.9   VCR

VCR is a gem that records your test suite's HTTP interactions and replays them during future test runs for fast, deterministic, accurate tests. It's also an essential companion to WebMock.

https://github.com/vcr/vcr

When you're using VCR with Factory Girl, you'll want to configure RSpec in such a way that the generated primary keys for your Active Record objects are deterministic, which is a fancy way of saying that they'll always start from 1 and therefore be the same for each spec suite run. Use the following Database Cleaner configuration to get that effect:

```
config.before(:suite) do
  DatabaseCleaner.strategy = :truncation, { pre_count: true }
  DatabaseCleaner.clean_with :truncation
end

config.around(:each) do |example|
  DatabaseCleaner.cleaning do
    example.run
  end
end
```

This configuration works because of the obscure `pre_count:  true` option, which makes Database Cleaner reset the database's primary key sequence generators for each example.

23.15   Conclusion

Over the course of this huge chapter you've gotten a taste of the testing experience delivered by RSpec Rails and its extensive ecosystem. At first glance, RSpec may have seemed like the same thing as Rails' native `MiniTest` with some words substituted and shifted around, but hopefully you now realize that it is so much more.

Importantly, RSpec is the best tool out there for doing BDD/TDD in earnest. It emphasizes that those philosophies are much more about code design than code testing, a difficult lesson that world-class developers generally learn through experience and mentoring. The way that RSpec embodies those philosophies in its syntax and vocabulary makes the learning curve easier.

RSpec

Active Model API Reference

Active Model

Active Model is a Rails library containing various modules used in developing frameworks that need to interact with the Rails Action Pack and Action View libraries. It came about by extracting common functionality that was not persistence specific out of Active Record, so that third party libraries would not have to copy code from Rails or use *monkey patching* anymore.

Out of this extraction came extremely useful reusable functionality to developers of Rails compatible libraries, such as dirty attributes, validations, and serialization into JSON or XML. And simply by using these modules developers could be DRY and not need to rewrite what has already been done before.

Section headings reflect the name of the Class or Module where each Active Model API method is located and are organized in alphabetical order for easy lookup. Sub-sections appear according to the name of the Ruby file in which they exist within Active Model's `lib` directory. Finally, the sub-sub-sections are the API methods themselves.

A.1 `AttributeAssignment`

A.1.1 Instance Public Methods

A.1.1.1 `assign_attributes(new_attributes)`

Enables you to set all the attributes by passing in a hash of attributes with keys matching the attribute names.

```
class Cat
  include ActiveModel::AttributeAssignment
  attr_accessor :name, :status
```

```
end

cat = Cat.new
cat.assign_attributes(name: "Gorby", status: "yawning")
cat.name # => 'Gorby'
cat.status => 'yawning'
cat.assign_attributes(status: "sleeping")
cat.name # => 'Gorby'
cat.status => 'sleeping'
```

This method invokes `permitted?` on the `new_attributes` hash if it is defined. The most notable object in Rails that does not permit mass-assignment is `Action-Controller::Parameters` (aka "strong parameters"). An `ActiveModel::ForbiddenAttributesError` exception will be raised if assignment is prevented.

A.2 AttributeMethods

This module adds the capability for your class to have custom prefixes and suffixes on its methods. It's used by adding the definitions for the prefixes and suffixes, defining which methods on the object will use them, and then implementing the common behavior for when those methods are called. An example implementation is as follows:

```
class Record
  include ActiveModel::AttributeMethods

  attribute_method_prefix 'reset_'
  attribute_method_suffix '_highest?'
  define_attribute_methods :score

  attr_accessor :score
  attr_accessor :previous_score

  private

  def reset_attribute(attribute)
    send("#{attribute}=", nil)
  end

  def attribute_highest?(attribute)
    attribute > 1000 ? true : false
  end
end
```

A.2.1   Instance Public Methods

A.2.1.1   `alias_attribute(new_name, old_name)`

This obscure, but super-useful, method enables you to easily make aliases for attributes, including their reader and writer methods.

```
class Person
  include ActiveModel::AttributeMethods
  attr_accessor :name
  alias_attribute :full_name, :name
end

person = Person.new
person.name = "John Smith"
person.name        # => "John Smith"
person.full_name   # => "John Smith"
```

A.2.1.2   `attribute_method_affix(*affixes)`

Defines a prefix and suffix that when used in conjuction with `define_attribute_methods`   creates an instance method with the prefix and suffix wrapping the previous method name.

A.2.1.3   `attribute_method_prefix(*prefixes)`

Defines a prefix that when used in conjuction with `define_attribute_methods` creates an instance method with the prefix and the previous method name.

A.2.1.4   `attribute_method_suffix(*suffixes)`

Defines a suffix that when used in conjuction with `define_attribute_methods` creates an instance method with the suffix and the previous method name.

A.2.1.5   `define_attribute_method(attr_name)`

Declares an attribute that will get prefixed and suffixed. The `define_attribute_method` should be defined *after* any prefix, suffix, or affix definitions or they will not hook in.

```
class Record
  include ActiveModel::AttributeMethods

  attribute_method_prefix 'reset_'
  define_attribute_methods :score

  attr_accessor :score

  private
```

```
   def reset_attribute(attribute)
     send("#{attribute}=", nil)
   end
end

record = Record.new
record.score = 1
record.reset_score # => nil
```

A.2.1.6 `define_attribute_methods(*attr_names)`

Declares the attributes that will get prefixed and suffixed. Note that `define_attribute_methods` should be defined *after* any prefix, suffix or, affix definitions.

A.2.1.7 `generated_attribute_methods`

Returns whether or not the dynamic attribute methods have been generated.

A.2.1.8 `undefine_attribute_methods`

Removes all the attribute method definitions previously defined.

A.3 Callbacks

This module gives any class Active Record style callbacks. It is used by first defining the callbacks that the model will use, and then in your model running the callbacks at the appropriate time. Once defined, you have access to `before`, `after`, and `around` custom methods.

```
class BaseRecord
  extend ActiveModel::Callbacks

  define_model_callbacks :create
  define_model_callbacks :update, only: :before

  def create
    run_callbacks :create do
      # Your create code here
    end
  end

  def update
    run_callbacks :update do
      # Your update code here
    end
  end
end

class Portfolio < BaseRecord
```

```
before_update :my_callback

...

private

def my_callback
  # code here will get run before update
end
end
```

A.3.1   Instance Public Methods

A.3.1.1   `define_model_callbacks(*callbacks)`

Defines the callback hooks that can be used in the model, which will dynamically provide you with a `before`, `after`, and `around` hook for each name passed.

Optionally, you can supply an `:only` option to specify which callbacks you want created.

```
define_model_callbacks :create, only: :after
```

Defined callbacks can accept a callback class by passing the given callback an object that responds to the name of the callback and takes the model object as a parameter.

```
class Record
  extend ActiveModel::Callbacks
  define_model_callbacks :create

  before_create SomeCallbackClass
end

class SomeCallbackClass
  def self.before_create(obj)
    # obj is the Record instance the callback is being called on
  end
end
```

When defining an around callback remember to yield to the block, otherwise it won't be executed:

```
around_create :log_status

def log_status
  puts 'going to call the block...'
  yield
  puts 'block successfully called.'
end
```

A.4 Conversion

A simple module that when included, gives the standard Rails conversion methods to your model. A couple of its methods expect your class to have an `id` attribute.

A.4.1 Instance Public Methods

A.4.1.1 `to_model`

Returns `self`. If your model does not act like an Active Model object, then you should define `to_model` yourself, returning a proxy object that wraps your object with Active Model compliant methods.

A.4.1.2 `to_key`

Returns an array containing your object's `id`, if it has one.

A.4.1.3 `to_param`

Return a URL friendly version of the object's primary key or `nil` if the object is not persisted.

A.4.1.4 `to_partial_path`

Returns a string identifying the path associated with the object.

```
record = Record.new
record.to_partial_path # => "records/record"
```

Used by Action View to find a suitable partial to represent the object.

A.5 Dirty

Provides a way to track changes in your object in the same way as Active Record does.

The requirements for implementing `ActiveModel::Dirty` are:

1. Include the `ActiveModel::Dirty` module in your object.
2. Call `define_attribute_methods` passing each method you want to track.
3. Call `[attr_name]_will_change!` before each change to the tracked attribute.
4. Call `changes_applied` after the changes are persisted.
5. Call `clear_changes_information` when you want to reset the changes information.
6. Call `restore_attributes` when you want to restore previous data.

A minimal implementation could be:

```
class Person
  include ActiveModel::Dirty

  define_attribute_methods :name

  def initialize(name)
    @name = name
  end

  def name
    @name
  end

  def name=(val)
    name_will_change! unless val == @name
    @name = val
  end

  def save
    # do persistence work

    changes_applied
  end

  def reload!
    # get the values from the persistence layer

    clear_changes_information
  end

  def rollback!
    restore_attributes
  end
end
```

A newly instantiated Person object is unchanged:

```
person = Person.new("Uncle Bob")
person.changed? # => false
```

Change the name:

```
person.name = 'Bob'
person.changed?       # => true
person.name_changed?  # => true
person.name_changed?(from: "Uncle Bob", to: "Bob") # => true
person.name_was       # => "Uncle Bob"
```

```
person.name_change    # => ["Uncle Bob", "Bob"]
person.name = 'Bill'
person.name_change    # => ["Uncle Bob", "Bill"]
```

Save the changes:

```
person.save
person.changed?       # => false
person.name_changed?  # => false
```

Reset the changes:

```
person.previous_changes          # => {"name" => ["Uncle Bob", "Bill"]}
person.name_previously_changed?  # => true
person.name_previous_change      # => ["Uncle Bob", "Bill"]
person.reload!
person.previous_changes          # => {}
```

Roll back the changes:

```
person.name = "Uncle Bob"
person.rollback!
person.name           # => "Bill"
person.name_changed?  # => false
```

Assigning the same value leaves the attribute unchanged:

```
person.name = 'Bill'
person.name_changed?  # => false
person.name_change    # => nil
```

Which attributes have changed?

```
person.name = 'Bob'
person.changed # => ["name"]
person.changes # => {"name" => ["Bill", "Bob"]}
```

If an attribute is modified in-place, then make use of [attribute_name]_
will_change! to mark that the attribute is changing. Otherwise Active Model
can't track changes to in-place attributes.

Note that Active Record can detect in-place modifications automatically.
You do not need to call [attribute_name]_will_change! on Active
Record models.

```
person.name_will_change!
```

```
person.name_change # => ["Bill", "Bill"]
person.name << 'y'
person.name_change # => ["Bill", "Billy"]
```

A.5.1   Instance Public Methods

A.5.1.1   changed
Returns an array of fields whose values have changed on the object.

A.5.1.2   changed?
Returns whether or not the object's attributes have changed.

As of Rails 4.1, you can determine whether an attribute has changed from one value to another by supplying hash options :from and :to.

```
user.name_changed?(from: 'Prince', to: 'Symbol')
```

A.5.1.3   changed_attributes
Returns a hash of the fields that have changed, with their original values.

A.5.1.4   changes
Returns a hash of changes, with the attribute names as the keys and the values being an array of the old and new value for that field.

A.5.1.5   previous_changes
Returns a hash of previous changes before the object was persisted, with the attribute names as the keys and the values being an array of the old and new value for that field.

A.6   Errors
A Hash class that you can use in your objects to provide a common interface for handling application error messages, in a way that is compatible with the rest of Rails.

❁ Note that including ActiveModel::Validations automatically adds an errors method to your instances initialized with a new Active-Model::Errors object, so there is no need for you to do this manually.

In order for your object to be compatible with the API with I18n and validations support, it needs to extend ActiveModel::Naming, ActiveModel::Translation, and include ActiveModel::Validations.

Active
Model

```
class User
  extend ActiveModel::Naming
  extend ActiveModel::Translation
  include ActiveModel::Validations

  attr_reader :errors
  attr_accessor :name

  def initialize
    @errors = ActiveModel::Errors.new(self)
  end
end
```

A.6.1   Class Public Methods

A.6.1.1 `new(instance)`

Passes in the instance of the object that is using the errors object.

```
class Person
  def initialize
    @errors = ActiveModel::Errors.new(self)
  end
end
```

A.6.2   Instance Public Methods

A.6.2.1 `[](attribute)`

Returns the errors for the supplied attribute as an array.

```
user.errors[:name] # => ["is invalid"]
```

A.6.2.2 `add(attribute, message = nil, options = {})`

Alternate (more comprehensive) way to add an error message for the supplied `attribute`. More than one error can be added to the same attribute. If no message is provided, `:invalid` is assumed. Options allowed are the following:

`:strict`

If set to `true`, will raise `ActiveModel::StrictValidationFailed` over adding an error.

```
>> user.errors.add(:name)
=> ["is invalid"]

>> user.errors.add(:name, 'must be implemented')
=> ["is invalid", "must be implemented"]
```

If message is a symbol, it will be translated using the appropriate scope (see generate_message).

If message is a proc, it will be called, enabling dynamic message generation.

```
>> person.errors.add(:name, -> { "Failed as of #{Time.now}" })
=> ["Failed as of 2016-01-02 12:12:54 -0500"]
```

If the :strict option is set to true, it will raise ActiveModel::StrictValidationFailed instead of adding the error. To raise a different exception, pass its class as the :strict parameter.

```
>> person.errors.add(:name, :invalid, strict: true)
=> ActiveModel::StrictValidationFailed: name is invalid
```

```
>> person.errors.add(:name, :invalid, strict: NameIsInvalid)
=> NameIsInvalid: name is invalid
```

```
person.errors.messages # => {}
```

The attribute should be set to :base if the error is not directly associated with a single attribute.

```
>> person.errors.add(:base, :username_or_email_blank,
     message: "either username or email must be present")
```

```
>> person.errors.messages
=> {:base=>["either username or email must be present"]}
```

```
>> person.errors.details
=> {:base=>[{error: :username_or_email_blank}]}
```

⚠ Probably a bad idea to use base as an attribute name in Rails.

A.6.2.3   added?(attribute, message = nil, options = {})
Returns true if an error on the attribute with the given message is present.

```
user.errors.add :name, :blank
user.errors.added? :name, :blank # => true
```

If the error message requires an option, then it returns true with the correct option or false with an incorrect or missing option.

```
>> person.errors.add :name, :too_long, { count: 25 }
```

```
>> person.errors.added? :name, :too_long, count: 25
=> true

person.errors.added? :name, "is too long (maximum is 25 characters)"
=> true

person.errors.added? :name, :too_long, count: 24
=> false

person.errors.added? :name, :too_long
=> false

person.errors.added? :name, "is too long"
=> false
```

A.6.2.4 `as_json(options=nil)`

Returns a hash that can be used as the JSON representation for this object. Available options are the following:

`:full_messages`

Defaults to `false`. If set to `true`, returns full errors messages for each attribute.

```
>> user.errors.as_json
=> {:name=>["can't be blank"]}

>> user.errors.as_json(full_messages: true)
=> {:name=>["Name can't be blank"]}
```

A.6.2.5 `blank?` / `empty?`

Returns `true` if there are no errors on the object, `false` otherwise.

A.6.2.6 `clear`

Clear the error messages.

```
person.errors.full_messages # => ["name cannot be nil"]
person.errors.clear
person.errors.full_messages # => []
```

A.6.2.7 `count`

Returns the total number of error messages.

A.6.2.8 `delete(key)`

Delete all messages for specified `key`.

```
user.errors[:name] # => ["can't be blank"]
user.errors.delete(:name)
user.errors[:name] # => []
```

A.6.2.9 `each`

Iterates through the error keys, yielding the attribute and the errors for each. If an attribute has more than one error message, it will yield for each one.

```
user.errors.each do |attribute, error|
  ...
end
```

A.6.2.10 `full_message(attribute, message)`

Returns a full message for a given attribute.

A.6.2.11 `full_messages`

Returns all the full error messages as an array.

A.6.2.12 `full_messages_for(attribute)`

Returns an array of all the full error messages for a given attribute.

A.6.2.13 `generate_message(attr, message = :invalid, options = {})`

Generates a translated error message under the scope `activemodel.errors.messages` for the supplied attribute. Messages are looked up via the following pattern: `models.MODEL.attributes.ATTRIBUTE.MESSAGE`. If a translation is not found, Active Model will then look in `models.MODEL.MESSAGE`. If that yields no translations, it will return a default message (`activemodel.errors.messages.MESSAGE`).

When using inheritance in your models, it will check all the inherited models too, but only if the model itself hasn't been found. Say you have a class `Admin` that extends `User` and you wanted the translation for the `:blank` error message for the `title` attribute. This is how it looks up translations:

- `activemodel.errors.models.admin.attributes.title.blank`

- `activemodel.errors.models.admin.blank`

- `activemodel.errors.models.user.attributes.title.blank`

- `activemodel.errors.models.user.blank`
- any default you provided through the options hash (in the `activemodel. errors` scope)
- `activemodel.errors.messages.blank`
- `errors.attributes.title.blank`
- `errors.messages.blank`

A.6.2.14 `has_key?(attribute)` / `include?(attribute)`
Returns `true` if the error messages include an error for the given `attribute`.

```
user.errors.include?(:name) # => true
```

A.6.2.15 `keys`
Return all message keys.

A.6.2.16 `size`
Returns the total number of error messages.

A.6.2.17 `to_a`
Returns an array of all the error messages, with the attribute name included in each.

A.6.2.18 `to_hash(full_messages = false)`
Returns a hash of all the error messages, with the attribute name set as the key and messages as values. If `full_messages` is set to `true`, it will contain full messages.

A.6.2.19 `to_xml`
Returns the errors hash as XML.

A.6.2.20 `values`
Returns all message values.

A.7 `ForbiddenAttributesError`
Defines the `ForbiddenAttributesError` exception class, which is raised when forbidden attributes are used for mass assignment.

```
params = ActionController::Parameters.new(name: 'Bob')
User.new(params) # => ActiveModel::ForbiddenAttributesError
params.permit!
User.new(params) # =>  #<User:0x007fefd4389020 ...>
```

A.8   `Lint::Tests`

You can check whether an object is compatible with the Active Model API by including `ActiveModel::Lint::Tests` in a test case. It contains assertions that tell you whether your object is fully compliant.

Note that an object is not required to implement all APIs in order to work with Action Pack. This module only intends to provide guidance in case you want all features out of the box.

These tests do not attempt to determine the semantic correctness of the returned values. For instance, you could implement `valid?` to always return `true`, and the tests would pass. It is up to you to ensure that the values are semantically meaningful.

Objects you pass in are expected to return a compliant object from a call to `to_model`. It is perfectly fine for `to_model` to return self.

A.8.1   Instance Public Methods

A.8.1.1   `test_errors_aref`

Passes if the object's model responds to errors and if calling `[]`(`attribute`) on the result of this method returns an array. Fails otherwise.

`errors[attribute]` is used to retrieve the errors of a model for a given attribute. If errors are present, the method should return an array of strings that are the errors for the attribute in question. If localization is used, the strings should be localized for the current locale. If no error is present, the method should return an empty array.

A.8.1.2   `test_model_naming`

Passes if the object's model responds to `model_name` both as an instance method and as a class method, and if calling this method returns a string with some convenience methods: `:human`, `:singular` and `:plural`.

A.8.1.3   `test_persisted?`

Passes if the object's model responds to `persisted?` and if calling this method returns either `true` or `false`. Fails otherwise.

The `persisted?` method is used when auto-generating the URL for a form. If the object is not persisted, a form for that object, for instance, will route to the `create` action. If it is persisted, a form for the object will route to the `update` action.

Active
Model

A.8.1.4 `test_to_key`

Passes if the object's model responds to `to_key` and if calling this method returns `nil` when the object is not persisted. Fails otherwise.

The `to_key` method returns an enumerable of all (primary) key attributes of the model and is used to a generate unique DOM id for the object.

A.8.1.5 `test_to_param`

Passes if the object's model responds to `to_param` and if calling this method returns `nil` when the object is not persisted. Fails otherwise.

The `to_param` is used to represent the object's key in URLs. Implementers can decide to either raise an exception or provide a default in case the record uses a composite primary key. There are no tests for this behavior in lint because it doesn't make sense to force any of the possible implementation strategies on the implementer.

A.8.1.6 `test_to_partial_path`

Passes if the object's model responds to `to_partial_path` and if calling this method returns a string. Fails otherwise.

The `to_partial_path` method is used for looking up partials. For example, a `BlogPost` model might return `"blog_posts/blog_post"`.

A.9 `MissingAttributeError`

Raised when you try to access an attribute that is known, but not defined in the current object. (This is a rare edge case.)

```
class User < ActiveRecord::Base
  has_many :pets
end

>> user = User.first
>> user.pets.select(:id).first.user_id
=> ActiveModel::MissingAttributeError: missing attribute: user_id
```

A.10 `Model`

`Model` is a module mixin that includes the required interface for a Ruby object to work with Action Pack and Action View. Classes that include `Model` get several other Active Model features out of the box, such as:

- Model name introspection
- Conversions

- Translations

- Validations

Like Active Record objects, `Model` objects can also be initialized with a hash of attributes.

```
class Contact
  include ActiveModel::Model

  attr_accessor :name, :email, :message

  validates :name, presence: true
  validates :email, presence: true
  validates :message, presence: true, length: { maximum: 300 }
end
```

The implementation of `Model` (minus comments) is only about 20 lines of code.

```
module ActiveModel
  module Model
    extend ActiveSupport::Concern
    include ActiveModel::AttributeAssignment
    include ActiveModel::Validations
    include ActiveModel::Conversion

    included do
      extend ActiveModel::Naming
      extend ActiveModel::Translation
    end

    def initialize(attributes={})
      assign_attributes(attributes) if attributes
      super()
    end

    def persisted?
      false
    end
  end
end
```

A.10.1 Class Public Methods

A.10.1.1 `new(attributes={})`

Initializes a new model with the given params.

A.10.2   Instance Public Methods

A.10.2.1 `persisted?`

Indicates whether the model is persisted. Default is `false`.

A.11   `Name`

The `Name` class wraps a bunch of logic around name information about your object so that it can be used with Rails.

How much name information could there be? Take a look at Name's constructor.

```
def initialize(klass, namespace = nil, name = nil)
  @name = name || klass.name

  raise ArgumentError, "Class name cannot be blank. You need to supply a
    name argument when anonymous class given" if @name.blank?

  @unnamespaced = @name.sub(/^#{namespace.name}::/, '') if namespace
  @klass        = klass
  @singular     = _singularize(@name)
  @plural       = ActiveSupport::Inflector.pluralize(@singular)
  @element      = ActiveSupport::Inflector.
    underscore(ActiveSupport::Inflector.demodulize(@name))
  @human        = ActiveSupport::Inflector.humanize(@element)
  @collection   = ActiveSupport::Inflector.tableize(@name)
  @param_key    = (namespace ? _singularize(@unnamespaced) : @singular)
  @i18n_key     = @name.underscore.to_sym

  @route_key      = (namespace ? ActiveSupport::Inflector.
    pluralize(@param_key) : @plural.dup)
  @singular_route_key = ActiveSupport::Inflector.singularize(@route_key)
  @route_key << "_index" if @plural == @singular
end
```

All of this information is calculated and stored at initialization-time, presumably since it's used all over Rails repeatedly.

A.11.1   Class Public Methods

A.11.1.1 `new(klass, namespace = nil, name = nil)`

Returns a new `ActiveModel::Name` instance.

```
module Foo
  class Bar
  end
end
```

```
ActiveModel::Name.new(Foo::Bar).to_s
# => "Foo::Bar"
```

A.11.2   Instance Public Attributes

A.11.2.1   `cache_key / collection`
Returns an underscored plural version of the model name.

A.11.2.2   `element`
Returns an underscored version of the model name.

A.11.2.3   `i18n_key`
Returns a symbol of the model name to be used as an I18n key.

A.11.2.4   `param_key`
Returns a version of the model name to be used for params names.

A.11.2.5   `plural`
Returns a pluralized version of the model name.

A.11.2.6   `route_key`
Returns a version of the model name to use while generating route names.

A.11.2.7   `singular`
Returns a singularized version of the model name.

A.11.2.8   `singular_route_key`
Returns a singularized version of the model name to use while generating route names.

A.11.3   Instance Public Methods

A.11.3.1   `=~(regexp) / !~(regexp)`
Equivalent to same methods on `String`. Matches whether class name does or does not match given `regexp`.

A.11.3.2   `<=>(other) / ==(other) / ===(other) / eql?(other)`
Equivalent to same methods on `String`. Compares class name against `other`.

A.11.3.3 `human(options={})`

Returns a translated human readable version of the model name using I18n. The basic recipe is to capitalize the first word of the name.

```
BlogPost.model_name.human # => "Blog post"
```

A.12 Naming

`Naming` is the module that you extend in your class to get name type information for your model.

A.12.1 Class Public Methods

A.12.1.1 `param_key(record_or_class)`

Returns string to use for params names, accounting for whether the class is inside an isolated Rails Engine or not.

```
# For isolated engine:
ActiveModel::Naming.param_key(Blog::Post) # => "post"

# For shared engine:
ActiveModel::Naming.param_key(Blog::Post) # => "blog_post"
```

A.12.1.2 `plural(record_or_class)`

Returns the plural class name of a record or class.

```
ActiveModel::Naming.plural(post)              # => "posts"
ActiveModel::Naming.plural(Highrise::Person)  # => "highrise_people"
```

A.12.1.3 `route_key(record_or_class)` / `singular_route_key(record_or_class)`

Returns string to use for generating route names, accounting for whether the class is inside an isolated Rails Engine or not.

A.12.1.4 `singular(record_or_class)`

Returns the singular class name of a record or class.

```
ActiveModel::Naming.singular(post)              # => "post"
ActiveModel::Naming.singular(Highrise::Person)  # => "highrise_person"
```

A.12.1.5 `uncountable?(record_or_class)`

Identifies whether the class name of a record or class is uncountable.

```
ActiveModel::Naming.uncountable?(Sheep)  # => true
ActiveModel::Naming.uncountable?(Post)   # => false
```

A.12.2   Instance Public Methods

A.12.2.1   `model_name`

Returns an `ActiveModel::Name` instance for the object. Used by Action Pack and Action View for naming-related functionality, such as routing.

A.13   **SecurePassword**

Including the `SecurePassword` module adds a single macro-style method `has_secure_password` to your class, which adds the capability to set and authenticate against a BCrypt password.

A full explanation of how to use `has_secure_password` is provided in the Chapter 14 section "has_secure_password."

A.14   **Serialization**

`Serialization` is a module to include in your models when you want to represent your model as a serializable hash. You only need to define an `attributes` method and the rest is handled for you.

```
class User
  include ActiveModel::Serialization
  attr_accessor :first_name, :last_name

  def attributes
    { 'first_name' => @first_name, 'last_name' => @last_name }
  end
end
```

A.14.1   Instance Public Methods

A.14.1.1   `serializable_hash(options = nil)`

Returns the serializable hash representation of your model. Options provided can be of the following:

:except

Do not include these attributes.

:methods

Include the supplied methods. The method name will be set as the key and its output the value.

:only

Only include the supplied attributes.

A.15   Serializers::JSON

`Serializers::JSON` is a module to include in your models when you want to provide a JSON representation of your object. It automatically includes the module and depends on the `attributes` and `attributes=` methods to be present.

```
class User
  include ActiveModel::Serializers::JSON
  attr_accessor :first_name, :last_name

  def attributes
    { 'first_name' => @first_name, 'last_name' => @last_name }
  end

  def attributes=(attrs)
    @first_name = attrs['first_name']
    @last_name = attrs['last_name']
  end
end
```

A.15.1   active_model/serializers/json.rb

A.15.1.1   as_json(options = nil)

Returns a hash representing the model. Some configuration can be passed through options.

The option `include_root_in_json` controls the top-level behavior of `as_json`. If `true`, `as_json` will emit a single root node named after the object's type. The default value for `include_root_in_json` option is `false`.

```
user = User.find(1)
user.as_json
# => { "id" => 1, "name" => "Konata Izumi", "age" => 16,
#      "created_at" => "2006/08/01", "awesome" => true}
```

Setting `ActiveRecord::Base.include_root_in_json = true` results in the addition of a root node named accordingly.

```
user.as_json
```

```
# => { "user" => { "id" => 1, "name" => "Konata Izumi", "age" => 16,
#                     "created_at" => "2006/08/01", "awesome" => true } }
```

This behavior can also be achieved by setting the :root option to true as in:

```
user = User.find(1)
user.as_json(root: true)
# => { "user" => { "id" => 1, "name" => "Konata Izumi", "age" => 16,
#                     "created_at" => "2006/08/01", "awesome" => true } }
```

Without any options, the returned hash will include all the model's attributes.

```
>> user = User.find(1)
>> user.as_json
=> { "id" => 1, "name" => "Konata Izumi", "age" => 16,
     "created_at" => "2006/08/01", "awesome" => true}
```

The :only and :except options can be used to limit the attributes included and work similarly to the attributes method.

```
>> user.as_json(only: [:id, :name])
=> { "id" => 1, "name" => "Konata Izumi" }


>> user.as_json(except: [:id, :created_at, :age])
=> { "name" => "Konata Izumi", "awesome" => true }
```

To include the result of some method calls on the model use :methods

```
>> user.as_json(methods: :permalink)
=> { "id" => 1, "name" => "Konata Izumi", "age" => 16,
     "created_at" => "2006/08/01", "awesome" => true,
     "permalink" => "1-konata-izumi" }
```

To include associations use :include

```
>> user.as_json(include: :posts)
=> { "id" => 1, "name" => "Konata Izumi", "age" => 16,
     "created_at" => "2006/08/01", "awesome" => true,
     "posts" => [ { "id" => 1, "author_id" => 1,
                    "title" => "Welcome to the weblog" },
                  { "id" => 2, "author_id" => 1,
                    "title" => "So I was thinking" } ] }
```

Second level and higher order associations work as well:

```
>> user.as_json(include: { posts: {
                           only: :title,
```

Active
Model

```
                          include: {
                          comments: { only: :body } },}})
```

```
=> { "id" => 1, "name" => "Konata Izumi", "age" => 16,
      "created_at" => "2006/08/01", "awesome" => true,
      "posts" => [ { "comments" => [ { "body" => "1st post!" },...
```

A.15.1.2 `from_json(json)`

Sets the model attributes from a JSON string. Returns `self`.

```
class Person
  include ActiveModel::Serializers::JSON

  attr_accessor :name, :age, :awesome

  def attributes=(hash)
    hash.each do |key, value|
      send("#{key}=", value)
    end
  end

  def attributes
    instance_values
  end
end
```

```
json = { name: 'bob', age: 22, awesome:true }.to_json
person = Person.new
person.from_json(json) # => #<Person:0x007fec5e7a0088 @age=22, @
                         #awesome=true, @name="bob">
person.name              # => "bob"
person.age               # => 22
person.awesome           # => true
```

The default value for `include_root` is `false`. You can change it to `true` if the given JSON string includes a single root node.

```
>> json = { person: { name: 'bob', age: 22, awesome:true } }.to_json
>> person = Person.new
>> person.from_json(json, true)
=> #<Person:0x007fec5e7a0088 @age=22, @awesome=true, @name="bob">
```

A.16 Translation

Provides integration between your object and the Rails internationalization (I18n) translation framework.

A minimal implementation could be:

```
class TranslatedPerson
  extend ActiveModel::Translation
end

>> TranslatedPerson.human_attribute_name('my_attribute')
=> "My attribute"
```

This also provides the required class methods for hooking into the Rails internationalization API, including being able to define a class based `i18n_scope` and `lookup_ancestors` to find translations in parent classes.

A.16.1   Instance Public Methods

A.16.1.1   `human_attribute_name(attribute)`

Transforms attribute names into a more human format, such as "First name" instead of "first_name".

A.16.1.2   `i18n_scope`

Returns the `i18n_scope` for the class. Can be overridden if you want a custom lookup namespace.

A.16.1.3   `lookup_ancestors`

Gets all ancestors of this class that support I18n. Used in `ActiveModel::Name#human`, `ActiveModel::Errors#full_messages`, and this module's `human_attribute_name` method.

A.17   Type

Provides functionality for adding new types to the registry, enabling them to be referenced as a symbol by `ActiveModel::Attributes::ClassMethods#attribute`.

A.17.1   Class Public Methods

A.17.1.1   `register(type_name, klass = nil, **options, &block)`

If your type is only meant to be used with a specific database adapter, you can do so by passing `adapter: :dbtype`.

If your type has the same name as a native type for the current adapter, an exception will be raised unless you specify an `override` option. Setting to `true` will cause your type to be used instead of the native type. Setting to `false` will cause the native type to be used over yours if one exists.

Active
Model

A.18 **ValidationError**

Raised by `validate!` when the model is invalid. Use the `model` method to retrieve the record which did not validate.

```
begin
  complex_operation_that_internally_calls_validate!
rescue ActiveModel::ValidationError => invalid
  puts invalid.model.errors
end
```

A.19 **Validations**

`Validations` adds a fully featured validations framework to your model. This includes the means to validate the following types of scenarios, plus the capability to create custom validators.

- Absence of a field
- Acceptance of a field.
- Confirmation of a field.
- Exclusion of a field from a set of values.
- Format of a field against a regular expression.
- Inclusion of a field in a set of values.
- Length of a field.
- Numericality of a field.
- Presence of a field.
- Size of a field.

See Chapter 8, "Validations," for a full explanation of how validations work.

The following minimal implementation would provide you with the full standard validation stack that you know from Active Record:

```
class User
  include ActiveModel::Validations

  attr_accessor :name

  validates_each :name do |record, attribute, value|
    record.errors.add(attribute, 'should be present') if value.nil?
  end
end
```

> ✎ Note that including `ActiveModel::Validations` automatically adds an errors method to your instances initialized with a new `Active-Model::Errors` object, so there is no need for you to do this manually.

A.19.1   Options

Note that available base options for validation macros that use options are as follows. If the specific validation has additional options they will be explained separately.

A.19.1.1   `:allow_nil`
Specify whether to validate `nil` attributes.

A.19.1.2   `:if`
Only run if the supplied method or proc returns `true`.

A.19.1.3   `:on`
Define when the validation will run.

A.19.1.4   `:strict`
If set to `true`, will raise `ActiveModel::StrictValidationFailed` over adding an error. It can also be set to any other exception.

A.19.1.5   `:unless`
Only run if the supplied method or proc returns `false`.

A.19.2   Class Public Methods

A.19.2.1   `attribute_method?(attribute)`
Returns `true` if a method is defined for the supplied attribute.

```
class User
  include ActiveModel::Validations

  attr_accessor :name
end

User.attribute_method?(:name) # => true
```

A.19.2.2   `clear_validators!`
Clears all of the validators and validations.

A.19.2.3 `validate(*args, &block)`

Adds a single validation to the model. Can be a method name as a symbol or a block with options. Additional option is:

`:allow_blank`

Specify whether to validate blank attributes.

A.19.2.4 `validates(*attributes)`

A method that enables setting all default validators and any custom validator classes ending in "Validator". To illustrate, with a single declaration to `validates`, we can set an attribute to validate presence and uniqueness.

```
validates :username, presence: true, uniqueness: true
```

The hash supplied to `validates` can also handle arrays, ranges, regular expressions, and strings in shortcut form.

```
validates :email, format: /@/
validates :gender, inclusion: %w(male female)
validates :password, length: 6..20
```

A.19.2.5 `validates!(*attributes)`

The `validates!` method enables setting all default validators and any custom validator classes ending in "Validator". The difference between `validates` and `validates!` is that in the latter all errors are considered exceptions. Essentially, it is the same as defining `validates` with the `:strict` option set to `true`.

A.19.2.6 `validates_each(*attrs, &block)`

Validates each of the attribute names against the supplied block. Options are passed in as a hash as the last element in the `attrs` argument. Additional options are

`:allow_blank`

Specify whether to validate blank attributes.

A.19.2.7 `validates_with(*args, &block)`

Passes the record off to the class or classes specified as `args` and enables them to add errors based on conditions that have been custom defined in a reusable fashion.

```
class Person
  include ActiveModel::Validations
  validates_with MyValidator
```

```
end

class MyValidator < ActiveModel::Validator
  def validate(record)
    if some_complex_logic
      record.errors.add :base, 'This record is invalid'
    end
  end

  private
    def some_complex_logic
      # ...
    end
end
```

You may also pass it multiple classes, like so:

```
class Person
  include ActiveModel::Validations
  validates_with MyValidator, MyOtherValidator, on: :create
end
```

Configuration options:

on Specifies the contexts where this validation is active. Runs in all validation contexts by default (`nil`). You can pass a symbol or an array of symbols (e.g., `on: :create` or `on: :custom_validation_context` or `on: [:create, :custom_validation_context]`).

if Specifies a method, proc or string to call to determine whether the validation should occur. Should return or evaluate to a `true` or `false` value.

unless Specifies a method, proc or string to call to determine whether the validation should not occur. Should return or evaluate to a `true` or `false` value.

strict Specifies whether validation should raise `ValidationError` on failure.

If you pass any additional configuration options, they will be passed to the class and made available as an `options` attribute:

```
class Person
  include ActiveModel::Validations
  validates_with MyValidator, my_custom_key: 'my custom value'
end

class MyValidator < ActiveModel::Validator
  def validate(record)
    options[:my_custom_key] # => "my custom value"
```

```
    end
end
```

A.19.2.8 `validators`

List all validators that are being used to validate the model using the `validates_with` method.

```
class Person
  include ActiveModel::Validations

  validates_with MyValidator
  validates_with OtherValidator, on: :create
  validates_with StrictValidator, strict: true
end

Person.validators
# => [
#       #<MyValidator:0x007fbff403e808 @options={}>,
#       #<OtherValidator:0x007fbff403d930 @options={on: :create}>,
#       #<StrictValidator:0x007fbff3204a30 @options={strict:true}>
#    ]
```

A.19.2.9 `validators_on(*attributes)`

Get all the validators for the supplied attributes.

A.19.3   Instance Public Methods

A.19.3.1 `errors`

Returns the Errors object that holds all information about attribute error messages.

```
class Person
  include ActiveModel::Validations

  attr_accessor :name
  validates_presence_of :name
end

person = Person.new
person.valid? # => false
person.errors # => #<ActiveModel::Errors:0x007fe603816640 @
                    #messages={name:["can't be blank"]}>
```

A.19.3.2 `invalid?(context = nil)`
Performs the opposite of `valid?`. Returns `true` if errors were added, `false` otherwise.

A.19.3.3 `valid?(context = nil)`
Runs all the specified validations and returns `true` if no errors were added, otherwise `false`. Aliased as `validate`.

```
class Person
  include ActiveModel::Validations

  attr_accessor :name
  validates_presence_of :name
end

person = Person.new
person.name = ''
person.valid? # => false
person.name = 'david'
person.valid? # => true
```

Context can optionally be supplied to define which callbacks to test against (the context is defined on the validations using the `:on` option).

```
validates_presence_of :name, on: :new

>> person = Person.new
>> person.valid?
=> true

>> person.valid?(:new)
=> false
```

A.19.3.4 `validate!(context = nil)`
Runs all the validations within the specified context. Returns `true` if no errors are found, raises `ValidationError` otherwise.

Validations with no `:on` option will run no matter the context. Validations with `:on` option will only run in the specified context.

A.19.3.5 `validates_with(*args, &block)`
Passes the record off to the class or classes specified and enables them to add errors based on their condition logic. Same as the class level method of the same name but operating on an instance.

A.19.4   Callbacks

Provides an interface for any class to have before_validation and after_ validation callbacks.

First, include ActiveModel::Validations::Callbacks into the class you are creating:

```
class MyModel
  include ActiveModel::Validations::Callbacks

  before_validation :do_stuff_before_validation
  after_validation  :do_stuff_after_validation
end
```

Like other before callbacks if before_validation raises :abort, then valid? will not be called. The interface is the same as ActiveModel::Callbacks covered earlier in this appendix.

A.20 **Validator**

Validator provides a class that custom validators can extend to seamlessly integrate into the ActiveModel::Validations API. It only requires that the new class defines a validate method.

A full explanation of how to use Validator and EachValidator is provided in the Chapter 8 section "Custom Validation Techniques."

```
class ScoreValidator < ActiveModel::Validator
  include ActiveModel::Validations

  def validate(object)
    # Perform validations and add errors here.
  end
end
```

A.20.1   Class Public Methods

A.20.1.1 **kind**

Returns the type of the validator, which is a symbol of the underscored class name without "Validator" included.

A.20.2   Instance Public Methods

A.20.2.1   `validate(record)`

Override this method in subclasses with validation logic, adding errors to the record's errors array where necessary.

Appendix B

Active Support API Reference

Active Support is a Rails library containing utility classes and extensions to Ruby's built-in libraries. It usually doesn't get much attention on its own—you might even call its modules the supporting cast members of the Rails ensemble.

However, Active Support's low profile doesn't diminish its importance in day-to-day Rails programming. To ensure that this book is useful as an offline programming companion, here is a complete, enhanced version of the Rails Active Support API reference, supplemented in many cases with realistic example usages and commentary. As you're reviewing the material in this appendix, note that many of the methods featured here are used primarily by other Rails libraries and are not particularly useful to application developers.

Section headings reflect the name of the Class or Module where the API method is located and are organized in alphabetical order for easy lookup.

Note that Active Support freely extends built-in Ruby classes such as `Array` and `Object` with its own extra functionality.

Sub-sections are the API methods themselves, in alphabetical order (or the order they appear in the file, depending on what we think is easier to understand). Methods are also grouped according to the name of the Ruby file in which they exist within Active Support's `lib` directory. File name headers are ommitted where a module is contained in a single file.

B.1 Array

B.1.1 `active_support/core_ext/array/access.rb`

The following methods add extra functionality for accessing array elements.

B.1.1.1 `from(position)`

Returns the tail of the array starting from the `position` specified. Note that the position is zero-indexed.

```
>> %w(foo bar baz quux).from(2)
=> ["baz", "quux"]
```

B.1.1.2 `to(position)`

Returns the beginning elements of the array up to `position` specified. Note that the position is zero-indexed.

```
>> %w(foo bar baz quux).to(2)
=> ["foo", "bar", "baz"]
```

B.1.1.3 `second`

Equivalent to calling `self[1]`.

```
>> %w(foo bar baz quux).second
=> "bar"
```

B.1.1.4 `third`

Equivalent to `self[2]`.

B.1.1.5 `fourth`

Equivalent to `self[3]`.

B.1.1.6 `fifth`

Equivalent to `self[4]`.

B.1.1.7 `forty_two`

Equivalent to calling `self[41]`—a humorous addition to the API by David. Also known as accessing "the reddit."

B.1.1.8 `second_to_last`

Equivalent to `self[-2]`

B.1.1.9   `third_to_last`
Equivalent to `self[-3]`

B.1.1.10   `without(*elements)`
Returns a copy of the Array without the specified elements.

```
>> people = ["David", "Rafael", "Aaron", "Todd"]
>> people.without "Aaron", "Todd"
=> ["David", "Rafael"]
```

> The `without` method is an optimization of `Enumerable#without` that uses `Array#-` instead of `Array#reject` for performance reasons.

B.1.2   `active_support/core_ext/array/conversions.rb`
The following methods are used for converting Ruby arrays into other formats.

B.1.2.1   `to_formatted_s(format = :default)`
Two formats are supported, `:default` and `:db`. The `:default` format delegates to the normal `to_s` method for an array, which just creates a string representation of the array.

```
>> %w(foo bar baz quux).to_s
=> "[\"foo\", \"bar\", \"baz\", \"quux\"]"
```

The much more interesting `:db` option returns `"null"` if the array is empty, or concatenates the `id` fields of its member elements into a comma-delimited string with code like this:

```
collect { |element| element.id }.join(",")
```

In other words, the `:db` formatting is meant to work with Active Record objects (or other types of objects that properly respond to `id`). If the contents of the array do not respond to `id`, a `NoMethodError` exception is raised.

```
>> %w(foo bar baz quux).to_s(:db)
NoMethodError: undefined method `id' for "foo":String
```

B.1.2.2   `to_s`
The `to_s` method of `Array` is aliased to `to_formatted_s`.

Active
Support

B.1.2.3 `to_default_s`

The `to_default_s` method of `Array` is aliased to `to_s`.

B.1.2.4 `to_sentence(options = {})`

Converts the array to a comma-separated sentence in which the last element is joined by a connector word.

```
>> %w(alcohol tobacco firearms).to_sentence
=> "alcohol, tobacco, and firearms"
```

The following options are available for `to_sentence`:

:**`words_connector`** The sign or word used to join the elements in arrays with two or more elements (default: `", "`).

:**`two_words_connector`** The sign or word used to join the elements in arrays with two elements (default: `" and "`).

:**`last_word_connector`** The sign or word used to join the last element in arrays with three or more elements (default: `", and "`).

:**`locale`** If `i18n` is available, you can set a locale and specify locale-specific connector options in the `support.array` namespace, like this:

```
es: support: array: words_connector: " o " two_words_connector:
        " y " last_word_connector: " o al menos "
```

The example locale (in Spanish) yields the following output:

```
>> ['uno', 'dos'].to_sentence(locale: :es)
=> "uno y dos"
>> ['uno', 'dos', 'tres'].to_sentence(locale: :es)
=> "uno o dos o al menos tres"
```

The `locale` feature can also be used to provide alternative sentence construction, like an *or* expression instead of *and*.

First, define a locale hash for the purpose (remembering that `I18n.translate` can be used to do bulk lookups, not just individual strings):

```
en:
  choices:
    words_connector: ', '
    two_words_connector: ' or '
    last_word_connector: ', or '
```

Then use it like this:

```
>> [:this, :that].to_sentence(I18n.translate('choices'))
=> "this or that"
>> [:this, :that, :another].to_sentence(I18n.translate('choices'))
=> "this, that, or another"
```

B.1.2.5 `to_xml(options = {}) |xml| ...`

Create an XML collection by iteratively calling `to_xml` on its members and wrapping the entire thing in an enclosing element. If the array element does not respond to `to_xml`, an XML representation of the object will be returned.

```
>> ["riding","high"].to_xml
=> "<?xml version=\"1.0\" encoding=\"UTF-8\"?>\n<strings type=\"array\">\n
   <string>riding</string>\n  <string>high</string>\n</strings>\n"
```

The following example yields the `Builder` object to an optional block so that arbitrary markup can be inserted at the bottom of the generated XML, as the last child of the enclosing element.

```
{foo: "foo", bar: 42}.to_xml do |xml|
   xml.did_it "again"
end
```

outputs the following XML:

```
<?xml version="1.0" encoding="UTF-8"?>
<hash>
  <bar type="integer">42</bar>
  <foo>foo</foo>
  <did_it>again</did_it>
</hash>
```

The options for `to_xml` are:

`:builder` Defaults to a new instance of `Builder::XmlMarkup`. Specify explicitly whether you're calling `to_xml` on this array as part of a larger XML construction routine.

`:children` Sets the name to use for element tags explicitly. Defaults to singularized version of the `:root` name by default.

`:dasherize` Whether or not to turn underscores to dashes in tag names (defaults to `true`).

:indent Indent level to use for generated XML (defaults to two spaces).

:root The tag name to use for the enclosing element. If no :root is supplied and all members of the array are of the same class, the dashed, pluralized form of the first element's class name is used as a default. An empty array will have nil-classes as its root. Otherwise the default :root is objects.

Given how variable Rails default behavior is, it's a good idea to always use the :root option and know for sure what you're going to get in the output.

:skip_instruct Whether or not to generate an XML instruction tag by calling instruct! on Builder.

:skip_types Whether or not to include a type="array" attribute on the enclosing element.

The options hash is passed downwards as XML is constructed:

```
>> Message.all.to_xml(skip_types: true)

<?xml version="1.0" encoding="UTF-8"?>
<messages>
  <message>
    <created-at>2008-03-07T09:58:18+01:00</created-at>
    <id>1</id>
    <name>1</name>
    <updated-at>2008-03-07T09:58:18+01:00</updated-at>
    <user-id>1</user-id>
  </message>
</messages>
```

B.1.3 active_support/core_ext/array/extract_options.rb

Active Support provides a method for extracting Rails-style options from a variable-length set of argument parameters.

B.1.3.1 extract_options!

Extracts options from a variable set of arguments. It's a bang method because it removes and returns the last element in the array if it's a hash; otherwise, it returns a blank hash and the source array is unmodified.

```
def options(*args)
  args.extract_options!
```

```
end

>> options(1, 2)
=> {}

>> options(1, 2, a: :b)
=> {:a=>:b}
```

B.1.4 `active_support/core_ext/array/grouping.rb`

Methods used for splitting array elements into logical groupings.

B.1.4.1 `in_groups(number, fill_with = nil) { |group| ... }`

The `in_groups` method splits an array into a `number` of equally sized groups. If a `fill_with` parameter is provided, its value is used to pad the groups into equal sizes.

```
%w(1 2 3 4 5 6 7 8 9 10).in_groups(3) { |group| p group }
["1", "2", "3", "4"]
["5", "6", "7", nil]
["8", "9", "10", nil]

%w(1 2 3 4 5 6 7).in_groups(3, ' ') { |group| p group }
["1", "2", "3"]
["4", "5", " "]
["6", "7", " "]
```

In the special case that you don't want equally sized groups (in other words, no padding) then pass `false` as the value of `fill_with`.

```
%w(1 2 3 4 5 6 7).in_groups(3, false) { |group| p group }
["1", "2", "3"]
["4", "5"]
["6", "7"]
```

B.1.4.2 `in_groups_of(number, fill_with = nil) { |group| ... }`

Related to its sibling `in_groups`, the `in_groups_of` method splits an array into groups of the specified `number` size, padding any remaining slots. The `fill_with` parameter is used for padding and defaults to `nil`. If a block is provided, it is called with each group; otherwise, a two-dimensional array is returned.

```
>> %w(1 2 3 4 5 6 7).in_groups_of(3)
=> [[1, 2, 3], [4, 5, 6], [7, nil, nil]]

>> %w(1 2 3).in_groups_of(2, ' ') { |group| puts group.to_s }
```

```
=> ["1", "2"]
   ["3", " "]
   nil
```

Passing `false` to the `fill_with` parameter inhibits the fill behavior.

```
>> %w(1 2 3).in_groups_of(2, false) { |group| puts group.to_s }
=> ["1", "2"]
   ["3"]
   nil
```

The `in_groups_of` method is particularly useful for batch-processing model objects and generating table rows in view templates.

B.1.4.3 `split(value = nil, &block)`

Divides an array into one or more subarrays based on a delimiting value:

```
>> [1, 2, 3, 4, 5].split(3)
=> [[1, 2], [4, 5]]
```

or the result of an optional block:

```
>> (1..8).to_a.split { |i| i % 3 == 0 }
=> [[1, 2], [4, 5], [7, 8]]
```

B.1.5 `active_support/core_ext/array/inquiry.rb`

Gives `Array` a Rails-style *inquirer* method.

B.1.5.1 `inquiry`

Returns the array wrapped in an `ArrayInquirer` object, which provides a friend-lier way to check string-like contents.

```
pets = [:cat, :dog].inquiry
pets.cat?       # => true
pets.ferret?    # => false
pets.any?(:cat, :ferret)     # => true
pets.any?(:ferret, :alligator) # => false
```

B.1.6 `active_support/core_ext/array/prepend_and_ append.rb`

Aliases for basic Ruby array operations that are subjectively more *human* according to DHH.

B.1.6.1 **append**

The append method of Array is aliased to <<.

B.1.6.2 **prepend**

The prepend method of Array is aliased to unshift.

B.1.7   **active_support/core_ext/array/wrap.rb**

B.1.7.1 **Array.wrap(object)**

Wraps the object in an Array unless it's an Array. If nil is supplied, an empty list is returned. Otherwise, the wrap method will convert the supplied object to an Array using to_ary (assuming it implements that method). It differs from the Kernel#Array method in that it does not try to call to_a on the argument if it does not implement to_ary.

This last point is most easily demonstrated with an instance of a Ruby hash.

```
Array(foo: :bar)          # => [[:foo, :bar]]
Array.wrap(foo: :bar)     # => [{:foo => :bar}] # to_a not called

Array("foo\nbar")         # => ["foo\nbar"]
Array.wrap("foo\nbar")    # => ["foo\nbar"]

Array(nil)                # => []
Array.wrap(nil)           # => []
```

B.2   **Autoload**

When doing Ruby coding outside of Rails, you have to require every file in your program in order for it to be executed. During development of a Rails app, whenever you run rails console or a server, etc. your program files are loaded lazily, on demand, as their constants are referenced. That behavior is fine for development but bad for production. In production, you want every single program file in your Rails application to be "eager loaded" on startup, so that even if it implies a longer startup time, you'll get more consistent performance.

Eager loading also tends to reveal syntax errors in your code that might otherwise pop up unexpectedly in production use.

The Autoload module enables you to define autoloading behavior for your own libraries based on Rails conventions (i.e., no need to define the path since it is automatically guessed based on the filename). It also provides a way to define a set of constants that you want to be eager loaded.

```
module MyLib
  extend ActiveSupport::Autoload

  autoload :Model

  eager_autoload do
    autoload :Cache
  end
end
```

Given the preceding example, `MyLib` can be eager loaded by calling:

```
MyLib.eager_load!
```

Note that this module is primarily useful inside of Rails framework source code and for writing Ruby libraries, versus your Rails application code, and is included here mainly for the sake of completeness.

B.2.1 `autoload(const_name, path)`
Declares that a particular constant should be autoloaded. Optionally, provide the `:path` option.

B.2.2 `autoloads`
Returns a collection of files registered to be autoloaded.

B.2.3 `autoload_at(path)`
Set an explicit path at which to autoload.

```
module ActionView
  extend ActiveSupport::Autoload

  autoload_at "action_view/template/resolver" do
    autoload :Resolver
    ...
  end
  ...
end
```

B.2.4   `autoload_under(path)`

Sets the name of a relative directory for all nested `autoload` declarations. For example, if the current file was `action_controller.rb`, and we call `autoload_under("metal")`, the path used to autoload from is `action_controller/metal`.

```
module ActionController
  extend ActiveSupport::Autoload

  autoload_under "metal" do
    autoload :Compatibility
    ...
  end
  ...
end
```

B.2.5   `eager_autoload`

Eagerly autoload any nested `autoload` declarations.

```
module ActionMailer
  extend ::ActiveSupport::Autoload

  eager_autoload do
    autoload :Collector
  end
  ...
end
```

B.2.6   `eager_load!`

Require each file defined in `autoloads`.

B.3   BacktraceCleaner

Many backtraces include too much information that's not relevant for the context. This makes it hard to find the signal in the backtrace and adds debugging time. With a custom `BacktraceCleaner`, you can set up filters and silencers for your particular context, so only the relevant lines are included.

If you want to change the setting of Rails' built-in `BacktraceCleaner`, to show as much as possible, you can call `BacktraceCleaner.remove_silencers!` in your console, specs or an application initializer. Also, if you need to reconfigure an existing `BacktraceCleaner` so that it does not filter or modify the paths of any lines of the backtrace, you can call `BacktraceCleaner#remove_filters!` These two methods will give you a completely untouched backtrace.

```
bc = ActiveSupport::BacktraceCleaner.new
bc.add_filter   { |line| line.gsub(Rails.root, '') }
bc.add_silencer { |line| line =~ /rubygems/ }

# will strip the Rails.root prefix and skip non-app lines of code
bc.clean(exception.backtrace)
```

Inspired by the Quiet Backtrace gem by Thoughtbot.

B.4 Benchmark

The following method provides additional functionality for returning benchmark results in a human readable format.

B.4.1 ms

Benchmark realtime in milliseconds.

```
>> Benchmark.realtime { User.all }
=> 8.0e-05

>> Benchmark.ms { User.all }
=> 0.074
```

B.5 Benchmarkable

Benchmarkable enables you to measure the execution time of a block in a template and records the result to the log.

B.5.1 benchmark(message = "Benchmarking", options = {})

Wrap this block around expensive operations or possible bottlenecks to get a time reading for the operation. For example, let's say you thought your file processing method was taking too long; you could wrap it in a benchmark block.

```
benchmark "Process data files" do
  expensive_files_operation
end
```

That would add an entry like "Process data files (345.2ms)" to the log, which can then be used to compare timings when optimizing your code.

You may give an optional logger level as the :level option. Valid options are :debug, :info, :warn, and :error. The default level is :info.

```
benchmark "Low-level files", level: :debug do
  lowlevel_files_operation
end
```

Finally, you can pass `true` as the third argument to silence all log activity inside the block. This is great for boiling down a noisy block to just a single statement:

```
benchmark "Process data files", level: :info, silence: true do
  expensive_and_chatty_files_operation
end
```

B.6   BigDecimal

B.6.1   active_support/core_ext/big_decimal/conversions.rb

B.6.1.1   to_formatted_s(*args)
Emits a string representation of the number without any scientific notation and without losing precision.

```
>> bd = BigDecimal.new("8439487874978349874983473987.839723497347")
=> #<BigDecimal:269fabc,'0.8439487874 9783498749 8347349878 3972349734 7E29',44(48)>
>> bd.to_s
=> "8439487874978349874983473987.839723497347"
```

B.6.1.2   to_s
The `to_s` method of `BigDecimal` is aliased to `to_formatted_s`.

B.6.2   active_support/json/encoding.rb
A BigDecimal would be naturally represented as a JSON number. Most libraries, however, parse non-integer JSON numbers directly as floats. Clients using those libraries would generally get a wrong number and no way to recover other than manually inspecting the string with the JSON code itself.

The JSON literal is not numeric, but if the other end knows by contract that the data is supposed to be a BigDecimal, it still has the chance to post-process the string and get the real value.

B.6.2.1   as_json
Returns `self.to_s`.

B.7   Cache::FileStore
A cache store implementation that stores everything on the filesystem. Selected via configuration using the following code:

```
config.cache_store = :file_store, "/path/to/cache/directory"
```

🔑 The `clear` method deletes all items from the cache. In this case it deletes all the entries in the specified file store directory except for `.keep` or `.git-keep`. Therefore, be careful which directory is specified in your config file since everything in that directory will be deleted.

B.8 Cache::MemCacheStore

A cache store implementation that stores data in Memcached[1] and is easily the most popular cache store for production Rails websites.

You can specify multiple memcached servers via configuration and `MemCache-Store` will load balance between all available servers. If a server goes down, then MemCacheStore will ignore it until it comes back up.

```
config.cache_store =
    :mem_cache_store, "cache-1.example.com", "cache-2.example.com"
```

The `write` and `fetch` methods on this cache accept two additional options that take advantage of features specific to memcached. You can specify `:raw` to send a value directly to the server with no serialization. The value must be a string or number. You can use memcached direct operations like `increment` and `decrement` only on raw values. You can also specify `:unless_exist` if you don't want memcached to overwrite an existing entry.

B.9 Cache::MemoryStore

This cache store keeps entries in memory in the same Ruby process. The cache store has a bounded size specified by sending the `:size` option to the initializer (default is 32Mb). When the cache exceeds the allotted size, a cleanup will occur and the least recently used entries will be removed.

```
config.cache_store = :memory_store, { size: 64.megabytes }
```

If you're running multiple Ruby on Rails server processes (which is the case if you're using Phusion Passenger or puma clustered mode), then your Rails server process instances won't be able to share cache data with each other.

This cache store is not appropriate for large application deployments. However, it can work well for small, low traffic sites with only a couple of server processes, as well as development and test environments.

---

1. http://memcached.org

B.10   `Cache::NullStore`

This implementation is only meant to be used in development or test environments and never stores anything. This can be very useful in development when you have code that interacts directly with `Rails.cache`, but caching may interfere with being able to see the results of code changes. All fetch and read operations on this cache will result in a miss.

```
config.cache_store = :null_store
```

See Chapter 17, "Caching and Performance," for a full discussion of caching in Rails. Also see the following section, `Cache::Store`, for full documentation of caching methods included in Active Support.

B.11   `Cache::Store`

An abstract cache store class. There are multiple cache store implementations, each having its own additional features. `MemCacheStore` is currently the most popular cache store for large production websites.

Some implementations may not support all methods beyond the basic cache methods of `fetch`, `read`, `write`, `exist?`, and `delete`.

`ActiveSupport::Cache::Store` can store any serializable Ruby object.

```
>> cache = ActiveSupport::Cache::MemoryStore.new
=> <#ActiveSupport::Cache::MemoryStore entries=0, size=0, options={}>
>> cache.read("city")
=> nil
>> cache.write("city", "Duckburgh")
=> true
>> cache.read("city")
=> "Duckburgh"
```

Keys are always translated into strings and are case-sensitive.

```
>> cache.read("city") == cache.read(:city)
=> true
```

When an object is specified as a key, its `cache_key` method will be called *if it is defined.* Otherwise, the `to_param` method will be called.

```
>> r = Report.first
=> #<Report id: 1, name: "Special", created_at: ...>
>> r.cache_key
=> "reports/1-20131001152655016228000"
```

```
>> r.to_param
=> "1"
```

Hashes and Arrays can also be used as keys. The elements will be delimited by slashes, and hash elements will be sorted by key so they are consistent.

```
>> cache.write ["USA","FL","Jacksonville"], "Obie"
=> true
>> cache.read "USA/FL/Jacksonville"
=> "Obie"
```

Nil values can be cached.

If your cache is on a shared infrastructure, you can define a namespace for your cache entries. If a namespace is defined, it will be prefixed on to every key. To set a global namespace, set the :namespace to the constructor of the cache store. The default value will include the application name and Rails environment.

```
cache = ActiveSupport::Cache::MemoryStore.new(namespace: 'tr5w')
```

All caches support auto expiring content after a specified number of seconds. To set the cache entry time to live, you can either specify :expires_in as an option to the constructor to have it affect all entries or to the fetch or write methods for just one entry.

```
cache = ActiveSupport::Cache::MemoryStore.new(expire_in: 5.minutes)
cache.write(key, value, expires_in: 1.minute) # Set a lower value for one entry
```

It's a recommended practice to set the :race_condition_ttl option in conjunction with :expires_in. When a cache entry is used frequently and the system is under a heavy load, a dog pile effect can occur during expiration. During this scenario, since the cache has expired, multiple processes will try to read the data natively and all attempt to regenerate the same cache entry simultaneously. Using :race_condition_ttl, you can set the number of seconds an expired entry can be reused while a new value is being regenerated. The first process to encounter the stale cache will attempt to write a new value, while other processes will continue to use slightly stale data for the period defined in :race_condition_ttl. Like the :expires_in option, :race_condition_ttl can be set globally or in the fetch or write methods for a single entry.

Caches can also store values in a compressed format to save space and reduce time spent sending data. Since there is some overhead, values must be large enough to warrant compression. To turn on compression either pass compress: true in the initializer or to `fetch` or `write`. To specify the threshold at which to compress values, set `:compress_threshold`. The default threshold is 16K.

B.11.1   `cleanup(options = nil)`

Clean up the cache by removing expired entries. Not all cache implementations may support this method. Options are passed to the underlying cache implementation.

B.11.2   `clear(options = nil)`

Clear the entire cache. Not all cache implementations may support this method. You should be careful with this method since it could affect other processes if you are using a shared cache. Options are passed to the underlying cache implementation.

B.11.3   `decrement(name, amount = 1, options = nil)`

Decrement an integer value in the cache. Options are passed to the underlying cache implementation.

B.11.4   `delete(name, options = nil)`

Delete an entry in the cache. Returns `true` if there was an entry to delete. Options are passed to the underlying cache implementation.

B.11.5   `delete_matched(matcher, options = nil)`

Delete all entries whose keys match a pattern. Options are passed to the underlying cache implementation.

```
>> Rails.cache.write :color, :red
=> true
>> Rails.cache.read :color
=> :red
>> Rails.cache.delete_matched "c"
=> ["city", "color", "USA/FL/Jacksonville"]
>> Rails.cache.read :color
=> nil
```

B.11.6   `exist?(name, options = nil)`

Return `true` if the cache contains an entry with this name. Options are passed to the underlying cache implementation.

B.11.7   `fetch(name, options = nil)`

Fetches data from the cache, using the given key. If there is data in the cache with the given key, then that data is returned.

If there is no such data in the cache (a cache miss occurred), then `nil` will be returned. However, if a block has been passed, then that block will be run in the event of a cache miss. The return value of the block will be written to the cache under the given cache key, and that return value will be returned.

```
cache.write("today", "Monday")
cache.fetch("today")    # => "Monday"

cache.fetch("city")     # => nil
cache.fetch("city") do
  "Duckburgh"
end
cache.fetch("city")     # => "Duckburgh"
```

You may also specify additional options via the options argument. Setting `:force => true` will force a cache miss:

```
cache.write("today", "Monday")
cache.fetch("today", force: true)    # => nil
```

Setting `:compress` will store a large cache entry set by the call in a compressed format.

Setting `:expires_in` will set an expiration time on the cache entry if it is set by call.

Setting `:race_condition_ttl` will invoke logic on entries set with an `:expires_in` option. If an entry is found in the cache that is expired, and it has been expired for less than the number of seconds specified by this option, and a block was passed to the method call, then the expiration future time of the entry in the cache will be updated to that many seconds in the future and the block will be evaluated and written to the cache.

This is very useful in situations where a cache entry is used very frequently under heavy load. The first process to find an expired cache entry will then become responsible for regenerating that entry while other processes continue to use the slightly out-of-date entry. This can prevent race conditions where too many processes are trying to regenerate the entry all at once. If the process regenerating the entry errors out, the entry will be regenerated after the specified number of seconds.

```
# Set all values to expire after one minute.
cache = ActiveSupport::Cache::MemoryStore.new(expires_in: 1.minute)

cache.write("foo", "original value")
val_1 = nil
```

```
val_2 = nil
sleep 60

Thread.new do
  val_1 = cache.fetch("foo", race_condition_ttl: 10) do
    sleep 1
    "new value 1"
  end
end

Thread.new do
  val_2 = cache.fetch("foo", race_condition_ttl: 10) do
    "new value 2"
  end
end

# val_1 => "new value 1"
# val_2 => "original value"
# sleep 10 # First thread extend the life of cache by another 10 seconds
# cache.fetch("foo") => "new value 1"
```

Other options will be handled by the specific cache store implementation. Internally, fetch calls `read_entry` and calls `write_entry` on a cache miss. Options will be passed to the read and write calls.

For example, MemCacheStore's write method supports the `:raw` option, which tells the memcached server to store all values as strings. We can use this option with `fetch` too:

```
cache = ActiveSupport::Cache::MemCacheStore.new
cache.fetch("foo", force: true, raw: true) do
  :bar
end
cache.fetch("foo")    # => "bar"
```

B.11.8   `increment(name, amount = 1, options = nil)`
Increment an integer value in the cache. Options are passed to the underlying cache implementation.

B.11.9   `mute`
Silence the logger within a block.

B.11.10   `options`
Get the default options set when the cache was created.

B.11.11 `read(name, options = nil)`

Fetches data from the cache, using the given key. If there is data in the cache with the given key, then that data is returned. Otherwise, `nil` is returned. Options are passed to the underlying cache implementation.

B.11.12 `read_multi(*names)`

Read multiple values at once from the cache. Options can be passed in the last argument. Some cache implementation may optimize this method.

Returns a hash mapping the names provided to the values found.

```
>> cache.write :color, :red
=> true
>> cache.write :smell, :roses
=> true
>> cache.read_multi :color, :smell
=> {:color=>:red, :smell=>:roses}
```

B.11.13 `silence!`

Silences the logger.

B.11.14 `write(name, value, options = nil)`

Writes the given value to the cache, with the given key.

You may also specify additional options via the `options` argument. The specific cache store implementation will decide what to do with options.

B.12 `CachingKeyGenerator`

`CachingKeyGenerator` is a wrapper around `KeyGenerator` that avoids re-executing the key generation process when it's called using the same salt and key_size.

B.12.1 `initialize(key_generator)`

Creates a new instance of `CachingKeyGenerator`.

B.12.2 `generate_key(salt, key_size=64)`

Returns a derived key suitable for use. The default `key_size` is chosen to be compatible with the default settings of `ActiveSupport::MessageVerifier`, such as `OpenSSL::Digest::SHA1#block_length`. Subsequent calls to `generate _key` will return a cached key if the supplied `salt` and `key_size` are the same.

B.13 Callbacks

Callbacks are hooks into the lifecycle of an object that enables you to trigger logic before or after an alteration of the object state. Mixing in this module enables you to define callbacks in your class.

For instance, assume you have the following code in your application:

```
class Storage
  include ActiveSupport::Callbacks

  define_callbacks :save
end

class ConfigStorage < Storage
  set_callback :save, :before, :saving_message

  def saving_message
    puts "saving..."
  end

  set_callback :save, :after do |object|
    puts "saved"
  end

  def save
    run_callbacks :save do
      puts "- running save callbacks"
    end
  end
end
```

Running the following code using

```
config = ConfigStorage.new
config.save
```

would output

```
saving...
- running save callbacks
saved
```

Note that callbacks defined on parent classes are inherited.

B.13.1 `active_support/callbacks`

The following methods are used to configure custom callbacks on your classes and are what Rails itself uses to create things such as `before_action` in Action Pack and `before_save` in Active Record. Note that this is rather advanced functionality, which you typically won't need in your day-to-day Rails programming.

B.13.1.1 `define_callbacks(*callbacks)`

Define callbacks types for your custom class.

```
module MyOwnORM
  class Base
    define_callbacks :validate
  end
end
```

The following options determine the operation of the callback:

`:terminator` Indicates when a before callback is considered to be halted.

```
define_callbacks :validate, terminator: "result == false"
```

In the preceding example, if any before validate callbacks return `false`, other callbacks are not executed. Defaults to `false`.

`:skip_after_callbacks_if_terminated` Determines whether after callbacks should be terminated by the `:terminator` option. By default, after callbacks are executed no matter whether callback chain was terminated or not.

`:scope` Specify which methods should be executed when a class is given as callback.

```
class Audit
  def before(caller)
    puts 'before is called'
  end

  def before_save(caller)
    puts 'before_save is called'
  end
end

class Account
  include ActiveSupport::Callbacks

  define_callbacks :save
  set_callback :save, :before, Audit.new

  def save
    run_callbacks :save do
      puts 'saving...'
```

```
      end
    end
  end
```

Calling `save` in the preceding example will execute `Audit#before`. If the callback is defined with a `[:kind, :name]` scope

```
define_callbacks :save, scope: [:kind, :name]
```

the method named `"#{kind}_#{name}"` would be invoked in the given class. In this case, `Audit#before_save` would be invoked.

The `:scope` option defaults to `:kind`.

B.13.1.2 `reset_callbacks(symbol)`
Remove all set callbacks for the given event.

B.13.1.3 `set_callback(name, *filter_list, &block)`
Set callbacks for a given event.

```
set_callback :save, :before, :before_method
set_callback :save, :after,  :after_method, if: :condition
set_callback :save, :around,
  ->(r, &block) { stuff; result = block.call; stuff }
```

The second argument indicates whether callback `:before`, `:after`, or `:around` is to be run. By default, if nothing is set, `:before` is assumed. The first example can also be expressed as:

```
set_callback :save, :before_method
```

The callback that the callback invokes can be specified as a symbol that references the name of an instance method or as a proc, lambda, or block. If a proc, lambda, or block is supplied, its body is evaluated in the context of the current object. A current object can optionally be set.

B.13.1.4 `skip_callback(name, *filter_list, &block)`
Skip a previously defined callback for a given type. The options `:if` or `:unless` may be passed in order to control when the callback is skipped.

B.14 Class
Rails extends Ruby's `Class` object with a number of class methods that then become available on all other classes in the runtime, regardless of type.

B.14.1 `active_support/core_ext/class/attribute.rb`

B.14.1.1 `class_attribute(*attrs)`

Declare one or more class-level attributes whose value is inheritable and overwritable by subclasses and instances, like so:

```
class Base
  class_attribute :setting
end

class Subclass < Base
end

>> Base.setting = "foo"
=> "foo"

>> Subclass.setting
=> "foo"

>> Subclass.setting = "bar"
=> "bar"

>> Subclass.setting
=> "bar"

>> Base.setting
=> "foo"
```

To be clear, the attribute can be of any type, not just a string.

What makes `class_attribute` more than just an attribute accessor on a class is that *instances* of the class get reader and writer methods for the attribute as well. Continuing the previous example

```
>> b = Base.new
>> b.setting
=> "foo"

>> sub = Subclass.new
>> sub.setting
=> "bar"
```

To opt out of instance reader methods, pass `instance_reader: false` like this:

```
class Example
  class_attribute :setting, instance_reader: false
end
```

```
>> e = Example.new
>> e.setting              # => NoMethodError
>> e.setting?             # => NoMethodError
```

To opt out of the instance writer method, pass `instance_writer: false` like this:

```
class Example
  class_attribute :setting, instance_writer: false
end
```

```
>> e = Example.new
>> e.setting = "qux"      # => NoMethodError: undefined method 'setting='
```

The `class_attribute` method also works with singleton classes, as can be seen in the following example:

```
class Example
  class_attribute :setting
end
```

```
>> Example.singleton_class.setting = "foo"
=> "foo"
```

As hinted in previous examples, a predicate method is defined as well, which enables you to see if an attribute has been set on a particular class instance.

```
class Example
  class_attribute :setting, instance_reader: false end
>> e = Example.new
>> e.setting?
=> false
```

```
>> e.setting = "foo"
=> "foo"
```

```
>> e.setting?
=> true
```

To opt out of defining a predicate method, set `instance_predicate` to `false`.

B.14.2 `active_support/core_ext/class/attribute_ accessors.rb`

Contains `cattr_accessor`, `cattr_reader`, and `cattr_writer` aliases to their `mattr_ -` counterparts in Module.

B.14.3 `active_support/core_ext/class/subclasses.rb`

Provides methods that introspect the inheritance hierarchy of a class. Used extensively in Active Record.

B.14.3.1 `descendents`

Returns an array of all class objects found that are subclasses of `self`.

B.14.3.2 `subclasses`

Returns an array with the names of the subclasses of `self` as strings.

```
Integer.subclasses # => ["Bignum", "Fixnum"]
```

B.15 Concern

B.15.1 `active_support/concern.rb`

The `Concern` module is only 26 lines of Ruby code. Using it, you can make your code more modular and have fewer dependency problems than ever before.

You use `Concern` to define common behavior that you want to mix into other application classes or into Rails itself in the case of plugins.

A `Concern` module has two elements: the `included` block and the `ClassMethods` module.

```
require 'active_support/concern'

module Foo
  extend ActiveSupport::Concern

  included do
    self.send(:do_something_in_mixin_class)
  end

  module ClassMethods
    def bar
      ...
    end
  end

  def baz
    ...
  end
end
```

To use your custom `Concern` module, just mix it into a class.

```
class Widget
  include Foo
end
```

The `included` block will be triggered at inclusion time. Methods in `ClassMethods` will get added to `Widget` as class methods. All other methods will get added to `Widget` as instance methods.

B.16 Configurable

The `ActiveSupport::Configurable` module is used internally by Rails to add configuration settings to `AbstractController::Base`. You can use it yourself to add runtime configuration to your classes.

```
require 'active_support/configurable'

class User
  include ActiveSupport::Configurable
end

user = User.new

user.config.allowed_access = true
user.config.level = 1

user.config.allowed_access      # => true
user.config.level      # => 1
```

B.16.1 active_support/configurable.rb

`Configurable` is implemented as a `Concern` that can be mixed into other classes.

B.16.1.1 config

Return the configuration of the object instance.

B.17 Date

Active Support provides a wide array of extensions to Ruby's built-in date and time classes to simplify conversion and calculation tasks in simple-to-understand language.

B.17.1 active_support/core_ext/date/calculations.rb

The following methods enable the use of calculations with `Date` objects.

B.17.1.1 `+(other)` / `-(other)`

Rails extends the existing + and − operator so that a `since` calculation is performed when the `other` argument is an instance of `ActiveSupport::Duration` (the type of object returned by methods such as `10.minutes` and `9.months`).

```
>> Date.today + 1.day == Date.today.tomorrow
=> true
```

B.17.1.2 `advance(options)`

Provides precise `Date` calculations for years, months, and days. The `options` parameter takes a hash with any of these keys: `:years`, `:months`, `:weeks`, and `:days`.

```
>> Date.new(2006, 2, 28) == Date.new(2005, 2, 28).advance(years: 1)
=> true
```

B.17.1.3 `ago(seconds)`

Converts `Date` to a `Time` (or `DateTime` if necessary) with the time portion set to the beginning of the day (0:00) and then subtracts the specified number of seconds.

```
>> Time.utc(2005, 2, 20, 23, 59, 15) == Date.new(2005, 2, 21).ago(45)
=> true
```

B.17.1.4 `at_beginning_of_day` / `at_midnight` / `beginning_of_day` / `midnight`

Converts `Date` to a `Time` (or `DateTime` if necessary) with the time portion set to the beginning of the day (0:00).

```
>> Time.utc(2005,2,21,0,0,0) == Date.new(2005,2,21).beginning_of_day
=> true
```

B.17.1.5 `at_beginning_of_month` / `beginning_of_month`

Returns a new `Date` object representing the start of the month (1st of the month). Objects will have their time set to 0:00.

```
>> Date.new(2005, 2, 1) == Date.new(2005,2,21).beginning_of_month
=> true
```

B.17.1.6 `at_beginning_of_quarter` / `beginning_of_quarter`

Returns a new `Date` object representing the start of the calendar-based quarter (1st of January, April, July, and October).

```
>> Date.new(2005, 4, 1) == Date.new(2005, 6, 30).beginning_of_quarter
=> true
```

B.17.1.7   **at_beginning_of_week**
Alias for beginning_of_week.

B.17.1.8   **at_beginning_of_year** / **beginning_of_year**
Returns a new Date object representing the start of the calendar year (1st of January).

```
>> Date.new(2005, 1, 1) == Date.new(2005, 2, 22).beginning_of_year
=> true
```

B.17.1.9   **at_end_of_day** / **end_of_day**
Converts Date to a Time (or DateTime if necessary) with the time portion set to the end of the day (23:59:59).

B.17.1.10   **at_end_of_month** / **end_of_month**
Returns a new Date object representing the last day of the calendar month.

```
>> Date.new(2005, 3, 31) == Date.new(2005,3,20).end_of_month
=> true
```

B.17.1.11   **at_end_of_quarter** / **end_of_quarter**
Returns a new Date object representing the end of the calendar-based quarter (31st March, 30th June, 30th September).

B.17.1.12   **at_end_of_week**
Alias for end_of_week.

B.17.1.13   **at_end_of_year** / **end_of_year**
Returns a new Date object representing the end of the year.

```
>> Date.new(2013, 12, 31) == Date.new(2013, 10, 1).end_of_year
=> true
```

B.17.1.14   **beginning_of_week**
Returns a new Date object representing the beginning of the week. By default, based on Date.beginning_of_week.

Active
Support

```
>> Date.new(2005, 1, 31) == Date.new(2005, 2, 4).beginning_of_week
=> true
```

B.17.1.15 `Date.beginning_of_week(start_day = :monday)`
Returns the week start for the current request/thread.

```
>> Date.beginning_of_week
=> :monday
```

The optional parameter defaults to `:monday`, but can be overriden. It's also possible to override on a per request/thread basis, or modified in an initializer for the entire application:

```
# per thread basis
Date.beginning_of_week = :sunday

# for the entire application
Rails.configuration.beginning_of_week = :sunday
```

B.17.1.16 `Date.beginning_of_week=(week_start)`
Sets `Date.beginning_of_week` to a week start for current request/thread. The method accepts the following symbols:

- `:monday`
- `:tuesday`
- `:wednesday`
- `:thursday`
- `:friday`
- `:saturday`
- `:sunday`

B.17.1.17 `change(options)`
Returns a new `Date` where one or more of the elements have been changed according to the options parameter.

The valid options are `:year`, `:month`, and `:day`.

```
>> Date.new(2007, 5, 12).change(day: 1) == Date.new(2007, 5, 1)
=> true
```

```
>> Date.new(2007, 5, 12).change(year: 2005, month: 1) == Date.new(2005, 1, 12)
=> true
```

B.17.1.18   `compare_with_coercion(other)` / `<=>`

Allow `Date` to be compared with `Time` by converting to `DateTime` and relying on the `<=>` from there.

B.17.1.19   `Date.current`

Returns `Time.zone.today` when `config.time_zone` is set, otherwise just returns `Date.today`. This is the preferred way to get the current date when your Rails application is timezone-aware.

B.17.1.20   `days_ago(days)`

Returns a new `Date` object, minus the specified number of days.

```
>> Date.new(2013, 10, 1).days_ago(5)
=> Thu, 26 Sep 2013
```

B.17.1.21   `days_since(days)`

Returns a new `Date` object representing the time a number of specified days into the future.

```
>> Date.new(2013, 10, 5) == Date.new(2013, 10, 1).days_since(4)
=> true
```

B.17.1.22   `days_to_week_start(start_day = Date.beginning_of_week)`

Returns the number of days to the start of the week.

```
>> Date.new(2013, 10, 10).days_to_week_start
=> 3
```

B.17.1.23   `end_of_week(start_day = Date.beginning_of_week)`

Returns a new `Date` object representing the end of the week.

```
>> Date.new(2013, 10, 13) == Date.new(2013, 10, 10).end_of_week
=> true
```

B.17.1.24   `Date.find_beginning_of_week!(week_start)`

Returns the week start day symbol or raises an ArgumentError if an invalid symbol is set.

```
>> Date.find_beginning_of_week!(:saturday)
=> :saturday
```

```
>> Date.find_beginning_of_week!(:foobar) ArgumentError: Invalid beginning of week: foobar
```

B.17.1.25 `future?`
Returns `true` if the `Date` instance is in the future.

```
>> (Date.current + 1.day).future?
=> true
```

B.17.1.26 `last_month` / `prev_month`
Convenience method for `months_ago(1)`.

B.17.1.27 `last_quarter` / `prev_quarter`
Convenience method for `months_ago(3)`.

B.17.1.28 `last_week(start_day = Date.beginning_of_week)` / `prev_week`
Returns a new `Date` object representing the given day in the previous week.

B.17.1.29 `last_year` / `prev_year`
Convenience method for `years_ago(1)`.

B.17.1.30 `middle_of_day` / `noon` / `midday`
Returns a new `Date` object representing the middle of the day.

B.17.1.31 `monday`
Convenience method for `beginning_of_week(:monday)`.

B.17.1.32 `months_ago(months)`
Returns a new `Date` object representing the time a number of specified months ago.

```
>> Date.new(2005, 1, 1) == Date.new(2005, 3, 1).months_ago(2)
=> true
```

B.17.1.33 `months_since(months)`
Returns a new `Date` object representing the time a number of specified months into the past or the future. Supply a negative number of months to go back to the past.

```
>> Date.today.months_ago(1) == Date.today.months_since(-1)
=> true
```

B.17.1.34   `next_month`
Convenience method for `months_since(1)`.

B.17.1.35   `next_quarter`
Convenience method for `months_since(3)`.

B.17.1.36   `next_week(given_day_in_next_week = Date` `.beginning_of_week))`
Returns a new `Date` object representing the start of the given day in the following calendar week.

```
>> Date.new(2005, 3, 4) == Date.new(2005, 2, 22).next_week(:friday)
=> true
```

B.17.1.37   `next_year`
Convenience method for `years_since(1)`.

B.17.1.38   `past?`
Returns `true` if `Date` is in the past.

```
>> (Date.current - 1.day).past?
=> true
```

B.17.1.39   `since(seconds)` / `in(seconds)`
Converts `Date` to a `Time` (or `DateTime` if necessary) with the time portion set to the beginning of the day (0:00) and then adds the specified number of seconds.

```
>> Time.local(2005, 2, 21, 0, 0, 45) == Date.new(2005, 2, 21).since(45)
=> true
```

B.17.1.40   `sunday`
Convenience method for `end_of_week(:monday)`.

B.17.1.41   `today?`
Returns `true` if the `Date` instance is today.

```
>> Date.current.today?
=> true
```

Active Support

B.17.1.42 `Date.tomorrow`
Convenience method that returns a new `Date` (or `DateTime`) representing the time one day in the future.

```
>> Date.tomorrow
=> Thu, 10 Oct 2013
```

B.17.1.43 `tomorrow`
Returns a new `Date` object advanced by one day.

```
>> Date.new(2007, 3, 1) == Date.new(2007, 2, 28).tomorrow
=> true
```

B.17.1.44 `weeks_ago(weeks)`
Returns a new `Date` object representing the time a number of specified weeks ago.

```
>> Date.new(2013, 10, 1) == Date.new(2013, 10, 8).weeks_ago(1)
=> true
```

B.17.1.45 `weeks_since(weeks)`
Returns a new `Date` object representing the time a number of specified weeks into the future.

```
>> Date.new(2013, 10, 8) == Date.new(2013, 10, 1).weeks_since(1)
=> true
```

B.17.1.46 `years_ago(years)`
Returns a new `Date` object representing the time a number of specified years ago.

```
>> Date.new(2000, 6, 5) == Date.new(2007, 6, 5).years_ago(7)
=> true
```

B.17.1.47 `years_since(years)`
Returns a new `Date` object representing the time a number of specified years into the future.

```
>> Date.new(2007, 6, 5) == Date.new(2006, 6, 5).years_since(1)
=> true
```

B.17.1.48 `Date.yesterday`
Convenience method that returns a new `Date` object representing the time one day in the past.

```
>> Date.yesterday
=> Tue, 08 Oct 2013
```

B.17.1.49 **yesterday**
Returns a new Date object subtracted by one day.

```
>> Date.new(2007, 2, 21) == Date.new(2007, 2, 22).yesterday
=> true
```

B.17.2 **active_support/core_ext/date/conversions.rb**
The following methods facilitate the conversion of date data into various formats.

B.17.2.1 **readable_inspect**
Overrides the default inspect method with a human readable one.

```
>> Date.current
=> Wed, 02 Jun 2010
```

B.17.2.2 **to_formatted_s(format = :default) / to_s**
Converts a Date object into its string representation, according to the predefined formats in the DATE_FORMATS constant.

The following hash of formats dictates the behavior of the to_s method.

```
DATE_FORMATS = {
  :short        => '%e %b',
  :long         => '%B %e, %Y',
  :db           => '%Y-%m-%d',
  :number       => '%Y%m%d',
  :long_ordinal => lambda { |date|
    day_format = ActiveSupport::Inflector.ordinalize(date.day)
    date.strftime("%B #{day_format}, %Y") # => "April 25th, 2007"
  },
  :rfc822       => '%e %b %Y'
}
```

Examples:

```
>> Date.today.to_s(:short)
=> "14 Jun"
>> Date.today.to_s(:long)
=> "June 14, 2017"
>> Date.today.to_s(:db)
=> "2017-06-14"
```

Active
Support

```
>> Date.today.to_s(:number)
=> "20170614"
>> Date.today.to_s(:long_ordinal)
=> "June 14th, 2017"
>> Date.today.to_s(:rfc822)
=> "14 Jun 2017"
```

B.17.2.3   Adding Your Own Standard Date Formats

You can add your own formats to the Date::DATE_FORMATS hash. Use the format name as the hash key and either a strftime string or Proc instance that takes a date argument as the value.

```
# config/initializers/date_formats.rb
Date::DATE_FORMATS[:month_and_year] = '%B %Y' Date::DATE_FORMATS[:short_ordinal] =
  -> (date) { date.strftime("%B #{date.day.ordinalize}") }
```

B.17.2.4   `to_time(timezone = :local)`

Converts a Date object into a Ruby Time object; time is set to beginning of day. The time zone can be :local or :utc.

```
>> Time.local(2005, 2, 21) == Date.new(2005, 2, 21).to_time
=> true
```

Note that Active Support explicitly removes the Date#to_time method in Ruby 2.0, as it converts localtime only.

B.17.2.5   `xmlschema`

Returns a string that represents the time as defined by XML Schema within the current time zone (also known as iso8601):

```
CCYY-MM-DDThh:mm:ssTZD
```

```
>> Date.today.xmlschema
=> "2017-06-14T00:00:00Z"
```

Note that Active Support explicitly removes the Date#xmlschema method in Ruby 2.0, as it converts a date to a string *without* the time component.

B.17.3   `active_support/core_ext/date/zones.rb`

B.17.3.1   `in_time_zone`

Converts Date object into a Ruby Time object in the current time zone. If Time.zone or Time.zone_default is not set, converts Date to a Time via #to_time.

```
>> Time.zone = "Eastern Time (US & Canada)"
=> "Eastern Time (US & Canada)"
>> Thu, 10 Oct 2013 00:00:00 EDT -04:00
```

B.17.4 `active_support/json/encoding.rb`

B.17.4.1 `as_json`

Returns `self` as a JSON string. The `ActiveSupport.use_standard_json_time_format` configuration setting determines whether the date string is delimited with dashes or slashes.

```
>> Date.today.as_json
=> "2010-06-03"
```

B.18 `DateAndTime`

Contains extended functionality common to `Date`, `DateTime`, and `Time` instances.

B.18.1 `active_support/core_ext/date_time/ calculations.rb`

The following methods permit easier use of `DateTime` objects in date and time calculations.

B.18.1.1 `<=> compare_with_coercion`

Layers additional behavior on `DateTime` so that `Time` and `ActiveSupport::-TimeWithZone` instances can be compared with `DateTime` instances.

B.18.1.2 `advance(options)`

Uses `Date` to provide precise `Time` calculations for years, months, and days. The `options` parameter takes a hash with any of the keys `:months`, `:days`, and `:years`.

B.18.1.3 `ago(seconds)`

Returns a new `DateTime` representing the time a number of seconds ago. The opposite of `since`.

B.18.1.4 `at_beginning_of_day` / `at_midnight` / `beginning_of_ day` / `midnight`

Convenience method that represents the beginning of a day (00:00:00). Implemented simply as `change(hour: 0)`.

B.18.1.5 at_beginning_of_hour / beginning_of_hour

Returns a new `DateTime` object representing the start of the hour (hh:00:00). Implemented simply as `change(min: 0)`.

B.18.1.6 at_beginning_of_minute / beginning_of_minute

Returns a new `DateTime` object representing the start of the minute (hh:mm:00). Implemented simply as `change(sec: 0)`.

B.18.1.7 at_end_of_day / end_of_day

Convenience method that represents the end of a day (23:59:59). Implemented simply as `change(hour: 23, min: 59, sec: 59)`.

B.18.1.8 at_end_of_hour / end_of_hour

Returns a new `DateTime` object representing the end of the hour (hh:59:59). Implemented simply as `change(min: 59, sec: 59)`.

B.18.1.9 at_end_of_minute / end_of_minute

Returns a new `DateTime` object representing the end of the minute (hh:mm:59). Implemented simply as `change(sec: 59)`.

B.18.1.10 change(options)

Returns a new `DateTime` where one or more of the elements have been changed according to the `options` parameter. The valid date options are `:year`, `:month`, `:day`. The valid time options are `:hour`, `:min`, `:sec`, `:offset`, and `:start`.

B.18.1.11 DateTime.current

Timezone-aware implementation of `Time.now` returns a `DateTime` instance.

B.18.1.12 future?

Tells whether the `DateTime` is in the future.

B.18.1.13 middle_of_day / noon

Returns a new `DateTime` object representing the middle of the day (12:00:00). Implemented simply as `change(hour: 12)`.

B.18.1.14 past?

Tells whether the `DateTime` is in the past.

B.18.1.15   `seconds_since_midnight`
Returns how many seconds have passed since midnight.

B.18.1.16   `seconds_until_end_of_day`
Returns how many seconds left in the day until 23:59:59.

B.18.1.17   `since(seconds) \ in(seconds)`
Returns a new `DateTime` representing the time a number of seconds since the instance time (aliased as `in`). The opposite of `ago`.

B.18.1.18   `utc`
Returns a new `DateTime` with the `offset` set to 0 to represent UTC time.

B.18.1.19   `utc?`
Convenience method returns `true` if the `offset` is set to 0.

B.18.1.20   `utc_offset`
Returns the offset value in seconds.

B.19.2   `active_support/core_ext/date_and_time/zones.rb`
The following method enables conversion of dates/times into different time zones.

B.19.2.1   `in_time_zone(zone = ::Time.zone)`
Returns the simultaneous time in `Time.zone`

```
>> Time.zone = 'Hawaii'
>> DateTime.new(2000).in_time_zone
=> Fri, 31 Dec 1999 14:00:00 HST -10:00
```

This method is similar to `Time#localtime`, except that it uses the `Time.zone` argument as the local zone instead of the operating system's time zone. You can also pass it a string that identifies a TimeZone as an argument, and the conversion will be based on that zone instead. Allowable string parameters are operating-system dependent.

```
>> DateTime.new(2000).in_time_zone('Alaska' )
=> Fri, 31 Dec 1999 15:00:00 AKST -09:00
```

Active Support

B.19   `DateTime`

The following methods extend Ruby's built-in `DateTime` class.

B.19.1   `active_support/core_ext/date_time/acts_like.rb`

Duck-types as a DateTime-like class. See `Object#acts_like?` for more explanation.

```
class DateTime
  def acts_like_date?
    true
  end

  def acts_like_time?
    true
  end
end
```

B.19.2   `active_support/core_ext/date_time/calculations.rb`

The following methods permit easier use of `DateTime` objects in date and time calculations.

B.19.2.1   `<=>` `compare_with_coercion`

Layers additional behavior on `DateTime` so that `Time` and `ActiveSupport::-TimeWithZone` instances can be compared with `DateTime` instances.

B.19.2.2   `advance(options)`

Uses `Date` to provide precise `Time` calculations for years, months, and days. The `options` parameter takes a hash with any of the keys `:months`, `:days`, and `:years`.

B.19.2.3   `ago(seconds)`

Returns a new `DateTime` representing the time a number of seconds ago. The opposite of `since`.

B.19.2.4   `at_beginning_of_day` / `at_midnight` / `beginning_of_day` / `midnight`

Convenience method that represents the beginning of a day (00:00:00). Implemented simply as `change(hour: 0)`.

B.19.2.5 `at_beginning_of_hour` / `beginning_of_hour`

Returns a new `DateTime` object representing the start of the hour (hh:00:00). Implemented simply as `change(min: 0)`.

B.19.2.6 `at_beginning_of_minute` / `beginning_of_minute`

Returns a new `DateTime` object representing the start of the minute (hh:mm:00). Implemented simply as `change(sec: 0)`.

B.19.2.7 `at_end_of_day` / `end_of_day`

Convenience method that represents the end of a day (23:59:59). Implemented simply as `change(hour: 23, min: 59, sec: 59)`.

B.19.2.8 `at_end_of_hour` / `end_of_hour`

Returns a new `DateTime` object representing the end of the hour (hh:59:59). Implemented simply as `change(min: 59, sec: 59)`.

B.19.2.9 `at_end_of_minute` / `end_of_minute`

Returns a new `DateTime` object representing the end of the minute (hh:mm:59). Implemented simply as `change(sec: 59)`.

B.19.2.10 `change(options)`

Returns a new `DateTime` where one or more of the elements have been changed according to the `options` parameter. The valid date options are `:year`, `:month`, `:day`. The valid time options are `:hour`, `:min`, `:sec`, `:offset`, and `:start`.

B.19.2.11 `DateTime.current`

Timezone-aware implementation of `Time.now`. Returns a `DateTime` instance.

B.19.2.12 `future?`

Tells whether the `DateTime` is in the future.

B.19.2.13 `middle_of_day` / `noon`

Returns a new `DateTime` object representing the middle of the day (12:00:00). Implemented simply as `change(hour: 12)`.

B.19.2.14 `past?`

Tells whether the `DateTime` is in the past.

Active Support

B.19.2.15 `seconds_since_midnight`
Returns how many seconds have passed since midnight.

B.19.2.16 `seconds_until_end_of_day`
Returns how many seconds left in the day until 23:59:59.

B.19.2.17 `since(seconds) \ in(seconds)`
Returns a new `DateTime` representing the time a number of seconds since the instance time (aliased as `in`). The opposite of `ago`.

B.19.2.18 `utc`
Returns a new `DateTime` with the `offset` set to 0 to represent UTC time.

B.19.2.19 `utc?`
Convenience method returns `true` if the `offset` is set to 0.

B.19.2.20 `utc_offset`
Returns the offset value in seconds.

B.19.3 `active_support/core_ext/date_time/ conversions.rb`
The following methods permit conversion of `DateTime` objects (and some of their attributes) into other types of data.

B.19.3.1 `formatted_offset(colon = true, alternate_utc_ string = nil)`
Returns the `utc_offset` as an HH:MM formatted string.

```
datetime = DateTime.civil(2000, 1, 1, 0, 0, 0, Rational(-6, 24))

>> datetime.formatted_offset
=> "-06:00"
```

The options provide for tweaking the output of the method by doing things like ommitting the colon character.

```
>> datetime.formatted_offset(false)
=> "-0600"
```

B.19.3.2 `nsec`
Returns the fraction of a second as nanoseconds.

B.19.3.3 `readable_inspect`
Overrides the default inspect method with a human-readable one that looks like this:

```
Mon, 21 Feb 2005 14:30:00 +0000
```

B.19.3.4 `to_date`
Converts `self` to a Ruby `Date` object, discarding time data.

B.19.3.5 `to_datetime`
Returns `self` to be able to keep `Time`, `Date`, and `DateTime` classes interchangeable on conversions.

B.19.3.6 `to_f`
Converts `self` to a floating-point number of seconds since the Unix epoch. Note the limitations of this method with dates prior to 1970.

```
>> Date.new(2000, 4,4).to_datetime.to_f
=> 954806400.0
>> Date.new(1800, 4,4).to_datetime.to_f
=> -5356627200.0
```

B.19.3.7 `to_formatted_s(format=:default)`
See the options on `to_formatted_s` of the `Time` class. The primary difference is the appending of the time information.

```
>> datetime.to_formatted_s(:db)
=> "2007-12-04 00:00:00"
```

B.19.3.8 `to_i`
Converts self to an integer number of seconds since the Unix epoch. Note the limitations of this methods with dates prior to 1970.

```
>> Date.new(2000, 4,4).to_datetime.to_i
=> 954806400
>> Date.new(1800, 4,4).to_datetime.to_i
=> -5356627200
```

B.19.3.9 `usec`
Returns the fraction of a second as microseconds.

Active
Support

B.19.4 `active_support/json/encoding.rb`

B.19.4.1 `as_json`

Returns `self` as a JSON string. The `ActiveSupport.use_standard_json_time_format` configuration setting determines whether the output is formatted using `:xmlschema` or the following pattern:

```
strftime('%Y/%m/%d %H:%M:%S %z')
```

B.20 Dependencies

This module contains the logic for Rails' automatic class loading mechanism, which is what makes it possible to reference any constant in the Rails varied load paths without ever needing to issue a `require` directive.

This module extends itself, a cool hack that you can use with modules that you want to use elsewhere in your codebase in a functional manner:

```
module Dependencies
  extend self
  ...
```

As a result, you can call methods directly on the module constant, à la Java static class methods, like this:

```
>> ActiveSupport::Dependencies.search_for_file('person.rb')
=> "/Users/obie/work/time_and_expenses/app/models/person.rb"
```

You shouldn't need to use this module in day-to-day Rails coding—it's mostly for internal use by Rails and plugins. On occasion, it might also be useful to understand the workings of this module when debugging tricky class-loading problems.

B.20.1 `active_support/dependencies.rb`

B.20.1.1 `autoload_once_paths`

The set of directories from which automatically loaded constants are loaded only once. Usually consists of your plugin `lib` directories. All directories in this set must also be present in `autoload_paths`.

B.20.1.2 `autoload_paths`

The set of directories from which Rails may automatically load files. Files under these directories will be reloaded on each request in development mode, unless the directory also appears in `load_once_paths`.

```
>> ActiveSupport::Dependencies.load_paths
=> ["/Users/kfaustino/code/active/example_app/app/assets",
    "/Users/kfaustino/code/active/example_app/app/controllers",
    "/Users/kfaustino/code/active/example_app/app/helpers",
    "/Users/kfaustino/code/active/example_app/app/mailers",
    "/Users/kfaustino/code/active/example_app/app/models",
    "/Users/kfaustino/code/active/example_app/app/controllers/concerns",
    "/Users/kfaustino/code/active/example_app/app/models/concerns"]
```

B.20.1.3 `constant_watch_stack`
An internal stack used to record which constants are loaded by any block.

B.20.1.4 `explicitly_unloadable_constants`
An array of constant names that need to be unloaded on every request. Used to allow arbitrary constants to be marked for unloading.

B.20.1.5 `history`
The set of all files ever loaded.

B.20.1.6 `loaded`
The Set of all files currently loaded.

B.20.1.7 `log_activity`
Set this option to `true` to enable logging of `const_missing` and file loads. (Defaults to `false`.)

B.20.1.8 `mechanism`
A setting that determines whether files are loaded (default) or required. This attribute determines whether Rails reloads classes per request, as in development mode.

```
>> ActiveSupport::Dependencies.mechanism
=> :load
```

B.20.1.9 `warnings_on_first_load`
A setting that determines whether Ruby warnings should be activated on the first load of dependent files. Defaults to `true`.

B.20.1.10 `associate_with(file_name)`
Invokes `depend_on` with `swallow_load_errors` set to `true`. Wrapped by the `require_association` method of `Object`.

B.20.1.11 `autoload_module!(into, const_name, qualified_ name, path_suffix)`

Attempts to autoload the provided module name by searching for a directory matching the expected `path suffix`. If found, the module is created and assigned to `into`'s constants with the name +const_name+. Provided that the directory was loaded from a reloadable base path, it is added to the set of constants that are to be unloaded.

B.20.1.12 `autoloadable_module?(path_suffix)`

Checks whether the provided `path_suffix` corresponds to an autoloadable module. Instead of returning a Boolean, the autoload base for this module is returned.

B.20.1.13 `autoloaded?(constant)`

Determines whether the specified `constant` has been automatically loaded.

B.20.1.14 `clear`

Clear all loaded items.

B.20.1.15 `constantize(name)`

Gets the reference for a specified class name. Raises an exception if the class does not exist.

B.20.1.16 `depend_on(file_name, message = "No such file to load -- %s.rb")`

Searches for the `file_name` specified and uses `require_or_load` to establish a new dependency. If the file fails to load, a `LoadError` is raised. Setting `message`, you can replace the error message set by `LoadError`.

B.20.1.17 `hook!`

Includes Rails specific modules into some Ruby classes.

- `Object` includes `Loadable`
- `Module` includes `ModuleConstMissing`
- `Exception` includes `Blamable`

B.20.1.18 `load?`

Returns `true` if `mechanism` is set to `:load`.

B.20.1.19   `load_file(path, const_paths = loadable_`
`                        constants_for_path(path))`

Loads the file at the specified `path`. The `const_paths` is a set of fully qualified constant names to load. When the file is loading, `Dependencies` will watch for the addition of these constants. Each one that is defined will be marked as autoloaded and will be removed when `Dependencies.clear` is next called.

If the second parameter is left off, `Dependencies` will construct a set of names that the file at `path` may define. See `loadable_constants_for_path` for more details.

B.20.1.20   `load_once_path?(path)`

Returns `true` if the specified `path` appears in the `load_once_path` list.

B.20.1.21   `load_missing_constant(from_mod, const_name)`

Loads the constant named `const_name`, which is missing from `from_mod`. If it is not possible to load the constant from `from_mod`, try its parent module by calling `const_missing` on it.

B.20.1.22   `loadable_constants_for_path(path, bases =`
`                        autoload_paths)`

Returns an array of constants, based on a specified filesystem `path` to a Ruby file, which would cause `Dependencies` to attempt to load the file.

B.20.1.23   `mark_for_unload(constant)`

Marks the specified `constant` for unloading. The constant will be unloaded on each request, not just the next one.

B.20.1.24   `new_constants_in(*descs, &block)`

Runs the provided block and detects the new constants that were loaded during its execution. Constants may only be regarded as new once. If the block calls `new_constants_in` again, the constants defined within the inner call will not be reported in this one.

If the provided block does not run to completion, and instead raises an exception, any new constants are regarded as being only partially defined and will be removed immediately.

Active
Support

B.20.1.25 `qualified_const_defined?(path)`

Returns `true` if the provided constant path is `defined?`

B.20.1.26 `qualified_name_for(parent_module, constant_name)`

Returns a qualified path for the specified `parent_module` and `constant_name`.

B.20.1.27 `reference(klass)`

Store a reference to a class.

B.20.1.28 `remove_constant(const)`

Removes an explicit constant.

B.20.1.29 `remove_unloadable_constants!`

Removes the constants that have been autoloaded and those that have been marked for unloading.

B.20.1.30 `require_or_load(file_name, const_path = nil)`

Implements the main classloading mechanism. Wrapped by the `require_or_load` method of `Object`.

B.20.1.31 `safe_constantize(name)`

Gets the reference for class named `name` if one exists. It returns `nil` when the name is not in CamelCase or is not initialized.

B.20.1.32 `search_for_file(path_suffix)`

Searches for a file in the autoload paths matching the provided `path_suffix`.

B.20.1.33 `to_constant_name(desc)`

Convert the provided constant description to a qualified constant name.

B.20.1.34 `will_unload?(constant)`

Returns `true` if the specified constant is queued for unloading on the next request.

B.20.1.35 `unhook!`

Exclude module `ModuleConstMissing` from `Module` and `Loadable` from `Object`.

B.21   **DescendantsTracker**

A module used internally by Rails to track descendants, which is faster than iterating through `ObjectSpace`.

B.21.1   **active_support/descendants_tracker.rb**

B.21.1.1   **DescendantsTracker.clear**

Clears all descendants.

B.21.1.2   **DescendantsTracker.descendants(klass)**

Returns a set of all the descendants of a class.

B.21.1.3   **descendants**

A convenience method for returning the descendants of a class. Implemented simply as `DescendantsTracker.descendants(self)`.

B.21.1.4   **DescendantsTracker.direct_descendants(klass)**

Returns a set of the direct descendants of a class.

B.21.1.5   **direct_descendants**

A convenience method for returning the direct descendants of a class. Implemented simply as `DescendantsTracker.direct_descendants(self)`.

B.21.1.6   **inherited(base)**

Sets a class as a direct descendant of another base class. Implemented simply as `DescendantsTracker.store_inherited(base, self)`.

B.21.1.7   **DescendantsTracker.store_inherited(klass, descendant)**

Adds a direct descendant to a class. Warning, this method is not thread safe, but is only called during the eager loading phase

B.22   **Digest::UUID**

Contains convenience methods for generating UUIDs (Universally Unique IDentifiers) also known as GUIDs (Globally Unique IDentifiers). A UUID is 128 bits long and can guarantee uniqueness across space and time.

B.22.1   `Digest::UUID.uuid_from_hash(hash_class, uuid_namespace, name)`

Generates the same UUID for a given `name` and `namespace` combination.

B.22.2   `Digest::UUID.uuid_v3(uuid_namespace, name)`

Convenience method for `uuid_from_hash` using `Digest::MD5`.

B.22.3   `Digest::UUID.uuid_v4`

Convenience method for `SecureRandom.uuid`.

B.22.4   `Digest::UUID.uuid_v5(uuid_namespace, name)`

Convenience method for `uuid_from_hash` using `Digest::SHA1`.

B.23   Duration

Provides accurate date and time measurements using the `advance` method of `Date` and `Time`. It mainly supports the methods on `Numeric`, such as in this example:

```
1.month.ago # equivalent to Time.now.advance(months: -1)
```

B.23.1   + (other)

Adds another `Duration` or a `Numeric` to this `Duration`. `Numeric` values are treated as seconds.

```
>> 2.hours + 2
=> 7202 seconds
```

B.23.2   - (other)

Subtracts another `Duration` or a `Numeric` from this `Duration`. `Numeric` values are treated as seconds.

```
>> 2.hours - 2
=> 7198 seconds
```

B.23.3   ago(time = Time.current)

Calculates a new `Time` or `Date` that is as far in the past as this `Duration` represents.

```
>> birth = 35.years.ago
=> Tue, 10 Oct 1978 16:21:34 EDT -04:00
```

B.23.4   `from_now(time = Time.current)`

Alias for `since`, which reads a little bit more naturally when using the default `Time.current` as the `time` argument.

```
>> expiration = 1.year.from_now
=> Fri, 10 Oct 2014 16:22:35 EDT -04:00
```

B.23.5   `inspect`

Calculates the time resulting from a `Duration` expression and formats it as a string appropriate for display in the console. (Remember that IRB and the Rails console automatically invoke `inspect` on objects returned to them. You can use that trick with your own objects.)

```
>> 10.years.ago
=> Fri, 10 Oct 2003 16:23:10 EDT -04:00
```

B.23.6   `since(time = Time.current)`

Calculates a new `Time` or `Date` that is as far in the future as this `Duration` represents.

```
expiration = 1.year.since(account.created_at)
```

B.23.7   `until(time = Time.current)`

Alias for `ago`. Reads a little more naturally when specifying a `time` argument instead of using the default value, `Time.current`.

```
membership_duration = created_at.until(expires_at)
```

B.23.8   `Duration.parse(iso8601duration)`

Parses an ISO 8601 formatted string representing the duration.

```
>> ActiveSupport::Duration.parse "PT24H"
=> 24 hours
```

B.23.9   `iso8601(precision: nil`

Returns an ISO 8601 formatted string representing the duration.

```
>> 24.hours.iso8601
=> "PT24H"
```

Active
Support

B.24 **Enumerable**

Extensions to Ruby's built-in `Enumerable` module, which gives arrays and other types of collections iteration abilities.

B.24.1 **exclude?**

The negative of the `Enumerable#include?`. Returns `true` if the collection does not include the object.

B.24.2 **index_by(&block)**

Converts an enumerable to a hash, based on a block that identifies the keys. The most common usage is with a single attribute name:

```
>> people.index_by(&:login)
=> { "nextangle" => <Person ...>, "chad" => <Person ...>}
```

Use full block syntax (instead of the `to_proc` hack) to generate more complex keys:

```
>> people.index_by { |p| "#{p.first_name} #{p.last_name}" }
=> {"Chad Fowler" => <Person ...>, "David Hansson" => <Person ...>}
```

B.24.3 **many?**

Returns `true` if the enumerable has more than one element.

Use full block syntax to determine whether there is more than one element based on a condition:

```
people.many? { |p| p.age > 26 }
```

B.24.4 **pluck(*keys)**

Convert an enumerable to an array/tuple based on the given key(s).

```
>> [{ name: "David" }, { name: "Rafael" }, { name: "Aaron" }].pluck(:name)
=> ["David", "Rafael", "Aaron"]

>> [{ id: 1, name: "David" }, { id: 2, name: "Rafael" }].pluck(:id, :name)
=> [[1, "David"], [2, "Rafael"]]
```

B.24.5 **sum(identity = 0, &block)**

Calculates a sum from the elements of an enumerable, based on a block.

```
payments.sum(&:price)
```

It's easier to understand than Ruby's clumsier `inject` method:

```
payments.inject { |sum, p| sum + p.price }
```

Use full block syntax (instead of the `to_proc` hack) to do more complicated calculations:

```
payments.sum { |p| p.price * p.tax_rate }
```

Also, `sum` can calculate results without the use of a block:

```
[5, 15, 10].sum # => 30
```

The default identity (a fancy way of saying, "the sum of an empty list") is 0. However, you can override it with anything you want by passing a default argument:

```
[].sum(10) { |i| i.amount } # => 10
```

B.24.6 `without(*elements)`

Returns a copy of the enumerable without the specified elements.

```
>> ["David", "Rafael", "Aaron", "Todd"].without "Aaron", "Todd"
=> ["David", "Rafael"]

>> {foo: 1, bar: 2, baz: 3}.without :bar
=> {foo: 1, baz: 3}
```

B.25   `ERB::Util`

A collection of utility methods added to ERb processing in Rails.

B.25.1 `html_escape(s)`

A utility method for escaping HTML tag characters. This method is also aliased as h.

In your templates, use this method to escape any unsafe (often, anything user-submitted) content, like this:

```
= h @person.name
```

The method primarily escapes angle brackets and ampersands.

```
>> puts ERB::Util.html_escape("is a > 0 & a < 10?")
=> "is a &gt; 0 &amp; a &lt; 10?"
```

B.25.2 `html_escape_once(s)`

A utility method for escaping HTML without affecting existing escaped entities.

```
>> puts ERB::Util.html_escape_once('1 < 2 &amp; 3')
=> "1 &lt; 2 &amp; 3"
```

B.25.3 `json_escape(s)`

A utility method for escaping HTML entities in JSON strings.

In your ERb templates, use this method to escape any HTML entities:

```
= json_escape @person.to_json
```

The method primarily escapes angle brackets and ampersands.

```
>> puts ERB::Util.json_escape("is a > 0 & a < 10?")
=> "is a \\u003E 0 \\u0026 a \\u003C 10?"
```

B.26 `EventedFileUpdateChecker`

Used by Rails development mode to "listen" to file system changes (like I18n locale files). Does not hit disk when checking for updates but, rather, uses platform-specific file system events to trigger state changes. Depends on the listen[2] RubyGem.

If you want to use this class with your own code, you can pass `EventedFile-Update.Checker#initialize` an array of files to watch or a hash specifying directories and file extensions to watch. It also takes a block that is called when `EventedFileUpdateChecker#execute` is run or when `EventedFileUp-dateChecker#execute_if_updated` is run and there have been changes to the file system.

Example:

```
>> spy = ActiveSupport::EventedFileUpdateChecker.new ["/tmp/efu"] { puts "changed" }
=> #<ActiveSupport::EventedFileUpdateChecker:0x007fdfaa898690...

>> spy.updated?
=> false

>> spy.execute_if_updated
=> nil

>> FileUtils.touch("/tmp/foo")
```

---

2. https://github.com/guard/listen

```
>> spy.updated?
=> true

>> spy.execute_if_updated
=> "changed"
```

See also `FileUpdateChecker`.

B.27   **FalseClass**

B.27.1   **active_support/core_ext/object/blank.rb**

B.27.1.1   **blank?**
Returns `true`.

B.27.2   **active_support/json/encoding.rb**

B.27.2.1   **as_json**
Returns `false`.

B.28   **File**
Provides an `atomic_write` method to Ruby's `File` class.

B.28.1   **atomic_write(file_name, temp_dir = Dir.tmpdir)**
Writes to a file atomically, by writing to a temp file first and then renaming to the target `file_name`. Useful for situations where you need to absolutely prevent other processes or threads from seeing half-written files.

```
File.atomic_write("important.file") do |file|
  file.write("hello")
end
```

If your `temp` directory is not on the same filesystem as the file you're trying to write, you can provide a different temporary directory with the `temp_dir` argument.

```
File.atomic_write("/data/something.important", "/data/tmp") do |f|
  file.write("hello")
end
```

B.29   **FileUpdateChecker**
Specifies the API used by Rails to watch files and control reloading. The API depends on four methods:

initialize Expects paths to watch and a block of code to execute on changes.

updated? Returns a boolean reporting if there were updates in the filesystem or not.

execute Executes the given block on initialization and updates the latest watched files and timestamp.

execute_if_updated Executes the initializer block if file(s) updated.

After initialization, a call to execute_if_updated must execute the block only if there was really a change in the filesystem.

The following code is used by Rails to reload the I18n framework whenever locale files are changed.

```
i18n_reloader = ActiveSupport::FileUpdateChecker.new(paths) do
  I18n.reload!
end

ActiveSupport::Reloader.to_prepare do
  i18n_reloader.execute_if_updated
end
```

B.29.1 initialize(files, dirs = {}, &block)

The first parameter files is an array of files and the second is an optional hash of directories. The hash must have directories as keys, and the value is an array of extensions to be watched under that directory.

This method must also receive a block that will be called once a path changes. The array of files and list of directories cannot be changed after FileUpdateChecker has been initialized.

B.29.1.1 updated?

Check if any of the entries were updated. If so, the watched and/or updated_at values are cached until the block is executed via execute or execute_if_updated methods.

B.29.1.2 execute

Executes the given block and updates the latest watched files and timestamp.

B.29.1.3 execute_if_updated

Execute the block given if updated. If a block is provided to this method, it will be executed first before calling execute to invoke the block passed to the initializer.

B.30   Gzip

A wrapper for the zlib standard library that allows the compression/decompression of strings with gzip.

B.30.1   Gzip.compress(source, level=Zlib::DEFAULT_ COMPRESSION, strategy=Zlib::DEFAULT_STRATEGY)

Compresses a string with gzip.

```
>> gzip = ActiveSupport::Gzip.compress('compress me!')
=> "\x1F\x8B\b\x00\x9D\x18WR\x00\x03K\xCE\xCF-
   (J-.V\xC8MU\x04\x00R>n\x83\f\x00\x00\x00"
```

B.30.2   Gzip.decompress(source)

Decompresses a string that has been compressed with gzip.

```
>> ActiveSupport::Gzip.
   decompress("\x1F\x8B\b\x00\x9D\x18WR\x00\x03K\xCE\xCF-
   (J- V\xC8MU\x04\x00R>n\x83\f\x00\x00\x00")
=> "compress me!"
```

B.31   Hash

Many additions and enhancements to Ruby's hash object.

B.31.1   active_support/core_ext/array/extract_ options.rb

B.31.1.1   extractable_options?

If a Hash is marked as *extractable* using this method, Array#extract_options! pops it from the Array when it is the last element.

By default, only instances of Hash itself are extractable. Subclasses of Hash may implement the extractable_options? method and return true to declare themselves as extractable.

```
class MyFancyOptions < Hash
  def extractable_options?
    true
  end
```

B.31.2   active_support/core_ext/hash/compact.rb

B.31.2.1   compact

Returns a hash with non nil values.

```
hash = { name: 'Marisa', email: nil }

=> hash.compact
>> { name: 'Marisa' }
```

B.31.2.2 `compact!`
Replaces current hash with non nil values.

B.31.3 `active_support/core_ext/hash/conversions.rb`
Contains code that adds the capability to convert hashes to and from xml.

B.31.3.1 `Hash.from_trusted_xml(xml)`
Builds a Hash from XML just like `Hash.from_xml`, but also allows Symbol and YAML.

B.31.3.2 `Hash.from_xml(xml)`
Parses arbitrary strings of XML markup into nested Ruby arrays and hashes. Works great for quick-and-dirty integration of REST-style web services.

Here's a quick example in the console with some random XML content. The XML only has to be well-formed markup.

```
>> xml = %(<people>
  <person id="1">
    <name><family>Boss</family> <given>Big</given></name>
    <email>chief@foo.com</email>
  </person>
  <person id="2">
    <name>
      <family>Worker</family>
      <given>Two</given></name>
    <email>two@foo.com</email>
  </person>
</people>)
=> "<people>...</people>"

>> h = Hash.from_xml(xml)
=> {"people"=>{"person"=>[{"name"=>{"given"=>"Big", "family"=>"Boss"},
"id"=>"1", "email"=>"chief@foo.com"}, {"name"=>{"given"=>"Two",
"family"=>"Worker"}, "id"=>"2", "email"=>"two@foo.com"}]}}
```

Now you can easily access the data from the XML:

```
>> h["people"]["person"].first["name"]["given"]
=> "Big"
```

An exception `DisallowedType` is raised if the XML contains attributes with `type="yaml"` or `type="symbol"`. If for some reason you want to be able to accept YAML and symbols as valid attributes, then use the variant `from_trusted _xml` instead.

B.31.3.3   `to_xml(options={})`

Collects the keys and values of a hash and composes a simple XML representation.

```
print ({greetings: {
              english: "hello",
              spanish: "hola"}}).to_xml


<?xml version="1.0" encoding="UTF-8"?>
<hash>
  <greetings>
    <english>hello</english>
    <spanish>hola</spanish>
  </greetings>
</hash>
```

B.31.4   `active_support/core_ext/hash/deep_merge.rb`

Enhancements to Ruby's built-in hash merging. Both methods accept a block to be invoked when merging values:

```
>> h1 = { a: 100, b: 200, c: { c1: 100 } }
>> h2 = { b: 250, c: { c1: 200 } }
>> h1.deep_merge(h2) { |key, this_val, other_val| this_val + other_val }
=> { a: 100, b: 450, c: { c1: 300 } }
```

B.31.4.1   `deep_merge(other_hash)`

Returns a new hash with self and `other_hash` merged recursively.

B.31.4.2   `deep_merge!(other_hash)`

Modifies `self` by merging in `other_hash` recursively.

B.31.5   `active_support/core_ext/hash/except.rb`

B.31.5.1   `except(*keys)`

Returns a hash that includes everything but the given keys. This is useful for limiting a set of parameters to everything but a few known toggles.

```
person.update(params[:person].except(:admin))
```

If the receiver responds to `convert_key`, the method is called on each of the arguments. This enables `except` to play nice with hashes with indifferent access.

```
>> {a: 1}.with_indifferent_access.except(:a)
=> {}
>> {a: 1}.with_indifferent_access.except("a")
=> {}
```

B.31.5.2 `except!(*keys)`
Removes the keys specified from the hash.

```
>> hash = { a: true, b: false, c: nil }
>> hash.except!(:c)  # => { a: true, b: false }
>> hash             # => { a: true, b: false }
```

B.31.6 `active_support/core_ext/hash/indifferent_access.rb`

B.31.6.1 `with_indifferent_access`
Converts a hash into an `Active Support::HashWithIndifferentAccess`.

```
>> {a: 1 .with_indifferent_access["a"]
=> 1
```

B.31.7 `active_support/core_ext/hash/keys.rb`
Provides methods that operate on the keys of a hash. The `stringify` and `symbolize` methods are used liberally throughout the Rails codebase, which is why it generally doesn't matter if you pass option names as strings or symbols.

You can use `assert_valid_keys` method in your own application code, which takes Rails-style option hashes.

B.31.7.1 `assert_valid_keys(*valid_keys)`
Raises an `ArgumentError` if the hash contains any keys not specified in `valid_keys`.

```
def my_method(some_value, options={})
  options.assert_valid_keys(:my_conditions, :my_order, ...)
  ...
end
```

Note that keys are NOT treated indifferently, meaning if you use strings for keys but assert symbols as keys, this will fail.

```
>> { name: "Rob", years: "28" }.assert_valid_keys(:name, :age)
=> ArgumentError: Unknown key(s): years
```

```
>> { name: "Rob", age: "28" }.assert_valid_keys("name", "age")
=> ArgumentError: Unknown key(s): name, age

>> { name: "Rob", age: "28" }.assert_valid_keys(:name, :age)
=> {:name=>"Rob", :age=>"28"} # passes, returns hash
```

B.31.7.2   `deep_stringify_keys`
Return a copy of the hash with all keys converted to strings. This includes the keys from the root hash and from all nested hashes.

B.31.7.3   `deep_stringify_keys!`
Destructively converts all keys in the hash to strings. This includes the keys from the root hash and from all nested hashes.

B.31.7.4   `deep_symbolize_keys`
Returns a new hash with all keys converted to symbols, as long as they respond to `to_sym`. This includes the keys from the root hash and from all nested hashes.

B.31.7.5   `deep_symbolize_keys!`
Destructively converts all keys in the hash to symbols, as long as they respond to `to_sym`. This includes the keys from the root hash and from all nested hashes.

B.31.7.6   `deep_transform_keys(&block)`
Return a copy of the hash with all keys converted by the block operation. This includes the keys from the root hash and from all nested hashes.

B.31.7.7   `deep_transform_keys!(&block)`
Destructively converts all keys in the hash by the block operation. This includes the keys from the root hash and from all nested hashes.

B.31.7.8   `stringify_keys`
Returns a new copy of the hash with all keys converted to strings.

B.31.7.9   `stringify_keys!`
Destructively converts all keys in the hash to strings.

B.31.7.10   `symbolize_keys` and `to_options`
Returns a new hash with all keys converted to symbols, as long as they respond to `to_sym`.

B.31.7.11   `symbolize_keys!` and `to_options!`

Destructively converts all keys in the hash to symbols.

B.31.7.12   `transform_keys(&block)`

Return a copy of the hash with all keys converted by the block operation.

B.31.7.13   `transform_keys!(&block)`

Destructively converts all keys in the hash by the block operation.

B.31.8   `active_support/core_ext/hash/reverse_merge.rb`

Enables reverse merging where the keys in the calling hash take precedence over those in the `other_hash`. This is particularly useful for initializing an incoming option hash with default values like this:

```
def setup(options = {})
  options.reverse_merge! size: 25, velocity: 10
end
```

In the example, the default `:size` and `:velocity` are only set if the options passed in don't already have those keys set.

B.31.8.1   `reverse_merge(other_hash)`

Returns a merged version of two hashes, using key values in the `other_hash` as defaults, leaving the original hash unmodified.

B.31.8.2   `reverse_merge!(other_hash)` and `reverse_update`

Destructive versions of `reverse_merge`; both modify the original hash in place.

B.31.9   `active_support/core_ext/hash/slice.rb`

B.31.9.1   `extract!(*keys)`

Removes and returns the key/value pairs matching the given keys.

```
>> { a: 1, b: 2 }.extract!(:a, :x)
=> {:a => 1}
```

B.31.9.2   `slice(*keys)`

Slice a hash to include only the given keys. This is useful for limiting an options hash to valid keys before passing to a method:

```
def search(criteria = {})
  assert_valid_keys(:mass, :velocity, :time)
```

```
end

search(options.slice(:mass, :velocity, :time))
```

If you have an array of keys you want to limit to, you should splat them:

```
valid_keys = %i(mass velocity time)
search(options.slice(*valid_keys))
```

B.31.9.3 `slice!(*keys)`

Replaces the hash with only the given keys.

```
>> {a: 1, b: 2, c: 3, d: 4}.slice!(:a, :b)
=> {:c => 3, :d =>4}
```

B.31.10 `active_support/core_ext/object/to_query.rb`

B.31.10.1 `to_param(namespace = nil)` / `to_query`

Converts a hash into a string suitable for use as a URL query string. An optional `namespace` can be passed to enclose the param names (see example below).

```
>> { name: 'David', nationality: 'Danish' }.to_param
=> "name=David&nationality=Danish"

>> { name: 'David', nationality: 'Danish' }.to_param('user')
=>"user%5Bname%5D=David&user%5Bnationality%5D=Danish"
```

B.31.11 `active_support/json/encoding.rb`

B.31.11.1 `as_json`

Returns `self` as a string of JSON.

B.31.12 `active_support/core_ext/object/blank.rb`

B.31.12.1 `blank?`

Alias for `empty?`

B.32 `HashWithIndifferentAccess`

A subclass of `Hash` used internally by Rails. Implements a hash where keys set as a string or symbol are considered to be the same. Probably one of the oldest and most iconic examples of Rails "magic."

```
>> hash = HashWithIndifferentAccess.new
=> {}
>> hash[:foo] = "bar"
```

```
=> "bar"
>> hash[:foo]
=> "bar"
>> hash["foo"]
=> "bar"
```

Although this class is compatible with non-string keys, this class is intended for use cases where strings or symbols are the expected keys and it is convenient to understand both as the same, the most common example being the params in Rails controllers.

B.33 Inflector

Methods in this module are covered in String inflections.

B.34 Inflector::Inflections

The Inflections class transforms words from singular to plural, class names to table names, modularized class names to ones without, and class names to foreign keys.

This API reference lists the inflections methods themselves in the modules where they are actually used: Numeric and String. The Inflections module contains methods used for modifying the rules used by the inflector.

The default inflections for pluralization, singularization, and uncountable words are kept in activesupport/lib/active_support/inflections.rb and reproduced here for reference.

```
module ActiveSupport
  Inflector.inflections(:en) do |inflect|
    inflect.plural(/$/, "s")
    inflect.plural(/s$/i, "s")
    inflect.plural(/^(ax|test)is$/i, '\1es')
    inflect.plural(/(octop|vir)us$/i, '\1i')
    inflect.plural(/(octop|vir)i$/i, '\1i')
    inflect.plural(/(alias|status)$/i,'\1es')
    inflect.plural(/(bu)s$/i, '\1ses')
    inflect.plural(/(buffal|tomat)o$/i, '\1oes')
    inflect.plural(/([ti])um$/i, '\1a')
    inflect.plural(/([ti])a$/i, '\1a')
    inflect.plural(/sis$/i, "ses")
    inflect.plural(/(?:([^f])fe|([lr])f)$/i, '\1\2ves')
    inflect.plural(/(hive)$/i, '\1s')
    inflect.plural(/([^aeiouy]|qu)y$/i, '\1ies')
    inflect.plural(/(x|ch|ss|sh)$/i, '\1es')
    inflect.plural(/(matr|vert|ind)(?:ix|ex)$/i, '\1ices')
    inflect.plural(/^(m|l)ouse$/i, '\1ice')
    inflect.plural(/^(m|l)ice$/i, '\1ice')
```

```
    inflect.plural(/^(ox)$/i, '\1en')
    inflect.plural(/^(oxen)$/i, '\1')
    inflect.plural(/(quiz)$/i, '\1zes')
    inflect.singular(/s$/i, "")
    inflect.singular(/(ss)$/i, '\1')
    inflect.singular(/(n)ews$/i, '\1ews')
    inflect.singular(/([ti])a$/i, '\1um')
    inflect.singular(/((a)naly|(b)a|(d)iagno|(p)arenthe|(p)
          rogno|(s)ynop|(t)he)(sis|ses)$/i, '\1sis')
    inflect.singular(/(^analy)(sis|ses)$/i, '\1sis')
    inflect.singular(/([^f])ves$/i, '\1fe')
    inflect.singular(/(hive)s$/i, '\1')
    inflect.singular(/(tive)s$/i, '\1')
    inflect.singular(/([lr])ves$/i, '\1f')
    inflect.singular(/([^aeiouy]|qu)ies$/i, '\1y')
    inflect.singular(/(s)eries$/i, '\1eries')
    inflect.singular(/(m)ovies$/i, '\1ovie')
    inflect.singular(/(x|ch|ss|sh)es$/i, '\1')
    inflect.singular(/^(m|l)ice$/i, '\1ouse')
    inflect.singular(/(bus)(es)?$/i, '\1')
    inflect.singular(/(o)es$/i, '\1')
    inflect.singular(/(shoe)s$/i, '\1')
    inflect.singular(/(cris|test)(is|es)$/i, '\1is')
    inflect.singular(/^(a)x[ie]s$/i, '\1xis')
    inflect.singular(/(octop|vir)(us|i)$/i, '\1us')
    inflect.singular(/(alias|status)(es)?$/i, '\1')
    inflect.singular(/^(ox)en/i, '\1')
    inflect.singular(/(vert|ind)ices$/i, '\1ex')
    inflect.singular(/(matr)ices$/i, '\1ix')
    inflect.singular(/(quiz)zes$/i, '\1')
    inflect.singular(/(database)s$/i, '\1')

    inflect.irregular("person", "people")
    inflect.irregular("man", "men")
    inflect.irregular("child", "children")
    inflect.irregular("sex", "sexes")
    inflect.irregular("move", "moves")
    inflect.irregular("zombie", "zombies")
    inflect.uncountable(%w(equipment information rice money
          species series fish sheep jeans police))
  end
end
```

As per the API documentation: These are the starting point for new projects and are not considered complete. The current set of inflection rules is frozen. This means, we do not change them to become more complete. This is a safety measure to keep existing applications from breaking.

A singleton instance of `Inflections` is yielded by `Inflector.inflections`, which can then be used to specify additional inflection rules in an initializer.

```
ActiveSupport::Inflector.inflections(:en) do |inflect|
  inflect.plural /^(ox)$/i, '\1en'
  inflect.singular /^(ox)en/i, '\1'
  inflect.irregular 'person', 'people'
  inflect.uncountable %w( fish sheep )
end
```

New rules are added at the top. So in the example, the irregular rule for octopus will now be the first of the pluralization and singularization rules that are checked when an inflection happens. That way Rails can guarantee that your rules run before any of the rules that may already have been loaded.

B.34.1   `acronym(word)`

Specifies a new acronym. An acronym must be specified as it will appear in a camel-ized string. An underscore string that contains the acronym will retain the acronym when passed to `camelize`, `humanize`, or `titleize`. A camelized string that contains the acronym will maintain the acronym when titleized or humanized, and will convert the acronym into a non-delimited single lowercase word when passed to underscore. An acronym word must start with a capital letter.

```
ActiveSupport::Inflector.inflections(:en) do |inflect|
  inflect.acronym 'HTML'
end

>> 'html'.titleize
=> "HTML"

>> 'html'.camelize
=> "HTML"

>> 'MyHTML'.underscore
=> "my_html"
```

The acronym must occur as a delimited unit and not be part of another word for conversions to recognize it:

```
ActiveSupport::Inflector.inflections(:en) do |inflect|
  inflect.acronym 'HTTP'
end

>> 'HTTPS'.underscore
=> "http_s"   # => 'http_s', not 'https'
```

```
# Alternatively
ActiveSupport::Inflector.inflections(:en) do |inflect|
  inflect.acronym 'HTTPS'
end
```

```
>> 'HTTPS'.underscore
=> "https"
```

B.34.2 `clear(scope = :all))`

Clears the loaded inflections within a given `scope`. Give the `scope` as a symbol of the inflection type: `:plurals`, `:singulars`, `:uncountables`, or `:humans`.

```
ActiveSupport::Inflector.inflections.clear
ActiveSupport::Inflector.inflections.clear(:plurals)
```

B.34.3 `human(rule, replacement)`

Specifies a humanized form of a string by a regular expression rule or by a string mapping. When using a regular expression-based replacement, the normal humanize formatting is called after the replacement. When a string is used, the human form should be specified as desired (example: "The name", not "the_name")

```
ActiveSupport::Inflector.inflections(:en) do |inflect|
  inflect.human /_cnt$/i, '\1_count'
  inflect.human "legacy_col_person_name", "Name"
end
```

B.34.4 `inflections(locale = :en)`

Yields a singleton instance of `Active Support::Inflector::Inflections` so you can specify additional inflector rules. If passed an optional locale, rules for other languages can be specified.

```
ActiveSupport::Inflector.inflections(:en) do |inflect|
  inflect.uncountable "rails"
end
```

B.34.5 `irregular(singular, plural)`

Specifies a new irregular that applies to both pluralization and singularization at the same time. The `singular` and `plural` arguments must be strings, not regular expressions. Simply pass the irregular word in singular and plural form.

```
ActiveSupport::Inflector.inflections(:en) do |inflect|
  inflect.irregular 'octopus', 'octopi'
  inflect.irregular 'person', 'people'
end
```

Active Support

B.34.6 `plural(rule, replacement)`

Specifies a new pluralization rule and its replacement. The `rule` can either be a string or a regular expression. The `replacement` should always be a string and may include references to the matched data from the rule by using backslash-number syntax, like this:

```
ActiveSupport::Inflector.inflections(:en) do |inflect|
  inflect.plural /^(ox)$/i, '\1en'
end
```

B.34.7 `singular(rule, replacement)`

Specifies a new singularization rule and its replacement. The `rule` can either be a string or a regular expression. The `replacement` should always be a string and may include references to the matched data from the rule by using backslash-number syntax, like this:

```
ActiveSupport::Inflector.inflections(:en) do |inflect|
  inflect.singular /^(ox)en/i, '\1'
end
```

B.34.8 `uncountable(*words)`

Adds uncountable words that should not be inflected to the list of inflection rules.

```
ActiveSupport::Inflector.inflections(:en) do |inflect|
  inflect.uncountable "money"
  inflect.uncountable "money", "information"
end
```

B.35 `Integer`

Extensions to Ruby's built-in `Integer` class.

B.35.1 `active_support/core_ext/integer/inflections.rb`

B.35.1.1 `ordinal`

Returns the suffix used to denote the position in an ordered sequence, such as 1st, 2nd, 3rd, 4th.

```
1.ordinal       # => "st"
2.ordinal       # => "nd"
1002.ordinal    # => "nd"
1003.ordinal    # => "rd"
```

B.35.1.2 `ordinalize`

Turns an integer into an ordinal string used to denote the position in an ordered sequence, such as 1st, 2nd, 3rd, 4th.

```
1.ordinalize      # => "1st"
2.ordinalize      # => "2nd"
1002.ordinalize   # => "1002nd"
1003.ordinalize   # => "1003rd"
```

B.35.2 `active_support/core_ext/integer/multiple.rb`

B.35.2.1 `multiple_of?(number)`

Returns `true` if the integer is a multiple of `number`.

```
9.multiple_of? 3 # => true
```

B.36 JSON

The JSON module adds JSON decoding and encoding support to Rails, using the JSON gem.

B.36.1 `decode(json)`

Parses a JSON string or IO object and converts it into a hash.

B.36.2 `encode(value, options = nil)`

Dumps object in JSON.

```
>> ActiveSupport::JSON.encode({a: 1, b: 2})
=> "{\"a\":1,\"b\":2}"
```

B.37 Kernel

Methods added to Ruby's `Kernel` class are available in all contexts.

B.37.1 `active_support/core_ext/kernel/reporting.rb`

B.37.1.1 `capture(stream)`

Captures the given stream and returns it.

```
stream = capture(:stdout) { puts 'notice' }
stream # => "notice\n"
```

B.37.1.2 `enable_warnings`

Sets `$VERBOSE` to `true` for the duration of the block provided and back to its original value afterward.

B.37.1.3 `quietly(&block)`

Silences both `STDOUT` and `STDERR`, even for subprocesses.

B.37.1.4 `silence_stream(stream)`

Silences any stream for the duration of the block provided.

```
silence_stream(STDOUT) do
  puts 'This will never be seen'
end

puts 'But this will'
```

B.37.1.5 `silence_warnings`

Sets `$VERBOSE` to `false` for the duration of the block provided and back to its original value afterward.

B.37.1.6 `suppress(*exception_classes)`

A method that should be named `swallow`. Suppresses raising of any exception classes specified inside of the block provided. Use with caution.

B.37.2 `active_support/core_ext/kernel/singleton_class.rb`

B.37.2.1 `class_eval`

Forces `class_eval` to behave like `singleton_class.class_eval`.

B.38 KeyGenerator

KeyGenerator is a simple wrapper around OpenSSL's implementation of PBKDF2. It can be used to derive a number of keys for various purposes from a given secret. This lets Rails applications have a single secure secret but avoid reusing that key in multiple incompatible contexts.

B.38.1 `initialize(secret, options = {})`

Creates a new instance. The `:iterations` option defaults to `2**16`—a number much higher than necessary for key derivation usages—just in case someone decides to use this code for password storage.

B.38.2 `generate_key(salt, key_size=64)`

Returns a derived key suitable for use. The default `key_size` is chosen to be compatible with the default settings of `ActiveSupport::MessageVerifier`, such as `OpenSSL::Digest::SHA1#block_length`.

```
>> key_generator = ActiveSupport::KeyGenerator.new('my_secret_key')
=> #<ActiveSupport::KeyGenerator:0x007fde6788b5d8
   @secret="my_secret_key", @iterations=65536>
>> key_generator.generate_key('my_salt')
=> "\xB6o5\xB2v\xBA\x03\x8E\xE0\xA0\x06[7<>\x81\xBB\xD6B\xB6,
   \xF3@a\x153\xB5\xC1\x8C\x8B\xEF\x04\x1C\xB9\x8D\x93I~`\
   xCD\xCB\"IKw\\u\xE9v\x15\xEE1\x99\"\xBD\xC7a\x92Y\x1EY\x94d\xFB"
```

B.39 LazyLoadHooks

Enables Rails to lazily load a lot of components in order to make the app boot process faster. This feature eliminates the need to require `ActiveRecord::Base` at boot time purely to apply configuration. Instead a hook is registered that applies configuration once `ActiveRecord::Base` is loaded.

Here is an example where the `on_load` method is called to register a hook:

```
initializer 'active_record.initialize_timezone' do
  ActiveSupport.on_load(:active_record) do
    self.time_zone_aware_attributes = true
    self.default_timezone = :utc
  end
end
```

When the entirety of `ActiveRecord::Base` has been evaluated then `run_load_hooks` is invoked. The very last line of `ActiveRecord::Base` is: `ActiveSupport.run_load_hooks(:active_record, ActiveRecord::Base)`.

B.39.1 `on_load(name, options = {}, &block)`

Declares a block that will be executed when a Rails component is fully loaded. Set `:yield` option to `true` if you want the block to be called with `base` as an argument, otherwise block will be `instance_eval` in `base`.

```
# File activesupport/lib/active_support/lazy_load_hooks.rb, line 41
def execute_hook(base, options, block)
  if options[:yield]
    block.call(base)
  else
    base.instance_eval(&block)
  end
end
```

B.39.2 `run_load_hooks(name, base = Object)`

Run block registered with a given `name`.

B.40 `Locale`

This section reproduces the standard Active Support locale file for reference purposes.

```
en:
  date:
    formats:
      # Use the strftime parameters for formats.
      # When no format has been given, it uses default.
      # You can provide other formats here if you like!
      default: "%Y-%m-%d"
      short: "%b %d"
      long: "%B %d, %Y"

    day_names: [Sunday, Monday, Tuesday, Wednesday, Thursday, Friday, Saturday]
    abbr_day_names: [Sun, Mon, Tue, Wed, Thu, Fri, Sat]

    # Don't forget the nil at the beginning; there's no such thing as a 0th month
    month_names: [~, January, February, March, April, May, June, July, August,
          September, October, November, December]
    abbr_month_names: [~, Jan, Feb, Mar, Apr, May, Jun, Jul, Aug, Sep, Oct, Nov, Dec]
    # Used in date_select and datetime_select.
    order:
      - year
      - month
      - day

  time:
    formats:
      default: "%a, %d %b %Y %H:%M:%S %z"
      short: "%d %b %H:%M"
      long: "%B %d, %Y %H:%M"
    am: "am"
    pm: "pm"

# Used in array.to_sentence.
  support:
    array:
      words_connector: ", "
      two_words_connector: " and "
      last_word_connector: ", and "
  number:
    # Used in NumberHelper.number_to_delimited()
    # These are also the defaults for 'currency', 'percentage', 'precision',
    # +9and 'human'
```

```
format:
  # Sets the separator between the units, for more precision
  # (e.g. 1.0 / 2.0 == 0.5)
  separator: "."
  # Delimits thousands (e.g. 1,000,000 is a million) (always
  # in groups of three)
  delimiter: ","
  # Number of decimals, behind the separator (the number 1
  # with a precision of 2 gives: 1.00)
  precision: 3
  # If set to true, precision will mean the number of
  # significant digits instead of the number of decimal digits
  # (1234 with precision becomes 1200, 1.23543 becomes 1.2)
  significant: false
  # If set, the zeros after the decimal separator will always
  # be stripped (eg.: 1.200 will be 1.2)
  strip_insignificant_zeros: false

# Used in NumberHelper.number_to_currency()
currency:
  format:
    # Where is the currency sign? %u is the currency unit, %n
    # the number (default: $5.00)

    format: "%u%n"
    unit: "$"
    # These five are to override number.format and are optional
    separator: "."
    delimiter: ","
    precision: 2
    significant: false
    strip_insignificant_zeros: false

# Used in NumberHelper.number_to_percentage()
percentage:
  format:
    # These five are to override number.format and are optional
    # separator:
    delimiter: ""
    # precision:
    # significant: false
    # strip_insignificant_zeros: false
    format: "%n%"

# Used in NumberHelper.number_to_rounded()
precision:
  format:
    # These five are to override number.format and are optional
    # separator:
```

```
    delimiter: ""
    # precision:
    # significant: false
    # strip_insignificant_zeros: false

# Used in NumberHelper.number_to_human_size() and
# NumberHelper.number_to_human()
human:
  format:
    # These five are to override number.format and are optional
    # separator:
    delimiter: ""
    precision: 3
    significant: true
    strip_insignificant_zeros: true
  # Used in number_to_human_size()
  storage_units:
    # Storage units output formatting.
    # %u is the storage unit, %n is the number (default: 2 MB)
    format: "%n %u"
    units:
      byte:
        one:     "Byte"
        other:   "Bytes"
      kb: "KB"
      mb: "MB"
      gb: "GB"
      tb: "TB"
      pb: "PB"
      eb: "EB"
  # Used in NumberHelper.number_to_human()
  decimal_units:
    format: "%n %u"
    # Decimal units output formatting
    # By default we will only quantify some of the exponents
    # but the commented ones might be defined or overridden
    # by the user.
    units:
      # femto: Quadrillionth
      # pico: Trillionth
      # nano: Billionth
      # micro: Millionth
      # mili: Thousandth
      # centi: Hundredth
      # deci: Tenth
      unit: ""
      # ten:
      #   one: Ten
      #   other: Tens
```

```
# hundred: Hundred
thousand: Thousand
million: Million
billion: Billion
trillion: Trillion
quadrillion: Quadrillion
```

B.41 **LogSubscriber**

Consumes `ActiveSupport::Notifications` events with the sole purpose of logging them. The log subscriber dispatches notifications to a registered object based on its given namespace. Every Rails component has its own implementation of a `LogSubscriber`.

For example, here is the Active Record log subscriber responsible for logging queries:

```
module ActiveRecord
  class LogSubscriber < ActiveSupport::LogSubscriber
    def sql(event)
      "#{event.payload[:name]} (#{event.duration}) #{event.payload[:sql]}"
    end
  end
end
```

It's registered as:

```
ActiveRecord::LogSubscriber.attach_to :active_record
```

Since we need to know all instance methods before attaching the log subscriber, the line above should be called after your `ActiveRecord::LogSubscriber` definition.

After being configured, whenever a `sql.active_record` notification is published, it will properly dispatch the event (`ActiveSupport::Notifications::Event`) to the `sql` method.

Log subscriber also has some helpers to deal with logging and automatically flushes all logs when a request cycle finishes.

The `color` method, available inside your own subclasses of `LogSubscriber`, makes highlighting terminal output using ANSI character sequences very easy.

B.41.1 **color(text, color, bold = false)**

The text parameter is the text to format. The color parameter is one of the following constant values: BLACK, RED, GREEN, YELLOW, BLUE, MAGENTA, CYAN, or WHITE. Finally, indicate whether output should be bold or not with a boolean value.

Active
Support

Here's the previous example, dressed up for Christmas.

```
def sql(event)
  "#{color(event.payload[:name],GREEN,true)} (#{color(event.duration,
        RED, true}) #{color(event.payload[:sql], WHITE, true)}"
end
```

B.41.2 `ActiveSupport::LogSubscriber::TestHelper`

Provides some helpers to deal with testing log subscribers by setting up notifications. Include the module in your test case or spec, and the test helper will take care of setting up the queue, subscriptions and turning colors in logs off. You'll get a `@logger` instance variable in your test cases or examples containing anything logged.

```
class SyncLogSubscriberTest < ActiveSupport::TestCase
  include ActiveSupport::LogSubscriber::TestHelper

  setup do
    ActiveRecord::LogSubscriber.attach_to(:active_record)
  end

  def test_basic_query_logging
    Developer.all.to_a
    wait
    assert_equal 1, @logger.logged(:debug).size
    assert_match(/Developer Load/,@logger.logged(:debug).last)
    assert_match(/SELECT \* FROM "developers"/, @logger.logged(:debug).last)
  end
end
```

B.42 Logger

Accessible via the `logger` property in various Rails contexts such as Active Record models and controller classes. Always accessible via `Rails.logger`. Use of the logger is explained in Chapter 1, "Rails Configuration and Environments."

B.42.1 `active_support/logger.rb`

B.42.1.1 `Logger.broadcast(logger)`

Generates an anonymous module that is used to extend an existing logger, which adds the behavior to broadcast to multiple loggers. For instance, when initializing a Rails console, `Rails.logger` is extended to broadcast to STDERR, causing Rails to log to both a log file and STDERR.

```
console = ActiveSupport::Logger.new(STDERR)
Rails.logger.extend ActiveSupport::Logger.broadcast(console)
```

B.42.2 `active_support/logger_silence.rb`

B.42.2.1 `silence(temporary_level = Logger::ERROR, &block)`

Silences the logger for the duration of the block.

B.43   MessageEncryptor

A simple way to encrypt values that get stored somewhere you don't trust. The cipher text and initialization vector are base64 encoded and returned to you.

Can be used in situations similar to the `MessageVerifier` but where you don't want users to be able to determine the value of the payload.

B.43.1 `active_support/message_encryptor.rb`

B.43.1.1 `MessageEncryptor.new(secret, *signature_key_or_options)`

Creates a new instance of `MessageEncryptor`. The supplied `secret` must be at least as long as the cipher key size. By default, the cipher is `aes-256-cbc`, which would require a cipher key size of at least 256 bits. If you are using a user-entered secret, you can generate a suitable key with `OpenSSL::Digest::SHA256.new(user_secret).digest`.

Available options are:

`:cipher` The cipher to use. Can be any cipher returned by `OpenSSL::Cipher.ciphers` Default is `'aes-256-cbc'`.

`digest` String of digest to use for signing. Default is `SHA1`. Ignored when using an AEAD cipher such as `'aes-256-gcm'`.

`:serializer` Object serializer to use (default is `Marshal`).

B.43.1.2 `MessageEncryptor.key_len(cipher = default_cipher)`

Given a cipher, returns the key length of the cipher to help generate a key of the desired size.

B.43.1.3 `encrypt_and_sign(value)`

Encrypt and sign a `value`. The `value` needs to be signed to avoid padding attacks.

B.43.1.4 `decrypt_and_verify(value)`

Decrypts and verifies a value. The value needs to be verified to avoid padding attacks.

Active Support

B.44   MessageVerifier

MessageVerifier makes it easy to generate and verify signed messages to prevent tampering. This is useful for cases like remember-me tokens and auto-unsubscribe links where the session store isn't suitable or available.

```
>> msg = v.generate([1, 2.weeks.from_now])
=> "BAhbB2kGVTogQWN0aXZlU3VwcG9ydDo..."
>> id, time = v.verify(msg)
=> [1, Fri, 25 Oct 2013 18:03:27 UTC +00:00]
```

B.44.1   active_support/message_verifier.rb

B.44.1.1   MessageVerifier.new(secret, options = {})

Creates a new MessageVerifier with the supplied secret. Available options are:

:digest Default is SHA1.

:serializer Object serializer to use (default is Marshal).

B.44.1.2   generate(value)

Generate a signed message.

```
cookies[:remember_me] = verifier.generate([user.id, 2.weeks.from_now])
```

B.44.1.3   verify(signed_message)

Verify a signed message.

```
id, time = @verifier.verify(cookies[:remember_me])
if time < Time.now
  self.current_user = User.find(id)
end
```

B.45   Module

Extensions to Ruby's Module class, available in all contexts.

B.45.1   active_support/core_ext/module/aliasing.rb

B.45.1.1   alias_attribute(new_name, old_name)

This super-useful method allows you to easily make aliases for attributes, including their reader, writer, and query methods.

In the following example, the Content class is serving as the base class for Email using STI, but emails should have a subject, not a title:

```
class Content < ActiveRecord::Base
  # has column named 'title'
end

class Email < Content
  alias_attribute :subject, :title
end
```

As a result of the `alias_attribute`, you can see in the following example that the title and subject attributes become interchangeable:

```
>> e = Email.find(:first)

>> e.title
=> "Superstars"

>> e.subject
=> "Superstars"

>> e.subject?
=> true

>> e.subject = "Megastars"
=> "Megastars"

>> e.title
=> "Megastars"
```

B.45.1.2 `alias_method_chain(target, feature)`
This method is *deprecated*. Please use `Module#prepend` that comes with Ruby 2.0 or newer instead.

B.45.2 `active_support/core_ext/module/anonymous.rb`
B.45.2.1 `anonymous?`
Returns `true` if `self` does not have a name.

A module gets a name when it is first assigned to a constant, either via the `module` or `class` keyword

```
module M
end

>> M.name
=> "M"
```

```
m = Module.new

>> m.name
=> ""
```

or by an explicit assignment

```
m = Module.new

>> M = m      # m gets a name here as a side-effect

>> m.name
=> "M"
```

B.45.3 `active_support/core_ext/module/attribute_accessors.rb`

Extends `Module` with class-level and instance accessors for attributes, just like the native `attr*` accessors do on instances. Aliased as `cattr_` methods on `Class`.

Also available in per-thread versions, as defined in `active_support/core_ext/module/attribute_accessors_per_thread.rb`.

B.45.3.1 `mattr_accessor(*syms)` / `thread_mattr_accessor(*syms)`

Creates both reader and writer methods for supplied method names `syms`.

```
class Person
  mattr_accessor :hair_colors
end

>> Person.hair_colors = [:brown, :black, :blonde, :red]

>> Person.new.hair_colors
=> [:brown, :black, :blonde, :red]
```

B.45.3.2 `mattr_reader(*syms)` / `thread_mattr_reader(*syms)`

Creates class and instance reader methods for supplied method names `syms`.

B.45.3.3 `mattr_writer(*syms)` / `thread_mattr_writer(*syms)`

Creates class and instance writer methods for supplied method names `syms`.

B.45.4 `active_support/core_ext/module/attr_internal.rb`

B.45.4.1 `attr_internal`

Alias for `attr_internal_accessor`.

B.45.4.2 `attr_internal_accessor(*attrs)`

Declares attributes backed by internal instance variables names (using an `@_` - naming convention). Basically just a mechanism to enhance controlled access to sensitive attributes.

For instance, `Object`'s `copy_instance_variables_from` will not copy internal instance variables.

B.45.4.3 `attr_internal_reader(*attrs)`

Declares an attribute reader backed by an internally named instance variable.

B.45.4.4 `attr_internal_writer(*attrs)`

Declares an attribute writer backed by an internally named instance variable.

B.45.5 `active_support/core_ext/module/delegation.rb`

B.45.5.1 `delegate(*methods)`

Provides a delegate class method to easily expose contained objects' methods as your own. Pass one or more methods (specified as symbols or strings) and the name of the target object via the `:to` option (also a symbol or string). At least one method name and the `:to` option are required.

Delegation is particularly useful with Active Record associations:

```
class Greeter < ActiveRecord::Base
  def hello
    "hello"
  end

  def goodbye
    "goodbye"
  end
end

class Foo < ActiveRecord::Base
  belongs_to :greeter
  delegate :hello, to: :greeter
end
```

```
Foo.new.hello # => "hello"
Foo.new.goodbye # => NoMethodError: undefined method `goodbye' for #<Foo:0x1af30c>
```

Multiple delegates to the same target are allowed:

```
class Foo < ActiveRecord::Base
  belongs_to :greeter
  delegate :hello, :goodbye, to: :greeter
end
```

```
Foo.new.goodbye # => "goodbye"
```

Methods can be delegated to instance variables, class variables, or constants by providing them as a symbols:

```
class Foo
  CONSTANT_ARRAY = [0,1,2,3]
  @@class_array  = [4,5,6,7]

  def initialize
    @instance_array = [8,9,10,11]
  end
  delegate :sum, to: :CONSTANT_ARRAY
  delegate :min, to: :@@class_array
  delegate :max, to: :@instance_array
end
```

```
Foo.new.sum # => 6
Foo.new.min # => 4
Foo.new.max # => 11
```

Delegates can optionally be prefixed using the :prefix option. If the value is true, the delegate methods are prefixed with the name of the object being delegated to.

```
Person = Struct.new(:name, :address)

class Invoice < Struct.new(:client)
  delegate :name, :address, to: :client, prefix: true
end

john_doe = Person.new("John Doe", "Vimmersvej 13")
invoice = Invoice.new(john_doe)
invoice.client_name    # => "John Doe"
invoice.client_address # => "Vimmersvej 13"
```

It is also possible to supply a custom prefix.

```
class Invoice < Struct.new(:client)
  delegate :name, :address, to: :client, prefix: :customer
end

invoice = Invoice.new(john_doe)
invoice.customer_name     # => "John Doe"
invoice.customer_address  # => "Vimmersvej 13"
```

If the delegate object is `nil` an exception is raised, and that happens no matter whether `nil` responds to the delegated method. You can get a `nil` instead with the `:allow_nil` option.

```
class Foo
  attr_accessor :bar
  def initialize(bar = nil)
    @bar = bar
  end
  delegate :zoo, to: :bar
end

Foo.new.zoo      # raises NoMethodError exception (you called nil.zoo)

class Foo
  attr_accessor :bar
  def initialize(bar = nil)
    @bar = bar
  end
  delegate :zoo, to: :bar, allow_nil: true
end

Foo.new.zoo      # returns nil
```

B.45.6 `active_support/core_ext/module/deprecation.rb`

B.45.6.1 `deprecate(*method_names)`

Provides a `deprecate` class method to easily deprecate methods. Convenience wrapper for `ActiveSupport::Deprecation.deprecate_methods(self, *method_names)`.

```
deprecate :foo
deprecate bar: 'message'
deprecate :foo, :bar, baz: 'warning!', qux: 'gone!'
```

B.45.7 `active_support/core_ext/module/introspection.rb`

B.45.7.1 `local_constants`

Returns the constants that have been defined locally by this object and not in an ancestor.

B.45.7.2 `parent`

Returns the module that contains this one; if this is a root module, such as `::MyModule`, then `Object` is returned.

```
>> ActiveRecord::Validations.parent
=> ActiveRecord
```

B.45.7.3 `parent_name`

Returns the name of the module containing this one.

```
>> ActiveRecord::Validations.parent_name
=> "ActiveRecord"
```

B.45.7.4 `parents`

Returns all the parents of this module according to its name, ordered from nested outward. The receiver is not contained within the result.

```
module M
  module N
  end
end
X = M::N

>> M.parents
=> [Object]

>> M::N.parents
=> [M, Object]

>> X.parents
=> [M, Object]
```

B.45.8 `active_support/core_ext/module/remove_method.rb`

B.45.8.1 `redefine_method(method, &block)`

The method `define_method` in Ruby enables the definition of methods dynamically. However, `define_method` doesn't check for the existence of the method beforehand, which issues a warning if it does exist. The method `redefine_method` resolves this by first removing the method definition if it exists, and internally calling `define_method`.

B.45.8.2 `remove_possible_method(method)`
Removes a method definition if it exists.

B.45.8.3 `remove_possible_singleton_method(method)`
Removes a singleton method definition if it exists.

B.45.9 `active_support/dependencies.rb`

B.45.9.1 `const_missing(const_name)`
The `const_missing` callback is invoked when Ruby can't find a specified constant in the current scope, which is what makes Rails autoclass loading possible. See the Dependencies module for more detail.

B.46 Module::Concerning
Proposed as a natural, low-ceremony way to separate bite-sized concerns. Include, then call `concerning` in the class context.

B.46.1 `concerning(topic, &block)`
Equivalent to defining an inline module within a class, having it extend `Active-Support::Concern`, and then mixing it into the class.

```
class Todo
  concerning :EventTracking do
    included do
      has_many :events
      before_create :track_creation
      after_destroy :track_deletion
    end

    private
      def track_creation
        ...
      end
  end
end

>> Todo.ancestors
=> [Todo, Todo::EventTracking, Object]
```

If a class is big enough to merit this technique, then it's probably violating traditional object-oriented guidelines such as the *Single Responsibility Principle*.

B.46.2 `concern(topic, &module_definition)`

Shorthand form of defining an `ActiveSupport::Concern`.

```
concern :Bar do
  ...
end

# equivalent to

module Bar
  extend ActiveSupport::Concern
  ...
end
```

B.47 `Multibyte::Chars`

The `chars` proxy enables you to work transparently with multibyte encodings in the Ruby `String` class without having extensive knowledge about encoding.

B.47.1 `active_support/multibyte/chars.rb`

A `Chars` object accepts a string upon initialization and proxies `String` methods in an encoding-safe manner. All the normal `String` methods are proxied through the `Chars` object and can be accessed through the `mb_chars` method. Methods that would normally return a `String` object now return a `Chars` object so that methods can be chained together safely.

```
>> "The Perfect String".mb_chars.downcase.strip.normalize
=> #<ActiveSupport::Multibyte::Chars:0x007ffdcac6f7d0
    @wrapped_string="the perfect string">
```

`Chars` objects are perfectly interchangeable with `String` objects as long as no explicit class checks are made. If certain methods do explicitly check the class, call `to_s` before you pass `Chars` objects to them to go back to a normal `String` object:

```
bad.explicit_checking_method("T".chars.downcase.to_s)
```

The default `Chars` implementation assumes that the encoding of the string is UTF-8. If you want to handle different encodings, you can write your own multibyte string handler and configure it through `ActiveSupport::Multibyte.proxy_class`

```
class CharsForUTF32
  def size
    @wrapped_string.size / 4
  end

  def self.accepts?(string)
    string.length % 4 == 0
  end
end

ActiveSupport::Multibyte.proxy_class = CharsForUTF32
```

Note that a few methods are defined on `Chars` instead of the handler because they are defined on `Object` or `Kernel` and `method_missing` (the method used for delegation) can't catch them.

B.47.1.1   `<=> (other)`

Returns -1, 0, or +1 depending on whether the `Chars` object is to be sorted before, equal to, or after the object on the right side of the operation. In other words, it works exactly as you would expect it to.

B.47.1.2   `capitalize`

Converts the first character to uppercase and the remainder to lowercase.

```
>> 'über'.mb_chars.capitalize.to_s
=> "Über"
```

B.47.1.3   `compose`

Performs composition on all the characters.

B.47.1.4   `decompose`

Performs canonical decomposition on all the characters.

B.47.1.5   `downcase`

Converts characters in the string to lowercase.

```
>> 'VĚDA A VÝZKUM'.mb_chars.downcase.to_s
=> "věda a výzkum"
```

B.47.1.6   `grapheme_length`

Returns the number of grapheme clusters in the string.

B.47.1.7 `limit(limit)`

Limits the byte size of the string to a number of bytes without breaking characters.

B.47.1.8 `method_missing(m, *a, &b)`

Tries to forward all undefined methods to the enclosed string instance. Also responsible for making the bang (!) methods destructive, since a handler doesn't have access to change an enclosed string instance.

B.47.1.9 `normalize(form = nil)`

Returns the KC normalization of the string by default. NFKC is considered the best normalization form for passing strings to databases and validations.

A normalization form can be one of the following:

- `:c`
- `:kc`
- `:d`
- `:kd`

Default is `ActiveSupport::Multibyte::Unicode#default_normal-ization_form`.

B.47.1.10 `reverse`

Reverses all characters in the string.

```
>> 'Café'.mb_chars.reverse.to_s
=> 'éfaC'
```

B.47.1.11 `slice!(*args)`

Works like `String`'s `slice!`, with the exception that the items in the resulting list are `Char` instances instead of `String`.

B.47.1.12 `split(*args)`

Works just like the normal `String`'s `split` method, with the exception that the items in the resulting list are `Chars` instances instead of `String`, which makes chaining calls easier.

```
>> 'Café périferôl'.mb_chars.split(/é/).map { |part| part.upcase.to_s }
=> ["CAF", " P", "RIFERÔL"]
```

B.47.1.13 `swapcase`
Converts characters in the string to the opposite case.

```
>> "El Cañón".mb_chars.swapcase.to_s
=> "eL cAÑÓN"
```

B.47.1.14 `tidy_bytes(force = false)`
Replaces all ISO-8859-1 or CP1252 characters by their UTF-8 equivalent resulting in a valid UTF-8 string.

Passing `true` will forcibly tidy all bytes, assuming that the string's encoding is entirely CP1252 or ISO-8859-1.

```
> "obie".mb_chars.tidy_bytes
=> #<ActiveSupport::Multibyte::Chars:0x007ffdcb76ecf8
    @wrapped_string="obie">
```

B.48 **Multibyte::Unicode**
Contains methods handling Unicode strings.

The `NORMALIZATION_FORMS` constant contains an array of all available normalization forms. See http://www.unicode.org/reports/tr15/tr15-29.html for more information about normalization.

Change the default normalization used for operations that require normalization by setting the value of `default_normalization_form` to any of the normalizations in `NORMALIZATION_FORMS`.

```
ActiveSupport::Multibyte::Unicode.default_normalization_form = :c
```

B.48.1 `Unicode.compose(codepoints)`
Compose decomposed characters to the composed form.

B.48.2 `Unicode.decompose(type, codepoints)`
Decompose composed characters to the decomposed form. The `type` argument accepts `:canonical` or `:compatability`.

B.48.3 `Unicode.downcase(string)`
Converts a unicode string to lowercase.

B.48.4 Unicode.in_char_class?(codepoint, classes)

Detect whether the codepoint is in a certain character class. Returns `true` when it's in the specified character class and `false` otherwise. Valid character classes are: `:cr`, `:lf`, `:l`, `:v`, `:lv`, `:lvt`, and `:t`.

B.48.5 Unicode.normalize(string, form = nil)

Returns the KC normalization of the string by default. NFKC is considered the best normalization form for passing strings to databases and validations. The form specifies the form you want to normalize in and should be one of the following: `:c`, `:kc`, `:d`, or `:kd`. Default form is stored in the `ActiveSupport::Multibyte.default_normalization_form` attribute and is overridable in an initializer.

B.48.6 Unicode.pack_graphemes(unpacked)

Reverse operation of `unpack_graphemes`.

B.48.7 Unicode.reorder_characters(codepoints)

Re-order codepoints so the string becomes canonical.

B.48.8 Unicode.swapcase(string)

Swapcase on a unicode string.

B.48.9 Unicode.tidy_bytes(string, force = false)

Replaces all ISO-8859-1 or CP1252 characters by their UTF-8 equivalent resulting in a valid UTF-8 string.

B.48.10 Unicode.unpack_graphemes(string)

Unpacks the string at grapheme boundaries. Returns a list of character lists.

```
>> ActiveSupport::Multibyte::Unicode.unpack_graphemes('ffff')
=> [[102], [102], [102], [102]]

>> ActiveSupport::Multibyte::Unicode.unpack_graphemes('Café')
=> [[67], [97], [102], [233]]
```

B.48.11 Unicode.upcase(string)

Converts a unicode string to uppercase.

B.49 NameError

Small enhancements to Ruby's built-in `NameError` exception.

B.49.1 `missing_name`

Extracts the name of the missing constant from the exception message.

```
begin
  HelloWorld
rescue NameError => e
  e.missing_name
end
# => "HelloWorld"
```

B.49.2 `missing_name?(name)`

Was this exception raised because the given name was missing?

```
begin
  HelloWorld
rescue NameError => e
  e.missing_name?("HelloWorld")
end
# => true
```

B.50 `NilClass`

Remember that everything in Ruby is an object, even nil, which is a special reference to a singleton instance of the `NilClass`.

B.50.1 `active_support/core_ext/object/blank.rb`

B.50.1.1 `blank?`

Returns `true`.

B.50.2 `active_support/core_ext/object/try.rb`

B.50.2.1 `try(*args)`

Calling `try` on `nil` always returns `nil`. It becomes especially helpful when navigating through associations that may return `nil`.

```
nil.try(:name)  # => nil
```

Without try:

```
@person && @person.children.any? && @person.children.first.name
```

With try:

```
@person.try(:children).try(:first).try(:name)
```

B.50.2.2 `try!(*args)`

Calling `try!` on `nil` always returns `nil`.

```
nil.try!(:name) # => nil
```

B.50.3 `active_support/json/encoding.rb`

B.50.3.1 `as_json`

Returns `"null"`.

B.51 Notifications

Provides a "pub/sub" instrumentation API for Ruby.

B.51.1 Instrumenters

To instrument something of interest, wrap it in a call to `ActiveSupport::Notifications.instrument` like this:

```
ActiveSupport::Notifications.instrument('render', extra: :information) do
  render plain: 'Foo'
end
```

In the example above, `'render'` is the name of the event, and the rest is called the *payload*. The payload is a mechanism that enables instrumenters to pass extra information to subscribers. Payloads consist of a hash whose contents are arbitrary and generally depend on the event.

First the block is executed, then subscribers to the `'render'` event are notified.

B.51.2 Subscribers

You can consume `Notifications` events and the information they provide by registering a subscriber.

```
ActiveSupport::Notifications.subscribe('render') do |name, start, finish, id, payload|
  name    # => String, name of the event (such as 'render' from above)
  start   # => Time, when the instrumented block started execution
  finish  # => Time, when the instrumented block ended execution
  id      # => String, unique ID for this notification
  payload # => Hash, the payload
end
```

For instance, let's store all `'render'` events in an array. We'll make use of the `ActiveSupport::Notifications::Event` class to encapsulate the event payload data in a clean fashion:

```
events = []

ActiveSupport::Notifications.subscribe('render') do |*args|
  events << ActiveSupport::Notifications::Event.new(*args)
end
```

That code returns right away; you are just subscribing to events. The block is saved and will be called whenever someone instruments `'render'`:

```
ActiveSupport::Notifications.instrument('render', extra: :information) do
  render plain: 'Foo'
end
```

```
>> event = events.first
>> event.name
=> "render"
>> event.duration
=> 10 (in milliseconds)
>> event.payload
=> { extra: :information }
```

The block in the subscribe call gets the name of the event, start timestamp, end timestamp, a string with a unique identifier for that event (something like "535801666f04d0298cd6"), and a hash with the payload, in that order.

The duration information is what makes this more than just a generic pub/sub event channel.

If an exception happens during a particular instrumentation the payload will get a key called `:exception` with an array of two elements: a string with the name of the exception class and the exception message. The `:exception_object` key of the payload will have the exception itself as the value.

As the previous example depicts, the class `ActiveSupport::Notifications::Event` is able to take the arguments as they come and provide an object-oriented interface to that data.

It is also possible to pass an object that responds to a `call` method as the second parameter to the `subscribe` method instead of a block:

```
module ActionController
  class PageRequest
    def call(name, started, finished, unique_id, payload)
      Rails.logger.debug ['notification:', name, started, finished, unique_
        id, payload].join(' ')
```

```
      end
   end
end
```

```
ActiveSupport::Notifications.subscribe('process_action.action_
         controller', ActionController::PageRequest.new)
```

The event processing of PageRequest in the example will result in the following output within the logs (including a hash with the payload):

```
notification: process_action.action_controller 2012-
         04-13 01:08:35 +0300 2012-04-13 01:08:35 +0300
         af358ed7fab884532ec7 {
   controller: "Devise::SessionsController",
   action: "new",
   params: {"action"=>"new", "controller"=>"devise/sessions"},
   format: :html,
   method: "GET",
   path: "/login/sign_in",
   status: 200,
   view_runtime: 279.3080806732178,
   db_runtime: 40.053
}
```

You can also subscribe to all events whose name matches a certain regular expression:

```
ActiveSupport::Notifications.subscribe(/render/) do |*args|
   ...
end
```

Calling `subscribe` without arguments will subscribe to all events.

B.51.3   Temporary Subscriptions

Sometimes you do not want to subscribe to an event for the entire life of the application. There are two ways to unsubscribe.

⚠️ The instrumentation framework is designed for long-running subscribers. Use temporary subscriptions sparingly, because it wipes some internal caches, causing a negative impact on overall performance.

B.51.3.1   Subscribe While a Block Runs

You can subscribe to some event temporarily while some block runs. For example, in

```
callback = lambda {|*args| ... }
   ActiveSupport::Notifications.subscribed(callback, "sql.active_record") do
      ...
```

the `callback` lambda will be called for all `sql.active_record` events instrumented during the execution of the block. The callback is unsubscribed automatically after that.

B.51.3.2   Manual Unsubscription

The `subscribe` method returns a subscriber object that can be used later to unsubscribe.

```
subscriber = ActiveSupport::Notifications.subscribe("render") do |*args|
  ...
end


ActiveSupport::Notifications.unsubscribe(subscriber)
```

You can also unsubscribe by passing the name of the subscriber object. Note that this will unsubscribe all subscriptions with the given name:

```
ActiveSupport::Notifications.unsubscribe("render")
```

 For a fantastic writeup on how to integrate `ActiveSupport::Notifications` with 3rd-party metrics collection services such as Datadog[3] or Librato[4] read this blog post from Ken Collins.[5]

B.51.4   `Notifications::Fanout`

The default queue implementation that powers `ActiveSupport::Notifications` by default. It just pushes events to all registered log subscribers in a thread-safe manner.

It's possible to replace `Fanout` with a different queue implementation by changing the value of `Notifications.notifier` in an initializer like this:

```
ActiveSupport::Notifications.notifier = MySpecialQueue.new(OPTS)
```

B.52   **NumberHelper**

See `NumberHelper` in Chapter 11, "All about Helpers."

---

3. https://www.datadoghq.com/

4. https://www.librato.com/

5. http://metaskills.net/2013/12/15/instrumenting-your-code-with-activesupport-notifications/

B.53   Numeric

Extensions to Ruby's Numeric class.

B.53.1   active_support/core_ext/object/blank.rb

B.53.1.1   blank?

Returns false.

B.53.2   active_support/json/encoding.rb

B.53.2.1   as_json

Returns self.

B.53.2.2   encode_json

Returns self.to_s.

B.53.3   active_support/core_ext/numeric/bytes.rb

Enables the use of byte calculations and declarations, like 45.bytes + 2.6.megabytes.

B.53.3.1   Constants

The following constants are defined in bytes.rb.

```
class Numeric
  KILOBYTE = 1024
  MEGABYTE = KILOBYTE * 1024
  GIGABYTE = MEGABYTE * 1024
  TERABYTE = GIGABYTE * 1024
  PETABYTE = TERABYTE * 1024
  EXABYTE  = PETABYTE * 1024
  ...
end
```

B.53.3.2   byte / bytes

Returns the value of self. Enables the use of byte calculations and declarations, like 45.bytes + 2.6.megabytes.

B.53.3.3   kilobyte / kilobytes

Returns self * 1024.

B.53.3.4   megabyte / megabytes

Returns self * 1024.kilobytes.

B.53.3.5 `gigabyte / gigabytes`
Returns `self * 1024.megabytes`.

B.53.3.6 `terabyte / terabytes`
Returns `self * 1024.gigabytes`.

B.53.3.7 `petabyte / petabytes`
Returns `self * 1024.terabytes`.

B.53.3.8 `exabyte / exabytes2`
Returns `self * 1024.petabytes`.

B.53.4   `active_support/core_ext/numeric/ conversions.rb`

B.53.4.1 `to_formatted_s(format = :default, options = {})`

Generates a formatted string representation of a number. Options are provided for phone numbers, currency, percentage, precision, positional notation, file size, and pretty printing.

Aliased as `to_s`.

:CURRENCY

Formats a number into a currency string. The `:currency` formatting option can be combined with the following additional options:

`:delimiter` Sets the thousands delimiter, defaults to `","`.

`:format` Sets the format for non-negative numbers, defaults to `"%u%n"`.

`:locale` Sets the locale to be used for formatting, defaults to current locale.

`:negative_format` Sets the format for negative numbers, defaults to prepending a hyphen to the formatted number.

`:precision` Sets the level of precision, defaults to 2.

`:separator` Sets the separator between the units, defaults to `"."`.

`:unit` Sets the denomination of the currency, defaults to `"$"`.

```
>> 1234567890.50.to_s(:currency)
=> $1,234,567,890.50

>> 1234567890.506.to_s(:currency)
```

```
=> $1,234,567,890.51

>> 1234567890.506.to_s(:currency, precision: 3)
=> $1,234,567,890.506

>> 1234567890.506.to_s(:currency, locale: :fr)
=> 1 234 567 890,51 €

>> -1234567890.50.to_s(:currency, negative_format: '(%u%n)')
=> ($1,234,567,890.50)

>> 1234567890.50.to_s(:currency, unit: '&pound;', separator: ',',
     delimiter: '')
=> &pound;1234567890,50
```

:DELIMITED

Formats a number with grouped thousands using delimiter. The :delimited formatting option can be combined with the following additional options:

:delimiter Sets the thousands delimiter, defaults to ",".

:locale Sets the locale to be used for formatting, defaults to current locale.

:separator Sets the separator between the units, defaults to ".".

```
>> 12345678.to_s(:delimited)
=> 12,345,678

>> 12345678.05.to_s(:delimited)
=> 12,345,678.05

>> 12345678.to_s(:delimited, delimiter: '.')
=> 12.345.678
```

:HUMAN

Formats a number that is more readable to humans. Useful for numbers that are extremely large. The :human formatting option can be combined with the following:

:delimiter Sets the thousands delimiter, defaults to "".

:format Sets the format for non-negative numbers, defaults to "%n %u". The field types are:

- %u: The quantifier
- %n: The number

:locale Sets the locale to be used for formatting, defaults to current locale.

:precision Sets the level of precision, defaults to 3.

:separator Sets the separator between fractional and integer digits, defaults to ".".

:significant If `true`, precision will be the number of significant_digits, otherwise the number of fractional digits are used. Defaults to `true`.

:strip_insignificant_zeros Setting to `true` removes insignificant zeros after the decimal separator, defaults to `true`.

:units A hash of unit quantifier names, or a string containing an I18n scope for where to find this hash. It might have the following keys:

- integers: `:unit, :ten, *:hundred, :thousand, :million, *:billion, :trillion, *:quadrillion`

- fractionals: `:deci, :centi, *:mili, :micro, :nano, *:pico, :femto`

```
>> 123.to_s(:human)
=> "123"

>> 1234.to_s(:human)
=> "1.23 Thousand"

>> 1234567.to_s(:human)
=> "1.23 Million"

>> 489939.to_s(:human, precision: 4)
=> "489.9 Thousand"
```

:HUMAN_SIZE

Formats a number of bytes into a more understandable string representation. Useful for reporting file sizes to users. The `:human_size` formatting option can be combined with the following additional options:

:delimiter Sets the thousands delimiter, defaults to "".

:format Sets the format for non-negative numbers, defaults to "%u%n".

:locale Sets the locale to be used for formatting, defaults to current locale.

:precision Sets the level of precision, defaults to 3.

:prefix Setting to `:si` formats the number using the SI prefix, defaults to `:binary`.

:separator Sets the separator between fractional and integer digits, defaults to ".".

:significant If `true`, precision will be the number of significant digits, otherwise the number of fractional digits are used. Defaults to `true`.

:strip_insignificant_zeros Setting to `true` removes insignificant zeros after the decimal separator, defaults to `true`.

:raise Setting to `true` raises `InvalidNumberError` when the number is invalid.

```
>> 123.to_s(:human_size)
=> 123 Bytes

>> 1234.to_s(:human_size)
=> 1.21 KB

>> 12345.to_s(:human_size)
=> 12.1 KB

>> 1234567.to_s(:human_size)
=> 1.18 MB

>> 1234567.to_s(:human_size, precision: 2)
=> 1.2 MB
```

:PERCENTAGE

Formats a number as a percentage string. The `:percentage` formatting option can be combined with the following additional options:

:delimiter Sets the thousands delimiter, defaults to `""`.

:format Sets the format of the percentage string, defaults to `"%n%"`.

:locale Sets the locale to be used for formatting, defaults to current locale.

:precision Sets the level of precision, defaults to 3.

:separator Sets the separator between the units, defaults to `"."`.

:significant If `true`, precision will be the number of significant digits, otherwise the number of fractional digits are used. Defaults to `false`.

:strip_insignificant_zeros Setting to `true` removes insignificant zeros after the decimal separator, defaults to `false`.

```
>> 100.to_s(:percentage)
=> 100.000%

>> 100.to_s(:percentage, precision: 0)
=> 100%
```

```
>> 1000.to_s(:percentage, delimiter: '.', separator: ',')
=> 1.000,000%

>> 302.24398923423.to_s(:percentage, precision: 5)
=> 302.24399%

>> 1000.to_s(:percentage, locale: :fr)
=> 1 000,000%

>> 100.to_s(:percentage, format: '%n    %')
=> 100 %
```

:PHONE

Formats a number into a U.S. phone number. The :phone formatting option can be combined with the following additional options:

:area_code Adds parentheses around the area code.

:country_code Sets the country code for the phone number.

:delimiter Specifies the delimiter to use, defaults to "-".

:extension Specifies an extension to add to the end of the generated number.

```
>> 5551234.to_s(:phone)
=> 555-1234

>> 1235551234.to_s(:phone)
=> 123-555-1234

>> 1235551234.to_s(:phone, area_code: true)
=> (123) 555-1234

>> 1235551234.to_s(:phone, delimiter: ' ')
=> 123 555 1234

>> 1235551234.to_s(:phone, area_code: true, extension: 555)
=> (123) 555-1234 x 555

>> 1235551234.to_s(:phone, country_code: 1)
=> +1-123-555-1234

>> 1235551234.to_s(:phone, country_code: 1, extension: 1343, delimiter: '.')
=> +1.123.555.1234 x 1343
```

:ROUNDED

Formats a number with the specified level of precision. The `:rounded` formatting option can be combined with the following additional options:

:delimiter Sets the thousands delimiter, defaults to "".

:locale Sets the locale to be used for formatting, defaults to current locale.

:precision Sets the level of precision, defaults to 3.

:separator Sets the separator between the units, defaults to ".".

:significant If `true`, precision will be the number of significant digits, otherwise the number of fractional digits are used. Defaults to `false`.

:strip_insignificant_zeros Setting to `true` removes insignificant zeros after the decimal separator, defaults to `false`.

```
>> 111.2345.to_s(:rounded)
=> 111.235

>> 111.2345.to_s(:rounded, precision: 2)
=> 111.23

>> 13.to_s(:rounded, precision: 5)
=> 13.00000

>> 389.32314.to_s(:rounded, precision: 0)
=> 389

>> 111.2345.to_s(:rounded, significant: true)
=> 111

>> 111.2345.to_s(:rounded, precision: 1, significant: true)
=> 100
```

B.53.5 `active_support/core_ext/numeric/inquiry.rb`

Adds a couple of predicates to numbers.

B.53.5.1 `positive?`

Returns `true` if the number is positive.

```
>> 1.positive?  # => true
>> 0.positive?  # => false
>> -1.positive? # => false
```

B.53.5.2 `negative?`
Returns `true` if the number is negative.

B.53.6 `active_support/core_ext/numeric/time.rb`
Enables the use of time calculations and declarations, like `45.minutes + 2.hours + 4.years`.

These methods use `Time#advance` for precise date calculations when using `from_now`, `ago`, etc. as well as adding or subtracting their results from a `Time` object. For example,

```
# equivalent to Time.now.advance(months: 1)
1.month.from_now
```

```
# equivalent to Time.now.advance(years: 2)
2.years.from_now
```

```
# equivalent to Time.now.advance(months: 4, years: 5)
(4.months + 5.years).from_now
```

While these methods return instances of `Duration` that provide precise calculation when used as in the examples above, care should be taken to note that this is not `true` if the result of 'months', 'years', etc. is converted before use:

```
# equivalent to 30.days.to_i.from_now
1.month.to_i.from_now
```

```
# equivalent to 365.25.days.to_f.from_now
1.year.to_f.from_now
```

It's totally unclear to us *why* you would ever want to convert the result of a duration expression to integer or float values, especially to use in a calculation.

B.53.6.1 `ago` and `until`
Appends to a numeric time value to express a moment in the past.

```
10.minutes.ago
```

B.53.6.2 `day` / `days`
A duration equivalent to `self * 24.hours`.

Active Support

B.53.6.3 `fortnight` / `fortnights`
A duration equivalent to `self * 2.weeks`.

B.53.6.4 `from_now(time = Time.current)` / `since(time = Time.current)`
An amount of time in the future, from a specified time (which defaults to `Time.current`).

B.53.6.5 `hour` / `hours`
A duration equivalent to `self * 3600.seconds`.

B.53.6.6 `in_milliseconds`
An equivalent to `self * 1000`. This value can be set in JavaScript functions like `getTime()`.

B.53.6.7 `minute` / `minutes`
A duration equivalent to `self * 60.seconds`.

B.53.6.8 `month` / `months`
A duration equivalent to `self * 30.days`.

B.53.6.9 `second` / `seconds`
A duration in seconds equal to `self`.

B.53.6.10 `week` / `weeks`
A duration equivalent to `self * 7.days`.

B.53.6.11 `year` / `years`
A duration equivalent to `self * 365.25.days`.

B.54 Object
Rails mixes quite a few methods into the `Object` class, meaning they are available via every other object at runtime.

B.54.1 `active_support/core_ext/kernel/agnostics.rb`
B.54.1.1 `` `(command)` ``
Makes backticks behave (somewhat more) similarly on all platforms. On win32 `nonexistent_command` raises `Errno::ENOENT`, but on Unix, the spawned shell prints a message to stderr and sets `$?`.

B.54.2 `active_support/core_ext/object/acts_like.rb`

B.54.2.1 `acts_like?(duck)`

A duck-type assistant method. For example, Active Support extends `Date` to define an `acts_like_date?` method and extends `Time` to define `acts_like_time?`. As a result, we can do `x.acts_like?(:time)` and `x.acts_like?(:date)` to do duck-type-safe comparisons, since classes that we want to act like `Time` simply need to define an `acts_like_time?` method.

B.54.3 `active_support/core_ext/object/blank.rb`

B.54.3.1 `blank?`

An object is blank if it's `false`, empty, or a whitespace string. For example, `""`, `" "`, `nil`, `[]`, and `{}` are blank.

This simplifies:

```
if !address.nil? && !address.empty?
```

to

```
unless address.blank?
```

B.54.3.2 `presence`

Returns object if it's `present?` otherwise returns `nil`. The expression `object.presence` is equivalent to `object.present? ? object : nil`.

This is handy for any representation of objects where blank is the same as not present at all. For example, this simplifies a common check for HTTP POST/query parameters:

```
state    = params[:state]    if params[:state].present?
country  = params[:country]  if params[:country].present?
region   = state || country || 'US'
```

becomes

```
region = params[:state].presence || params[:country].presence || 'US'
```

B.54.3.3 `present?`

An object is present if it's not `blank?`.

B.54.4 `active_support/core_ext/object/deep_dup.rb`

Returns a deep copy of object if it's duplicable. If it's not duplicable, returns `self`.

B.54.5 `active_support/core_ext/object/duplicable.rb`

Classes may signal their instances are not duplicable by removing `dup` and `clone` or raising exceptions from them. The normal Ruby idiom for calling `dup` on an arbitrary object is to be ready to rescue an exception:

```
arbitrary_object.dup rescue object
```

That `rescue` is very expensive (around 40 times slower than calling an extra predicate method), which is why the Rails team decided to check `duplicable?` instead of using the rescue idiom mentioned above.

B.54.5.1 `duplicable?`

Answers the question: "Is it possible to safely duplicate this object?"

Returns `false` for `nil`, `false`, `true`, `symbols`, `numbers`, class and module objects, `true` otherwise.

B.54.6 `active_support/core_ext/object/inclusion.rb`

B.54.6.1 `in?(object)`

Returns `true` if this object is included in the argument. The argument must respond to `include?`.

```
characters = %w(Hulk Thor Hawkeye)

>> "Thor".in?(characters)
=> true
```

B.54.6.2 `presence_in(another_object)`

Returns the receiver if it's included in the argument, otherwise returns `nil`. Argument must be any object that responds to `include?` (else `ArgumentError` is raised).

```
params[:bucket_type].presence_in %w(project calendar)
```

B.54.7 `active_support/core_ext/object/instance_variables.rb`

B.54.7.1 `instance_values`

Returns a hash that maps instance variable names without "@" to their corresponding values. Keys are strings both in Ruby 1.8 and 1.9.

```
class C
  def initialize(x, y)
```

```
    @x, @y = x, y
  end
end

C.new(0, 1).instance_values # => {"x" => 0, "y" => 1}
```

B.54.7.2 `instance_variable_names`
Returns an array of instance variable names including "@".

```
class C
  def initialize(x, y)
    @x, @y = x, y
  end
end

C.new(0, 1).instance_variable_names # => ["@y", "@x"]
```

B.54.8 `active_support/core_ext/object/json.rb`
B.54.8.1 `to_json`
A basic definition of `to_json` which prevents calls to `to_json` from going directly to the `json` gem on the following core classes:

- `Object`
- `Array`
- `FalseClass`
- `Float`
- `Hash`
- `Integer`
- `NilClass`
- `String`
- `TrueClass`

B.54.9 `active_support/core_ext/object/to_param.rb`
B.54.9.1 `to_param`
Calls `to_param` on all of its elements and joins the result with slashes. This is used by the `url_for` method in Action Pack.

```
>> ["riding","high","and","I","want","to","make"].to_param
=> "riding/high/and/I/want/to/make"
```

B.54.10 `active_support/core_ext/object/to_query.rb`

B.54.10.1 `to_query(key)`

Converts an object into a string suitable for use as a URL query string, using the given `key` as the param name.

B.54.11 `active_support/core_ext/object/try.rb`

B.54.11.1 `try(*a, &block)`

Attempts to call a public method whose name is the first argument. Unlike `public_send`, if the object does not respond to the method, `nil` is returned rather than an exception being raised.

This simplifies:

```
@person ? @person.name : nil
```

to

```
@person.try(:name)
```

If `try` is invoked without arguments, it yields the receiver unless it's `nil`.

```
@person.try do |p|
  ...
end
```

Arguments and blocks are forwarded to the method if invoked:

```
@posts.try(:each_slice, 2) do |a, b|
  ...
end
```

B.54.11.2 `try!(*a, &block)`

The hipster alternative to `try` raises a `NoMethodError` exception if the receiver is not `nil` and does not implement the tried method.

```
>> "a".try!(:upcase)
=> "A"

>> nil.try!(:upcase)
=> nil

>> 123.try!(:upcase)
=> NoMethodError: undefined method `upcase' for 123:Integer
```

B.54.12 `active_support/core_ext/object/with_options.rb`

B.54.12.1 `with_options(options)`

An elegant way to refactor out common options. Each method called in the block, with the block variable as the receiver, will have its options merged with the default `options` hash provided. Each method called on the block variable must take an options hash as its final argument.

```
class Post < ActiveRecord::Base
  with_options(dependent: :destroy) do |post|
    post.has_many :comments
    post.has_many :photos
  end
end
```

B.54.13 `active_support/dependencies.rb`

B.54.13.1 `load(file, *extras)`

Rails overrides Ruby's built-in `load` method to tie it into the `Dependencies` subsystem.

B.54.13.2 `require(file, *extras)`

Rails overrides Ruby's built-in `require` method to tie it into the `Dependencies` subsystem.

B.54.13.3 `require_dependency(file_name, file_name, message = "No such file to load -- %s")`

Used internally by Rails. Invokes `Dependencies.depend_on(file_name)`.

B.54.13.4 `require_or_load(file_name)`

Used internally by Rails. Invokes `Dependencies.require_or_load(file_name)`.

B.54.13.5 `unloadable(const_desc)`

Marks the specified constant as unloadable. Unloadable constants are removed each time dependencies are cleared.

Note that marking a constant for unloading need only be done once. Setup or init scripts may list each unloadable constant that will need unloading; constants marked in this way will be removed on every subsequent `Dependencies.clear`, as opposed to the first clear only.

Active Support

The provided constant descriptor `const_desc` may be a (nonanonymous) module or class or a qualified constant name as a string or symbol.

Returns `true` if the constant was not previously marked for unloading, `false` otherwise.

B.55 OrderedOptions

A subclass of `Hash` that adds a method-missing implementation so that hash elements can be accessed and modified using normal attribute semantics, aka dot-notation.

Usually key value pairs are handled something like this:

```
h = {}
h[:boy]  = 'John'
h[:girl] = 'Mary'
h[:boy]  # => 'John'
h[:girl] # => 'Mary'
h[:dog]  # => nil
```

Using `OrderedOptions`, the preceding code could be reduced to:

```
opts = ActiveSupport::OrderedOptions.new(h)
opts.boy  = 'John'
opts.girl = 'Mary'
opts.boy  # => 'John'
opts.girl # => 'Mary'
opts.dog  # => nil
```

To raise an exception when the value is blank, append a bang to the key name, like this:

```
opts.dog! # => raises KeyError: key not found: :dog
```

B.56 ProxyObject

A class with no predefined methods that behaves similarly to Builder's `Blank-Slate`. Used for proxy classes and can come in handy when implementing domain-specific languages in your application code.

The implementation of `ProxyObject` inherits from `BasicObject`, un-defines two methods, and allows exceptions to be raised. The implementation is reproduced here for your reference.

```
class ProxyObject < ::BasicObject
  undef_method :==
```

```
    undef_method :equal?

    # Let ActiveSupport::ProxyObject at least raise exceptions.
    def raise(*args)
      ::Object.send(:raise, *args)
    end
  end
end
```

B.57 Railtie

Contains Active Support's initialization routine for itself and the I18n subsystem.

If you're depending on Active Support outside of Rails, you should be aware of what happens in this Railtie in case you end up needing to replicate it in your own code.

```
module ActiveSupport
  class Railtie < Rails::Railtie # :nodoc:
    config.active_support = ActiveSupport::OrderedOptions.new

    config.eager_load_namespaces << ActiveSupport

    initializer "active_support.deprecation_behavior" do |app|
      if deprecation = app.config.active_support.deprecation
        ActiveSupport::Deprecation.behavior = deprecation
      end
    end

    # Sets the default value for Time.zone
    # If assigned value cannot be matched to a TimeZone, an
    # exception will be raised.
    initializer "active_support.initialize_time_zone" do |app|
      require 'active_support/core_ext/time/zones'
      zone_default = Time.find_zone!(app.config.time_zone)

      unless zone_default
        raise 'Value assigned to config.time_zone not recognized. ' \
          'Run "rake -D time" for a list of tasks for finding
          appropriate time zone names.'
      end

      Time.zone_default = zone_default
    end

    # Sets the default week start
    # If assigned value is not a valid day symbol
    # (e.g., :sunday, :monday, ...), an exception will be raised.
    initializer "active_support.initialize_beginning_of_week" do |app|
      require 'active_support/core_ext/date/calculations'
      beginning_of_week_default = Date.
```

```
          find_beginning_of_week!(app.config.beginning_of_week)

      Date.beginning_of_week_default = beginning_of_week_default
    end

    initializer "active_support.set_configs" do |app|
      app.config.active_support.each do |k, v|
        k = "#{k}="
        ActiveSupport.send(k, v) if ActiveSupport.respond_to? k
      end
    end
  end
end
```

B.58 Range

Extensions to Ruby's Range class.

B.58.1 `active_support/core_ext/enumerable.rb`

B.58.1.1 `sum(identity = 0)`

Optimize range sum to use arithmetic progression if a block is not given and we have a range of numeric values.

B.58.2 `active_support/core_ext/range/conversions.rb`

B.58.2.1 `to_formatted_s(format = :default)`

Generates a formatted string representation of the range.

```
>> (20.days.ago..10.days.ago).to_formatted_s
=> "Fri Aug 10 22:12:33 -0400 2007..Mon Aug 20 22:12:33 -0400 2007"
>> (20.days.ago..10.days.ago).to_formatted_s(:db)
=> "BETWEEN '2007-08-10 22:12:36' AND '2007-08-20 22:12:36'"
```

You can add your own formats to the `Range::RANGE_FORMATS` hash. Just use the format name as the hash key and a lambda as the value.

```
# config/initializers/range_formats.rb
Range::RANGE_FORMATS[:short] = ->(start, stop) { "Between
        #{start.to_s(:db)} and #{stop.to_s(:db)}" }
```

B.58.3 `active_support/core_ext/range/include_` `range.rb`

B.58.3.1 `include?(value)`

Extends the default `Range#include?` to support range comparisons.

```
>> (1..5).include?(1..5)
=> true

>> (1..5).include?(2..3)
=> true

>> (1..5).include?(2..6)
=> false
```

The native `include?` behavior is untouched.

```
>> ("a".."f").include?("c")
=> true

>> (5..9).include?(11)
=> false
```

B.58.4 `active_support/core_ext/range/overlaps.rb`

B.58.4.1 `overlaps?(other)`

Compare two ranges and see if they overlap each other.

```
>> (1..5).overlaps?(4..6)
=> true

>> (1..5).overlaps?(7..9)
=> false
```

B.59 Regexp

Extensions to Ruby's `Regexp` class.

B.59.1 `active_support/core_ext/regexp.rb`

B.59.1.1 `multiline?`

Returns `true` if a multiline regular expression.

B.59.2 `active_support/json/encoding.rb`

B.59.2.1 `as_json`

Returns `self.to_s`.

B.60 Rescuable

The `Rescuable` module is a `Concern` that adds support for easier exception handling. Used within Rails primarily in controller actions but potentially useful in your own libraries too.

B.60.1 `rescue_from(*klasses, &block)`

The `rescue_from` method receives a series of exception classes or class names and a trailing `:with` option with the name of a method or a `Proc` object to be called to handle them. Alternatively a block can be given.

Handlers that take one argument will be called with the exception, so that the exception can be inspected when dealing with it.

Handlers are inherited. They are searched from right to left, from bottom to top, and up the hierarchy. The handler of the first class for which `exception is_a?(klass)` returns `true` is the one invoked, if any.

Here's some example code taken from Action Controller.

```
class ApplicationController < ActionController::Base
  rescue_from User::NotAuthorized, with: :deny_access
  rescue_from ActiveRecord::RecordInvalid, with: :show_errors

  rescue_from 'MyAppError::Base' do |exception|
    render xml: exception, status: 500
  end

  protected
    def deny_access
      ...
    end

    def show_errors(exception)
      exception.record.new? ? ...
    end
end
```

B.60.2 `rescue_with_handler(exception, object: self, visited_exceptions: [])`

Matches an exception to a handler based on the exception class.

If no handler matches the exception, check for a handler matching the (optional) `exception.cause`. If no handler matches the exception or its cause, this method returns `nil`.

Don't forget the possibility of having to re-raise unhandled exceptions.

```
begin
  ...
rescue => exception
```

```
    rescue_with_handler(exception) || raise
end
```

B.61 SecureRandom

B.61.1 base58(n = 16)

Generates a random base58 string. The argument n specifies the length of the random string to be generated. The result may contain alphanumeric characters except 0, O, I, and l

```
p SecureRandom.base58 # => "4kUgL2pdQMSCQtjE"
p SecureRandom.base58(24) # => "77TMHrHJFvFDwodq8w7Ev2m7"
```

B.62 SecurityUtils

B.62.1 secure_compare(a, b)

Used internally by Rails to do *constant-time* string comparison in authentication and message verification routines.

If you're going to use this method in your own secure applications, make sure that the values compared are of fixed length, such as strings that have already been processed by HMAC. This method should not be used on variable length plaintext strings because it could leak length info via timing attacks.

B.63 String

Extensions to Ruby's String class.

B.63.1 active_support/json/encoding.rb

B.63.1.1 as_json

Returns self.

B.63.1.2 encode_json

Returns JSON escaped version of self.

B.63.2 active_support/core_ext/object/blank.rb

B.63.2.1 blank?

Returns true if the string consists of only whitespace.

```
class String
  def blank?
    self !~ /\S/
  end
end
```

B.63.3 `active_support/core_ext/string/access.rb`

B.63.3.1 `at(position)`

Returns the character at `position`, treating the string as an array (where 0 is the first character). Returns `nil` if the position exceeds the length of the string.

```
>> "hello".at(0)
=> "h"

>> "hello".at(4)
=> "o"

>> "hello".at(10)
=> nil
```

B.63.3.2 `first(number)`

Returns the first `number` of characters in a string.

```
"hello".first        # => "h"
"hello".first(2)     # => "he"
"hello".first(10)    # => "hello"
```

B.63.3.3 `from(position)`

Returns the remaining characters of a string from the `position,` treating the string as an array (where 0 is the first character). Returns `nil` if the position exceeds the length of the string.

```
"hello".at(0)   # => "hello"
"hello".at(2)   # => "llo"
"hello".at(10)  # => nil
```

B.63.3.4 `last(number)`

Returns the last `number` of characters in a string.

```
"hello".last        # => "o"
"hello".last(2)     # => "lo"
"hello".last(10)    # => "hello"
```

B.63.3.5 `to(position)`

Returns the beginning of the string up to the `position`, treating the string as an array (where 0 is the first character). Doesn't produce an error when the `position` exceeds the length of the string.

```
"hello".at(0)  # => "h"
"hello".at(2)   # => "hel"
"hello".at(10)   # => "hello"
```

B.63.4   `active_support/core_ext/string/` `conversions.rb`

B.63.4.1   `to_date`
Uses Date.parse to turn a string into a Date.

B.63.4.2   `to_datetime`
Uses Date.parse to turn a string into a DateTime.

B.63.4.3   `to_time(form = :local)`
Uses Date.parse to turn a string into a Time either using either :utc or :local (default).

B.63.5   `active_support/core_ext/string/exclude.rb`

B.63.5.1   `exclude?(other)`
The inverse of include?. Returns true if self does not include the other string.

B.63.6   `active_support/core_ext/string/filters.rb`

B.63.6.1   `remove(pattern)`
A convenience method for gsub(pattern, ''). It returns a new string with all occurrences of the pattern removed.

B.63.6.2   `remove!(pattern)`
Performs a destructive remove. See remove.

B.63.6.3   `squish`
Returns the string, first removing all whitespace on both ends of the string, and then changing remaining consecutive whitespace groups into one space each.

```
>> %{ Multi-line
   string }.squish
=> "Multi-line string"
>> " foo bar \n \t boo".squish
=> "foo bar boo"
```

B.63.6.4 `squish!`

Performs a destructive squish. See `squish`.

B.63.6.5 `truncate(length, options = )`

Truncates a given `text` after a given `length` if `text` is longer than `length`. The last characters will be replaced with the `:omission` (which defaults to "...") for a total length not exceeding `:length`.

Pass a `:separator` to truncate `text` at a natural break.

```
>> "Once upon a time in a world far far away".truncate(30)
=> "Once upon a time in a world..."

>> "Once upon a time in a world far far away".truncate(30, separator: ' ')
=> "Once upon a time in a world..."

>> "Once upon a time in a world far far away".truncate(14)
=> "Once upon a..."

>> "And they found that many people were sleeping better.".
      truncate(25, omission: "... (continued)")
=> "And they f... (continued)"
```

B.63.7 `active_support/core_ext/string/indent.rb`

B.63.7.1 `indent(amount, indent_string=nil, indent_empty_lines=false)`

Indents a string by the given `amount`.

```
>> "foo".indent(2)
=> " foo"

=> "foo\nbar"
>> " foo\n bar"
```

The second argument `indent_string` specifies what indent string to use. If no `indent_string` is specified, it will use the first indented line, otherwise a space is used. If `indent_empty_lines` is set to `true`, empty lines will also be indented.

B.63.7.2 `indent!`

Performs a destructive indent. See `indent`.

B.63.8 `active_support/core_ext/string/inflections.rb`

String inflections define new methods on the `String` class to transform names for different purposes. For instance, you can figure out the name of a database from the name of a class:

```
>> "ScaleScore".tableize
=> "scale_scores"
```

If you get frustrated by the limitations of Rails inflections, try the most excellent Linguistics library by Michael Granger at https://github.com/ged/linguistics. It doesn't do all of the same inflections as Rails, but the ones that it does do, it does better. (See `titleize` for an example.)

B.63.8.1 `camelcase`

Alias for `camelize`.

B.63.8.2 `camelize(first_letter = :upper)`

By default, `camelize` converts strings to UpperCamelCase. If the argument to `camelize` is set to `:lower`, then `camelize` produces lowerCamelCase. Also converts "/" to "::", which is useful for converting paths to namespaces.

```
>> "active_record".camelize
=> "ActiveRecord"

>> "active_record".camelize(:lower)
=> "activeRecord"

>> "active_record/errors".camelize
=> "ActiveRecord::Errors"
>> "active_record/errors".camelize(:lower)
=> "activeRecord::Errors"
```

B.63.8.3 `classify`

Creates a class name from a table name. Used by Active Record to turn table names to model classes. Note that the `classify` method returns a string and not a `Class`. (To convert to an actual class, follow `classify` with `constantize`.)

```
>> "egg_and_hams".classify
=> "EggAndHam"

>> "post".classify
=> "Post"
```

Active Support

B.63.8.4 `constantize`

The `constantize` method tries to find a declared constant with the name specified in the string. It raises a `NameError` if a matching constant is not located.

```
>> "Module".constantize
=> Module

>> "Class".constantize
=> Class
```

Also available in a `safe_constantize` version that returns `nil` instead of raising
`NameError`.

B.63.8.5 `dasherize`

Replaces underscores with dashes in the `string`.

```
>> "puni_puni"
=> "puni-puni"
```

B.63.8.6 `demodulize`

Removes the module prefixes from a fully qualified module or class name.

```
>> "ActiveRecord::CoreExtensions::String::Inflections".demodulize
=> "Inflections"

>> "Inflections".demodulize
=> "Inflections"
```

B.63.8.7 `foreign_key(separate_class_name_and_id_with_`
`underscore = true)`

Creates a foreign key name from a class name.

```
"Message".foreign_key # => "message_id"
"Message".foreign_key(false) # => "messageid"
"Admin::Post".foreign_key # => "post_id"
```

B.63.8.8 `humanize(options = {})`

Capitalizes the first word of a string, turns underscores into spaces, and strips `_id`.
Similar to the `titleize` method in that it is intended for creating pretty output.

```
>> "employee_salary".humanize
=> "Employee salary"
>> "author_id".humanize
=> "Author"
```

Setting the :capitalize option to false results in the string being humanized without being capitalized.

```
>> "employee_salary".humanize(capitalize: false)
=> "employee salary"
```

B.63.8.9 `parameterize(sep = '-')`
Replaces special characters in a string with sep string so that it may be used as part of a *pretty* URL.

B.63.8.10 `pluralize`
Returns the plural form of the word in the string.

```
"post".pluralize # => "posts"
"octopus".pluralize # => "octopi"
"sheep".pluralize # => "sheep"
"words".pluralize # => "words"
"the blue mailman".pluralize # => "the blue mailmen"
"CamelOctopus".pluralize # => "CamelOctopi"
```

B.63.8.11 `safe_constantize`
The safe_constantize method tries to find a declared constant with the name specified in the string. It returns nil when the name is not in CamelCase or is not initialized.

B.63.8.12 `singularize`
The reverse of pluralize; returns the singular form of a word in a string.

```
"posts".singularize # => "post"
"octopi".singularize # => "octopus"
"sheep".singularize # => "sheep"
"word".singularize # => "word"
"the blue mailmen".singularize # => "the blue mailman"
"CamelOctopi".singularize # => "CamelOctopus"
```

B.63.8.13 `tableize`
Creates a plural and underscored database table name based on Rails conventions. Used by Active Record to determine the proper table name for a model class. This method uses the pluralize method on the last word in the string.

```
"RawScaledScorer".tableize # => "raw_scaled_scorers"
"egg_and_ham".tableize # => "egg_and_hams"
"fancyCategory".tableize # => "fancy_categories"
```

Active
Support

B.63.8.14 `titlecase`
Alias for `titleize`.

B.63.8.15 `titleize`
Capitalizes all the words and replaces some characters in the string to create a nicer-looking title. The `titleize` method is meant for creating pretty output and is not used in the Rails internals.

```
>> "The light on the beach was like a sinus headache".titleize
=> "The Light On The Beach Was Like A Sinus Headache"
```

It's also not perfect. Among other things, it capitalizes words inside the sentence that it probably shouldn't, like "a" and "the" and "on".

B.63.8.16 `underscore`
The reverse of `camelize`. Makes an underscored form from the expression in the string. Changes "::" to "/" to convert namespaces to paths.

```
"ActiveRecord".underscore # => "active_record"
"ActiveRecord::Errors".underscore # => active_record/errors
```

B.63.9 `active_support/core_ext/string/inquiry.rb`
B.63.9.1 `inquiry`
Wraps the current string in the `ActiveSupport::StringInquirer` class, providing an elegant way to test for equality.

```
env = 'production'.inquiry
env.production? # => true
env.development? # => false
```

B.63.10 `active_support/core_ext/string/multibyte.rb`
Defines a mutibyte safe proxy for string methods.

B.63.10.1 `mb_chars`
The `mb_chars` method creates and returns an instance of `ActiveSupport::-Multibyte::Chars`, encapsulating the original string. A Unicode safe version of all the `String` methods is defined on the proxy class. If the proxy class doesn't respond to a certain method, it's forwarded to the encapsulated string.

```
>> name = 'Claus Müller'

>> name.reverse
=> "rell??M sualC"
```

```
>> name.length
=> 13

>> name.mb_chars.reverse.to_s
=> "rellüM sualC"
>> name.mb_chars.length
=> 12
```

All the methods on the Chars proxy that normally return a string will return a Chars object. This enables method chaining on the result of any of these methods.

```
>> name.mb_chars.reverse.length
=> 12
```

The Chars object tries to be as interchangeable with String objects as possible: sorting and comparing between String and Char work like expected. The bang! methods change the internal string representation in the Chars object. Interoperability problems can be resolved easily with a to_s call.

For more information about the methods defined on the Chars proxy see Active-Support::Multibyte::Chars. For information about how to change the default Multibyte behavior see ActiveSupport::Multibyte.

B.63.10.2 is_utf8?(suffix)
Returns true if the string has UTF-8 semantics, versus strings that are simply being used as byte streams.

B.63.11 active_support/core_ext/string/output_ safety.rb

B.63.11.1 html_safe
Returns an html-escaped version of self. See ERB::Util#html_escape for more information.

B.63.12 active_support/core_ext/string/starts_ ends_with.rb
Provides String with additional condition methods.

B.63.12.1 starts_with?(prefix)
Alias for start_with?.

B.63.12.2 `ends_with?(suffix)`

Alias for `end_with?`.

B.63.13 `active_support/core_ext/string/strip.rb`

B.63.13.1 `strip_heredoc`

Strips indentation in heredocs. For example,

```
if options[:usage]
  puts <<-USAGE.strip_heredoc
    This command does such and such.

    Supported options are:
      -h         This message
    ...
  USAGE
end
```

would cause the user to see the usage message aligned against the left margin.

B.63.14 `active_support/core_ext/string/in_time_zone.rb`

B.63.14.1 `in_time_zone(zone = ::Time.zone)`

Converts the string to a `TimeWithZone` in the current zone if `Time.zone` or `„,Time.zone_default` are set. Otherwise returns `String#to_time`.

B.64 `StringInquirer`

Wrapping a string in this class gives you a prettier way to test for equality. The value returned by `Rails.env` is wrapped in a `StringInquirer` object so instead of calling this:

```
Rails.env == "production"
```

you can call this:

```
Rails.env.production?
```

This class is really simple, so you only really want to do this with strings that contain no whitespace or special characters.

```
>> s = ActiveSupport::StringInquirer.new("obie")
=> "obie"
>> s.obie?
=> true
```

B.65 Subscriber

The `ActiveSupport::Subscriber` object is used to consume `Active-Support::Notifications`. The subscriber dispatches notifications to a registered object based on its given namespace.

For example, a subscriber could collect statistics about Active Record queries:

```
module ActiveRecord
  class StatsSubscriber < ActiveSupport::Subscriber
    def sql(event)
      Statsd.timing("sql.#{event.payload[:name]}", event.duration)
    end
  end
end
```

To attach a subscriber to a namespace, use the `attach_to` method.

```
ActiveRecord::StatsSubscriber.attach_to :active_record
```

B.66 TaggedLogging

Wraps any standard Logger object to provide tagging capabilities.

B.66.1 active_support/tagged_logger.rb

B.66.1.1 flush
Clear all tags and invoke the parent definition if it exists.

B.66.1.2 tagged(*tags, &block)
Prefix `tags` to each log message in the yielded block.

```
logger = ActiveSupport::TaggedLogging.new(Logger.new(STDOUT))
logger.tagged("tr5w") { logger.info "Stuff" } # [tr5w] Stuff
```

B.67 TestCase

Inheriting from `MiniTest::Unit::TestCase`, adds Rails specific testing methods and behavior.

B.67.1 active_support/test_case.rb

B.67.1.1 assert_no_match
Alias for `refute_match` for `Test::Unit` backwards compatibility.

B.67.1.2 `assert_not_empty`
Alias for `refute_empty` for `Test::Unit` backwards compatibility.

B.67.1.3 `assert_not_equal`
Alias for `refute_equal` for `Test::Unit` backwards compatibility.

B.67.1.4 `assert_not_in_delta`
Alias for `refute_in_delta` for `Test::Unit` backwards compatibility.

B.67.1.5 `assert_not_in_epsilon`
Alias for `refute_in_epsilon` for `Test::Unit` backwards compatibility.

B.67.1.6 `assert_not_includes`
Alias for `refute_includes` for `Test::Unit` backwards compatibility.

B.67.1.7 `assert_not_instance_of`
Alias for `refute_instance_of` for `Test::Unit` backwards compatibility.

B.67.1.8 `assert_not_kind_of`
Alias for `refute_kind_of` for `Test::Unit` backwards compatibility.

B.67.1.9 `assert_not_nil`
Alias for `refute_nil` for `Test::Unit` backwards compatibility.

B.67.1.10 `assert_not_operator`
Alias for `refute_operator` for `Test::Unit` backwards compatibility

B.67.1.11 `assert_not_predicate`
Alias for `refute_predicate` for `Test::Unit` backwards compatibility

B.67.1.12 `assert_not_respond_to`
Alias for `refute_respond_to` for `Test::Unit` backwards compatibility

B.67.1.13 `assert_not_same`
Alias for `refute_same` for `Test::Unit` backwards compatibility

B.67.1.14 `assert_nothing_raised(*args)`
Tests whether the block doesn't raise an exception.

B.67.1.15   `assert_raise`

Alias for `assert_raises` for `Test::Unit` backwards compatibility.

B.68   `Testing::Assertions`

B.68.1   `active_support/testing/assertions.rb`

Rails adds a number of assertions to the basic ones provided with `MiniTest`.

B.68.1.1   `assert_changes(expression, message = nil, from:, to:, &block)`

Asserts that the result of evaluating an expression is changed before and after invoking the passed in block.

```
assert_changes 'Status.all_good?' do
  post :create, params: { status: { ok: false } }
end
```

You can pass the block as a string to be evaluated in the context of the block. A lambda can be passed for the block as well.

```
assert_changes -> { Status.all_good? } do
  post :create, params: { status: { ok: false } }
end
```

The assertion is useful for testing side effects. The passed block can be anything that can be converted to string with `to_s`.

```
assert_changes :@object do
  @object = 42
end
```

The keyword arguments `:from` and `:to` can be given to specify the expected initial value and the expected value after the block was executed.

```
assert_changes :@object, from: nil, to: :foo do
  @object = :foo
end
```

An optional error message can be specified.

```
assert_changes -> { Status.all_good? }, 'Expected the status to be bad' do
  post :create, params: { status: { incident: true } }
end
```

Inverse version available as `assert_no_changes`.

B.68.1.2 `assert_difference(expressions, difference = 1, message = nil, &block)`

Tests whether a numeric difference in the return value of an expression is a result of what is evaluated in the yielded block. (Easier to demonstrate than to explain!)

The following example evaluates the expression `Article.count` and saves the result. Then it yields to the block, which will execute the `post :create` and return control to the `assert_difference` method. At that point, `Article.count` is evalaluated again, and the difference is asserted to be 1 (the default difference).

```
assert_difference 'Article.count' do
  post :create, article: {...}
end
```

Any arbitrary expression can be passed in and evaluated:

```
assert_difference 'assigns(:article).comments(:reload).size' do
  post :create, comment: {...}
end
```

Arbitrary difference values may be specified. The default is 1, but negative numbers are okay too:

```
assert_difference 'Article.count', -1 do
  post :delete, id: ...
end
```

An array of expressions can also be passed in—each will be evaluated:

```
assert_difference [ 'Article.count', 'Post.count' ], 2 do
  post :create, article: {...}
end
```

A lambda or a list of lambdas can be passed in and evaluated:

```
assert_difference ->{ Article.count }, 2 do
  post :create, article: {...}
end
```

```
assert_difference [->{ Article.count }, ->{ Post.count }], 2 do
  post :create, article: {...}
end
```

An error message can be specified:

```
assert_difference 'Article.count', -1, "Article should be destroyed" do
  post :delete, id: ...
end
```

B.68.1.3 `assert_no_difference(expressions, message = nil, &block)`

Tests that the return value of the supplied expression does not change as a result of what is evaluated in the yielded block.

```
assert_no_difference 'Article.count' do
  post :create, article: invalid_attributes
end
```

B.68.1.4 `assert_not(object, message = nil)`

Assert that an expression is not truthy.

```
assert_not nil          # => true
assert_not false        # => true
assert_not 'foo'        # => 'foo' is not nil or false
```

B.68.1.5 `assert_nothing_raised()`

Assertion that the block should not raise an exception. Passes if evaluated code in the yielded block raises no exception.

```
assert_nothing_raised do
  perform_service(param: 'no_exception')
end
```

B.68.2 `active_support/testing/declarative.rb`

B.68.2.1 `test(name, &block)`

Helper to define a test method using a String ala RSpec. Under the hood, it replaces spaces with underscores and defines the test method.

```
test "verify something" do
  ...
end
```

B.68.3 `active_support/testing/file_fixtures.rb`

Adds simple access to sample files called file fixtures. File fixtures are normal files stored in `ActiveSupport::TestCase.file_fixture_path`.

File fixtures are represented as `Pathname` objects. This makes it easy to extract specific information:

```
file_fixture("example.txt").read # get the file's content
file_fixture("example.mp3").size # get the file size
```

Active
Support

B.68.3.1 `file_fixture(fixture_name)`

Returns a Pathname to the fixture file named `fixture_name`. Raises `Argument-Error` if it can't be found.

B.68.4 `active_support/testing/setup_and_teardown.rb`

Adds support for setup and teardown callbacks. These callbacks serve as a replacement to overwriting the #setup and #teardown methods of your TestCase.

```
class ExampleTest < ActiveSupport::TestCase
  setup do
    # ...
  end

  teardown do
    # ...
  end
end
```

B.68.5 `active_support/testing/time_helpers.rb`

Mostly eliminates the need for third-party time management gems such as TimeCop.[6]

B.68.5.1 `travel(duration, &block)`

Changes the current time to the time in the future or in the past by a given time difference. This is accomplished by stubbing `Time.now` and `Date.today`.

```
Time.current # => Sat, 09 Nov 2013 15:34:49 EST -05:00
travel 1.day
Time.current # => Sun, 10 Nov 2013 15:34:49 EST -05:00
Date.current # => Sun, 10 Nov 2013
```

B.68.5.2 `travel_to(date_or_time, &block)`

Changes the current time to the supplied date or time. This is accomplished by stubbing `Time.now` and `Date.today`.

B.69 Thread

Extensions to Ruby's built-in `Thread` class.

B.69.1 `active_support/core_ext/thread.rb`

B.69.1.1 `freeze`

Freeze thread local variables.

---

6. https://github.com/travisjeffery/timecop

B.69.1.2 `thread_variable?(key)`

Returns `true` if the given string (or symbol) exists as a thread local variable.

```
>> current_thread = Thread.current
=> #<Thread:0x007fd2c08c0da8 run>

>> current_thread.thread_variable?(:tr5w)
=> false

>> current_thread.thread_variable_set(:tr5w, 'is awesome')
=> "is awesome"

>> current_thread.thread_variable?(:tr5w)
=> true
```

B.69.1.3 `thread_variable_get(key)`

Returns the value of a thread local variable that has been set.

B.69.1.4 `thread_variable_set(key, value)`

Set a thread local variable .

```
>> Thread.current.thread_variable_set(:tr5w, 'is awesome')
=> "is awesome"
```

B.69.1.5 `thread_variables`

Returns an array of thread local variables represented as symbols.

```
>> Thread.current.thread_variables
=> [:tr5w]
```

B.70 Time

Extensions to Ruby's built-in `Time` class.

B.70.1 `active_support/json/encoding.rb`

B.70.1.1 `as_json`

Returns `self` as a JSON string. The `ActiveSupport.use_standard_json_time_format` configuration setting determines whether the output is formatted using `:xmlschema` or the following pattern:

```
%(#{strftime("%Y/%m/%d %H:%M:%S")} #{formatted_offset(false)})
```

```
>> Time.now.as_json
=> "2017-06-14T12:43:36.881-04:00"
```

B.70.2 `active_support/core_ext/time/acts_like.rb`

Duck-types as a Time-like class. See `Object#acts_like?` for more explanation.

```
class Time
  def acts_like_time?
    true
  end
end
```

B.70.3 `active_support/core_ext/time/calculations.rb`

Contains methods that facilitate time calculations.

B.70.3.1 `===(other)`

Overriding case equality method so that it returns `true` for `ActiveSupport::-TimeWithZone` instances.

B.70.3.2 `+ (other)`

Implemented by the `plus_with_duration` method. Enables addition of times like this:

```
expiration_time = Time.now + 3.days
```

B.70.3.3 `- (other)`

Implemented by the `minus_with_duration` method. Enables addition of times like this:

```
two_weeks_ago = Time.now - 2.weeks
```

B.70.3.4 `<=>`

Implemented by the `compare_with_coercion` method. Layers additional behavior on `Time#eql?` so that `ActiveSupport::TimeWithZone` instances can be compared with `Time` instances.

B.70.3.5 `advance(options)`

Provides precise `Time` calculations. The `options` parameter takes a hash with any of the keys `:months`, `:days`, `:years`, `:hours`, `:minutes`, and `:seconds`.

B.70.3.6 `ago(seconds)`

Returns a new `Time` representing the time a number of seconds into the past; this is basically a wrapper around the `Numeric` extension of the same name. For the best accuracy, do not use this method in combination with `x.months`; use `months_ago` instead!

B.70.3.7   `all_day`

Convenience method for `beginning_of_day..end_of_day`. Returns a Range representing the whole day of the current time.

B.70.3.8   `all_month`

Convenience method for `beginning_of_month..end_of_month`. Returns a Range representing the whole month of the current time.

B.70.3.9   `all_quarter`

Convenience method for `beginning_of_quarter..end_of_quarter`. Returns a Range representing the whole quarter of the current time.

B.70.3.10   `all_week(start_day = Date.beginning_of_week)`

Convenience method for `beginning_of_week(start_day)..end_of_week(start_day)`. Returns a Range representing the whole week of the current time.

B.70.3.11   `all_year`

Convenience method for `beginning_of_year..end_of_year`. Returns a Range representing the whole year of the current time.

B.70.3.12   `at_beginning_of_day` / `at_midnight` / `beginning_of_day` / `midnight`

Returns a new `Time` object representing the "start" of the current instance's day, hard-coded to 00:00 hours.

B.70.3.13   `at_beginning_of_hour` / `beginning_of_hour`

Returns a new `Time` object representing the start of the hour (hh:00:00). Implemented simply as `change(min: 0)`.

B.70.3.14   `at_beginning_of_minute` / `beginning_of_minute`

Returns a new `Time` object representing the start of the minute (hh:mm:00). Implemented simply as `change(sec: 0)`.

B.70.3.15 `at_beginning_of_quarter` / `beginning_of_quarter`

Returns a new `Time` object representing the start of the calendar quarter (1st of January, April, July, October, 00:00 hours).

B.70.3.16 `at_beginning_of_week`

Alias for `beginning_of_week`.

B.70.3.17 `at_beginning_of_year` / `beginning_of_year`

Returns a new `Time` object representing the start of the year (1st of January, 00:00 hours).

B.70.3.18 `at_end_of_day` / `end_of_day`

Returns a new `Time` object representing the end of a day (23:59:59). Implemented simply as `change(hour: 23, min: 59, sec: 59)`.

B.70.3.19 `at_end_of_hour` / `end_of_hour`

Returns a new `Time` object representing the end of the hour (hh:59:59). Implemented simply as `change(min: 59, sec: 59)`.

B.70.3.20 `at_end_of_minute` / `end_of_minute`

Returns a new `Time` object representing the end of the minute (hh:mm:59). Implemented simply as `change(sec: 59)`.

B.70.3.21 `at_end_of_month` / `end_of_month`

Returns a new `Time` object representing the end of the month (last day of the month at 23:59:59 hours).

B.70.3.22 `at_end_of_quarter` / `end_of_quarter`

Returns a new `Time` object representing the end of the quarter (31st March, 30th June, 30th September, 31st December, at 23:59:59 hours)

B.70.3.23 `at_end_of_week`

Alias for `end_of_week`.

B.70.3.24 `at_end_of_year` / `end_of_year`

Returns a new `Time` object representing the end of the year (last day of the year at 23:59:59 hours).

B.70.3.25 beginning_of_week(start_day = Date.beginning _of_week)

Returns a new Time object representing the "start" of the current instance's week, defaulting to Date.beginning_of_week.

B.70.3.26 change(options)

Returns a new Time where one or more of the elements have been changed according to the options parameter. The valid date options are :year, :month, :day. The valid time options are :hour, :min, :sec, :offset, and :start.

B.70.3.27 Time.current

Returns Time.zone.now when Time.zone or config.time_zone are set, otherwise returns Time.now.

B.70.3.28 days_ago(days)

Returns a new Time object, minus the specified number of days.

B.70.3.29 Time.days_in_month(month, year = nil)

Returns the number of days in the given month. If a year is given, February will return the correct number of days for leap years. Otherwise, this method will always report February as having 28 days.

```
>> Time.days_in_month(7, 1974)
=> 31
```

B.70.3.30 days_since(days)

Returns a new Time object representing the time a number of specified days into the future.

B.70.3.31 days_to_week_start(start_day = Date.beginning_ of_week)

Returns the number of days to the start of the week.

B.70.3.32 end_of_week(start_day = Date.beginning_of_week)

Returns a new Time object representing the "end" of the current instance's week, with the week start_day defaulting to Date.beginning_of_week.

B.70.3.33 future?

Returns true if the Time instance is in the future.

B.70.3.34 `middle_of_day` / `noon`

Returns a new `Time` object representing the middle of the day (12:00:00). Implemented simply as `change(hour: 12)`.

B.70.3.35 `last_month` / `prev_month`

Convenience method for `months_ago(1)`.

B.70.3.36 `last_quarter` / `prev_quarter`

Convenience method for `months_ago(3)`.

B.70.3.37 `last_week(start_day = Date.beginning_of_week)` / `prev_week`

Returns a new `Time` object representing the given day in the previous week, with the week `start_day` defaulting to `Date.beginning_of_week`.

B.70.3.38 `last_year` / `prev_year`

Convenience method for `years_ago(1)`.

B.70.3.39 `monday`

Convenience method for `beginning_of_week(:monday)`.

B.70.3.40 `months_ago(months)`

Returns a new `Time` object representing the time a number of specified `months` into the past.

B.70.3.41 `months_since(months)`

The opposite of `months_ago`. Returns a new `Time` object representing the time a number of specified `months` into the future.

B.70.3.42 `next_month`

Convenience method for `months_since(1)`.

B.70.3.43 `next_quarter`

Convenience method for `months_since(3)`.

B.70.3.44 `next_week(given_day_in_next_week =` `Date.beginning_of_week)`

Returns a new `Time` object representing the start of the given day in the following calendar week.

B.70.3.45 `next_year`

Convenience method for `years_since(1)`.

B.70.3.46 `seconds_since_midnight`

Returns the number of seconds that have transpired since midnight.

B.70.3.47 `seconds_until_end_of_day`

Returns how many seconds left in the day until 23:59:59.

B.70.3.48 `since(seconds) / in(seconds)`

Returns a new `Time` representing the time a number of `seconds` into the future starting from the instance time. This method is basically a wrapper around the `Numeric` extension of the same name. For best accuracy, do not use this method in combination with x.`months`; use `months_since` instead!

B.70.3.49 `sunday`

Convenience method for `end_of_week(:monday)`.

B.70.3.50 `today?`

Returns `true` if the `Time` is today.

B.70.3.51 `tomorrow`

Returns a new `Time` object advanced by one day.

B.70.3.52 `weeks_ago(weeks)`

Returns a new `Time` object representing the time a number of specified weeks ago.

B.70.3.53 `weeks_since(weeks)`

Returns a new `Time` object representing the time a number of specified weeks into the future.

Active Support

B.70.3.54 `years_ago(years)`

Returns a new `Time` object representing the time a number of specified `years` into the past.

B.70.3.55 `years_since(years)`

The opposite of `years_ago`. Returns a new `Time` object representing the time a number of specified `years` into the future.

B.70.3.56 `yesterday`

Returns a new `Time` object subtracted by one day.

B.70.4 `active_support/core_ext/time/conversions.rb`

Extensions to Ruby's `Time` class to convert time objects into different convenient string representations and other objects.

B.70.5 `DATE_FORMATS`

The `DATE_FORMATS` hash constant holds formatting patterns used by the `to_formatted_s` method to convert a `Time` object into a string representation:

```
DATE_FORMATS = {
  :db            => '%Y-%m-%d %H:%M:%S',
  :number        => '%Y%m%d%H%M%S',
  :nsec          => '%Y%m%d%H%M%S%9N',
  :time          => '%H:%M',
  :short         => '%d %b %H:%M',
  :long          => '%B %d, %Y %H:%M',
  :long_ordinal => lambda { |time|
    day_format = ActiveSupport::Inflector.ordinalize(time.day)
    time.strftime("%B #{day_format}, %Y %H:%M")
  },
  :rfc822        => lambda { |time|
    offset_format = time.formatted_offset(false)
    time.strftime("%a, %d %b %Y %H:%M:%S #{offset_format}")
  }
}
```

B.70.5.1 `formatted_offset(colon = true, alternate_utc_string = nil)`

Returns the UTC offset as an `HH:MM` formatted string.

```
Time.local(2000).formatted_offset          # => "-06:00"
Time.local(2000).formatted_offset(false)   # => "-0600"
```

B.70.5.2 `to_formatted_s(format = :default)`

Converts a `Time` object into a string representation. The `:default` option corresponds to the `Time` object's own `to_s` method.

```
>> time = Time.now
=> Thu Jan 18 06:10:17 CST 2007

>> time.to_formatted_s(:time)
=> "06:10"

>> time.to_formatted_s(:db)
=> "2007-01-18 06:10:17"

>> time.to_formatted_s(:number)
=> "20070118061017"

>> time.to_formatted_s(:short)
=> "18 Jan 06:10"

>> time.to_formatted_s(:long)
=> "January 18, 2007 06:10"

>> time.to_formatted_s(:long_ordinal)
=> "January 18th, 2007 06:10"

>> time.to_formatted_s(:rfc822)
=> "Thu, 18 Jan 2007 06:10:17 -0600"
```

B.70.5.3 `to_s`

Aliased to `to_formatted_s`.

B.70.6 `active_support/core_ext/time/marshal.rb`

Rails layers behavior on the `_dump` and `_load` methods so that utc instances can be flagged on dump and coerced back to utc on load.

Ruby 1.9.2 adds `utc_offset` and zone to `Time`, but marshaling only preserves `utc_offset`. Rails preserves zone also, even though it may not work in some edge cases.

B.70.7 `active_support/core_ext/time/zones.rb`

Extensions to `Time` having to do with support for time zones.

B.70.7.1 `find_zone(time_zone)`

Returns a `TimeZone` instance or `nil` if it does not exist.

```
>> Time.find_zone("Eastern Time (US & Canada)")
=> #<ActiveSupport::TimeZone:0x007fd2c0bc49c8
   @name="Eastern Time (US & Canada)", ...>
```

B.70.7.2 `find_zone!(time_zone)`

Same as `find_zone`, except it raises an `ArgumentError` if an invalid `time_zone` is provided.

B.70.7.3 `in_time_zone(zone = ::Time.zone)`

Returns the simultaneous time in the supplied `zone`.

```
>> Time.zone = 'Hawaii'
=> "Hawaii"
>> Time.utc(2000).in_time_zone
=> Fri, 31 Dec 1999 14:00:00 HST -10:00
```

B.70.7.4 `use_zone(time_zone, &block)`

Enables override of `Time.zone` locally inside supplied block; resets `Time.zone` to existing value when done.

```
>> Date.today
=> Wed, 02 Jun 2010

>> Time.use_zone(ActiveSupport::TimeZone['Hong Kong']) { Date.today }
=> Thu, 03 Jun 2010
```

B.70.7.5 `zone`

Returns the `TimeZone` for the current request, if this has been set (via `Time.zone=`). If `Time.zone` has not been set for the current request, returns the `TimeZone` specified in `config.time_zone`.

B.70.7.6 `zone=(time_zone)`

Sets `Time.zone` to a `TimeZone` object for the current request/thread. This method accepts any of the following:

- A Rails `TimeZone` object.
- An identifier for a Rails `TimeZone` object (e.g., "Eastern Time (US & Canada)", `-5.hours`).
- A `TZInfo::Timezone` object.
- An identifier for a `TZInfo::Timezone` object (e.g., "America/New_York").

Here's an example of how you might set `Time.zone` on a per request basis. The code assumes that `current_user.time_zone` returns a string identifying the user's preferred `TimeZone`:

```
class ApplicationController < ActionController::Base
  before_action :set_time_zone

  def set_time_zone
    Time.zone = current_user.time_zone
  end
end
```

B.71 TimeWithZone

A `Time`-like class that can represent a time in any time zone. Necessary because standard Ruby `Time` instances are limited to UTC and the system's `ENV['TZ']` zone.

You shouldn't ever need to create a `TimeWithZone` instance directly via `new`. Rails provides the methods `local`, `parse`, `at`, and `now` on `TimeZone` instances, and `in_time_zone` on `Time` and `DateTime` instances, for a more user-friendly syntax.

```
>> Time.zone = 'Eastern Time (US & Canada)'
=> 'Eastern Time (US & Canada)'

>> Time.zone.local(2007, 2, 10, 15, 30, 45)
=> Sat, 10 Feb 2007 15:30:45 EST -05:00

>> Time.zone.parse('2007-02-01 15:30:45')
=> Sat, 10 Feb 2007 15:30:45 EST -05:00

>> Time.zone.at(1170361845)
=> Sat, 10 Feb 2007 15:30:45 EST -05:00

>> Time.zone.now
=> Sun, 18 May 2008 13:07:55 EDT -04:00

>> Time.utc(2007, 2, 10, 20, 30, 45).in_time_zone
=> Sat, 10 Feb 2007 15:30:45 EST -05:00
```

`TimeWithZone` instances implement the same API as Ruby `Time` instances, so that `Time` and `TimeWithZone` instances are interchangeable. See `Time` and `Active-Support::TimeZone` for further documentation of these methods.

```
>> t = Time.zone.now
=> Sun, 18 May 2008 13:27:25 EDT -04:00
```

Active
Support

```
>> t.class
=> ActiveSupport::TimeWithZone

>> t.hour
=> 13

>> t.dst?
=> true

>> t.utc_offset
=> -14400

>> t.zone
=> "EDT"

>> t.to_s(:rfc822)
=> "Sun, 18 May 2008 13:27:25 -0400"

>> t + 1.day
=> Mon, 19 May 2008 13:27:25 EDT -04:00

>> t.beginning_of_year
=> Tue, 01 Jan 2008 00:00:00 EST -05:00

>> t > Time.utc(1999)
=> true

>> t.is_a?(Time)
=> true
```

B.72 `TimeZone`

The `TimeZone` class serves as a wrapper around `TZInfo::Timezone` instances. It enables Rails to do the following:

- Limit the set of zones provided by `TZInfo` to a meaningful subset of 146 zones

- Retrieve and display zones with a friendlier name (e.g., "Eastern Time (US & Canada)" instead of "America/New_York")

- Lazily load `TZInfo::Timezone` instances only when they're needed

- Create `ActiveSupport::TimeWithZone` instances via TimeZone's `local`, `parse`, `at`, and `now` methods.

If you set `config.time_zone` in an initializer, you can access this `TimeZone` object via `Time.zone`:

```
config.time_zone = "Eastern Time (US & Canada)"

Time.zone        # => #<TimeZone:0x514834...>
Time.zone.name   # => "Eastern Time (US & Canada)"
Time.zone.now    # => Sun, 18 May 2008 14:30:44 EDT -04:00
```

B.72.1 `active_support/values/time_zone.rb`

The version of `TZInfo` bundled with Active Support only includes the definitions necessary to support the zones defined by the `TimeZone` class. If you need to use zones that aren't defined by `TimeZone`, you'll need to install the `TZInfo` gem. If a recent version of the gem is installed locally, this will be used instead of the bundled version.

This file also contains the mapping of Rails time zones to `TZInfo` identifiers as a hash assigned to `MAPPING`.

B.72.1.1 `<=> (other)`

Compares this timezone to the parameter. The two are compared first based on their offsets and then by name.

B.72.1.2 `=~(re)`

Compare name and `TZInfo` identifier to a supplied regexp. Returns `true` if a match is found.

B.72.1.3 `TimeZone[] (arg)`

Locates a specific timezone object. If the argument is a string, it is interpreted to mean the name of the timezone to locate.

```
>> ActiveSupport::TimeZone['Dublin']
=> #<TimeZone:0x3208390 @name="Dublin", @utc_offset=nil ...>
```

If it is a numeric value it is either the hour offset, or the second offset, of the timezone to find. (The first one with that offset will be returned.)

Returns `nil` if no such timezone is known to the system.

B.72.1.4 `TimeZone.all`

Returns an array of all 146 `TimeZone` objects. There are multiple `TimeZone` objects per timezone (in many cases) to make it easier for users to find their own timezone.

```
>> ActiveSupport::TimeZone.all
=> [#<ActiveSupport::TimeZone:0x551c34...
```

B.72.1.5 `at(seconds)`

Creates a new `ActiveSupport::TimeWithZone` instance in time zone of `self` from the number of seconds since the Unix epoch.

```
Time.zone = 'Hawaii'         # => "Hawaii"
Time.utc(2000).to_f          # => 946684800.0
Time.zone.at(946684800.0)    # => Fri, 31 Dec 1999 14:00:00 HST -10:00
```

B.72.1.6 `TimeZone.create(name, offset)`

Creates a new `TimeZone` instance with the given name and offset.

```
>> ActiveSupport::TimeZone.create("Atlanta", -5.hours)
=> #<ActiveSupport::TimeZone:0x007fd2c136b118 @name="Atlanta",
    @utc_offset=-18000 seconds, @tzinfo=#<TZInfo::TimezoneProxy: Atlanta>,
    @current_period=nil>
```

B.72.1.7 `TimeZone.find_tzinfo(name)`

Returns a `TZInfo` instance matching the specified `name`.

B.72.1.8 `formatted_offset(colon=true, alternate_utc_string = nil)`

Returns the offset of this timezone as a formatted string, in the format `HH:MM`. If the `offset` is zero, this method will return an empty string. If `colon` is `false`, a colon will not be inserted into the output.

B.72.1.9 `initialize(name, utc_offset = nil, tzinfo = nil)`

Create a new `TimeZone` object with the given `name` and `offset`. The `offset` is the number of seconds that this time zone is offset from UTC (GMT). Seconds were chosen as the offset unit because that is the unit that Ruby uses to represent time zone offsets (see `Time#utc_offset`). The `tzinfo` parameter can be explicitly passed in, otherwise the `name` will be used to find it: `TimeZone.find_tzinfo(name)`.

B.72.1.10 `local(*args)`

Creates a new `ActiveSupport::TimeWithZone` instance in time zone of `self` from given values.

B.72.1.11   `local_to_utc(time, dst=true)`

Adjusts the given time to the simultaneous time in UTC. Returns a `Time.utc()` instance.

B.72.1.12   `now`

Returns `Time.now` adjusted to this timezone.

```
>> Time.now
=> 2013-10-16 17:45:49 -0400
>> ActiveSupport::TimeZone['Hawaii'].now
=> Wed, 16 Oct 2013 11:46:05 HST -10:00
```

B.72.1.13   `parse(str, now=now)`

Creates a new `ActiveSupport::TimeWithZone` instance in time zone of `self` from parsed string.

```
>> Time.zone = 'Hawaii'
=> "Hawaii"
>> Time.zone.parse('1999-12-31 14:00:00')
=> Fri, 31 Dec 1999 14:00:00 HST -10:00
```

B.72.1.14   `period_for_local(time, dst=true)`

Method exists so that `TimeZone` instances respond like `TZInfo::Timezone`.

B.72.1.15   `period_for_utf(time)`

Method exists so that `TimeZone` instances respond like `TZInfo::Timezone`.

B.72.1.16   `TimeZone.seconds_to_utc_offset(seconds, colon = true)`

Assumes `self` represents an offset from UTC in seconds (as returned from `Time#utc_offset`) and turns this into a +HH:MM formatted string.

```
ActiveSupport::TimeZone.seconds_to_utc_offset(-21_600) # => "-06:00"
```

B.72.1.17   `to_s`

Returns a textual representation of this timezone.

```
ActiveSupport::TimeZone['Dublin'].to_s     # => "(GMT+00:00) Dublin"
```

B.72.1.18   `today`

Returns the current date in this timezone.

```
>> Date.today
=> Wed, 16 Oct 2013
>> ActiveSupport::TimeZone['Darwin'].today
=> Thu, 17 Oct 2013
```

B.72.1.19 `TimeZone.us_zones`

A convenience method for returning a collection of `TimeZone` objects for timezones in the USA.

```
>> ActiveSupport::TimeZone.us_zones.map(&:name)
=> ["Hawaii", "Alaska", "Pacific Time (US & Canada)", "Arizona",
"Mountain Time (US & Canada)", "Central Time (US & Canada)", "Eastern
Time (US & Canada)", "Indiana (East)"]
```

B.72.1.20 `utc_offset`

Returns the offset of this time zone from UTC in seconds.

B.72.1.21 `utc_to_local(time)`

Adjust the given time to the simultaneous time in the timezone.

B.73 `TrueClass`

B.73.1 `active_support/core_ext/object/blank.rb`

B.73.1.1 `blank?`

Returns `false`.

B.73.2 `active_support/json/encoding.rb`

B.73.2.1 `as_json`

Returns `true`.

B.74 `XmlMini`

The `XmlMini` module contains code that enables Rails to serialize/deserialize and parse XML using a number of different libraries.

- JDOM (requires JRuby)
- LibXML (fast native XML parser)
- Nokogiri (requires `nokogiri` gem)

B.74.1 `active_support/xml_mini.rb`

If you're doing anything of significance with XML in your application, you should definitely use the super-fast native `libxml` parser. Install the binaries (instructions vary depending on platform), then the Ruby binding:

```
gem 'libxml-ruby', '=0.9.7'
```

Set XmlMini to use `libxml` in `application.rb` or an initializer.

```
XmlMini.backend = 'LibXML'
```

B.74.2 Constants

The `TYPE_NAMES` constant holds a mapping of Ruby types to their representation when serialized as XML.

```
TYPE_NAMES = {
  "Symbol"      => "symbol",
  "Fixnum"      => "integer",
  "Bignum"      => "integer",
  "BigDecimal"  => "decimal",
  "Float"       => "float",
  "TrueClass"   => "boolean",
  "FalseClass"  => "boolean",
  "Date"        => "date",
  "DateTime"    => "dateTime",
  "Time"        => "dateTime",
  "Array"       => "array",
  "Hash"        => "hash"
}
```

The `FORMATTING` constant holds a mapping of lambdas that define how Ruby values are serialized to strings for representation in XML.

```
FORMATTING = {
  "symbol"      => Proc.new { |symbol| symbol.to_s },
  "date"        => Proc.new { |date| date.to_s(:db) },
  "dateTime"    => Proc.new { |time| time.xmlschema },
  "binary"      => Proc.new { |binary| ::Base64.encode64(binary) },
  "yaml"        => Proc.new { |yaml| yaml.to_yaml }
}
```

The `PARSING` constant holds a mapping of lambdas used to deserialize values stored in XML back into Ruby objects.

```
PARSING = {
  "symbol"        => Proc.new { |symbol| symbol.to_sym },
```

```
  "date"           => Proc.new { |date| ::Date.parse(date) },
  "datetime"       => Proc.new {
    |time| Time.xmlschema(time).utc rescue ::DateTime.parse(time).utc },
  "integer"        => Proc.new { |integer| integer.to_i },
  "float"          => Proc.new { |float|    float.to_f },
  "decimal"        => Proc.new { |number|      BigDecimal(number) },
  "boolean"        => Proc.new {
    |boolean| %w(1 true).include?(boolean.strip) },
  "string"         => Proc.new { |string|    string.to_s },
  "yaml"           => Proc.new { |yaml|    YAML::load(yaml) rescue yaml },
  "base64Binary"   => Proc.new { |bin|       ::Base64.decode64(bin) },
  "binary"         => Proc.new { |bin, entity| _parse_binary(bin, entity) },
  "file"           => Proc.new { |file, entity| _parse_file(file, entity) }
}


PARSING.update(
  "double"       => PARSING["float"],
  "dateTime"     => PARSING["datetime"]
)
```

Appendix C

Rails API

> I kind of somehow get carried away sometimes, and get fired up about integrated software, but at the same time, if [microservices is] what you want to do, if that floats your boat, fantastic! Rails 5 [is] the mother of frameworks for microservices. Woo-hoo!!! If you wanna use Rails to make that setup and have a lot of different things that derive off of one API base and its really neat and structured that's wonderful, we're gonna bake it into Rails 5 and you're gonna love it on day 5 and you're gonna hate it on Year 2, but it's all good because in the meantime you won't be blaming me, and umm, we can still work together! That's the thing I really love about the Ruby and the Rails community—even if we feel so passionate about certain things, and I feel so passionate about the majestic monolith and integrated software, I can also think: "That's fine, but if someone wants to collaborate on Active Record, I don't give a hoot what deity they pray to at night, whether it's the altar of microservices or the 'one true monolith', we can still work together and it can still be wonderful."
>
> —DHH—2015 Railsconf Keynote, https://youtu.be/KJVTM7mE1Cc?t=25m12s

First, let's review some context and history. It's become incredibly popular in the last few years to write rich client applications using React or Angular (instead of just JavaScript-enriched, server-rendered HTML). These kinds of projects still need application server backends but dispense with the need for server-based view templating and a whole lot of the kind of controller logic that goes into more traditional web applications.

Taken a step further, these rich client applications may not even have a monolithic backend anymore, instead being *serverless* (one of my favorite topics, actually[1]) or

---

1. http://leanpub.com/serverless

943

relying on a constellation of *microservices* that provide functionally isolated chunks of business logic, communications, and data persistence.

C.1 Rails API Mode

Now Rails is undoubtedly the king of traditional web applications, but even I have to admit that it has lost mindshare for newer architecture patterns to competing technologies such Node.js and others. That's why DHH, despite his avowed aversion to these trends, used a chunk of his 2015 Railsconf keynote to announce a new feature called Rails API Mode—easy bootstrapping of applications meant to function as microservices.

Want to see what the fuss is about? Invoke API mode by adding an `--api` flag to the main Rails generator command.

```
$ rails new microservice --api
```

The generated application will be configured to start with a more limited set of middleware than usual. It leaves out middleware meant for browser applications (like cookies support).

```
$ rails middleware
use Rack::Sendfile
use ActionDispatch::Static
use ActionDispatch::Executor
use ActiveSupport::Cache::Strategy::LocalCache::Middleware
use Rack::Runtime
use ActionDispatch::RequestId
use Rails::Rack::Logger
use ActionDispatch::ShowExceptions
use ActionDispatch::DebugExceptions
use ActionDispatch::RemoteIp
use ActionDispatch::Reloader
use ActionDispatch::Callbacks
use ActiveRecord::Migration::CheckPending
use Rack::Head
use Rack::ConditionalGet
use Rack::ETag
run Microservice::Application.routes
```

Signficantly, `ApplicationController` will inherit from `ActionController::API` instead of `ActionController::Base`, again leaving out functionality that is primarily meant for traditional web applications.

```
class ApplicationController < ActionController::API
end
```

Finally, the generators will default to skipping creation of view templates, helpers, and assets whenever you generate a new resource.

```
$ rails g resource Purchase total_cents:integer status shipping_address:text
Expected string default value for '--jbuilder'; got true (boolean)
     invoke  active_record
     create    db/migrate/20170214004746_create_purchases.rb
     create    app/models/purchase.rb
     invoke    rspec
     create      spec/models/purchase_spec.rb
     invoke      factory_girl
     create        spec/factories/purchases.rb
     invoke  controller
     create    app/controllers/purchases_controller.rb
     invoke    rspec
     create      spec/controllers/purchases_controller_spec.rb
     invoke  resource_route
      route    resources :purchases
```

C.1.1   Serving JSON by Default

The term *media type* in the HTTP 1.1 specification is what we refer to as format in Rails. If the Rails router is not provided with a format (i.e., .html or .json), it will usually pick HTML. However, a request that doesn't specify a format in Rails API mode will get served JSON by default. It's one of the bigger differences between the two modes.

C.2   JSON

The dominant *lingua franca* of single-page applications and microservices is undoubtedly JSON (JavaScript Object Notation). Thanks to the work of Ruby Heroes such as Steve Klabnik and Yehuda Katz, it even has its own API specification.

> JSON API is a specification for how a client should request that resources be fetched or modified, and how a server should respond to those requests.
>
> JSON API is designed to minimize both the number of requests and the amount of data transmitted between clients and servers. This efficiency is achieved without compromising readability, flexibility, or discoverability.[2]

Adopting the JSON API specification on your project gives you a set of conventions to work with so that you don't have to invent them yourself and is highly recommended.

Of course, creating JSON API-based applications means needing to generate JSON. There are two major options available: Jbuilder and, of course, creating JSON API-based applications means needing to generate JSON and Active-Model Serializers.

---

2. "Introduction," http://jsonapi.org/format/

Rails API

C.2.1   Jbuilder

Rails API nudges you in the direction of its sister project: Jbuilder (https://github
.com/rails/jbuilder). Note that it's included in the boilerplate Gemfile but commented out.

```
# Use Puma as the app server
gem 'puma', '~> 3.0'
# Build JSON APIs with ease. Read more: https://github.com/rails/jbuilder
# gem 'jbuilder', '~> 2.5'
```

Uncomment and bundle to enable the generation of JSON data structures using a
Ruby-based domain-specific language (DSL). You can use the DSL directly in your
Ruby code or to write templates in the `app/views` directory tree, much as you
would do in a normal Rails application.

Here's what a template looks like:

```
# app/views/messages/show.json.jbuilder
json.(auction, :final_price_cents, :created_at, :updated_at)

json.item do
  json.name auction.item.name
  json.url url_for(auction.item, format: :json)
end

json.number_of_bids auction.bids.count

json.bids auction.bids, :bid_amount, :created_at
```

You might be wondering about that weird "dot-parens" syntax used in
Jbuilder. It's shorthand syntax for `Proc#call`. See http://stackoverflow
.com/questions/19108550/how-does-rubys-operator-work for more information about it.

The preceding sample code would generate JSON looking something like this:

```
{
  "final_price": 12400,
  "created_at": "2011-10-29T20:45:28-05:00",
  "updated_at": "2011-10-29T20:45:28-05:00",

  "item": {
    "name": "Beats by DRE (2014 Edition, Red)",
    "url": "http://example.com/items/7305434b2308-beats-by-dre.json"
  },
```

```
  "number_of_bids": 15,

  "bids": [
    { "bid_amount_cents": 12400, "created_at": "2011-10-
        29T20:45:28-05:00" },
    { "bid_amount_cents": 3400, "created_at": "2011-10-
        29T20:47:28-05:00" },
    ... // and so on
  ],
}
```

Top-level, unnamed arrays can be handled directly in a way that's useful for index and other collection actions.

```
json.array! comments do |c|
  next if c.marked_as_spam_by?(current_user)

  json.body markdown(c.body)
  json.author do
    json.first_name c.author.first_name
    json.last_name c.author.last_name
  end
end
```

 # ⇒ [{ "body": "great post...", "author": { "first_name": "Joe", "last_name": "Bloe" }}]

🔧 The use of `markdown` to transform `c.body` in the preceding example illustrates that it's possible to call helper methods, just like you would in a regular Rails view template.

C.2.1.1 Partials

Continuing the similarities to view templates, Jbuilder gives you the capability to break complicated JSON rendering tasks into sub-components using partials.

The following example code will render the file `views/comments/comments.json.jbuilder`, and set a local variable comment with all of the message comments, to use inside the partial.

```
json.partial! 'comments/comments', comments: message.comments
```

It's also possible to render collections of partials. Both lines of code in the following example do the same thing:

```
json.array! posts, partial: 'posts/post', as: :post
json.partial! 'posts/post', collection: posts, as: :post
```

Rails API

You can also pass a partial as an argument to a normal builder method call:

```
json.comments @post.comments, partial: 'comments/comment', as: :comment
```

Just like their view template counterparts, Jbuilder partials accept variables with or without `:locals` option.

```
json.partial! 'settings', locals: { user: user }
json.partial! 'settings', user: user
```

C.2.1.2   Null Values
You can explicitly make Jbuilder object return `null` if you want:

```
json.extract! @post, :id, :title, :content, :published_at
json.author do
  if @post.anonymous?
    json.null! # or json.nil!
  else
    json.first_name @post.author_first_name
    json.last_name @post.author_last_name
  end
end
```

To prevent Jbuilder from including null values in the output, you can use the `ignore_nil!` method:

```
json.ignore_nil!
json.foo nil
json.bar "bar"
# => { "bar": "bar" }
```

C.2.1.3   Caching
One of the most powerful features of the Jbuilder Rails integration, at least for high-traffic deployments, is support for fragment caching. Again, it should be very familiar to those of you familiar with how it works in view templates—it uses `Rails.cache` under the covers.

```
json.cache! ['v1', @person], expires_in: 10.minutes do
  json.extract! @person, :name, :age
end
```

You can also conditionally cache a block by using `cache_if!` like this:

```
json.cache_if! !admin?, ['v1', @person], expires_in: 10.minutes do
  json.extract! @person, :name, :age
end
```

<img> If you are rendering fragments for a collection of objects, have a look at the `jbuilder_cache_multi` gem. It uses `fetch_multi` to fetch multiple keys from the cache at once.

C.2.2 Active Model Serializers

If you don't like Jbuilder, a different (perhaps slightly more popular) option is called Active Model Serializers (AMS). It claims to adhere to Rails' convention over configuration philosophy and, according to some of its advocates, encourages consistency in a way that results in easier to maintain code than Jbuilder.

https://github.com/rails-api/active_model_serializers

Contrary to Jbuilder's templating approach, with AMS you define classes that extend `ActiveModel::Serializer`. They look kind of like Active Record models and have similar macro methods for defining attributes and associations.

```
class AuctionSerializer < ActiveModel::Serializer
  attributes :name, :description, :ends_at
  has_many :bids
end
```

Once you define serializers, Rails will use them by convention whenever you render JSON in your controllers.

Unfortunately, a couple of factors came together to prevent us from doing much more than mentioning AMS in *The Rails 5 Way*. One is that the API is somewhat in flux, which made us worry that the information would get outdated quickly. The second factor is that it is a large library and would take many pages to even scrape the surface. Your best bet at the moment is to start by studying the guides provided by the project authors at https: // github.com/rails-api/active_model_serializers/tree/master/docs.

Rails API

Index

Register Your Product at informit.com/register

Access additional benefits and **save 35%** on your next purchase

- Automatically receive a coupon for 35% off your next purchase, valid for 30 days. Look for your code in your InformIT cart or the Manage Codes section of your account page.

- Download available product updates.

- Access bonus material if available.*

- Check the box to hear from us and receive exclusive offers on new editions and related products.

Registration benefits vary by product. Benefits will be listed on your account page under Registered Products.

InformIT.com—The Trusted Technology Learning Source

InformIT is the online home of information technology brands at Pearson, the world's foremost education company. At InformIT.com, you can:

- Shop our books, eBooks, software, and video training
- Take advantage of our special offers and promotions (informit.com/promotions)
- Sign up for special offers and content newsletter (informit.com/newsletters)
- Access thousands of free chapters and video lessons

Connect with InformIT—Visit informit.com/community

the trusted technology learning source

Addison-Wesley · Adobe Press · Cisco Press · Microsoft Press · Pearson IT Certification · Prentice Hall · Que · Sams · Peachpit Press

 Pearson